Major Problems in American History, 1920–1945

DOCUMENTS AND ESSAYS

EDITED BY

COLIN GORDON

UNIVERSITY OF IOWA

HOUGHTON MIFFLIN COMPANY   Boston   New York

Editor-in-Chief: Jean L. Woy
Senior Associate Editor: Frances Gay
Associate Project Editor: Amy Johnson
Associate Production/Design Coordinator: Jodi O'Rourke
Senior Marketing Manager: Sandra McGuire
Assistant Manufacturing Coordinator: Andrea Wagner

Cover Designer: Sarah Melhado
Cover Image: Untitled, 1930s. Collection of Leonard Bates, New York.

Printed in the U.S.A.

Library of Congress Catalog Card Number: 98-72031

ISBN: 0-395-87074-7

7 8 9-QF-08 07 06 05 04

For Susan, Izzy, and Alex

Contents

CHAPTER 10
Private Lives in Hard Times
Page 273

CHAPTER 11
Shaping the New Deal: Recovery and Reform Politics
Page 303

CHAPTER 12
Race, Gender, and the Rise of the CIO
Page 338

CHAPTER 13
Contesting the New Deal
Page 370

C H A P T E R   1 4
The Social Impact of World War II
Page 398

C H A P T E R   1 5
The Political Economy of World War II
Page 428

Major Problems
in
American History, 1920–1945

American Politics and
Society Between the Wars

The history of the interwar era is not marked by an overarching set of issues or interpretations. Indeed, traditional political history invariably approaches the era as two discrete chronological episodes. On one side of 1929, we have the "roaring" 1920s, a decade of cultural excess, political corruption, mass production, and mass consumption. On the other side, we have the "dirty" 1930s, a decade of economic privation and political innovation.

But behind the neat chronological divide provided by the economic crash and the launching of the New Deal, historians have explored (and are exploring) a complex narrative of continuity and change that spans the first half of the twentieth century. Social and labor historians have suggested the ways in which ordinary Americans experienced waves of industrialization and urbanization. Cultural historians have traced the ways in which the institutions and ideology of mass consumption emerged alongside the technological advance of mass production. Intellectual historians have explored the ambiguities and dilemmas of American liberalism in a setting increasingly dominated by concentrations of private and public power. And historians of gender and race relations have examined the transformation of private lives and political rights across an era in which two world wars and an unprecedented economic crisis recast the very terms and expectations of citizenship.

What commands the attention of historians of this era, in other words, is a tangle of questions that are tied in different ways to the premises, promises, and performance of American democracy. From a variety of angles and perspectives, historians have portrayed the interwar era as a transformative moment. For some, this moment came early in the era—in the post-World War I battles over the meaning the war's democratic rhetoric, for example, or in the collective postwar realization that the United States (in its cultural values, its social organization, and its economic development) was now a "modern" society. For some, this moment came a decade later, with the fundamental cultural, economic, and political shock of the Great Depression. For some, this moment came later still—not with the onset of the Depression itself, but with the political and cultural reaction to it that began with the New Deal and continued through the Second World War.

These three essays, in different ways, place the events of the interwar era in a larger historical context. In the first essay, Robert McElvaine underscores the historical importance of the Depression by placing both the economic crisis and the reforms it generated into a broad historical context. In the second essay, Lynn Dumenil suggests both the attraction and the limitations of the conventional scholarly divide between the bathtub gin of the 1920s and the breadlines of the 1930s. In the third essay, Alan Dawley sees the emergence of New Deal liberalism as a response to the Great Depression but, more important, as the culmination of a multifaceted popular struggle and the reflection of a deeply seeded incongruity between "the ways Americans lived and the ways they were governed."

The Great Depression in Historical Perspective

ROBERT McELVAINE

One need not be a devotee of astrology or sunspot theories to recognize that certain rhythms seem to exist in our history. Many different types of business cycles have been traced over the years. During the nineteenth century, for example, major economic slumps occurred with disturbing regularity: 1819, 1837, 1857, 1873, 1893. Another economic collapse was beginning "on schedule" in 1914, when the outbreak of war in Europe revived the American economy.

Less universally accepted, but hard to deny when our history is viewed in its entirety, are periodic swings of mood, opinion, and values among the American people. An oscillation between the dominance of reform sentiment and standpattism has taken place throughout American history, with each wave of reform and each trough of reaction usually lasting between ten and twenty years. The opposing moods have been called by many names: Jeffersonian and Hamiltonian, democratic and aristocratic, liberal and conservative. The terms inevitably lead to confusion, because their meanings are so imprecise that the opposing names are sometimes used to describe the same policy. Jefferson's famous declaration in his first inaugural address, "We are all republicans—we are all federalists," hinted at the ambiguity. In a speech during his 1928 presidential campaign, Herbert Hoover restated the point: "We are a nation of progressives; we differ as to what is the road to progress." Precisely. But the differences over the meaning of progress and the best road to reach it are often great.

The fundamental difference was well stated by Jefferson. Some men, he declared, "fear the people, and wish to transfer all power to the higher classes of society." Others "consider the people as the safest depository of power in the last resort." Despite the frequent confusion over means, the goals of the former group are conveniently labeled conservative; those of the latter, who have been more concerned with the wrongs done to people than with the rights of property, are generally termed liberal. Given this admittedly loose distinction, American history in its broadest outline can be seen as consisting of periods of liberal reform punctuated by conservative breathing spaces. The peaks of reform were reached during the American Revolution, the ages of Jefferson and Jackson, the crusade against slavery, the Progressive era, the New Deal, and Lyndon Johnson's Great Society. The motive forces in the decline of reform eras seem to have been principally three: First, people eventually grow weary of social problems. They choose instead to withdraw into more personal interests. This sentiment was best summed up by the slogan Republicans used in the 1946 congressional campaign and several times since: "Had enough?" When a majority is sufficiently tired of the activism of such leaders as Jefferson, Lincoln, the Roosevelts, Wilson, Kennedy, or Johnson to answer "yes," a period of reaction sets in. Such notable ages in American history have been the Federalist era, the Era of Good Feelings, the 1840s and early 1850s, the Gilded Age, the 1920s, the 1950s, and the 1980s.

The second main factor in bringing a period of liberalism to a close is that the pace of change in our society outdistances a generation of reformers. Their ideas become dated. Much of their program has been put into effect, yet old problems remain and new ones arise. Some of those who seek change in their youth come to favor the status quo as they grow older.

A third reason for the decline of reform eras is that political leaders who start out committed to principles are likely, after time, to come to prefer, unlike Henry Clay, to be president (or congressman) to being right. Thus their zeal for the cause diminishes, and with it the reform era itself cools.

New reform eras arise for reasons similar to those that lead to the demise of their predecessors: a rejection of the dominant mood and a generational change. Just as people tire of calls for self-sacrifice, they eventually become upset with themselves after a period of hedonism and disregard for others. For some, at least, a time of reform offers an opportunity for personal redemption as well as for social change. If the public ultimately grows weary of activist leaders, it finally becomes bored or disgusted with the Adamses, Fillmores, Coolidges, Eisenhowers, and Reagans, too. Zealots of the right come to find office-holding as comfortable as do their liberal counterparts. And as a new generation arises the old battles are history and new configurations of problems bring forth new attempts at solutions.

The fact that at least some *new* solutions are sought in each wave of reform indicates that the often-used metaphor of a swinging pendulum is not quite suitable for describing changes in America's mood. No conservative era succeeds in wiping out all the gains of the preceding period of reform. The Republicans in the Eisenhower years were unable (and in many cases unwilling) to repeal the New Deal. The Reagan Republicans appeared for a time to be on the verge of dismantling the Great Society, if not the New Deal, but the public has proved unwilling to follow its reactionary leaders that far. Each liberal age is able to build upon some accomplishments of those that came before it. Some positions of the Reagan administration that are today considered extremely conservative would have been denounced as liberal in the 1920s.

The limits of the pulsations of national opinion here under discussion must be made clear. They do not, of course, involve everyone. Nearly 17 million Americans voted against Franklin Roosevelt in 1936; more than 27 million voted for Barry Goldwater in 1964. We are speaking of shifts between about 40 and 60 percent of the electorate, which seem to be the lower and upper limits of support for one viewpoint or the other. Nor are the shifts of mood usually as dramatic as we sometimes make them seem. The continued strength of some items on the progressive agenda during the 1920s, the "white backlash" of the 1960s, and the surprising popularity in opinion polls of many social programs in the 1980s are cases in point. It should also be plain that this is no simple argument about "history repeating itself." There has been a substantial variation in the length and intensity of periods of reform and reaction. All sorts of external factors ranging from economic conditions to wars to individual leadership can affect the timing and strength of reform waves. None of these qualifications, however, detracts from the usefulness of the concept of oscillations of public sentiment to an understanding of the American past. Those who remain skeptical of the idea may be persuaded by noting the startling accuracy of the following prediction Arthur Schlesinger, Sr., made in 1949: "We may expect the recession from liberalism which began in 1947 to last till 1962, with a possible margin of a year or two in one direction or the other. The next conservative epoch will then be due around 1978." And, it might now be added, liberalism can be expected to be in the ascendancy again in the 1990s, if not before.

I have taken the time to go into this discussion of tides of public sentiment in some detail because the concept is vitally important to an understanding of Depression America. It is notable that the cycles of opinion appear to be unrelated to those of the economy. The two worst depressions in American history prior to the 1930s occurred in the long conservative period of the late nineteenth century. Populism was already strong when the Panic of 1893 hit, but it remained an overwhelmingly agrarian movement and did not become nationally dominant during the nineties. When reform did win majority support after the turn of the century, the United States was again enjoying prosperity. Prosperity gives middle-class reformers the security they feel is necessary to undertake change. The last great liberal uprising we have experienced, that of the 1960s, also took place in a period of great prosperity for middle-class Americans. Clearly hard times are not a prerequisite for reform. Indeed, only one of the major reform eras in American history occurred during a depression and, to state the same point differently, all of the major economic collapses save one happened during conservative eras. The one exception is the Great Depression of the 1930s, our worst depression, during which the New Deal, our most significant era of liberalism, took place. The so-far unique coincidence of the nation's economic and values cycles in the 1930s is a little-noted but critical fact about the history of Depression America.

Superimposed upon the economic and mood shifts are basic differences in class values. These are far from absolute, but as a rule of thumb, working-class people have been more likely to hold values centered on cooperation, sharing, equity, fairness, and justice than have their affluent countrymen. The latter have, throughout our history, been more likely to defend the marketplace as the sole determinant of the distribution of the economy's fruits. The poor—whether farmers or industrial workers—have generally been less willing worshipers at the shrine of Adam Smith. So long as the marketplace economy provided reasonable opportunities, they were likely to accept it. But during hard times or when maldistribution was especially evident, working-class people have tended to call for community or government action to supplement—or counteract—the marketplace. In short, they have believed that morality ought to have a role in the workings of the economy.

The basic reason for this difference is not hard to find. The self-interest of have-nots is better served by a more equitable distribution, whereas the self-interest of the wealthy is obviously better served by keeping things as they are. This in no sense makes the two positions ethically equivalent. The self-interest of the poor coincides with justice, that of the rich with injustice. The significance of this for the Great Depression is that it, like previous depressions, led the lower classes to demand government action to help them. Workers and farmers had made similar protests in the 1870s and 1890s. The key differences in the 1930s were that the country was "due" for a swing to more humanitarian values and that the depression was so much deeper, wider, and longer than previous slumps that a far larger segment of the middle class was directly affected and hence came to identify its interests with those of the poor. The combination of all these ingredients made the 1930s the time in which the values of compassion, sharing, and social justice became the most dominant that they have ever been in American history.

Each periodic depression that plagued the United States from the early nineteenth century through the 1930s was worse than the one before it. Many reasons for this could be cited, but one stands out as by far the most important. As the United States became less agrarian and more industrial, less rural and more urban, an ever-increasing percentage of its population became susceptible to the vagaries of the market economy. This is not to say that farmers were not victims of economic collapse—much of the history of the late nineteenth century and of the 1920s and 1930s makes plain that they were—but that people who *owned* farms and were not deeply in debt could at least feed their families during hard times. Stated simply, more and more people became *dependent* as the national industrialized. Urban working-class people who rented their living quarters and whose income was derived entirely from wages found themselves in desperate straits when they lost their jobs and could find no other employment.

The Panic of 1893 was America's worst depression in the nineteenth century. Real income of Americans is estimated to have dropped some 18 percent between 1892 and 1894. That depression led to massive unemployment, which in turn fueled protest. Workers were angry and ready to undertake cooperative and, in some cases, radical action. These facts alarmed middle-class Americans, some of whom believed revolution might be imminent, particularly since the farm belts of the nation were seething with populism. Under the circumstances, middle America chose to cast its lot with business and dig in to defend economic orthodoxy. No quarrel on this would come from President Cleveland who, in vetoing the Texas Seed bill of 1887, which would have provided a scant $10,000 for relief of farmers hard-hit by drought, uttered the immortal words, "though the people support the Government the Government should not support the people." Cleveland, like most others in power in the 1890s, believed that depressions were natural events, part of the working of the business cycle, and therefore the government could do little about them. His formula for recovery (which was continued in all its essentials by his Republican successor, William McKinley) was to maintain sound money, preserve the sanctity of contracts, and cut federal spending. It has an uncannily familiar ring.

If the effects of the Panic of 1893 on the economy, workers, and business were dramatic, the depression's impact on American politics was equally spectacular.

Although only one Democrat (Cleveland) had been elected president between 1860 and 1892, the Republicans had failed to establish themselves as a clear-cut majority party. Democrats won decisively in the House elections in 1890 and 1892, and Cleveland regained the White House in the latter year. This was the first time since Reconstruction that *either* party had held the White House and both houses of Congress simultaneously. But what seemed a happy occasion for the Democrats soon proved to be quite otherwise. It meant that thier party was fully "in charge" when the panic struck. They were blamed, as the Republicans would be four decades later, for the economic collapse and had to pay the price at the polls. The elections of 1894 and 1896 saw what has been called "one of the greatest bloodless political realignments that this country has ever experienced." The shift of House seats from Democrats to Republicans in 1894 was the largest in modern history, exceeding even the transfer in the other direction in 1932. The political results of the Panic of 1893 clearly foreshadowed those of the Great Depression: the party in power was devastated and the opposition party became dominant for more than a generation. Woodrow Wilson's two victories under unusual circumstances notwithstanding, the Republicans remained the majority party from 1894 until a new economic collapse turned the tables on them in the early 1930s. For an earlier generation, Grover Cleveland and the Democrats represented what Herbert Hoover and the Republicans have stood for to so many Americans in the last half century. "I was a child of four during the Panic of '93," Walter Lippmann wrote two decades later, "and Cleveland has always been a sinister figure to me. His name was uttered with monstrous dread in the household . . . And to this day I find myself with a subtle prejudice against Democrats that goes deeper than what we call political conviction."

Preindustrial America was, in historian Robert Wiebe's apt phrase, a nation of "island communities." What was dominant in the lives of people of all classes was the local community. Each community was to a large extent self-contained, its significant contacts with the rest of the nation infrequent. Given the large number of limited stages on which Americans performed, there was an abundance of leading roles. Each town had its local elite—its merchants, bankers, clergymen, attorneys, physicians, editors, and so forth—to whom the community looked for leadership. These elites, of course, enjoyed their status. But the existence of tight-knit communities with a shared set of values was also beneficial to other groups. Several social and labor historians have shown in recent years that nineteenth-century workers were often able to use shared values to gain community support for strikes and fair treatment.

The rapid industrialization of the United States during the late nineteenth century upset this world. The development of national systems of transportation and communications, of highly concentrated industrial and financial systems, and of mass circulation newspapers and magazines, along with the explosion of urban populations, submerged the independence of the nation's separate local communities. In the useful concept developed by nineteenth-century German sociologist Ferdinand Tönnies, *Gemeinschaft*—the small, personal community of the nineteenth century—was replaced by *Gesellschaft,* a large, anonymous society in which the importance of one's place and achievements in the local context nearly dissolved.

The Progressive era in the broadest sense was an attempt to regain the old values or construct new ones. Progressivism may have meant many different things, but what tied it together was that all its manifestations were responses to a common stimulus: the myriad effects of industrialization on traditional American values. Because of the vast changes, even true conservatives found it necessary to become reformers. The only way to preserve at least some of the old world in the face of the upheaval being wrought by industrialization was to try to make social changes that would compensate for some of the economic changes. Paradoxically, by the beginning of the twentieth century, it was necessary for a sincere conservative (that is, someone genuinely interested in preserving the old values, not simply an apologist for concentrated wealth) to become a reformer, a "progressive." Such people saw "certain radical but strictly limited reforms as the only way to salvage the system."

For the middle-class reformer, alterations might be needed, but they could not be undertaken safely during the economic crisis of the 1890s. By the turn of the century, though, both prosperity and optimism had returned. The United States had recovered from its worst depression to that time, had won a "splendid little war," the Spanish-American War, that most believed was fought for the highest, most unselfish objectives, and was emerging as a world power. Under such conditions, it was possible for the "better sort" to attempt to guide the discontent that had been so evident among farmers and workers in the nineties into acceptable channels. Middle America could rediscover poverty, as it seems to do once a generation. Thus, while progressivism had important working-class, farmer, and corporate components, its dominant form represented a "cautious uprising of the better classes." There can be little doubt that most of these people sincerely wanted the "uplift" of the lower classes and a better, more honest, just, and moral society. They also wanted the beneficiaries to know to whom they should be thankful. Improvements were not to be won by the struggles of the lower classes, but to be bestowed as gifts from the moral, disinterested people above them. Much of what passed for progressivism was pushed by people who saw themselves as altruistic—they wanted to do good for others, not themselves. As Richard Hofstadter pointed out, populism had been a reform dictated by empty stomachs, while progressivism was a reform movement guided by the mind and heart.

World War I not only brought the culmination of the Progressive era and intensified the reaction that followed, it also provided in several important ways the soil in which the seeds of the Great Depression and New Deal would germinate.

When the basically pacifist Woodrow Wilson finally took his country into the war in April 1917 he justified it, as he had to in order to convince himself and the American people, in the moralistic rhetoric of progressivism. "There is not a single selfish element, so far as I can see," Wilson said, "in the cause we are fighting for." Unlike other belligerents, Wilson insisted, the United States fought for altruistic purposes.

In addition to demonstrating to himself and a majority of his countrymen that it was "right" for the United States to enter the war, Wilson's use of the language of idealistic self-sacrifice as a rationale for participation had at least two other notable effects. It tied the war so tightly to progressive values that, if people became disillusioned with the war, they would also lose their faith in reform. Wilson's rhetoric also made the war seem an unprecedented example of national self-sacrifice and hence it served finally to release the combined guilt and moral energy that had been at the base of much of middle-class progressivism. Having at last paid their dues and made their sacrifices, Americans after the war could turn with somewhat clear consciences to personal concerns. The hedonistic, greedy, self-centered norms of the twenties, which played no small part in the coming of the Depression, were at least intensified by the wrapping of the war in the mantle of progressive moralism.

The war also created an international economic situation that helped bring on the Great Depression. Following Versailles there was an "unquenchable jingoism" throughout the industrial world. The reparations and war debts questions fueled dangerous international tension and weakened both the domestic economies of some European nations and the international economic structure. European countries became debtors to, rather than creditors of, the United States. Among other factors, this meant that these nations were no longer in a position to provide a good market for the surplus farm production of the United States.

The contraction of Europe's ability to buy American agricultural products aggravated another fundamental economic problem produced by the war. Wartime demand for food was great and the normal supply in Europe had been cut sharply. Both market forces and government policies led during the war to a vast increase in America's farm output. When wartime Food Administrator Herbert Hoover allowed the price of wheat to be set at $2.20 a bushel, farmers increased wheat acreage by nearly 40 percent and output by almost 50 percent. This in turn meant chronic "overproduction" in the 1920s, a massive agricultural depression during America's "prosperity decade," and a further dislocation in the world economic structure.

The First World War had other results with a direct bearing on the Great Depression. It represented what historian Henry May has called "the end of American innocence." The great optimism of the progressive years, as well as most of what was left of the old familiar values, was shattered by the war and the disillusionment of Versailles and the struggle over the League of Nations. Unmistakable clouds now hung over the previously sunny American horizon. "Those of you who did not live in that period before 1914, or are not old enough to remember it," clergyman John Haynes Holmes reminisced years later, "cannot imagine the security we enjoyed and the serenity we felt in that old world." Like most old worlds when they are gone, prewar America took on more of a glow than reality warranted, but the feeling of loss was a significant part of the mood of the twenties and the motive for the desire to return to "normalcy." The word itself, coined accidentally by Warren Harding during his 1920 campaign for the presidency, symbolized perfectly what the nation sought after the war: a return to a golden age that, like Harding's word, only resembled what had existed before.

To carry on the war effort, the United States government had embarked, for the first time, on serious social and economic planning. Indeed, it has been persuasively argued that the models for many programs and practices of the New Deal are to be found in wartime Washington rather than in the proposals of progressive reformers.

John Dewey, for one, took note in 1918 of "the social possibilities of war." The American economy was controlled in a completely unprecedented fashion during

World War I. The War Industries Board, when placed under the leadership of Wall Street speculator Bernard Baruch early in 1918, held extensive powers over business during the war. The WIB tightly regulated and managed the economy, achieving remarkable results that many observers believed were proof of the efficacy of a planned economy.

Other precedents for New Deal actions are readily discernible in wartime practices. The National War Labor Board mediated labor conflicts. Workers were guaranteed the right to bargain collectively. Union membership increased by more than 40 percent between 1915 and the Armistice, and real earnings for laborers increased a modest 4 percent during the same period.

Major wars are sufficiently grave that orthodox thinkers are willing to suspend their dogma for the duration. Most American leaders who would not consider having an unbalanced budget in peacetime saw no alternative during the war. About half of the more than $32 billion cost of the war was met by borrowing. The rest was paid for through sharply increased taxes, including levies on corporate profits and a sharply graduated income tax (the latter made possible by the ratification of the Sixteenth Amendment in 1913). All of these wartime precedents were rummaged through for useful ideas when a different but equally momentous crisis had to be faced more than a decade later.

The fanatical patriotism of World War I left a legacy that would play an important part in the decade ahead. The insistence on "100 percent Americanism" helped turn many people against anything with a hint of "internationalism" about it. This included Communists, Catholics, and Jews, all of whom became prime targets of the new Ku Klux Klan. The Klan of the 1920s represented a carry-over of the intolerance and reaction against progressivism, the war, and internationalism that had become so popular in 1919–20. It cannot be blamed for creating these feelings. Indeed it was, like so much else in the twenties, a business dictated by the marketplace. Its organizers were interested in nothing so much as making money through the sale of memberships. It was organized rather like a modern fast-food franchise, but in this case the product was not hamburgers but hatred. Accordingly, the Klan had to be willing to be intolerant of anyone the potential consumers did not like. Basically it was: "You don't like Group X? Well we don't either. Join us." This meant that while the KKK certainly exacerbated intergroup tensions in the twenties, it did not manufacture them. That a sizable part of the nation—principally in rural and small-town regions—continued for so long the passionate intolerance of the postwar period is closely related to another of the prominent realities of the twenties: the decline of rural America and its values.

The war itself was the last and greatest example of the progressive spirit of sacrifice. It was a mood that dissolved rapidly after the war. But the progressive-wartime state of mind carried through one last sacrifice before it expired: the Eighteenth Amendment. Although the fact would be forgotten quickly in the twenties, prohibition enjoyed solid majority support when the amendment sailed through state legislatures to ratification in January 1919. "Prohibition," *The New York Times* accurately observed, "seems to be the fashion, just as drinking once was."

By definition, fashions change. Few have changed more rapidly than this one. The shift of opinion on drinking was one of the more dramatic examples of how, by the fall of 1920, much of America had tired of the whole idea of self-sacrifice. The temper of the twenties was to be vastly different from what had gone before.

The Modern Temper

LYNN DUMENIL

"The world broke in two in 1922 or thereabouts," announced novelist Willa Cather. Journalist Mark Sullivan picked 1914, the beginning of World War I, as the point "of fundamental alteration, from which we would never go back." That these astute observers were joined by many others in offering different dates to mark the watershed of the twentieth century should call into question the historian's penchant for precise periodization. U.S. history covering the last hundred years has tended to fall into neat divisions by decade, a fate especially true of the 1920s. World War I's end in 1918 seemed a natural break, signifying the close of one era and the beginning of a new one that in turn was closed by the stock market crash in 1929. The war's timing encouraged contemporaries and historians to see a sharp break between prewar and postwar America. Moreover, it contributed to a sense that the war had been causal in transforming American cultural and intellectual life by bringing about the alienated, lost generation of intellectuals, creating the new woman, and pushing Americans into hedonism. Recent scholarship has challenged this vision; social historians in particular have made it increasingly clear that many of the changes so evident in the 1920s predated the war. The thrust of social history has been to challenge conventional periodization and to emphasize as well the unevenness of social change and the continuities that characterized the private worlds of individuals.

Why have historians persisted in viewing the period as so distinctive? Is it perhaps that historians cannot escape the fascination for the decade's drama any more than their students can lose their romantic vision of the twenties filtered through the lens of *The Great Gatsby*? In part. It is also because the richness of the newer research—on women, ethnicity, and leisure, for example—makes an attempt at a new synthesis almost irresistible. And it is because an analysis of the decade's events and concerns reveals so clearly the transformation of American culture as it emerged as a "modern" society.

In characterizing the 1920s as modern, I recognize that the essential transformations began in the late nineteenth century, with the triad of rapid industrialization, sprawling urbanization, and massive immigration. Industrial development changed the nature of work and daily life and gave rise to an extensive network of corporations that integrated the country into a national economy. The result, as Robert Wiebe has suggested in *The Search for Order, 1877–1920,* was to erode the isolation of "island communities"—the towns of antebellum America that while part of a market economy had nonetheless maintained a degree of local autonomy and order based on "modesty in women, rectitude in men, and thrift, sobriety, and hard work in both." But the spread of railroads and national corporations after the Civil War transformed American communities. The multiplication of national bureaucratic structures—of voluntary associations, professional organizations, and corporations—led to an organized society in which both individuals and communities found themselves powerfully affected by forces outside their control and increasingly removed from the locus of economic and political power.

The growth of cities added to the complexity of life, as urban dwellers experienced impersonal relationships that replaced the intimate nature of smaller communities. Skyscrapers, elevators, streetcars, and the noise of the metropolis also contributed to a more mechanized, regimented life. And despite the nationalizing trends in the economy that had a certain homogenizing effect, the cities also became bastions of cultural pluralism. A highly visible working class increasingly subjected to the power of corporate employers made urban areas the site of notable episodes of class conflict, such as the Chicago Haymarket Riot of 1886. These tensions invaded the arena of culture as well when working-class saloons, dance halls, and other leisure-time venues became the focus of middle- and upper-class elites' fears about declining morality and disintegrating social order.

These fears were closely associated with the pervasive presence of immigrants in the city. By 1900, "new" immigrants from Southern and Eastern Europe were the target of intense nativism, and in the early twentieth century, two other groups joined the streams of people migrating to American cities. Mexican immigration into the Southwest and Midwest dramatically increased in the teens, and African American migration from the South to the cities of the North accelerated with the beginning of World War I, adding still further diversity to the urban matrix.

The late nineteenth century witnessed other significant transformations. The massacre at Wounded Knee in 1890 signaled the final military conquest of Native Americans. With the displacement of indigenous people and the extension of the railroad, settlement and corporations moved west, leading historian Frederick Jackson Turner to reflect in 1893 on the meaning of the closing of the frontier. At the same time, the trajectory of conquest moved beyond the continent. Through diplomatic negotiations and the Spanish-American War, the United States had acquired an empire and become an international power, a position confirmed by its role in World War I.

Other changes stemmed from the challenges to traditional religious faith embodied in Darwinian science and the new biblical criticism that resulted in denominational upheavals for the churches and spiritual crises for individuals. Assaults on an older order emerged on the gender front as well, as working-class women increasingly entered paid employment and middle-class women began a campaign for women's rights that coalesced in the suffrage amendment of 1919. Both were harbingers of major changes in women's roles and the family itself.

Many Americans were of two minds about these transformations. On the one hand, they were fearful about urban poverty, decay, and disorder. The decline in individual and community autonomy and the hardening of class lines prompted anxieties about social mobility and democratic politics. Pluralism threatened the nineteenth-century Victorian worldview that valued hierarchy, order, and a single standard of culture, morality, and values. On the other hand, many people were excited about progress. Breakthroughs in technology, the increase in material wealth, and the beginning of an empire seemingly heralded the upward march of civilization, with America in the forefront. Thus despite prevailing fears about challenges to their ordered world, for the most part Victorians remained optimistic.

In the 1920s, the same broad forces that had so powerfully transformed the nineteenth century continued the process of making America more "modern"— more organized, more bureaucratic, more complex. . . . But despite strong links with the past, we can identify distinctive qualities as well. For example, the sense of unprecedented prosperity—made all the more striking by its dramatic collapse in the stock market crash of 1929—helped to give the decade its singular tone. By 1922 the country had recovered from a debilitating postwar depression and entered a period of stunning industrial productivity, neatly symbolized by auto manufacturer Henry Ford, whose use of mechanization and innovative management helped him to churn out affordable cars at such a spectacular rate that his success earned the label "The Ford Miracle." This productivity, coupled with war-inflicted devastation of European economies, made the United States the dominant world economic power. At home, most Americans enjoyed a higher standard of living. Not everyone shared in the fabled prosperity, however. Many sectors of the economy, especially farming, never truly recovered from the postwar depression, and African Americans and other minorities continued to live in poverty. In general, the aura of wealth obscured a highly skewed distribution of income that placed the bulk of the country's assets in the hands of a few. Nonetheless, the 1920s were marked by a sense of prosperity and a get-rich-quick mentality, evident not only in the stock market but also in giddy land booms in Florida and Los Angeles that reflected prosperous Americans' sense of a new era of unlimited material progress.

The faith in prosperity powerfully shaped the politics of the decade. The Progressive reform era (1900–14) that had preceded World War I gave way in the 1920s to a period of conservatism in which politicians and pundits alike celebrated Big Business as the savior of American democracy and enterprise. The period's Presidents—Warren Harding (1921–23), who died in office, Calvin Coolidge (1923–29), and Herbert Hoover (1929–33)—were Republicans who successfully identified their party with the promise of peace and prosperity. Differing dramatically in temperament and skill, they shared a commitment to promoting strong business/government cooperation that led to almost unbridled corporate power. Their approach to what they called the "New Era" underwrote a sense of complacency and preoccupation with material progress that is one facet of the characteristic tone of the 1920s.

But another key image, and perhaps the most enduring, is that of the roaring twenties—of a fast life, propelled by riches and rapidly changing social values. Dubious get-rich-quick schemes and fads like flagpole sitting contributed to a tone of feverish frivolity. Flappers dancing the Charleston and participating in a sexual revolution, movie stars in already decadent Los Angeles setting the pace for the rest of the country, and speakeasies trafficking in illegal liquor, all suggested a world far removed from Victorian restraint.

One group that contributed to this stereotype was the Lost Generation, a term used to describe the young artists and writers of the decade whose works embodied so much of the spirit of the times. Poets like Edna St. Vincent Millay celebrated the new—and sexually liberated—woman. Novelists like F. Scott Fitzgerald and Ernest Hemingway depicted a generation's cynicism and disillusionment which seemed to explain the escapism that fueled the excesses of the jazz age. Somewhat older writers like Sinclair Lewis also figured importantly in creating the literary portrait of the twenties. Lewis's *Babbitt* serves as such an enduring critique of middle-class life that "Babbitt" entered dictionaries as a term connoting a businessman caught up in almost ritualistic consumerism and conformity. These writers made a lasting mark, shaping a scenario of the twenties for generations to come. While there is some truth to these images—especially among the urban, white, prosperous middle and upper classes—they overshadow the average Americans who led far more quiet lives and ignore those excluded from the prosperity of the times.

This depiction of the roaring twenties also obscures the complexities lying beneath the surface, especially the considerable social tensions that permeated the culture. After a major period of industrial unrest in 1919–20, in which corporations ruthlessly repressed strikes, labor was for the most part quiescent in the twenties and subject to increased regimentation. But if class conflict for the most part was muted, ethnic and racial tensions came roiling to the surface. Race riots in Chicago and other cities in 1919 signified new dynamics in urban areas that had experienced significant African American migration during the war years. Migration to the North as well as wartime military service helped to create a militant spirit among African Americans. Both the artistic movement termed the Harlem Renaissance and the black nationalism of Marcus Garvey and his Universal Negro Improvement Association symbolized what was popularly called the New Negro. Empowering for African Americans, the new spirit was unsettling to whites who wished to maintain a repressive racial order.

White Anglo-Saxon Protestants also continued to resent the rising influence of immigrants, Catholics, and Jews, and the 1920s were a particularly virulent period of nativism. The decade had been ushered in by the 1919–20 Red Scare, a product of Americans' fears that the 1919 Bolshevik Revolution in Russia might spread to the United States. That fear, coupled with the postwar wave of strikes, unspent wartime nationalism, and long-standing hostility to immigrants, led to a widespread hysteria about radicals and dissenters, with much of the focus on aliens. After a witch hunt marked by massive violations of civil liberties, the extremes of the Red Scare died down, but the animus toward immigrants did not, and Congress passed a series of laws that severely restricted European and Asian immigration. A new Ku Klux Klan modeled after the southern Reconstruction Klan contributed to the nativist furor. Targeting African Americans, immigrants, Catholics, and Jews, it spread its racist and xenophobic ideology and became a potent force in local and national politics until its demise in the mid-twenties.

Nativism also figured in another distinctive facet of the 1920s: prohibition. The Eighteenth Amendment outlawing the sale of intoxicating beverages had passed in 1919, but it continued to be a highly contested issue until its repeal in 1933. Supporters viewed prohibition not only as a means of promoting morality and sobriety but as a symbol of the dominance of white Anglo-Saxon Protestant cultural values. Critics assailed it for violating personal liberties while ethnic groups resented its cultural imperialism. Prohibition persisted as a disruptive issue in politics, most notably in the 1928 presidential contest between Hoover and Al Smith, where Smith's immigrant background, Catholicism, and opposition to prohibition figured prominently in the campaign.

Specific events, people, and social movements helped to define the 1920s, but the decade was also distinguished by Americans' growing consciousness of change, a perception that a yawning gulf separated them from the world of only a decade before. World War I set the stage for this shift in tone. Older interpretations of the impact of war centered on the way it crushed the progressive reform movement that had sought to ameliorate problems of industrial, urban society. The war allegedly left in its wake disillusionment and reaction, as indicated by the Red Scare's repression of aliens and radicals. Disillusionment with war and a concomitant search for escape in amusements also suggested an explanation for the nation's retreat from world politics and the Senate's failure to ratify the Covenant of the League of Nations, Woodrow Wilson's cherished plan for an international organization to prevent future wars. In this view, Americans in the 1920s appear to be reactionary, hedonistic, and self-centered, and the stock market crash brings to an end a morality play, with the Great Depression the nation's punishment for its sins of excess and selfishness.

Revisionist historians have long since corrected this image of the jazz age (although it seems quite resilient in popular culture and memory and thus worth addressing here). The 1920s were not a period of unrelieved hedonism, nor did reform completely disappear. Partisan politics, Wilson's intransigence, and the public's ambivalence about internationalism had as much to do with killing the League as did disillusionment. Nor does World War I account for the tremendous social forces transforming American life—industrialization, immigration, urbanization, and changing patterns in work, politics, religion, leisure, and the family were in place well before 1914–18.

Yet, if the impact of the war has been misstated, it was nonetheless a major watershed that is central to understanding the decade. it contributed to the economic boom that made the prosperity of the twenties possible, and also promoted significant population movement—especially the rural-to-urban migration of African Americans, Mexicans, and native whites—thus underscoring the ethnic and racial heterogeneity of the society. Many contemporaries were also convinced that the war, by giving women opportunities in formerly male jobs, had created the liberated woman. Other popular views held that war undermined religious faith and set in motion the secular trends that many observers noted in the 1920s. Although both of these perceptions greatly overstated the impact of the war, nonetheless they point to the way in which the public viewed the war as undermining traditional values, religious faith, and sexual mores.

Indeed, "since the war" emerged as a persistent refrain that people invoked to describe a wide range of changes in daily life and cultural values. Everything from rising divorce rates, "flaming youth," African American militancy, increased standardization and regimentation, and the vogue for fads like crossword puzzles was chalked up to the war. Most commonly, Americans used it to try to pin down a troubling change in mood. From the pages of *Presbyterian Magazine* came the announcement: "The world has been convulsed . . . and every field of thought and action has been disturbed. . . . The most settled principles and laws of society . . . have been attacked." In the popular journal *World's Work,* one author announced that "the World War has accentuated all our differences. It has not created those differences, but it has revealed and emphasized them." The war, in short, became a key metaphor for major changes transforming modern civilization: a marker that helped to explain and thus make more manageable the emergence of a modern society.

A watershed of a different kind was reflected in the U.S. Census Bureau's findings that marked 1920 as the turning point of the country's urbanization: fully one-half of America's 105 million people now lived in cities. To some extent, this was a dubious statistic, since the Census Bureau used a population of 2,500 people as the cutoff for "urban," not a very meaningful measure of urbanization. But the census data formed part of the contemporary assessment of the growth and influence of cities. Observers in the 1920s had a sense—at times oversimplified—that they were witnessing an urban/rural conflict, a battle between the forces of change and the forces of reaction. Prohibition, the Ku Klux Klan, and immigration restriction were just the most well-known manifestations of this tension, and signified native white Protestants' anxious concern that the cities and the culture itself risked being dominated by immigrants and African Americans. For their part, more than ever before, African Americans and other minorities were challenging the status quo, and were demanding a pluralistic vision of American identity that would accord them cultural influence and political power.

In addition to pluralism, the cities also embodied the power of large corporations, their economic influence, and the continued transformation of work. The metropolis was also the home of mass culture—of popular magazines, newspaper syndications, advertising, and the movies. Leisure and consumption provided some of the most visible, modern changes of the 1920s. An urban, cosmopolitan culture, shaped by its pluralism and the agencies of mass culture, spread to the hinterlands and helped to promote new social values. Technology and mass production resulted in a flood of consumer products. Automobiles, electric irons, refrigerators, and radios, a fraction of the goods available to increasingly more Americans, helped to transform daily life dramatically.

The new values and new products signaled the clear emergence of a consumer culture characterized by an emphasis on leisure, purchasing, sociability, expressiveness, and personal pleasure. Changing sexual morality, modified ideas about success and how to achieve it, and mounting secularism merged with the values of consumerism to form a major challenge to the Victorian ethos of restraint, frugality, and order. All of these changes were contested, as some Americans embraced the freedom implied in the new social order while others bemoaned the corruption of the old culture. And for many, both sentiments played a part. As Lawrence W. Levine has suggested, Americans in the twenties harbored feelings of both "progress and nostalgia." . . .

It is hard not to picture the crash as a fault line running between the prosperity of the New Era and the economic collapse that characterized the 1930s. Following a period of humdrum and conservative politics that had dampened the reform spirit, the thirties were enlivened by the energetic administration of Franklin D. Roosevelt. His New Deal programs of extensive federal social services and increased regulation of the economy seemed the fruition of much of what progressive reformers had envisioned. The ebbing of the conservative tide was also evident in a changing climate for labor. After the reversals of the 1920s, the 1930s witnessed militant strikes, a burgeoning labor movement, and unprecedented recognition of the rights of labor unions by the federal government. This labor militancy was part of what encouraged many intellectuals once again to be optimistic about social change and political activism. Also inspired by what they viewed as the remarkable progress of the Soviet Union, many writers and artists, while not abandoning the potent theme of the alienated individual in modern society, became much more concerned with issues of social conscience and class conflict. The wave of interest in documentaries further spoke to a new tone of social realism and seriousness that made Fitzgerald's flappers seem frivolous.

The tone of the two decades suggests a sharp dissonance. Bathtub gin gave way to breadlines. The image of the ticker-tape welcome for aviator hero Charles A. Lindbergh was superseded by representations of a new American icon: the haunting portraits of forgotten men and women like the famous "Migrant Mother" that the photographer Dorothea Lange captured. The "era of wonderful nonsense," as one popular historian called the 1920s, seemed to many to give way, almost inevitably, to retribution for the decade's sins of excess: the grim and harsh Great Depression.

. . . [T]his view of the roaring twenties is in many ways a false one that obscures the considerable tensions surrounding social and cultural change that permeated the period. It distorts the lives of most ordinary Americans and in particular negates the experiences of poor people, of African Americans and ethnic minorities. The image perpetuates a notion of extremes, contrasting the "decadence" of the twenties with the despair of the next ten years. Although the differences between the decades are indeed striking, there are strong continuities as well that defy convenient periodization.

To a great extent, the sources of the Depression are to be found in specific economic developments of the preceding period. In addition, the international nature of the Depression brings into sharp relief the interdependence of the world economy and is a compelling example of the developments that had for many decades been transforming economic life in the United States. Corporations and other large bureaucratic structures had been integrating the nation into a web of interdependence, bringing about a decline in local and individual autonomy, and an environment in which remote decisions and events could have far-reaching, rippling effects. In this context, the Great Depression represents not a break from the past, but rather an almost logical consequence of the organization and complexity of a modern economy.

In the 1920s, as Americans grappled with the implications of this more "organized" society, social tensions emerged that reflected a nostalgia for rugged individualism, for a harmonious society undisturbed by class tensions or ethnic diversity. As we have seen, the nativism of the decade stemmed in part from the search for scapegoats to explain disruptive forces that were unseating traditional forms of community. Although nativism in the 1930s was not as virulent as in the preceding period, it nonetheless persisted, with Father Coughlin, the demagogic "radio priest," the most notable exemplar. Using a rhetoric laced with an appeal to tradition and community, Coughlin repeatedly invoked the disappearance of the small merchant who had been swamped by the octopus of giant corporations and chain stores, a problem intensified with the economic collapse. In offering his explanation for the Depression, Coughlin emphasized a stereotype made familiar by the *Dearborn Independent*—the villainous international Jewish banker—and helped to keep alive a popular anti-Semitism that was also evident in the refusal by Congress to modify the National Origins Act to permit the entry of Jewish refugees from Hitler's Germany. Hostility to Mexican immigrants deepened in the 1930s as well.

Fears of competition in a scarce job market, anxiety about the radicalism of foreign workers, and a desire to keep welfare rolls down led to the large-scale deportation of immigrants and sometimes citizens back to Mexico with little attention to the niceties of legal procedures or civil rights. Discrimination against African Americans constituted another continuity with the 1920s. Lowest on the economic totem pole, they experienced devastating poverty in both the South and the North during the Depression. Although New Deal programs helped many African Americans weather some of the hardships of the period, the New Deal's emphasis on reform did not encompass a drive to topple the country's racial caste system.

The efforts of minorities to stake their claims to recognition and power that were so evident in the 1920s also persisted in the next decade. As the Democratic Party's identification with urban liberalism and social reform sharpened, European ethnic voters became extremely important to the New Deal coalition. Although African Americans were not yet important players in the party, the 1930s marked the shift of black voters from the Republicans to the Democrats, a development that had long-range implications for black political influence. The recognition of the country's pluralism was also evident in the changing face of organized labor. In contrast to the restrictive policies of the American Federation of Labor, the fledgling Congress of Industrial Organizations, founded in 1935, acknowledged the necessity of organizing a diverse workforce. In tackling the mass production industries, it incorporated ethnic workers, African Americans, and women into its organization drives. Particularly for European ethnics, the more inclusive stance of organized labor, as well as the changed constituency of the Democratic Party, helped diminish their sense of marginality and legitimate their claims to equal citizenship.

The presence of women in the Congress of Industrial Organizations, even though their numbers were limited, points to another continuation with the 1920s. Women's participation in the workforce continued to climb, despite intense public hostility to working women that had been exacerbated by the economic crisis and the fear that working women robbed men of employment. Women were also active participants in the New Deal, finding new opportunities in an expanding federal bureaucracy and helping to shape the New Deal's social welfare policy. In the final analysis, although we can chart women's "progress," including the increased use and availability of birth control, changes were still, as they had been in the 1920s, within narrow limits. Discrimination and the ideology about women's roles that underwrote it continued unabated.

Women's involvement in the New Deal underlines the return in politics to a social reform agenda, at first glance a sharp contrast with the 1920s. The federal government expanded in unprecedented ways. New regulatory agencies such as the Federal Deposit Insurance Corporation indicated a federal government more involved in the economy to protect the interests of ordinary Americans. Legislation like the 1935 Social Security Act signaled the beginnings of a modest welfare state that acknowledged federal responsibility for the well-being of its citizens. Despite these innovations, the New Deal was powerfully affected by New Era themes. Ideas about individualism and local democracy, as well as hostility to federal bureaucracy and power, remained very potent. The legacy of the Red Scare also ran deep and encouraged the association of government activism with foreign radicalism. Traditional ideology, thus buttressed, was a powerful influence that helped to keep the New Deal constrained and to maintain the structure of corporate power.

The New Deal also embodied the continued development of the interest group politics that so clearly characterized the 1920s. Lobbying groups proved extremely influential in shaping legislation. Moreover, the legitimacy that New Deal legislation accorded to organized labor and to the representatives of the farming sector led to the emergence of "big labor" and "big agriculture" as important players in shaping public policy. The Depression thus helped to cement the role of the federal government as a broker state mediating between contending interests.

Another political innovation that marked the 1930s was the extensive use of the radio to reach citizens and potential voters. Roosevelt proved a master at it as he used his homey "fireside chats" to explain his programs and drum up support for the New Deal. Father Coughlin's impassioned radio addresses brought in even more mail than the President's and made him one of the most prominent men in the country. The radio thus became a powerful new tool that highlighted the political implications of mass culture. Just as radio illustrated the power of the media, advertising, movies, and commercial sports continued, as they had in the 1920s, to play a central role in entertaining Americans, while at the same time serving to articulate and shape their values.

These continuities between the 1920s and the 1930s serve as signposts for key developments in twentieth-century America. The[se] themes . . . —the implications for personal and community autonomy in an increasingly organized and corporate-dominated society; the importance of interest group politics for shaping public policy; the tensions implicit in racial and ethnic pluralism; the social and cultural meanings of changing roles for women; the significance of mass media in helping to construct a consumer culture; the way in which the search for meaning in the modern world engaged religious leaders and intellectuals—emerged sharply in the 1920s. These issues not only set the tone for the decade but also formed central motifs that have shaped the modern American temper.

American Liberalism and the Struggle for Justice Between the Wars

ALAN DAWLEY

When it came time to celebrate the semicentennial of the Statue of Liberty on October 28, 1936, President Roosevelt was nearing the end of his first reelection campaign. Not one to pass up a chance for political advantage, he boated out to Liberty Island to rededicate the country's most hallowed public monument. Speaking over a nationwide radio hookup, he quoted President Cleveland's original dedication speech to say that the nation needed to renew its covenant with liberty, especially now after so many new immigrants had entered the country. Welcoming the huddled masses to the "place of the second chance," he boasted that the multitude of Old World cultures had finally found "their common destiny in America."

Roosevelt's theme that day was as old as the republic. Like his ceremonial counterpart fifty years earlier, he looked to history for the common values that would unite a divided people. There was no doubt about the division. Even as he spoke, one-third of the nation still suffered the worst effects of the Great Depression, ethnic groups warily eyed one another, and labor and farmer movements demanded radical action against the rich. Seeking a way through these troubled times, Roosevelt called upon the tradition of Jefferson and Lincoln to give the current generation a sense of common destiny.

The great irony of renewing the covenant with liberty in the 1930s was that Roosevelt's New Deal had done more to change the liberal tradition than anything since the Revolution. Whether one looked at managerial institutions such as the National Recovery Administration or social reforms such as the Social Security system, it was clear that a new liberalism had come into being. Extensive government regulation of the market and the coming of the welfare state marked a permanent turn away from laissez faire.

Although it is impossible to speak about the "causes" of this transformation with anything like scientific precision, it is possible to say something about the central dynamics of American life. In one aspect, the dynamics arose out of internal contradictions among opposing social forces, and, in another, out of the imbalance between the changing life of the society and the existing form of the state. In either case, the growing incongruity between the way Americans lived and the way they were governed forced them into a reckoning with their traditional forms of liberty.

Tracing the matter to its roots, one is drawn deep into the subsoil of the material environment. From the relentless pace of Henry Ford's assembly line to the hustle and bustle of Montgomery Ward's home office, Americans were busy inventing new techniques of mass production and mass distribution and new forms of bureaucratic organization to manage them. Flocking to the roller-coaster thrills of Coney Island and the bewitching images of the silver screen, they also pioneered the development of mass culture. Indeed, they were changing the very way they handed down their way of life across the generations—that is, changing the way they *reproduced* in a social sense—as they patronized public schools, mass entertainments, and big city hospitals.

The fact that Americans increasingly worked and lived en masse did not make America a mass society of interchangeable individuals. To the contrary, the chasm of class and culture that separated the college-educated executive at a firm such as Armour & Company from the immigrant packinghouse workers of Upton Sinclair's *The Jungle* guaranteed that modern society would be divided against itself. As America rushed headlong through the second Industrial Revolution and as family capitalism gave way to corporate capitalism, the rift between corporate elites and working classes spread into every crevice of social life. With the social weight of industrial workers mounting to its all-time peak, it is not surprising that industrial conflict climaxed in 1919–1920 with the largest strike wave in all of American history. It is not too much to say that the tension between corporate elite and laboring mass was the main dynamic of social change in this period.

That is not to say it was the only one. The fact that every aspect of the society was changing at once was a measure of the depth of social transformation. Something as basic as the relation between the sexes was put on a new footing as increasing numbers of men and women threw over the ways of their Victorian forebears. Breaking free from her gilded cage, the New Woman claimed sexual equality as a human right against the more conventional assertion of women's special virtue and peculiar needs. As the middle-class family collapsed toward its nuclear core and as women increasingly entered the job market and public life, the old doctrine of separate spheres increasingly became an anachronism.

Another set of tensions swirled around the question of American identity. Passions ran high in bitter clashes between Protestant and Catholic, Anglo-Saxon and Jew, white supremacist and Negro nationalist, and a good deal of argument went to decide the best basis for a common national identity. The larger significance of this debate lay in its relation to the high-stakes game of wealth, power, and prestige. The fact that corporate elites were largely college-educated Yankee Protestants whereas the mass of urban wage earners were culturally diverse and poorly educated meant that the relative strength of the various groups hung in the balance around the outcome of political battles such as those over immigration restriction and Prohibition.

If the leading public issues of the day arose from the cockpits of social conflict, then the place to look for an explanation for the rise of the new liberalism is in the impact of contending social forces upon the governing system. For the more American society changed the more it outgrew the existing form of the liberal state. The old governing system—that is, legislatures and courts devoted to laissez faire, buttressed by Victorian forms of gender, and imbued with Social Darwinist myths of race—lost its capacity to govern.

The first inkling that a great transformation was in store came in the Progressive Era when social reformers first laid siege to laissez faire. According to the conventional wisdom, any meddling with the market to equalize social conditions inevitably curbed individual liberty. In other words, there was a choice between liberty and equality.

If so, progressive reformers were ready to restrain individual liberty for the good of society. In the springtime of the twentieth century, it was still possible to be full of optimism about human progress, and they mounted crusades for a new social conscience that made inroads on laissez faire upon which there was no turning back. When social consciousness revived in the 1930s, New Deal reformers only had to pick up where progressives had left off.

Not to be overlooked in the accounting, U.S. entrance onto the world stage laid heavy strains on the existing governing system. Even more than the acquisition of an overseas empire, the exigencies of the First World War proved that the old state structures were simply not up to the task of mobilizing, regulating, and propagandizing the civilian population. The Wilson administration's new battery of hastily improvised wartime administrations resembled the kind of corporatist institutions emerging in Europe in that they gave representation to broad interest groups—business, labor, the public—instead of to elected parliamentary representatives. Although the war ended before these exotic hothouse plants could develop into permanent state bureaucracies, they set an example that would be imitated in the response to depression in the 1930s.

The inadequacy of old-fashioned liberalism was also revealed in the aftermath of the war. Repelled by the unsettling turns of events in Versailles and Russia, the United States abandoned the spirit of crusading liberalism that had served it so well in the Spanish-American War and in the mobilization to "make the world safe for democracy." But Europe proved to be off-limits to the empire of liberty. Wilson's high hopes for a liberal world order as embodied in the Fourteen Points ran aground on the imperial ambitions of America's allies and were dealt another blow by the Bolshevik Revolution. Recoiling from the sticky entanglements of European power politics, crusading liberalism turned inward upon itself in the Red Scare and collapsed in a heap of isolationist reaction.

At home, the fact that liberal restoration could come only through repression showed a similar failing. In response to social tumult many progressives joined old-fashioned liberals to show their teeth in violent suppression of strikes and scandalous violations of the Bill of Rights. Frightened by the prospect of sexual emancipation, they set out to restore Victorian virtue through the discipline of Prohibition and the abolition of prostitution. Determined to restore the waning privileges of Anglo-Saxon Protestants, they closed the gates on Catholic and Jewish immigrants. If all this amounted to the revenge of nineteenth-century liberalism upon the twentieth century, the resort to vigilantism and state coercions only showed how far the old-time liberalism was out of step with the mass of the population. Thus in both foreign and domestic affairs, the country had not yet found the formula to restore the balance between the state and modern society.

By the time the Great Depression came along, the Gilded Age republic had become a hollow shell. So when political experiments resumed under the emergency conditions of economic collapse, Presidents Hoover and Roosevelt had no choice but to change the form of the state if they wished to regain consent of the governed to the governing system.

Even before the Depression, Hoover had begun to draw government into the affairs of the marketplace, and his pace only quickened in the face of economic calamity. Although he did not move nearly fast or far enough, he set the stage for many of the reforms enacted by his successor. Contrary to much worshipful mythology, Roosevelt began by following in his predecessor's managerial footsteps, and only when government-assisted corporate planning failed to end the Depression did he embark on new experiments of his own. Wedded to no particular philosophy, he supported the Wagner Act and Social Security, which, along with numerous other innovations, curbed private property and gave birth to a welfare state.

In terms of consequences, one must not expect mathematical exactitude, either. Much of what happened after the 1930s was not readily traceable to the New Deal or the New Era, and other influences would leave their mark on the years to come. Certainly, the Second World War had a major impact, as did such far-off events as the revolutions in China and Vietnam. Yet it is possible to say that the changes of the 1930s laid the foundation for a hegemonic system that lasted through the next four decades.

The New Deal reformed capitalism in ways that preserved both liberalism and capitalism. Never before had the federal government imposed so many restraints on the individual and so many curbs on private property; never again would the state absent itself from the market. State capitalism and the welfare state were here to say. Yet somehow these changes were carried out in the name of preserving individual opportunity, and New Dealers stole the liberal banner from free-market conservatives.

Because the New Deal struck just the right political chord, its immense popularity went a long way toward replenishing the legitimacy that was slowly hemorrhaging away during the Depression. Out of the conflict of the depression-wracked 1930s came a new consensus.

In evaluating that achievement, there is something to be said for humanizing a system that, left to its own devices, invariably put profits ahead of people. The social-democratic reforms of liberalism undoubtedly improved the conditions of life for the majority of the working population, provided a certain dignity in retirement, and, for the first time, introduced a modicum of liberty inside the factory gate. Whereas crusading liberals at the time of the Red Scare had seen socialism as their mortal enemy, the new liberals of the "Red Decade" were willing to use watered-down socialist ideas against the would-be tyranny of archconservative industrialists. It may have been the case that the best in liberal values could no longer be realized within a capitalist society; even so, a more humane capitalism was better than a less humane one.

If there was any doubt on that score, one had only to look at Germany. Certainly, a capitalism that honored liberal values was more benign than one that drew the fascist gun. Although the United States was not entirely free of the ugliness that characterized Germany's response to depression, it successfully resisted the strong pull of racial nationalism, masculine swagger, militarist expansion, and authoritarianism. Although the U.S. response to the rise of fascism can be faulted on many counts, including its head-in-the-sand diplomacy in the face of fascist aggression and its cold shoulder to many ordinary victims of Nazi persecution, the fact remains that America did not succumb to its own worst impulses.

But neither did it yield to its best impulses. The new liberalism incorporated privileges of gender and race that mocked the ideal of equality. With feminism at its lowest ebb since the turn of the century, the New Deal simply ducked the issue of equality between the sexes. Indeed, in excluding many of the poorest wage earners—often female—from state protection and in seeking to shore up the consumer family, it displaced many of the burdens of inequality onto women. With respect to race relations, although New Deal social programs won support from the black community, the New Deal never confronted "the American dilemma" head on. As a consequence, the unanswered questions of sex and race were left to become the burning issues of the 1960s.

For that matter, the New Deal's reform of liberty was never intended to usher in the reign of equality. Roosevelt was determined at all times to save the capitalist system, even if that meant saving it from the capitalists themselves. He certainly stopped far short of emancipating the working class for anything like full participation in social decision making. In truth, the aim was never to realize social equality but rather to promote social security.

That intent was summed up by Roosevelt himself in a revealing parable. Borrowing from Abraham Lincoln, the all-time master of the political parable, Roosevelt told the story of the shepherd (FDR) and the wolf (conservative businessmen of the Liberty League): "The shepherd drives the wolf from the sheep's throat, for which the sheep thanks the shepherd as his liberator, while the wolf denounces him for the same act, as the destroyer of liberty." The parable speaks volumes about

Roosevelt's conception of the federal government as the protector of a nation of sheep.

The new governing system that emerged by the eve of the Second World War was something more than the social programs associated with New Deal liberalism. Although it included safeguards and securities for the weak, it also incorporated protections for the strong. Whatever one may choose to call it—corporate liberalism, liberal capitalism, or interest-group liberalism—the fact was that the new system was more congruent with corporate dominance and the contending forces within American society than was the old.

The main proof of that fact lies in the longevity of the settlement. Having experimented for several decades with a variety of half-way solutions, the country settled down to live within the limits of the new hegemony for almost a half century. Although the 1960s witnessed profound challenges to the New Deal's acceptance of racial segregation and women's subordination, the rest of the system was simply taken for granted. While successive Democratic administrations from Truman's Fair Deal to Johnson's Great Society added new wings to the house the New Deal built, even Republican presidents from Eisenhower to Nixon and Ford were content to dwell within it. Indeed, the system built around state capitalism and the welfare state was so solid, even Ronald Reagan could not knock down the whole thing.

Today, in the waning years of the twentieth century, we are as far away in time from the 1930s as the New Deal was from the Gilded Age. In the interim, the relentless evolution of American society has radically altered material conditions to create computers, nuclear weapons, and other forms of hypertechnology unknown to previous generations. Great changes in production and reproduction have taken place, including a massive restructuring of the global economy, a tidal wave of women workers, and the growth of megalopolis. Their effect has been as significant as those of changes in the previous era.

The difference is that instead of going along with American ascendancy, they accompany American decline. Formerly the unchallenged colossus of world capitalism, the United States has shrunk relative to Japan and Germany. Once the world's leading creditor and prime exporter of industrial goods, it has become the world's largest debtor and a declining industrial power. Given the collapse of communism in Eastern Europe and the end of the Cold War, it has lost influence in what used to be called the "free world." With amazing speed, the "American Century" has come and gone, a casualty of deindustrialization, defeat in Vietnam, and the rise of Western Europe and Eastern Asia.

At home, the system built in response to the Great Depression has started to fall apart. New Deal policies that once stabilized the distribution of income gave way to policies under President Reagan that widened the gap between rich and poor. The removal of state regulations in the 1980s precipitated an orgy of speculation and the biggest rash of business failures since the 1930s. Even the core institutions of state capitalism became overburdened as a result of the crisis in banks and savings institutions. The loss of American hegemony in world affairs has been paralleled at home by the declining hegemony of the modern governing system.

Given these sharp discontinuities with the past, is there anything the earlier period has to say to the late twentieth century? Maybe not. Maybe the rusting factories and worn-out social programs from the era of industrial capitalism are just things of the past, and the long reckoning with liberty is merely a story to tell our grandchildren.

And yet, surely there is something worth remembering in the way the Depression generation accepted its rendezvous with destiny and in the fact that common people played no lesser role in this than elites.

It still may be that the only lessons are negative ones. The twentieth century has become understandably engulfed in pessimism. After the cataclysmic events of the modern era, it was no longer possible to believe with all one's heart in the kind of limitless optimism about human progress that prevailed at the dawn of the century. American innocence has died many deaths, but none so convincing as those of the two world wars and the Great Depression.

And yet, why should that mean there was no progress at all? If one asks whether four decades of struggle humanized the harshest aspects of the competitive market, reaffirmed liberty against authoritarianism, and advanced the social goals of a truly human community—in short, if one asks whether there was social progress, then, surely, the answer ought to be yes.

And what of the future? In the age of the "uncertainty principle," not even hard science is confident about prediction, so the Queen of the Humanities had best leave prediction to fortune tellers. Yet the inescapable fact is that understanding the past inevitably changes the future. People gain identity and purpose through individual and collective memory. They feel empowered by a sense of mission or destiny and may gain a certain power to shape a more rational future by understanding the logic of cause and effect. It may be impossible to predict the future, but it is equally certain that consciousness of the past affects the way people will shape it. They may not be able to shape it just as they please, but they can certainly judge for themselves what will make things better or worse and act accordingly.

SUGGESTED READING

Cohen, Wilbur J., ed. *The New Deal: Fifty Years Later: A Historical Assessment* (1984).
Dawley, Alan. *Struggles for Justice: Social Responsibility and the Liberal State* (1991).
Dumenil, Lynn. *The Modern Temper: American Culture and Society in the 1920s* (1995).
Eisenach, Eldon. *The Lost Promise of Progressivism* (1994).
Fearon, Peter. *War, Prosperity, and Depression: The U.S. Economy, 1917–45* (1987).
Fink, Leon. *Progressive Intellectuals and the Dilemmas of Democratic Commitment* (1997).
Fraser, Steve, and Gary Gerstle, eds. *The Rise and Fall of the New Deal Order* (1989).
Hawley, Ellis. *The Great War and the Search for a Modern Order, 1917–1933.* 2d ed. (1992).
Karl, Barry. *The Uneasy State: The United States from 1915–1945* (1983).
Leuchtenberg, William. *The Perils of Prosperity, 1914–1932.* 2d ed. (1993).
Levine, Lawrence. "American Culture and the Great Depression." *Yale Review* 74 (January 1985): 196–223.
Livingston, James. *Pragmatism and the Political Economy of Cultural Revolution, 1850–1940* (1994).
Marquis, Alice. *Hopes and Ashes: The Birth of Modern Times, 1929–1939* (1986).
Painter, Nell. *Standing at Armageddon: The United States, 1877–1919* (1987).
Parrish, Michael. *Anxious Decades: America in Prosperity and Depression, 1920–1941* (1992).
Perret, Geoffrey. *America in the Twenties: A History* (1982).
Potter, Jim. *The American Economy Between the World Wars* (1985).
Schaffer, Ronald. *America in the Great War: The Rise of the War Welfare State* (1991).
Sitkoff, Harvard, ed. *Fifty Years Later: The New Deal Evaluated* (1985).
Weinstein, James. *The Corporate Ideal in the Liberal State: 1900–1918* (1968).

CHAPTER 2

Reform and Reaction:
Public Policy in the Republican Era

✊

Historians have viewed the public policy of the 1920s from a number of angles. For some, the politics of the 1920s are best captured by Calvin Coolidge's dour observation that "the business of America is business." In this view, the Republican decade is marked by the corruption of the Harding Administration (particularly the infamous "Teapot Dome" oil lease scandal) and by the laissez-faire policies pursued by Presidents Coolidge and Hoover. For some, the Republican era is best understood against the backdrop of the New Deal. In this respect, scholarly admirers of the New Deal usually focus on what the respective Republican Administrations did to cause (or hasten) the Great Depression, and on what they failed to do in response to the Depression (and in contrast to the New Deal). Increasingly, however, scholars have looked to the 1920s for the intellectual and political origins of the New Deal—finding in Republican labor, welfare, and economic policies important precedents for the landmark reforms of the 1930s. And for some, the 1920s is marked by the persistence of the Progressive effort to balance public and private interests. In this view, Republican policies share the central dilemma of the Progressive Era, which acknowledged many of the problems of modern urban and industrial society but hoped that private or local solutions would be enough.

In all, the Republican era is suspended uneasily between two great reform movements: the Progressive Era (circa 1900–1916) and the New Deal (circa 1933–1945). Some Republican policies stand in stark contrast to these movements; some mark important political and ideological connections between the two. This is apparent, in different ways, in the trajectory of economic policy and social provision. Herbert Hoover personified Republican economic policy, serving Harding and Coolidge as Secretary of Commerce and assuming the Presidency himself in 1928. Tellingly, various historians have pegged Hoover as a "forgotten Progressive" and early New Dealer for his innovations as Secretary of Commerce; blasted his meager response to the Great Depression; and celebrated his Administration as the last gasp of the American ideals of individualism and limited government. In social policy, Republican Administrations merely responded, in a piecemeal fashion, to the programmatic efforts of local and national activists. While national social policy in the 1920s would pale beside the frantic innovations of the New Deal, the persistence of reform would serve as a reminder that public policy could both percolate up from popular demands and trickle down from the ideology of national leaders.

D O C U M E N T S

In some respects, the Republican era began as a backlash against the "starry-eyed" liberalism of the Progressive Era and the war. This is captured in Document 1, in which Attorney General Mitchell Palmer suggests the anxieties of the postwar "Red Scare"; and in Document 2, in which then-Secretary of Commerce Hoover lays out the basic philosophy of Republican individualism. Document 3 suggests some of the dilemmas of economic policy: while Republicans trumpeted voluntary cooperation and minimal federal regulation, many saw trade associations and other forms of private organization as futile. In Document 4, Sinclair Lewis uses a speech by George Babbitt (the protagonist of his 1922 novel *Babbitt*) to caricature the business ethic of the 1920s. Importantly, the Republican 1920s also marked the first postsuffrage decade and featured an ongoing debate over the terms and fruits of women's political participation. In Document 5, a leading "suffragette" urges newly enfranchised women to avoid the established political parties. In Document 6, two feminists continue an ongoing debate over "difference" and "equality," over the importance of balancing formal legal equality against legislated protections for women and mothers. Document 7, excerpting a woman's letter to the federal Children's Bureau, suggests how ordinary women looked to public institutions for support.

1. Attorney General Palmer's Case Against the "Reds," 1920

In this brief review of the work which the Department of Justice has undertaken, to tear out the radical seeds that have entangled American ideas in their poisonous theories, I desire not merely to explain what the real menace of communism is, but also to tell how we have been compelled to clean up the country almost unaided by any virile legislation. . . .

Like a prairie-fire, the blaze of revolution was sweeping over every American institution of law and order a year ago. It was eating its way into the homes of the American workman, its sharp tongues of revolutionary heat were licking the altars of the churches, leaping into the belfry of the school bell, crawling into the sacred corners of American homes, seeking to replace marriage vows with libertine laws, burning up the foundations of society. . . .

Upon these two basic certainties, first that the "Reds" were criminal aliens, and secondly that the American Government must prevent crime, it was decided that there could be no nice distinctions drawn between the theoretical ideals of the radicals and their actual violations of our national laws. An assassin may have brilliant intellectuality, he may be able to excuse his murder or robbery with fine oratory, but any theory which excuses crime is not wanted in America. This is no place for the criminal to flourish, nor will he do so, so long as the rights of common citizenship can be exerted to prevent him. . . .

From *The Forum* 63 (February 1920): 173–176, 181–182.

It has always been plain to me that when American citizens unite upon any national issue, they are generally right, but it is sometimes difficult to make the issue clear to them. If the Department of Justice could succeed in attracting the attention of our optimistic citizens to the issue of internal revolution in this country, we felt sure there would be no revolution. The Government was in jeopardy. . . .

My information showed that communism in this country was an organization of thousands of aliens, who were direct allies of Trotzky. Aliens of the same misshapen caste of mind and indecencies of character, and it showed that they were making the same glittering promises of lawlessness, of criminal autocracy to Americans, that they had made to the Russian peasants. How the Department of Justice discovered upwards of 60,000 of these organized agitators of the Trotzky doctrine in the United States, is the confidential information upon which the Government is now sweeping the nation clean of such alien filth. . . .

Behind, and underneath, my own determination to drive from our midst the agents of Bolshevism with increasing vigor and with greater speed, until there are no more of them left among us, so long as I have the responsible duty of that task, I have discovered the hysterical methods of these revolutionary humans with increasing amazement and suspicion. In the confused information that sometimes reaches the people, they are compelled to ask questions which involve the reasons for my acts against the "Reds." I have been asked, for instance, to what extent deportation will check radicalism in this country. Why not ask what will become of the United States Government if these alien radicals are permitted to carry out the principles of the Communist Party as embodied in its so-called laws, aims and regulations?

There wouldn't be any such thing left. In place of the United States Government we should have the horror and terrorism of bolsheviki tyranny such as is destroying Russia now. Every scrap of radical literature demands the overthrow of our existing government. All of it demands obedience to the instincts of criminal minds, that is, to the lower appetites, material and moral. The whole purpose of communism appears to be a mass formation of the criminals of the world to overthrow the decencies of private life, to usurp property that they have not earned, to disrupt the present order of life regardless of health, sex or religious rights. By a literature that promises the wildest dreams of such low aspirations, that can occur to only the criminal minds, communism distorts our social law.

2. Herbert Hoover on American Individualism, 1922

Five or six great social philosophies are at struggle in the world for ascendency. There is the Individualism of America. There is the Individualism of the more democratic states of Europe with its careful reservations of castes and classes. There are Communism, Socialism, Syndicalism, Capitalism, and finally there is Autocracy—whether by birth, by possessions, militarism, or divine right of kings. Even the Divine Right still lingers on although our lifetime has seen fully two-thirds of the earth's population, including Germany, Austria, Russia, and China, arrive at a state of angry disgust with this type of social motive power and throw it on the scrap heap.

From Herbert Hoover, *American Individualism* (New York: Doubleday, 1922), 4–9.

All these thoughts are in ferment today in every country in the world. They fluctuate in ascendency with times and places. They compromise with each other in daily reaction on governments and peoples. Some of these ideas are perhaps more adapted to one race than another. Some are false, some are true. What are we interested in is their challenge to the physical and spiritual forces of America.

The partisans of some of these other brands of social schemes challenge us to comparison; and some of their partisans even among our own people are increasing in their agitation that we adopt one or another or parts of their devices in place of our tried individualism. They insist that our social foundations are exhausted, that like feudalism and autocracy America's plan has served its purpose—that it must be abandoned. . . .

For myself, let me say at the very outset that my faith in the essential truth, strength, and vitality of the developing creed by which we have hitherto lived in this country of ours has been confirmed and deepened by the searching experiences of seven years of service in the backwash and misery of war. Seven years of contending with economic degeneration, with social disintegration, with incessant political dislocation, with all of its seething and ferment of individual and class conflict, could but impress me with the primary motivation of social forces, and the necessity for broader thought upon their great issues to humanity. And from it all I emerge an individualist—an unashamed individualist. But let me say also that I am an American individualist. For America has been steadily developing the ideals that constitute progressive individualism.

No doubt, individualism ran riot, with no tempering principle, would provide a long category of inequalities, of tyrannies, dominations, and injustices. America, however, has tempered the whole conception of individualism by the injection of a definite principle, and from this principle it follows that attempts at domination, whether in government or in the processes of industry and commerce, are under an insistent curb. If we would have the values of individualism, their stimulation to initiative, to the development of hand and intellect, to the high development of thought and spirituality, they must be tempered with that firm and fixed ideal of American individualism—*an equality of opportunity.* If we would have these values we must soften its hardness and stimulate progress through that sense of service that lies in our people.

3. A Business Analyst Explains Why Trade Associations Don't Work, 1933

The difficulties in the way of a trade agreement come both from the companies that are outside the combination and from those that are in. To control production, it is necessary to hold in line substantially all the producing units. Otherwise the restriction of output, with a presumed enhancement of price, will be taken advantage of by competitors who do not play the game. We need only recall the situation in the Kentucky tobacco fields. A large surplus had been carried over, and the cooperatives tried to reduce the amount of tobacco grown. Before long, night riders were going through the country, destroying the crops of neighbors who persisted in planting a larger acreage. Trade agreements among manufacturers and wholesalers have

---

From Edgar Heermance, *Can Business Govern Itself?* (New York: Harper & Brothers, 1933), 18–20, 54–55.

shown the same weakness. The only difference was that they could not employ the night-rider method, though some of the boycott cases under our anti-trust laws came pretty close to it.

Even if outside competition is negligible, the trade agreement tends to break down through treachery or suspicion. Competitors do not trust one another. Often it comes to be a race to see who can break it first. I have known of cases where a general curtailment was voted with enthusiasm by an industry's representatives. In the midst of the conference, a man would excuse himself for a moment; he would go to the telephone and wire his factory to start up full blast. There seems to be something in the nature of an agreement which tempts the weak-kneed competitor to break it, in order to reap an immediate advantage.

Looking at the matter from another angle, production agreements do nothing to reduce surplus capacity. If there are too many machines in the industry—and generally that is why they try to slow them down—a competitive situation develops which would make any agreement unworkable. Each company is too hungry for business.

There may be certain industries where voluntary combination might possibly be made to operate and be of general advantage, provided the monopoly, for that is what it would amount to, exercised enough self-restraint. The secret of success lies there. Much the same results would be obtained without any agreement, if all the competitors followed an intelligent business policy. I shall have more to say on that at a later point. Trade agreements are not a panacea for overproduction and ruinous price. Most of the demand for modification is an attempt to escape the consequences of poor business management. I have come to regard the Sherman Law as a protection to the ordinary business group. They are saved from abortive experiments that would only make matters worse. Common effort is forced into more fruitful lines of attack on the problem of overcapacity. One reason why the trade association movement in Great Britain is ten years behind ours is because they have no Sherman Law. . . .

. . . Probably three-quarters of . . . [trade associations] are of little practical service to their members. They have only meager funds to work with, and a cheap secretary, whose chief interest is in keeping up the membership so that he may draw his salary. The activities carried on in common are more or less of a farce. The convention is a big debauch, and in my observation the efficiency of such a body varies inversely with the amount of liquor that is in circulation when they meet. There is the same need as in other industries, perhaps an even greater need, for a strong service agency. But about all they receive for their dues is a more friendly feeling between competitors and some exchange of experience. The leaders have not sensed the possibilities in trade organization. The rank and file are not ready to pay the price.

4. "Babbitt" Sketches "Our Ideal Citizen," 1922

"Our Ideal Citizen—I picture him first and foremost as being busier than a bird-dog, not wasting a lot of good time in day-dreaming or going to sassiety teas or kicking about things that are none of his business, but putting the zip into some store or profession or art. At night he lights up a good cigar, and climbs into the

---

From Sinclair Lewis, *Babbitt* (Harcourt, Brace & World, 1922), 150, 152–155.

little old 'bus, and maybe cusses the carburetor, and shoots out home. He mows the lawn, or sneaks in some practice putting, and then he's ready for dinner. After dinner he tells the kiddies a story, or takes the family to the movies, or plays a few fists of bridge, or reads the evening paper, and a chapter or two of some good lively Western novel if he has a taste for literature, and maybe the folks next-door drop in and they sit and visit about their friends and the topics of the day. Then he goes happily to bed, his conscience clear, having contributed his mite to the prosperity of the city and to his own bank-account.

"In politics and religion this Sane Citizen is the canniest man on earth; and in the arts he invariably has a natural taste which makes him pick out the best, every time. In no country in the world will you find so many reproductions of the Old Masters and of well-known paintings on parlor walls as in these United States. No country has anything like our number of phonographs, with not only dance records and comic but also the best operas, such as Verdi, rendered by the world's highest-paid singers.

"In other countries, art and literature are left to a lot of shabby bums living in attics and feeding on booze and spaghetti, but in America the successful writer or picture-painter is indistinguishable from any other decent business man; and I, for one, am only too glad that the man who has the rare skill to season his message with interesting reading matter and who shows both purpose and pep in handling his literary wares has a chance to drag down his fifty thousand bucks a year, to mingle with the biggest executives on terms of perfect equality, and to show as big a house and as swell a car as any Captain of Industry! But, mind you, it's the appreciation of the Regular Guy who I have been depicting which has made this possible, and you got to hand as much credit to him as to the authors themselves. . . .

"Some time I hope folks will quit handing all the credit to a lot of moth-eaten, mildewed, out-of-date, old, European dumps, and give proper credit to the famous Zenith spirit, that clean fighting determination to win Success that has made the little old Zip City celebrated in every land and clime, wherever condensed milk and pasteboard cartons are known! Believe me, the world has fallen too long for these worn-out countries that aren't producing anything but bootblacks and scenery and booze, that haven't got one bathroom per hundred people, and that don't know a loose-leaf ledger from a slip-cover; and it's just about time for some Zenithite to get his back up and holler for a show-down!

"I tell you, Zenith and her sister-cities are producing a new type of civilization. There are many resemblances between Zenith and these other burgs, and I'm darn glad of it! The extraordinary, growing, and sane standardization of stores, offices, streets, hotels, clothes, and newspapers throughout the United States shows how strong and enduring a type is ours. . . .

"Yes, sir, these other burgs are our true partners in the great game of vital living. But let's not have any mistake about this. I claim that Zenith is the best partner and the fastest-growing partner of the whole caboodle. I trust I may be pardoned if I give a few statistics to back up my claims. If they are old stuff to any of you, yet the tidings of prosperity, like the good news of the Bible, never become tedious to the ears of a real hustler, no matter how oft the sweet story is told! Every intelligent person knows that Zenith manufactures more condensed milk and evaporated cream, more paper boxes, and more lighting-fixtures, than any other city in the

United States, if not in the world. But it is not so universally known that we also stand second in the manufacture of package-butter, sixth in the giant realm of motors and automobiles, and somewhere about third in cheese, leather findings, tar roofing, breakfast food, and overalls! . . .

"But the way of the righteous is not all roses. Before I close I must call your attention to a problem we have to face, this coming year. The worst menace to sound government is not the avowed socialists but a lot of cowards who work under cover—the long-haired gentry who call themselves 'liberals' and 'radicals' and 'non-partisan' and 'intelligentsia' and God only knows how many other trick names! Irresponsible teachers and professors constitute the worst of this whole gang, and I am ashamed to say that several of them are on the faculty of our great State University! The U. is my own Alma Mater, and I am proud to be known as an alumni, but there are certain instructors there who seem to think we ought to turn the conduct of the nation over to hoboes and roustabouts.

"Those profs are the snakes to be scotched—they and all their milk-and-water ilk! The American business man is generous to a fault, but one thing he does demand of all teachers and lecturers and journalists: if we're going to pay them our good money, they've got to help us by selling efficiency and whooping it up for rational prosperity! And when it comes to these blab-mouth, fault-finding, pessimistic, cynical University teachers, let me tell you that during this golden coming year it's just as much our duty to bring influence to have those cusses fired as it is to sell all the real estate and gather in all the good shekels we can.

"Not till that is done will our sons and daughters see that the ideal of American manhood and culture isn't a lot of cranks sitting around chewing the rag about their Rights and their Wrongs, but a God-fearing, hustling, successful, two-fisted Regular Guy, who belongs to some church with pep and piety to it, who belongs to the Boosters or the Rotarians or the Kiwanis, to the Elks or Moose or Red Men or Knights of Columbus or any one of a score of organizations of good, jolly, kidding, laughing, sweating, upstanding, lend-a-handing Royal Good Fellows, who plays hard and works hard, and whose answer to his critics is a square-toed boot that'll teach the grouches and smart alecks to respect the He-man and get out and root for Uncle Samuel, U.S.A.!"

5. Alva Belmont Urges Women Not to Vote, 1920

"Today men celebrate their political independence. Today I appeal to you women voters of the United States to rise and assert your political independence that future generations may celebrate our victory.

"Women voters, strong in numbers and potential power, you can be, if you will, a new force in modern civilization. Beware of political pitfalls. Don't let either of the two old parties use you as catspaws. Ignore their flattery. Be strong and self-respecting. Hand back to the wily leaders the empty honors offered bribing for your servitude. They are but crumbs from the bosses' table.

From "Mrs. Belmont Begs Women Not to Vote," *New York Times,* July 6, 1920, 15.

"After nineteen centuries of man's government the only way that they have found to settle international questions affecting the lives and happiness of the human race is by recognized international murder.

"After nineteen centuries of man's government the world is terribly in the grip of pestilence, poverty, hunger, discontent, corruption and tyranny.

"After nineteen centuries of man's government, with the opportunity for learning over this extended period, the only way they have found to settle domestic problems like the high cost of living is by regulating profiteering. By protecting and condoning the whole system of exploitation, which practically denies to the multitude the necessities of every day life. Does this indicate work for the betterment of the human race?

"I ask you women, are you going to be content to become servants of the two old parties in our country, to try to bolster up their system of corruption? Are you able to recognize fraud, deception, stupidity and dishonesty? If you are you will not be found allied with a system which is decayed.

"Put a high price on your freedom! Keep away from the Democratic and Republican Parties. You women have had nothing to do with selecting their candidates. You have had nothing to do with writing their platforms. You ought to have nothing to do with putting them in power. Your vote now means simply strengthening a power that is not with the human race, nor for its betterment, and does not represent its needs, but merely upholds the power of the boss system. Don't vote!

"By this refusal to consort with admitted evils, you will get new strength. You will cleanse your own power for good. You will be free to act at the right moment. Don't vote! Husband your new power!"

6. Florence Kelley and Elsie Hill Debate Equal Rights for Women, 1922

Yes!

The removal of all forms of the subjection of women is the purpose to which the National Woman's Party is dedicated. Its present campaign to remove the discriminations against women in the laws of the United States is but the beginning of its determined effort to secure the freedom of women, an integral part of the struggle for human liberty for which women are first of all responsible. Its interest lies in the final release of woman from the class of a dependent, subservient being to which early civilization committed her.

The laws of various States at present hold her in that class. They deny her a control of her children equal to the father's; they deny her, if married, the right to her own earnings; they punish her for offenses for which men go unpunished; they exclude her from public office and from public institutions to the support of which her taxes contribute. These laws are not the creation of this age, but the fact that they are still tolerated on our statute books and that in some States their removal is

From "Shall Women Be Equal Before the Law?" *The Nation* 114 (April 12, 1922): 421.

vigorously resisted shows the hold of old traditions upon us. Since the passage of the Suffrage Amendment the incongruity of these laws, dating back many centuries, has become more than ever marked. . . .

The National Woman's Party believes that it is a vital social need to do away with these discriminations against women and is devoting its energies to that end. The removal of the discriminations and not the method by which they are removed is the thing upon which the Woman's Party insists. It has under consideration an amendment to the Federal Constitution which, if adopted, would remove them at one stroke, but it is at present endeavoring to secure their removal in the individual States by a blanket bill, which is the most direct State method. . . .

> *Section 1.* Women shall have the same rights, privileges, and immunities under the law as men, with respect to the exercise of suffrage; holding of office or any position under the government, either State or local or for which government funds or subsidies are used, and with respect to remuneration for services in such office or position; eligibility to examination for any position affected by civil-service regulations; jury service; choice of domicile, residence, and name; acquiring, inheriting, controlling, holding, and conveying property; ownership and control of labor, services, and earnings within and without the home, and power to recover damages for loss of such labor, services, and earnings; freedom of contract, including becoming a party in any capacity to negotiable instruments or evidence of indebtedness, or becoming surety or guarantor; becoming parties litigant; acting as executors or administrators of estates of decedents; custody and control of children, and control of earnings and services of such children; grounds for divorce; immunities or penalties for sex offenses; quarantine, examination, and treatment of diseases; and in all other respects.
>
> *Section 2.* This article shall be construed as abrogating in every respect the common-law disabilities of women.
>
> *Section 3.* This act shall not affect laws regulating the employment of women in industry.
>
> *Section 4.* All acts and parts of acts in conflict with any of the provisions of this statute are hereby repealed. . . .

Elsie Hill

No!

Sex is a biological fact. The political rights of citizens are not properly dependent upon sex, but social and domestic relations and industrial activities are. All modern-minded people desire that women should have full political equality and like opportunity in business and the professions. No enlightened person desires that they should be excluded from jury duty or denied the equal guardianship of children, or that unjust inheritance laws or discriminations against wives should be perpetuated.

The inescapable facts are, however, that men do not bear children, are freed from the burdens of maternity, and are not susceptible, in the same measure as women, to poisons now increasingly characteristic of certain industries, and to the universal poison of fatigue. These are differences so far reaching, so fundamental, that it is grotesque to ignore them. Women cannot be made men by act of the legislature or by amendment of the Federal Constitution. This is no matter of today or tomorrow. The inherent differences are permanent. Women will always need many laws different from those needed by men.

The effort to enact the blanket bill in defiance of all biological differences recklessly imperils the special laws for women as such, for wives, for mothers, and for wage-earners. The safeguarding clause affords no adequate safeguard for these protective measures. . . .

Why should wage-earning women be thus forbidden to get laws for their own health and welfare and that of their unborn children? Why should they be made subject to the preferences of wage-earning men? Is not this of great and growing importance when the number of women wage-earners, already counted by millions, increases by leaps and bounds from one census to the next? And when the industries involving exposure to poisons are increasing faster than ever? And when the overwork of mothers is one recognized cause of the high infant death-rate? And when the rise in the mortality of mothers in childbirth continues?

If there were no other way of promoting more perfect equality for women, an argument could perhaps be sustained for taking these risks. But why take them when every desirable measure attainable through the blanket bill can be enacted in the ordinary way?

Is the National Woman's Party for or against protective measures for wage-earning women? Will it publicly state whether it is for or against the eight-hour day and minimum-wage commissions for women? Yes or No?

Florence Kelley

7. A Mother's Letter to the Children's Bureau, 1916

Mrs. H. B., Illinois (February 28, 1916)

Sirs:

After reading your editorial in the paper Daily News entitled Save the babies, I cant help but sit down and write you. I wonder how many of you Gentlemen have ever stopped to consider the cause of infants deaths and why most mothers do not nurse their babies.

5 years ago, 13 Nov, I gave birth to a baby boy. After having been obliged to go without food myself so my other 2 little girls could have enough to eat and not go hungry, then my baby was born. And there I was, no food for me, only what was given to me by kind neighbors. The 4th day after birth I had to get up of my sick [bed] and then [on the] tenth day [I] went out to look for work, obtained it, [and] went to work on the 11th day.

I nursed my baby mornings and night, at night time after working all day then nursing my child. Every drop it s[w]ollowed it would throw up. At the same [time] I [was] suffering the awful torture with my milk, pumping it and throwing it into the sink, while my *baby starved* and my husband *refused* to *provide* for us. At the end of

From Molly Ladd-Taylor, ed., *Raising a Baby the Government Way: Mothers' Letters to the Children's Bureau, 1915–1932* (New Brunswick, N.J.: Rutgers University Press, 1986), 148–152.

one month my milk had dried up. There [I] was without the fountain nature had provided me with to feed my child. After Christmas, the loss of my position [made me] now unable to buy food for the baby, I must starve and also see the rest of the children do the same. At the end of 3 months my chubby little fellow that weighed 11 lbs at birth now was just merely a skeleton. When the nurse from the welfare Ass. was sent to me [she] asked me to bring the baby to the conference which I did. I exsplained the case and they were kind enough to ask the united Charities to supply me with 1 Pt. of certified [milk]. And following the instructions and [this] help I have raised my boy. He will be 5 years old next Nov. This is only one reason why mothers cant nurse their babies.

Now. Sirs, I am to become a mother again this coming month, and just what I have endured I must go through again. No food for the ones I already have, and nothing to nourish the coming. Only *abuse* and *torture* at the hands of the man who *promised to provide and protect woman*. And *no law to enforce this promise.*

Now, your advice as to regards of clothing. God forbid the mother who wont properly cloth[e] her baby if she can afford it. Mine coming would be without any clothing if the United Charities did not furnish me with a baby layette. Thats is the reason for not [having] proper clothing: We mothers can't afford to buy cloths. Yet each one who sees us will say *why* do you have *children* for such a *man*. Dear Sirs we cant help ourselves. As the saying goes, any fool can have them but it takes a wise one to keep from it; and the law has given man that right. What can us mothers do? Nothing. Only suffer and suffer. With no hand outstretch[ed] to help us. . . . Dirt and dust, how many mothers as well as myself cant afford soap to help clean with? And then Prenatal care during Pregnancy. My god all that I have had to suffer and endure these eight months. No dog need suffer as I have.

I love my children and willing would have as many as possible but never before have I dreaded the ordeal of child birth, as I am afraid to look upon its little face. How can it be human and a perfect child after all that I have been through this last time? Each place I have asked for advice what to do, or for to compel my husband to work and provide for me and the children, the best I receive is, "why do you live with him and have children for such a man? You deserve no pity." Nice advice to poor mothers, who are nothing but fools for men but to bear their children for them, and then afterwards neglect them to go out to work for to buy their food.

God help the poor mothers of today. The cry is Save the babies, but what about the mothers who produce these babies? Now, Dear Sirs, No hard feelling for what I have written. But would it not be better to enact a law that, when a man marries a woman and she bears his children for him, that he be compelled to provide for the babies he caused to be brought into the world, and permit mothers to properly care for their babies, and give [a man] a life sentence for bringing home disease and inflicting his wife with it. And if possible start an association to protect mothers who are to give birth and after that help them to help themselves, and enable them to do for their babies. The Soldier receive his pension. What do mothers' receive? Abuse, torture, slurs, that is the best they receive. Men in long service receive their pension. Mothers deserving receiv[e] nothing.

Now I hope some evening to pick up a newspaper and be able to read that your department, that you will punish men so severely who neglect their wife and children that their will be less need of advice to *mothers*. Only I beg of you to do something to protect mothers in the pitfall I find myself in. When my baby is born, will I be able to feed it? Or will I be compelled again to leave my infant and work, for to buy for the other 3 as well as the new one—and have to pay some one else to look after the little one I love to put to my breast and let it grow and live? Or will it mean starvation again as before? The time is drawing near, but I would sooner go through the fires of H than the misery I have had to go through.

Now please excuse me for writing this to your dept. but I just could not help doing so. You may send me all the reading matter you have on prenatal care, and infant care. It may give me a little encouragement. So thanking you many times for reading this, and [I hope] that through your help all mothers the same as myself will get some consideration.

I also have a little girl 8 years old who is frail, and the school doctor tells her to eat fresh eggs and drink fresh milk and lots of it, but where am I to get it? I can see her going into decline right along, but what am I to do? Think it over gentlemen. Se[e] if you cant make men do a little different, and then there will be better babies, better mothers, better grown children, and a better country, and less human beings in the penaten[t]ierey.

I trust you will look at this in the right light and excuse for crying out my soul to you. Sincerely yours.

Please do not use my name in publication as the children would be jeered at by the neighbors children.

E S S A Y S

In the first essay, Ellis Hawley carefully dissects the intellectual premises of Republican economic policy. In their pursuit of "associationalism," Hawley argues, Hoover and others were carving out a middle ground that both anticipated the New Deal in important respects and consistently championed private cooperation over political intervention. In the second essay, Molly Ladd-Taylor uses the example of the Sheppard-Towner Infant and Maternity Act to suggest both the impact of suffrage on the progress of "maternal" policies, and the promises and limits of New Era social policy.

Herbert Hoover and the "Associational" State

ELLIS HAWLEY

In recent years, the traditional image of American governmental activity in the 1920s has been substantially altered. Delving beneath the older stereotypes of "normalcy" and "retrenchment," scholars have found unsuspected survivals of progressivism, a growing federal bureaucracy that tried to use as well as serve business groups, and an incipient form of "indicative planning" based on corporatist rather

Excerpts from "Herbert Hoover, the Commerce Secretariat and the Vision of an 'Associative State,' 1921–28," by Ellis Hawley. *Journal of American History*, 61 (1974) pp. 116–140. Reprinted by permission of Organization of American Historians and the author.

than classical economics. In many respects, they have concluded, the period should be viewed as the beginnings of the "modern era," not as a reversion to past patterns or as a frivolous and wasted interlude between progressivism and the New Deal. . . .

[Herbert] Hoover in 1921 saw himself as the protagonist of a new and superior synthesis between the old industrialism and the new, a way whereby America could benefit from scientific rationalization and social engineering without sacrificing the energy and creativity inherent in individual effort, "grass-roots" involvement, and private enterprise. Such a synthesis, he argued, would make the "American system" superior to any other, particularly in its ability to raise living standards, humanize industrial relationships, and integrate conflicting social elements into a harmonious community of interests. And the key to its achievement, he had concluded on the basis of his wartime, engineering, and personal experience, lay in the development and proper use of cooperative institutions, particularly trade associations, professional societies, and similar organizations among farmers and laborers. These, Hoover and other associationists believed, would form a type of private government, one that would meet the need for national reform, greater stability, and steady expansion, yet avoid the evils long associated with "capital consolidations," politicized cartels, and governmental bureaucracies. Unlike the earlier trusts, these newer institutions would preserve and work through individual units, committing them voluntarily to service, efficiency, and ethical behavior and developing for them a new and enlightened leadership capable of seeing the larger picture. And unlike governmental bureaus, they would be flexible, responsive, and productive, built on service and efficiency rather than coercion and politics, and staffed by men of expertise and vision, not by self-serving politicians or petty drudges.

To some extent, too, Hoover believed that the components of this associational order were evolving naturally and had been for the past thirty years. Within the womb of the old industrialism there had developed not only the associational structures around which the new system was taking shape but also the moral awakening, the commitment to science and productivity, and the mutuality of interests that would convert such structures into instruments of social progress. As these developments continued, the new private government would take shape on its own and bring with it the superior synthesis that Hoover envisioned. Yet there was no assurance that it would do so, or that it would develop fast enough to meet national needs. There was, so Hoover also believed, a need to manage, speed up, and guide this evolutionary process, both to help realize its full potentialities and to prevent those impatient with persisting social and economic problems from turning to undesirable statist solutions. And to meet this need, he envisioned an "associative state," tied to, cooperating with, and helping to develop and guide the new associational order. Paradoxically, he saw himself both as an anti-statist and as an ardent champion of one form of positive government and national planning.

For two reasons, however, Hoover did not regard these positions as being inconsistent. In the first place, the structure and methods of the associative state would be different, thus enabling it to escape the torpor and rigidity characteristic of most governmental structures. In so far as possible, it would function through promotional conferences, expert inquiries, and cooperating committees, not through public enterprise, legal coercion, or arbitrary controls; and like the private groupings to which it would be tied, it would be flexible, responsive, and productive, staffed by men of talent, vision, and expertise, and committed to nourishing individualism and local initiative rather than supplanting them. In the second place, the associative state would be needed only during a transitional phase. Like the Marxist state or those posited by some European corporatists, it would theoretically serve as midwife to a new, non-statist commonwealth and, having performed this function, would either wither away or revert to the status of umpire, caretaker, and symbol of unity.

Hoover's New Era activities were in part efforts to implement his vision of an associative state. For him the vision defined the difference between constructive and undesirable activism. Although some of what he did can be attributed to his ambivalent personality, his adjustment of an engineering approach to political realities, his recognition of new technological problems, or his accommodation of business groups desirous of governmental services but reluctant to give up their own autonomy, many of his activities flowed logically from his postwar plans for associative "reconstruction" and particularly from his conviction that the commerce department, if properly expanded and transformed, could become the central agency for implementing such plans. When offered more prestigious positions, he chose and stuck with the secretaryship of commerce, chiefly he implied, because no other department had the same potential for guiding the associational activities that were transforming American society. With Harding's assurance that he could remake the department and have a voice in labor, farm, financial, and foreign policies, he moved into it, as Arthur Schlesinger, Jr., says, much "as he might have into a bankrupt mining company a decade earlier," determined to convert a collection of miscellaneous technical bureaus into the governmental apparatus needed for an assured transition to an American utopia.

Hoover must have realized at the outset that such a task was not likely to be easy. He was beginning with one of the smallest and newest of the federal departments, one whose appropriations for 1920, exclusive of those for the census, had totaled only $17,000,000. He could hardly be encouraged by the inability of his predecessor, William Redfield, to salvage some of the cooperative machinery established during the war. And his plans were bound to collide with the strong sentiment for governmental retrenchment, the popular disdain for overly ambitious bureaucrats, and the entrenched positions of established bureaucratic domains. Yet there was also ground for optimism. Hoover's vision was an attractive and timely one, admirably suited to make him the "old order's candidate for ushering in the new"; and against the obstacles in his path, he could pit his immense prestige and formidable administrative talents, his following of dedicated personal associates, and his extensive ties to like-minded men in the worlds of business, engineering, journalism, scholarship, and social uplift.

Before long, too, by drawing on a variety of recommendations, Hoover was mapping out specific plans for departmental expansion. As visualized, his agency would eventually consist of three great divisions: one for industry, one for trade, and one for transportation and communication. Into the first, in addition to this own bureaus of fisheries and standards, should go the interior department's Bureau of Mines and patent office, plus a new Bureau of Federal Statistics, formed by joining the Census Bureau with the statistical programs of several other departments. Into the trade division, as adjuncts to his Bureau of Foreign and Domestic Commerce, should go the Bureau of Markets from the agriculture department, the foreign trade service and economic consulates from the state department, the Latin-American activities of the treasury department, and the research work of the Federal Trade Commission. And into the transportation and communication division, along with the lighthouse, steamboat, and mapping services, should go a part of the Coast Guard, the navy's Observatory, Hydrographic Office, and Steamboat Movement Service, the army's Lake Survey and Harbor Supervisors, the Panama Canal, the inland waterways, the shipping subsidies, and a new Bureau of Aeronautics. In essence, the commerce department was to become a department of economic development and management; other agencies would still be responsible for special sectors of the economy, but commerce would serve as a general policy coordinator. In effect, as S. Parker Gilbert once put it, Hoover would be "Under-Secretary of all other departments."

Reaching out from this expanded governmental base would be an extensive net of promotional activities, cooperating committees, and other ad hoc structures, all tied to private groupings and associations and all designed to energize private or local collectivities and guide them toward constructive solutions to national problems. From Hoover's standpoint, governmental reorganization was intended not only to reduce wasteful overlap and unwise expenditures, but also to provide the necessary base on which an associative state could be built. Hand in hand with his drive for new jurisdictional boundaries went a series of conferences, negotiations, and "missionary activities," designed to forge cooperative links with the "community at large" and develop the associational apparatus that could speed up and manage socioeconomic progress. Assuming top priority in 1921 were the problems of housing, unemployment, industrial waste, stagnating foreign trade, and inadequate business planning; and in each of these problem areas, Hoover and his deputies were soon moving to resurrect and expand the voluntaristic-cooperationist side of the war government. . . .

Under his tutelage, for example, the Bureau of Foreign and Domestic Commerce was reorganized along commodity lines, staffed with men from the export industries themselves, and made the center of an associational system for gathering and disseminating commercial intelligence, dealing with foreign governments and cartels, and organizing trade and investment activities into a rational and integrated set of operations. Tied to and working in conjunction with each commodity division was a cooperating industrial committee, chosen typically by the trade and export associations in the field; and ideally it was these cooperating private groups that would build and develop the steadily expanding market needed for permanent prosperity. The state would act only as a clearing house, inspirational force, and protector of international rights, not as a trader, investor, or detailed regulator. And it was for the former functions that Hoover won larger and larger appropriations, set up one appendage after another, and kept expanding his network of trade commissioners, researchers, and public relations men. By 1925 the bureau's appropriations had risen 140 percent; services rendered, so it claimed, were up 600 percent; and in six months, according to its energetic director, Julius Klein, it had issued "more than enough" press releases "to put 18 columns of type up and down the Washington Monument."

In attempting to expand its jurisdictional boundaries, the Bureau of Foreign and Domestic Commerce was less successful. In the areas of economic diplomacy and international finance, its role remained a limited one, thus hampering Hoover's efforts to guide overseas investment into proper channels. Nor did it ever succeed in taking over the foreign economic services of the Department of State and the Department of Agriculture. Yet its domain did expand. Its new financial division offered advice on foreign loans and investments; its research and public relations arms assumed responsibility for a new program of domestic market analysis, a massive publicity campaign against foreign "monopolies," and a world-wide search for independent sources of raw materials; and its foreign service, to the accompaniment of much friction with the state department, kept expanding and strengthening its intelligence apparatus. In 1922, in return for giving suitable credit to consular officials, it secured the right to request information from them through the diplomatic head of mission. In 1924, it secured an executive order directing all representatives abroad to meet and exchange information at least every two weeks. In 1927, it was given permanent legislative status. And repeatedly, when state department critics struck back by charging it with wasteful duplication and diplomatic bungling, the bureau was able to defend successfully its claim to special expertise. . . .

Building on existing bureaus, Hoover was moving to implement his original designs, both of an expanded departmental jurisdiction and of an associational bureaucratic structure. And while a few critics charged that he was fostering either "big government" or "monopoly," he and his publicists were highly successful in bucking the sentiment for "economy in government" and selling their programs to the President, the budget bureau, the appropriations committees, the business community, and the general public. Their bureaucracy, they kept saying, was "different." Unlike the typical variety, with its tax eating propensities, red tape, and rigid controls, this new species paid returns on the money "invested" by generating new expansion and new revenue, delivered efficient and businesslike service, and functioned under "responsive" and competent men, who understood national needs and "cooperated" instead of "meddling." Besides, its whole purpose differed. By building industrial self-government and thus reducing the need for governmental controls, it was actually checking the whole movement toward big government; and by fostering and nourishing the grassroots activities of private groups and local communities, it was promoting democratic decentralization rather than bureaucratic centralism. . . .

At the same time, in further efforts to implement his original plans, Hoover was trying either to convert other departments into cooperative satellites, preempt their domains through the sponsorship of new associational bureaucracies, or fill "power vacuums" into which they had been slow to move. In his relations with the interior department, he pursued all three approaches; and once Albert Fall had been replaced by the cooperative and colorless Hubert Work, the efforts of the secretary of commerce to set up associational machinery in such areas as power and waterway development, transportation improvement, and construction planning met with little resistance. In each of these areas, Hoover soon established networks of cooperating committees and allied associations, and in each of them the commerce secretariat assumed new responsibilities for making policy, stimulating "grass-roots" activity, and fostering "industrial self-government."

In the power field, Hoover tried to devise a "middle way" by seizing on the idea of "superpower," the notion of regionally coordinated and technically advanced power networks developed by a cooperative alliance of state agencies, private groups, and public-minded engineers. First set forth in "superpower surveys" sponsored by the interior and war departments, this vision received wide publicity in the early 1920s. Beginning as a member of the interior department's Superpower Advisory Committee, Hoover quickly assumed leadership, worked with the surveyors, especially with engineer William S. Murray, to promote the idea, and began organizing the necessary cooperative alliance. The practical results of his efforts were minimal, partly because of the increasingly acrimonious polarization of power politics. But by 1924 he had set up a Northeastern Super Power Committee with himself as chairman and assistant Paul Clapp as secretary, surrounded this with an apparatus of study groups and publicity campaigns, and tied the governmental activities to interlocking private committees representing the power producers and consumers, the Chamber of Commerce, and the utility engineers. . . .

In many respects, too, Hoover functioned as the real secretary of labor and proceeded to organize associational reform efforts in that field. It was Hoover, not "Puddler Jim" Davis, who sponsored the Unemployment Conference and tried to meet the unemployment crisis through expanded construction activities. Even more indicative of his role, it was Hoover rather than Davis who took the lead in pressuring the steel industry into giving up its twelve-hour day, urging business and labor groups to develop programs of unemployment insurance, and trying to substitute cooperation for conflict in the railroad and coal industries. Davis thought it more important to be at a meeting of the Loyal Order of Moose than at the Unemployment Conference. And while he sometimes complained about Hoover's expanding machinery and activities, he was usually content to echo Hoover's policies and allow what remained of the labor department to atrophy.

Although the labor department retained its welfare agencies and efforts to create a new department in the welfare field had been blocked, a new welfare "adhocracy" was taking shape, attached, appropriately enough in an era of welfare capitalism, to the Department of Commerce. To deal with problems of housing, child welfare, and emergency relief, Hoover put together associational structures similar to those used to tackle economic problems. At the centers of these structures, stimulating and guiding them toward "constructive action," were men who were also serving as officials or associates of the commerce secretariat.

In the housing field, for instance, Hoover was concerned not only with stabilizing the construction industries and breaking the "blockade" against mass production but also with relieving a national housing shortage, fostering urban zoning and planning, and securing the social stability and "spiritual values" inherent in widespread home ownership. John Gries, who headed the Building and Housing Division, came to think of his organization not only as a "division of construction" but also as a housing expediter, "bureau of municipalities," and social stabilizer. And to fulfill these added responsibilities, new campaigns of associational reform were constantly launched. The division was soon working with the Chamber of Commerce to devise community housing plans, with the American Institute of Architects to set up small house service bureaus, with a network of expert committees and cooperating interest groups to develop model building codes and model zoning and planning laws, and with realtors, loan associations, and interested philanthropists to educate prospective home owners and develop better methods of mortgage and construction financing.

In addition, Hoover utilized an organization known as Better Homes in America to carry on a massive educational campaign, one that reached out through some 3,600 local committees and a host of affiliated groups to provide exhibits of model homes, foster better "household management," promote research in the housing field, and generate a "greater, steadier, and more discriminating demand for improved dwellings," especially for families with "small incomes." Originally founded by Marie Meloney of the *Delineator,* Better Homes had first operated independently. But in late 1923, seeing the potentialities in the organization and taking advantage of Meloney's desire to reduce her own role and to keep what she had started from being "commercialized," Hoover reorganized it as a public service corporation with himself as president, thus converting it, in his words, into a "collateral arm" of the commerce department. He then secured operating funds from private foundations, persuaded James Ford, a professor of social ethics at Harvard, to serve as executive director, and tied the whole apparatus to his Housing Division by having the directors of that agency serve as officers in the new corporation. Again, by building another dependent "adhocracy" that could stimulate and work through private groups, he was able to reconcile his conflicting roles as a bureaucratic expansionist who was also a declared foe of "big government."

Similar, too, were the secretary's operations along a second welfare front, that of improving child health and well being. Here the major vehicle, analogous to Better Homes, was the American Child Health Association, formed in 1922 when Hoover arranged a merger between the American Child Hygiene Association and the Child Health Organization of America, installed himself as president of the new body, and brought in his lieutenants from the American Relief Administration to direct it. After a fund raising campaign failed, financing was also arranged through the A.R.A. Children's Fund. And since Hoover and his lieutenants, at the expense of some internal friction and several reorganizations, managed to impose their program and priorities on the association, it too became a "collateral arm" of the commerce secretariat, filling another "vacuum" and in the process colliding at times with the Children's Bureau of the labor department and the treasury department's Public Health Service. By 1927 the American Child Health Association was working to survey, rate, and upgrade municipal health services, to assist and coordinate local health programs, to promote health education, both in the schools and through demonstration and publication projects, and to secure comprehensive birth registration, cleaner milk, improved prenatal care, and better control of communicable diseases.

Given Hoover's previous experience, it seemed logical for him and his department to handle federal relief activities and thus to broaden still further their responsibilities in the welfare field. The Unemployment Conference was largely a Hoover production, and its subsequent Committee on Civic and Emergency Measures, which tried to provide unemployment relief during the winter of 1921 and 1922, functioned essentially as a departmental appendage and model of how an associative state should function. Its approach was not to provide jobs or funds but to organize, coordinate, and inform a "cooperative" effort, thus enabling a grassroots network of mayors' emergency committees, public-minded business groups, concerned social organizations, and ad hoc employment bureaus to meet the needs of the jobless. And similarly in 1927, during the decade's greatest natural disaster, it was the secretary of commerce who took charge of a special Mississippi Flood

Committee and drew on both personal and departmental resources to construct another special bureaucratic apparatus, one that worked with and through a network of local citizens' committees, Red Cross chapters, and cooperating private organizations and public agencies to provide systematic coordination, make available the needed refugee centers and rehabilitation credits, and consider future flood prevention and social "reconstruction."

While constructing new bureaucracies in areas that might more logically have been left to the secretaries of labor or interior, Hoover was also trying, with somewhat greater difficulty, to convert other departments into cooperative satellites or friendly allies. In the antitrust realm, for example, where "outmoded" interpretations of the law threatened to wreck Hoover's cooperative machinery and undermine his vision of an associational order, the commerce department appeared at first to be losing the battle but by the mid-1920s had emerged victorious. Initially, efforts to secure a new interpretation of antitrust regulations through proposed amendments, expanded governmental cooperation, clarifying letters, and "friendly criticism" from sympathetic Federal Trade Commissioners all seemed ineffective. But after Harry Daugherty's resignation in 1924, the picture changed rapidly. The new attorneys general, first Harlan Stone and later John Sargent, were more sympathetic. The Supreme Court in June 1925 sanctioned the associational activities of the maple flooring and cement industries. And following the reorganization of the Federal Trade Commission and the appointment of William Donovan to head the Antitrust Division, these agencies became friendly allies. The former, through its trade practice conferences, was soon promoting numerous codes of ethical behavior, devices that Hoover regarded as highly "constructive," and Donovan was ready to give friendly advice to business cooperators on how to stay within the law.

By the mid-1920s, too, another Hoover protégé, William Jardine, had succeeded Henry C. Wallace as secretary of agriculture and was trying, although only with limited success, to win support for Hoover's associational approach to the farm problem. Initially, attempts to expand in this direction met with stiff resistance, resulting in bitter jurisdictional conflicts over export promotion, lumber standards, and farm processing statistics, and in heated policy debates, with each side impugning the motives of the other. As Hoover saw it, he was fighting socialists and petty bureaucrats, men who could see nothing but the pernicious McNary-Haugen bill and the preservation of their own domains and men who were ready to use "smear tactics" to achieve their ends. To Wallace, the struggle was a defensive battle against business aggression, particularly against a cooperative marketing plan intended to cripple genuine cooperatives, divert attention from real relief measures, and shift marketing activities to a farm board dominated by the commerce department. For a time, Hoover's offensive scored few gains, but with the death of Wallace in 1924 he was able to select the new secretary, shape the recommendations of Coolidge's Agricultural Conference, secure a "purge" of the "petty bureaucrats," and bring the Department of Agriculture into alignment with his vision of agricultural self-government through cooperative marketing associations. Given the new relationship, he was even ready to establish sharp boundaries between forestry activities and his own wood utilization program, conceding while doing so that his Lumber Standards Committee had "embarrassed" him by trying to move into areas which did not "rightfully belong in the Department of Commerce."

Hoover had less success in his efforts to influence the state department, the treasury department, and the Federal Reserve Board, partly because in these areas he came into conflict with powerful men. He was forced to accept a continued division of foreign economic activities, and in the face of strong opposition from the treasury department, state department, and banking leaders, he was unable to establish the qualitative standards and purposeful controls that he hoped to use in guiding American investments abroad. He was also reluctant to challenge Andrew Mellon's dismantling of the progressive tax system. He was unable to do much about the "pro-British," "easy money" policy of the Federal Reserve Board. And although his role in the making of foreign policy was far from insignificant, he was frequently unable to move the diplomatic establishment in directions he felt desirable.

In later years, Hoover would attribute some of the difficulties after 1929 to the resistance that he had encountered from financial and foreign policy makers. But at the time he did not seem to regard his failures in these fields as constituting major threats to the continued development of a superior socioeconomic order. Although some of his initial plans had miscarried, he had succeeded in raising the commerce department to the "first rank" and transforming a collection of technical bureaus into a unified, purposeful, and rapidly expanding organization, with a strong sense of esprit de corps and with a far-flung apparatus that was attempting to guide socioeconomic development as well as serve business groups. Essentially, he believed, he had created the type of governmental tool that he had envisioned in 1921, one that functioned as an economic "general staff," business "correspondence school," and national coordinator, all rolled into one, yet preserved the essentials of American individualism by avoiding bureaucratic dictation and legal coercion, implementing its plans through nearly 400 cooperating committees and scores of private associations, and relying upon appeals to science, community, and morality to bridge the gap between the public interest and private ones. It was a tool, moreover, whose use was hastening the day when "functional self-government" through a "cooperative system" of self-regulating "organisms" would meet the needs of industrial democracy without statist interference. Like the war to end all wars, it was the bureaucratic empire to end future bureaucratic empires; and in theory at least it was supposed to wither away once the new order was built.

As Hoover surveyed the state of associational development in the late 1920s, he was also optimistic about the progress that had been made toward his ultimate goal. The number of national associations had multiplied from approximately 700 in 1919 to over 2,000 by 1929. Inspired and coordinated by the right kind of governmental structures—those fostering "associational activities" imbued with "high public purposes"—these associations had in Hoover's eyes become "legitimate" and "constructive" instruments for advancing the "public interest" and ushering in a "fundamentally new" phase in the nation's economic evolution. The dream of an associational order, it seemed, was on the way to realization; and as if to symbolize the role of the commerce secretariat in making such a superior system possible, a new "temple of commerce" was under construction, which, except for the Capitol, would be the largest building in Washington.

The next few years, of course, would demonstrate that Hoover's utopia was not to be. Viewed from the altered perspective that took shape after 1929, his emerging private government seemed increasingly undemocratic, oppressive, and unresponsive. Associationalism, once widely accepted as a new and superior formulation of the "American way," became for many a mere facade behind which "selfish monopolists" had abused their power and plunged the nation into depression. And the leaders of his new order, revealed now to be far less altruistic and far less prescient than Hoover had hoped they would be, seemed unable either to sustain expansion, solve festering social problems, or check the greatest economic contraction in the nation's history. As conflict mounted, moreover, demands for more effective "coordination" were soon transforming Hoover's efforts at associational direction and reform into programs and agencies he had never intended. Ironically, by demonstrating that they could not achieve the sustained expansion, rising living standards, and decentralized, non-coercive planning that they were supposed to achieve, he helped open the way for "big government" and state-enforced market controls in the 1930s.

Viewed in terms of its utopian goals and assumptions, Hoover's approach can only be adjudged a tragic failure. Yet this should not obscure the fact that he and his New Era associates, far from being mere tools of rapacious business interests or unimaginative proponents of laissez-faire, drift, and governmental inaction, were groping their way toward a form of American corporatism and indicative planning, were engaged in imaginative processes of state building and bureaucratic expansion, and were wrestling actively with the still unsolved problem of reconciling techno-corporate organization with America's liberal-democratic heritage. If historians are to understand either the men involved or the era in which they operated, it seems imperative that their associational structures and activities be explored in greater depth. And viewed from the perspective of the 1970s, from a time of disenchantment with the solutions flowing from the 1930s and of a search by "neo-federalists," "new radicals," and "postliberals" for new organizational arrangements that will liberate and humanize rather than mechanize and oppress, such explorations may be more relevant and more instructive than most historians have previously assumed.

Maternalism, Feminism, and the Politics of Reform in the 1920s

MOLLY LADD-TAYLOR

"Of all the activities in which I have shared during more than forty years of striving," reflected Florence Kelley in 1926, "none is, I am convinced, of such fundamental importance as the Sheppard-Towner Act." The Maternity and Infancy Protection Act was the first federally funded social welfare measure and the first "women's" legislation to pass after the suffrage amendment. Its enactment in 1921 marked the climax of the maternalist campaign to create and control a welfare system that protected the health of mothers and children. Its repeal less than eight years later brought women's efforts to secure federal responsibility for child welfare to a discouraging end.

Designed by Children's Bureau chief Julia Lathrop, the Sheppard-Towner Act exemplified the political philosophy and program of maternalism. Maternalists' high regard for mothers' work and service to the state was evident in their call for

---

Excerpt from *Mother-Work: Women, Child Welfare, and the State, 1890–1930.* Copyright 1994 by the Board of Trustees of the University of Illinois. Used with permission of the University of Illinois Press.

the government protection of motherhood; their belief that women had a special sensitivity to child welfare was manifest in their insistence that Sheppard-Towner health programs be run by women. The maternalist commitment to all children's welfare motivated Sheppard-Towner workers to extend the principles of scientific childrearing into every community and racial ethnic group, while the maternalist adherence to the family wage system was reflected in the bill's concern for women only in their maternal role. Sheppard-Towner was intended to protect the health of women and children within the family; it did not challenge married women's economic dependence on men or try to empower mothers in other social roles. . . .

More than any other maternalist reform, the campaign for maternal and child health care reveals the intersection of women's private and public mother-work. The Maternity and Infancy Act grew out of women's personal concerns about their children's health and fears that they or their children would die. The campaign to secure the bill's passage brought these "private" concerns about infant and prenatal care into the world of politics. In turn, as we shall see, Sheppard-Towner programs altered many women's personal experience of mothering by improving and med-icalizing health services, accelerating the decline of traditional beliefs about infant death and maternal suffering, and raising women's expectations for care.

Although its passage was a major victory, the Sheppard-Towner Act was a compromise measure that was far from achieving all of the maternalists' goals. The final version of the bill, sponsored by Texas Senator Morris Sheppard and Iowa Congressman Horace Towner, provided federal matching grants to the states for information and instruction on nutrition and hygiene, prenatal and child health clinics, and visiting nurses for pregnant women and new mothers. It furnished no financial aid or medical care, and limited appropriations to a period of five years. Yet despite its narrow provisions, Sheppard-Towner was vigorously opposed by a coalition of medical associations and right-wing organizations who claimed it was a Communist-inspired step toward state medicine that threatened the home and violated the principle of states' rights. By 1926, when Sheppard-Towner funding was to be renewed, the bill's opponents had gained so much strength that they succeeded in forcing the bill's supporters to accept a compromise that extended funding for two more years, but repealed the law itself in 1929, thereby ensuring that all federal appropriations for maternal and infant care would cease. . . .

The 1920s was a decade of fiscal conservatism and a backlash to feminism and progressive reform. Partly because activist women played such a large role in creating the U.S. welfare system, right-wing opposition to social welfare programs was tied to antifeminist hostility to changing gender roles and to women's visibility in public life. . . . In this environment, the adamantly political objective of the Sheppard-Towner Act—to educate women with an eye toward mobilizing them to demand more extensive welfare services—could hardly be more controversial. Indeed, the highly politicized character of the Sheppard-Towner Act, evident in its unusual reliance on volunteer labor and its (for the government) relatively democratic administration, may be one reason that the maternity bill—in contrast to the mothers' aid bureaucracy—did not survive the decade. . . .

. . . Sheppard-Towner supporters defended the maternity bill in the progressive reform vocabulary of efficiency, scientific progress, and justice. Julia Lathrop insisted that modern science had established health care as a "minimum standard" for child welfare, to be "provided as the public schools are provided, to be used by all with dignity and self-respect." Florence Kelley contended that the large number of preventable deaths betrayed the low value society placed on women's and children's lives. In eloquent testimony in congressional hearings, she declared that women deeply resented the fact that Congressmen legislated salary and pension increases for postal employees and veterans, but claimed that the government could not afford to provide health care for women and children. "No woman in the United States would begrudge those increases of salaries," she said angrily, "but when we are told that this country is so poor and this Congress so harassed by things of greater importance than the deaths of a quarter of a million children a year . . . we say to ourselves, 'Surely we are not to take this seriously? . . . Why does Congress wish women and children to die?' "

Like the earlier debate over mothers' pensions, the battle over Sheppard-Towner turned on sharp differences over the state's obligation for child welfare and the politicization of motherhood. However, because the Sheppard-Towner debate took place in the midst of the anticommunist hysteria of the 1920s, disagreements over state responsibility for child welfare were muddied by accusations of bolshevism and feminism. Moreover, while the influence of private charities was evident in the discussion of mothers' aid, the tone of the Sheppard-Towner debate was set by the powerful American Medical Association, which combined an attack on "state medicine" with hostility to the "lay" women in the Children's Bureau. The fight over the maternity bill occurred after progressive maternalists had achieved considerable success at establishing a women-controlled welfare system, and thus Sheppard-Towner opponents made a direct and powerful challenge to women's authority over child welfare.

Right-wing associations and medical societies objected to the proposed Maternity Act on three counts: it made a political issue of women's and children's health; it expanded the social welfare function of the state; and it increased professional women's authority over public health and welfare programs. Like opponents of mothers' pensions, the foes of the Sheppard-Towner Act portrayed it as an invasion of privacy that would replace the authority of the father with that of the state. "It is an invasion of the castle of the American citizen," warned a former antisuffragist. "This idea is to take care of all alike, or, in other words, to substitute the State for the father," deplored the editor of the right-wing *Woman Patriot.* If maternal mortality was to be stopped, declared Elizabeth Lowell Putnam, a conservative clubwoman who pioneered the development of private-sector prenatal services but was a vigorous opponent of the Sheppard-Towner Act, "the husbands and fathers of the country must see that this is done, and it is their duty to their wives to take hold of the situation and to demand proper care for them." Women should not demand care for themselves.

Like the charity workers who lobbied against state mothers' pensions, foes of the Sheppard-Towner Act feared that government aid would undermine individual men's responsibility for their families. The maternity bill might save a few lives, they conceded, but it would do more harm than good by "discouraging private initiative, responsibility, and thrift." State responsibility for social welfare "tends to pauperize the people," insisted a right-wing opponent of the bill; "it tends to make the mothers believe that Uncle Sam instead of their own husbands, ought to take care of them." A conservative Congressman warned, "When the Government itself goes beyond instructing and enters into the business of taking care of the individuals constituting American citizenship, it has made a leap into the arena of paternalism from which it can never escape."

Right-wingers considered communism and politicized motherhood two sides of the same coin, and they objected to both in the Sheppard-Towner Act. The family was "the very foundation of our national life," declared the president of the Massachusetts Anti-Suffrage Association; "those who would overturn present Governments consider it the first point of attack. Abolish the family and the whole structure must fall." Insisting that Sheppard-Towner was a step to motherhood endowment and birth control, superpatriots quoted statements advocating motherhood endowment by feminists Helen Todd and Harriot Stanton Blatch to discredit the bill. A reference in a Children's Bureau publication on maternity benefits to a study by Soviet feminist Alexandra Kollontai was widely cited as an example of the Bureau's ties to Bolshevik leaders. "No one in this House can deny that those who have propagated this maternity bill really advocate the maintenance of indigent, pregnant women, both before, during, and after labor; child control by the State; mothers' pensions; the doctrine of eugenics; birth control; and other notions of the sort born out of purely socialistic brains," one Congressman warned.

Right-wing patriots attacked the main proponents of the Maternity Act as feminists, communists, and unwomanly spinsters incapable of caring for children. One opponent of the bill objected that Julia Lathrop was "one of the Hull House crowd," while another accused her of endorsing the "feminist ideals of the unspeakable Madam Kollontai." The caustic remarks of Missouri Senator James Reed, a leading critic of the bill, illustrate right-wingers' hostility to women in public life: "It is now proposed to turn the control of the mothers of the land over to a few single ladies holding Government jobs at Washington. I question whether one out of ten of these delightful reformers could make a bowl of buttermilk gruel that would not give a baby the colic in five minutes. [Laughter.] We would better reverse the proposition and provide for a committee of mothers to take charge of the old maids and teach them how to acquire a husband and have babies of their own. [Laughter.]"

Significantly, the earliest statements of medical opposition to Sheppard-Towner played as much on popular fears of feminism and communism as on the issue of medical expertise. Dominated by male specialists engaged in private practice, the AMA objected to public health programs—especially when provided by women—as a threat to male doctors' incomes and control over the health care system. The AMA campaign against Sheppard-Towner began in February 1921 with an editorial in the *Journal of the American Medical Association,* and it grew stronger and more effective over the course of the decade.

Doctors also questioned the ability of the "lay" women on the Children's Bureau staff to administer maternity and infancy programs. Overlooking the fact that a female physician headed the Maternity and Infancy Division of the Children's Bureau, medical leaders argued that, if passed, the maternity bill should be administered by the (male) doctors in the Public Health Service, rather than by the (female) social workers at the Bureau. Conservative health reformer Elizabeth Lowell Putnam, a close ally of the medical establishment and an energetic foe of the Children's Bureau staff, explained this position: "Everyone of knowledge and wisdom when confronted with a case of childbirth in their own family would call in a skilled obstetrician and not a social worker for the management of the case." Interestingly, the question of Sheppard-Towner administration also divided the Children's Bureau from sentimental maternalists, who had more traditional ideas about gender roles and accorded male experts greater authority over the science of child study. Yet although National Congress of Mothers president Hannah Schoff believed that Sheppard-Towner should be administered by the Public Health Service, she agreed to actively support the bill wherever its administration was placed.

The Children's Bureau focus on the social and economic dimensions of infant mortality incensed doctors and right-wingers alike. Elizabeth Lowell Putnam, who headed up an innovative experiment in prenatal care under the auspices of the Boston Women's Municipal League between 1909 and 1914, insisted that infant mortality was "a medical question, pure and simple;" the best way to reduce maternal and infant death was to require better medical school training in obstetrics. In keeping with the denigration of maternal skills by childrearing experts of the 1920s, Sheppard-Towner opponents asserted that mothers were capable of being educated only to the extent of finding good medical care and "of cooperating with it by carrying out the doctor's orders." The only purpose of health education was to convince women of the "enormous benefit of proper medical care," Putnam remarked, for the mother "cannot possibly be educated to take care of herself to any further extent than this."

Putnam's conception of women's intelligence presents a striking contrast to that of the bill's supporters, who insisted that women had a right to know what to expect during pregnancy and childbirth. Women activists who were pro Sheppard-Towner believed that educating women about infant and prenatal care would remove the mystique surrounding reproduction and give them more control of their health during pregnancy and childbirth. "One of the opinions I have always fought is that a woman is too delicate or too sensitive to know about her chief function—child bearing—and her chief contribution to civilization—the bearing and rearing of children," Bureau physician Dorothy Reed Mendenhall remarked. Maternalists and grassroots mothers, living at a time when many women were not taught vital information about reproduction, supported Sheppard-Towner for the same reason some doctors resisted it: it promised them more knowledge about reproduction and their bodies.

In spite of its vigorous campaign against the bill, the anti–Sheppard-Towner coalition made little headway in 1921. Congress passed the Maternity and Infancy Act by a wide margin—63–7 in the Senate and 279–39 in the House of Representatives—and President Warren G. Harding signed it into law on November 23, 1921. Congressmen may have been afraid of provoking the wrath of newly enfranchised women voters or the powerful maternalist lobby, or they may have heeded women's requests for the "protection of maternity and infancy" out of chivalry and sentimentalism. In any case, most observers agreed that congressional support for the bill was soft. "On a secret ballot I don't think it would have got 50 votes," observed Alice Robertson, the only woman in Congress and a staunch opponent of the bill. "Nineteen men who voted for it—so one of them told me—were cursing it and themselves at once in the cloak room."

Although unable to prevent passage of the bill, Sheppard-Towner opponents did manage to effect compromise. Even though the bill originally designed by

Lathrop provided medical and nursing care in addition to instructional programs, the final bill was purely educational. Moreover, the Children's Bureau chief took pains to disassociate herself from socialism and to reaffirm her commitment to the family wage when she testified in congressional hearings on the bill. Admitting that cash maternity benefits might be necessary for poor families in Europe, Lathrop said that the preferred solution in the U.S. was to increase men's wages so that they could support their wives and children. "If the country has that it will not have to endow motherhood," she explained.

Children's Bureau officials went to great lengths to quell the medical opposition to the bill. In an attempt to placate doctors worried that Sheppard-Towner would lead to state medicine, they carefully distinguished between publicly funded health education and private medical care. Sheppard-Towner clinics would only advise parents on the care of healthy children, they contended; doctors still cured the sick. "We are not giving medicines"; Josephine Baker testified during Congressional hearings, "we are not treating sick people; we do nothing of that kind. We simply teach people how to keep well and readjust as far as we are able the bad effects of wrong environment. . . . Infant mortality is very largely a social problem and an economic problem." The Bureau maintained (correctly, as it turned out) that prenatal and child health clinics would increase doctors' patients, not compete for them. "Your private practice should immediately reflect its [Sheppard-Towner's] work, which is to discover remediable conditions and stir up parents to visit their doctors for the necessary treatment and supervision," read a letter distributed to physicians by Sheppard-Towner administrators in Pennsylvania.

As a result of the need for compromise, the final version of the Sheppard-Towner Act was considerably weaker than the initial bill introduced in 1918 by Representative Jeannette Rankin and Senator Joseph Robinson. The Rankin-Robinson bill provided "medical and nursing care at home or at a hospital when necessary," as well as instruction in hygiene, and it specifically targeted rural areas, where mortality was thought highest. By contrast, Sheppard-Towner furnished no hospital or medical care, reduced the Children's Bureau's authority over administration, and sharply cut appropriations. Although the original Sheppard-Towner bill requested an appropriation of 4 million dollars, the version that passed allocated only 1.48 million for fiscal year 1921–22 and 1.24 million for the next five years. No more than fifty thousand dollars was given to the U.S. Children's Bureau for administrative expenses. Five thousand dollars went to each state outright and an additional five thousand to states that provided matching funds. Furthermore, funds were only appropriated for five years, requiring the bill to be approved again in 1927.

The administrative structure of the Sheppard-Towner Act was another compromise. Unlike the Rankin-Robinson bill, which invested administrative authority in the Children's Bureau, Sheppard-Towner kept responsibility for the bill's daily administration with the Children's Bureau, but transferred ultimate authority to a newly created Federal Board of Maternity and Infant Hygiene, composed of the Surgeon General of the Public Health Service, the U.S. Commissioner of Education, and the Children's Bureau chief. It gave states wide discretion in the development of maternity and infancy programs and required each state to pass special enabling legislation and provide a plan for implementing the program before it could receive funds. The bill also prohibited government agents from entering any home or taking charge of any child over the objection of either parent. Finally, in re-action to feminist advocates of motherhood endowment, it explicitly prohibited us-ing Sheppard-Towner funds "for the payment of any maternity or infancy pension, stipend, or gratuity." . . .

Most maternalists were thrilled with the passage of even a moderate Sheppard-Towner Act. However, some feminists thought the compromise had been too great. Writing in the National Woman's Party journal *Equal Rights,* Madeleine Doty judged the bill's passage to be "in reality a defeat." In her view, women had been duped but were "too dazed and weary to protest" a compromise bill that reduced ap-propriations and gave mothers only instruction, and no real help, with child care. "If a woman hadn't money, she must die without aid, clutching the *knowledge* of what ought to have been done and hadn't, to save her and the child," she wrote. Another writer argued that the initial bill would do little in the way of dignifying mother-hood: "Requests for grants of money to teach rules which the mother had no money to carry out are futile. Much more than that will have to be gained before the mother takes her place beside her self-supporting sister, a complete and self-respecting per-sonality." Unlike mothers' pensions, which some feminists saw as a step toward women's independence, the educational programs of the Sheppard-Towner Act did not challenge women's dependent position in the family.

Still, most mothers appear to have welcomed the bill. Those who lacked vital information about reproduction and their bodies, who had suffered a difficult preg-nancy or birth, or who had lost a child, were desperate for any information that could give them more control over their health. Some women wrote the Children's Bureau to express their appreciation of its work and to find out how the bill might benefit them. "I do hope it will help us Poor Country people who need help," a Texas mother wrote. "I am 27 yrs. old and have Five little one's to Care for besides my husban[d] and his Father." . . .

The attacks on Sheppard-Towner and the Children's Bureau staff continued through the 1920s. There were two constitutional challenges to the bill's legality, both dismissed by the U.S. Supreme Court in 1923, and the medical establishment conducted an energetic campaign against the bill. Medical opposition was probably the major reason Illinois and Massachusetts refused to accept Sheppard-Towner funds in the first place. Moreover, although thousands of small-town doctors coop-erated with the Children's Bureau, the state directors of maternity and infancy pro-grams found that AMA opposition to Sheppard-Towner had a growing impact on local doctors. The director of the Minnesota Division of Child Hygiene complained that the head of the state medical association with discrediting Sheppard-Towner work. It was "disgusting" that one man could create such a disturbance, she wrote. . . .

Women's enthusiasm for Sheppard-Towner services is documented in the let-ters they wrote to the federal and state children's bureaus. "I trust you'll find by many letters that your work is doing much and will continue it," wrote a West Vir-ginia mother of twins. "There are many who do not Pay attention But It Is a great Benefit to those that do." A Georgia woman agreed. "I don't see how we poor moth-ers could do without them [prenatal clinics]. It has meant so much to me and so many more mothers to[o]. . . . I am the mother of 14 children, and I never was cared for till I begin going to the good will center clinic. . . . We mothers do learn a lot from the kind nurses. We are so glad the day has come when we have someone to care for our babies when they get sick."

A further indication of the program's success was the significant decrease in infant mortality during the Sheppard-Towner years. According to the Children's Bureau, infant deaths in the birth registration area dropped from 76 to 69 per 1,000 live births between 1921 and 1928, and declined by 11 percent in states that had been in the birth registration area before Sheppard-Towner began. Deaths due to gastrointestinal disease, most easily prevented by educational programs, dropped 47 percent. The Bureau attributed a slight rise in maternal deaths (from 68 per 10,000 live births in 1921 to 69 in 1929) to the inclusion of predominantly African American counties with high death rates into the birth registration area for the first time. Maternal mortality declined from 67 to 64 per 10,000 live births in states that had been in the birth registration area the entire time.

Yet deaths remained high among babies of color. When Sheppard-Towner began in 1921, 108 babies of color died for every 1,000 live births; by 1928, the infant death rate had fallen only slightly, to 106 (compared to 64 for whites). The 1921 statistics were probably artificially low since several states with high African American death rates had not yet joined the birth registration area. Moreover, most rural people of color were so poor, and conditions in their communities so dire, that the meager resources of the Sheppard-Towner Act were unable to make much more than a dent in improving their health. The decentralized administration of the Sheppard-Towner Act and maternalists' bias against traditional healing probably also reduced the effectiveness of maternity and infancy work among racial ethnic groups.

White farm wives appear to have been the chief beneficiaries of the Sheppard-Towner Act—unlike mothers' pensions programs, which principally benefited white widows in cities. This is partly because health agencies were already established in cities, but it is also no doubt because Julia Lathrop and her staff had been profoundly influenced by their correspondence and personal contacts with rural women, who were the main audience for *Infant Care* and *Prenatal Care*. Indeed, the original maternity bill specifically targeted rural areas, even though Children's Bureau statistics actually showed a slightly higher infant mortality rate in cities than in the country (possibly because birth registration lagged behind there). Targeting the country was astute not only because white farm women already shared the Bureau's cultural values regarding family life and science but also because there was less danger of conflict with the medical profession, since the specialists who dominated the AMA had less influence in rural areas.

The popularity and moderate success of the Sheppard-Towner Act notwithstanding, activist women were unable to win its renewal. The 1924 elections brought into power President Calvin Coolidge, an ally of big business and critic of a strong federal government, and a Congress more concerned with cutting taxes than with providing for social welfare. Furthermore, politicians who supported the maternity bill in 1921 because of the sentimental appeal to motherhood and their fear of the unknown female vote knew by the end of the 1920s that women did not vote as a bloc and that they had nothing to fear. Consequently, when the Children's Bureau tried to extend Sheppard-Towner appropriations (which were to expire in June 1927), the American Medical Association and the right-wing Sentinels of the Republic and Woman Patriots moved to defeat the bill itself. Using basically the same arguments as they had in 1921, opponents described Sheppard-Towner as an "entering wedge" to socialism and an attack on the sanctity of the family. They denounced Lathrop, Abbott, and Kelley as Bolsheviks. These allegations, which carried little weight in 1921, apparently seemed more convincing after the defeat of the child labor amendment in mid-decade. The Catholic church, which was initially indifferent to the Sheppard-Towner bill, began speaking out against government intervention into family affairs, and the Daughters of the American Revolution, a warm supporter of the Maternity Act in 1921, became a vigorous opponent in 1926.

Although the bill to renew Sheppard-Towner passed the House easily by a vote of 218 to 44, right-wing senators blocked it in the Senate for eight months, forcing the Children's Bureau to agree to a compromise measure that extended appropriations for two years until 1929, and then automatically repealed the law itself. Between 1928 and 1932, fourteen bills that would reverse the repeal of the Sheppard-Towner Act were introduced in Congress. All of them failed. The Children's Bureau itself opposed many of the renewal bills because they transferred responsibility for overseeing maternity and infancy work to the Public Health Service.

The tensions between maternalists and their adversaries in the medical profession exploded at the 1930 White House Conference on Child Health and Protection. Called by President Herbert Hoover, the conference was clearly intended to establish medical authority over child health and to rescue public health services from "lay" women's control. Secretary of the Interior Ray Lyman Wilbur, a past president of the AMA and outspoken opponent of the Sheppard-Towner Act, was the conference chair. Children's Bureau chief Grace Abbott, who had been secretary of the 1919 White House conference, was given only a minor role. In contrast to 1919, when maternalists set the conference agenda, the 1930 White House conference was shaped by male physicians who rejected the Bureau's belief in children's right to federally funded health care and who wanted to return responsibility for child welfare to the private sector. In the midst of the Depression, they virtually ignored the economic causes of ill health.

Maternalists were furious when conference officials tried to sneak through a resolution recommending the transfer of maternity and infancy programs from the Children's Bureau (and women's control) to the medically run Public Health Service. Hundreds of women attending the conference protested the proposal and forced its withdrawal. They made it plain that they preferred no maternity bill at all to one that asserted men's authority over women's and children's welfare, that was administered by doctors who had a narrowly medical conception of children's health needs, and that intended ultimately to depoliticize maternal and child health programs and return them to the private sector. Yet although maternalists managed to stop the transfer of Sheppard-Towner programs to the Public Health Service, they no longer had the political clout necessary to pass their own maternity bill. The White House Conference signaled the triumph of the medical profession over maternalists and the defeat of politicized motherhood.

Ironically, the success of the Maternity and Infancy Act contributed to its eventual defeat. By raising individual women's expectations for their health and making them more knowledgeable about prenatal and well-baby care, Sheppard-Towner convinced physicians to incorporate preventive health education into their private practices and to improve obstetrical training in medical schools. The improvements in—and easier access to—both private- and public-sector prenatal and well-baby health services were important factors in the drop of the white infant mortality rate. Sadly, when the health of white women and children improved, publicly funded health care appeared less urgent to middle-class voters and stopped being an important political concern of women activists.

Contrary to the intentions of its female supporters, the Sheppard-Towner Act also hastened women's loss of control over health policy and care. Because of maternalists' faith in modern science and desire to maintain good relations with the medical profession—and because of their failure to secure a bill that provided publicly funded medical or nursing care—Sheppard-Towner clinics encouraged women to seek private medical care and thus accelerated the medicalization of childbirth and infant care. In the process, they inadvertently undermined both the Bureau's holistic approach to child welfare and "lay" women's claim to expertise in the field. Although individual women continued to play a prominent role in the development and administration of child health services, by the mid 1930s male physicians and public health bureaucrats dominated both public- and private-sector health services. Once maternity and infancy programs were professionalized and rendered part of the government bureaucracy, they were no longer considered a special women's concern. All but three of the forty-eight state directors of child welfare programs had been women when Sheppard-Towner began in 1922, but by 1939 three-quarters of them were men.

The repeal of the Sheppard-Towner Act in 1929 reasserted the principle that Progressive-era maternalists and feminists had spent their lives trying to change: that children's welfare was primarily the responsibility of individual mothers, not of society. Although twenty-one states tried to continue maternity and infancy work after Sheppard-Towner was repealed, the removal of federal funds reduced public support for the program. "In other words," observed the Children's Bureau, "the participation of the Federal Government contributed something else as important as money." The financial constraints of the Depression forced some states to drop maternity and infancy work entirely, making health care once again unavailable to women who could not afford private physicians or who lived in remote areas—the women who benefited most from the Maternity and Infancy Act. Federal monies for maternal and infant care were restored under the 1935 Social Security Act, but maternal and child health services were no longer considered an entitlement for women of all classes. Instead, they were needs-based and limited to the poor.

Maternalists lost their battle to dignify motherhood and make children's welfare a societal concern, but their campaign for the state protection of mothers and children left a permanent mark on women's work of reproduction and caregiving and on the future welfare state. The Sheppard-Towner Act eased the burden of countless mothers by improving the health of their children, and it served as a bridge between Progressive-era maternalism and public welfare expansion during the New Deal. Yet, like maternalism itself, it left an ambiguous legacy. Sheppard-Towner expanded employment opportunities for professional women while leaving women's responsibility for child care unquestioned. It extended some health services to women and children of color, but demanded that they follow Anglo-American prescriptions about childrearing and medicine. It created a women-controlled public health system and mobilized thousands of women activists to help run it, but set up a public health bureaucracy that eventually supplanted them. Ironically, the Children's Bureau's success at one goal—professionalizing maternal and child welfare services—contributed to the failure of another—sustaining a broad-based women's movement to demand further welfare reform. Maternalism's greatest achievement thus inadvertently paved the way for its final defeat.

S U G G E S T E D   R E A D I N G

Anderson, Kristi. *After Suffrage: Women in Partisan and Electoral Politics Before the New Deal* (1996).

Brown, Dorothy. *Setting a Course: American Women in the 1920s* (1987).

Chambers, Clarke. *Seedtime of Reform: American Social Service and Social Action, 1918–1933* (1963).

Cott, Nancy. *The Grounding of Modern Feminism* (1987).

Freedman, Estelle. "The New Woman: Changing Views of Women in the 1920s." *Journal of American History* 61 (1974): 372–393.

Goodwin, Joanne. *Gender and the Politics of Welfare Reform: Mothers' Pensions in Chicago, 1911–1929* (1997).

Gordon, Linda. *Pitied But Not Entitled: Single Mothers and the History of Welfare* (1994).

Hawley, Ellis. "Economic Inquiry and the State in New Era America." In *The State and Economic Knowledge: The American and British Experiences,* ed. Barry Supple and Mary O. Furner, 287–324 (1990).

Hawley, Ellis, ed. *Herbert Hoover as Secretary of Commerce, 1921–1928: Studies in New Era Thought and Practice* (1974).

Himmelberg, Robert. *The Origins of the National Recovery Administration: Business, Government, and the Trade Association Issue, 1921–1933* (1976).

Himmelberg, Robert, ed. *Business-Government Cooperation, 1917–1932: The Rise of Corporatist Policies* (1994).

Keller, Morton. *Regulating a New Economy: Public Policy and Economic Change in America, 1900–1933* (1990).

Lunardini, Christine. *From Equal Suffrage to Equal Rights: Alice Paul and the National Woman's Party, 1910–1928* (1986).

Mink, Gwendolyn. *The Wages of Motherhood: Inequality in the Welfare State, 1917–1942* (1995).

Muncy, Robyn. *Creating a Female Dominion in American Reform, 1890–1935* (1991).

Murray, Robert K. *The Politics of Normalcy: Governmental Theory and Practice in the Harding-Coolidge Era* (1973).

Scharf, Lois, and Joan Jensen, eds. *Decades of Discontent: The Women's Movement, 1910–1940* (1983).

Wilson, Joan Hoff. *Herbert Hoover: Forgotten Progressive* (1975).

CHAPTER
3

Labor and Welfare
Capitalism in the 1920s

~✊~

In labor policy and labor relations, the Republican era hung loosely between the Progressive Era and the New Deal. Many workers, labor leaders, and reformers hoped that economic mobilization for World War I would deliver the Progressive Era promise of "industrial democracy." But 1919 and the subsequent decade brought bitter disappointment. Bolstered by the "Red Scare" and the federal government's retreat from war era labor regulations, employers quickly and brutally rolled back war era gains. The year 1919 alone saw over thirty-five hundred strikes involving four million workers, highlighted by an industrywide strike that devastated fledgling unions in the steel industry. By the middle of the 1920s, unionization of the nation's workers had collapsed nearly to prewar levels. Despite the relative prosperity of the "roaring" 1920s, workers suffered continued job insecurity, deteriorating job conditions, and a widening gap between stagnating wages and the rising expectations of a "culture of consumption." Employers protected their managerial stake in mass production industries with an open-shop campaign against unionization, and an array of meager and discretionary benefits (dubbed "welfare capitalism") designed to encourage workers to identify with the firm rather than with fellow employees.

The participation of women (especially married women) in the labor force increased steadily through the decade, but long-standing assumptions about the propriety of women's working persisted. Women, employers, labor unions, and the state all juggled questions of special protection and equal pay. Even as slipping family incomes, the rise of new service industries, and the new consumerism pushed and pulled women into the paid labor force, few disputed the "family wage" assumption that men were breadwinners and women were not. As a result, working women occupied a tenuous and ambiguous status in the eyes of male workers, unions, and employers, and under the terms of both private and public labor policies.

Understanding the labor movement's "lean years" is important for understanding both the limits of New Era prosperity and the consequences of the decade's deference to business needs and business values. In turn, the private and public labor policies of the 1920s set the stage for the upheaval of the 1930s. The growing gap between productivity growth and wage growth contributed directly to a crisis of

56

"underconsumption" and the severity of the Great Depression. And the employer strategies of company unionism and welfare capitalism would, by their limits in the 1920s and their utter failure after 1929, contribute directly to popular support for industrial unionism and the welfare state in the 1930s.

DOCUMENTS

The first two documents underscore the postwar collapse of labor relations, highlighted by the steel strike (Document 1) and the labor implications of the "Red Scare" (Document 2). The next four documents trace the debate between labor and management over the terms of postwar labor relations. In Document 3, the National Industrial Conference Board argues for welfare capitalism. In Document 4, a labor reporter sees welfare capitalism as an insincere and thinly veiled anti-union ploy. In Document 5, the National Association of Manufacturers argues that the open shop protects the democratic ideal of individualism. In Document 6, the American Federation of Labor (AFL) counters that the open shop violates the democratic ideal of representative, majority rule. The final three documents suggest the response to women's participation in the labor force. In Document 7, an employers' group argues that women deserve special "maternal" protection. Document 8 traces the AFL's ambivalence about women workers. And in Document 9, the Women's Bureau tries to puncture some myths about women's work.

1. The Interchurch World Movement Investigates the Steel Strike, 1920

In normal times the Steel Corporation's system of industrial relations functioned under the dominating idea of opposition to workers' organization. In strike times the Corporation's opposition was more actively supplemented by similar repression by organized society. . . .

Blacklists as an integral part of the anti-union alternative of course are ordinarily kept secret by the companies. The steel plant in Monessen, however, which freely lent its "labor file" to an investigator to study, included among the detectives' reports, etc., several blacklists. To most actual plant managers, as distinguished from Mr. Gary, blacklists seem after all too common to be deeply concealed. With the lists examined by the Commission are evidences of the system of inter-company exchange like the detective reports where the names of "independent" and Corporation mills were mixed together. . . .

Great systems of espionage are an integral part of the anti-union alternative; spies are integral to warfare.

Espionage was of two general classes: spies directly in the employ of the steel companies; and spies hired from professional "labor detective" agencies. The Steel Corporation plants have their own detective forces; one case of hiring outside agencies by a Corporation subsidiary was charged publicly during the strike.

From Interchurch World Movement of North America. Commission of Inquiry. *Report on the Steel Strike of 1919* (New York: Da Capo Press, 1971), 200, 219, 221, 234–235. Originally published ca. 1920.

Espionage was of two general characters: spies pure and simple who merely furnished information; and spies who also acted as propagandist strike breakers, mingling with the strikers and whispering that the strike was failing, that the men in other towns had gone back, that the union leaders were crooks, etc. The Monessen "labor file" contained some six hundred daily reports by "under-cover" spies of both characters, mere detectives and strike-breaking propagandists.

These company spy-systems carry right through into the United States Government.

Federal immigration authorities testified to the Commission that raids and arrests, for "radicalism," etc., were made especially in the Pittsburgh District on the denunciations and secret reports of steel company "under-cover" men, and the prisoners turned over to the Department of Justice. . . .

. . . Many workingmen, especially steel workers, have come to suspect that the government, *as government,* has taken sides in industrial warfare; has taken sides against workingmen. . . .

The maintenance of the non-unionism alternative, therefore, entailed for the steel companies activities running from spies in church offices in New York to sealed carloads of negroes shipped into Pittsburgh plant yards at night. For communities and for states the alternative entailed activities of greater import and greater menace. These affected civil liberties in whole communities, local legislative bodies, police authorities, judges, state police troops, Federal government departments and the U.S. Army.

The consequences . . . are perhaps most important in regard to the abrogation of civil liberties. War-experiences especially have accustomed the American people to the thought that the right of assembly, the right of free speech, and traditional personal rights can be abrogated when the cause is deemed sufficiently great. The practise of western Pennsylvania proved that these rights were abrogated for the purpose of preventing the organization of trade unions among steel workers, or of defeating organized unions. The abrogations largely persist four months after the strike.

2. Ralph Chaplin Recalls the Clampdown of the "Red Scare" of the 1920s

Trouble had been brewing for a long time. The whole country was aroused against us. Public opinion was being lashed into fury as reports from European battle fronts became more disturbing. We were on record as having denounced the war as another capitalist slaughterfest. That didn't help.

Our most intensive organizational drive was under way. We were getting a break at last in our efforts to line up "wage slaves" in support of the "One Big Union" program. Metal miners, longshoremen, seamen, as well as harvest, oil, and construction workers, were flocking to the I.W.W. [Industrial Workers of the World] in droves. Starting with the boxcars, we were obtaining job control in several basic industries. . . . It looked like our inning. We had waited a long time for it. But, while

Excerpted from *Wobbly* by Ralph Chaplin, University of Chicago Press, pp. 219, 223, 225. Copyright © 1948 University of Chicago Press. Reprinted by permission.

this was going on, the information of our strikes, picket lines, and utterances as it reached the public was distorted and exaggerated out of all proportion. There were dark hints about machinery, bridges, and trains that had been "sabotaged." Whenever a haystack or a barn burned down, a posse of good citizens started to look for the Wobbly in the woodpile. Itinerant workers and I.W.W. organizers were every man's game. Local hoosegows were full of "I.W.W. dynamiters." I.W.W. prisoners dragging ball-and-chain were a common sight in many otherwise tranquil towns and cities. . . .

Edith told me the story when I reached home. After giving Vonnie his lunch and seeing him off to school, Edith had gone downtown to do some shopping. Shortly afterward the federal men had arrived. Finding no one at home, they inquired from the janitor where Vonnie attended school. There was much excitement and embarrassment when the teacher turned the little fellow over to the federal agents. "Get into the car, little boy," they urged, "and we'll drive you home." But Vonnie was obdurate. "I'll walk," he insisted. When pressed for a reason, he stated simply, "I know what happened to Frank Little when he went riding with fellows like you!" Later, the special agent asked Edith what he meant by that.

Vonnie walked home with a Department of Justice man on either side of him and another driving the long black limousine. When Edith came home, the car was parked in front of the building. She knew full well what it meant. Vonnie told her breathlessly what had happened. He held her hand tightly. Just as she put the key in the outer lock, three men got out of the car. They were polite, but firm, explaining that they were government men. They merely wanted to search the apartment. Edith asked to see the search warrant. They pushed past her and entered the hallway. Edith mentioned the Bill of Rights. "This is a war emergency," the chief "investigator" answered gruffly. "We had a right to break down that door. You are lucky we didn't."

"Maybe you're lucky my husband isn't here," Edith said. "After all, an American's home is still his castle, and a citizen has a right to defend that home from unlawful entry."

The federal men ransacked our little apartment from one end to the other. They played every phonograph record on the old Victrola and opened our many books separately, fluttering the pages to shake out any loose secret documents. They rolled up carpets, seeking incriminating "charts and diagrams." They took the pictures off the walls and searched every drawer and file for "revolutionary plots and plans."

They discovered a *Ladies' Home Journal* dress pattern, still in its envelope, which the investigators opened up and spread out on the dining-room table. One of them pointed to the perforations and said something in an undertone to the other two. "Surely you don't want that!" Edith said.

"I'm sorry, but the United States Government will have to decide," the special agent answered. . . .

. . . They went to Vonnie's playbox and took out the tinfoil ball which Taro had made for him. This was too much for the youngster. As the special agent reached for the ball, Vonnie said, "You can't have that, it's mine." But the toy was placed with the other "evidence" and carted away in the long black limousine. None of the papers or drawings were ever returned. Nor was any item, seized without search warrant in my home, ever used in the trial. . . .

As the tons of literature and records at the Federal Building were sifted, a fabulous but strangely convincing case was built up against Bill Haywood and key men of the I.W.W. After reading the sensational newspaper accounts of our villainy, I sometimes doubted my own innocence. At least I could understand why some of my acquaintances preferred not to see me on the streets and why neighbors ducked into doorways if I met them in the dimly lit hall coming home from the office.

Things finally reached such a pass that the corner grocer refused to wait on Edith, and Vonnie was shunned by teacher and playmates alike. Even Ida and my father came under the shadow of my evil notoriety. After all, good citizens couldn't afford to take a chance on the sort of people who burned bridges and haystacks or obstructed the war effort with strikes and sabotage.

3. The Employer's Case for Welfare Capitalism, 1925

A variety of purposes move employers to institute pension plans. In setting forth these purposes many employers are inclined to stress their purely benevolent aspect. . . .

Benevolence on its own account, however, cannot long be indulged by the management of a business, particularly when it begins to involve substantial expenditures. To be a legitimate charge on the corporation's income, it must be subordinated to other objects—such as are at least of potential advantage to the business. . . .

First and most common among the avowed purposes of pension programs is the desire to recognize and reward long and faithful service on the part of employees. . . . What distinguishes this view from the ostensibly charitable one referred to above is the recognition that a pension is something earned by the employee, not merely the free gift of the employer. It is earned by dint of length of service, which is of definite value to the business. The granting of a pension is, to be sure, a voluntary act of the employer who, in most cases, admits no contractual obligation on his own part nor any legal right thereto on the part of the employee. But he does acknowledge a moral obligation and a corresponding moral claim to the payment of a pension actually "earned." . . .

While the elements of appreciation and reward are stressed in reference to those employees who have attained the age of retirement, the emphasis as regards the members of the active force is upon earning the reward. For the latter the purpose of the pension is that of encouraging them to give the kind of service which is of greatest value to the company. Primarily this means long and continuous service. This concrete aim is often present, though unexpressed. Sometimes it is suggested, sometimes frankly stated, as in the announcement of a pension plan by a large automobile manufacturing concern, which says:

> These plans will be considered . . . as a participation in the profits of the corporation, rewarding employees for the increased value of their services which result from continuous employment, and from cooperative effort. . . .

From *Industrial Pensions in the United States,* National Industrial Conference Board, 1925, pp. 24–30. Reprinted by permission of The Conference Board.

The reduction in labor turnover, which is implied in long and continuous service records, is a material saving to the company. Every change in personnel involves some temporary loss in efficiency, while unbroken service makes for familiarity with the task and proficiency in performing it. . . . The promise of a pension as the reward of constancy logically, if not actually in every case, carries with it such a recognition of obligation on the part of the employer. It presupposes, moreover, that the expectation of earning the pension will operate as an inducement upon the employee to forgo other advantages elsewhere and to cling to his job to the end. . . .

The manner in which employees may be expected to "earn" their pension reward may include, besides length and continuity of service, also quality of service. Here belong those appeals to loyalty and efficiency which are frequently incorporated in pension plans as the purpose or expectation of the employer in establishing them. . . .

The aim of promoting loyalty, efficiency and a cooperative spirit on the part of the employees by virtue of the pension prospect is expressed with varying degrees of directness in different plans. One states it thus: "The Roll of Honor awaits those who loyally and faithfully serve." Another sets forth that the plan has been adopted by the company—a life insurance company—"in the expectation that economic efficiency in the administration of the business of the Company will thereby be promoted." . . .

It is a significant fact that most pension plans, as at present conducted, make the award in every case dependent on the discretion of the employer. In view of this fact, it is but a step from using the promise of a pension as an incentive to using it as a deterrent. Indeed, the efficacy of the promise for stimulating continuity or quality of service depends in large measure on the employee's realization that the pension may be withheld in the event of his service falling short of expectation on either score. . . .

The use of a pension system as a deterrent or disciplinary device is directed, among other things, against strike action by the employees. A great many plans contain a rule like the following:

> Persons who leave the service thereby relinquish the pension privilege, and if they re-enter the service they shall be considered, for pension record purposes, as new employees.

The intention is less veiled in the following phrasing of the rule:

> If an employee, after leaving the service voluntarily, or by participating in a strike, shall be re-employed, he shall be considered in his relation to the Pension System as a new employee.

The same end is accomplished indirectly in many plans by making the test of "loyalty" and "morale" include the employee's behavior at a time of unrest in the force.

4. Labor's Case Against Welfare Capitalism, 1927

The corporations and their spokesmen as usual claim the very best intentions and the very highest purposes. They talk about "Contact, Conference, Confidence and Cooperation" as the guide posts of personnel work. They express very generous

Source: *The Americanization of Labor* by Robert Dunn, International Publishers Co., Inc. Copyright © 1927, pp. 197–207.

sentiments about "service and profit walking hand in hand," about "human engineering" and team work and the Golden Rule. One hears that the "employees' transcendental ethical sense" is being developed. Industry is being "humanized"; the "man factor is being intelligently handled"; the spirit of cooperation and family unity is said to be at work in the plant, and the "remedy" is to be found "not in any one reform, but in the gradual readjustment of our relations with each other, with the physical world around us, and with God." . . .

Leaving aside for the moment these magnanimous intentions and noble words let us examine some other welfare motives both hidden and expressed. The first one might be summarized in the words of the head of the Steel Corporation—"welfare work pays." Of course some of the items more than pay for themselves, the only expense being for the initial "sales talks" or for the personnel director who supervises the installation. The average corporation using welfare would probably phrase the results in much the same words as an official of the Marion Steam Shovel Co., "We consider all the activities eminently worth while and productive of the spirit of goodwill and cooperation far beyond the expenses which they entail." Others call it a "good investment." The *Nation's Business,* published by the United States Chamber of Commerce, puts it more bluntly: "Every attempt at patronage by employers is resented by 100% Americans. Welfare work of employers has been a failure except when the employer frankly admitted that his motive was selfish." This is probably not strictly true but it represents a more realistic attitude toward welfare which contrasts favorably with the sentimental attitudes expressed above.

That welfare work is often used to keep down wages is another charge that cannot be denied. Even the conservative *Commerce and Finance* (Feb. 4, 1925, p. 243) admits that "some of the attempts at welfare were spurious in that they were substitutes for an adequate wage, were devised principally to tie the worker more firmly to his job, and were to a great extent empty forms devoid of spirit." . . .

In addition to being a good investment and a dividend-paying proposition as the big companies, such as the Eastman Kodak Co. contend, welfare work can always be pointed to in an emergency as an indication of what the company *has done* for its workers even though many of the devices are properly a part of the business itself and have been recommended by engineers as a necessary expense on behalf of efficiency and production. Every time the wage increase question comes up before the company union committee, for example, the company representative can say in effect: "Look what we pay out for welfare. How can you expect us to do more than this?" Then he reels off the impressive figures representing the amounts spent for safety, housing, polo fields and plant cafeterias. To the public also the publicity agents of the corporation address their releases concerning the generosity of the company. In case of a strike or a threat of strike the company by complaining of its workers' "ingratitude" thus publicly admits that its handouts were made in the hope of cashing in on them during a crisis. The cant and hypocrisy involved in these maneuvers can scarcely be exaggerated. With the welfare spade the company can quite easily dig itself out of an embarrassing wage situation where, other things being equal, the public might incline to the side of the workers. . . .

"Loyalty" is, of course, the first word that falls from the employer's lips when the reasons for welfare are asked. "We must have the worker's loyalty. Welfare, properly applied, will strengthen it." One personnel manager, employed by a big Insull public utility company in the Middle West has declared that he adopted the machine politician's policy of "personal contacts" in building up his industrial relations department. Help the employees out in small things, when they are in personal trouble, and they will stand behind you loyally in the crisis. He says, "They come to us for advice on all sorts of questions and we help them out." The ideal situation to be attained may be put in the words of the *Manufacturers' Record* (July 22, 1926), in describing the southern textile serfs: "These people, inherently proud even in poverty, possessed a keen sense of honor, and this character is reflected in their intense patriotism and loyalty to their employers." There can be no doubt that welfare breeds this kind of "loyalty" which in the minds of editors of manufacturers' journals, means a nice blend of subordination, subserviency, humility, feudal allegiance, respectful homage, and, as the *New Republic* puts it, "the dutiful respect of the inferior for the superior, the unthinking response of the true and faithful and rather stupid servant, who shall not be without his reward." This abject surrender to an emotional identification with the employer, this sycophantic relationship to the corporation is the ideal pursued by most of the practitioners of welfare. It stands out clearly in every strike situation where the scabs are proudly referred to by the proprietors of the factory as "loyal employees." It is implied in all the "happy family" propaganda issued by the human relations experts.

Welfare work is also one very good way to keep workers from discussing their real grievances. In his book on *Representative Government in Industry,* James Myers, formerly Executive Secretary of the Board of Operatives of the Dutchess Bleachery, and a liberal churchman, writes: "The Manager of Industrial Relations in a large and well-known electrical concern in the East asked me if we employed motion pictures in the plant with which I was connected. I said that we had them occasionally. 'Well,' he said, 'we have them every day at noon. They are remarkably successful. There is something about the movies that the employees can't resist. Even if they think that you are trying to put something over on them, they come in anyway. In this way we fill up the employees' time during the noon hour and keep them from getting together in little groups and talking about their troubles.' " . . .

Care and strategy are needed to prevent workers from unionizing—and this is the primary purpose of much welfare and personal activity. "Labor shortage and the fear of unionization during the period in which organization was spreading rapidly have been principally responsible for the sudden interest in personnel administration." H. C. Metcalfe, now Vice-President of the Continental Baking Co., phrases this motive more skillfully. Writing on the introduction of personnel practices in industry he says, "Many employers doubtless desired less irritating and indirect dealings with the working force than were possible through union agents." In other words the unions were asked to retire and permit the personnel manager to become the "labor leader" in the plant. . . .

Preventing trade unionism and "driving out the radicals" have become almost synonymous functions, for the radicals today are among the most tireless workers for the unionization of the unorganized. Some of the advocates of welfare make it clear that they aim directly at the radicals when they introduce their schemes. In an article in *Industrial Management* (Feb. 1925, p. 92) headed "Management's Greatest Opportunity—Personnel Directors Tell How Common Sense Management Policies are Driving the Radicals out of the Ranks of Labor," Will G. Caldwell says that during an unemployment period when there is a plentiful supply of labor, "it is indeed a great opportunity for management to prove to labor that the agitator, the organizer and the 'red' has no place in American laboring circles—that labor's best bet is in management itself." . . .

Another point stressed by employers in discussing welfare work is that it prevents what they consider restrictive and unfavorable legislation and regulation. To be able to point to a certain amount of spurious welfare work is often to deceive the legislators and to convince them that state action to protect the workers is unnecessary. Undoubtedly a great many such services are inspired by the fear of what the "uplifters," as they call persons working for decent social legislation, health, insurance, workmen's compensation, etc., may do to the corporations if they fail to grant a few apparent concessions to their workers.

5. The National Association of Manufacturers Defends the Open Shop, 1922

I. Definition.   "A shop in which there is no discrimination against workers because of membership or non-membership in a lawful organization operating in a lawful manner." . . .

. . . As you know in the past two years our chief effort has been to convince the public that the open shop was for its best interests. We have not argued primarily that the open shop would benefit the employer or even that it would benefit the worker. We have, on the contrary, asserted their interests are secondary to the interests of the general public. The value of this line of argument is shown not only in the fact that it has been extremely successful, but that closed shop apologists nearly always refuse to discuss the question from that angle.

. . . In their efforts to convince the public, local associations have to a larger extent than ever before, resorted to the use of advertising and to public lectures upon the subject.

. . . It has been recognized the educators are very important molders of public opinion. And as we must attempt to consider the future as well as the present we recognize also that the opinions of our professional teachers of future years are to a large extent based upon the social philosophy they are taught at present. Our own Open Shop Department has upon its mailing lists practically all the college and university teachers of economics, government, and sociology in the country.

The importance of debating contests has also been recognized. High school and college debates are heard in the aggregate by millions of people yearly. In Texas alone last year 1,000,000 persons attended debates on the open shop. Such contests, therefore, provide a fertile field for the providing of sound information which will be heard by many members of the general public. During the past year our Open Shop Department has furnished direct information to at least 1500 debaters. Some State Associations have also recognized the importance of such debates and have endeavored to foster them in every legitimate manner. . . .

From "Status of the Open Shop" (1922), Box 251, National Association of Manufacturers Papers, Hagley Museum and Library, Wilmington, Del.

. . . Especially with the advent of woman suffrage, the clergyman as a molder of public opinion has become extremely important. We have, therefore, devoted a great deal of attention to the furnishing of sound information to the clergy. Last Labor Day, for example, we especially urged all local associations to provide their ministers with sound data for their Labor Day sermons. This request met with a very wide and favorable response. . . .

VII. Arguments of the Opposition.   The open shop is non-union.

. . . This is the most frequent claim made by closed shop advocates. It is aimed to bring conviction to the general public. Labor mis-leaders know that the public is opposed to any restrictions of the right to organize for lawful aims, and that if the public can be persuaded the closed shop is the only way to retain organization, that the public will be alienated from the open shop. Constant reiteration will, it is believed, bring conviction.

. . . The argument must, therefore, be constantly denied, both in words and practice. Employers have no right to organize and to refuse that right to others. They have only the right to oppose organizations which are not representative of their own employees, which are not lawful in their purpose, which do not use lawful methods, and whose practices are uneconomic and wasteful and hence unfair and burdensome to the general public.

. . . The Philadelphia Public Ledger rendered a valuable service to the open shop in its symposium of July 3, 1921, completely disapproving the argument that the open shop is only a non-union shop.

Many employers' associations operate employment bureaus which do not inquire about or discriminate because of union membership, thus giving assurance to the workers that the claims of their own leaders are false. The effect, of course, is to weaken reliance upon and membership in the unions—but because of the latter's weaknesses and unreliability. . . .

VIII. Where Is Our Danger.

. . . We must constantly make our real position known to the general public.

. . . We must back up our words with reality. We say that open shop plants are not non-union. Do we mean it? Can the public know we mean it? One national association issued repeated bulletins announcing belief in and adherence to the open shop—and at the same time said that no unionists should be allowed to work unless they tore up their cards. Mr. Edgerton, as President of our Association, issued a statement asserting that while employers had a right to operate non-union shops if they desired, they had no claim to be operating "open" shops.

6. The AFL Condemns the Open Shop, 1921

The drive now on for the "open shop" is a drive against unionism. Nothing else. No one need be fooled in this respect except those who want to be fooled. It is the old Bourbon fight. It is the wearisome, reactionary cry of those who "learn nothing and

From James Lord, "The 'Open Shop,'" *American Federationist*, 28 (January 1921), 49–50.

forget nothing." To anticipate industrial peace and orderly progress through this misguided and misleading tenet is worse than useless. The entire argument is as misleading as the term "open shop," or the purpose of its sponsors.

The real purpose of the "open shop" is to destroy the efforts of all effective labor unions and subject the workers to the complete selfish domination of the employers. This idea, old, antiquated as the bow and arrow, inadequate in all the processes of industrial history, can never find an abiding place in the minds of a free people. What right have one set of citizens in our Republic to say to another set: "We shall not recognize *your* associations, we shall be guided by the wisdom of *our* association in dealing with *your* affairs." Just the same right they would have to say that this government should be conducted on the "open shop" basis, and that those who remained aloof from membership or participation in the government, or who refused to subscribe to taxation, would have the right to enjoy a full measure of the benefits of the government.

The men and women in industry, like the citizens of the Republic, can only make their desires and aspirations known through collective action, and by collectively selecting their spokesmen and representatives. Industrial peace will be maintained in the same proportion as adequate joint relations and understandings are established between employer and employe through their respective organizations. With each side privileged to put forward any idea in joint conference that seems fit and proper, with no undue restraint or advantage on either side, and where nothing can be adopted except it receives the unit vote of both sides, intelligent and orderly peace may be achieved in industry. A joint agreement reached in this manner, is the property and concern of both sides, and is subject to amendment and perfection as time and experience warrant. The erection of adequate machinery for the peaceful settlement of disputes, guarantees that industry will be kept in operation during the life of the agreement, are questions for joint consideration by both parties. To write an agreement, with either side refusing to recognize the equity or association of the other side is as futile as walking on the hands to save shoe leather.

The union shop is the real "open shop." It is open to all workers, in every trade and industry, who desire to join and lend their efforts to an intelligent solution of their affairs. No matter what their past attitude has been, no matter what they in their ignorance have done to retard progress in their own and other men's affairs, the past is wiped out that minute they exhibit a desire to carry their share of the burden and costs of their own movement, as well as share in its achievements and blessings.

The non-union shop is the real "closed shop," closed to any measure of democratic action by the workers. Under the policy generally known as the "open shop," the employes have no power to resist any changes detrimental to their interests the employer wants to force on them. True, in some instances, some form of joint relations appear to exist, where grievances are considered "jointly," but they amount to just as much as "playing horse" as far as any real results are concerned. It is just a pitiful pretence. On the employers' side is a complete organization, as complete in every respect as they are able or desire to make it, while on the other side is disorganization, lack of any considered policy, and simply the privilege of taking part in a pretence of joint relations which are absolutely set up by the employers. As far as getting the collective advice or desires of the workers in the industry, or conferring with them in the event they ought to resist some particular decision emanating from the employers, they are as helpless as galley slaves. The entire procedure is an empty farce. To give these "open shop" movements some appearance of being genuine, the particular clauses dealing with the handling of grievances, are invariably copied from existing joint agreements between unions of workers and their employers. They read alike, word for word, but always, when the interval for "playing horse" is over, the terms of the employers are final and there is no appeal. This joint movement, agreement and all, is their creation and property.

There are two kinds of shops in vogue, and they are properly termed union shop and non-union shop. Under the union shop plan, the controversial matters that arise in industry are brought into a real joint conference and dealt with intelligently. This method naturally brings to the workers, not only an interest in their own affairs, but an interest in the industry itself, and the desire to keep up a sensible, sane relationship and continuity of production. The human equation is recognized and the atmosphere is altogether clearer for both sides. Better cooperation and greater efficiency is manifested all along the line, and the workers under such conditions will watch with jealous eyes any attempt to jeopardize these relations, coming from either side. Where full opportunity to express their views is denied the workers, every semblance of mutuality is swept from the situation and the most intelligent and thoughtful of the workers realize that they are up against an absolute dictation of terms by their industrial taskmasters, from which there is no escape other than by force.

Industry, in the hands of workers who are denied full expression of their desires and needs, is carried on in a desultory or dissatisfied way, a sullen or open spirit of enmity is prevalent in all phases of industry all the time, and the irreconcilable in the ranks of the workers can get a fuller play and more attention from the workers than in any other situation. He has been furnished with the reason, or the ammunition, for inflaming his fellows, preaching discontent and often bringing about industrial chaos and stagnation.

Those who are carrying on the fight for the "open shop," whether because they are paid for it, are dependent on social or business patronage through it, or simply because they know no better, are working in one of the surest ways possible to bring about an industrial upheaval in America. The fact that they can put across some phase of their program for the minute, or that they are the recipients of momentary applause, signifies nothing but the fact that they have made a contribution to the most uncertain situation that has ever existed in this world.

The workers know, by bitter experience, what the terms "open shop" and "closed shop" mean. They know that their hope for the future rests in their ability to make progress now in the thinly veiled fight for the non-union shop as against the union shop, or free action as against suppression, and I was never more sincere in my life when I say that nothing in the world can stop the men and women who do the useful work of our country, by hand or brain, from forging ahead with such measures of freedom as they now have, to a greater and better environment, and to try to block or sidetrack this desire is to try to dam the forces of Niagara, to later meet these pent up forces with the additional power gained by being held back from their natural course.

The future of industry will be largely determined by what is done today. Intelligent analysis and action today mean better relations and understanding tomorrow, while beclouding and misrepresenting the issues of today mean widening the breach and adding to the uncertainty and unrest for tomorrow.

Nothing in the world has ever permanently stopped the desire for truth and freedom in the mind of man. Nothing ever can. Then where is the gain in temporizing with a situation that anyone who desires may fully understand? The workers are demanding the full, unrestricted rights of citizenship in this country equal in all things, to any other class of citizens, and the rights of free speech, a free press, the right of peaceful assembly and the right to form their own association, according to the constitution of these United States, are rights that they will defend now just as quickly as they did at Lexington and Concord, at Shiloh and at Gettysburg. And the workers are also a part of *the public.*

7. Employers Consider the Regulation of Women's Work, 1920

The Chairman: Mr. Secretary, we are ready to proceed to the next paragraph.

Secretary Boudinot: "We do not believe in the regulation by legislation of hours, rates and conditions of employment, excepting in the case of child or female labor, or where peculiar occupational conditions affecting the health, safety, and welfare of the worker exist, and that any regulation or legislation by the government beyond such necessities are not consistent with the highest interest of all concerned."

The Chairman: Are there any objections? If not, a motion to approve will be in order.

Mr. Harry Sharp, Kansas: Mr. President, I would like to move an amendment to that by striking out the word "female" and leave it stand at child labor. The legislation in the state of Kansas with regard to restrictions on hours of service and the establishment of minimum wages and sanitary conditions surrounding employment of women in industry has reached the point where we have had to appeal to the Courts for protection and I think it should be discouraged. That is a matter of contractual right, wherein, perhaps, the rights of women would be best served to let it remain as such. The women of the state of Kansas, to a very general degree, are supporting us in our contention.

Mr. L. J. Williams, Michigan: Mr. President, I will say that the committee has no very set conclusions as to the inclusion of the limitation on females. We put it in there so that it could be considered and discussed by the committee of the whole. We did have in mind the fact that women are the mothers of our men, and we considered the matter of maternity, and we considered the fact that the conditions under which women should work are matters involving a peculiar public interest, as is the matter of child labor, and I think it is something that we should give most careful consideration before we make such an amendment as has been proposed.

From "Stenographer's Minutes of Special Conference of Delegates" (May 1920), 195–196, Accession 1412, National Association of Manufacturers Papers, Hagley Museum and Library, Wilmington, Del.

8. The AFL Ignores Women, 1927

Although there are some eleven million women in industry in the United States, only a small proportion, perhaps 250,000, are in the trade unions. The common attitude of most union leaders is that women cannot be organized. Actually, the problem is a different one: how to fit women into the trade unions. The admission of women involves new policies, new responsibilities, and new difficulties. Rather than face them and make the necessary adjustments, union officials have preferred to "let the women alone."

The life of a union official is hard. The work is discouraging and exhausting. The reward for a man is a higher office, with increasing responsibility. He becomes manager of his local union or joint board. He becomes a national officer. There are no such opportunities for women. Women have successfully held minor offices in their local unions. They have been efficient business agents and organizers. Rarely have they held offices of importance. A few women have been international officers, but no woman has ever been on the Executive Council of the American Federation of Labor. Most of the few women who have attained prominence in the trade-union movement have discreetly tried to play the union game as men play it. They have realized that their prestige and position were at stake. On the theory that a poor union is better than no union they have steadily refused to embarrass labor officials by a vigorous protest at the discriminations and inequalities to which women have been subjected in the unions. As a result they have been unable to achieve any outstanding leadership among the rank and file of trade-union women.

When women come into the unions they are, generally speaking, controlled by men officials, particularly when the women in the trade, both organized and unorganized, outnumber the men. I remember one prominent international officer who said, referring to a woman's local which had made remarkable strides under the leadership of women officers: "These women need to be protected. They have a membership now which is ample to pay a good salary to a man official whom we shall appoint. From now on we are going to have iron control over this local." Another official bitterly condemned workers' education classes in his union. The attendance had been largely made up of women. "They have all become lefts," said he indignantly. "That is what education for women does. Now see the trouble they are making us."

The struggles of promising rank-and-file girls for recognition have met not only lack of cooperation but often direct sabotage from their trade-union brothers. . . .

In Newark, New Jersey, last summer, a campaign was initiated to try out the American Federation of Labor's Tentative Plan to Organize Women which had been adopted at the 1925 convention. It was the first move on the part of the federation to face the problem of the unorganized women. The plan provided that the various unions in a given locality should make a joint intensive drive to organize women under their jurisdiction. Each union was to supply its own organizers and its own technique and the particular literature necessary for its special trade problems. The impetus given by such systematic and thorough work progressing simultaneously in

Reprinted with permission from the March 23, 1927 issue of *The Nation* magazine.

different industries would create a trade-union consciousness among women workers and have a tremendous educational value in the entire community.

A legislative agent of the federation—Edward F. McGrady—sent from Washington as an "observer," was in charge of the drive. But neither he nor the unions involved cared whether it was successful, and consequently it was a failure. Another woman and myself, both experienced in organization work, made an effort to take part in the Newark campaign. The legislative agent agreed to consider us as organizers and made an appointment to discuss the campaign with us. He took us to lunch at his favorite restaurant in the theatrical district of New York. We selected a modest lunch, appalled at the high prices, while he consumed a most elaborate one. It was apparent that he had repented of his rashness in interviewing us, for now he would not have us. He used all the old arguments to discourage us: women could not be organized; women did not want to be organized; women had been organized, at great trouble and expense, and their unions had not lasted. We countered on every point.

By this time, he was smoking expensive cigars. "You say you want to work with women; I know a good place for you—go work for the Y. W. C. A."

"We want to work with women in the Newark campaign," we answered promptly.

He was much annoyed, but he made another effort: "Why don't you forget all this business and leave the labor movement to men? It's too rough for women. Why don't you get married?"

"Perhaps we are married," we answered cheerfully; "we still want to organize women into trade unions in Newark."

"You are hopeless," he said angrily. He fled from us in a taxi. His parting words were no more encouraging: "If you want to organize women, you'll have to wait until the federation gets around to it. We think the time isn't ripe yet. It will not be for another twenty-five or fifty years. The trouble with you is that you are ahead of your time."

Must the millions of exploited women, miserably underpaid and overworked, wait until the A. F. of L. gets around to them—in twenty-five or fifty years? The slogan "Organize the Unorganized" was not raised in vain in the Passaic strike. Passaic has proved beyond doubt that the organization of men and women can take place side by side, if the purpose exists and the work is undertaken on a large scale in the basic industries. Let it be upon an equal footing, so that a new spirit and new standards may rebuild the trade unions and create a vigorous, honest, and progressive American labor movement.

9. The Women's Bureau Exposes the Myths About Women's Work, 1924

The time has come when facts not fancies must regulate the position of wage-earning women. Women are in industry to stay, for industry needs women to produce the world's goods, and women need industry to enable them to earn a living. . . .

From U.S. Department of Labor, Women's Bureau. *Radio Talks on Women in Industry.* Bulletin No. 36 (Washington D.C.: Government Printing Office, 1924), 32–34.

Among the first great troubles to be fought are the false ideas and old preju-dices about women in industry that are firmly rooted in the minds of many people. These old-fashioned ideas are a hangover from several scores of years ago when a few scattered women first ventured to work outside the home. Now, when there are more than eight and a half million working women, when one-fifth of the wage earners in the United States are women, these old theories are fast being exploded, for antiquated traditions about women in industry are as much out of place as hoop skirts, and are just as useless and cumbersome. If these prejudices are cluttering up your minds like cobwebs, there is no better time than the present for a good mental housecleaning.

The first prejudice to discard is the "pin-money theory." What mischief it has wrought in keeping women's wages low! Are you guilty? Have you believed that women work in order to get money for feminine fripperies? Or have you re-alized that the great bulk of women who work in stores, factories, mills, laun-dries, and restaurants must earn money for the bare essentials of life? Cold, hard facts and statistics collected by the Women's Bureau and by many other organi-zations prove that women have to work to buy food and pay rent and frequently to support dependents as well, and that the size of their earnings is of real social significance.

Following closely on the heels of the pin-money theory is the idea that girls who live at home can get along on very low wages, since their families will help to support them. This idea is not only wrong—it is vicious. When unscrupulous em-ployers offer it as an excuse for low pay the public is satisfied and the girls them-selves suffer. Frequently, instead of the family income serving to supplement the girl's wage, it is the girl's wage that must supplement the family income to make ends meet. . . .

Another theory to be discarded—the sooner the better—is that all women are transients in the industrial world. Are you one of the many people who believe that girls go into stores and factories only until they marry? The truth is a number of women never marry, but work 40 or 50 years in industry. Furthermore, many mar-ried women must continue to work after marriage to keep the wolf from the door. . . . Also, in the ranks of industrial toilers are many widows who must be fa-thers as well as mothers to their children, who must be breadwinners as well as home-makers. . . .

There is another mistaken theory that glibly falls from the lips of those who don't know. Those folks who call themselves old-fashioned and are always harping on the idea that woman's place is in the home, believe that women go into stores, factories, and mills because they prefer that kind of labor to housework. If these same old-fashioned theorists could take a peep into the homes of most wage-earning women they would discover these same women, after 8 or 10 hours of in-dustrial work, toiling in the home, at the stove, dish-pan, wash-tub, or sewing machine. Housework must be done before and after factory work each day, even though women get up at 4 a.m. and go to bed at midnight.

There are many more fallacies about women in industry, enough to fill a vol-ume or two—they can not all be given in a short radio talk. Instead, everyone must be constantly on the lookout for themselves, to be sure that they are not encouraging theories based on prejudices rather than on facts.

E S S A Y S

In the first essay, Rick Halpern suggests how welfare capitalists employed a carrot and a stick—the promise of fringe benefits coupled with dismal and coercive working conditions—to fend off the threat of unionization. In the case of the packinghouses, as Halpern documents, managers and unions maintained starkly divergent views of the sincerity and efficacy of private welfare programs. In the second essay, Alice Kessler-Harris examines the tensions between the labor movement and women workers. Even in the female-dominated garment trades, as Kessler-Harris shows, male unionists feared that women workers threatened the sanctity of male wages and the security of the labor movement.

Welfare Capitalism in
the Packinghouses

RICK HALPERN

The large packing firms joined the most progressive segment of American business in advancing a new variety of welfare capitalism in the 1920s. The packers had first experimented with pension plans, stock ownership, and recreational activities earlier in the century. Initially, these programs were designed to win the loyalty of a narrow segment of the workforce—the elite butcher aristocracy whose skills remained essential to production, or the black workers whose reserve labor figured critically into the packers' calculations. In the 1920s, a more ambitious program was put in place. It encompassed all hourly workers and, unlike the earlier effort, aimed to increase efficiency and productivity as well as inculcate a sense of allegiance to the employer. Far more complex than the modest programs that preceded it, welfare capitalism in the twenties had a contradictory impact upon labor relations.

Swift, the most paternalistic of the large packers, led the way, hiring industrial relations expert John Calder to design and implement programs for all of the company's eighteen plants. Armour and Wilson followed this lead, modeling their respective plans on Swift's. The creation of a joint Committee on Industrial Relations under the auspices of the Institute of American Meatpackers lent a certain degree of coordination to these efforts. Although the brands of welfare capitalism practised by the large packers were not identical, they shared several basic features: employee representation through company unions, a restructuring of work relations through wage incentive schemes and foreman training, and an expanded range of benefits and recreational activities designed to reduce turnover. Each of these areas merits investigation, for in each case reality differed significantly from capital's original intent.

In each plant, the company union functioned as the centerpiece of welfare capitalism. The packers hoped this institution would resolve shop floor conflict and counter more threatening forms of workers' organization. In each department workers elected delegates who met regularly with management representatives in a

Excerpted from "The Iron Fist and the Velvet Glove: Welfare Capitalism in Chicago's Packinghouses, 1921–1933" by Rick Halpern, *Journal of American Studies*, v. 26 (Aug. 1992), pp. 171–183. Copyright © 1992. Reprinted by permission of Cambridge University Press.

"joint conference" or "assembly." The assembly oversaw company sponsored recreational activities, attended to its own procedures and elections, and, most importantly, considered grievances brought to its attention by disgruntled workers.

Most of these cases concerned wage adjustments, disputes with foremen, and working conditions. Hearing between 500 and 800 cases a year, the conference decided in favor of the employee in three-quarters of the disputes. This surprising figure prompts one to question both the nature of grievances which found their way from the shop floor to the conference board as well as the kinds of workers elected to serve as representatives. At least half of the cases heard by the board involved relatively trivial matters. Wage adjustments often referred to instances in which a worker's paycheck was short a few cents, a frequent occurrence for those performing piecework in which complex calculations were required. The far more important question of wage *rates* was outside the board's jurisdiction.

Other cases concerning safety, recreation, and food service posed little threat to power relations in the plant and could safely be decided in favor of the employee. "I could have asked for a new towel, or for some new soap in the wash basin," one worker recalled, but "if I would have asked for a raise would I have gotten that?" Moreover, at both Armour and Swift, plant superintendents exercised veto power over the board's rulings, making it unlikely that matters of substance would be decided as a result of the grievance process. At Wilson, the grievance mechanism was a transparent sham. Soon after going to work in the plant, John Wrublewski appealed a two-day suspension received for "sassing" his foreman. Nothing was done. When he pressed the matter, his representative shrugged, saying "we can't have workers bossing the bosses now can we?"

At the other end of the spectrum were cases in which the grievance system upheld management's authority. Here the involvement of workers' representatives helped legitimate unpopular policies and diffuse resentment. When women in Armour's canning department asked for rubber mats upon which to stand, their representative reported back that "the company couldn't afford mats but they would consider putting out some rags and old papers." Workers realized that this pecuniary rationale was preposterous, but in the weeks that had elapsed "the matter just kind of died." By handling grievances on an individual rather than a collective basis, the system had the effect of isolating workers from one another. Plainly the company union never served as any kind of bargaining agent, even if it could act within the joint council as a workers' advocate.

How individual representatives in the company unions voted in these matters is not known, but workers who served in this capacity tended to be older, male, skilled employees who had demonstrated their loyalty to the company. A majority of the representatives were native-born; and those who immigrated hailed from Ireland, Canada, or Germany. Numerous restrictions on eligibility—including U.S. citizenship and fluency in English—ensured that few Slavs served as delegates. Other workers, whose loyalty was suspect, were prevented from serving by bureaucratic subterfuge or outright prohibition. Describing these delegates, one Armour manager stated that the company, "picked out and selected people throughout the plant who were . . . respected." Workers elected their representatives, "but they had to be agreed upon by management," thus ensuring that "hot-heads" and trouble-makers remained out of positions of authority.

Black workers were especially active in company unions. They, too, tended to be older men who wielded considerable influence in their community. "Big" Mitchell, the representative from the Armour pork trim, was a respected churchman who had worked for the company since 1916. Sometimes these black delegates were cultivated by the company. Lowell Washington, who remained at work during the 1921–22 strike and made no effort to disguise his aversion to "the white man's union," was repeatedly badgered by his foreman to run for office. Other blacks participated not so much out of loyalty to their employers, but because, as one delegate explained, there was considerable "prejudy" against colored men in the independent unions while this was largely absent within company-sponsored representation schemes.

The preponderance of "company men" involved in employee representation plans turned many workers away from participation. C. H. Talley, the treasurer of Armour's Conference Board, also held an appointed position in the company's credit union where he reviewed workers' applications for loans. Intensely disliked, his presence on the Board discredited it. Many workers refused to have anything to do with the company unions, even when subject to punishment or fines for refusing to vote in elections. Although the companies claimed that over eighty percent of their employees were active members, many workers cast ballots or paid their dues under duress. The weekly ten cent dues payment was "like a bribe," recalled Milt Norman, and often was extracted under threat of layoff.

Although employers heralded the company unions as "new institutions of freedom" which would render obsolete the "old aristocracy of unionism," most packinghouse workers placed little stock in them. While on the surface their structure appeared democratic, in reality they were not very representative and possessed a limited ability to meet workers' needs. However, employee representation was not inconsequential. Although lacking independent power or authority, company unions exerted an important influence upon workers' lives. Beyond their limited ability to secure on-the-job improvements, they gave many future CIO activists their first organizational experience, providing them with practical training in parliamentary procedure, grievance writing, and bargaining. Organized on an industrial rather than craft basis, these bodies had the unintended consequence of bringing workers together across the divisions of skill, ethnicity, and race. In the short run, such unions may have contributed to the maintenance of capital's hegemony, in the long term they functioned as foils for bona fide unionism and as "schools" for workers.

The second element of the packers' welfare capitalism, the restructuring of work relations, had greater impact upon workers' lives. Here the rise of personnel departments and the introduction of wage incentives changed the nature of labor in many departments. Again, the actual results of these reforms were vastly different from those anticipated by the packers. Centralized hiring offices and training programs might have reduced the power of foremen, but they continued to dominate the shop floor. "Fitting the workers to the job" sounded good in the companies' annual reports, but meant little when most jobs were interchangeable and fluctuating production levels necessitated frequent layoffs. Bonus plans may have enticed some workers to labor more diligently, but they allowed very few of them to take home larger paychecks. Instead of creating a community of interest, they produced confusion, discord, and resentment.

These attempts to rationalize labor policy resulted from management's realization that past unrest stemmed largely from workers' resentment over the treatment they received at the hands of immediate superiors. By standardizing jobs and wages, and by investing control of hiring and firing in centralized personnel departments, the packers hoped to improve the way in which workers experienced company authority. While the near total autonomy exercised by foremen was necessary during the earlier struggle to deprive skilled craftsmen of control over production, it now jeopardized the company's hold over its employees. Accordingly, special training programs designed to sensitize supervisors to the "human factor" when handling workers and to familiarize them with the "executive viewpoint" were instituted. At the same time, trained engineers armed with stopwatches and slide rules began making many of the production decisions previously determined by departmental foremen.

Yet the policies formulated by the "I-R" specialists rarely translated into rational, scientific practice in the rough and tumble world of the shop floor. Despite training programs and courses, foremanship largely remained a matter of brawn. The selection of straw bosses and foremen "wasn't really what you call a corporate operation," recalled one worker. "It was just who was the toughest guy down there." Tommy Megan, a kill floor foreman at a Swift subsidiary plant, thought that company's pamphlets and guidelines were "a load of crap. . . . You knew how to get the job done because you'd been out there yourself, you'd come up through the ranks, not because some book said to do it one way and not the other." Many foremen resented the intrusions of college-educated time-study engineers and ignored the "eggheads" who "knew how to make numbers dance but couldn't tell a steer from a sow."

The "foreman's empire" did not collapse in the face of reform. In the key areas of hiring, firing, and promotion, departmental foremen continued to wield significant power. As far as hiring was concerned, two parallel processes emerged. The centralized employment office managed the daily "roustabout," selecting common labor from the morning crowd of job seekers and assigning the hirees to departments in need of additional hands. Although the companies devoted lip-service to the use of specialists and the distribution of proper "types" of workers in the labor force, the hiring of casual labor remained a simple matter of physically sizing up potential recruits. Typically, the employment manager tapped an applicant's chest, felt his muscles, and even checked his teeth. "You'd think he was buying a horse," one worker recalled.

Since foremen were more likely to reside in the "Back-of-the-Yards" neighborhood than white-collar specialists, they continued to play the major role in hiring. Their personal contacts among packinghouse workers were a more valuable resource than the files of the employment manager. This was especially true for skilled labor. When Tommy Megan's gang was short, he would send a runner to the homes of neighbors whom he knew would appreciate the opportunity to fill in. Moreover, many workers hired through the personnel office gained entry there by waving a foreman's recommendation or by referring to him by name.

Job security and promotion were equally dependent upon the foreman's good will even though company policy supposedly dictated such matters. Favoritism did not decline in the 1920s; foremen continued to reward workers they liked and penalize those whom they did not. Armour workers commonly referred to "half-pint" seniority. "On all the holidays . . . you'd see the men coming to work with their pockets bulging and taking the foremen off in corners, handing over their half pints. Your job wasn't worth much if you didn't observe the holiday custom." At other times of the year a cigar, a cash bribe, or other gift often meant the difference between work and layoff.

Women contended with another kind of pressure; their accounts are filled with stories about unwanted sexual advances and the threats which followed their rejection. "You could get along swell if you let the boss slap you on the behind and feel you up," grumbled Anna Novak. Married women were not immune from this kind of harassment. "They'd tell you you was going out with them, *tell you*," remembered Gertie Kamarczyk. "And if you didn't, they'd make it rough . . . they'd put you on a tough job, or they wouldn't let you leave to go to the john, or they would fool with your pay. . . . What could you do? They was the boss, the union was gone, we were scared and needed those jobs so bad."

The most important change in packinghouse work that occurred in the 1920s was the introduction of wage-incentive schemes in almost all of the Chicago plants. Each of the large houses and several of the independents replaced straight time and piecework remuneration with some kind of bonus system. At first a number of methods were employed—"Manchester Piecework," "the Halsey Premium," "Taylor Differential Piecework"—each of which involved the calculation, using time and motion studies, of an hourly standard for each job. Workers exceeding the standard received a cash bonus tied to their individual production. By the end of the decade, however, the system devised by French industrial engineer Charles Bedaux had been universally adopted.

The Bedaux System reduced each job to a unit termed a 'B'—the amount of work performed in one minute by a normally skilled operator working under normal conditions at his normal rate of speed. A 'B' value then was assigned to each job, with sixty 'B's established as the normal amount of work per hour. While workers continued to earn their base hourly wage, they received a premium if their production during eight hours exceeded 480 'B's. At the end of the week, each employee received two paychecks—one for straight time and another which reflected 75 percent of the bonus. The other 25 percent went to the company which, in turn, shared its gain with the worker's foreman.

Within each plant, the Bedaux System was applied in different ways. Swift, the first to implement the system, was the most committed to it. All production workers stood to earn bonuses if they exceeded established rates. Armour initially followed Swift's example, but soon retreated, applying incentives only to those tasks originally performed on a piecework basis. Wilson appears to have done the same, although there the system was abandoned in 1929 on all but a few select jobs. The packers hoped that incentive plans would simultaneously boost productivity and provide workers with a sense of investment in the company. They also expected that the lure of bonuses would break down group solidarity, discourage restriction of output, and isolate individual workers from one another. "When each worker is paid according to his record there is not the same community of interest," one executive stated.

To a certain extent, incentive systems encouraged competition between employees and pushed workers to increase their productivity. But they did not improve workers' self-image about their status as wage-earners. Part of the problem was that it became difficult for workers to earn sizeable bonus payments. As production rates increased, management revised the standards downward. One study found that over twenty percent of those workers in a position to earn premiums failed to do so, while 85 percent took home less than five dollars a week in bonus pay. Another study revealed that in many departments, net pay actually decreased after the introduction of the bonus system.

Even when workers benefited from wage incentives, they rarely evinced an understanding of the complex calculations that determined the size of their payment. "I never could understand how it worked," admitted Porter Jackson, "I dunno how they actually figger it, those bonus hours. Because I know some men get a higher bonus 'n another 'n for doin' the same job." Many employers tried to explain how they arrived at the incentive, but the complex calculations were beyond the limited mathematical abilities of most workers. Thus, instead of recognizing a correlation between exertion and remuneration, workers regarded bonus pay as a fickle occurrence which "seems to rain upon them as a gift from the gods." Bill Voorhis put it this way: "the bonus is like playing the horses. You work hard an' you expect him. You get nothing. You work easy. You get a lot." Another mystified worker concluded simply, "you get just what the bosses want you to have."

Like piecework, wage incentive plans could have a deleterious effect upon group solidarity. Complaints about cut-throat competitiveness abound in workers' testimony. Marian Simmons, who experienced the incentive system in a Kansas City packinghouse, recounted that women in the casings department remained at their stations when their menstrual periods arrived, working in feverish pursuit of the bonus while blood ran down their legs.

Yet workers did not all become unabashed individualists. Instead they found collective ways to protect themselves from the system's excesses. In Swift's sliced bacon department, workers agreed not to exceed the limit of 144 packages per hour, even though larger bonuses beckoned. "A new girl would come in and the oldtimers would train her. They would help her out so that gradually by the end of a certain period of time she was doing the 144. But they would never let anyone go beyond the 144 packages," remembered Vicky Starr. When one "smart-aleck" newcomer attempted to break the limit, co-workers sabotaged her efforts by sending unusable scrap bacon to her station. "We took a loss just to show her," Starr recalled.

Almost every job had certain tricks and shortcuts which workers passed along to one another. When the time-study man entered the department, the shortcuts were left aside and extra, unnecessary motions added to the routine. On certain jobs, the calculation of the bonus involved weighing workers' buckets of trimmed meat. Here, cheating was widespread and often engaged in collectively—workers buried bones or gristle in the bottom of their pails "to make it come out on the heavy side." In some gangs, workers cooperated, storing extra meat that then was used to stretch the output of slower workers. In this way each member received the same pay. This kind of informal organization stemmed from workers' intimate knowledge of the production process. It was a defensive measure that did not subvert the system, or even challenge it. It did yield a sense of control and power—however circumscribed—that helped workers survive from day to day.

The final element of the packing companies' welfare capitalism consisted of the various benefits and amenities provided to workers. Some of these were, in theory, available to all who desired them—medical care for workplace injuries, company credit unions, and an expanded range of recreational activities. Other benefits, such as vacations and pensions, were available only after certain service qualifications were met. Obviously these programs did not directly affect worker productivity. Whether inspired by a sense of noblesse oblige or a more calculating desire to woo workers away from their own institutions, they were designed to promote a feeling of loyalty to the company. In some cases this undoubtedly occurred, but as the packers soon discovered, allegiance to the company could co-exist with allegiance to a host of other sources—family, church, ethnic community, or class. Many workers took advantage of company sponsored benefits but at the same time continued their membership in fraternal orders, kept up their insurance policies, and retained their subscriptions to labor periodicals. Sensing that the programs offered by their employers were unreliable, they hedged their bets, demonstrating a certain savvy while looking out for their families' welfare.

The packing companies' provision of health care for their employees provides a good example of the limited nature of benefits which encouraged workers to take a rather jaundiced view of welfare capitalism. Packinghouse work has always been among the most dangerous kinds of industrial labor, and injuries occurred daily in Chicago's packinghouses. Before the reforms of the 1920s, injured workers were simply sent home. Early in the decade, the large plants opened infirmaries and hired physicians and nurses to staff them. In addition to treating the cuts, bruises, and broken bones that resulted from on the job accidents, medical staff provided lunch hour talks on hygiene and diet, oversaw safety campaigns, and even made house calls.

However, workers soon came to suspect and resent the ministrations of the company doctor. Lectures on health and nutrition often were tinged with nativist condescension towards ethnic cultures and foodways. While some distrust was born out of old world suspicion of modern science, many workers had good reason to avoid the company doctor. A negative health report, a slight heart murmur, or the suspicion of tuberculosis could mean discharge.

Moreover, the quality of the care frequently left much to be desired. Armour workers nicknamed the plant infirmary the "butcher shop," and bemoaned the treatment provided there. "The doctors are lousy in that place," Jean Solter declared,

> They don't give a hang about you. The girls always joke about the 'treatments' they give you. Got a headache? Here you are. White pill. Dizzy spell? Take a pink pill. Cold? Take an aspirin. Sore throat? Take an aspirin.

More serious ailments rarely received adequate attention. Pulmonary and dermatological diseases were rampant in the yards and resulted from working conditions themselves. The dusty wool houses and fertilizer departments produced a kind of infectious brown lung; and hundreds of workers suffered from "pickle hands" and "hog itch", debilitating eczema-like conditions caused by constant contact with brine or entrails. Unwilling to take preventive measures, the medical care the packers provided was inadequate. Workers recognized the hypocrisy involved. "If they really cared about us, they would have cleaned up some of the filthy hell holes in that plant. What good was a band-aid or an aspirin when I was standing up to my ankles in cold water, freezing half to death?" reasoned Laura Rutkowski.

Of course, poor medical attention was better than none. Some workers benefited from the company infirmary, such as the man whose life was saved when a doctor revived him after a freak electrocution or (in a somewhat different vein) the woman who pilfered medicine for her sick child. Other programs had similar effects. Loans from the company credit union helped some workers afford to purchase homes or to see their families through hard times, even as the burden of debt tied them more firmly to their employers. Likewise, company baseball teams gave workers recreational opportunities and the chance to wear "real uniforms that matched," even if that meant ceding leisure time to the employer and having his name emblazoned on their jerseys. Sometimes the trade off was a minor one; at other times it involved greater compromise.

By and large workers were cognizant of their employers' intention to "attach strings" to them through welfare programs. When they applied for a loan or bought into a pension plan, they did so in a calculating way. If welfare capitalism complicated the relationship between capital and labor, it also had unintended consequences. By instituting paid vacations and pensions for long service employees, the packers planted in workers' minds the belief that they had a right to such benefits. This became especially clear after 1929 when, responding to fiscal crisis, the companies abandoned many of the welfare programs they had so proudly instituted earlier and in so doing sharpened the edge of workers' bitterness.

In her study of Chicago's mass production workers Lizabeth Cohen notes that welfare capitalism gave workers new reasons and methods for communicating with one another. Employer sponsored activities engendered more than the "family feeling" that management intended. Such events could just as easily intensify collective identity as diffuse it. In meatpacking, where working-class fragmentation reached a level far exceeding other industries, welfare capitalism ironically provided vehicles that could point in the direction of unity. Company-sponsored glee clubs, sports teams, social clubs, provided packinghouse workers with a bit of common ground upon which they could come together across lines of ethnicity and race. . . .

The very existence of company unions, ineffectual as they were, prompted workers to think about the form that bona fide unionism might assume. Later, in imagining the form their own collective institutions might take, the major lesson to emerge from the 1921–22 defeat was the overriding need for interracial solidarity. Regardless of their racial attitudes or inherited prejudices, workers realized that a divided movement stood little chance of success against the power and resources of the packers. Gertie Kamarczyk explained, "there was a . . . kind of feeling that we just had to work together . . . or the bosses were just gonna let us have it in the neck again." Similar sentiments were expressed by others. Joe Zabritski, who worked at Reliable Packing in the early 1930s, recalled that the old timers in that plant, including many blacklisted veterans of past struggles, resigned themselves to including blacks in the new campaign. "They didn't come in and hug 'em and kiss 'em," he quickly admitted. "But they knew they had to be together, period. Even though some of them were anti-Negro, they still knew you had to be together to form a union and to win some of their demands." Thus, while the defeat of the Amalgamated Meat Cutters resulted in a legacy of fear and distrust, it also spelled the end of exclusionary, craft-based unionism in the stockyards.

The packing companies' policy of placing black workers in strategic departments and advancing them into skilled positions became, as Paul Street has aptly if inelegantly put it, "a dialectical boomerang." Unlike the black migrants who were newcomers to the yards in the 1917–22 period, the blacks who labored alongside whites at the close of the decade were seasoned packinghouse veterans. They shared the work-related grievances of other workers and this provided the most important common ground for the movement that emerged in the 1930s. Especially on the killing floors, where the pace of work was most intense, blacks and whites cooperated in order to survive. When the cattle pens were full, foremen, feeling pressure from their own superiors, pushed these workers to the limits of their endurance. Job actions in these departments continued unabated throughout the 1920s without benefit of formal organization. Here, and in other areas of the packinghouses, the relations of production sustained a tradition of militancy and promoted solidarity among workers. During the twenties, this tradition remained submerged. It required the shock of the Depression and a shift of class forces as a result of the New Deal to bring it to the surface.

The Uneasy Relationship Between Labor and Women

ALICE KESSLER-HARRIS

Tensions between women and men in trade unions were not new in the 1920s. A hundred years earlier, organized men had complained that wage-earning women deprived breadwinners of jobs, reduced wages and lowered standards. Repeatedly in the nineteenth century, they debated the efficacy of organizing women as opposed to excluding them from their trades, and they appealed to the state to regulate women's work lest their own efforts to raise standards be hindered. But I have chosen the 1920s as the focus for exploration and illustration for several reasons. It was a decade when issues posed by the spread of waged work, especially for married women, were the subject of national debate. Trade unions not only participated in the debate, but accepted women for the first time as a permanent factor in the labor force. Women had, after all, just won the vote—a circumstance many thought would move them quickly toward economic equality. Moreover, the decade followed a period of rapid and heady organization by women, such that in 1920 nearly 400,000 women (6.6 percent of all non-agricultural wage-earning women, and 18 percent of all women in industry) belonged to trade unions. Although these figures may seem tiny by present standards, they reflect a quintupling of the absolute numbers of women in trade unions over the preceding ten years, and that alone should have laid to rest prevailing skepticism about the possibility of organizing wage-

From *Women, Work, and Protest: A Century of U.S. Women's Labor History,* edited by Ruth Milkman. © 1985. Reprinted by permission of Routledge Ltd., London, England.

earning women. Indeed, one can argue that by this time most trade unionists involved in female-employing industries had stopped asking whether to organize women and started wondering which women. Given the corporate assault on trade unions in general and an unsympathetic national mood, the possibility for a successful coalition between men and women existed. That this did not occur certainly contributed to (though it by no means explains) declining trade union membership nationwide and the labor movement's relative weakness throughout the decade.

Despite incentives, male trade union leaders failed to create fruitful alliances with the women in their organizations. In an embattled period, one expects little effective organizing activity of men or women, but the record shows a pattern of treatment of women that can be described at best as an uneasy truce. Trade union leaders paid little attention to the methods needed to organize or service their female members. The labor movement as a whole (the rhetoric of American Federation of Labor presidents Gompers and Green notwithstanding) welcomed women no more than in the period before they had demonstrated their effectiveness. Even in the face of the great garment and textile strikes with their militant demonstrations of female commitment and leadership, women remained on the periphery of trade union structures. They were recruited, sometimes reluctantly, as dues-paying members, tolerated as shop-level leaders, and occasionally advanced to become business agents and local and international officers. But incentives or inducements designed to create a loyal and effective female membership were virtually nonexistent.

Instead, we find the opposite. Where it could have fostered harmony, cooperation and a sense of belonging, the trade union movement, persistently mistrusted its female members. It created friction, resentment and defensiveness among them, reducing their value and undermining their ability to do good work. Why would a labor movement aware of, and articulate about, the problems posed by female members, consciously perpetuate divisions between these workers and others? . . .

As the political realm altered, so women's relationships to trade unions changed. [Before 1920,] women had won the protective arm of organized labor on the grounds that they were different. Primarily out of self-interested fear of female competition, reinforced by their perception of the male role, trade union leaders had taken advantage of women's need for protection. Now women threatened to take jobs away from organized men. Bitter postwar struggles by women to defend places they had earned during the war effort raised questions about whether women would utilize trade unions to serve their own ends in ways that violated societal norms. In an environment in which political access had reduced the value of moral arguments, leaving economic clout as the only viable weapon to win strikes and improve the position of workers, how were trade unions to treat women? From the male trade union perspective, the demands of women for continued protection as future mothers, on the one hand, and their insistence on equality in the competition for jobs, on the other, seemed irreconcilable. The editor of *Advance,* the official journal of the ACW [Amalgamated Clothing Workers of America], put it this way:

> the social inferiority of women . . . is a sequence of tens of thousands of years of recorded history and development. In a world based upon fierce individual competition, . . . there is no escape from the truth that if women want an improvement of their status, *they must fight for the improvement of their status, not appeal to men.*

In the new environment of the 1920s, protection would come from legislation, while trade unions would reduce competition for jobs by organizing those women who competed directly with their male members. Women inside unions would continue to be treated as 'different' but now not because they required protection, but because they lacked economic power.

From the perspective of the female trade unionist, in contrast, membership was an invitation to struggle for equal pay and access to good jobs. Believing that their new political voice could be translated into economic power, women expected to participate fully in union activities. They abandoned the tactics of moral suasion as well as the security of their own 'communitas,' hoping to join trade union structures as full-fledged political participants. Yet the continuing belief in women's special place, coupled with the realities of discrimination, led trade union women to resist attempts to dismantle the hard-won privileges of legislative protection—a solution that yielded divided loyalties. Where wage-earning women were concerned, the trade union was only one avenue for increasing well-being. The other, which was heir to the higher morality of the pre-war period, was protective labor legislation. Their ambiguity about the relationship between equality and difference left women who were inside the trade union movement vulnerable in struggles for power and, because ambiguity provided an alternative means for regulating job competition, encouraged male trade unionists to treat women as 'outsiders.'

Women's own perceptions of the work experience explain how easily that happened. . . . Women, as a group, bring to the work experience a socialization, a set of values, roots in home and family—in short, a *culture*—that shares class, ethnic and racial characteristics with their menfolk, but that differs in terms of gender. While workers with similar traditions and roots share many work values, the 'cultural baggage' associated with gender enters into a woman's sense of 'dignity' or 'honor' at work, ordering her perceptions of what she is willing to tolerate, and what violates her sense of dignity. How women acted on that sense of honor or dignity accounts for much of the strength of their organizing campaigns between 1910 and 1920, and the power of moral suasion in that decade. Their failure to pay attention to these aspects of difference accounts for women's relative weakness in the labor movement of the 1920s. For just as allegiance to trade union discipline among men addresses the cultural factors unique to them, so organizing among women and maintaining their loyalty to the trade union require special attention to the cultural factors unique to wage-earning women. . . .

The assertion of a separate culture that served women so well in organizational campaigns of 1910–20 ran foul of the internal politics of the trade union movement in the 1920s, which adopted a more pessimistic outlook and perceived a heightened need for loyalty. . . . Craft-oriented, protective of special interests, concerned more for its membership than for the whole class of workers, by 1920 the AFL (with which 80 percent of all organized workers were affiliated) had developed a primary commitment to job security and bread-and-butter gains. With the dismemberment of the Industrial Workers of the World in World War I, and the intense divisions within the American left that resulted from the Russian Revolution, unions with a social agenda found themselves operating defensively. In 1920, only 20 percent of US workers belonged to trade unions, and that number was declining. Survival of the institution was key. Battling communism, one side, and the 'American System,' on the other, the AFL and its international affiliates drew the wagons into a tight circle.

By 1920, most US trade unionists had become what they have remained since: agents of 'social closure,' to use Frank Parkin's felicitous phrase. Seeing their major task as preserving or extending the socio-economic position of their members, they operated primarily to increase (or usurp) authority and social place from those above them. Any union's capacity to provide increasing benefits depended on the loyalty of its members, and membership loyalty, conversely, rested on the degree to which leadership came through for them. Leaders had to insure that they could control a job and had the economic resources to sustain lengthy strikes. Weak or potentially weak members were unwelcome, except when leaving such people out might increase labor-market competition and lead to the loss of job control. Then, when closing the doors to membership threatened the possibilities for increased usurpation, trade unions accepted new recruits. Parkin calls this phenomenon 'dual closure.' The trade union's primary gain comes from utilizing the economic power of a strong and united constituency to gain more benefits for its members. A secondary gain derives from keeping out those whose presence would tend to weaken the organization's bargaining power—that is, those who are readily replaceable in the workforce.

Applied to male-dominated trade unions in the 1920s, the concept of dual closure illuminates the persistent tension between the labor movement and wage-earning women. To engage in activities calculated to usurp, the trade union movement required a tight political structure and loyalty on which it could rely. But women as wage-earners were perceived as different—a perception of which women themselves had taken advantage of in the past, and which they were still reluctant to abandon. Could they then be relied upon for the solidarity necessary for successful usurpationary activities? In industries where jobs were largely male-defined, unions preferred simply to exclude them. In other industries, where women competed directly with male members for jobs, unions admitted them to membership and then protected usurpationary struggles by relegating women to special places justified in the same language of difference that women used to protect themselves. To rally women to membership in such female-employing industries as those manufacturing garments, textiles and shoes, unions appealed to shared notions of social justice. In male-dominated industries and crafts, these appeals were unnecessary and unions sought solidarity through exclusion. The conception of woman as outsider served both kinds of unions well. AFL president William Green testified to its continuing value in a 1929 *American Federationist* editorial. 'When there were hand industries in the home,' Green argued, 'women were definitely a part of production undertakings. But when industries left homes to go into factories, men were the first to follow. They made the factory their job before women entered to any appreciable extent.'

If male trade unionists, fearing that women would reduce internal strength or loyalty, could divest themselves of the responsibility of chivalry, they could not so easily shed the burden of a potentially competitive female labor force. The notion of dual closure illuminates some of the discrepancies between the rhetoric of the AFL regarding women and the actions of its constituent members. For while an exclusionary demand relies on the integrity of the group as it already exists, usurpation often involves appeals to some higher authority and morality, such as to the principle of justice or to the right to a living wage. Exclusion calls for internal unity and cohesion against an unwitting Trojan horse; usurpation requires solidarity in the cause of right, and must appear at least to represent all workers. The AFL, representing the labor movement as a whole, could and did take strong moral positions in favor of organizing and integrating women. Not to do so would drive away the support of friendly social reform groups such as the League of Women Voters, the National Consumers' League and the Women's Trade Union League. Introduction and passage of the AFL's well-known resolution and program for organizing women in 1925 must be seen in this light. Cognizant of competition, as well as of the permanent place of women in industry, the AFL asked its affiliates to support an extensive organizing campaign among them. But the campaign foundered, scuttled by local resistance. For, as Theresa Wolfson noted in her classic volume on women workers in the trade unions, the AFL 'has had a far more liberal and far-sighted official attitude than the unions which it depended on for carrying into operation its official attitude.'

The constituent members responsible for carrying out the program had their own protective interests in mind. In their capacity as agents of exclusion, unions in such male-dominated industries as iron-molding continued to refuse to admit women to membership, using legalistic tactics whenever possible and reverting to moral arguments about propriety and a woman's place when it was not. When employers tried to substitute women for male workers, unions too weak to resist the change were forced to confront the issue of solidarity. The Journeymen Barbers' Union provides a good example. Young women began to 'bob' their hair after the war, and barber shops added women to their staff. The union refused to admit 'lady barbers' under a constitutional provision that denied females the right to membership. As shop after shop became 'open' and then moved out of union hands altogether, the union realized it had a problem. Theresa Wolfson records the 1924 convention debate which ranged from questions about whether women's sense of honor from a pecuniary standpoint 'would be as strong as a man's' to whether the presence of several 'ladies in a shop of ten or twelve chairs would be conducive to good discipline.' But the nub of the matter seems to have been whether an attractive woman would 'not have a tendency to create discord among the men, who, up to the time of her admittance to membership, were real working brothers.' Women, in other words, would disrupt the solidarity of male members, interfering with the smooth running of the organization to become, in the end, 'nothing but a blithering liability.' The Brotherhood of Electrical Workers solved this problem by isolating a strong union of female telephone operators into a separate local, where they were relegated to second-class status. Other internationals relied on their ability to control access to the job, or, like the railway clerks and printers, appealed directly to the state to declare their jobs off limits to women. . . .

More complicated issues arose within female-dominated industries where women were of necessity inside the unions. There, the same sense of women's place that excluded women from other unions blinded labor leaders, eager to close ranks in the service of a militant fighting force, to the desirability of community for women. Indeed, they often insisted that women accede to the prevailing male methods and goals, and interpreted women's attempts to find new paths to loyalty and participation as subversive. The ILGWU [International Ladies' Garment Workers' Union] leadership offers repeated examples. Its women leaders insisted, and some of its male vice-presidents recognized, that who organized and the manner of organization had consequences. But the union's General Executive Board (GEB) persisted in attributing failure and success to the character of women, rather than to union policy. So, for example, in 1921, the board decided to suspend 'out of town organization work in the waist and dress industry' because 'to attempt to organize largely gentile girls in the small towns would, under the present conditions, be a waste of money and energy.' This sort of sexism could inhibit a union's growth, for, as one vice-president who successfully organized gentile girls reported, 'Most of them are married which makes them independent and full of fighting spirit. The girls in the little cities, it seems, are the best element.' In 1917, President Benjamin Schlesinger recommended reducing the union's involvement in Toronto because the majority of workers in the industry there were 'women, and largely Gentile, and consequently not an organizable element.' Not everyone agreed with him. When the predictable stagnation happened, the leaders of three Toronto locals chastised the GEB. They asked for an English-speaking woman organizer because 'men organizers appointed by the union failed to achieve satisfactory results . . . and only women organizers can have access to this unorganized element.' Repeatedly, the ILGWU ignored requests such as the one for 'a girl organizer' to go to St Louis; or, in one case, for fifteen unemployed Philadelphia union girls to go to Baltimore where organizer Hortense Powdermaker was sure they could successfully recruit the most difficult American-born women.

ILGWU policies came not out of a failure to understand the need to recruit women for the union's own protection, but rather out of a conviction that women did not constitute a 'fighting force.' Incredibly, this view persisted despite the ILGWU's own history of militant female activity. . . .

Suspicion and doubt about female commitment to unionization undermined women's efforts to make their own demands. It meant that women would spend enormous energies simply convincing men that they belonged in a common struggle. . . .

Being part of, and yet not part of—this was the dilemma of the woman trade unionist of the 1920s. In 1924, at the ILGWU's biennial convention, Cohn introduced a motion instructing the union's delegates to the forthcoming AFL meeting to 'introduce resolutions and work for the adoption [of] . . . a plan of organization of workingwomen that shall include an educational campaign among women directly and through organized men indirectly.' The committee to which the resolution was referred rejected it reprovingly. 'It can be stated without contradiction,' the committee noted, 'that as yet no successful methods of organizing women workers have been found.' And then it went on to argue that the union's delegates 'possess a quite satisfactory acquaintance with the principles, policies and method sof our International Union and can be fully relied upon to carry out such policies during conventions of the AFL without any specific instructions to do so.'

Female rank and filers who failed to support women implicitly acknowledged the real power structure and simultaneously protected their own interests. Women who supported male leadership faced fewer accusations of disloyalty. And since female trade union officials did not speak for women or to their particular issues, and had minimal voice in the union as a whole, women members reasonably felt they deserved better representation than that offered by women. This explains the seeming paradox of Jennie Silverman. An ILGWU business agent, she was rejected by a women's shop as its representative. A manager of the local recalled that the shop refused to be persuaded by the argument that 'you are all women. Jennie is a woman . . . She and you will work together.' The workers simply replied, 'never mind this, we want a man.' Here, workers acknowledged the power of the formal political structure as they did in a similar instance recorded by the New York *World* in 1922. Before women got the vote, a Massachusetts shoe-workers' local had consistently selected a woman to be their manager. Afterward, they repeatedly chose men. A woman stitcher explained why: 'The business man,' she said, 'is getting so he doesn't pay as much attention to the requests of women as he did before we were given the franchise.'

The practical manifestation of this set of dilemmas was the extraordinarily awkward place in which women in the labor movement found themselves. Ann Washington Craton, after she had left her position as organizer with the ACW, despaired of the situation. In an article written for the *Nation* in 1927, she noted that in order to maintain even minor official positions in the trade union movement, women 'have discreetly learned to play the union game as men play it . . . On the theory that a poor union is better than no union, they steadily refused to embarrass labor officials by a vigorous protest at the discriminations and inequalities to which women have been subjected in the unions.' The result, as she correctly observed, was that 'they have been unable to achieve any outstanding leadership among the rank and file of trade-union women.' . . .

Ironically, the struggle against the 1923 Equal Rights Amendment (ERA)—called the 'Blanket Amendment' by trade union women—provides the most successful example of the resuscitation of the spirit of community that prevailed in the pre-war period. The labor movement's unmitigated antagonism to this first ERA illustrates the remaining strength of moral suasion. For here was an amendment that proclaimed the equality of men and women—an equality that trade union women knew had no economic reality but which, if it were asserted, would threaten even their limited organizational position. Eager to affirm their sense that women still required the special protection offered by labor laws, women labor leaders joined with middle-class allies and the Women's Bureau to renew once again the spirit of struggle. Acting now as a community of women seeking not to usurp the prerogatives of men but to acknowledge their own special place, they drew on trade union support to bring the ERA to a standstill. Male trade union leaders, of course, understood protective labor legislation as a way of restraining women's demands for admission into their organization, and opposed the amendment all too willingly.

Self-definition as outsiders and the development of a notion of community without a politics of its own enabled individual women to continue to function within the trade union movement, extracting some benefits from it. Those who became spokespeople won more social and economic mobility for themselves than most working women could hope to achieve. With the Women's Bureau as their vehicle, they were able to bring public attention to many of the problems facing women wage-earners, and they succeeded in gaining the tacit support of the male-dominated trade unions for issues that concerned women. But the trade union movement offered women no access to the power structure and insisted that women in its ranks accept male assumptions about their role and place. It thus undermined whatever female leadership developed within the movement, leaving women like Rose Pesotta, who rebelled, without support (labeled 'unstable') and those like Cohn, Newman and O'Connor, who conformed, without power.

What then of the power of difference? The material presented here suggests that two intersecting factors have to be acknowledged if we are to understand the past and present relationships of women to trade unions. Between 1910 and 1920, a sense of women's culture was joined with the more open stance of some trade unions to create successful alliances. By the 1920s, the alliance had broken down on two fronts. Some elements of the feminist coalition looked to a new equality with men to transcend women's confined place. And the labor movement, no longer convinced that appeals to women's place worked as well as economic struggle, and itself battling to survive, perceived women as a source of weakness better taken care of by the state. Ambivalent about an equality that seemed illusory, and now without the organized feminist support that had sustained the struggle for difference, trade union women floundered or, as Jennie Matyas put it, 'ran away.'

Failure was not so much a result of bad faith as of conflicting perceptions. For women to come to terms with the changing social values of the 1920s, to integrate their worldview with the decade's new realities, was a difficult task. To do so in the context of a defensive and harassed trade union movement might have been impossible. At the same time, to expect an embattled trade union movement to recognize women's cultural space seems equally difficult. But such were the conflicts of the 1920s.

They give us cause to hope that the dual purposes of feminism and trade unionism are not irreconcilable. In the contemporary period, when socio-economic forces have confronted wage-earning women with profound challenges to their perceptions of themselves as wage-earners, and when trade unions are beginning to recognize the workforce shifts that demand organization of new groups of women workers, the culture of women might yet find a place in the politics of unions.

SUGGESTED READING

Benson, Susan Porter. *Counter Cultures: Saleswomen, Managers, and Customers in American Department Stores, 1890–1940* (1986).

Bernstein, Irving. *The Lean Years: A History of the American Worker, 1920–1933* (1960).

Brandes, Stuart. *American Welfare Capitalism: 1880–1940* (1976).

Brody, David. *Labor in Crisis: The Steel Strike of 1919* (1965).

———. *Workers in Industrial America: Essays on the Twentieth Century Struggle,* 2d ed. (1993).

Cohen, Lizabeth. *Making a New Deal: Industrial Workers in Chicago, 1919–1939* (1990).

Fraser, Steve. *Labor Will Rule: Sidney Hillman and the Rise of American Labor* (1991).

Gordon, Colin. *New Deals: Business, Labor, and Politics in America, 1920–1935* (1994).

Jacoby, Sanford. *Employing Bureaucracy: Managers, Unions, and the Transformation of Work in American Industry, 1900–1945* (1985).

Kessler-Harris, Alice. *Out to Work: A History of Wage-Earning Women in the U.S.* (1982).

Lichtenstein, Nelson, and Stephen Meyer, eds. *On the Line: Essays in the History of Auto Work* (1989).

McCartin, Joseph. *Labor's Great War: The Struggle for Industrial Democracy and the Origins of Modern American Labor Relations, 1912–1921* (1998).

Montgomery, David. *The Fall of the House of Labor: The Workplace, the State, and American Labor Activism, 1865–1925* (1987).

———. "Thinking About American Workers in the 1920s." *International Labor and Working Class History* 32 (1987): 1–12.

Nelson, Daniel. "The Company Union Movement: A Re-examination, 1900–1937." *Business History Review* 56 (1982): 335–357.

Rotella, Elyce. *From Home to Office: U.S. Women at Work, 1870–1930* (1981).

Stricker, Frank. "Affluence for Whom? Another Look at Prosperity and the Working Class in the 1920s." *Labor History* 24 (1983): 5–33.

Tone, Andrea. *The Business of Benevolence: Industrial Paternalism in Progressive America* (1997).

Wandersee, Winifred. *Women's Work and Family Values, 1920–1940* (1981).

Weiner, Lynn. *From Working Girl to Working Mother: The Female Labor Force in the United States, 1820–1980* (1985).

Zahavi, Gerald. *Workers, Managers, and Welfare Capitalism: The Shoeworkers and Tanners of Endicott Johnson, 1890–1950* (1988).

Zieger, Robert. *Republicans and Labor, 1919–1929* (1969).

CHAPTER
4

The Politics and Culture
of Consumption

After 1920, popular culture and economic life were increasingly reoriented around consumption. The decade saw the emergence of new industries (such as automobile and electrical manufacturing) that sold their products directly to the public, technological developments (such as the rapid spread of domestic electrification and refrigeration) that further encouraged domestic consumption, and a popular culture that was increasingly dominated by commercial advertising. In many respects, the new "culture of consumption" was typified by the automobile. Personal mobility transformed patterns of leisure and consumption: the 1920s saw the rise of movies, spectator sports, and the tourist industry. As a major consumer purchase, the car also introduced the idea of consumer credit. Consumption according to style and fashion, previously the domain of the higher classes, came to middle America: many felt pressed to purchase this year's Chevrolet, the latest household appliance, or nationally advertised foodstuffs. And the complex relationship between mass production and mass consumption—what some observers dubbed "Fordism"—captured both the promise and the limits of the interwar economy. Indeed, consumption would emerge as a political issue after 1929: many saw the Depression as a crisis of underconsumption, and the New Deal (especially in the late 1930s) increasingly turned its attention to the problem of restoring mass purchasing power as the key to recovery.

In turn, the new emphasis on material possessions and consumption was perhaps most important in the impact it had on the development of mass culture—radio, newspapers, and magazines. More and more, the shape and purpose of mass culture would be shaped by advertising. Consumers did not pay for radio signals or for the full cost of publishing newspapers and magazines. Instead, advertisers paid part of the costs of programming in exchange for the ability to not only reach millions of potential buyers with their message, but also shape the content and coverage of the new "mass" media. In all, the "culture of consumption" reorganized both leisure time and the social and material expectations of consumers. The new consumer goods industries not only met consumer demands but—through advertising and social pressures—also created them. A producers' ethic of thrift, work, and sacrifice, as some historians have suggested, was being gradually displaced by a consumers' ethic of "buy now, pay later" leisure and gratification.

The new consumer economy was also important for the impact it had on women— in part because the demands and expectations of the new consumerism pushed and pulled women into the workforce and in part because consumption fell within the domestic sphere. The 1920s, accordingly, also saw the emergence of "home economics," the managerial notion of running an efficient home based on educated and practical consumption. Producers and advertisers understood this but were unsure how to appeal to women—seeing or portraying them sometimes as practical and powerful consumers, sometimes as capricious and unpredictable. And while consumption was widely understood as an extension of domestic responsibilities, the culture and economics of the new consumer economy also meant new public roles for women—both as consumers and as workers in the production and sale of consumer goods.

D O C U M E N T S

Contemporary observers were torn over the cultural and political implications of the new consumer culture. Some (as in Document 1) assailed the intoxicating promises of advertising. Some (as in Document 2) celebrated the new techniques and forms by which producers and sellers could inform a consuming public. In Document 3, two advertisements from 1929 and 1930 illustrate some of these techniques, including an emphasis on lifestyle or status. Document 4, excerpting a famous sociological study of Muncie, Indiana, in the 1920s, suggests the singular impact of the automobile. In Document 5, a leader of the American Federation of Labor (AFL) suggests the importance of the connection between working and consuming, an argument that could carry either radical implications for labor and community organizing (see the essay by Dana Frank) or, as is the case here, very traditional overtones of the "family wage." In Document 6, the business writer Bruce Barton underscores the impact of the new business and consumer culture by reinterpreting the Bible as a sort of advertising manual.

1. A Critic Sees Advertising as a Narcotic, 1934

I went into a chain store recently, and asked for wheat.

"Wheat?" repeated the clerk. 'Oh, you mean 'Wheaties.' "

I did not mean "Wheaties." Nor did I mean any of the sixteen varieties of trademarked, packaged, blown-from-guns, puffed, radiated, neutered and otherwise degraded wheat derivatives which the clerk offered me, at prices ranging from ten to fifty cents a pound.

I wanted wheat, grains of wheat, and the clerk sent me to a feed store. There I got my wheat, shoveled out of a bin, at three cents a pound. That is a spread of about 600 percent from the farm, where wheat has sold this year at twenty cents a bushel. But that is another story.

I took my wheat home, and ground ten pounds of it quickly in a large coffee grinder. I made muffins. They were praised heartily by one of our guests that weekend—a hospital dietitian. She praised, also, the boiled cereal made next morning from the ground whole wheat. We made bread, too—bread containing all the vitamins extracted from wheat before it is sold to constipated consumers as a packaged specialty. . . .

From James Rorty, "Advertising: America's Narcotic," in *Challenge to the New Deal,* ed. Alfred Bingham and Selden Rodman, 48–52 (New York: Falcon, 1934).

What, you ask, has this to do with advertising? Well, what else is responsible? The wheat, in the grain, is available. Anyone can get it, grind it and cook it.

Why do we not, in this period of drastic economy in the kitchen, go back to the grain? Why do millions go hungry for bread, while farmers have a surfeit of wheat which they sell for twenty cents a bushel?

Basically, of course, it is because of the breakdown of capitalistic economy. But before that, it was because of the opium of advertising—advertising of bread, advertising of trick brands of flour, advertising of patented cereals of great expense and little nutritive value. Because of a pretty package, because of a mere reiteration of the name, because of a radio hour based on a comic strip, the housewife and her husband and her children demand their special brands of prepared cereal, or a special species of bakery-sliced bread.

Recently in the Argentine, the government became critical of the "service" of commercial bakers. It took over the baking industry and cut the price of bread from 3.5 cents to two cents a pound.

Compare this with what happened when an advertising expert, Mr. Claude C. Hopkins, took over the marketing of Puffed Rice and Wheat Berries, which he rechristened Puffed Wheat. Puffed Rice was then selling at ten cents a package and Puffed Wheat at seven. Hopkins raised the prices to fifteen cents for Puffed Rice and ten cents for Puffed Wheat. In describing the exploit in Advertising and Selling, Mr. Hopkins remarks, "This added an average of $1.25 a case to the billing price. This gave us an advertising appropriation."

2. An Enthusiast Applauds Advertising, 1928

A young man who had just joined the staff of one of the larger advertising agencies sought his boss in some perturbation. "I wish you would tell me the truth about this advertising business, chief. Is it all bunk?" To which his employer replied, "There is just as much bunk in advertising as there is in law or medicine, or for that matter, in literature and life, but it is never necessary to use bunk to practise advertising successfully."

That young man's state of mind was the natural result of his reading. He had been recruited from the profession of writing, and he still followed the animadversions of the ultra-intellectual world, which has lately concerned itself with the inconsistencies, the waste, and the smugness of advertising. In short, with the bunk. . . .

In considering the value and necessity of advertising, we must accept the present civilization in which we live. . . . Since most people live by making and selling goods, can they go on making and selling goods without advertising? You see we are all in the same boat. We cannot divide ourselves into two classes, a large one consisting of ultimate consumers and a small one exploiting them by advertising. We each live by making and selling something, and the more we make and sell the better we live. We cannot say, "I will sell my goods to you by advertising, but you cannot sell your goods to me." It is the right of each to advertise and sell. This interchange of goods constitutes what we call business. When we say business is good, we mean there is a brisk exchange of commodities and money. When it is slack, the interchange has slowed

From *Business the Civilizer* by Earnest Elmo Calkins, Little Brown & Co., pp. 1, 8, 11–12, 15–17. Reprinted by permission of the Estate of Earnest Elmo Calkins.

up. There is just as much money in existence, and, except for the fact that production is slowed up in dull times, just as much goods in existence, but both are static. The money remains in the pocket, the goods remain on the shelves. . . .

. . . The question before the house is simply this: Is advertising a benefit to the public as a whole, is it necessary to retain the desirable phases of our present system of living, does it impose an unnecessary burden of cost on the ultimate consumers of goods, becoming thereby an economic waste, or does it, in short, add to the sum of human happiness? . . .

Sometimes advertising supplies a demand, but in most cases it creates demand for things that were beyond even the imagination of those who would be most benefited by them. A woman knew the use of a broom, but she could not imagine a vacuum cleaner. Therefore she could not demand one, save with that vague unspoken desire which has existed from the beginning for some lightening of the terrible drudgery of keeping a house livable. The vacuum cleaner was introduced by educational advertising. The advertising was done partly by manufacturers anxious to sell vacuum cleaners, and partly by electric-light companies anxious to sell current. The spread of electrical housekeeping devices has followed the increase in the number of houses wired for electricity, and that too has been brought about by advertising, by the selfish desire to do more business, to sell more goods. But the result has been a public benefit, an increasing willingness to spend money to lighten the human burden, to cut down the waste of human energy spent in the operation of living. . . .

I do not think I am claiming too much in giving to advertising the credit of the great change in housekeeping that we have seen. I have had to observe it very closely for thirty years, and I have to some extent helped to bring it about. Some may be inclined to think it is due to the women's magazines. It is true that they have directed their editorial energies to the same ends and with remarkable results.

But it should not be forgotten that it is advertising that makes such magazines possible. It is the revenue from the advertisers that pays for the services of domestic economists, physicians, interior decorators, cooks, dressmakers, and other experts who teach women better ways of doing things. More than that, while such department ments are conducted with the primary purpose of being helpful to readers, they furnish an excellent background for the advertising. Magazines with constructive departments on the care of babies, cooking, furnishing, housekeeping, dressmaking, laundry work, and all the other activities which go into home-making are preparing audiences to listen to manufacturers who sell sanitary nursing bottles, infants' wear, prepared foods, salad oils, paints, fabrics, wall papers, electric mangles, and washing powders. This is no reflection on those departments. It is meant for praise. The editors of such departments are frequently men and women of the highest professional character, and the advertisers who are permitted to use space in such magazines are often subjected to rigid censorship, not only as to the real utility or value of what they sell, but also as to the way they talk about it. Some magazines maintain laboratories for testing utensils and foods for household use offered in their columns.

Behind the successful and intelligently conducted magazine is the advertiser, who buys space and makes the magazine profitable; and so the educational work of home-making magazines should be credited largely to him.

Advertising is not an end. It is a means to an end. So the question is not, Is advertising desirable, but Are those ends desirable, and is advertising too great a price to pay for them?

3. Two Magazine Advertisements, 1929 and 1930

CHRYSLER

BEAUTY *is no chance creation*

FOR the first time *in the history of motor car design an authentic system has been devised based upon the canons of ancient classic art*

The most modern thing in motor car design —Chrysler's matching of slender-profile radiator with cowl bar moulding—has its artistic origin in the repetition of motif in the historic frieze of the ancient Parthenon.

Note the dynamic symmetry of Chrysler fender contours and wheels, counterparts of the "wave border" of the classic masterpieces of architecture and design.

The Chrysler front elevation indicates the influence of the Egyptian lotus leaf pattern. Applied with consummate artistry in blending beauty and utility.

Artists know this as a "rising, diminishing series." The level road, the bumper, the tie-rod above, and radiator form a series in perfect harmony.

CHRYSLER designers realize fully that beauty is an elusive thing and that the pursuit of it in motor car design must not be hampered by too rigid adherence to laws and conventions . . . But Chrysler also has found that there are so many glorious precedents and inspirations in art, architecture and design, that the search for authentic and harmonious symmetry can actually be reduced to something like a scientific system in which results are certain . . . Chrysler has left nothing to chance . . . Chrysler has not relied alone upon the inspiration of individual designers . . . Chrysler has sought instead to do something never done before in motor car design — to search out *authentic* forms of beauty which have come down the centuries unsurpassed and unchallenged and *translate* them in terms of motor car beauty and motor car utility . . . The lengths to which Chrysler designers have gone in this patient pursuit of beauty will doubtless prove a revelation to those who have probably accepted Chrysler symmetry and charm as fortunate but more or less accidental conceptions . . . The Chrysler process goes far deeper than any charming but accidental conception.

New Chrysler "75" Coupe (with rumble seat) $1535. Wire wheels extra

All Chrysler models will be exhibited at the National Automobile Shows; and at special displays in the Commodore Hotel during the New York Show, January 5th to 12th and in the Balloon Room and entire lobby space of the Congress Hotel during the Chicago Show, January 26th to February 2nd.

1929 Chrysler advertisement from *Literary Digest*, January 12, 1929.

Some WIVES DO IT but I wouldn't dare!

SOME wives I know treat their husbands shamefully. Off they're sent—every morning—with little more than a cup of coffee, a few bites of toast and a kiss. They show it, too! They have that lean and hungry look.

Not so with *my* husband. I wouldn't dare serve him such a flimsy breakfast. His health—and our happiness—are too precious for me to gamble with.

Early morning appetites *simply have to be pampered*—so I try to select breakfast dishes that are not only nourishing but also enticing. And that's why I serve Wheatena *regularly*. It's the only cereal my husband really enjoys—and the children just love it, too.

My discovery of Wheatena is due entirely to our doctor. He recommended Wheatena when my first baby reached the cereal age. He said Wheatena was not robbed—like so many cereals—of the minerals, vitamins, and other valuable food elements of the whole wheat.

For variety sake—I prepare Wheatena in a number of delicious ways. Sometimes I cook it with just water—other times with half milk and half water—and in summer I often serve it chilled with fruit.

And one of the nicest things about Wheatena is that it is so *quick cooking*. In just 2 minutes of boiling and bubbling, it's ready for the table.

Perhaps you, too, have this problem of selecting breakfast dishes that are not only nourishing but also enticing.

Wheatena is one of the most delicious and nourishing foods you can serve your family. It supplies all the precious health, strength and growth materials that nature pours into the sun-ripened wheat . . . roasted and toasted to give it a delicious nut-like flavor.

And no matter how you serve Wheatena—steaming hot or chilled, with fruit—it's equally delicious, equally nourishing, equally easy to digest and assimilate.

Wouldn't YOU like to try this wonderful cereal? Just mail the coupon below and we'll send you 3 generous servings. Or, better still, get a full-size package from your grocer today so you'll have it for breakfast tomorrow.

3 *Delicious Servings*

FREE

THE WHEATENA CORPORATION
Wheatenaville, Rahway, N. J.

Gentlemen: Please send me, by return mail, one of your friendly little packages of Wheatena . . . the sun-browned wheat cereal . . . sufficient to make three generous servings.

Name ....

Address .... TS 5-30

Wheatena advertisement from *True Story Magazine,* May, 1930.

4. The Automobile Comes to Middletown, 1929

The first real automobile appeared in Middletown in 1900. About 1906 it was estimated that "there are probably 200 in the city and county." At the close of 1923 there were 6,221 passenger cars in the city, one for every 6.1 persons, or roughly two for every three families. . . . For some of the workers and some of the business class, use of the automobile is a seasonal matter, but the increase in surfaced roads and in closed cars is rapidly making the car a year-round tool for leisure-time as well as getting-a-living activities. As, at the turn of the century, business class people began to feel apologetic if they did not have a telephone, so ownership of an automobile has now reached the point of being an accepted essential of normal living.

Into the equilibrium of habits which constitutes for each individual some integration in living has come this new habit, upsetting old adjustments, and blasting its way through such accustomed and unquestioned dicta as "Rain or shine, I never miss a Sunday morning at church"; "A high school boy does not need much spending money"; "I don't need exercise, walking to the office keeps me fit"; "I wouldn't think of moving out of town and being so far from my friends"; "Parents ought always to know where their children are." . . . No one questions the use of the auto for transporting groceries, getting to one's place of work or to the golf course, or in place of the porch for "cooling off after supper" on a hot summer evening; however much the activities concerned with getting a living may be altered by the fact that a factory can draw from workmen within a radius of forty-five miles, or however much old labor union men resent the intrusion of this new alternate way of spending an evening, these things are hardly major issues. But when auto riding tends to replace the traditional call in the family parlor as a way of approach between the unmarried, "the home is endangered," and all-day Sunday motor trips are a "threat against the church"; it is in the activities concerned with the home and religion that the automobile occasions the greatest emotional conflicts.

Group-sanctioned values are disturbed by the inroads of the automobile upon the family budget. A case in point is the not uncommon practice of mortgaging a home to buy an automobile. Data on automobile ownership were secured from 123 working class families. Of these, sixty have cars. Forty-one of the sixty own their homes. Twenty-six of these forty-one families have mortgages on their homes. Forty of the sixty-three families who do not own a car own their homes. Twenty-nine of these have mortgages on their homes. Obviously other factors are involved in many of Middletown's mortgages. That the automobile does represent a real choice in the minds of some at least is suggested by the acid retort of one citizen to the question about car ownership: "No, sir we've *not* got a car. *That's* why we've got a home." According to an officer of a Middletown automobile financing company, 75 to 90 per cent of the cars purchased locally are bought on time payment, and a working man earning $35.00 a week frequently plans to use one week's pay each month as payment for his car. . . .

Many families feel that an automobile is justified as an agency holding the family group together. "I never feel as close to my family as when we are all to-gether in the car," said one business class mother, and one or two spoke of giving up Country Club membership or other recreations to get a car for this reason. "We don't spend anything on recreation except for the car. We save every place we can and put the money into the car. It keeps the family together," was an opinion voiced more than once. Sixty-one per cent of 337 boys and 60 per cent of 423 girls in the three upper years of the high school say that they motor more often with their parents than without them.

But this centralizing tendency of the automobile may be only a passing phase; sets in the other direction are almost equally prominent. "Our daughters [eighteen and fifteen] don't use our car much because they are always with somebody else in their car when we go out motoring," lamented one business class mother. And an-other said, "The two older children [eighteen and sixteen] never go out when the family motors. They always have something else on." "In the nineties we were all much more together," said another wife. "People brought chairs and cushions out of the house and sat on the lawn evenings. We rolled out a strip of carpet and put cush-ions on the porch step to take care of the unlimited overflow of neighbors that dropped by. We'd sit out so all evening. The younger couples perhaps would wander off for half an hour to get a soda but come back to join in the informal singing or lis-ten while somebody strummed a mandolin or guitar." "What on earth *do* you want me to do? Just sit around home all evening!" retorted a popular high school girl of to-day when her father discouraged her going out motoring for the evening with a young blade in a rakish car waiting at the curb. The fact that 348 boys and 382 girls in the three upper years of the high school placed "use of the automobile" fifth and fourth respectively in a list of twelve possible sources of disagreement between them and their parents suggests that this may be an increasing decentralizing agent. . . .

The threat which the automobile presents to some anxious parents is suggested by the fact that of thirty girls brought before the juvenile court in the twelve months preceding September 1, 1924, charged with "sex crimes," for whom the place where the offense occurred was given in the records, nineteen were listed as having committed the offense in an automobile. Here again the automobile appears to some as an "enemy" of the home and society.

5. The AFL on the "Living Wage," 1919

The worker today is a free man. He has equal rights with all other citizens. He is no longer a creature of the soil. However, the full and free exercise of his rights is limited by his economic standing in the community. If he be rich and freed from the pangs of hunger, he may exercise his rights in full. If his means of livelihood be limited, his rights are correspondingly restricted. The great problem of the workers, the great task of all lovers of freedom and of democratic nations, is to provide all peoples with ample opportunities to assure their economic independence, which in turn will enable the full and free exercise of their rights as free men in all their relations of life and activity. . . .

From "Insist on the Living Wage," *American Federationist* 26 (February 1919): 151–153.

The great object of the workers today in resisting a wage reduction is not to prove or disprove any particular philosophy of economics. The workers are not interested in which particular economic theory shall be given preference. They have no faith in the theory advanced by Adam Smith that wages like anything else are governed by the law of supply and demand. There is at hand too much conclusive evidence that the law of supply and demand is not immutable and that it readily lends itself to manipulation and control. The wage-earners are no longer bewildered by the subtle logic of the wage-fund theory advanced by David Ricardo, James Mill or John Stuart Mill. No one in this enlightened age would attempt to advance this theory as a fitting answer to the wage-earners' yearning and craving for a better and happier life. Neither does Labor accept the conclusion advanced by La Salle in the so-called "iron law of wages" or find solace and satisfaction in the idealistically expounded theory of the cooperative commonwealth. The present movement of the wage-earners is more than a resistance to the artful demand to bring down the prices of commodities. It is an onward march to carry the rights of the workers to a new and greater height.

The demand of the workers is for a wage which will maintain the American standard of living. This demand for a living wage is in fact a rebellion against the maladministration of life and labor by others. It is an insurrection against the decree of business that wages shall follow prices when prices know no law but competition between traders. The workers are tired of having themselves, their wives and children used as chips for our commercial, financial and industrial gamblers. Having accepted the principle of a living wage, the next step is to maintain this living wage where it is established and to secure it for all workers where it does not now obtain. . . .

After all, the question may be well asked: What does it cost to produce an American, a man fitted to be your fellow-citizen and to help administer the institutions of liberty left us by our forefathers? What is the price we pay for children free from factory life, for mothers burdened by no duties outside of home, for fathers who have leisure for home and families? All these elements of human well-being should be taken into consideration of the estimate upon which to base the cost of producing an American.

The best American authority tells us that men are born equal with inalienable rights to life, liberty and the pursuit of happiness. Alienate one right, be it the humblest and smallest right of life, of liberty or of happiness, and the wage received is less than the living wage. The living wage is the right to be a man and to exercise freely and fully the rights of a free man. That is the living wage and to realize it is the sure and true destiny of organized labor.

6. Bruce Barton Sees Jesus as an Advertising Man, 1925

Every advertising man ought to study the parables of Jesus . . . , schooling himself in their language and learning these four big elements of their power.

1. First of all they are marvelously condensed, as all good advertising must be. . . . A single sentence grips your attention; three or four more tell the story; one

---

or two more and the application is driven home. When he wanted a new disciple he said simply "Follow me." When he sought to explain the deepest philosophic mystery—the personality and character of God—he said, "A king made a banquet and invited many guests. God is that king and you are the guests; the Kingdom of Heaven is happiness—a banquet to be enjoyed." . . .

2. His language was marvelously simple—a second great essential. There is hardly a sentence in his teaching which a child can not understand. His illustrations were all drawn from the commonest experiences of life; "a sower went forth to sow"; "a certain man had two sons"; "a man built his house on the sands"; "the kingdom of heaven is like a grain of mustard seed." The absence of adjectives is striking. . . .

Jesus used few qualifying words and no long ones. . . . [Recall] those three literary masterpieces, The Lord's Prayer, The Twenty-Third Psalm, The Gettysburg Address. Recall their phraseology:

Our Father which art in Heaven, hallowed be thy name

The Lord is my shepherd; I shall not want

Four score and seven years ago

Not a single three-syllable word; hardly any two-syllable words. All the greatest things in human life are one-syllable things—love, joy, hope, home, child, wife, trust, faith, God—and the great advertisements generally speaking, are those in which the most small words are found.

3. Sincerity glistened like sunshine through every sentence he uttered; sincerity is the third essential. . . . The public has a sixth sense for detecting insincerity; they know instinctively when words ring true. . . .

Jesus was notably tolerant of almost all kinds of sinners. . . . But for one sin he had no mercy. He denounced the *insincerity* of the Pharisees in phrases which sting like the lash of a whip. They thought they had a first mortgage on the Kingdom of Heaven, and he told them scornfully that only those who become like little children have any chance of entering in. . . .

Much brass has been sounded and many cymbals tinkled in the name of advertising; but the advertisements which persuade people to act are written by men who have an abiding respect for the intelligence of their readers, and a deep sincerity regarding the merits of the goods they have to sell. . . .

4. Finally he knew the necessity for repetition and practised it. . . .

It has been said that "reputation is repetition." No important truth can be impressed upon the minds of any large number of people by being said only once. The thoughts which Jesus had to give the world were revolutionary, but they were few in number. "God is your father," he said, "caring more for the welfare of every one of you than any human father can possibly care for his children. His Kingdom is happiness! his rule is love." This is what he had to teach, but he knew the necessity of driving it home from every possible angle. So in one of his stories God is the shepherd searching the wilds for one wandering sheep; in another, the Father welcoming home a prodigal boy; in another a King who forgives his debtors large amounts and expects them to be forgiving in turn—*many* stories, *many* advertisements, but the same big Idea.

E S S A Y S

The essays touch on different elements of the "culture of consumption." In the first essay, Roland Marchand suggests some of the "parables" that advertisers used to shift attention from consumer products themselves to their apparent ability to enhance the
buyer's social status, bring the buyer love or popularity, or save the buyer from profound personal embarrassment. In the second essay, Dana Frank describes how workers
in Seattle politicized consumption—seeing cooperatives and boycotts as a logical and
necessary complement to more conventional union organizing.

The Culture of Advertising

ROLAND MARCHAND

No era provides such revealing insights into the cultural values of both producers
and consumers of American advertising as the 1920s and 1930s, when admen not
only claimed the status of professionals but also saw themselves as missionaries of
modernity.

During the era, advertising came to focus less on the product that was for sale
and more on the consumer who would do the buying. (An ad in the *Ladies' Home
Journal* of the late 1920s assured each reader that "Elizabeth Arden is personally interested in you.") The scale and tempo of contemporary life left the average citizen
anxious, advertisers saw, and they offered their products as palliatives. What made
advertising "modern" was the advertisers' discovery of techniques for both responding to and exploiting the public's insecurities.

Advertisers regularly created detailed vignettes of social life to arouse empathy, envy, or guilt—with huge sums of money riding on their effectiveness. And
since these ad agents worked with ingenuous self-assurance, they filled the trade
press with gossip about their techniques. Their own enthusiastic naïveté and their
facile assumptions about the masses they addressed make the ads of this era particularly revealing—about the men and women who wrote them, the consumers who
responded to them, and the cultural anxieties they reflected. . . .

During a single year in the early 1920s, major advertising campaigns rescued
two fading products so successfully that the entire advertising industry had to pon-
der the lessons they offered in modern advertising technique.

Fleischmann's Yeast, the first of these advertising legends, had been "something merely to bake bread with—until Fleischmann advertisements said otherwise," the copywriter claimed. Prohibition had destroyed one sales outlet for yeast,
and in the fact of a steady decline in home baking, even Fleischmann's lofty characterization of its product as the "Soul of Bread" could not stem declining sales.
Could a product with such specific functions be salvaged by promoting it for some
new use?

Within a year, with the impetus supplied by its new agency, the J. Walter
Thompson Company, Fleischmann's advertising had transformed yeast into a

potent source of vitamins, a food to be eaten directly from the package. Two years later, when the market had become saturated by new vitamin products, Fleischmann's Yeast evolved once again, this time into a natural laxative. A prize contest brought in hundreds of testimonials for the product's newly advertised properties. From 153 of the winners, the agency gained permission to use their letters and "illustrate them in any way we saw fit."

Capturing the tempo of popular journalism, the J. Walter Thompson copywriters established a brash format for the Fleischmann campaign and placed their ads in the high-priced rotogravure sections. They injected as much human interest and eye appeal as possible by using multiple "candid" photographs and succinct, first-person testimony. Sometimes the ads so closely copied the layout of the magazine or newspaper that the reader might become thoroughly immersed in one before discovering that it was not an editorial feature.

By 1926 the Fleischmann Company had become one of the nation's ten largest magazine advertisers and a major purchaser of newspaper space. By the spring of 1926, sales had increased 130 percent over 1923, when the candid, man-in-the-street testimonials had begun.

When sales threatened to recede, the Thompson agency called doctors to the rescue. Authoritative physicians in white coats explained how the pressures of modern civilization had led to constipation and advised readers to eat half a cake of yeast three times a day to counteract "intestinal fatigue." "Fatigue is universal," one agency executive explained. "We simply have to credit it to the intestines, that's all." The agency dramatized the role of the intestines by superimposing bold diagrams of "where the trouble starts" over photographs of lovely young women. The American Medical Association was outraged and prohibited its members from testifying for Fleischmann. Undaunted, the agency turned for paid testimonials to European doctors, whose impressively unpronounceable names and prestigious hospital affiliations were most effective.

The success of Fleischmann's Yeast in the 1920s—in spite of the product's high price, its repulsive taste, and, according to the agency, "the almost complete absence of *quickly apparent* results"—seemed to confirm the power of advertising. One pleased copywriter reflected that advertising alone had increased sales, and had done so even though the home baking market had declined sharply.

The success of the Fleischmann campaign was overshadowed, however, by the even more spectacular story of Listerine. The profits of its manufacturer, the Lambert Pharmacal Company, mushroomed from approximately $100,000 per year in 1920 and 1921 to over $4,000,000 in 1927. Not surprisingly the company's strategy gave rise to a whole school of advertising practice.

Listerine was not a new product in 1920. For years it had been merchandised perfunctorily as a general antiseptic. Initially, the three men who transformed Listerine into the marvel of the advertising world—the copywriters Milton Feasley and Gordon Seagrove and the company president, Gerard B. Lambert—did not so much convert the product to a new use as induce the public to discover a new need. After a year of comparatively awkward ads for Listerine as a mouthwash, the copywriters hit upon a winning formula. The picture of a lovely girl introduced a story cryptically entitled "He Never Knew Why." The hero, a rising young businessman, was spurned by the "luminous" but "charming demure" girl of his dreams after a single romantic encounter. He seemed to have every advantage in life—wealth, good looks, charm—but he labored under one insurmountable handicap. He had "halitosis."

The term *halitosis* (exhumed from an old medical dictionary) had a scientific sound and took some of the coarseness out of a discussion of bad breath. The ads mimicked the tabloids' personal-interest stories and advice-to-the-lovelorn columns. As the advertising industry's journal *Printers' Ink* reflected in a tribute to Feasley: "He dealt more with humanity than with merchandise. He wrote advertising dramas rather than business announcements—dramas so common to everyday experience that every reader could easily fit himself into the plot as the hero or culprit of its action."

By 1926 *Printers' Ink* went so far as to eulogize Feasley for having transformed behavior patterns. He had "amplified the morning habits of our nicer citizenry—by making the morning mouthwash as important as the morning shower or the morning shave." But Gerard Lambert was not content to wed the fortunes of his product to *one* new habit. To maintain advertising momentum, he kept finding new uses for Listerine. Halitosis had hardly become an advertising byword before Lambert began to proclaim Listerine's virtues as a cure for dandruff. Between 1921 and 1929 the American public also learned the virtues of Listerine as an after-shave tonic, a cure for colds and sore throats, an astringent, and a deodorant. Lambert capitalized on the new fame of his product to market a Listerine toothpaste, which brought even greater financial returns. The Listerine advertising budget mounted from $100,000 in 1922 to $5,000,000 in 1928.

The financial feats of the Listerine campaign held the advertising trade enthralled. Phrases like "the halitosis style," "the halitosis appeal," and "the halitosis influence" became standard advertising jargon. Copywriters soon discovered and labeled over a hundred new diseases, including such transparent imitations as "bromodosis" (sweaty foot odors), "homotosis" (lack of attractive home furnishings), "acidosis" (sour stomach), and such inventive afflictions as "office hips," "ashtray breath," and "accelerator toe."

The promoters of Listerine were not the first to discover the sociodrama as an advertising technique—just as they had not pioneered the appeal to social shame or personal fear. In advertisements headlined "Within the Curve of a Woman's Arm," the deodorant Odo-ro-no had earlier confronted the threats to romance posed by underarm perspiration. But Listerine purchased larger space in a wider variety of publications. Its expanding appropriations and spectacular profits impressed the business community. The J. Walter Thompson Company summarized the new perception of proper advertising techniques in 1926: "To sell *goods* we must also sell *words*. In fact we have to go further: we must sell *life*." . . .

How, then, did the creative elite of American advertising in the 1920s and 1930s characterize its audience?

First, the consumer was a "she." As one ad in *Printers' Ink* succinctly put it, "The proper study of mankind is man . . . but the proper study of markets is *woman*." No facet of the advertiser-audience relationship held such consequence for advertising content as the perception by the overwhelmingly male advertising elite that it was engaged primarily in talking to masses of women.

Demographically, of course, women composed no more than a razor-thin majority of the nation's population, but contemporary statistics indicated that they—the family "purchasing agents"—did about 80 to 85 percent of the nation's retail buying.

Once the audience was understood to be overwhelmingly female, certain implications for copy content and selling appeal seemed evident. In a tone of scientific assurance, advertising leaders of the 1920s and 1930s asserted that women possessed a "well-authenticated greater emotionality" and a "natural inferiority complex." Since women were "certainly emotional," advertisements must be emotional. Since women were characterized by "inarticulate longings," advertisements should portray idealized visions rather than prosaic realities. Copy should be intimate and succinct, since "women will read anything which is broken into short paragraphs and personalized."

Although the articles in the quality women's magazines pictured their sophisticated readers as leading busy, diversified, action-packed lives, advertising agencies generally adopted a very different model of the typical woman consumer, one that owed more to the contemporary stereotypes of the *True Story* reader. "We must remember," wrote a *Printers' Ink* contributor, "that most American women lead rather monotonous and humdrum lives. . . ." The advertising pages, he argued, should become the "magical carpets on which they may ride out to love."

The second advertising man's assumption was about the consumer's level of intelligence. Army tests during World War I had recently startled Americans. New techniques of evaluation revealed that a shocking percentage of prospective inductees had not possessed the minimal level of intelligence to qualify for military service. Advertising writers followed these reports avidly and reminded their colleagues of the latest figure that had lodged in their memory: "Remember, the average citizen has the mentality of a child of twelve"—or "ten" or "thirteen."

The content of the popular press reinforced this image of an unintelligent public. Several advertising writers recalled that Arthur Brisbane, the editorial genius of the Hearst papers and the guiding spirit of the tabloid *Daily Mirror,* had posted a sign in the Hearst city rooms that read, "You *cannot* underestimate the intelligence of the American public."

Movie content, also, offered a measure of public intelligence. "We say Hollywood people are stupid, the pictures are stupid," reflected one agency representative. "What we are really saying is the great bulk of people are stupid." The Ruthrauff and Ryan advertising agency, flaunting its own success in following the example of "editors, movie directors, and popular novelists," instructed the trade in the deplorable but inescapable facts of life: "After all, men and women in the mass are apt to have incredibly shallow brain-pans. In infancy they are attracted by bright colors, glitter, and noise. And in adulthood they retain a surprisingly similar set of basic reactions."

A third assumption, closely related to the theory of the limited mental capacity of advertising's audience, was the assumption of public lethargy. "The mass mind is averse to effort," an experienced woman copywriter warned agency novices. "Women don't like to think too much when buying," added a contributor to *Advertising Age.* George Gallup, reporting on his polling information for the Young and Rubicam advertising agency, suggested that the success of the New York *Daily*

News was related to the tendency of "whole legions of women to read only the headlines except in the case of a juicy crime story where their interest overcomes their mental inertia." The prolific advertising writer Kenneth Goode reminded the trade in *How to Turn People into Gold* that "man in the mass," except when caught up in emotion, "won't exert himself beyond the line of least resistance."

Advertising men associated consumer lethargy with weak-kneed conformity. The masses, the copywriters were convinced, never looked beyond the need for immediate gratification. They would greet with suspicion any invitation to differ from the crowd. Subtleties entirely escaped their "careless, uncomprehending mentality." They refused to respond to anything but the most blatantly sensational stimuli. In trying to capture a sense of the culture of the "people," a Ruthrauff and Ryan ad verbally panned across the advertising audience for a quick, cinematic impression: "Perspiring thousands at Coney Island. . . . Gaudy pennants. The crunch of peanut shells underfoot. Chewing gum. Mustard dripping from hot dogs. People struggling for a view of some queer freak in a side show. Red-faced men elbowing and crowding for a vicarious thrill of a cooch dancer. . . . Stopping for the shudder of gaping at a gory accident. . . . Women tearing other women's clothing in the scramble at a bargain counter . . . huddling at a radio to hear a crooner drone Tin Pan Alley's latest potion of vapid sentimentality. . . . Waiting in line for hours to view the saccharine emotional displays of a movie idol. Taking a daily dose of culture from the comic strips." . . .

Unlike the varied ways in which women were depicted in advertising tableaux, men usually appeared in nondescript, standardized parts as husbands or businessmen. But their occupational roles were more varied than women's—an accurate reflection of social realities.

As doctors, dentists, or business executives, they might endorse the product; as truckers, deliverymen, house painters or gas-station attendants they entered the tableaux only when it was necessary to demonstrate the product's manufacture or use. But working-class men never appeared as consumers: an unspoken law decreed that the protagonist in every ad must be depicted as a prosperous member of the middle class, dressed in a suit, tie, and hat or fashionable sporting togs.

When merchandising strategy did not call for a particular occupational function, the leading man tended to conform to a single stereotype: he was a businessman. Remedies for nerves, fatigue, and constipation regularly attributed such ills to the stress of business. Among the hundreds of thousands of advertisements that appeared during the 1920s and 1930s, I have yet to discover a single one in which the husband or the ambitious young man is defined as a factory worker, policeman, engineer, professor, architect, or government official, and only one in which he is a lawyer. Even such solid citizens as doctors and dentists appear only in their functional roles, duly proclaimed by a white coat—not as typical husbands.

Within the role of businessman, some slight differentiations emerged. Older men were likely to be cast as business executives. Young men were often salesmen, aspiring to the intermediate step on the business ladder of sales manager. When husbands telephoned their wives to prepare for an unexpected dinner guest, they always brought home either a "sales manager" or a "client." The spectrum of men's activities was described in one tableau in the phrase "wherever they may be, at their desks or on the golf course."

Ads also suggested that, in the struggle of business, the man had often lost "a bit of the sentiment that used to abide in his heart." He had been "shackled to his desk" and might even need to slacken his pace, get to know his wife and children again, and experience those softer sentiments preserved within the shelter of the home. But only for a brief respite. The competitive world of business helped make him a true man, and advertisers occasionally worried that the attempt to pretty him up for the collar ads and the nightclub scenes would sissify and weaken man's image, tailoring it too much to feminine tastes. Edgeworth Smoking Tobacco even suggested that the growing number of women smokers had effeminized cigarettes; men should respond by giving them up and turning to pipes. An Edgeworth ad proclaimed: "A man looks like a man when he smokes a pipe." . . .

A flush of anticipation colored the cheeks of the beautiful young lady as her escort seated her at the elegant table. It was her first important dinner among the city's smart set. But as the butler served the first course, her excitement turned to terror. "From that row of gleaming silver on either side of her plate, which piece shall she pick up?" Suddenly she sensed that her chance of being invited to such an affair again—in fact, her whole future popularity—would be determined by this first impression of her "presence." As her social destiny hung in the balance, "she could feel every eye on her *hesitating hand*."

Even if she passed the test of the "Hesitating Hand," a young lady was certain to encounter many other fateful first-impression judgments. In the episode of the "Open Door," she and her husband faced the greatest social crisis of their five-year marriage: they had taken the bold step of inviting the vice-president-in-charge-of-sales and his wife to dinner. For days the eager young wife planned the dinner menu. Her husband researched and rehearsed several topics for appropriate conversation. But both completely forgot about their tasteless front doorway, with its lack of beautifully designed woodwork. And neither realized how dreary and out-of-date the furniture they had purchased soon after their marriage had become. Thus, all their efforts at preparation came to naught, for their guests formed an indelible impression during "those few seconds" from the "touch of the bell" to their entrance into the living room. . . .

These dramas from advertisements of the late 1920s suggest the pathos with which copywriters could recount the popular parable of the First Impression. According to such tableaux, first impressions brought instantaneous success or failure. In a relatively mobile society, where business organizations loomed ever larger and people dealt far more often with strangers, the reasons one man gained a promotion or one woman suffered a social snub had become less explicable on grounds of long-standing favoritism or old family feuds. One might suspect that almost anything—especially a first impression—had made the crucial difference.

Sensing their power in these circumstances, advertisers made use of the parable of the First Impression. Often they modified the basic formula of the tableau slightly to fit their particular product. Clothing manufacturers stressed overall appearance; makers of gum, toothpaste, and toothbrushes promised a "magic road to popularity in that first winning smile." Williams Shaving Cream stressed that powerful initial impact of the "face that's fit" for the "double-quick march of business." All agreed that "it's the 'look' of you by which you are judged most often." One of the most important effects of preparing carefully for that crucial first impression, many ads suggested, was the sense of self-confidence it created. A lovely frock, washed in Lux, would enable any woman to overcome an inferiority complex and feel a "deep, sure, inner conviction of being charming," Dorothy Dix counseled readers of the *Ladies' Home Journal.* The House of Kuppenheimer confided to the up-and-coming young man that "someday your father may tell you how a certain famous letter *k* in his inner coat pocket . . . put confidence in his heart . . . the confidence born of good appearance. And so helped him land his first job."

The parable of the First Impression taught that these impressions were being formed constantly and almost instantaneously. Only because she was constantly prepared could the heroine of a Dr. West's toothbrush tableau pass the "Smile Test" during that moment when a handsome man picked her up from a fall off a speeding toboggan. A charming hostess who failed to obtain stylish new furnishings would henceforth be condemned to "lonely afternoons, dreary evenings" for being unprepared for acquaintances who called once out of courtesy but never came again. One ardent suitor completely destroyed the good impression he had built up over months "when she noticed a hint of B.O." as he knelt to pop the question. There was no appeal from such judgments; no way to escape the constant surveillance. The Cleanliness Institute of the Association of American Soap and Glycerine Producers counseled: "Everywhere we go the people we meet are sizing us up. Very quickly they decide whether we are, or are not, from nice homes." . . .

Advertisers of bathroom furnishings and fixtures boldly applied the parable of the First Impression to the innermost recesses of the home. If every room told a story, then this most hidden and intimate of rooms would clearly reveal family character. In "The Room You Do Not Show," discerning visitors would find a quick index to your standards and "beliefs on how a civilized person should live," a Kohler Company ad proclaimed.

The C. F. Church Manufacturing Company narrowed the focus ever further: "The bathroom, most of all, is a clue to the standards of the household and the most conspicuous thing in the bathroom is the toilet seat." Little wonder that the man in the Brunswick-Balke-Collender Company tableau, who had just learned of the impending visit of an influential business associate, thought first of the "old-fashioned wood toilet seat" as his mind's eye quickly scanned his house for social flaws.

No other medium of popular culture preached the parable of the First Impression with the insistence of advertising or accepted its validity so unquestioningly. Whereas movies and soap operas often provided vicarious experiences of triumphs over society's false accusations, advertisements emphasized the power, validity, and pervasiveness of the world's judgmental scrutiny. With headlines such as "When they look at YOUR FEET ON THE BEACH," "Suppose you could follow yourself up the street. . . . What would you see?" and "more searching than your mirror . . . your husband's eyes," they encouraged the transformation of this scrutiny into self-accusation. Their cumulative effect was more likely to reinforce the readers' impression of being surrounded by a host of accusing eyes than to reassure them that new furniture, familiarity with good silverware, or a "face that's fit" would testify to their "innocence" and spare them social shame. . . .

During the summer of 1931, an irreverent new magazine entitled *Ballyhoo* exploded like a bombshell on the advertising scene. An overnight financial success, this unlikely Depression phenomenon offered vivid evidence of a latent public skepticism of all advertising. Launched as a humor magazine, *Ballyhoo* relied for laughs entirely on lampoons of notorious advertisements. Its parody of Listerine toothpaste's what-you-can-buy-with-the-money-you-save campaign proclaimed the wonders of "Blisterine": "Buy yourself some false teeth with the money you save on toothpaste." In "How Georgie Cursed when Milktime Came," *Ballyhoo* lampooned the new Cocomalt style with a worried-mother ad for Creme de Cocoa: "Georgie's weight has gone up a pound a week . . . since I began giving him milk this easy way. . . . You'll be surprised what Creme de Cocoa will do for your baby. It will darn near knock him outen his little bassinet!" Movie star "La Belle Zilch" kept her girlish figure by bathing "every fortnight" with "Lox Toilet Soap."

With ad copy of this character, the initial edition of *Ballyhoo* (August 1931) sold out the entire run of 150,000 copies in a few days. It simply burst into existence, an agency executive complained, "like some rank tropical flower." The September issue sold almost double that number—275,000 copies. October brought another sellout, this time of all 650,000 copies. Within five months *Ballyhoo* magazine, with a circulation of a million and a half, had become one of the most sensational new business enterprises to defy the Depression. The publisher began accepting paid ads at $3,750 a page but insisted that all adopt an appropriate satirical approach.

Ballyhoo also gained overnight success within the advertising trade. Everyone talked about it, joked about it, and shuddered a bit at its ultimate implications. "Anyone with two eyes in his head can see that the public is getting restive," warned H. A. Batten of N. W. Ayer and Son. *Advertising and Selling* sensed a growing public skepticism that regarded advertising as a "great joke." It was all right for advertising agents to enjoy private lampoons at their own expense, but quite a different story when the paying customers reacted to high-priced ads with a "coarse and disrespectful horse-laugh."

An even more disturbing symptom of rising public distrust of advertising emerged in the form of a fledgling consumer movement. In 1927 the flustered advertising trade had reacted with a flurry of censure, ridicule, and counterattack to Stuart Chase and F. J. Schlink's muckraking book, *Your Money's Worth*. Chase and Schlink had suggested that consumers create a test service to provide an objective source of information about products. Public response to the book encouraged them to expand their initial Consumers Club in White Plains, New York, into a national organization known as Consumers' Research. Its membership reached twelve thousand by 1930, and with the impetus of the Depression, membership doubled in 1931.

Meanwhile, other consumer-education organizations had emerged. A consumers' cooperative movement was expanding. In 1933 F. J. Schlink and Arthur Kallet published *1,000,000 Guinea Pigs,* a sensational account of the misleading advertising of drugs and cosmetics. The trade press erupted with furious denials. But some advertising leaders interpreted the incipient consumers' movement as a symptom of a public skepticism induced by the heavy-handed advertising of the early 1930s. Devoting its first page of copy to an unprecedented lead editorial, *Advertising and Selling* alerted readers that its October 1931 article on the work of Consumers Research had evoked more concerned responses than any article since a paid testimonials controversy of the late 1920s. The psychologist Henry Link reported survey results that indicated that only 4 to 5 percent of the public believed certain current advertising assertions. Even the most credible assertions convinced only 37 percent of those surveyed. *Printers' Ink Monthly* noted the growth of consumer councils and warned the smug creators of "misleading, vulgar advertising" that a "movement of this kind grows with the geometrical rapidity of a snowball."

By the mid-1930s the tiny new consumer organizations were inspiring fear in the advertising trade because they threatened to pursue their objectives through the new regulatory powers of the federal government. The Roosevelt administration proposed to extend the powers of the Food and Drug Administration to cover cosmetics and to regulate advertising as well as labeling. It also called for government-enforced grade labeling of food. What would happen to brand-name advertising, many advertising leaders wondered, if people were induced to base their buying decisions on a grading system defined by the government? Would it destroy all advertising that celebrated, by implication, the superiority of Jones's grade-A canned peaches over the grade-A peaches canned by Brown? And once the regulation of drug and cosmetic advertising began, would not other inhibiting forms of regulation follow?

As early as the fall of 1932, *Advertising and Selling* had begun to warn that such "pseudo-scientific" scare campaigns as the Scott Tissue ads, which dramatically warned of the dire results of using the arsenic-laden brands of toilet paper sold by competitors, were a "direct invitation to government regulation." The New Deal proposals for the expansion of FDA regulation inspired calls for preventive self-regulation within the industry. A contributor to *Advertising and Selling* warned that the 1934 elections would bring a new Congress and a "flood of social legislation which will place advertising on a hotter seat than it has ever been on before." In an editorial entitled "Let's Face the Music," *Printers' Ink* noted the growing number of dignified organizations now testifying to their skepticism of advertising before the Senate Commerce Committee. The specter of advancing government regulation provoked the editor to call upon "honest, intelligent, and high-minded advertisers" to silence the "fakers, charlatans, and crooks" of their trade.

The Golden Age was over. Never again would advertising be so uncritically accepted by the public or so unabashedly composed by the agencies.

Or would it?

Workers as Consumers in Seattle

DANA FRANK

"Food wins all struggles," cooperative activist Oscar McGill told the Seattle Metal Trades Council in November 1919. If Seattle's trade unions would organize cooperatives, they would have access to enough food to hold out indefinitely during strikes, and would then "be able to win any fight" they undertook. A visitor from the East that same year found ideas such as McGill's ubiquitous in the Seattle American Federation of Labor (AFL) movement: "Out in Seattle now they have what they call

Excerpted from "'Food Wins All Struggles': Seattle Labor and the Politicization of Consumption," by Dana Frank in *Radical History Review* 51 (1991): 65–89. Copyright © MARHO: The Radical Historian's Organization. Reprinted with the permission of Cambridge University Press.

the 'Big Idea'. This means that the trade unionists do not stop with organizations merely at the point of production. They believe they must use their cooperative power and resources as consumers as well as producers."

Between 1919 and 1929 members of Seattle's AFL and their families took up organizing activities with great zeal, hoping to deploy their "power and resources as consumers." Three thousand working-class families joined consumer cooperatives; over 50,000 wage earners belonged to unions that formed or owned stock in consumer and producer cooperatives; 100,000 subscribers to the labor-owned *Seattle Union Record* could read columns on cooperation every day. Thousands observed a union-sponsored boycott of Seattle's largest department store in 1920. Equal numbers at least heard their union officials exhort them to look for the union label and shop card, especially in the second half of the decade. Although the exact numbers are impossible to know, labor-sponsored consumer organizing campaigns touched the lives of tens of thousands of Seattle workers in the post-World War I decade.

The AFL movement in Seattle, then, deeply politicized consumption. Trade unionists used boycotts, cooperatives, and union-label promotion in order to advance what they perceived as their class interests. Through these campaigns working people came to understand consumption in specifically articulated class terms, and then consciously shaped their consumption choices to serve political ends. In postwar Seattle, consumption proved to be inseparable from class conflict—it became a deliberate and often effective extension of politics from the shopfloor to the grocery store. As others have demonstrated with respect to working-class leisure, consumption itself became an arena of class struggle.

The manner in which Seattle unionists brought class consciousness to their shopping carts nonetheless varied widely. For a few, class-understood shopping evinced class consciousness in the classic revolutionary sense, in which workers hoped each purchase would contribute to the overthrow of the capitalist class and the workers' rise to power. Far more commonly, though, organized workers and their families envisioned prounion shopping in service to the gradual collective advancement of their class, bringing more evolutionary benefits—perhaps within the capitalist system, perhaps not. Still others viewed the politicization of consumption in far narrower terms. Consumer tactics would serve working people as members of trade unions, which had found a comfortable nest within capitalist society and could utilize prounion shopping to better feather it.

Envisioning politicized consumption and actually deploying it, however, were two very different things. Food did not, in fact, win *all* struggles for the working class of postwar Seattle, even when thousands mobilized in behalf of consumer tactics. Equally important, the AFL movement did not fully mobilize the Seattle working class as consumers. Some of the forces limiting its success came from without. Repression and economic depression ate away at the movement, undermining the breadth of its aspirations as well as its ability to realize them. Other limits the AFL unions brought upon themselves. Racial exclusion, male unionists' inability to understand and reach women either as wage earners or unwaged workers in the home, and a growing chasm between leaders and rank-and-file members all sharply constrained the unions' ability to persuade working people to shop according to union precepts. A careful look at consumer organizing campaigns in Seattle reveals that women and men, socialists and business unionists, leaders and rank-and-file members, white workers and those they defined as racially "other" constantly renegotiated the strategies with which the labor movement would use its consumer powers. That process of negotiation over consumer strategies, moreover, was part and parcel of the development of the Seattle labor movement as a whole in the 1920s. Throughout the process, workers and their families analyzed the political economy of consumption from a working-class point of view, always with an eye to manipulating it to their own advantage.

The story of consumer organizing in the postwar Seattle AFL movement, in sum, provides a rare glimpse into working-class people's encounter with consumer society, from their own perspective. The story of the trade unions' campaigns raises as many questions as it answers about the ideological and practical concerns of rank-and-file workers. But it nonetheless underscores how deeply linked production and consumption have been in the history of U.S. class relations, just as it reminds us that working people have been shrewd participants in the development of modern American consumer society. . . .

As trade unionism and class consciousness expanded in postwar Seattle, labor activism spilled over into efforts by workers to politicize consumption. The first impulse was toward cooperation, both producer and consumer. Working-class cooperatives boomed in Seattle in the years just after the war. One cross-city chain, the Seattle Consumers' Co-operative Association, identified itself with strict principles of one member, one vote, and patronage dividends to members, following guidelines established in Rochdale, England, in the nineteenth century. By 1920 the association counted 1,200 member-families, with nine consumer branches plus a cooperative jewelry store, tailors' shop, and fuel yard. Local unions and farmers directly owned and managed a second chain, the Co-operative Food Products Association (CFPA). It began with a meat market sponsored by the butchers' union, then expanded to include sausage production, a slaughterhouse, a milk condensary, and five neighborhood distributive branches off a central downtown market. Over 1,000 families joined by late 1919. Plumbers, steamfitters, and municipal employees started independent consumers' cooperatives; Scandinavian workers formed a cooperative bakery, restaurant, and reading room that employed 25 people; 1,000 joined the "Co-operative Campers" "to make our mountains accessible at low cost." Barbers, auto mechanics, longshoremen, painters, carpenters, shoe repairers and fishermen all formed producers' cooperatives.

A 1919 drive to create a worker-owned department store indicated the breadth of the Seattle cooperative movement's vision. Union locals from trades throughout the city sent delegates to a series of meetings at which they plotted fundraising activities, debated the best economic structure for the store, and planned ways for it to interlock with existing cooperatives. One enthusiast explained: "The THING Organized Labor wants in Seattle is a modern Department Store, with its numerous branches and service stations, so that we can buy from ourselves, anything we may want, from a paper of pins or a cup of coffee, to a fine suit of clothes, a fine coat for the wife, an automobile or a $2.00 dinner."

Mass enthusiasm for cooperative institution-building grew directly out of the workplace concerns of Seattle unionists. After the great shipyard strike that had precipitated the General Strike, many workers in the metal trades became convinced that consumers' cooperatives could help unions win strikes—they could extend credit to locked-out workers, for example, and lower food costs through self-management. Many unions formed cooperatives as an organizing wedge with which to break employers' lockouts or to win strikes, using producer cooperatives to harbor union activists or siphon business away from anti-union firms. This was the impetus behind the butchers' cooperative that began the Food Products Association, and behind a cooperative organized by cleaning and dye-work employees.

Indeed, the General Strike increased the popularity of cooperatives immensely. During the strike, government officials raided the Co-operative Food Products Association in a fake liquor raid, producing a landslide of support for the cooperatives. The actual strike experience contributed still further: during the four-day strike, labor-managed kitchens fed an estimated 30,000 people a day, while another worker-managed system supplied milk throughout the city. Cooperative membership burgeoned in the weeks following the strike, and cooperative ideas gained ascendance in the movement's strategic debates. At the same time, the failure of the General Strike to force the shipyards to capitulate lent the cooperatives a secessionist character. If employers could not be bested through a head-on confrontation at the point of production, then perhaps workers could secede from the union of labor and capital and retreat to their own autonomous world.

According to the theorists and managers of Seattle cooperatives, cooperation could create an independent working-class sector of the economy that would ultimately supplant capitalist institutions. "Cooperation penetrates steadily into the business of the capitalistic world and crowds it out," one advocate explained. Central to this process was "eliminating the middleman"—otherwise known as "the profiteer"—who interposed himself between producer and consumer, skimmed off an inappropriate profit, and drove prices up. According to these theories, cooperatives would wipe out the middleman (always a "he") by supplying products "direct from producer to consumer," and thus achieve greater "efficiency" than the "present private profit system." Victory would be possible if the cooperatives mobilized "this great weapon, the purchasing power of the worker, which up to this time he has literally thrown away," as the CFPA newsletter argued. The concept of the workers' purchasing power was central to the cooperative movement, as it was to all the consumer campaigns undertaken by the Seattle labor movement in the postwar decade.

In discussing cooperation, Seattle workers became embroiled in constant dialogue about the relationship between wages, prices, and profits. "Wages are not fixed alone in the workshop. They are fixed quite as much in the grocery store," wrote a national cooperative enthusiast in the CFPA newsletter. A local activist elaborated: "When your workers get an increase of wages, the employers add just that amount to the cost of production, and prices are increased to you at the counter, and the cost of living goes up." Only by eliminating profiteering "at the point of consumption" as well could workers protect the flanks of both wages and prices. For Seattle cooperative advocates, the key for workers was to "organize their purchasing power," spend working-class dollars to support both consumer and producer cooperatives, and thus usher in "the cooperative commonwealth." Cooperation would restructure the political economy of both consumption and production as part of an integrated strategic approach.

Both women and men participated in the cooperatives, but not on equal terms. The original boards of directors of both chains included only one woman, and it was there that real decisionmaking power within the coops lay. Key managers were also male, as were all the original members of key committees. When hiring employees, the cooperatives appear to have replicated the sexual division of labor in the regular labor force. The cooperative fuel yard, for example, employed a woman to take orders, a man to make deliveries.

Nonetheless, the cooperative movement's leaders envisioned a special place for women within the movement. "The labor man fights at the point of production, where he is robbed; the labor woman fights at the point of consumption, where she is robbed," one female staff member summed up tidily. Excluded from most formal channels of powers with the cooperatives, women activists in both chains started networks of women's clubs, organized on a neighborhood-by-neighborhood basis. The clubs, designed initially as the seeds for neighborhood buying clubs, which would evolve into local branches, soon became educational and social organizations. Female cooperative members discussed key texts on cooperation, listened to local and visiting cooperative enthusiasts, and strengthened social ties. From 1919 through 1921 they developed the clubs' activities beyond the usual social occasions to include charity work, a dry-goods operation within the Food Products Association's main store, and a daycare center for wage-earning mothers. Throughout these activities, cooperative women spoke of using cooperatives to make the world more ideally "homelike"—through decorations at teas in members' homes, through furnishings at a "women's lounge" at the cooperative store, and by extending women's roles as caretakers for their families to political activities in behalf of those younger or less well off than themselves. One woman summed up her point of view on the movement: "Anything that is for the good, for the humane, the noble, and unselfish, ideas and principles, we the women of the co-operative clubs, are interested in helping and patronizing."

To make these activities happen, women donated their own unwaged labor as volunteers, whether to bake cakes for fundraisers or sew quilts for the dry goods department to sell. Yet the women's activities indicate that they understood that all this was work, and that they turned to cooperation in part to address their own concerns as unwaged workers whose job it was to consume. Meetings of the cooperative clubs might include a demonstration of how to can green beans, for example. The women created their downtown lounge so tired shoppers could rest their feet. Most centrally, women turned to cooperation because it promised a relief to the unrelenting inflation of the war and immediate postwar years. Prices nationwide increased from a July 1914 index of 100 to 165 by November, finally peaking in July 1920 at 204 percent of July 1914 levels. Cooperative activists specifically promoted their movement as an answer to this "high cost of living"—a problem so omnipresent that the labor press commonly abbreviated it as the "h.c. of l." For married women especially, inflation meant more work, searching for bargains, cooking cheaper and cheaper meals, and satisfying increasingly disgruntled family members. With one or two exceptions all the women identified as active in the cooperative movement were married and presumably responsible for their families' food budgets. Working-class women involved in the cooperatives came to the movement to address their own workplace concerns, just as did the men. And like the men, they quickly moved beyond that to a vision of a differently structured, self-managed world. . . .

In the immediate postwar years, as the cooperatives burgeoned, the politicization of consumption became part of the frontal battle between Seattle labor and capital. For employers, the 1919 General Strike threatened the triumph of bolshevism on American soil. In response, they organized a new employers' association, the Associated Industries, and launched a massive and effective open-shop drive in the late summer of 1919. By pooling funds, refusing to negotiate, and promoting the "American Plan," they were able to defeat one by one Seattle's unions. What had been promised to be a routine Labor Day strike by the building trades ended disastrously in mid-fall with the open shop in most building-trade workplaces. Two other early fall strikes, by the tailors and printers, also wore on disastrously. By Christmas the closed shop had been shattered in the building trades, printing, much service work, and the metal trades. Meanwhile, government repression mounted. City officials shut down the *Union Record* in late November (albeit temporarily) in response to the massacre of Wobblies in nearby Centralia. Deportations of foreign-born dissidents continued. Orders stood to arrest on sight anyone who passed out a pamphlet, called a meeting, or gave a speech on behalf of the IWW.

Initially, the labor movement was at sea in the face of this offensive, groping for an effective tactical response. Clearly, organized labor's traditional basic weapon, the strike, no longer served. First the unions turned to politics, but a November mobilization failed to elect any labor-sponsored working-class candidates.

A second strategic turn looked to the sphere of consumption. Beginning in December, the movement's leadership began to experiment with consumer boycotts to retaliate against the Associated Industries. After the Centralia-inspired raids, the Central Labor Council called upon members of organized labor and their families to refuse to buy Christmas presents, especially from the city's department stores. Unionists identified owners of those stores as "in the vanguard of the movement to crush labor." Two prominent radical activists, one from the longshoremen, the other from the shipyard laborers, toured the city's union locals promoting the boycott, not only linking the department store owners to the open-shop drive, but also analyzing their marketing tactics from a shrewd perspective. Prices were jacked up for Christmas, they noted, and the stores were dependent on profits obtained from high sales during the holidays. By waiting until after Christmas to buy presents, workers could not only cut store owners' profits, but also "secure toys ninety percent lower" and liberate themselves from a "puzzling of your brains to find a present, to match the one you may get."

Over the course of the weeks before Christmas, however, the campaign swiftly narrowed from a refusal to buy Christmas presents altogether, to a boycott of department stores, to a smaller boycott of four department stores particularly hostile to labor. By mid-December ads in the *Record* urged workers to buy presents that would support labor's cause, such as stock in the labor-owned Mutual Laundry, cooperatives, or the *Record* itself. Advertisements appeared for regular businesses (though not the department stores), the texts of which implicitly acknowledged labor's campaign while nonetheless promoting the purchase of presents. Usually they stressed their product's usefulness; thus, an ad for furniture promised "Practical

Common Sense CHRISTMAS GIFTS." By 19 December the campaign had eroded, and the paper ran a full-page Christmas-present advertising spread, complete with wreaths and holly about the margins, that allured readers with a jewelry store's reminder that there were "only Four Days Before Xmas" and an offer of "FURS FOR CHRISTMAS AT HALF PRICE."

What can we learn from this campaign? The original boycott calls reveal an awareness of merchants' economic weaknesses and a willingness to manipulate those vulnerabilities. In their arguments promoting the boycott, unionists identified the relationship between the employers' association, anti-union campaigns, working-class shopping habits, and retailers' marketing strategies. Equally important, the boycott shows the links the Seattle labor movement forged between struggles over production—the General Strike and capital's response—and those over consumption. Organized labor retaliated against the employers' association drive through an explicit economic link to those employers' investments in consumption. To do so meant viewing something as ostensibly "consumerist" as Christmas-present buying sprees in explicitly political class terms, in which individual workers' acts of consumption were understood collectively. The gradual narrowing of the campaign's scope, though, also shows the resistance of many rank-and-file union members to abandoning Christmas spending. With only a smattering of evidence, it is difficult to ascertain more about the boycott's reception or demise.

The Christmas-present boycott was only a dress rehearsal for a much larger boycott campaign that organized labor commenced in March 1920 against Seattle's largest department store, the Bon Marche. The decision to call the boycott came on the heels of another round of tactical defeats. The Associated Industries' open-shop drive still raged while a second mass electoral mobilization, in February, failed to win the mayoral seat for labor. The Central Labor Council turned to the Bon Marche boycott as a final vehicle through which to dispatch the Associated Industries. Frank Waterhouse, owner of the Bon Marche, was president of the Associated Industries, while Broussais C. Beck, the store's manager, also was an active leader in the open-shop drive. The Bon Marche, moreover, despite its substantial working-class patronage (unionists estimated it to be around 75 percent), was in the process of constructing a lavish new downtown store rather ostentatiously with nonunion labor.

The Bon Marche boycott involved trade unions from throughout the city and began with a citywide advertising campaign against the store. Leaflets, billboards across the state, and resolutions from trade-union bodies all discouraged shopping at the store. A publicity committee regularly visited meetings of locals to exhort members to join the boycott. Most prominently, the *Record* ran an almost daily series of articles vilifying the store. The paper attacked the Bon Marche on four counts: (a) the store's hostility to the building trades and alliance with the employers' association, (b) its cruel treatment of female clerks—who were refused chairs and forced to toil in "foul smelling basements," (c) its "excess profits," and finally, (d) its manipulative bait-and-switch-selling practices. The *Record* charged, for example, that Bon Marche lured shoppers with ostensible "bargains" in a special basement storeroom, and then, when unsuspecting customers discovered only off-sizes available, sold them the same article upstairs at a high mark-up.

These accusations against the Bon Marche thus freely mixed charges of exploitation of wage earners, as workers, with charges of exploitation of customers, as consumers. Bait-and-switch, union busting, and overworking employees were equally heinous. Moreover, readers of the *Record* were well apprised of the Bon Marche's manipulation of its customers; through the *Record*'s pages they could learn to see through bait-and-switch tactics, just as they had earlier read of department stores' tendency to raise prices at Christmas time. Through their locals they envisioned ways to politicize a critique of such practices in service to a class-based movement, and they plotted their own quite effective ways of manipulating the Bon Marche right back—again, in their own capacities as workers *and* as patrons at the store.

Yet the Bon Marche boycott revealed limits to the ability of the trade unions to politicize consumption effectively. Working-class women involved in the labor movement, at least at the upper organizational levels, failed to support the boycott campaign enthusiastically. Labor's male leadership, conscious of its need to reach women, had designed the campaign specifically with them in mind—stressing the store's high prices, advertising the boycott through the *Union Record,* which enjoyed a mass female readership, and selecting a single store to boycott rather than targeting all department stores. "For the women will buy in these stores," Labor Council Secretary Charles Doyle admitted.

Despite these efforts, the city's highly organized leadership of women trade unionists and activist wives never came forward to support the boycott. Women of labor chose, instead, to place their organizational energies behind a quite different campaign in the time period of the Bon boycott—a campaign to increase the state minimum wage for women. They traveled constantly to the state capital, Olympia, to lobby and testify on behalf of that cause. Key women activists in the labor movement, in other words, chose to promote the interests of women wage workers at the point of production, rather than actively promote a boycott that they themselves did not initiate. With one exception, women were completely excluded from the leadership of the Central Labor Council, which was responsible for the decision to boycott the Bon.

The success of the boycott is difficult to assess. If we only had the *Record*'s word for it, we would see nothing but success. The labor paper marshaled an array of statistics to bolster its argument that the boycott devastated the Bon Marche. Profits had plummeted, it claimed; store crowds were thinner. A department head at the store, it reported, had confided to a friend that the store's business was down 50 percent from the previous year. A *Record* reporter stationed at three department stores' entrances counted few shoppers entering the Bon Marche, in contrast to the numbers shopping at its rivals.

Seattle employers' internal literature makes clear that the boycott did, indeed, hurt the Bon Marche and prompt caution on the part of the city's employers. In the fall of 1920, the Associated Industries acknowledged that "there is little question but that [the Bon Marche] is being injured." They complained of "dastardly" boycotts, and noted that firms were being selected for their "vulnerability"—thus granting that firms were, indeed, vulnerable to boycotts. The employers' protests indicate that some working-class men and women, at the rank-and-file level, did boycott the Bon Marche. Although the leadership stratum of women within the AFL movement lacked enthusiasm for the boycott, some sympathetic women affiliated with the unions, whether members themselves or family members, probably observed the Central Labor Council's boycott.

Concrete evidence can be found in the employers' change in behavior. By the fall and winter of 1920–21 they had backed off their open-shop drive. One significant indication was a split in the chamber of commerce, which, in a September 1920 about-face, came out for profit-sharing and company unions rather than a frontal assault on labor. As the city's economy contracted, moreover, many smaller firms rebelled against the Associated Industries' hard-line strictures. With unemployment still on the rise, employers could gain many of their demands without needlessly antagonizing the unions with a hostile approach. The General Strike only a year and a half behind them, and the IWW by no means dead, many employers feared that the situation could easily explode. As a result, business leaders encouraged firms to hire large numbers of part-time workers to reduce the total number of unemployed workers and lessen possible tensions. The outcome, on the eve of the 1921–22 recession, was essentially a stalemate between labor and capital: employers were no longer interested in an outright showdown that might backfire, while labor was tired, on the defensive, and in no mood for aggressive posturing. . . .

The story of consumer organizing in postwar Seattle shows working people as critical actors. Organized workers in Seattle developed theories about the political economy of consumption, analyzed their place as both workers and shoppers within that economy, and tried to use their powers in both capacities to shape American society. Cooperative activists debated the relationship between prices and wages, railed against "profiteering" of many sorts, and advocated an alternative model for the structure of consumption in U.S. society. Promoters of both the Christmas-present and Bon Marche boycotts identified links between organized capital's anti-union activities and employers' investment in merchandising, and then zeroed in on merchandisers' economic vulnerabilities. Label and shop-card advocates, from a quite different perspective, analyzed the relationship between capital and labor only to conclude that their interests were harmonious, that working-class shopping could dovetail happily with employers' goals both economically and politically. In all cases, though, organized labor understood working-class consumption as a linchpin in the realization of employers' profits. In all cases, unionists spoke of "the workers' purchasing power" as a resource for struggle. And in all cases they not only theorized about power "at the point of consumption," but also deployed it.

SUGGESTED READING

Benson, Susan Porter. *Counter Cultures: Saleswomen, Managers, and Customers in American Department Stores, 1890–1940* (1986).

Berger, Michael. *The Devil Wagon in God's Country: The Automobile and Social Change in Rural America, 1893–1929* (1979).

Brooks, Dwight Ernest. *Consumer Markets and Consumer Magazines: Black America and the Culture of Consumption, 1920–1960* (1991).

Cohen, Lizabeth. "The Class Experience of Mass Consumption." In *The Power of Culture: Critical Essays in American History,* ed. T. J. Jackson Lears, 135–160 (1993).

Davis, Donald Finlay. *Conspicuous Production: Automobiles and Elites in Detroit* (1988).

Douglas, Susan. *Inventing American Broadcasting, 1899–1922* (1987).

Edsforth, Ronald. *Class Conflict and Cultural Consensus: The Making of a Mass Consumer Society in Flint, Michigan* (1987).

Ewen, Stuart. *Captains of Consciousness: Advertising and the Social Roots of Consumer Culture* (1976).

Fink, James. *The Car Culture* (1975).

———. *The Automobile Age* (1988).

Fox, Stephen R. *The Mirror Makers: A History of American Advertising and Its Creators* (1984).

Frank, Dana. *Purchasing Power: Consumer Organizing, Gender, and the Seattle Labor Movement, 1919–1929* (1994).

Gamber, Wendy. *The Female Economy: the Millinery and Dressmaking Trades, 1860–1930* (1997).

Garvey, Ellen Gruber. *The Adman in the Parlor: Magazines and the Gendering of Consumer Culture* (1996).

Horowitz, Daniel. *The Morality of Spending: Attitudes Toward the Consumer Society in America, 1875–1940* (1985).

Leach, William. *Land of Desire: Merchants, Power and the Rise of a New American Culture* (1993).

Lears, T. J. Jackson. *Fables of Abundance: A Cultural History of Advertising in America* (1994).

Lears, T. J. Jackson, and Richard Wightman Fox, eds. *The Culture of Consumption* (1983).

Lebergott, Stanley. *Pursuing Happiness: American Consumers in the Twentieth Century* (1993).

Ling, Peter. *America and the Automobile: Technology, Reform, and Social Change* (1990).

Marchand, Roland. *Advertising the American Dream: Making Way for Modernity, 1920–1940* (1985).

May, Larry. *Screening Out the Past: The Birth of Mass Culture and the Motion Picture Industry* (1980).

McChesney, Robert. *Telecommunications, Mass Media, and Democracy: The Battle for the Control of U.S. Broadcasting, 1928–1935* (1993).

Nasaw, David. *Going Out: The Rise and Fall of Public Amusements* (1993).

Olney, Martha. *Buy Now, Pay Later: Advertising, Credit, and Consumer Durables in the 1920s* (1991).

Peiss, Kathy. *Cheap Amusements: Working Women and Leisure in Turn of the Century New York* (1986).

Scanlon, Jennifer. *Inarticulate Longings: The Ladies' Home Journal, Gender, and the Promises of Consumer Culture* (1995).

Scharff, Virginia. *Taking the Wheel: Women and the Coming of the Motor Age* (New York: Free Press, 1991).

Sklar, Robert. *Movie-Made America: A Cultural History of American Movies* (1994).

Strasser, Susan. *Satisfaction Guaranteed: The Making of the American Mass Market* (1989).

Susman, Warren. "Culture Heroes: Ford, Barton, Ruth." In *Culture as History: The Transformation of American Society in the Twentieth Century*, 122–149 (1984).

CHAPTER
5

Intellectual and Cultural Currents

Beyond the common experience of mass consumption, American culture followed diverse paths between the wars. In some respects, writers, artists, and intellectuals lashed out against, or withdrew from, the horror of the war and the commercialism of the postwar decade. This was evident in the expatriate writings of Ernest Hemingway and Gertrude Stein, in the chronicles of the Jazz Age penned by F. Scott Fitzgerald and others, and in the caustic social commentary of H. L. Mencken and Sinclair Lewis—indeed Lewis's 1922 novel Babbitt *remains perhaps the most biting and bittersweet portrait of America in the 1920s. For some, this sense of alienation would deepen with the onset of the Great Depression in 1929. Indeed many American writers became involved in radical politics in the 1930s, supporting the New Deal (or radical alternatives to it) and participating in the "popular front" against fascism in the late 1930s.*

At the same time, economic, technological, and demographic change opened new cultural and intellectual vistas. One of the fruits of the "great migration" of African Americans to the urban North in the years surrounding World War I was the flowering of cultural life in settings such as Harlem. While patronage remained segregated in many ways, the Harlem Renaissance marked the emergence of a new generation (the "New Negro," as the critic Alain Locke put it at the time) of African American writers, poets, artists, and musicians. This new sense of cultural autonomy and community spilled into politics as well as many African Americans, especially in the urban North, turned to nationalist organizations such as Marcus Garvey's United Negro Improvement Association.

While many intellectuals scorned the institutions of mass culture, others held out some hope for the democratic and educational promise of media such as popular magazines and radio. Through the 1920s and 1930s, for example, many fought the commercialization of radio and tried vainly to cobble together some semblance of a public broadcasting system. And through the 1930s and 1940s, many saw in the New Deal an opportunity for federal patronage and promotion of the arts. In debates over both New Deal art programs and the regulation of radio, however, advocates of public solutions found it difficult to balance the promise of democratic control against the threat of state domination.

👊 *D O C U M E N T S*

While it is difficult to impart a sense of intellectual life or culture with a few short selections, the documents attempt to capture a range of debates and experiences. Document 1, two poems by Langston Hughes, serves as an example of the literary world of the Harlem Renaissance and comments upon African American life in the 1920s. Document 2 is a distillation of the Jazz Age by F. Scott Fitzgerald, the author of *The Great Gatsby* and other works. Document 3, a 1930 editorial from the *New Republic,* presents some sense of the hope that radio would serve as more than a vehicle for light entertainment and advertising. The final documents trace the response of writers and artists to the turmoil of the 1930s. In Document 4, the author and critic Granville Hicks suggests the attraction of radical politics for intellectuals in the 1930s. Document 5 reproduces two typical examples of public art sponsored by the Works Progress Administration (WPA); and Document 6 lampoons the proliferation of such images. In Document 7, an artist recalls the importance of the New Deal programs.

1. Langston Hughes, Two Poems of the 1920s

One-Way Ticket

> I pick up my life
> And take it with me
> And I put it down in
> Chicago, Detroit,
> Buffalo, Scranton,
> Any place that is
> North and East—
> And not Dixie.
>
> I pick up my life
> And take it on the train
> To Los Angeles, Bakersfield,
> Seattle, Oakland, Salt Lake,
> Any place that is
> North and West—
> And not South.
>
> I am fed up
> With Jim Crow laws,
> People who are cruel
> And afraid,
> Who lynch and run,
> Who are scared of me
> And me of them.
>
> I pick up my life
> And take it away

From *Collected Poems* by Langston Hughes. Copyright © 1994 by the Estate of Langston Hughes. Reprinted by permission of Alfred A. Knopf, Inc.

On a one-way ticket—
Gone up North,
Gone out West,
Gone!

Refugee in America

There are words like *Freedom*
Sweet and wonderful to say.
On my heart-strings freedom sings
All day everyday.

There are words like *Liberty*
That almost make me cry.
If you had known what I knew
You would know why.

2. F. Scott Fitzgerald on the Jazz Age, 1931

It is too soon to write about the Jazz Age with perspective, and without being suspected of premature arteriosclerosis. Many people still succumb to violent retching when they happen upon any of its characteristic words—words which have since yielded in vividness to the coinages of the underworld. It is as dead as were the Yellow Nineties in 1902. Yet the present writer already looks back to it with nostalgia. It bore him up, flattered him and gave him more money than he had dreamed of, simply for telling people that he felt as they did, that something had to be done with all the nervous energy stored up and unexpended in the War.

The ten-year period that, as if reluctant to die outmoded in its bed, leaped to a spectacular death in October, 1929, began about the time of the May Day riots in 1919. When the police rode down the demobilized country boys gaping at the orators in Madison Square, it was the sort of measure bound to alienate the more intelligent young men from the prevailing order. We didn't remember anything about the Bill of Rights until Mencken began plugging it, but we did know that such tyranny belonged in the jittery little countries of South Europe. If goose-livered business men had this effect on the government, then maybe we had gone to war for J. P. Morgan's loans after all. But, because we were tired of Great Causes, there was no more than a short outbreak of moral indignation, typified by Dos Passos' "Three Soldiers." Presently we began to have slices of the national cake and our idealism only flared up when the newspapers made melodrama out of such stories as Harding and the Ohio Gang or Sacco and Vanzetti. The events of 1919 left us cynical rather than revolutionary, in spite of the fact that now we are all rummaging around in our trunks wondering where in hell we left the liberty cap—"I know I *had* it"— and the moujik blouse. It was characteristic of the Jazz Age that it had no interest in politics at all. . . .

The Jazz Age had had a wild youth and a heady middle age. There was the phase of the necking parties, the Leopold-Loeb murder (I remember the time my wife was arrested on Queensborough Bridge on the suspicion of being the "Bob-haired Bandit") and the John Held Clothes. In the second phase such phenomena as sex and murder became more mature, if much more conventional. Middle age must be served and pajamas came to the beach to save fat thighs and flabby calves from competition with the one-piece bathing-suit. Finally skirts came down and every-thing was concealed. Everybody was at scratch now. Let's go—

But it was not to be. Somebody had blundered and the most expensive orgy in history was over.

It ended two years ago, because the utter confidence which was its essential prop received an enormous jolt and it didn't take long for the flimsy structure to set-tle earthward. And after two years the Jazz Age seems as far away as the days be-fore the War. It was borrowed time anyhow—the whole upper tenth of a nation living with the insouciance of grand ducs and the casualness of chorus girls. . . .

Now once more the belt is tight and we summon the proper expression of hor-ror as we look back at our wasted youth. Sometimes, though, there is a ghostly rum-ble among the drums, an asthmatic whisper in the trombones that swings me back into the early twenties when we drank wood alcohol and every day in every way great better and better, and there was a first abortive shortening of the skirts, and girls all looked alike in sweater dresses, and people you didn't want to know said "Yes, we have no bananas," and it seemed only a question of a few years before the older people would step aside and let the world be run by those who saw things as they were—and it all seems rosy and romantic to us who were young then, because we will never feel quite so intensely about our surroundings any more.

3. The Educational Promise of Radio, 1930

From the beginning of radio, ten years ago, high hopes have been held out for its use in education. We were told then, as we are told now, that this marvelous device will prove a mighty tool in teaching old and young. Yet in ten years' time so little progress has been made that it is scarcely visible to the naked eye. Most of the at-tempts which have been made in the meantime to use the radio in education, in the United States, have failed for one reason or another and have been abandoned.

This failure should not be mourned with too much vehemence. Other means of education continue to be used, and, however unsatisfactory they may be to the ide-alist, they are probably more efficient, and certainly more universally employed, than ever before. The radio is a valuable medium for entertainment, and its use in that field is not to be despised. Moreover, the present trend of educational theory is away from learning by mere sitting back and listening—all that the radio has thus far been able to provide. It may prove to be true, as Miss Katherine Ludington of the National League of Women Voters believes, that the ultimate serious function of the

Excerpted from "The Radio and Education," *The New Republic* August 13, 1930, pp. 357–358.

radio is as a substitute for the old-fashioned New England town meeting, rather than the classroom.

Yet the radio undoubtedly has some definite possibilities as an educational force, as is proved by the successful experience of European countries. The failure in the United States is partly due to the fact that we have turned over this device to private interests which exploit it purely for making money. The pretense that radio is conducted in the public interest is no more genuine, in America, than is the similar pretense in the case of the newspaper or popular magazine, both of which are private business institutions existing in order to sell advertising space wherein merchants and others may seek to change the buying habits of the general population. The radio broadcasters hardly consider at all what, from the public standpoint, ought to be sent over the etherial waves; they consider only what is to their own greatest immediate advantage to disseminate. It is true that not every moment of every program is paid for by someone with goods to sell; there are also what are called "sustaining programs," supplied by the stations or chains of stations. While some of this material is excellent of its kind, on the whole only the musical parts of the programs are to be taken seriously; the broadcasters are inferior as a group, in traditions and general culture, to the newspaper and magazine editors, and they are terrorized by the size and the supposed low mental level of their audiences. . . .

Educational broadcasting has been treated with brutal indifference both by the Federal Radio Commission and the commercial broadcasters. The Commission has been reluctant to give adequate power or desirable channels to stations owned by educational institutions. The broadcasters who have loaned their facilities have hardly ever donated time which they could sell to anybody else, and the educational work has therefore been done at bad hours, when there are few listeners. No one in this country has inquired into the technique of teaching by radio. No serious attempt has been made to study the listeners and see just what they get out of the material dumped upon them. . . .

This failure in the United States, as we have said, is the more humiliating when it is compared with the success achieved in education by radio in Europe, and notably in Great Britain and Germany. In both these countries broadcasting is a government monopoly and a strictly controlled one. The English owner of a radio set pays an annual license fee of $2.50 and this provides a large revenue out of which musicians and speakers are paid for their appearances before the microphone. In 1929, the sum thus available was $4,200,000. The educational activities are directed by a distinguished committee, and the actual results are checked as carefully as possible. Several magazines are published for listeners, and these carry the printed material which supplements the lectures. In many communities "group listening" is practised. A number of people meet, hear a radio speaker, and then talk the matter over among themselves. Courses are given each year in a wide range of subjects, and they constitute in effect a popular university of the air. Much attention is also paid to formal academic work; last year more than 2,300 schools used the radio as a part of their regular instruction. . . .

It has been assumed, in the United States, that the radio must be left in private hands because that means "individual initiative," the American way of doing things. But whatever may be true in other fields of endeavor, in that of broadcasting this theory is working badly. It is ridiculous that into 12,000,000 homes should come, for several hours each evening, information and amusement dictated by the manufacturers of tooth paste, soap, ginger ale and gasoline, and circumscribed both by their intellectual limitations and their greed. When you add to this the ultra-conservatism, timidity and lack of initiative of the broadcasters themselves, you have a situation which urgently needs reconsideration. Broadly speaking, the radio in America is going to waste. How shall it be salvaged—and by whom?

4. Granville Hicks on Writers in the 1930s

I was one of the lucky ones, for I had a job in the bad years; but my father lost his job, and he and my mother moved in with us. Everybody in the middle class, however lucky he may have been himself, knew someone—and, if he had any compassion, was helping someone—who was less fortunate. Everyone knew that something had to be done.

In the twenties, as I have said, few writers were political in any very specific sense. (There were some exceptions.) By 1931, however, more and more writers were saying that they had a responsibility for the state of the nation. After all, they had emphatically and sometimes stridently called attention to the shortcomings of our business civilization, and, now that that civilization had come close to collapse, they could not pretend that it was no business of theirs.

It may help you to understand what happened if you remember that artists are not temperamentally inclined to moderation. They aren't likely to say, "Oh, let's give a little here, and change a little there, and tinker with this and play around with that." They are, for better or for worse, more likely to demand that something fundamental be done and be done here and now. And to many writers in 1932 nothing seemed more fundamental than the program of the Communist party. . . .

It is sometimes hard to remember how pervasive social discontent was in the thirties. It affected many of the older writers. Theodore Dreiser, for example, was active in a variety of communist causes, and he wrote a book of left-wing propaganda, *Tragic America.* (He quarreled with the Communist party after that, but he was a member of it when he died in 1945.) Sherwood Anderson was hit hard by communism for a brief time, and his concern showed itself in a book of essays, *Puzzled America,* and in such novels as *Kit Brandon.* Sinclair Lewis was wary about the Communists, but he did write an anti-fascist novel, *It Can't Happen Here,* which Communist critics welcomed. (He also wrote an anti-Communist novel, *The Prodigal Parents.*)

But it was, naturally, the new writers who reacted most sharply to the depression, and in the middle thirties there was a great spate of so-called proletarian novels. Most of them have long since been forgotten, and deservedly so. Who remembers the names Myra Page, James Steele, Grace Lumpkin, William Rollins, Arnold B. Armstrong, Clara Weatherwax, or Philip Stevenson?

Yet it is a mistake to suppose that the radical fiction of the thirties was all negligible. There was Jack Conroy, whose novel about a poor miner's family, *The Disinherited,* was recently issued in a paperback edition and proved to be not so irrelevant to life in the year 1965 as we should like to believe. There was Robert Cantwell's *Land of Plenty,* which described with skill and authority a strike in the West Coast lumber industry. . . . There was Josephine Herbst, who wrote a trilogy describing the decline of the middle class—*Pity Is Not Enough, The Executioner Waits,* and *Rope of Gold*—three excellent titles and three excellent books. There was Richard Wright, a Communist for a time, though not a pious one; his first and most powerful novel, *Native Son,* dramatized the racial struggle rather than the class struggle, though Wright tried to show that they were one and the same. There was Henry Roth, whose *Call It Sleep,* first published in 1934, has recently been revived; this was, among other things, a true proletarian novel, though its Marxist critics did not recognize it as such. . . .

Only a few of the writers I have thus far named were members of the Communist party, but most of them followed the party line at least for a time. The question is often asked: What was the effect of the Communist party on the writers and other artists who were either members or fellow-travelers? There is no doubt in my mind now that the influence was harmful. I do not believe that artists can accept the direction of any political organization, and the direction of the Communist party was particularly dangerous because of its dogmatic and dictatorial character. But we must not assume that all the left-wing writers of the thirties bowed to the dictates of Earl Browder or any other party official. Even the few of us who were party members were not so subject to party discipline as we were supposed to be. If the Soviet Union, after decades of dictatorship, could not eliminate the possibility of a Pasternak, a Zoshchenko, or an Abram Tertz, we should not exaggerate the power of the Communist party in the United States, even in the thirties.

5. Two WPA Posters, 1935 and 1938

"Work Promotes Confidence" WPA poster (Library of Congress).

"Register Now: Informal Study Group" WPA poster (Library of Congress).

6. A Magazine Cover Comments on Public Art, 1941

Cover drawing by Virginia Snedeker © 1941 The New Yorker Magazine, Inc.

7. An Artist Remembers the WPA, 1935–1939

The golden years of the WPA New York Federal Art Project were about four—from 1935 to 1939—the years, naturally, when I was employed by the "Project."

They seem golden to me now, loaded with nostalgia. That was another life and I am now another person, living a different life. Some of us remember our grandparents or even a great-grandmother. It is what that kind of distance in time that I now remember the project. Recently I unearthed some of the sketches of that period and remarked to myself, somewhat surprised by the young man's ability, as though it were someone else's work, "Not bad, not bad at all!" A little choke of wistfulness comes over me at what might have been if my career had taken another turn. But I have no regrets. Everything balances out.

The Great Depression fostered a generation of young people in New York City who knew what they were about because evidently their elders didn't. They had all the answers. Zeal was a measure of certainty. The Establishment represented the left-over stupidities of the last century. A good number who were concerned about the justice and dilemmas of the world were revolutionaries, although they didn't ape the Bolsheviks. They had their own shade of red. The ghost of John Reed hovered about. There was even a John Reed Club that held dances, socials, and esoteric lectures and discussions on Art and Society. The fiery speeches of Norman Thomas and Earl Brower and the cocksureness of their causes had some of the flavor of the romantic stories of the barricades of 1848 Paris.

There were benefit parties for unions in trouble. I remember Zero Mostel as the life of the party with his clown pokerface. There were also "pay the rent" parties, especially where a group of artists used the same loft. The Artists' Union was in the front lines. One of its presidents, Paul Bloch, went off to Spain to join the Abraham Lincoln Brigade. He never came back.

The predominant intellectual milieu surrounding the Federal Art Project may have been somewhat as sketched above, but there were also many artists who were nonpolitical, who desperately wanted to pursue their careers, and who looked neither to the left or right. It was good to know your work went somewhere, gracing the walls of some public building. It gave you purpose and helped out a faltering self-esteem. It was not until years later you learned there was excess production and that, sadly, most of the work was eventually junked. . . .

Art philosophies were constantly argued, often quite passionately. One continuing controversy was "social significance" vs. "art for art's sake." Many, like myself, didn't follow either side. We felt that the individual artist was the best judge of his own work. Those who worked realistically or moderately stylized or impressionistically tended to "social significance," whereas the many abstract schools called their own work "visual music." Ad Reinhardt, Hananiah Harari, Eugene Morley and many others were advocates for abstraction. The others felt that not only should the themes comment on social problems, but that the work itself should be readily appreciated by the hoi polloi, the masses, the culturally impoverished.

Excerpted from "A Remembrance of the WPA" by Anthony Velonis in *Posters of the WPA* by Christopher De Noon. Copyright © 1987 The Wheatley Press, pp. 72–75.

This controversy reached a high point at a meeting held in the auditorium of the New School for Social Research. I remember the atmosphere hazily. The "Baroness" (some connection with Guggenheim) presented a series of large paintings by a German artist she thought was the greatest. The paintings were more than abstract, they were "nonobjective," all based on mathematical and geometric forms. Needless to say, the meeting was quite turbulent. The majority seemed to feel abstract art was arguable: it was human; it was play; it had occasional symbolism. But this nonobjective stuff had no content at all: it was cold and plodding. To this day, though, I can't see why it made so many artists angry. Many spoke up, but I remember the dashing, handsome figure of Byron Browne making an impassioned speech from the floor, after which half of the audience walked out. Informal panels continued to argue in the local coffee houses and cafeterias far into the night.

The various art philosophies made their imprint on me. I had decided early that I would learn as much as I could from everybody. I felt the FAP was a golden opportunity. There had never been an art school as dynamic with so many crosscurrents.

E S S A Y S

In the first essay, David Levering Lewis traces the artistic richness and political and cultural importance of the Harlem Renaissance. In the second essay, Robert McChesney argues that an opportunity to build an open and democratic broadcasting system was lost in the debate over radio regulation in the 1920s and 1930s. In the third essay, Jane S. De Hart suggests the democratic implications of New Deal art programs.

When Harlem Was in Vogue

DAVID LEVERING LEWIS

The Harlem Renaissance was a somewhat forced phenomenon, a cultural nationalism of the parlor, institutionally encouraged and directed by leaders of the national civil rights establishment for the paramount purpose of improving race relations in a time of extreme national backlash, caused in large part by economic gains won by Afro-Americans during the Great War. W.E.B. Du Bois labeled this mobilizing elite the "Talented Tenth" in a seminal 1903 essay. He fleshed out the concept that same year in "The Advance Guard of the Race," a piece in *Booklover's Magazine* in which he identified the poet Paul Laurence Dunbar, the novelist Charles W. Chestnut, and the painter Henry O. Tanner, among a small number of other well-educated professionals, as representatives of this class. The Talented Tenth formulated and propagated a new ideology of racial assertiveness that was to be embraced by the physicians, dentists, educators, preachers, businesspeople, lawyers, and morticians who comprised the bulk of the African American affluent and influential—some ten thousand men and women out of a total population in 1920 of more than ten million. (In 1917, traditionally cited as the natal year of the Harlem Renaissance, there were 2,132 African Americans in colleges and universities, probably no more than fifty of them attending "white" institutions.)

It was, then, the minuscule vanguard of a minority—a fraction of 0.1 percent of the racial total—that jump-started the New Negro Arts Movement, using as its vehicles the National Association for the Advancement of Colored People (NAACP) and the National Urban League (NUL), and their respective publications, *The Crisis* and *Opportunity* magazine. The Harlem Renaissance was not, as some students have maintained, all-inclusive of the early twentieth-century African American urban experience. Not everything that happened between 1917 and 1935 was a Renaissance happening. The potent mass movement founded and led by the charismatic Marcus Garvey was to the Renaissance what nineteenth-century populism was to progressive reform: a parallel but socially different force related primarily through dialectical confrontation. Equally different from the institutional ethos and purpose of the Renaissance was the Black Church. If the leading intellectual of the race, Du Bois, publicly denigrated the personnel and preachings of the Black Church, his animadversions were merely more forthright than those of other New Negro notables James Weldon Johnson, Charles S. Johnson, Jessie Redmon Fauset, Alain Locke, and Walter Francis White. An occasional minister (such as the father of poet Countee Cullen) or exceptional Garveyites (such as Yale-Harvard man William H. Ferris) might move in both worlds, but black evangelism and its cultist manifestations, such as Black Zionism, represented emotional and cultural retrogression in the eyes of the principal actors in the Renaissance.

When Du Bois wrote a few years after the beginning of the New Negro movement in arts and letters that "until the art of the black folk compels recognition they will not be rated as human," he, like most of his Renaissance peers, fully intended to exclude the blues of Bessie Smith and the jazz of "King" Oliver. Spirituals sung like *Lieder* by the disciplined Hall Johnson Choir—and, better yet, *Lieder* sung by conservatory-trained Roland Hayes, 1924 recipient of the NAACP's prestigious Spingarn Medal—were deemed appropriate musical forms to present to mainstream America. The deans of the Renaissance were entirely content to leave discovery and celebration of Bessie, Clara, Trixie, and various other blues-singing Smiths to white music critic Carl Van Vechten's effusions in *Vanity Fair.* When the visiting Russian film director Sergei Eisenstein enthused about new black musicals, Charles S. Johnson and Alain Locke expressed mild consternation in their interview in *Opportunity* magazine. As board members of the Pace Phonograph Company, Du Bois, James Weldon Johnson, and others banned "funky" artists from the Black Swan list of recordings, thereby contributing to the demise of the African American–owned firm. But the wild Broadway success of Miller and Lyles's musical *Shuffle Along* (which helped to popularize the Charleston) or Florence Mills's *Blackbirds* revue flouted such artistic fastidiousness. The very centrality of music in black life, as well as of black musical stereotypes in white minds, caused popular musical forms to impinge inescapably on Renaissance high culture. Eventually, the Renaissance deans made a virtue out of necessity; they applauded the concert-hall ragtime of "Big Jim" Europe and the "educated" jazz of Atlanta University graduate and big-band leader Fletcher Henderson, and took to hiring Duke Ellington or Cab Calloway as drawing cards for fund-raising socials. Still, their relationship to music remained beset by paradox.

New York ragtime, with its "Jelly Roll" Morton strides and Joplinesque elegance, had as much in common with Chicago jazz as Mozart did with "Fats" Waller.

Although the emergence of the Harlem Renaissance seems much more sudden and dramatic in retrospect than the historic reality, its institutional elaboration was, in fact, relatively quick. Because so little fiction or poetry had been produced by African Americans in the years immediately prior to the Harlem Renaissance, the appearance of a dozen or more poets and novelists and essayists seemed all the more striking and improbable. Death from tuberculosis had silenced poet-novelist Dunbar in 1906, and poor royalties had done the same for novelist Chesnutt after publication the previous year of *The Colonel's Dream*. Since then, no more than five African Americans had published significant works of fiction and verse. There had been *Pointing the Way* in 1908, a flawed, fascinating civil rights novel by the Baptist preacher Sutton Griggs. Three years later, Du Bois's sweeping sociological allegory *The Quest of the Silver Fleece* appeared. The following year came James Weldon Johnson's well-crafted *The Autobiography of an Ex–Colored Man*, but the author felt compelled to disguise his racial identity. A ten-year silence fell afterward, finally to be broken in 1922 by Claude McKay's *Harlem Shadows*, the first book of poetry since Dunbar.

Altogether, the Harlem Renaissance evolved through three stages. The first phase, ending in 1923 with the publication of Jean Toomer's unique prose poem *Cane*, was deeply influenced by white artists and writers—Bohemians and Revolutionaries—fascinated for a variety of reasons with the life of black people. The second phase, from early 1924 to mid-1926, was presided over by the Civil Rights Establishment of the NUL and the NAACP, a period of interracial collaboration between Zora Neale Hurston's "Negrotarian" whites and the African American Talented Tenth. The last phase, from mid-1926 to the Harlem Riot of March 1935, was increasingly dominated by the African American artists themselves—the "Niggerati," in Hurston's pungent phrase. The movement, then, was above all literary and self-consciously an enterprise of high culture well into its middle years. When Charles S. Johnson, new editor of *Opportunity*, sent invitations to some dozen young and mostly unknown African American poets and writers to attend a celebration at Manhattan's Civic Club of the sudden outpouring of "Negro" writing, on March 21, 1924, the Renaissance shifted into high gear. . . .

If they were adroit, African American civil rights officials and intellectuals believed they stood a fair chance of succeeding in reshaping the images and repackaging the messages out of which Mainstream racial behavior emerged. Bohemia and the Lost Generation suggested to the Talented Tenth the new approach to the old problem of race relations, but their shared premise about art and society obscured the diametrically opposite conclusions white and black intellectuals and artists drew from them. Harold Stearns's Lost Generation *revoltés* were lost in the sense that they professed to have no wish to find themselves in a materialistic, mammon-mad, homogenizing America. [Alain] Locke's New Negroes very much wanted full acceptance by Mainstream America, even if some, like Du Bois, McKay, and the future *enfant terrible* of the Renaissance, Wallace Thurman, might have immediately exercised the privilege of rejecting it. For the whites, art was the means to change society before they would accept it. For the blacks, art was the means to change society in order to be accepted into it. For this reason, many of the Harlem intellectuals found the white vogue in Afro-Americana troubling, although they usually feigned enthusiasm about the new dramatic and literary themes. Despite the insensitivity, burlesquing, and calumny, however, the Talented Tenth convinced itself that the civil rights dividends were potentially greater than the liabilities. Benjamin Brawley put this potential straightforwardly to James Weldon Johnson: "We have a tremendous opportunity to boost the NAACP, letters, and art, and anything else that calls attention to our development along the higher lines." . . .

Two preconditions made this unprecedented mobilization of talent and group support in the service of a racial arts-and-letters movement more than a conceit in the minds of a handful of leaders: demography and repression. The Great Black Migration from the rural South to the industrial North produced the metropolitan dynamism undergirding the Renaissance. The Red Summer of 1919, a period of socialist agitation and conservative backlash following the Russian Revolution, produced the trauma that led to the cultural sublimation of civil rights. In pressure-cooker fashion, the increase in its African American population caused Harlem to pulsate as it pushed its racial boundaries south below 135th Street to Central Park and north beyond 139th ("Strivers' Row"). In the first flush of Harlem's realization and of general African American exuberance, the Red Summer of 1919 had a cruelly decompressing impact upon Harlem and Afro-America in general. Charleston, South Carolina, erupted in riot in May, followed by Longview, Texas, in July, and Washington, D.C., later in the month. Chicago exploded on July 27. Lynchings of returning African American soldiers and expulsion of African American workers from unions abounded. In the North, the white working classes struck out against perceived and manipulated threats to job security and unionism from blacks streaming north. In Helena, Arkansas, where a pogrom was unleashed against black farmers organizing a cotton cooperative, and outside Atlanta, where the Ku Klux Klan was reconstituted, the message of the white South to African Americans was that the racial *status quo ante bellum* was on again with a vengeance. Twenty-six race riots in towns, cities, and counties swept across the nation all the way to Nebraska. The "race problem" became definitively an American dilemma in the summer of 1919, and no longer a remote complexity in the exotic South.

The term "New Negro" entered the vocabulary in reaction to the Red Summer, along with McKay's poetic catechism—"Like men we'll face the murderous, cowardly pack/Pressed to the wall, dying, but fighting back!" There was a groundswell of support for Marcus Garvey's UNIA [Universal Negro Improvement Association]. Until his 1924 imprisonment for mail fraud, the Jamaican immigrant's message of African Zionism, anti-integrationism, working-class assertiveness, and Bookerite business enterprise increasingly threatened the hegemony of the Talented Tenth and its major organizations, the NAACP and NUL, among people of color in America (much of Garvey's support came from the West Indians). "Garvey," wrote Mary White Ovington, one of the NAACP's white founders, "was the first Negro in the United States to capture the imagination of the masses." *The Negro World,* Garvey's multilingual newspaper, circulated throughout Latin America and the African empires of Britain and France. Locke spoke for the alarmed "respectable" civil rights leadership when he wrote, in his introductory remarks to the special issue of *Survey Graphic,* that, although "the thinking Negro has shifted a little to the left with the world trend," black separatism (Locke clearly had Garveyism in mind) "cannot be—even if it were desirable." Although the movement was its own worst enemy, the Talented Tenth was pleased to help the Justice Department speed its demise.

No less an apostle of high culture than Du Bois, initially a Renaissance enthusiast, vividly expressed the farfetched nature of the arts-and-letters movement as early as 1926: "How is it that an organization of this kind [the NAACP] can turn aside to talk about art? After all, what have we who are slaves and blacks to do with art?" It was the brilliant insight of the men and women associated with the NAACP and NUL that, although the road to the ballot box, the union hall, the decent neighborhood, and the office was blocked, there were two untried paths that had not been barred, in large part because of their very implausibility, as well as irrelevancy to most Americans: arts and letters. They saw the small cracks in the wall of racism that could, they anticipated, be widened through the production of exemplary racial images in collaboration with liberal white philanthropy, the robust culture industry primarily located in New York, and artists from white Bohemia (like themselves marginal and in tension with the status quo). If, in retrospect, then, the New Negro Arts Movement has been interpreted as a natural phase in the cultural evolution of another American group, as a band in the literary continuum running from New England, Knickerbocker New York, Hoosier Indiana, to the Village's Bohemia, to East Side Yiddish drama and fiction, and then on to the Southern Agrarians, such an interpretation sacrifices causation to appearance. Instead, the Renaissance represented much less an evolutionary part of a common experience than it did a generation-skipping phenomenon in which a vanguard of the Talented Tenth elite recruited, organized, subventioned, and guided an unevenly endowed cohort of artists and writers to make statements that advanced a certain conception of the race, a cohort of men and women most of whom would never have imagined the possibility of artistic and literary careers. . . .

The third phase of the Harlem Renaissance began even as the second had only just gotten under way. The second phase (1924 to mid-1926) was dominated by the officialdom of the two major civil rights organizations, with its ideology of civil rights advancement of African Americans through the creation and mobilization of an artistic-literary movement. Its essence was summed up in blunt declarations by Du Bois that he didn't care "a damn for any art that is not used for propaganda" or in exalted formulations by Locke that the New Negro was "an augury of a new democracy in American culture." The third phase of the Renaissance, from mid-1926 to the end of 1934, was marked by rebellion against the Civil Rights Establishment on the part of many of the artists and writers whom that Establishment had assembled and promoted. Three publications during 1926 formed a watershed between the genteel and the demotic Renaissance. Hughes's "The Negro Artist and the Racial Mountain," which appeared in the June 1926 issue of *The Nation,* served as manifesto of the breakaway from the arts-and-letters party line. Van Vechten's *Nigger Heaven,* released by Knopf that August, drove much of literate Afro-America into a dichotomy of approval and apoplexy over "authentic" versus "proper" cultural expression. Wallace Thurman's *Fire!!,* available in November, assembled the rebels for a major assault against the Civil Rights Ministry of Culture. . . .

. . . There was considerable African American displeasure; and it was complex. Much of the condemnation of the license for expression Hughes, Thurman,

Hurston, and other artists arrogated to themselves was generational or puritanical, and usually both. "Vulgarity has been mistaken for art," Brawley spluttered after leafing the pages of the new magazine *Fire!!,* which contained among other shockers Richard Bruce Nugent's extravagantly homoerotic short story "Smoke, Lilies and Jade." Du Bois was said to be deeply aggrieved.

But much of the condemnation stemmed from racial sensitivity, from sheer mortification at seeing uneducated, crude, and scrappy black men and women depicted without tinsel and soap. Thurman and associate editors John Davis, Aaron Douglas, Gwendolyn Bennett, Arthur Huff Fauset, Hughes, Hurston, and Nugent took the Renaissance out of the parlor, the editorial office, and the banquet room. With African motifs by Douglas and Nordic-featured African Americans with exaggeratedly kinky hair by Nugent; poems to an elevator boy by Hughes; a taste for the jungle by Edward Silvera; short stories about prostitution ("Cordelia the Crude") by Thurman, gender conflict between black men and women at the bottom of the economy ("Sweat") by Hurston, and a burly boxer's hatred of white people ("Wedding Day") by Gwendolyn Bennett; a short play about pigment complexes within the race (*Color Struck*) by Hurston—the focus shifted to Locke's "peasant matrix," to the sorrows and joys of those outside the Talented Tenth. . . .

Superficially, Harlem itself appeared to be in fair health well into 1931. James Weldon Johnson's celebration of the community's strengths, *Black Manhattan,* was published near the end of 1930. "Harlem is still in the process of making," the book proclaimed, and the author's confidence in the power of the "recent literary and artistic emergence" to ameliorate race relations was unshaken. In Johnson's Harlem, redcaps and cooks cheered when Renaissance talents won Guggenheim and Rosenwald fellowships; they rushed to newsstands whenever the *American Mercury* or *New Republic* mentioned activities above Central Park. It was much too easy for Talented Tenth notables like Johnson, White, and Locke not to notice in the second year of the Great Depression that, for the great majority of the population, Harlem was in the process of unmaking. Still, there was a definite prefiguration of Harlem's mortality when A'Lelia Walker suddenly died in August 1931, a doleful occurrence shortly followed by the sale of Villa Lewaro, her Hudson mansion, at public auction. By the end of 1929, African Americans lived in the five-hundred block of Edgecombe Avenue, known as "Sugar Hill." The famous "409" overlooking the Polo Grounds was home at one time or another to the Du Boises, the Fishers, and the Whites. Below Sugar Hill was the five-acre Rockefeller-financed Dunbar Apartments complex, its 511 units fully occupied in mid-1928. The Dunbar eventually became home for the Du Boises, E. Simms Campbell (illustrator and cartoonist), Fletcher Henderson, the A. Philip Randolphs, Leigh Whipper (actor), and (briefly) Paul and Essie Robeson. The complex published its own weekly bulletin, the *Dunbar News,* an even more valuable record of Talented Tenth activities during the Renaissance than the *Inter-State Tattler.*

The 1931 *Report on Negro Housing,* presented to President Hoover, was a document starkly in contrast to the optimism found in *Black Manhattan.* Nearly 50 percent of Harlem's families would be unemployed by the end of 1932. The syphilis rate was nine times higher than white Manhattan's; the tuberculosis rate was five times greater; pneumonia and typhoid were twice that of whites. Two African American mothers and two babies died for every white mother and child. Harlem

General Hospital, the single public facility, served 200,000 African Americans with 273 beds. A Harlem family paid twice as much of their income for rent as a white family. Meanwhile, median family income in Harlem dropped 43.6 percent by 1932. The ending of Prohibition would devastate scores of marginal speakeasies, as well as prove fatal to theaters like the Lafayette. . . .

The literary energies of the Renaissance finally slumped. McKay returned to Harlem in February 1934 after a twelve-year sojourn abroad, but his creative powers were spent. The last novel of the movement, Hurston's beautifully written *Jonah's Gourd Vine,* went on sale in May 1934. Charles Johnson, James Weldon Johnson, and Locke applauded Hurston's allegorical story of her immediate family (especially her father) and the mores of an African American town in Florida called Eatonville. Fisher and Thurman could have been expected to continue to write, but their fates were sealed by professional carelessness. Thurman died a few days before Christmas 1934, soon after his return from an abortive Hollywood film project. Ignoring his physician's strictures, he hemorrhaged after drinking to excess while hosting a party in the infamous house at 267 West 136th Street. Four days later, Fisher expired from intestinal cancer caused by repeated exposure to his own X-ray equipment.

Locke's *New Negro* anthology had been crucial to the formation of the Renaissance. As the movement ran down, another anthology, English heiress Nancy Cunard's *Negro,* far more massive in scope, recharged the Renaissance for a brief period, enlisting the contributions of most of the principals (though McKay and Walrond refused, and Toomer no longer acknowledged his African American roots), and captured its essence in the manner of expert taxidermy. A grieving Locke wrote Charlotte Mason from Howard University, "It is hard to see the collapse of things you have labored to raise on a sound base."

Arthur Fauset, Jessie's perceptive brother, attempted to explain the collapse to Locke and the readers of *Opportunity* at the beginning of 1934. He foresaw "a socio-political-economic setback from which it may take decades to recover." The Renaissance had left the race unprepared, Fauset charged, because of its unrealistic belief "that social and economic recognition will be inevitable when once the race has produced a sufficiently large number of persons who have properly qualified themselves in the arts." Du Bois had not only turned his back on the movement, he had left the NAACP and Harlem for a university professorship in Atlanta after an enormous row over civil rights policy. Marxism had begun to exercise a decided appeal for him, but as the 1933 essay "Marxism and the Negro Problem" had made abundantly clear, Du Bois ruled out collaboration with American Marxists because they were much too racist. James Weldon Johnson's philosophical *tour d'horizon* appearing in 1934, *Negro Americans, What Now?,* asked precisely the question of the decade. Most Harlemites were certain that the riot exploding on the evening of March 19, 1935, taking three lives and costing two million dollars in property damage, was not an answer. By then, the Works Progress Administration (WPA) had become the major patron of African American artists and writers. Writers William Attaway, Ralph Ellison, Margaret Walker, Richard Wright, and Frank Yerby would emerge under its aegis, as would painters Romare Bearden, Jacob Lawrence, Charles Sebree, Lois Maillou Jones, and Charles White. The Communist Party was another patron, notably for Richard Wright, whose 1937 essay "Blueprint for Negro

Writing" would materially contribute to the premise of Hughes's "The Negro Artist and the Racial Mountain." For thousands of ordinary Harlemites who had looked to Garvey's UNIA for inspiration, then to the Renaissance, there was now Father Divine and his "heavens."

In the ensuing years, much was renounced, more was lost or forgotten, yet the Renaissance, however artificial and overreaching, left a positive mark. Locke's *New Negro* anthology featured thirty of the movement's thirty-five stars. They and a small number of less gifted collaborators generated twenty-six novels, ten volumes of poetry, five Broadway plays, countless essays and short stories, three performed ballets and concerti, and a considerable output of canvas and sculpture. If the achievement was less than the titanic expectations of the Ministry of Culture, it was an arts-and-letters legacy, nevertheless, of which a beleaguered and belittled Afro-America could be proud, and by which it could be sustained. If more by osmosis than conscious attention, Mainstream America was also richer for the color, emotion, humanity, and cautionary vision produced by Harlem during its Golden Age.

The Battle for the Airwaves

ROBERT McCHESNEY

U.S. broadcasting in the mid-1920s was far different from the system that would be entrenched only a few years later. Several hundred nonprofit broadcasters had commenced operations in the first half of the decade, the majority affiliated with colleges and universities, and well over 200 of these (approximately two-fifths of all stations) remained on the air in 1925. Although still largely overlooked in mass communications literature, these nonprofit broadcasters are now recognized as the true pioneers of U.S. broadcasting, who were, as one of the leading radio engineers of the period observed, "at the start of things distinctly on the ground floor." As for the ostensibly for-profit broadcasters, they were hardly professional broadcasters in the modern sense of the term. The majority were owned and operated by newspapers, department stores, power companies, and other private concerns, and their *raison d'être* was to generate favorable publicity for the owner's primary enterprise. Indeed, as late as 1929, few if any private broadcasters were thought to be earning profits from the business of broadcasting, and there was little sense, in public discourse at least, that they ever would.

The National Broadcasting Company (NBC), established in 1926, and the Columbia Broadcasting System (CBS), established in 1927, did not have much of an impact until after the passage of the Radio Act of 1927. Throughout the late 1920s, NBC presented itself not as a traditional for-profit corporation but as a public service corporation that would sell advertising only as necessary to subsidize high-quality noncommercial fare. And commercial advertising, the other pillar of the emerging status quo, did not begin its stampede to the ether in earnest until 1928.

Excerpted from "The Battle for the U.S. Airwaves, 1928–1935," by Robert McChesney from *Journal of Communication,* v. 40 (Autumn 1990), pp. 30–34, 38–44, 46–47. Reprinted by permission of Oxford University Press, Oxford, England.

As has been amply documented in the major studies of the period, commercial advertising was very controversial and more than a little unpopular throughout the 1920s. Few contemporary observers foresaw the role that NBC, CBS, and commercial advertising would assume in short order. Indeed, in all public discourse on the matter prior to 1927, there was general agreement that nonprofit broadcasting should play a significant and perhaps even a dominant role in the U.S. system and that commercial advertising's potential contributions to the field should be regarded with great skepticism.

Hence there is little reason, on the surface, to regard the passage of the Radio Act of 1927 as some sort of mandate for network-dominated, advertising-supported broadcasting, as that system barely existed at the time and absolutely no one was discussing the issue in those terms. Moreover, the Act was hurriedly passed in February after a federal judge had ruled the Department of Commerce's licensing of stations unconstitutional in 1926. With any effort at regulation discontinued, the ether had become a mass of chaos; 200 new broadcasters immediately commenced operations, the total wattage increased by nearly 75 percent, and few stations respected the frequencies occupied by other broadcasters. The committee deliberations and floor debate concerning the Radio Act of 1927 were what one might expect of emergency legislation; there was almost no discussion of what the legislation would mean for the type of broadcast system to be created. . . .

. . . The law gave the FRC [Federal Radio Commission] only one directive in its allocation determinations: to favor those station applicants that best served the "public interest, convenience or necessity." The primary reason that even these criteria were put in the statute was to ensure the bill's constitutionality; otherwise, the bill's sponsors argued that it was essential to give the FRC complete latitude to operate as it saw fit. The commercial broadcasters were vocal in their support of having the FRC, rather than Congress, determine licensing criteria. . . .

The FRC crystallized the dominant trends within broadcasting over the previous two years and made no effort to counteract them. The allocating committee held a number of meetings with radio engineers and representatives of the networks and the commercial broadcasters' trade association, the National Association of Broadcasters (NAB), as they determined their plan. These conferences and sessions were barely publicized, and the nonprofit broadcasters and concerned nonbroadcasters did not have an opportunity to present their opinions. . . .

In August 1928, the FRC announced its reallocation plan under General Order 40. Forty of the 90 available channels were set aside to be 50,000-watt clear channels that would have only one occupant nationally. The other 50 channels would house the remaining 600 or so broadcasters who could operate simultaneously on the same channel at much lower power levels; broadcasters in the same region would share a frequency by using it at different times of day. Anyone could challenge existing broadcasters for their frequency assignments at the end of their three-month terms. In general, the FRC had competing applicants share the contested frequency, with the station deemed most worthy allocated the majority of the hours. In the long run, the station accorded the fewest hours on a shared channel often found it very difficult to stay on the air. This direct head-to-head competition for the scarce broadcast channels created great antipathy between the contending applicants, particularly, as was often the case, when commercial broadcasters successfully challenged nonprofit broadcasters. In any case, without the FRC actually having to turn down many license renewal applications, there were 100 fewer stations on the air by the autumn of 1929.

With General Order 40, all stations, except for a handful of network-affiliated clear channel stations that had been established by the FRC the previous year, were assigned to new frequencies and new power levels. The networks were the big winners. In 1927 NBC had 28 affiliates and CBS 16, for a combined 6.4 percent of the broadcast stations; within four years they together accounted for 30 percent of the stations. And this alone vastly understates their new role, as all but three of the 40 clear channel stations were owned by or affiliated with one of the two networks. Indeed, when the number of hours broadcast and the level of power are considered, NBC and CBS accounted for nearly 70 percent of U.S. broadcasting by 1931. By 1935, only four of the 62 stations that broadcast at 5,000 or more watts did not have a network affiliation. Moreover, commercial advertising, which barely existed on a national level prior to 1928, grew by leaps and bounds to an annual total of $72 million by 1934. One commentator noted in 1930 regarding the emerging status quo that "nothing in American history has paralleled this mushroom growth." . . .

The other side of the coin, however, was reflected in the equally dramatic decline in nonprofit and noncommercial broadcasting. Nonprofit broadcasters found themselves in a vicious cycle. The FRC, noting the nonprofit broadcasters' lack of financial and technological prowess, lowered their hours and power (to the advantage of well-capitalized private broadcasters) and thus made it that much more difficult for them to generate the funds to become successful. "Now the Federal Radio Commission has come along and taken away all of the hours that are worth anything and has left us with hours that are absolutely no good for commercial programs or for educational programs," wrote the despondent director of the soon-to-be-extinct University of Arkansas station. "The Commission may boast that it has never cut an educational station off the air. It merely cuts off our head, our arms, and our legs, and then allows us to die a natural death." The number of stations affiliated with colleges and universities declined from 95 in 1927 to less than half that number by 1930, while the total number of nonprofit broadcasters declined from some 200 in 1927 to less than a third that total in 1934. Moreover, almost all of these stations operated with low power on shared frequencies. By 1934, nonprofit broadcasting accounted for only two percent of total U.S. broadcast time.

As the contours of modern U.S. broadcasting fell into place with astonishing speed, a coherent and unrepentant opposition to the emerging capitalist domination of the airwaves developed for the first time. "The battle was begun in earnest," noted one of the leading groups that arose to oppose the status quo, "in the summer of 1928 soon after the enactment of the Commission's General Order 40." The primary opposition came from the ranks of the displaced and harassed nonprofit broadcasters, particularly those affiliated with colleges and universities. Many educators felt their stations were being left "unprotected" by the FRC as they were "attacked constantly by commercial broadcasters." . . .

Three themes underscored virtually all criticism of the status quo by the various elements of the opposition movement. First, the opposition movement argued that the airwaves should be regarded as a public resource and broadcasting as a public utility. By this reasoning, turning broadcasting over to a relative handful of private broadcasters who sought to satisfy selfish goals was a scandalous misuse of a public resource. Moreover, the FRC had established the existing system entirely outside of public view; even Congress seemed largely oblivious to what had taken place. Hence, the public had yet to exercise its right and duty to determine broadcast policy.

Second, and perhaps most crucially, the opposition movement argued that a network-dominated, for-profit, advertising-supported broadcast system would invariably shade its programming to defend the status quo and would never give fair play to unpopular or radical opinions. The entire opposition movement was propelled by a profound desire to create a broadcasting system that would better promote its vision of a democratic political culture.

Third, the reformers criticized the nature of broadcast advertising and the limitations of advertising-subsidized programming, particularly in regard to the lack of cultural, educational, and public affairs programming that the system seemed capable of profitably generating. Some of this criticism had a distinctly elitist tone. . . .

Armed with this critique and perspective, the opposition movement advocated any number of plans to recreate U.S. broadcasting, but three in particular received the most attention in the early 1930s. One plan was to have the government set aside a fixed percentage of channels—generally either 15 percent or 25 percent—for the exclusive use of nonprofit broadcasters. The second plan was to have Congress authorize an extensive and independent study of broadcasting with the aim of providing for an entirely new broadcast system. This plan was based on what had transpired in Britain and, particularly, Canada, which in 1932 announced—to no small extent due to its distaste for what it saw taking place to its south—the establishment of a nonprofit and noncommercial broadcasting system. To the opposition movement, it was axiomatic that any independent study of broadcasting would resolve to alter the status quo. The third plan was to have the government establish a series of local, regional, and national nonprofit and noncommercial stations that would be subsidized through taxes and operated by a congressionally approved board of directors of prominent citizens. This plan also was inspired by the experiences in Britain and Canada and, indeed, in most of the world. The government stations would supplement, not replace, the existing commercial networks.

Indeed, with the exception of one or two isolated comments, none of the elements of the opposition movement advocated the complete nationalization and decommercialization of broadcasting. All the plans pointedly created what the opposition movement regarded as a dual system. "And out of the competition between them," one reformer told Congress in 1934 as he outlined his plan for a series of government stations, "there would unquestionably issue a much higher program standard and far less discrimination against vast sections of the public who are now substantially excluded from genuine enjoyment of radio." The NCER [National Committee on Education by Radio] characterized Australia, which had one commercial network and one noncommercial network, as a "listener's utopia." Interestingly, with but one exception, throughout the early 1930s no proponent of the status quo took seriously the opposition movement's proposals for a mixed system; all efforts to create space for nonprofit and noncommercial broadcasting were approached as if they were specific efforts to eliminate for-profit, commercial broadcasting in its entirety.

One basic and overriding problem plagued the opposition movement throughout its existence: how to subsidize high-quality nonprofit broadcasting. Clearly, the existing system of nonprofit stations with dilapidated facilities, restricted hours, and low power, attempting to rely upon donations from listeners, handouts from philanthropists, and grants from nonprofit groups, had proven unsatisfactory, particularly as the economy was grinding to a halt. To many members of the opposition movement the answer was obvious: Have the government subsidize nonprofit broadcasting by establishing a series of government stations (à la Britain) to be bankrolled by annual license set fees. "A charge of $1.00 per set would provide America ten times the funds which we would need for a generous program of broadcasting," the NCER's Morgan informed a convention of educators in 1932. This was a touchy subject in U.S. politics, however. Some elements of the opposition movement, like the ACLU [American Civil Liberties Union], were more than a little skeptical of granting the government a larger role in communications. Even those that did not share the ACLU's innate skepticism toward the state, like the NCER, began lobbying for a state-subsidized system only years after most of their leaders, including Morgan, had gone on record in its favor. "A government-controlled radio system," two members of the opposition movement noted in 1931, "whether or not hypothetically desirable, is highly impracticable, almost impossible."

The only real alternative to having the government play a larger role was having advertising subsidize nonprofit broadcasting. This idea was anathema to the NCER, the ACLU, and much of the opposition movement, which regarded advertising as every bit as bad as network domination. But nonprofit stations like WCFL and WLWL repeatedly defended their right to sell advertising to subsidize their operations. This became the basis of the fundamental tactical split in the opposition movement. The NCER, the ACLU, and the *Ventura Free Press,* among others, dropped the fixed percentage idea to promote a government study or a government network. WCFL and WLWL, on the other hand, were not especially interested in schemes that did not address the specific plight of their stations. Hence, they showed little enthusiasm for the government plans or for any program that might restrict their sale of advertising.

In addition to the opposition movement being divided over tactics, it faced at least three other major barriers. First, the radio lobby—NBC, CBS, and the NAB—had quickly emerged "as one of the most effective trade associations in the United States" and one of the most powerful lobbies in Washington. Its control of the airwaves gave the radio lobby greater than customary leverage over publicity-conscious politicians—a point lost on neither the commercial broadcasters nor the opposition movement.

In addition, the commercial broadcasters spared no expense in the early 1930s in a public relations campaign to establish the status quo as the only innately "American" and only truly "democratic" method for organizing broadcasting services. With their abundant resources, the radio lobby was able to overwhelm the underfunded communications of the angered opposition movement. . . .

Second, given the clear contrast between the political strength and financial wherewithal of the radio lobby and that of the opposition movement, the reformers obviously needed extensive (and preferably sympathetic) print coverage. Unfortunately, what little coverage the press offered was strongly oriented toward presenting the position of the commercial broadcasters. This delighted the radio lobby, which provided the press with a continual stream of press releases. It angered and puzzled the opposition movement, for the most part, which could not understand why their cause seemed to be getting short shrift. . . .

Third, the legal community, with few exceptions, rallied to the defense of the status quo. The American Bar Association (ABA) established a Standing Committee on Communications in the late 1920s with "the duty of studying and making recommendations on proposed radio legislation." This ABA committee was chaired by Louis G. Caldwell, who had been the FRC's first General Counsel during the implementation of General Order 40 and had emerged as one of the leading commercial broadcasting attorneys in the nation. The ABA committee, staffed almost entirely by commercial broadcasting attorneys, turned out annual reports ranging from 40 to 100 pages that argued in no uncertain terms that any reform of the status quo would be disastrous. Although these reports were never voted upon by the ABA, they were relied upon by Congress and presented to Congress and the public as the expert, neutral opinion of the U.S. legal community. The opposition movement was appalled by this apparent conflict of interest but had little success in challenging the ABA committee's legitimacy. . . .

The campaign to restructure U.S. broadcasting experienced three distinct phases over the period 1930–1935. The first stage, from 1930 until President Herbert Hoover left office in the spring of 1933, was clearly the high watermark for popular discontent with U.S. broadcasting, far surpassing anything that would develop subsequently. Public distaste for commercial broadcast fare was being repeatedly communicated to members of Congress. "Many members on both sides of the Capitol are aroused by local conditions," *Broadcasting* informed its readers, and they "have heard protests from constituents" regarding the nature of the U.S. system. . . .

Nevertheless, reform legislation failed to get through Congress during this period, for two reasons. First, this was the trough of the Great Depression, and the preponderance of congressional activity was dedicated to legislation for economic recovery. "Were it not for the disturbing economic situation," *Broadcasting* observed in 1931, "Congress might blunder into the political radio morass camouflaged by these lobbying factions." Second, while there was considerable support for reform among the rank and file members of Congress, relevant committee leaders were nearly unanimously opposed. "We have been lucky," modestly observed NAB president Harry Shaw in a speech to the NAB Board of Directors on the legislative situation in 1932. "We have been content to leave the protection of this industry to a few of our friends in certain places." "If it were not for a little group of reactionary leaders in both branches of Congress," an incensed Nockels observed in 1931, reform "legislation would have been passed by this time." . . .

The second stage of the campaign, which lasted from March 1933 until the Communications Act of 1934 was signed into law in June of that year, was the decisive period when Congress finally enacted permanent broadcasting legislation. The opposition movement was initially quite encouraged by the change in administrations and hoped that President Roosevelt would assist their cause. Indeed, many key members of the New Deal were outspoken critics of commercial broadcasting and advocates of sweeping reform. Moreover, one of Roosevelt's closest political and personal friends, Ambassador to Mexico Josephus Daniels, was an unabashed proponent of completely nationalized broadcasting. "There is no more reason why other communications industries should be privately owned than the mails," he wrote the president in one of numerous letters on the subject. Nevertheless, Roosevelt chose not to take a public position on the broadcast debate, while his aides worked behind the scenes to assist the commercial broadcasters with their legislative agenda. Clearly Roosevelt was in no mood to take on an uphill fight against a powerful and entrenched communications industry, particularly when he enjoyed less than perfect relations with the nation's largely Republican newspaper industry. As even Daniels advised him, he had more important battles to fight. . . .

With the passage of the Communications Act of 1934, Congress effectively removed itself from substantive broadcast policy issues for the balance of the century. The only "legitimate" opportunity remaining for the opposition movement to present its case was in the October 1934 FCC [Federal Communications Commission] hearings mandated by section 307(c), which required the FCC to evaluate the Wagner-Hatfield fixed percentage concept. The outcome of the hearings was never in doubt; most elements of the opposition movement regarded them as a "setup for the broadcasters," and, indeed, two of the three FCC members who would be at the hearings announced to the NAB convention in September that there was no way they would alter the status quo, regardless of what transpired at the upcoming hearings. In January 1935, the FCC formally issued its report to Congress: There was no need to alter the status quo, and efforts should be made to assist disenfranchised nonprofit groups in utilizing commercial broadcasting facilities. In effect, this was the cooperation thesis advanced by the Wilbur Committee in 1930 and rejected at the time on its face. The opposition movement had, at best, delayed the full stabilization of the airwaves from 1929 or 1930 to 1935. . . .

In the second half of the decade, as the industry became economically and politically consolidated, the commercial broadcasters strove for ideological closure. In this campaign they triumphantly located commercial broadcasting next to the newspaper industry as an icon of American freedom and culture and, with considerable historical revisionism if not outright fabrication, removed it from critical contemplation. The opposition movement was correspondingly written out of the dominant perspective on the development of U.S. broadcasting, and the conflict of the early 1930s was erased from the historical memory. "Our American system of broadcasting," Radio Corporation of America president David Sarnoff informed a nationwide audience over NBC in 1938,

> is what it is because it operates in the American democracy. It is a free system because this is a free country. It is privately owned because private ownership is one of our national doctrines. It is privately supported, through commercial sponsorship of a portion of its program hours, and at no cost to the listener, because ours is a free economic system. No special laws had to be passed to bring these things about. They were already implicit in the American system, ready and waiting for broadcasting when it came.

The implications of this logic were not always left unspoken. "He who attacks the fundamentals of the American system," of broadcasting, CBS president Paley informed an audience in 1937, "attacks democracy itself."

A New Deal for Art

JANE S. DE HART

"Life is drab and ugly. Life can be beautiful" if only we can "reshuffle the constituent parts that formed the dreary design of our national life" into a "picture of democratic justice and spiritual beauty." The words are those of George Biddle, American artist, mural painter, and Groton schoolmate of that master reshuffler and reshaper of American life, Franklin Delano Roosevelt, and they reflect the faith of those who believed that inherent in the American dream of a more abundant life was the promise not only of economic and social justice but also of cultural enrichment—in short, "Arts for the Millions."

Individuals sharing that belief expressed it in a variety of phrases. "People's Theatre" was the term of those who saw in the federal theatre project the seeds of a national institution belonging to all the people. In the same spirit, Federal Art Project directors entitled a collection of essays on that project, "Art for the Millions." But it is the term "cultural democracy" which best encompasses the ideas and aspirations of a New Deal élite who sought to integrate the artist into the mainstream of American life and make the arts both expressive of the spirit of a nation and accessible to its people. . . .

. . . The progressive thrust to integrate the arts and democracy would have had relatively little impact had it not been for the Depression and the creation of the New Deal cultural projects. As economic conditions worsened, private patronage virtually ceased, as did those peripheral odd jobs on which artists depended for subsistence. By the early 1930s, the question was simply this: were artists important enough to use the power of the federal government to shield them from a depression which, without federal interference, would surely force them into nonartistic activities. Many people were indifferent; others thought artists were not a matter of legitimate government concern. But a few New Dealers dissented. In 1933, Harry Hopkins began funneling Federal Emergency Relief Agency (FERA) funds to a few unemployed artists, actors, and musicians. The following year, Secretary of the Treasury Henry Morgenthau authorized the creation of a Section of Fine Arts, under Edward Bruce, which put visual artists to work decorating public buildings. And in 1935, a major relief appropriation created the Works Progress Administration (WPA) and nationwide work relief projects for visual artists, musicians, theatrical and literary people.

The task of Bruce and his staff at the treasury was to secure for federal buildings "the best art" this country could produce and to select artists to do that work solely on the basis of quality. But for the directors of "Federal One," as the four WPA cultural projects were known, humanitarian considerations were paramount—90 percent of their clientele had to come from welfare rolls. Yet neither they, Hopkins, nor the President regarded these WPA projects as the simple relief measures Congress intended. Rather they were the means to more important ends: the fulfillment of a long-standing desire to bring together artist and people and to use the uplifting

Excerpted from "A New Deal for the Arts" by Jane S. De Hart, *Journal of American History,* Sept. 1975, pp. 316, 318–328, 337–339. Reprinted by permission of the Organization of American Historians and the author.

power of art to enrich the lives of ordinary citizens. Translated into New Deal terminology, this meant creating a nation of cultural consumers, for, if recovery were to be achieved in the arts as well as the economy, government would have to provide potential consumers access to the arts. Only through accessibility would people come to regard the arts, not as an expendable luxury, but as a community asset.

Although New Dealers shared this commitment to aesthetic accessibility, the nature of the commitment varied considerably. For the President, the conviction that people were entitled to cultural enrichment as well as economic and social justice stemmed in part from his concern for the quality of life in this country. Although Roosevelt himself had no real aesthetic sense, as a patrician who had been exposed to culture in childhood and to the stimulus of artists, musicians, and theatre people in later years, he assumed that classical music, legitimate theatre, and the masterpieces of art were a part of the good life. For Roosevelt, access to the arts seemed as logical as access to the ballot box or school house. Hopkins shared this assumption, but he also saw the arts as instruments of reform. In moments of idealistic fervor, Hopkins talked not only of carrying music and plays to children in city parts but also of using the power of theatre to spotlight tenements so as to encourage the building of decent houses for all people.

For Hopkins' four cultural projects directors, concern for the state of the arts was paramount, but even here the level of commitment was uneven. Henry Alsberg, with his state guides and heterogenous assortment of writers, was perhaps least concerned with the need of a creative intelligensia for a public. Music project director Nikolai Sokoloff was more so. A cultural élitist prepared neither by temperament nor training to exchange his conductor's baton for the role of musical evangelist, he nonetheless had 15,000 unemployed musicians for whom new employment opportunities had to be generated, and that brought a keen awareness of the need to expand the national audience. For the federal theatre's Hallie Flanagan, art project director [Holger] Cahill, and their associates, "Arts for the Millions" became an ideological imperative. Neither director would restrict audiences to the traditional forms associated with "high" art—a decision indicative of the imagination and flexibility which would distinguish them both.

Whatever their differing perspectives, New Deal cultural enthusiasts shared with other liberals and some leftists a belief that the fine arts had become the property of the monied few to the detriment of arts, arts institutions, and the public. Painting, sculpture, even drama had become luxury items—superfluous and expendable. Museums, like the objects they exhibited, had become "fragments of the past . . . legacies from rich men's houses," instead of inviting, accessible public institutions. The ultimate loss was that of the American people, for, outside a few metropolitan centers, original works of art, accomplished orchestras, and professionally competent theatre groups were few indeed. Roosevelt himself estimated that only one out of ten Americans had ever had a chance to see a "fine picture." The estimate was probably optimistic. Aside from museums, there were in New York City in the 1930s only about two dozen art galleries. Although the American Federation of Arts had been sending exhibits throughout the country since 1909, vast areas of the South and Midwest remained virtually untouched. And while the burgeoning of community and university theatres had helped to compensate for the demise of touring companies, thousands of people had never seen live actors.

Thus denied access to "high" culture, most of this nation's citizens subsisted on the aesthetically deficient pap served up as entertainment—a later generation would call it *kitsch*. Although New Deal cultural enthusiasts rejected the cultural élitism of such critics of mass culture as José Ortega y Gasset or T. S. Eliot, they were well aware that by the 1930s the nation had become addicted to mass culture: movies, radio, the tabloid newspaper, *Life* magazine. Predictably, "high" culture had suffered. As Dwight Macdonald subsequently observed, there was a Gresham's Law in cultural as well as monetary circulation: "bad stuff drives out the good, since it is more easily understood and enjoyed." These developments were not lost on Hopkins and his associates, who were also aware of the technological unemployment which resulted when motion pictures displaced live actors and stage technicians and when sound film and records abolished orchestras. They knew, for example, that in 1926 there had been 22,000 musicians involved in the production of silent movies and that by 1934 that number had dwindled to just over 4,000.

To put unemployed artists to work, the cultural resources of the nation would have to become accessible. Theatrical production units and symphony orchestras would have to be established in regional centers from which touring companies could be dispatched. Local art centers would have to be founded to house workshops and traveling exhibits. In short, the arts would have to be freed from a cultural milieu that kept them as "high" culture—a thing apart—and returned to the healthy channels of everyday life. This the "cleansing waters of the depression" now made possible.

The directors of New Deal cultural projects reflected on potential contributions. Flanagan and her fellow enthusiasts spoke of the federal theatre as a true people's theatre. Rejecting the idea of the stage as a place "where sophisticated secrets are whispered to the blasé initiate," she insisted that federal players could bring to huge new audiences not only the classics but also experimental plays, religious plays, dance drama, and children's theatre. More important, they could produce plays that would reflect regional and ethnic differences and plays that would be boldly relevant to contemporary problems. The other arts could do no less. Sokoloff believed that orchestras and chamber groups could take "fine music" to "the masses." And while Bruce and his associate Forbes Watson talked of the murals that would advance American art, improve the nation's taste, and weld its people into a whole, Cahill elaborated on the potential contribution of the federal art project: gallery tours, free art classes, exhibits that would bring the works of the graphic, easel, and sculpture divisions to the people and finally an allocation program that would keep art on extended display in public buildings across the country. But Cahill knew that exposure alone was not enough—not even exposure to the easily accessible scene painting, largely representational works which derived their inspiration from contemporary life and culture.

If these Depression-born ventures were to achieve institutional permanence, the arts must not only be physically accessible but also intellectually and emotionally accessible. The arts must have social meaning if they were to elicit response. And it is in the probing of artistic process and response that Cahill in particular went beyond his New Deal colleagues in developing the concept of a cultural democracy.

For Cahill, an ardent follower of John Dewey, the key was primarily "process" and only secondarily "product." "Art," wrote the director of the federal art project,

"is not a matter of rare occasional masterpieces. . . . [G]reat art arises only in situations where there is a great deal of art activity, and where the general level of art expression is high." To produce such a climate and, more important, to create the "free and enriching communion" of which Dewey spoke, Cahill, like his former professor, believed in the primacy and pervasiveness of experience. Real understanding of art, he insisted, came not from passive observation but from intense participation in the creative process. The task of the federal art project, therefore, was to make possible "democracy in the arts" through "community participation."

The public art of the mural provided unexpected opportunities for just such participation as onlookers queried painters about subject matter and technique, volunteered criticism and suggestions, and thus turned the production of a mural into a community endeavor. Still more valuable were those participation-oriented classes where sympathetic teachers in the progressive tradition neglected the principles of "correct" drawing in order to encourage the kind of experience that would make their students "eye-minded." Through project-sponsored classes in technique, media, and design, Cahill was convinced that aesthetic sensitivity could be enhanced, expressiveness encouraged, audiences created, and the quality of life improved.

The institutions which best exemplified the kind of physical and intellectual accessibility that would create an arts-conscious public were the community art centers. Physical symbols of the New Deal effort to decentralize the nation's cultural resources, they were scattered across the country in small cities where they were directed by qualified artists-teachers. An arts-conscious public would be born in these centers, Cahill believed, as children and adults, irrespective of technical fluency, became amateur artists. In the process of creation they would discover that art was not something preserved in elaborate institutions, but "beauty for use"—use in the "broadest human sense." In emphasizing artistic process and public response, Cahill groped for a definition of art which Dewey had supplied only the year before. By providing access to what the philosopher called "art as experience," the New Deal could perhaps create the mass audience—the hallmark of cultural democracy.

With access would also come the integration of artist and public—one of the sought-after goals of creative intellectuals throughout the 1930s. As the arts became necessary, so, too, would the artist. No longer an extraneous, alienated member of society, he would find his livelihood more secure. More important, his works, whether literary, visual, or performing, would change as communication with the public stimulated his imagination and inspired a deeper interpretation of life. The arts would become infused with a new vitality, commitment, and maturity. Watson would have said meaning; Flanagan, relevance; Cahill, use. What they envisioned were the arts "interwoven with the very stuff and texture of human experience, intensifying that experience, making it more profound, rich, clear, and coherent."

Such works could affect and even transform men's hearts and minds, it was hoped. They could also reflect the spirit of a nation. For New Deal cultural enthusiasts, who were also aesthetic nationalists, the promise of arts which were distinctly American was tantalizing indeed. With characteristic confidence, Hopkins predicted that from the federal theatre "a vital new American drama" would emerge. To fulfill that pledge, Flanagan urged directors to search for plays which probed America's past, its present, and the richness of its regional diversity. To New England directors she even suggested dramatization of portions of the New England guides. With equal zeal, the music project's Charles Seeger called for the integration of popular, folk, and academic music into a distinctively American idiom. As initiator of that superb pictorial survey of early decorative arts, the "Index of American Design," Cahill was concerned with the sources and development of American art. To be sure, he and his fellow directors never went to such lengths as Bruce, who confined section artists to realistic depictions of wholesome American themes, but neither would they have quarrelled with the poster in a Massachusetts art center which proclaimed: "OUT OF THE SPIRIT OF A PEOPLE ARISES ITS ART." Indeed, such assumptions were basic to all who hoped that interaction of artist and public would evoke a quality which, however elusive, was unmistakably American.

The actual process of interaction—the precise nature of this new communication—was never spelled out. Nor was there any acknowledgment of the perennial tension existing between the artist's desire for rapprochement with society and the defiant individualism, which has so often culminated in social alienation and aesthetic privatism. There are reasons why limited theorizing was devoted to these questions. Administrators—and artists—are seldom aestheticians. Moreover, the belief that the union of artist and the people would create a revitalized American art was in the 1930s a rhetorical commonplace and almost an article of faith. It also reflected the renewed interest in national values and traditions which permeated American thought in this troubled Depression decade.

These three elements then comprised the concept of a cultural democracy: cultural accessibility for the public, social and economic integration for the artist, and the promise of a new national art. Inspired as much by commitment to the arts as to democracy, it was also part of the 1930s effort to create and document an American culture—and the word is used here in the anthropological sense. But whatever its inspiration, this quest for a cultural democracy was one which had to be pursued in a context complicated by relief, bureaucracy, and politics—and there, of course, was the rub.

The task of bringing "Arts to the Millions" was formidable. Physical access demanded decentralization—getting the arts out of a few metropolitan centers where artists had congregated and dispersing them across the nation. It also meant providing access to the millions who had never attended a museum, symphony concert, or a play—and to the thousands more who could no longer afford the price of a ticket. For culturally starved New Yorkers, these projects meant free concerts in the park, a new municipal art gallery, Shakespeare in the schools, and inexpensive tickets to such varied dramatic fare as Eliot's *Murder in the Cathedral* or at the Orson Welles–John Houseman production of *Horse Eats Hat*.

White New Yorkers were not the only beneficiaries. With an absence of racism not always characteristic of other New Deal agencies, the cultural projects hired unemployed black artists and carried their work to an expanding black audience. Under WPA auspices, Harlem's old Lafayette Theatre again became a theatrical magnet with a variety of productions, including a resplendent *Macbeth* which ultimately played to 130,000 people. And at the Harlem Art Center children and adults encountered the works of black artists, often for the first time. A young black girl later wrote to WPA alumnus Jacob Lawrence: "Even though I have had a very limited acquaintance with art, I was immediately struck by the power of your paintings of Negro life. As soon as I saw them, there was a shock of recognition and the feeling that this is just right, just as it should be."

Cultural élitists might dismiss Lawrence and his fellow artists as "sorry daubers, ham actors, spavined dancers and radical scribners luxuriating on the dole," but elated New Dealers knew better. As similar encounters occurred, project directors found tangible evidence of vastly expanded audiences. But the shortcoming of the federal theatre, and to some degree the other cultural projects, was that this was still predominantly a metropolitan audience. Plans to send theatre companies and orchestras to the other areas of the nation foundered on WPA regulations prohibiting sending relief personnel across state lines. An attempt was then made to establish local projects where there were enough musicians or actors on relief to comprise a performing unit, but many such units had to be disbanded because of reduced appropriations. Thus the number of states producing WPA music and drama declined. Roosevelt and Hopkins repeatedly urged Flanagan and Sokoloff to tour, but touring was expensive, complicated, and unpopular in Congress. As one congressman so bluntly put it, the purpose of the federal theatre was to relieve distress and prevent suffering by providing employment; it was not to go "touring over the country, from place to place, charging admissions at cut rates in open competition with the theatrical industry. . . ." Thus economic distress, bureaucratic restrictions, and political opposition confined WPA's performing artists to a few major cities, inaccessible to millions of people for whom these theatres and orchestras had been intended.

Access to the visual arts proved easier. Although 75 percent of art project personnel were employed in eight metropolitan areas, Cahill boasted of operations in thirty-eight states. These figures, of course, indicated community art centers. Manned by small staffs—sometimes only a single artist-teacher—these gallery-workshops could be set up inexpensively throughout the hinterland. Beginning with North Carolina, Cahill oversaw the creation of over 100 centers throughout the country. Stretching from Salem, Oregon, to Key West, Florida, they were initially housed in vacant stores, abandoned restaurants and undertakers' parlors, and in the assorted garages and basements provided by local communities. Some quickly acquired spacious, well-equipped quarters, but all opened their doors to the entire community. "High-hatting," observed a *Time* reporter, was "taboo." As residents of middle America discovered in these centers opportunities to participate as well as observe, attendance figures climbed into the millions. Moreover, those who attended WPA exhibits were getting quality art. In addition to work by project artists, Washington headquarters circulated works on loan from such institutions as the Whitney, the Pennsylvania Academy of Fine Arts, the Denver Museum, and the American Federation of Arts. Perhaps more important, people grew to appreciate what they saw. Visitors to the Raleigh Art Center were a case in point. Objecting to an early exhibit of abstract and surrealist paintings from the Corcoran, they demanded what the center's director could only describe as "realistic paintings of the most saccharine type." Within less than a year, some of these viewers responded to a watercolor exhibit with a new openness to experimentation in subject matter and style. In similar centers across the country where art was becoming accessible, "Arts for the Millions" seemed a reality.

But to suggest that the New Deal quest for a cultural democracy had been realized would be folly. In 1939, a mere four years after its creation, the federal theatre was abolished by a hostile Congress amidst charges of subversion, inefficiency, and immorality. The other cultural projects were allowed to limp along into the war years, when they too were disbanded. Cultural enthusiasts failed to convince the Congress that support of the arts or the provision of access to them was a legitimate function of government. Cultural democracy never became public policy. Even tangible remains were few: paintings, graphics, and sculptures of varying quality on loan to public institutions, over one million dollars worth of theatrical equipment consigned to storage, and the seemingly endless boxes of records. For most Americans this federal foray into the arts was one of the more ephemeral episodes in an era of bread and circuses. . . .

. . . To conclude that this outpouring of Americana was mere aesthetic boondoggling, however, is to miss the mark. Quite apart from their immediate value, the vast quantity of "American stuff" amassed by these New Deal cultural projects constituted the raw material for new creative works. Artists and critics, noted [Archibald] MacLeish, need no longer assume that each artistic beginning in America was "a beginning *de novo.*" Indeed, amassing the material was significant for artists such as Ralph Ellison and Ben Shahn. Ellison in his research for the New York City guide had so immersed himself in the Harlem of *Invisible Man* that his novel acquired a substance and authenticity lacking in many of the works associated with the Harlem Renaissance. In much the same fashion, the photographic trips around the country which Shahn made for the Farm Security Administration provided him with photographs as well as the mental images which dominated his subsequent works. If the act of amassing material was important, so, too, was the mode of presentation. In their efforts to let ordinary people tell their own stories or to dramatize evidence about contemporary problems, New Deal artists were taking part in the creation of a new genre, the documentary. Evident in film, photography, journalism, and broadcasting, as well as the arts, the documentary captured the "tone, mood, and concerns of a decade." It was, according to William Stott, distinctively "thirties America." And nowhere is it better exemplified than in the federal theatre's living newspapers. Combining factual data and live actors with such diverse techniques as loudspeakers, film clips, lights, and music, these documentary explorations of public issues stimulated the emotions as well as the intellect. Influenced by such disparate sources as the "March of Time" and the "agitprops" of the Russian Blue Blouses, the living newspaper nonetheless constituted the "most original" form of drama developed in the United States and as a product of the New Deal, it was quintessential people's theatre.

What then of this quest for cultural democracy? Scholars must conclude that it was only partially realized, perhaps because it was only partially articulated. New Deal cultural enthusiasts did bring arts to the people, even pioneering in a new genre that was eminently accessible. But most people never fully accepted the arts as a public right and personal necessity. And in the postwar climate of disengagement, the vision of integration which had once been so inspiring seemed as dated as a 1935 copy of *New Masses.* In a characteristic expression of rejection, the painter Adolph Gottlieb, once a proponent of cultural democracy, denounced the "sentimental attitude that longs for a reconciliation between artist and public in the false hope that the artist can, in some nebulous fashion, be in touch with the grass roots of human aspirations."

The notion of an "organic society" within which the artist could exist harmoniously was, in his view, a "Utopian fantasy." As for aesthetic nationalism, Gottlieb and his fellow art project colleagues would soon agree that attempts to establish a national character for the American arts were, at best, "misguided." But these old visions and the economic crisis which spawned them had served Gottlieb and his compatriots better than they realized. To be sure, fundamental questions about the relationship between artist and public were never resolved in the 1930s—this had, after all, been a persistent problem. But by their very existence, New Deal projects provided, however briefly, symbolic legitimization of the arts and public patronage. More important, they provided the artist with a livelihood, an artistic milieu, and objective affirmation of his professional identity and worth. In short, they brought the two concepts of "culture" into greater association with each other and both into closer identification with the living concept of democracy; and that, in a nation historically so indifferent to its cultural resources, was a matter of no small consequence.

SUGGESTED READING

Baker, Houston. *Modernism and the Harlem Renaissance* (1987).

Bindas, Kenneth. *All of This Belongs to the Nation: The WPA's Federal Music Project and American Society* (1996).

Coben, Stanley. *Rebellion Against Victorianism: The Impetus for Cultural Change in 1920s America* (1991).

De Hart, Jane S. *The Federal Theater, 1935–1939: Plays, Relief, and Politics* (1967).

De Noon, Christopher. *Posters of the WPA* (1987).

Douglas, Ann. *Terrible Honesty: Mongrel Manhattan in the 1920s* (1994).

Erenberg, Lewis. *Stepping Out: New York City Nightlife and the Transformation of American Culture* (1981).

Fass, Paula. *The Damned and the Beautiful: American Youth in the 1920s* (1977).

Jongh, James de. *Vicious Modernism: Black Harlem and the Literary Imagination* (1990).

Lewis, David Levering. *When Harlem Was in Vogue* (1989).

Mangione, Jerre. *The Dream and the Deal: The Federal Writers' Project, 1935–1943* (1972).

Marling, Karal Ann. *Wall-to-Wall America: A Cultural History of Post Office Murals in the Great Depression* (1982).

McChesney, Robert. *Labor and the Marketplace of Ideas: WCFL and the Battle for Labor Radio Broadcasting, 1927–1934* (1992).

———. *Telecommunications, Mass Media, and Democracy: The Battle for Control of U.S. Broadcasting, 1928–1935* (1994).

Melosh, Barbara. *Engendering Culture: Manhood and Womanhood in New Deal Public Art and Theater* (1991).

O'Connor, Francis. *Federal Art Patronage, 1933 to 1943* (1966).

O'Connor, Francis, ed. *Art for the Millions: Essays from the 1930s by Artists and Administrators of the WPA Federal Art Project* (1973).

Ogren, Kathy. *Jazz Revolution: Twenties America and the Meaning of Jazz* (1989).

Park, Marlene, and Gerald E. Markowitz. *Democratic Vistas: Post Offices and Public Art in the New Deal* (1984).

Smulyan, Susan. *Selling Radio: The Commercialization of American Broadcasting* (1994).

Steele, Richard W. *Propaganda in an Open Society: The Roosevelt Administration and the Media, 1933–1941* (1985).

Susman, Warren. *Culture as History* (1984).

Wall, Cheryl. *Women of the Harlem Renaissance* (1995).

CHAPTER
6

"100 Percent Americanism": Race and Ethnicity Between the Wars

American society—reflecting the immigration boom of the late nineteenth century, the first "great migration" of African Americans from the rural South in the years surrounding World War I, and the continued internal migration across the porous Northern and Southern borders—boasted a remarkably diverse racial and ethnic fabric in the interwar years. But race and ethnic relations—reflecting nativist reactions to new immigration, the long shadow of slavery, and postwar fears of "foreign" radicalism—were marked by renewed anxieties and intolerance. The wartime rhetoric of "100% Americanism" became after 1920 a defense of a "biological republic," which floated a narrow racial definition of true citizenship, defining white Protestant stock as "American" and all others as "alien" threats to be assimilated or resisted.

Nativism and racism took a variety of forms, including the continued popularity of various Americanization campaigns and a fascination with the racial science eugenics. Perhaps most important, the postwar mood contributed to a marked deterioration in race relations in North and South, and to political efforts to restrict new immigration. In many ways, the Second Ku Klux Klan (which emerged in the 1920s) served as a nasty caricature of New Era race relations. The Second Klan was not simply a white supremacist organization but also inveighed against Roman Catholicism, Judaism, bolshevism, and—more broadly—the threats of modern society where, as one Klan paper put it, "money rules and morals rot." Similarly, the immigration restrictions of 1924—which curtailed new immigration with a quota system aimed largely at Eastern and Southern Europeans, Asians, and Africans— underscored both simple nativism and a broader anxiety about social change. After 1924 the population did not change as radically as it had in previous decades. The new and distinctly American consumer culture absorbed many second-generation immigrants (whose ethnic or racial communities had stopped growing). And the size of many immigrant communities (especially the Chinese and Japanese) was frozen by immigration quotas. The new immigration laws could not stem informal migration within the Americas, however, particularly the movement of Mexicans through the expanding agricultural economy of the Southwest and the continued migration of African Americans (almost 1 million through the 1920s) from the rural South.

*In this atmosphere, racial and ethnic groups did their best to adapt and re-
spond. Asian American communities, circumscribed by the immigration restrictions
and hampered by state laws restricting political and property rights, relied heavily
on their own cultural and economic institutions, including Japanese social and
farming associations and the development of Chinatowns. The barrios of New York,
Los Angeles, and elsewhere provided some stability and community for a growing
Latino population, but most working people in the migrant farm economy of the
Southwest suffered not only the indignities of "Jim Crow" but the uncertainty and
exploitation that followed from their immigration status. Growing African American communities in many northern cities breathed new life into the struggle for civil
rights, marked by the antilynching campaign of the National Association for the
Advancement of Colored People (NAACP) and the emergence of Marcus Garvey's
Universal Negro Improvement Association (UNIA). And all these struggles were
transformed by the Depression, which worsened conditions, and by a political response that at least promised more fundamental federal protection of basic civil
rights.*

DOCUMENTS

These documents suggest both the logic and ferocity of the postwar backlash against
immigrants and African Americans, and the response of these communities. In Document 1, the noted African American intellectual W.E.B. Du Bois argues that the democratic rhetoric of the war should underscore—for African Americans and the state—the
racial limits of American citizenship. In Document 2, the Governor of California tries
to explain the anti-Asian sentiment in his state. Document 3 captures the tone and tenor
of the congressional debate over immigration restriction; in Document 4, a Jewish
leader bemoans the nativist drift toward restriction. In Document 5, the Ku Klux Klan
offers its own peculiar definition of true citizenship. In Document 6, NAACP leader
Walter White documents the consequences of these views: a brutal lynching. In Document 7, Marcus Garvey, the leader of UNIA, advocates black nationalism. The writer
Richard Wright recalls the social and psychological conditions of "Jim Crow" segregation in Document 8. And in Document 9, journalist Carey McWilliams suggests the
economic logic of American immigration policy, which paid little attention to the influx of Mexican migrant laborers until the Depression transformed a labor shortage in
Southwest agriculture into a surplus.

1. W.E.B. Du Bois on the Meaning of the War for African Americans, 1919

We are returning from war! The Crisis and tens of thousands of black men were
drafted into a great struggle. For bleeding France and what she means and has
meant and will mean to us and humanity and against the threat of German race arrogance, we fought gladly and to the last drop of blood; for America and her highest

From "Returning Soldiers," *The Crisis* (May 19, 1919): 13–14.

ideals, we fought in far-off hope; for the dominant southern oligarchy entrenched in Washington, we fought in better resignation. For the America that represents and gloats in lynching, disfranchisement, caste, brutality and devilish insult—for this, in the hateful upturning and mixing of things, we were forced by vindictive fate to fight, also.

But today we return! We return from the slavery of uniform which the world's madness demanded us to don to the freedom of civil garb. We stand again to look America squarely in the face and call a spade a spade. We sing: This country of ours, despite all its better souls have done and dreamed, is yet a shameful land.

It *lynches*.

And lynching is barbarism of a degree of contemptible nastiness unparalleled in human history. Yet for fifty years we have lynched two Negroes a week, and we have kept this up right through the war.

It *disfranchises* its own citizens.

Disfranchisement is the deliberate theft and robbery of the only protection of poor against rich and black against white. The land that disfranchises its citizens and calls itself a democracy lies and knows it lies.

It encourages *ignorance*.

It has never really tried to educate the Negro. A dominant minority does not want Negroes educated. It wants servants, dogs, whores and monkeys. And when this land allows a reactionary group by its stolen political power to force as many black folk into these categories as it possibly can, it cries in contemptible hypocrisy: "They threaten us with degeneracy; they cannot be educated."

It *steals* from us.

It organizes industry to cheat us. It cheats us out of our land; it cheats us out of our labor. It confiscates our savings. It reduces our wages. It raises our rent. It steals our profit. It taxes us without representation. It keeps us consistently and universally poor, and then feeds us on charity and derides our poverty.

It *insults* us.

It has organized a nation-wide and latterly a world-wide propaganda of deliberate and continuous insult and defamation of black blood wherever found. It decrees that it shall not be possible in travel nor residence, work nor play, education nor instruction for a black man to exist without tacit or open acknowledgment of his inferiority to the dirtiest white dog. And it looks upon any attempt to question or even discuss this dogma as arrogance, unwarranted assumption and treason.

This is the country to which we Soldiers of Democracy return. This is the fatherland for which we fought! But it is *our* fatherland. It was right for us to fight. The faults of *our* country are *our* faults. Under similar circumstances, we would fight again. But by the God of Heaven, we are cowards and jackasses if now that that war is over, we do not marshal every ounce of our brain and brawn to fight a sterner, longer, more unbending battle against the forces of hell in our own land.

We *return*.

We *return from fighting*.

We *return fighting*.

Make way for Democracy! We saved it in France, and by the Great Jehovah, we will save it in the United States of America, or know the reason why.

2. The Governor of California on the "Oriental Problem," 1920

The Japanese in our midst have indicated a strong trend to land ownership and land control, and by their unquestioned industry and application, and by standards and methods that are widely separated from our occidental standards and methods, both in connection with hours of labor and standards of living, have gradually developed to a control of many of our important agricultural industries. Indeed, at the present time they operate 458,056 acres of the very best lands in California. The increase in acreage control within the last decade, according to these official figures, has been 412.9 per cent. In productive values—that is to say, in the market value of crops produced by them—our figures show that as against $6,235,856 worth of produce marketed in 1909, the increase has been to $67,145,730, approximately tenfold.

More significant than these figures, however, is the demonstrated fact that within the last ten years Japanese agricultural labor has developed to such a degree that at the present time between 80 and 90 per cent of most of our vegetable and berry products are those of the Japanese farms. Approximately 80 per cent of the tomato crop of the state is produced by Japanese; from 80 to 100 per cent of the spinach crop; a greater part of our potato and asparagus crops, and so on. So that it is apparent without much more effective restrictions that in a very short time, historically speaking, the Japanese population within our midst will represent a considerable portion of our entire population, and the Japanese control over certain essential food products will be an absolute one. . . .

These Japanese, by very reason of their use of economic standards impossible to our white ideals—that is to say, the employment of their wives and their very children in the arduous toil of the soil—are proving crushing competitors to our white rural populations. The fecundity of the Japanese race far exceeds that of any other people that we have in our midst. They send their children for short periods of time to our white schools, and in many of the country schools of our state the spectacle is presented of having a few white children acquiring their education in classrooms crowded with Japanese. The deep-seated and often outspoken resentment of our white mothers at this situation can only be appreciated by those people who have struggled with similar problems.

It is with great pride that I am able to state that the people of California have borne this situation and seen its developing menace with a patience and self-restraint beyond all praise. California is proud to proclaim to the nation that despite this social situation her people have been guilty of no excesses and no indignities upon the Japanese within our borders. No outrage, no violence, no insult and no ignominy have been offered to the Japanese people within California. . . .

But with all this the people of California are determined to repress a developing Japanese community within our midst. They are determined to exhaust every power in their keeping to maintain this state for its own people. This determination is

From California State Board of Control, *California and the Oriental* (Sacramento: State Printing Office, June 1920), 8–13.

based fundamentally upon the ethnological impossibility of assimilating the Japanese people and the consequential alternative of increasing a population whose very race isolation must be fraught with the gravest consequences. . . .

In dealing with this problem, we cannot very well take precedent out of the experience of the nation with the previous race question which so bitterly aroused all the sectional feelings of our people and led to the Civil War. There is one vital difference. The Japanese, be it said to their credit, are not of servile or docile stock. Proud of their traditions and history, exultant as they justly are at the extraordinary career of their country, they brook no suggestion of any dominant or superior race. Virile, progressive and aggressive, they have all the race consciousness which is inseparable from race quality.

And it is just because they possess these attributes in such marked degree and feel more keenly the social and race barriers which our people instinctively raise against them that they are driven to that race isolation and, I fear ultimately will reach that race resentment, which portend danger to the peace of our state in the future. In extending to them the just credit which is theirs, the thought does not occur to our people that because the Japanese come from a puissant nation, whose achievements on the field have brought it renown, that therefore our attitude should be moulded by pusillanimity or temporary expediency. We have faith in the willingness and power of our common country to protect its every part from foreign danger.

3. Congress Debates Immigration Restriction, 1921

Mr. Parrish We should stop immigration entirely until such a time as we can amend our immigration laws and so write them that hereafter no one shall be admitted except he be in full sympathy with our Constitution and laws, willing to declare himself obedient to our flag, and willing to release himself from any obligations he may owe to the flag of the country from which he came.

It is time that we act now, because within a few short years the damage will have been done. The endless tide of immigration will have filled our country with a foreign and unsympathetic element. Those who are out of sympathy with our Constitution and the spirit of our Government will be here in large numbers, and the true spirit of Americanism left us by our fathers will gradually become poisoned by this uncertain element.

The time once was when we welcomed to our shores the oppressed and downtrodden people from all the world, but they came to us because of oppression at home and with the sincere purpose of making true and loyal American citizens, and in truth and in fact they did adapt themselves to our ways of thinking and contributed in a substantial sense to the progress and development that our civilization has made. But that time has passed now; new and strange conditions have arisen in the countries over there; new and strange doctrines are being taught. The Governments of the Orient are being overturned and destroyed, and anarchy and bolshevism are threatening the very foundation of many of them, and no one can foretell

From *Congressional Record* (April 20, 1921), 66th Congress, 2nd session, vol. 59, 511–512, 515.

what the future will bring to many of those countries of the Old World now struggling with these problems.

Our country is a self-sustaining country. It has taught the principles of real democracy to all the nations of the earth; its flag has been the synonym of progress, prosperity, and the preservation of the rights of the individual, and there can be nothing so dangerous as for us to allow the undesirable foreign element to poison our civilization and thereby threaten the safety of the institutions that our forefathers have established for us.

Now is the time to throw about this country the most stringent immigration laws and keep from our shores forever those who are not in sympathy with the American ideas. It is the time now for us to act and act quickly, because every month's delay increases the difficulty in which we find ourselves and renders the problems of government more difficult of solution. We must protect ourselves from the poisonous influences that are threatening the very foundation of the Governments of Europe; we must see to it that those who come here are loyal and true to our Nation and impress upon them that it means something to have the privileges of American citizenship. We must hold this country true to the American thought and the American ideals. . . .

Mr. London. . . . This bill is a continuation of the war upon humanity. It is an assertion of that exaggerated nationalism which never appeals to reason and which has for its main source the self-conceit of accumulated prejudice.

At whom are you striking in this bill? Why, at the very people whom a short while ago you announced you were going to emancipate. We sent 2,000,000 men abroad to make the world "safe for democracy," to liberate these very people. Now you shut the door to them. Yes. So far, we have made the world safe for hypocrisy and the United States incidentally unsafe for the Democratic Party, temporarily at least. [Laughter.] The supporters of the bill claim that the law will keep out radicals. The idea that by restricting immigration you will prevent the influx of radical thought is altogether untenable. . . .

Ideas can neither be shut in nor shut out. There is only one way of contending with an idea, and that is the old and safe American rule of free and untrammeled discussion. Every attempt to use any other method has always proven disastrous.

While purporting to be a temporary measure, just for a year or so, this bill is really intended to pave the way to permanent exclusion.

To prevent immigration means to cripple the United States. Our most developed industrial States are those which have had the largest immigration. Our most backward States industrially and in the point of literacy are those which have had no immigration to speak of.

The extraordinary and unprecedented growth of the United States is as much a cause as the effect of immigration.

Defenders of this bill thoughtlessly repeat the exploded theory that there have been two periods of immigration, the good period, which the chairman of the committee fixes up to the year 1900, and the bad period since. The strange thing about it is that at no time in history has any country made such rapid progress in industry, in science, and in the sphere of social legislation as this country has shown since 1900.

The new immigration is neither different nor worse, and besides that, identically the same arguments were used against the old immigration.

By this bill we, who have escaped the horrors of the war, will refuse a place of refuge to the victims of the war.

I repeat, this is an attempt at civilization. Progress is by no means a continuous or uninterrupted process. Many a civilization has been destroyed in the tortuous course of history and has been followed by hundreds or thousands of years of darkness. It is just possible that unless strong men who love liberty will everywhere assert themselves, the world will revert to a state of savagery. Just now we hear nothing but hatred, nothing but the ravings of the exaggerated I—"I am of the best stock, I do not want to be contaminated; I have produced the greatest literature; my intellect is the biggest; my heart is the noblest"—and this is repeated in every parliament, in every country, by every fool all over the world. [Applause.]

4. A Jewish Leader Laments the Rise of Nativism, 1922

. . . It occurred to me that it might be of service to you if I give you a purely personal view of what seems to me to have happened in the American public mind during the last few years on the subject of immigration. I may be wrong in my analysis, of course, but I think you may assume I have watched the situation and am at least in as good a position to reach a conclusion as another.

There has, of course, for a long time, been an uneasiness in certain sections of the country with regard to the large influx of foreign non-English speaking population. In the South this has for many years assumed the complection of a race question; the southern whites have said in effect: "We have a negro problem on our hands and we do not want another problem." In the South there was no Jewish migration to speak of, but the migration that the people there objected to was that of the Italian and Syrian. I state this to indicate that the Jewish question had nothing to do with the strong growth of anti-immigration sentiment in the Southern part of the United States. Nor was it an economic question, because as you know, the South is still very sparsely settled. . . .

The War caused the spread of an anti-immigration sentiment to practically every part of the United States. This according to my diagnosis was due to the following causes: During the period that America was not in the War, the Austrian and German ambassadors were organizing their former nationals in the United States just as though they had been on their own territory. The Austrian ambassador did this openly, the German ambassador secretly. As a result, a wave of uneasiness spread throughout the entire native population.

A great many people, however, still cherished the idea of America as an asylum for the persecuted and oppressed and had also conceived the notion that through our public school system, the immigrants, who had reached as much as a million a year or over, were being surely molded into the American body politic. When the draft law was passed and our Army was assembled, this theory, which had been strengthened by Mr. [Israel] Zangwill's phrase of the "melting pot," was rudely overthrown. It was found that we had tens of thousands of citizens who did not know enough

From "To Lucien Wolf, August 22, 1922" in *Cyrus Adler: Selected Letters,* vol. 2, ed. Ira Robinson (New York: Jewish Publication Society of America, 1985), 51–52.

English to get the word of command: that even in a state like Massachusetts there were two entire regiments of which this was true. One of [Theodore] Roosevelt's last phrases was that it appeared that we had not developed a nation, but a polyglot boarding house. In other words, America drew back in affright at the great numbers of what it considered undigested human material in its midst, and for good or ill, and I believe without reference whatever to any economic advantages or disadvantages, it has decided that this country is no longer a field for immigration. The present limit of three percent may become two percent or even less. The forces that are operating toward this restriction are too numerous and powerful to be overcome. The American Federation of Labor, in spite of its fine phrases, is one of the most potent of these influences. The old line families of New England and the South are just as determined. Right here in Philadelphia, all of the publications controlled by Mr. [Cyrus H.] Curtis, himself a New England man, are militantly restrictionist. By that, I do not mean solely the *Public Ledger,* which is one of the most read papers in Philadelphia though local in its influence, but the *Saturday Evening Post,* which is said to circulate two million copies and is read in every city, town and village in the United States, has practically as its sole editorial policy the restriction of immigration. . . .

These views, you will see, therefore are being spread not only among the masses through a five-cent paper like the *Saturday Evening Post,* but in college and university circles by leading professors. All of this, whether mistaken or not, is I think honest; that is to say, the people who are promulgating these ideas are sincere in their conviction that the American people, the American spirit, and the English language are seriously threatened.

5. The Ku Klux Klan Defines Americanism, 1926

The Klan . . . has now come to speak for the great mass of Americans of the old pioneer stock. We believe that it does fairly and faithfully represent them, and our proof lies in their support. To understand the Klan, then, it is necessary to understand the character and present mind of the mass of old-stock Americans. The mass, it must be remembered, as distinguished from the intellectually mongrelized "Liberals."

These are, in the first place, a blend of various peoples of the so-called Nordic race, the race which, with all its faults, has given the world almost the whole of modern civilization. The Klan does not try to represent any people but these. . . .

. . . The Nordic American today is a stranger in large parts of the land his fathers gave him. Moreover, he is a most unwelcome stranger, one much spit upon, and one to whom even the right to have his own opinions and to work for his own interests is now denied with jeers and revilings. "We must Americanize the Americans," a distinguished immigrant said recently. Can anything more clearly show the state to which the real American has fallen in this country which was once his own? . . .

Thus the Klan goes back to the American racial instincts, and to the common sense which is their first product, as the basis of its beliefs and methods. . . .

From "The Ku Klux Klan's Fight for Americanism" by Hiram Wesley Evans from *North American Review* (March–May 1926), pp. 38–39, 52–54. Reprinted by permission of *North American Review.*

There are three of these great racial instincts, vital elements in both the historic and the present attempts to build an America which shall fulfill the aspirations and justify the heroism of the men who made the nation. These are the instincts of loyalty to the white race, to the traditions of America, and to the spirit of Protestantism, which has been an essential part of Americanism ever since the days of Roanoke and Plymouth Rock. They are condensed into the Klan slogan: "Native, white, Protestant supremacy."

First in the Klansman's mind is patriotism—America for Americans. He believes religiously that a betrayal of Americanism or the American race is treason to the most sacred of trusts, a trust from his fathers and a trust from God. He believes, too, that Americanism can only be achieved if the pioneer stock is kept pure. There is more than race pride in this. Mongrelization has been proven bad. It is only between closely related stocks of the same race that interbreeding has improved men; the kind of interbreeding that went on in the early days of America between English, Dutch, German, Hugenot, Irish and Scotch.

Racial integrity is a very definite thing to the Klansman. It means even more than good citizenship, for a man may be in all ways a good citizen and yet a poor American, unless he has racial understanding of Americanism, and instinctive loyalty to it. It is in no way a reflection on any man to say that he is unAmerican; it is merely a statement that he is not one of us. It is often not even wise to try to make an American of the best of aliens. What he is may be spoiled without his becoming American. The races and stocks of men are as distinct as breeds of animals, and every boy knows that if one tries to train a bulldog to herd sheep, he has in the end neither a good bulldog nor a good collie. . . .

The second word in the Klansman's trilogy is "white." The white race must be supreme, not only in America but in the world. This is equally undebatable, except on the ground that the races might live together, each with full regard for the rights and interests of others, and that those rights and interests would never conflict. Such an idea, of course, is absurd; the colored races today, such as Japan, are clamoring not for equality but for their supremacy. The whole history of the world, on its broader lines, has been one of race conflicts, wars, subjugation or extinction. This is not pretty, and certainly disagrees with the maudlin theories of cosmopolitanism, but it is truth. The world has been so made that each race must fight for its life, must conquer, accept slavery or die. The Klansman believes that the whites will not become slaves, and he does not intend to die before his time.

Moreover, the future of progress and civilization depends on the continued supremacy of the white race. The forward movement of the world for centuries has come entirely from it. Other races each had its chance and either failed or stuck fast, while white civilization shows no sign of having reached its limit. Until the whites falter, or some colored civilization has a miracle of awakening, there is not a single colored stock that can claim even equality with the white; much less supremacy.

The third of the Klan principles is that Protestantism must be supreme; that Rome shall not rule America. The Klansman believes this not merely because he is a Protestant, nor even because the Colonies that are now our nation were settled for the purpose of wresting America from the control of Rome and establishing a land of free conscience. He believes it also because Protestantism is an essential part of

Americanism; without it America could never have been created and without it she cannot go forward. Roman rule would kill it.

Protestantism contains more than religion. It is the expression in religion of the same spirit of independence, self-reliance and freedom which are the highest achievements of the Nordic race. It sprang into being automatically at the time of the great "upsurgence" of strength in the Nordic peoples that opened the spurt of civilization in the fifteenth century. It has been a distinctly Nordic religion, and it has been through this religion that the Nordics have found strength to take leadership of all whites and the supremacy of the earth. Its destruction is the deepest purpose of all other peoples, as that would mean the end of Nordic rule.

6. Walter White Documents a Lynching, 1925

My dear Gov. McLeod:

I have just left Aiken which I visited along with other cities in South Carolina as a representative of *The New York World*. My purpose in going there was to cover the recent lynching at Aiken of Clarence, Demon and Bertha Lowman. . . .

. . . [Here are the facts.] [E]arly in the morning of October 8th around three o'clock, Sheriff Mollie Robinson, Deputy Sheriff R. L. McElheny, Deputy Sheriff A. D. Sheppard and Traffic Officer John B. Salley of Aiken went to Bertha Lowman's cell, Sheriff Robinson unlocking the door. Bertha Lowman asked them, "What do you want now?" They told her to put on her clothes as she was wanted downstairs. When she was reluctant to leave her cell, suspecting something amiss, I am informed that she was dragged from her cell by Robinson and Salley. She was taken down stairs and with Clarence and Demon Lowman delivered to the mob. Two shots were fired after the mob had gotten possession of the prisoners, so I am informed, and not as Sheriff Robinson claims, when he was resisting entrance of the mob into the jail.

May I at this point call attention in corroboration of these facts that the jail at Aiken is only four years old and well constructed. It shows little if any signs of the struggle which Robinson claims he made in trying to defend the prisoners. . . .

I also want to mention at this point that plans had been made to remove the prisoners hastily from Aiken to Columbia should they be convicted. But when Demon Lowman was freed of a murder charge, a circumstance certain to inflame lynchers if there was fear of a lynching following a conviction, they were placed in the jail and only one man put there to guard them. This action, I feel safe in asserting, is concrete evidence of extreme carelessness if not of nonfeasance on the part of Sheriff Robinson and his Deputies. . . .

Returning again to the lynching—on the way from the jail Clarence Lowman, 14 years of age at the time Sheriff Howard was killed and 15 years old when he was lynched, jumped from the car which was taking him from the jail to the scene of his

From the Yale Collection of American Literature, Beinecke Rare Book and Manuscript Library, Yale University.

death. Clarence was shot and recaptured. I am informed that to keep blood from getting in the car a rope was tied to Clarence and to the car and his body was dragged in this manner to the scene of the execution. The mob went out York Street on the Dixie Highway to a point about $1\frac{1}{2}$ to 2 miles from Aiken near a Tourist Camp. I am informed that Bertha Lowman begged so piteously for her life that members of the mob had a hard time killing her. After being shot she dragged herself over the ground pleading piteously not to be killed moving about as she did so. A number of shots had to be fired before one of the bullets mercifully ended her agony and caused her death.

Pierce Howard, so I am informed, was to have had the honor of being the Executioner but his nerve failed him. I am informed that Deputy Sheriffs McElheny and Walter Sheppard and Marion Bell, Chain gang Captain, were chief executioners assisted by Pink Gaddy (or Gady) and Gary Seigler. . . .

Several men were invited to come to the lynching who were not members of the Klan. This, it is believed in Aiken, was done in an effort to establish the fact subsequent to the lynching that it was not a Klan affair. I am informed that this effort met with no success. The late Sheriff Howard, the present Sheriff Robinson, his deputies and all of the members of the mob were members of the Klan. I can furnish you with documentary proof from South Carolina sources of the correctness of this statement.

A responsible and well known citizen of South Carolina further stated to me that as soon as the news got out about the murders certain people involved in them in an effort to cover up their guilt and to "muddy the waters" tried to precipitate a race riot. These persons, I am informed went about frightening the white people, telling them that the Negroes were armed and were going to rise at night and kill all of the white people. It is unnecessary for me to state that there was no evidence whatever to substantiate such a charge. . . .

This entire trouble at Aiken appears to be an outgrowth of the Klan and its activities. The element of the membership which acted as a restraining influence from the early days of the organization of the Klan has largely resigned, leaving it in the hands of an irresponsible, vicious and criminal element. There is in the vicinity of Aiken and in the towns nearby a very extensive business of distilling of liquor and transportation and sale of same as well as other criminal practices. There have been floggings and even murders as result of this reign of lawlessness and barbarity. A number of white men as well as Negroes have been flogged and killed and the more law abiding and respectable element is living in constant terror. In all my experience, I have never before seen such a reign of lawlessness as exists in and near Aiken.

I am placing these facts before you at such great length that you may have the benefit of my investigation and that you and the state of South Carolina may take such steps as you feel disposed to take to apprehend the lynchers of the three Lowmans, to punish them adequately for the murder and to end the state of lawlessness that now exists. I have reasons to believe that as set forth above many of the law enforcement officers who should be apprehending criminals are not only protecting these criminals but engaged in criminal practices themselves. . . .

Respectfully submitted,

(Signed) Walter White

7. Marcus Garvey Makes a Case for Black Nationalism, 1925

For five years the Universal Negro Improvement Association has been advocating the cause of Africa for the Africans—that is, that the Negro peoples of the world should concentrate upon the object of building up for themselves a great nation in Africa. . . .

A "Program" at Last

I trust that the Negro peoples of the world are now convinced that the work of the Universal Negro Improvement Association is not a visionary one, but very practical, and that it is not so far fetched, but can be realized in a short while if the entire race will only co-operate and work toward the desired end. Now that the work of our organization has started to bear fruit we find that some of these "doubting Thomases" of three and four years ago are endeavoring to mix themselves up with the popular idea of rehabilitating Africa in the interest of the Negro. They are now advancing spurious "programs" and in a short while will endeavor to force themselves upon the public as advocates and leaders of the African idea.

It is felt that those who have followed the career of the Universal Negro Improvement Association will not allow themselves to be deceived by these Negro opportunists who have always sought to live off the ideas of other people.

The Dream of a Negro Empire

It is only a question of a few more years when Africa will be completely colonized by Negroes, as Europe is by the white race. What we want is an independent African nationality, and if America is to help the Negro peoples of the world establish such a nationality, then we welcome the assistance.

It is hoped that when the time comes for American and West Indian Negroes to settle in Africa, they will realize their responsibility and their duty. It will not be to go to Africa for the purpose of exercising an over-lordship over the natives, but it shall be the purpose of the Universal Negro Improvement Association to have established in Africa that brotherly co-operation which will make the interests of the African native and the American and West Indian Negro one and the same, that is to say, we shall enter into a common partnership to build up Africa in the interests of our race. . . .

The Basis of an African Aristocracy

The masses of Negroes in America, the West Indies, South and Central America are in sympathetic accord with the aspirations of the native Africans. We desire to help them build up Africa as a Negro Empire, where every black man, whether he was

From Marcus Garvey, "Africa for the Africans," *The Portable Harlem Renaissance Reader*, ed. David Levering Lewis (New York: Penguin, 1994), 17–25.

born in Africa or in the Western world, will have the opportunity to develop on his own lines under the protection of the most favorable democratic institutions. . . .

An Eye for an Eye

Men may spurn the idea, they may scoff at it; the metropolitan press of this country may deride us; yes, white men may laugh at the idea of Negroes talking about government; but let me tell you there is going to be a government, and let me say to you also that whatsoever you give, in like measure it shall be returned to you. . . .

. . . When we come to consider the history of man, was not the Negro a power, was he not great once? Yes, honest students of history can recall the day when Egypt, Ethiopia and Timbuctoo towered in their civilizations, towered above Europe, towered above Asia. When Europe was inhabited by a race of cannibals, a race of savages, naked men, heathens and pagans, Africa was peopled with a race of cultured black men, who were masters in art, science and literature; men who were cultured and refined; men who, it was said, were like the gods. Even the great poets of old sang in beautiful sonnets of the delight it afforded the gods to be in companionship with the Ethiopians. Why, then, should we lose hope? Black men, you were once great; you shall be great again. Lose not courage, lose not faith, go forward. The thing to do is to get organized; keep separated and you will be exploited, you will be robbed, you will be killed. Get organized, and you will compel the world to respect you. If the world fails to give you consideration, because you are black men, because you are Negroes, four hundred millions of you shall, through organization, shake the pillars of the universe and bring down creation, even as Samson brought down the temple upon his head and upon the heads of the Philistines.

An Inspiring Vision

So Negroes, I say, through the Universal Negro Improvement Association, that there is much to live for. I have a vision of the future, and I see before me a picture of a redeemed Africa, with her dotted cities, with her beautiful civilization, with her millions of happy children, going to and fro. Why should I lose hope, why should I give up and take a back place in this age of progress? Remember that you are men, that God created you Lords of this creation. Lift up yourselves, men, take yourselves out of the mire and hitch your hopes to the stars; yes, rise as high as the very stars themselves. Let no man pull you down, let no man destroy your ambition, because man is but your companion, your equal; man is your brother; he is not your lord; he is not your sovereign master.

We of the Universal Negro Improvement Association feel happy; we are cheerful. Let them connive to destroy us; let them organize to destroy us; we shall fight the more. Ask me personally the cause of my success, and I say opposition; oppose me, and I fight the more, and if you want to find out the sterling worth of the Negro, oppose him, and under the leadership of the Universal Negro Improvement Association he shall fight his way to victory, and in the days to come, and I believe not far distant, Africa shall reflect a splendid demonstration of the worth of the Negro, of the determination of the Negro, to set himself free and to establish a government of his own.

8. Richard Wright Recalls "Living Jim Crow," 1937

Negroes who have lived South know the dread of being caught alone upon the streets in white neighborhoods after the sun has set. In such a simple situation as this the plight of the Negro in America is graphically symbolized. While white strangers may be in these neighborhoods trying to get home, they can pass unmolested. But the color of a Negro's skin makes him easily recognizable, makes him suspect, converts him into a defenseless target.

Late one Saturday night I made some deliveries in a white neighborhood. I was pedaling my bicycle back to the store as fast as I could, when a police car, swerving toward me, jammed me into the curbing.

"Get down and put up your hands!" the policemen ordered.

I did. They climbed out of the car, guns drawn, faces set, and advanced slowly.

"Keep still!" they ordered.

I reached my hands higher. They searched my pockets and packages. They seemed dissatisfied when they could find nothing incriminating. Finally, one of them said:

"Boy, tell your boss not to send you out in white neighborhoods this time of night."

As usual, I said:

"Yes, sir." . . .

[Later] . . . my Jim Crow education assumed quite a different form. It was no longer brutally cruel, but subtly cruel. Here I learned to lie, to steal, to dissemble. I learned to play that dual role which every Negro must play if he wants to eat and live.

For example, it was almost impossible to get a book to read. It was assumed that after a Negro had imbibed what scanty schooling the state furnished he had no further need for books. I was always borrowing books from men on the job. One day I mustered enough courage to ask one of the men to let me get books from the library in his name. Surprisingly, he consented. I cannot help but think that he consented because he was a Roman Catholic and felt a vague sympathy for Negroes, being himself an object of hatred. Armed with a library card, I obtained books in the following manner: I would write a note to the librarian, saying: "Please let this nigger boy have the following books." I would then sign it with the white man's name.

When I went to the library, I would stand at the desk, hat in hand, looking as unbookish as possible. When I received the books desired I would take them home. If the books listed in the note happened to be out, I would sneak into the lobby and forge a new one. I never took any chances guessing with the white librarian about what the fictitious white man would want to read. No doubt if any of the white patrons had suspected that some of the volumes they enjoyed had been in the home of a Negro, they would not have tolerated it for an instant.

From Richard Wright, "The Ethics of Living Jim Crow," in *American Stuff: An Anthology of Prose and Verse by Members of the Federal Writers' Project* (New York: Viking Press, 1937), 47–48, 50–51.

9. Carey McWilliams Accuses California of "Getting Rid of the Mexicans," 1933

For a long time Mexicans had regarded Southern California, more particularly Los Angeles, with favor, and during the decade from 1919 to 1929, the facts justified this view. At that time there was a scarcity of cheap labor in the region and Mexicans were made welcome. When cautious observers pointed out some of the consequences that might reasonably be expected to follow from a rash encouragement of this immigration, they were shouted down by the wise men of the Chamber of Commerce. Mexican labor was eulogized as cheap, plentiful, and docile. . . .

But a marked change has occurred since 1930. When it became apparent last year that the program for the relief of the unemployed would assume huge proportions in the Mexican quarter, the community swung to a determination to oust the Mexican. Thanks to the rapacity of his overlords, he had not been able to accumulate any savings. He was in default in his rent. He was a burden to the taxpayer. At this juncture, an ingenious social worker suggested the desirability of a wholesale deportation. But when the federal authorities were consulted, they could promise but slight assistance, since many of the younger Mexicans in Southern California were American citizens, being the American-born children of immigrants. Moreover, the federal officials insisted on, in cases of illegal entry, a public hearing and a formal order of deportation. This procedure involved delay and expense, and, moreover, it could not be used to advantage in ousting any large number.

A better scheme was soon devised. Social workers reported that many of the Mexicans who were receiving charity had signified their "willingness" to return to Mexico. Negotiations were at once opened with the social-minded officials of the Southern Pacific Railroad. It was discovered that, in wholesale lots, the Mexicans could be shipped to Mexico City for $14.70 *per capita.* This sum represented less than the cost of a week's board and lodging. And so, about February 1931, the first trainload was dispatched, and shipments at the rate of about one a month have continued ever since. A shipment consisting of three special trains left Los Angeles on December 8. The loading commenced at about six o'clock in the morning and continued for hours. More than twenty-five such special trains had left the Southern Pacific station before last April.

No one seems to know precisely how many Mexicans have been "repatriated" in this manner to date. The Los Angeles *Times* of November 18 gave an estimate of eleven thousand for the year 1932. The monthly shipments of late have ranged from thirteen hundred to six thousand. The *Times* reported last April that altogether more than 200,000 *repatriados* had left the United States in the twelve months immediately preceding, of which it estimated that from fifty to seventy-five thousand were from California, and over thirty-five thousand from Los Angeles County. Of those from Los Angeles County, a large number were charity deportations.

From Carey McWilliams, "Getting Rid of the Mexicans," *American Mercury* 28 (March 1933). Excerpted from Matt S. Meier and Feliciano Rivera, eds., *Readings on La Raza: The Twentieth Century* (New York: Hill and Wang, 1974), 87–90.

The repatriation program is regarded locally as a piece of consummate state-craft. The average per family cost of executing it is $71.14, including food and transportation. It cost Los Angeles County $77,249.29 to repatriate one shipment of 6,024. It would have cost $424,933.70 to provide this number with such charitable assistance as they would have been entitled to had they remained—a saving of $347,684.41.

One wonders what has happened to all the Americanization programs of yester-year. The Chamber of Commerce has been forced to issue a statement assuring the Mexican authorities that the community is in no sense unfriendly to Mexican labor and that repatriation is a policy designed solely for the relief of the destitute—even, presumably, in cases where invalids are removed from the County Hospital in Los Angeles and carted across the line. But those who once agitated for Mexican exclusion are no longer regarded as the puppets of union labor. . . .

The Los Angeles industrialists confidently predict that the Mexican can be lured back, "whenever we need him." But I am not so sure of this. He may be placed on a quota basis in the meantime, or possibly he will no longer look north to Los Angeles as the goal of his dreams. At present he is probably delighted to abandon an empty paradise.

E S S A Y S

In the first essay, Nancy MacLean argues that the Second Ku Klux Klan was born of economic insecurities; that racist and anti-Semitic words and actions, in other words, often reflected the displacement of class and regional anxieties. In the second essay, David Montejano documents the ways in which Southwestern politicians and agricultural interests exploited immigration law and labor controls to ensure a dependable, and politically weak, supply of migrant labor.

The Class Anxieties of the Ku Klux Klan

NANCY MacLEAN

"For the first time in the history of our country," E. D. Rivers, a Great Titan of the Klan, state senator, and now candidate for governor, warned in 1930, "we are faced with being ruled by an oligarchy [of] centralized wealth." Rivers joined other Klansmen as spokespeople in a campaign being waged in Clarke County against "the invasion of these minions of monopoly—the alien chain stores." Employing a traditional idiom of popular protest, Rivers identified chain stores with "the taking away of the freedom of government from the masses." "The Little Group of Kings in Wall Street," one campaign advertisement admonished, is "very deliberately wiping out your independence." Another prominent Klan speaker expressed concern for the "young men of the country who will become 'automatons'" with no choice but to work for such monopolies. "Are your Sons and Daughters for sale?" the Citizens' Protective League demanded of local parents. "Do you realize you are gradually selling them into slavery?" The League implored residents not to let "Wall Street [continue] . . . destroying the community life of America." It was vital, an Athens Klan lecturer had earlier warned, to "break up [the] MONOPOLY that is now RUIN[IN]G and CRUSHING DOWN ON THE ENTIRE POPULATION of the world."

In the fight against chain stores, radical rhetoric roused popular support for restorationist ends. The critique of economic concentration aimed, not to promote radical democratic change, but to avert it. The Speaker of the Georgia House, Richard B. Russell, Jr., warned that "if the monopolistic tendency is allowed to continue unchecked, it will result in socialism or communism." The Citizens' Protective League agreed. If the mergers weren't stopped, "we are going to face exactly the situation that has been gone through with Russia." River's claim that this was the "first time" that concentrated capital endangered the welfare of the people made a mockery of the very populism it evoked. When he said the trusts aimed to take away popular sovereignty, he clearly had in mind the middling groups the Klan represented, since blacks and many poor whites had lost long ago what little sovereignty they had. Most telling, perhaps, of the Klan's reactionary motives in the anti–chain store campaign were its associations. Rivers attacked "atheism, communism, chain stores and companionate marriage" as though they were of a piece.

Local Klan lecturers on "Americanism," for their part, blamed Jews and Catholics for the chain-store peril. One speaker dared his listeners to "find out who owns stock" in companies like the "A & P Grocery stores." Jews and Catholics, it seems, hid behind the initials. He further complained that "department stores, all of which are principally owned by Jews or foreigners," were pushing out "American" businesses. He raved against the inroads made into Georgia by Sears & Roebuck, which he insisted was owned by "JEWS. JEWS. JEWS." Its entrenchment would "spell ruination" for the state's independent merchants. He told listeners to find out whether their druggists, undertakers, grocers, butchers, and clothing and shoe merchants were "JEWS OR CATHOLICS," and if so, to boycott them and organize others to do the same. National Klan leaders concurred. If present trends continued, Imperial Wizard Simmons warned, immigrants from Southern and Eastern Europe and their children would soon crowd native-born whites out of "the business class." Such charges struck a chord with local members, several of whom operated in competition with Jews and immigrants from Italy and Greece. The Bernstein Brothers, for example, prospered in undertaking and furniture sales, where Klansmen *Chester Morton* and Bela Dunaway and his sons struggled to acquire a footing; the Michael Brothers owned the local department store, and Joseph Costa and family ran a flourishing ice cream and soda business.

The campaign against chain stores illustrates how impossible it is to understand the Klan if one conceives of it as a simple conservative force. The Klan was indeed conservative, fiercely so, as the anti-Semitism and nativism of the chain-store struggle make clear. Yet the order's politics were different from those of the usual standard-bearers of conservatism, "the better people" in Clarke County as elsewhere. The Klan put forward a populist critique of American society suited to the middling men who made up the core of its following. They resented, sometimes vociferously, "the silk hat crowd" and the social transformation their reign had wrought. Yet the Klan's was no ordinary populism. While it gave voice to middle-class fears of economic concentration and political disempowerment, it also put up ferocious opposition to social reconstruction from the left.

In this dualism lay the appeal of the Klan's class politics to the lower-middle-class men who flocked to the order in such numbers. It articulated the animosity petit-bourgeois whites felt toward *both* capital and labor—and it spoke in idioms at the core of American culture. From classical liberalism, the Klan drew its anti-statist economics. From republicanism, the Klan drew many of its assumptions about the good society and the prerequisites of citizenship. From evangelical Protestantism, it drew a structure of feeling that expressed its members' feelings of being embattled from above and below and that sanctified aggressive self-defense. The composite is best described as reactionary populism.

Klan leaders prided themselves on their fidelity to the vision of the founding fathers. On one hand, they exalted the old liberal tradition of possessive individualism. That property was the basis of freedom was the grounding assumption of the Klan's political theory. In this line of reasoning, as C. B. MacPherson observed, the individual could only be "free inasmuch as he was proprietor of his person and capacities." Politics thus became "a calculated device for the protection of this property and for the maintenance of an orderly relation of exchange." Klan propaganda often manifested such assumptions. "The function of the government," wrote a Klan-recommended writer, "is to protect individuals in their right of person and right of property." The great merit of the United States Constitution was that it had "established individual property rights more securely" than any other form of government, guarding against the twin dangers of "feudalism" and "all forms of socialism or communism." . . .

Klansmen committed themselves to what they understood as the social vision of Thomas Jefferson: a republic of small proprietors. According to Simmons, the "real America has always been a country America." "The farmer is the wealth producer of the nation," concurred the *Imperial Night Hawk,* "the backbone of all industry." Simmons saw urgent danger in contemporary population trends. In 1920, for the first time, most Americans lived in urban areas, and city residents cast the majority of votes. "Ignore the problem of the white small farming class yet a little longer," Simmons warned, "and we shall be driven into farming on a great scale, with armies of stolid peasants doing the work." Simmons found the prospect of the day "when the countryside, like the city, shall have lost its free independent population" horrible to contemplate.

Although Klansmen shared Jefferson's adulation of independent farmers, they modified his vision to suit a modern class structure. They extended their loyalties to "the middle class" as a whole, among whom Klansmen also included small businessmen, white-collar workers, independent professionals, and skilled craftsmen. Common to both the yeoman ideal and its broad petit-bourgeois variant was the belief that the future of the republic depended on those with a stake in society. Simmons asserted that the success of early American democracy was attributable to the homogenous interests of "the small property-holders and skilled workers" who made up the citizenry. "The importance of the middle class in history," declared

Charles Gould, "cannot be overestimated." As a mediating force between ruling and exploited classes, the middle class had provided stability to hierarchical social orders, from the ancient slave states forward. When the middle class was "depressed" or "destroyed," the ruin of whole societies ensued. Another Klan author cited "the failure of the middle class" as the preeminent reason for the problems of all nations—most immediately, his own.

Now, it seemed, sinister forces imperiled the fragile balance a republic depended on. Far more than their contemporaries, Klan representatives gloomily foresaw the end of the republic. The rhetoric of republican alarm and despair "luxury," "corruption," and "decay"—and morbid analogies between the contemporary United States and the declines of ancient Greece, Rome, and Old World Europe regularly peppered Klan propaganda. Simmons predicted "a steady drift toward monarchy," a "natural outgrowth" for "a decadent republic" that had spawned "a great class of the rich on the one hand and a great class of the poor on the other." Both of these classes tended "toward corruption"; neither could be trusted to serve the commonweal. *"As a people and as a nation,"* he warned, *"we are face to face with dissolution."* "Democracy [was] threatened from every side" in the contemporary United States, "by greedy and designing powers above, as by a great mass of incompetent, unprincipled and undemocratic voters from below." "Both plutocracy and Bolshevism," announced Simmons, "are new forms of tyranny" the Klan would combat. The Klan, said Simmons' successor, Hiram Evans, was a tool for "the common people . . . to resume control of their country," implying they had already lost it.

The foremost threat to the republic, in the Klan's view, came from below. The order's press and many of its leaders, North and South, saw the "labor question" as *the* critical one in their society in the early 1920s. They were terrified about how it would be answered. According to an Arkansas Klan leader, the "grave industrial unrest" of the era had driven men into the Klan. "Look at the list of our strikes," explained Klan propagandist and preacher Charles Jefferson. "In no other country is the conflict between labor and capital so implacable and so bitter." "Everybody who reads the newspapers or talks with his neighbors," agreed Imperial Wizard Simmons, "knows that the conflict between labor and capital is drifting us into another civil war. . . . And how much more deadly is disunity between classes than between sections." Creating "a closer relationship between capital and labor" was one of the Klan's oft-stated goals.

So, too, was fighting the left. Indeed, nothing else elicited from Klan members quite the same distemper. Socialism was "without a possible exception . . . the most destructive philosophy preached by thinking men." "The 'Red' is the most dastardly creature infesting the earth," intoned the *Searchlight* in 1923, "the worst menace to civilization." The activities of the Industrial Workers of the World and the Communist Party proved that "America Needs the Klan." In later years, Klan leaders would boast that it was their organization that had first "discovered Communism in the United States and which first assailed it." . . .

Such vehement anti-communism seems odd in light of the weakness of the American left relative to its European counterparts, particularly after the Red Scare, and its virtual absence in the Southeast. But the paradox is more apparent than real. Communism condensed into a single entity all the leveling influences Klansmen perceived in the contemporary world—from economic concentration to the organization of African Americans, immigrants, women, and youth. Hence the depiction of it as "the extreme of Democracy." Anti-communism became a sign expressing Klansmen's belief that all these hierarchies were linked: tampering with one would unloose all the others. In order to rouse mass popular opposition to changes in any one area, Klan leaders situated them in a worldwide conspiracy. The threat of "anarchy" from Bolshevism was thus discovered "even in villages and hamlets where it would be least expected."

Not surprisingly, then, combatting communism—in all its faces—appeared an urgent task to Klansmen, particularly in the early 1920s, but even thereafter. "Klan Declares War on Radical Forces in U. S.," one headline thus proclaimed, while the Klan press published a whole series on the theme "Bolshevism—Menace to America." After the first World War, socialism ceased to be only "a remote threat" in the United States; "Never was the Red Peril so real." "Labor strikes take on the nature of social revolutions," complained Simmons. "The advocacy of Bolshevism arouses mighty crowds to wild enthusiasm." If such subversion continued, he predicted, native-born Americans would "probably divide and civil war will result." . . .

In interpreting the threat from below, Klansmen reminded their compatriots of Jefferson's fear of the unskilled wage-earners. "Jefferson was right," affirmed Simmons. "Unless" the cities were "reformed they will destroy both democracy and civilization." Simmons believed that "real Americans" simply could not survive factory discipline or urban life; farm life was an essential component of American manhood. "Factory work," he said, calling on Social Darwinism to brand the unskilled as biologically inferior, "progressively selects those who are more and more unfit to be Americans." Like the "idle rich," they were "physical weaklings," "fit only to be the subject of a more or less absolute monarch." Indeed, in the view of the Imperial Commander of the Women's Klan, workers were "those least fitted by blood and training to rule."

Such open hostility toward workers was rare, however; more commonly it was packaged in racism. Klansmen blamed virtually all labor trouble on immigrants and "foreign agitators"—those its publications depicted as "the riff-raff and outcasts of Europe." Simmons maintained that already, in the cities of the North and East, ethnic lines had become class lines. The urban working class was split between skilled tradesmen from Britain, Germany and Scandinavia, whom he respected as the modern heirs of artisans, and unskilled workers from Southern and Eastern Europe, whom he detested. The new immigrants lacked the capacity to appreciate republican institutions. "Rebellion against tyrants to them," said Simmons, "means acceptance of Anarchism or Bolshevism, or at least German state Socialism." "Just as long as there is a tendency of foreign domination in any industrial section of this country," concluded Leroy Curry, "there will be war—eternal warfare." . . .

Yet, as their fears of changes in the federal government suggested, the threats Klansmen discerned came from above as well as below. "Increasing economic inequalities," Evans warned, *"threaten the very stability of society."* The Klan's involvement in the Athens anti–chain store campaign drew on a critique of economic concentration the national organization had developed over the decade. Just as Rivers charged chain stores with failure to contribute to the churches like local businesses did, so another Klan lecturer told his audience that "THE WALL ST[.] CRACKER TRUST . . . [was] encroach[ing] on your city without paying TAXES."

The allegation that trusts lacked civic commitment flowed from a more general condemnation of "materialism" or "Mammon" worship in American culture, which the Klan adapted from nineteenth-century popular protest movements. Klansmen complained that contemporary society, as Imperial Wizard Simmons put it, valued "money above manhood." This "love of money," asserted E. F. Stanton, was "the root of all evil." "Who loves Mammon, hates God." "In the strenuous rush of big business," Klan leader Edward Young Clarke mourned, "we have forgotten the spirit from which came . . . this great nation."

The order held the unbridled quest for wealth responsible for the decay of communal ethos. Klan propagandist Leroy Curry thus accused "materialism" of "poisoning the minds and shriveling the hearts" of America's young men, who looked out only for themselves now with no thought for "the advancement of the common weal." Such criticisms suggest Klansmen's nostalgia for the nineteenth-century petty-producer ideal, in which communal obligations and a sense of fair practice tempered the voracious self-seeking that private enterprise might otherwise promote. Looking back to the turn of the century from the 1930s, the wife of a local Klansmen gave voice to that yearning. "Everybody used to be neighborly," she reminisced, "helping them that couldn't help themselves. Now unless you are organized or belong to some club, nobody pays any attention to whether you're starving, half-clothed, or sick." "Times sure have changed something terrible," she concluded. In short, in the scramble for progress, society had lost its humane features.

Klansmen sought to compensate for that loss by practicing what they called "vocational Klannishness." It entailed "trading, dealing with and patronizing Klansmen in preference to all others," even if that meant sacrifice of time, money, or former friendships. At least ninety-one local Klansmen had co-workers in the order, a number in businesses owned or supervised by Klansmen. Some perhaps hoped that membership would secure their employment or promotion. Combining commitment to the order with a bid for the trade of members, many Klan employers instituted—and advertised—"100% American" employment policies: they would only hire Klan members. Others made their sympathies clear with firm names such as Kwik Kar Wash, Kountry Kitchen, or Kars, Kars, Kars. Athens Klansmen, for their part, contracted work out to chapter members, backed fellow Klansmen for appointive jobs, employed Klan members, and urged residents to boycott "alien" capital.

The Klan also gave voice to apprehension that middling folks would lose power in the emerging political order. On the local level, Klansmen often pitted themselves against the élite sponsors of municipal "reform." Klansmen saw in so-called Progressive proposals for appointed city managers and commission governments attempts to constrict popular control over the state so that it could better serve business interests. In Georgia, Klansmen in several cities butted heads with wealthy élites over such "reform" proposals. The Atlanta-based *Searchlight* denounced those in its city as "imperialistic" maneuvers for the benefit of "the big interests through their well-organized commercial clubs and autocratic Chamber of Commerce." To thwart the Columbus plan, Klansmen beat up the new city manager and bombed the mayor's home. . . .

A similar spirit of reactionary populist dissent infused the Klan's hostility to the League of Nations and the World Court. In Athens, as elsewhere in the United States, Klan chapters fought against these initiatives. Such efforts, in the view of the *Kourier,* aimed at establishing a "Super State," a "gigantic trust" that would "rule the world . . . in the interest of a few." As the self-appointed representatives of small, local business, Klansmen perceived that they would lose out if large capital in the United States cooperated with its counterparts in Europe and Japan for a less contested division of the world's spoils. Klansmen felt keenly their "inability to compete . . . with great corporations . . . who do not hold their allegiance to one flag and government." They believed the World Court and like efforts at international cooperation were plots by "the international bankers."

As had the Populists, Klansmen thus charged finance capital and its political allies with responsibility for public policies inimical to the interests of petit-bourgeois Americans. Hence a Grand Klokard (lecturer) wrote to Tom Watson in 1922 to hone his own arguments about how "the Wall St. Bankers" and Federal Reserve policy had "brought hard times upon us." Watson's protégé, Klansman and state secretary of agriculture J. J. Brown, blamed the agricultural disaster in 1920 on the Federal Reserve's refusal to ease credit for farmers. Other Klan politicians earned accolades from their fellows for continuing Watson's attacks on President Harding and his alleged Wall Street paymasters for having produced the "wrecked farmers, banks, [and] small merchants of the South and West." More generally, the Klan accused "big financiers" of "robbing the people." The damage caused by the boll weevil was said to pale compared to that inflicted by "gamblers and speculators in manipulating the market."

Klansmen inherited hatred of Wall Street from nineteenth-century petit-bourgeois radicals who located the sources of inequality not in the economic system itself, but in relations of exchange and unjust laws. The analysis they held in common maintained, as Watson put it in 1921, that "the money question . . . is the greatest of all economic questions." "In all ages," *The Searchlight*'s editor explained, "the financiers have been able to completely rule and ruin the nations." The source of the current troubles in the economy was that the United States had been "turned . . . over to the great financiers and the transportation companies." "And when the government loses control of those two things," the editor explained, "the citizens have but little to hope for."

Like the resentments against Democratic Party élites, the critique of finance capital had deep roots in the South. Farmers ensnared by crop liens, mortgages, and monopoly control of the marketing and transportation of their crops had good cause to hate financiers and trusts. The economic crisis of the 1920s helped revive this antipathy as the banks' tight-fisted credit policies exacerbated the plight of hard-pressed residents. Local Klan leaders gave voice to the resulting popular hostility. Klansman George D. Bennett, for example, campaigned in 1926 on a platform that included "better banking laws." "I feel sure," Bennett intoned, that "the people of Georgia have suffered enough from high finance and rascality in high places."

Klan leaders employed these complaints to their own ends. They made finance capital the scapegoat for a corporate order in which it was inseparable from industrial capital. Klansman E. D. Rivers thus implicitly exonerated industry when he told an Athens audience that unemployment and hard times resulted from mergers of big banking institutions. Over and over again, the Klan counterposed "the genuine Americanism of Henry Ford"—not coincidentally a virulent anti-Semite—to the alleged cupidity of John D. Rockefeller and his fellow "international money sharks."

On the rare occasions when the Klan criticized not just monopolists or financiers but capitalists as a group, the charge was usually that they were insufficiently patriotic and racist. Capital's "love of money," the Klan alleged, had led it to import people of "inferior races" to the United States. A meeting of Grand Dragons denounced opposition to immigration restriction by "the big employers of pauper labor" reliant on this "European 'riff-raff' . . . the very scum of the earth." Employers used this imported "cheap labor," according to the Klan, to lower the living standards of white, Protestant Americans. Klansmen's criticisms of large employers thus centered, not on their exploitation of workers, but their infidelity to their "race" and nation.

The communalist spirit of "vocational Klannishness" was similarly double-edged. While its advocates condemned the dominance of market values, they did so in a calculated effort to drive out Catholic, Jewish, and African-American entrepreneurs whom Klansmen otherwise had to weigh in against in an impersonal marketplace. Klansmen's criticisms of Mammon had the same quality: insubstantial at best, reactionary at worst. Like "selfishness," "materialism" was a moral failing. Combatting it required, not systemic change in the economy, but rather a spiritual awakening.

The "Mexican Problem"

DAVID MONTEJANO

In the midst of the confident and ambitious mood that accompanied the sweeping agricultural transformation of Texas and the greater Southwest lingered a somber realization—a hesitant, reluctant acknowledgment of a significant Mexican presence. The recognition was necessarily ambivalent: the rapid development of the region was dependent on Mexican labor, yet this type of labor brought with it unknown and potentially troublesome social costs. Politicians, educators, and concerned citizens warned that Mexicans were the cause of political corruption and fraud, the destruction of homogeneous rural communities, labor problems, crime, and disease, among other social problems. What was to be done with the Mexican?

There were opposing views on the question. Growers argued that the feared social costs of Mexican immigration could be regulated; small farmers and workers, on the other hand, predicted the "undoing" of America. The end result, after a decade of frequently bitter discussion, was a compromise—Mexicans were to be kept in the fields and out of industry. The proper place for Mexicans in modern Texas was that of farm laborers. . . .

The discussion of the Mexican question was not exactly new. A similar discussion, carried publicly in national magazines and major newspapers, had occurred immediately in the aftermath of annexation. The solution of the period lay in the optimistic faith that the backward Mexican race would disappear before the energetic

Anglo-Saxon. Labor economist Victor Clark, for example, referring to physicians who believed that the Mexican race had "low powers of resistance" to disease, noted in 1908 that "the impression of Americans here [Los Angeles] and in the Territories [Arizona and New Mexico] accords with the opinions given from Colorado, that the American-born Mexicans are a decadent race, yielding before the physically more vigorous immigrants from Europe and the East." The prediction never came to pass, although it was widely held among Anglo-Americans in the Southwest. The great increase in Mexican immigration, in any case, made such beliefs irrelevant. In 1910–1919, 173,663 Mexicans immigrated to the United States, compared to only 23,991 for the previous decade. In 1920–1929, the number of Mexicans crossing into the United States rose dramatically to 487,775. The Mexican presence again commanded the attention of the Anglo.

Warnings about the dire consequences of Mexican immigration appeared rather regularly in the popular and academic literature of the early twentieth century. University professors, ministers, social workers, politicians, and eugenicists warned of grave social problems; some even envisioned an ominous clash between blacks and Mexicans for "second place" in Anglo-American society. In a 1921 issue of the *Annals of the American Academy,* Congressman James Slayden of San Antonio criticized growers and businessmen for failing to look "beyond the next cotton crop or the betterment of railway lines." As Slayden put it, "large planters short of labor . . . welcome the Mexican immigrants as they would welcome fresh arrivals from the Congo, without a thought of the social and political embarrassment to their country." Substituting the Mexican for the black, moreover, was "jumping from the frying pan into the fire." What this might mean, Slayden concluded, "no one can tell. Probably our safety and peace lie in the fact that as yet so few of them, comparatively, are coming."

Slayden's assessment of the situation, however, came before the "deluge" of Mexican immigrants in the 1920s. As they kept coming, and in increasing numbers, the outcry about social decay reached near-hysterical levels. Eugenicists pointed out with alarm that Mexicans were not only intellectually inferior—they were also quite "fecund." Imaginative calculations were formulated to drive home the point. C. M. Goethe, president of the Immigration Study Commission, speaking of a Los Angeles Mexican with thirty-three children, figured that "it would take 14,641 American fathers . . . at a three-child rate, to equal the descendants of this one Mexican father four generations hence." One journalist who traveled through the midwestern and Rocky Mountain states in 1926 reported that this type of hysteria—what he called "statistical terrorism"—had gripped the region. "Nearly every street-corner nativist could prove," wrote the journalist tongue in cheek, that "the last Nordic family in the republic will have to choose between starvation and emigration to Greenland on or about October 17, 2077 A.D."

The same message was presented in the popular literature by other "experts" on the subject of Mexicans. The Reverend Robert McLean, for example, in a highly recommended "first-hand account" of life among Mexicans in the Southwest, conveyed his reservations about the "average Juan Garcia" through a colorful homily: "But this *chili con carne!!* Always it seems to give Uncle Sam the heart-burn; and the older he gets, the less he seems to be able to assimilate it. Indeed it is a question whether *chili* is not a condiment to be taken in small quantities rather than a regular article of diet." All the law and prophets, concluded the Reverend McLean, ought to hang on this dietary lesson so far as Mexican immigration was concerned. Uncle Sam simply had no stomach for Juan Garcia.

In short, the Mexican problem had nothing to do with integration or assimilation; rather, it was a question of locating another inferior race in American society. There was general agreement, in Texas and elsewhere, that Mexicans were not a legitimate citizenry of the United States. They were outside the civic order, and references to American national integrity and Texas history were often ill-disguised claims of Anglo supremacy. A comparison with the "Negro problem" seemed natural.

In Texas, where most Mexican immigrants went, the discussion about Mexicans was especially sharp and intense. As early as 1916, University of Texas Professor William Leonard had predicted that the coming of Mexicans would have disastrous effects for rural Texas. Already community life was dying "a lingering death" and whole neighborhoods were "slowly passing into decay." Leonard, a newcomer from the Midwest, described the nature of the problem as follows: "Society in the Southwest cannot easily adapt itself to the handling of a second racial problem . . . for Mexican immigrants, there is no congenial social group to welcome them. . . . They are not Negroes. . . . They are not accepted as white men, and between the two, the white and the black, there seems to be no midway position." The same position was argued by Texas sociologist Max Handman in a 1930 issue of the *American Journal of Sociology.* American society simply had no place for "partly colored races." What might result from this, Handman conceded, he was not sure— "but I know that it may mean trouble." Texas labor historian Ruth Allen, in another commentary of the period, voiced a similar concern eloquently: "When the Negro had begun to rise out of the semi-peonage of the one-crop farm and a vicious credit system, we brought across the Rio Grande horde after horde of Mexican peons even more ignorant and helpless than the Negro. One can only marvel at the temerity of a people who, faced with the gravest race question of all time, have injected into their civilization a second group, alien in background and language, and not readily assimilable." Allen ended her rather grim assessment by saying that Anglo-Saxons must face the race problem or "let the Negro and the Mexican take upon us a terrible vengeance for years of exploitation, deprivation, and oppression."

If Mexicans were a racial menace, an unassimilable alien presence, why increase their ranks by encouraging immigration? Class interests divided the Anglo population into opposed positions on the issue. . . .

There were major disagreements among Anglos on the course that economic development should take and what social costs were acceptable. Generally speaking, growers and their business allies held that Mexican labor was necessary for continued growth, and thus favored an "open border" with Mexico. The other side, composed of working farmers and urban workers, claimed that Anglo labor and small farmers could develop the area and called for a closed border and for repatriation of those Mexicans already in the Southwest. The stand of merchants and businessmen in this debate depended on the composition of their clientele. Most bankers and big businessmen saw their fortunes tied with the success of commercial farming and thus usually aligned themselves behind the growers. A minority opinion, however, apparently the view of retailers and others dependent on the local domestic trade, held that agribusiness threatened to ruin the country and that small, diversified farming should be the model to pursue. These opposed views of development provided the framework for approaching most major political and social issues, including those dealing with the Mexican presence. . . .

Through the 1920s national policy making was decidedly in favor of agribusiness interests in the Southwest. Although the restrictionist immigration acts of 1917, 1921, and 1924 had effectively barred immigration from certain sections of Europe and Asia, growers and other southwestern employers had successfully lobbied to have Mexico (under the guise of the "Western Hemisphere") exempted or excluded. The results for working farmers in Texas were disastrous. In Central Texas, tenant farming was on the point of total collapse, and tenant farmers in South and West Texas recognized that the same fate was in store for them.

Not surprisingly, many Texans were quite conscious of "a gulf between classes" on the issue of Mexican immigration. Sociologist Charles Hufford, in a 1929 survey of West Texas ranchers, farmers, and tenant farmers, provided some measure of the class-related differences. Of the forty-four ranchers and farmers interviewed, thirty-three believed their business to be favorably affected by Mexican labor and thirty-five thought Mexican labor to be satisfactory. Tenant farmers thought otherwise. Of the twenty-two surveyed, fifteen believed Mexican laborers to be an unfavorable influence, and eighteen believed them to be inefficient. In South Texas the division of opinion ran along similar lines. Anglo working farmers and wage laborers did not hesitate to place the blame for the Mexican problem on the grower: "The small farmer and laboring man wishes the Mexicans were out of the country. The big grafting man fancies them; they work cheaper." Small cotton farmers and Anglo cotton pickers were unanimously against further immigration of Mexican laborers, denied that Anglo laborers would not pick cotton, and emphasized the prevailing low wages—"Mexican wages"—of the area. Even the working farmers, however, were compelled to hire Mexicans because, as another tenant explained, they could only afford to pay Mexican wages: "A lot of white men would come down from the north and set onions, but they can't do it at Mexican prices, and we can't afford to pay more at the present prices of onions. At smaller acreages and better prices we could pay white men's wages. Nearly any working man would do any of this work if he got a white man's price. Millionaires are ruining the working man." One Anglo laborer in Nueces County expressed the common sentiment of his class when he told Taylor he wished the Mexicans could be put back in their own country. "Of course," added the laborer, "it is to the interest of the wealthy to have them here, and they run the government."

The growers, of course, disagreed. "Without the Mexican," one West Texas grower noted, "the laboring class of white people, what there is, would demand their own ages and without doing half the labor the Mexican does." Or as one Nueces County grower put the familiar argument, "We big farmers can produce cheaper than the family on 100 acres." Mexicans, in any case, were well suited to perform the task of agricultural labor. Nueces County cotton growers were lavish in their praise of the Mexican's qualities as field labor: "You can't beat them as labor." "I prefer Mexican labor to other classes of labor. It is more humble and you get more for your money." "The Mexicans have a sense of duty and loyalty, and the qualities that go to make a good servant." "They are the best labor we have." "No other class we could bring to Texas could take his place. He's a natural farm laborer."

The position of businessmen on the question of Mexican immigration depended on whether they were tied in some way with agribusiness or were "independent." Those merchants with grower connections understood that a low-wage,
mobile labor force was necessary to continue farm development in the region and
thus supported unrestricted immigration. When confronted with the negative consequences of unrestricted immigration, such as the presence of large, conspicuous
Mexican settlements, these progrower merchants were quick to defend the Mexicans and to point out their positive qualities. Much like the growers who praised the
Mexicans for their qualities as laborers, merchants were likely to comment on the
positive qualities of Mexican buying habits. One merchant in South Texas, for example, explained to Taylor why he preferred Mexican immigration over that of European stock: "Let me tell you that the Mexicans buy out of the stores of South
Texas more John B. Stetson hats than the whites; they don't think anything of paying $16 for a hat. I don't want the damn Sicilians to come in."

In contrast, most independent retailers sensitive to the buying habits and spending power of their Mexican clientele were well aware that farm development placed
critical limits on the growth of a domestic market. It was not difficult to see, when
Mexicans constituted a significant portion of the retail trade, that unrestricted immigration had serious consequences for the store. Thus, independent retailers generally opposed continued Mexican immigration, advocated the diversification of the
farm economy, and even proposed the paying of higher wages to the present work
force. A controversial statement circulated by the Laredo Chamber of Commerce
spoke to the point: "We have got about as far as we can with cheap labor. . . . Our
merchants have no trading territory. Labor with $1.25 wages can't buy." After char-
acterizing South Texas farmers as "onion speculators" who live in hotels, the statement went on to call for an alternative to big agribusiness: "What we need is more
white farmers and more capital, and we can't go ahead until we get them. We don't
need more cheap labor. We should not drive out our own labor in the North to provide ourselves with cheap labor here." The Laredo chamber was somewhat of a
"maverick" business organization in South Texas, a characteristic that can be attributed, in part, to the powerful position of merchants in that border city. In border
counties with no major trading center, however, only the Anglo merchants serving
the Mexican trade, Anglos who were already marginal in any case, would openly
espouse the Laredo position. In areas where growers had both the money and the
power, most businessmen supported the dominant line. Thus, the Laredo statement
was quickly repudiated by other South Texas businessmen. The president of the Del
Rio Chamber of Commerce said that the Laredo chamber president did not understand the situation in the farm counties because he was an oil man who used high-
priced labor and not "this cheap labor." Thus, concluded the Del Rio businessman,
"he does not represent us." To stress the point, the Del Rioan added that the secretary of the Laredo chamber, the apparent author of the statement, was married to a
Mexican woman.

As the 1920s wore on, the line between the opposing sides was drawn fairly
clearly. Restrictionists counted small farmers, progressives, labor unionists, and eugenicists among their ranks; the antirestrictionists, meanwhile, were spearheaded
by large-scale growers, railroad executives, and businessmen. The conflicting eco-

nomic interests of the two sides were quite evident, but the immigration question also raised the question of "national integrity" so far as race was concerned. . . .

What gave the national and regional discussion of Mexican immigration its highly charged, controversial character stemmed from the social and political implications involved. European and Asian immigration had been barred in large part for such nationalist reasons, and the same reasoning dictated that Mexican immigration be stopped.

Those opposed to Mexican immigration repeatedly emphasized, with great effect, the moral and political dangers presented by Mexicans. In the 1920 congressional debates over immigration policy, Representative John C. Box from East Texas, then still a stronghold for small Anglo farmers, warned the House about the perils of "deAmericanization" and of a "hyphenated citizenship," as well as the dangers of political unrest, for the people who were coming from Mexico and Europe "have not been trained in the schools of order but have stewed in disorder." Importing this type of labor, moreover, would change the "relationship and spirit of American industrial life . . . to the undoing of America." "We want no peasant or peon or coolie class nor caste system," added Box, "dividing us into an upper and lower world."

Those who defended the policy of unrestricted Mexican immigration, the antirestrictionists, understood well the talk about the social ills presented by the Mexican race. When it came to assessing the Mexican, in fact, Texas growers outdid the Anglo nativists supporting the Box Bill. The president of the Ysleta Farm Bureau in West Texas, for example, was curt but straightforward when asked for his opinion of Mexicans: "The Chilis are creatures somewhere in between a burro and a human being." But, added the agribusinessman, "We would hate to lose this junk we've got now." The Ysleta bureau accordingly had passed a resolution against the Box Bill. Growers throughout Texas generally found themselves in the same dilemma—not found of Mexicans but heavily dependent on them for labor. "More Mexicans are not best for the country," one Nueces cotton grower told Taylor; "it isn't good for the country because we expect to live here." Paul Taylor, sensing the irony of the grower's position, asked why he wanted unrestricted immigration if he did not want to associate with Mexicans. Because, answered the grower, "We can never get the whites to live and work as we have it here. The whites who would work on halves would not be any good. You could not handle them as easily." One Dimmit County resident, nonplussed by Taylor's probing questions, failed to see any contradiction in his position: "We don't want them to be associated with us, we want them for labor. I don't know how we would get along without Mexican labor." Another Dimmit County resident said that they "would be blowed up" if Mexicans were stopped from coming, and that they could keep things under control; but still he was worried: "They don't vote, but they increase like rats. If something is not done we will soon be shoved out of the picture. There ought to be a law passed that every (white) married couple should have so many children and if they don't, they ought to find out why."

Such considerations had moved a few growers to support restrictionist legislation and to encourage diversification, but economic interests generally outweighed social principles. One farmer summed up the situation nicely. His principles, as he explained to Taylor, ruled out Mexican immigration because Mexicans "haven't the mentality" of Anglos and "are an inferior race." But principles are one thing and interests another, noted the farmer: "My principles rule my selfishness, but I am kind of weak on that. We need them and they need us."

The antirestrictionists, then, were quite mindful of the possible social consequences of continued Mexican immigration. As a rule, however, they felt confident that they could control the situation—and in a manner that would satisfy both social principles and economic needs. Agribusinessmen, after all, only wanted laborers, not neighbors or fellow citizens. To those who warned of dire consequences, the progrower politicians presented the familiar argument that strict measures could be taken to guarantee that Mexican agricultural laborers would not "wander off" into other work or stay beyond the term of the harvest. In one memorable exchange before a congressional committee in 1926, for example, restrictionist Robert L. Bacon of New York pointed out to the progrower witness from Corpus Christi, S. Matson Nixon, that nearly half his district was Mexican and that a high proportion of these were voters. The New York congressman then asked Mr. Nixon for his opinion of that type of situation. Nixon handled the delicate question rather well:

> Mr. Nixon: I think that they [the Mexicans] offer excellent material for American citizenship. . . . I believe I can truthfully say that American civilization and American ideals are as high in Texas as any state in the United States.
> Mr. Bacon: That is what I am in favor of. I am in favor of keeping Texas white.
> Mr. Nixon: That is all right. But I think Texans who are thoroughly familiar with Mexican influence feel satisfied that they are fully capable of maintaining their superiority over the Mexican.

There was no contradiction in having Mexican American citizens and in safeguarding the Anglo-Saxon character of Texas and the United States. One distinguished professional man from Corpus Christi explained to Taylor how the two were reconcilable: "If the Mexicans came in and demanded social equality the case would be entirely different. But the Mexicans have sense, and innate courtesy, and they don't demand social equality like the Negro. There never will be any race question with the Mexicans." A cotton grower from the same county appraised the Mexicans in similar terms: "They are docile and law-abiding. They are the sweetest people in this position that I ever saw." Unlike the alarmist nativists, then, growers and their allies were not overly worried about any Mexican menace. Their modest proposals, which were essential for the continued development of the region, would not jeopardize Anglo-American society. . . .

By 1930 the decay that so many had predicted had progressed beyond hope, and the social commentaries about the Mexican in Texas were no longer warnings but eulogies and resigned statements of fact. Writing in 1930 University of Texas Professor Robert Montgomery described the changes in rural life as "a sad chapter in the history of the state." Speaking of a typical Central Texas town, fictitiously named Keglar Hill, Montgomery portrayed its fate after the coming of Mexicans as follows: "Keglar Hill, as a way of life, was one with Carthage and Thebes. The Nordic-American tenants, who for twenty years had tilled the farms, . . . had educated their children in school and church, and had contributed fairly to the building of a healthy and pleasant community, were uprooted utterly." Through the early twentieth century, this story of Keglar Hill, a story about the displacement of Anglo tenant farmers by Mexican sharecroppers and laborers, repeated itself throughout Central, West, and South Texas. Anglo tenant farmers and laborers, of course, understood what was happening. With the matter of land tenure completely in the hands of the landlord, it was only a question of time before the switch to the "cheaper" Mexicans came. One West Texas tenant summed up the situation in 1928 as follows: "Mexican labor forces our farm boys to the cities. Mexicans take their work at a rate lower than American boys can live at. A few more years will give it all over to the Mexicans."

Away from the fields, the situation of the Anglo nonfarm worker was not much different. The position of most Anglo workers, if one judges from the statements and actions of organized labor, was completely unsympathetic to Mexicans. Not only were more Mexicans coming every year, reported one worried labor official to the AFL [American Federation of Labor] Executive Council in 1919, but they also were now moving out of agriculture and accepting employment in "different lines of efforts" to the detriment of labor standards and the best interests of the country. In Texas, the state chapter of the AFL refused to recognize the existence of a wage-earning class in agriculture, and its various affiliates made it clear that they would not work alongside Mexicans and that they opposed the hiring of unskilled Mexican workers. Texas oil workers, many of them ex-cowboys and ex-tenants, were likewise quite upset about the "immigrant increase" in the industry. At the convention of the International Oil Workers in 1920, the oil unions passed a resolution asking for "an investigation of the situation, the sending back to Mexico of immigrants illegally in the United States, and return to agricultural work of those remaining." In some oil fields, the tense situation exploded into riots against Mexicans. In 1921, oil workers in the Ranger and Island Oil fields in Mexia (North Central Texas) clubbed and threatened Mexican workers and their families with death unless they left within twelve hours. Governor Pat Neff imposed martial law in Mexia and sent eighty state troopers to end the brutalities. The Rangers arrived too late, however, to save several women and children from dying of exposure. This was no isolated incident; similar episodes occurred in mines and manufacturing plants through the 1940s.

The overwhelming sentiment among nonfarm workers, organized and unorganized, was for the expulsion or regulation of Mexican workers. Already by the early 1920s, many unions in the Southwest had formulated "gentlemen's agreements" to blackball all Mexican workers. Texas unions handled Mexican workers in much the same way that they dealt with blacks: through outright exclusion, through segregated locals, and through racial quotas in employment. As the decade wore on, these exclusionary proposals became more strident as organized labor joined eugenicist associations in decrying the "alien" danger that Mexicans posed for the nation. The political direction provided by the American labor movement pointed clearly toward maintaining skilled work as a preserve for Anglo workers. Especially in Texas, Anglo workers saw the "color bar" as an important concession to be won from employers.

And so on went the regional and national debates on Mexican immigration through the 1920s. The progrower interests, with their considerable influence in Congress, were able to defeat the restrictionist efforts repeatedly. By the end of the decade, however, the restrictionists had built a strong national movement and had found an unexpected ally in President Herbert Hoover. In 1928 executive orders to enforce existing immigration law effectively closed the border, and the president and Congress appeared stalemated, at least momentarily, on the Mexican issue.

It was perhaps fitting that a compromise solution to this stalemate should come from Texas in the form of a proposal to "restrain" the movement of its Mexican workers to state boundaries. This proposal, embodied in the Emigrant Labor Agency Laws of 1929, received the endorsement of both the AFL and the chambers of commerce of the state. Such significant consensus was not difficult to understand; the labor agency laws represented the first step to deal with the mutual inter ests of Anglo workers and growers. Organized labor in the state was ready to concede agriculture to Mexicans—an already accomplished fact by this time—if it could work out some arrangement that would protect the status of nonfarm workers. Texas growers, for their part, found themselves competing with major out-of-state interests for Mexican labor and were amenable to a plan that would keep Mexicans in the fields and out of industry.

For the farm counties, the end result was that agricultural labor became defined as "Mexican work." One Dimmit County resident put the matter clearly: "Onion transplanting is distinctly the work of Mexicans. There are quite a few whites who would do it and who need the work, but they are too proud to do it because it classes them as onion setters." A ranch manager in the same county agreed and provided an example: "The Americans can usually get something better, for example, filling station work. My brother took $1 a day there rather than $1.50 from my father on the farm." A Nueces County farmer remarked similarly that "when some whites see Mexicans doing farm work, they don't want to do it." And in West Texas, according to one tenant farmer, tenants opposed Mexican labor "because you have to work with them." Other reports from farmers and workers throughout the state repeatedly point to the sensitivity of Anglos to these matters of race and class.

S U G G E S T E D   R E A D I N G

Acuna, Rodolfo. *Occupied America: A History of Chicanos* (1981).

Balderrama, Francisco E. *Decade of Betrayal: Mexican Repatriation in the 1930s* (1995)

Blee, Kathleen M. *Women of the Klan: Racism and Gender in the 1920s* (1991).

Camarillo, Al. *Chicanos in a Changing Society* (1979).

Chan, Sucheng, ed. *Entry Denied: Exclusion and the Chinese Community in America* (1991).

Cohen, Lizabeth. *Making a New Deal: Industrial Workers in Chicago, 1919–1939* (1990).

Daniels, Roger. *Asian America: Chinese and Japanese in the United States* (1988).

Deutsch, Sarah. *No Separate Refuge: Culture, Class, and Gender on an Anglo-Hispanic Frontier in the American Southwest, 1880–1940* (1987).

Forrest, Suzanne. *The Preservation of the Village: New Mexico's Hispanics and the New Deal* (1989).

Gerstle, Gary. *Working-Class Americanism: The Politics of Labor in a Textile City, 1914–1960* (1989).

Goodman, James E. *Stories of Scottsboro* (1994).

Harris, William. *The Harder We Run: Black Workers Since the Civil War* (1982).

Harrison, Alferdteen, ed. *Black Exodus: The Great Migration from the American South* (1991).

Hauptman, Laurence. *The Iroquois and the New Deal* (1981).

Higham, John. *Strangers in the Land: Patterns of American Nativism, 1860–1925* (1955).

Kelley, Robin. *Hammer and Hoe: Alabama Communists During the Great Depression* (1990).

Kersey, Harry. *The Florida Seminoles and the New Deal, 1933–1942* (1989).

Kirby, John B. *Black Americans in the Roosevelt Era* (1980).

Kwong, Peter. *Chinatown, N.Y.: Labor and Politics* (1979).

Lay, Shawn, ed. *The Invisible Empire in the West* (1992).

Lewis, Earl. *In Their Own Interests: Race, Class, and Power in Twentieth-Century Norfolk, Virginia* (1991).

Lewis, Earl, and Joe Trotter, eds. *African Americans in the Industrial Age* (1996).

MacLean, Nancy. *Behind the Mask of Chivalry: The Making of the Second Ku Klux Klan* (1994).

Marks, Carole. *Farewell—We're Good and Gone: The Great Black Migration* (1989).

Montejano, David. *Anglos and Mexicans in the Making of Texas, 1836–1986* (1987).

Moore, Leonard. *Citizen Klansmen: The Ku Klux Klan in Indiana, 1921–1928* (1991).

Parman, Donald L. *The Navajos and the New Deal* (1976).

Reisler, Mark. *By the Sweat of Their Brow: Mexican Immigrant Labor in the United States* (1976).

Romo, Ricardo. *East Los Angeles: History of a Barrio* (1983).

Ruiz, Vicki. *Cannery Women, Cannery Lives* (1987).

Sanchez, George J. *Becoming Mexican American: Ethnicity, Culture, and Identity in Chicano Los Angeles, 1900–1945* (1993).

Sitkoff, Harvard. *A New Deal for Blacks* (1978).

Stein, Judith. *The World of Marcus Garvey* (1986).

Takaki, Ronald T. *Strangers from a Different Shore: A History of Asian-Americans* (1989).

———. *A Different Mirror: A History of Multicultural America* (1993).

Taylor, Graham D. *The New Deal and American Indian Tribalism* (1980).

Trotter, Joe. *Black Milwaukee: The Making of an Industrial Proletariat, 1915–1945* (1985).

Trotter, Joe, ed. *The Great Migration in Historical Perspective* (1991).

Tsai, Henry Shih-shan. *The Chinese Experience in America* (1986).

Tuttle, William. *Race Riot: Chicago in the Red Summer of 1919* (1971).

Weiss, Nancy. *Farewell to the Party of Lincoln: Black Politics in the Age of FDR* (1983).

Responding to the Crash

The Great Depression defies easy description. From the market crash of late 1929 to the trough of the Depression in 1932, the lives and livelihoods of millions of Americans fell apart. Between 1929 and 1932, national income fell 40 percent, wages fell over 60 percent, and real weekly earnings—despite deflation and falling consumer prices—dropped from twenty-five dollars to barely twenty dollars. Facing slipping demand, companies cut wages or laid off workers. Because this happened virtually everywhere, workers had few alternatives and often accepted huge wage cuts in exchange for continued work. By 1933 the unemployment rate had risen from a pre-Depression low of 3 percent to almost 25 percent. An average of one hundred thousand workers lost their jobs every week between 1929 and 1932. In heavy-industry centers, unemployment reached dizzying heights: 50 percent in Cleveland, 60 percent in Akron, 80 percent in Toledo. In large cities, sheer numbers overwhelmed relief agencies: six hundred sixty thousand in Chicago, over one million in New York.

The causes of the Depression remain a matter of some controversy. According to their political leanings, economists and historians have argued the merits of a range of economic and political explanations, some focusing on the events of 1929–1930, some focusing on the deeper dilemmas of the interwar economy (the persistence of cutthroat competition, the problem of underconsumption, and the tenuous structure of the international economy). For their part, contemporaries also struggled to understand what had happened to the boom of the 1920s, what the economic crisis meant for the future of American democratic capitalism, and what the federal government should (or should not) do to bring about recovery. Two elements of politics of the early 1930s stand out: the political and intellectual caution of leading politicians and business interests on the one hand and the growing uncertainty and expectations of ordinary Americans on the other. Indeed, over the next decade, the tension between conventional politics and popular demands would reshape American political culture and political economy.

The immediate political response was shaped by prevailing political and economic understanding of economic depression, and by ideological and legal limits on federal responsibility. Business interests responded to the Depression by cynically blaming it on others, optimistically pretending that misery and deprivation constituted a minor "correction" or claiming that recovery was just around the corner. Business urged anyone with cash left to "buy now" and revive the economy. For their part, President Hoover and his advisers accepted the common view that such crises were self-correcting, even a means of "cleansing the economy" of inflated stock values and inefficiency. And they largely accepted (and believed in) constitutional restrictions on a direct federal role in economic regulation or the provision of relief. In all, however, few historians still hold to the sharp contrast between a "do-nothing" Hoover Administration and the innovations of the New Deal. The Hoover Administration launched a number of experiments that would be adapted by the New Deal after 1932. And the Roosevelt Administration, at least initially, echoed the basic political and economic premises (especially regarding federal intervention and spending) of its Republican predecessor. In the end, it was the persistence of the Depression and the urgency of popular demands, rather than the election of 1932, that turned the tide of reform.

Ordinary Americans responded (and demanded that their government respond) much more urgently to the economic crisis. There was no provision for mass unemployment by companies, cities, states, or the federal government. Immediately, relief fell to private (mostly religious) agencies that were equipped to deal with sporadic unemployment and a few hard-luck cases but were scarcely prepared to care for half or two-thirds of the population of a large city. As charities faltered, relief fell to local governments, but these too were unprepared to administer or raise the money necessary for even minimal levels of relief, and they actually began suspending relief as the Depression persisted. In response, a variety of citizen, consumer, worker, and farmer organizations emerged to provide immediate support for their members and to press all levels of government to address the suffering of the Depression. Such efforts included the proliferation of Unemployed Councils (particularly active on tenant and employment rights) in urban settings, the famous Bonus Army March of World War I veterans on Washington, rural opposition (typified by the short-lived Farmer's Holiday Association) to tumbling farm prices and foreclosures, and the first organizational stirrings of the industrial and agricultural unions that would emerge in the mid-1930s.

☞ D O C U M E N T S

These documents capture the range of popular and political response to the early Depression. In Document 1, President Hoover offers a version of his monotonous plea for calm and caution, and warns against the dangers of federal intervention. Document 2 captures the tentative optimism of much of the business community, which was reluctant to admit either that its system had failed or that political solutions were called for. In Document 3, Henry Ford extends this logic to the problem of unemployment. Documents 4 and 5 recall the political urgency of Depression-era protest: the first recalls the 1932 Ford Hunger March; the second recalls the 1932 Bonus Army March. In Document 6, a group of leading retailers concludes (not surprisingly) that the key to recovery lies in increased consumer spending.

1. Herbert Hoover Reassures the Nation, 1931

The Federal Government has assumed many new responsibilities since Lincoln's time, and will probably assume more in the future when the states and local communities can not alone cure abuse or bear the entire cost of national programs, but

From Herbert Hoover, "Radio Address on Lincoln's Birthday" (February 12, 1931), in *The State Papers and Other Public Writings of Herbert Hoover,* collected and edited by William Starr Myers (Garden City, N.Y.: Doubleday, 1934), Vol. 1, 503–505.

there is an essential principle that should be maintained in these matters. I am convinced that where Federal action is essential then in most cases it should limit its responsibilities to supplement the states and local communities, and that it should not assume the major role or the entire responsibility, in replacement of the states or local government. To do otherwise threatens the whole foundations of local government, which is the very basis of self-government.

The moment responsibilities of any community, particularly in economic and social questions, are shifted from any part of the Nation to Washington, then that community has subjected itself to a remote bureaucracy with its minimum of understanding and of sympathy. It has lost a large part of its voice and its control of its own destiny. Under Federal control the varied conditions of life in our country are forced into standard molds, with all their limitations upon life, either of the individual or the community. Where people divest themselves of local government responsibilities they at once lay the foundation for the destruction of their liberties.

And buried in this problem lies something even deeper. The whole of our governmental machinery was devised for the purpose that through ordered liberty we give incentive and equality of opportunity to every individual to rise to that highest achievement of which he is capable. At once when government is centralized there arises a limitation upon the liberty of the individual and a restriction of individual opportunity. The true growth of the Nation is the growth of character in its citizens. The spread of government destroys initiative and thus destroys character. Character is made in the community as well as in the individual by assuming responsibilities, not by escape from them. Carried to its logical extreme, all this shouldering of individual and community responsibility upon the Government can lead but to the superstate where every man becomes the servant of the State and real liberty is lost. Such was not the government that Lincoln sought to build.

There is an entirely different avenue by which we may both resist this drift to centralized government and at the same time meet a multitude of problems. That is to strengthen in the Nation a sense and an organization of self-help and cooperation to solve as many problems as possible outside of government. We are today passing through a critical test in such a problem arising from the economic depression.

Due to lack of caution in business and to the impact of forces from an outside world, one-half of which is involved in social and political revolution, the march of our prosperity has been retarded. We are projected into temporary unemployment, losses, and hardships. In a Nation rich in resources, many people were faced with hunger and cold through no fault of their own. Our national resources are not only material supplies and material wealth but a spiritual and moral wealth in kindliness, in compassion, in a sense of obligation of neighbor to neighbor and a realization of responsibility by industry, by business, and the community for its social security and its social welfare.

The evidence of our ability to solve great problems outside of Government action and the degree of moral strength with which we emerge from this period will be determined by whether the individuals and the local communities continue to meet their responsibilities.

Throughout this depression I have insisted upon organization of these forces through industry, through local government and through charity, that they should meet this crisis by their own initiative, by the assumption of their own responsibilities. The Federal Government has sought to do its part by example in the expansion of employment, by affording credit to drought sufferers for rehabilitation, and by cooperation with the community, and thus to avoid the opiates of Government charity and the stifling of our national spirit of mutual self-help.

We can take courage and pride in the effective work of thousands of voluntary organizations for provision of employment, for relief of distress, that have sprung up over the entire Nation. Industry and business have recognized a social obligation to their employees as never before. The State and local governments are being helpful. The people are themselves succeeding in this task. Never before in a great depression has there been so systematic a protection against distress; never before has there been so little social disorder; never before has there been such an outpouring of the spirit of self-sacrifice and of service. . . .

We are going through a period when character and courage are on trial, and where the very faith that is within us is under test. Our people are meeting this test. And they are doing more than the immediate task of the day. They are maintaining the ideals of our American system. By their devotion to these ideals we shall come out of these times stronger in character, in courage, and in faith.

2. A Business Leader Responds (Hopefully) to the Crash, 1929

The recent collapse of stock market prices has no significance as regards the real wealth of the American people as a whole. It has had unfortunate effects in shifting the rights of ownership from some hands to others. But the basic economic concept relating to the welfare of the community is income, not capital. And of itself the stock market deflation has no direct connection with the current income from industrial production. There have been real losses for some individuals. There have been real gains for others. There have been paper losses for still others, and by far the greater part of the calculated reduction in security values have been of this character. Those who owned stocks outright and did not sell them are still entitled to the same income to which they would have been entitled if deflation had not occurred. Their current purchasing power will be in no way affected by the reduction in the capital value of their securities. The individuals who have suffered real losses, on the other hand, are those who had extended their claims to income by acquisition of securities beyond the limits of their own capital. By borrowing, they had purchased capital value with the funds of others, and with the shrinkage of these capital values their own margin of ownership has been completely wiped out. . . . Last week's disturbance in the market may well be characterized as a "margin speculator's panic"; a rectification of fictitious values and unrealizable paper profits. In essence, it has no relation to what has happened, or is happening in business. On the very day that stocks declined most, I noticed, the United Steel Corporation declared an extra dividend and the American Can Company increased its dividend rate. According to the newspapers, stocks lost billions in value, yet at the same time the income from two

---

Excerpted from "Suggested Telegram to Magnus Alexander" dated October 31, 1929, Series 6, Box 1, Records of The National Industrial Conference Board. Reprinted by permission.

such leading industrial stocks, which is the measure of their present real value to investors, actually increased. It is highly significant, furthermore, that the financial and credit situation in the United States is unusually sound at the present time. Stock speculation during the past few years has been stimulated by the very fact that bank credit has been easy, there being ample money at low rates available. The very fact that the Federal Reserve system at the present time has a higher reserve ratio than at any time since the war indicates the fundamental soundness of the financial situation, as well as emphasizes the fact that the stock market collapse was due to mob-psychology, the same as the previous unprecedented rise in security prices was due to speculative fever which fed on easy money and the prospects of making money easily. The United States has prospered because of its increasing efficiency and productivity. There is therefore no reason whatever for American businessmen to let stock market upsets influence them in their business policies. Adam Smith's famous definition, that the wealth of nations consists not of the unconsumable riches of money but of the consumable goods annually produced by society, still holds true, and the stock market cannot make it any less true. Productivity alone creates purchasing power, a lesson well ingrained in American business philosophy by experience during the past decade. It is now up to American businessmen not to allow a stock quotation flurry to becloud their vision. It is true that stock speculation in earlier years often was able to stimulate or depress business. Business men pyschologically then were more easily influenced; the stock market, indeed, was considered a reliable index of future business conditions. Business today has better indices. . . . On the basis of such authentic, reliable and prompt information as is available to modern businessmen through their trade associations, the government and through such organizations as the National Industrial Conference Board and Chambers of Commerce, American industry and trade may well proceed on their course to satisfy the normal wants of the population of the United States and of foreign countries. Paper profits and paper losses in stocks will not change people's total demand for either necessities or luxuries to any considerable extent; and as far as actual stock transactions are concerned, at whatever prices, they can only result in transfers of money from one to another, not in any diminution of the total resources of wealth. Future business prosperity therefore will continue to rest, as it has in the past, on our industrial productivity and well-informed business leadership.

3. Henry Ford on Unemployment and Self-Help, 1932

I have always had to work, whether any one hired me or not. For the first forty years of my life, I was an employe. When not employed by others, I employed myself. I found very early that being out of hire was not necessarily being out of work. The first means that your employer has not found something for you to do; the second means that you are waiting until he does.

From *Literary Digest,* June 18, 1932. Reprinted courtesy of Ford Motor Company.

We nowadays think of work as something that others find for us to do, call us to do, and pay us to do. No doubt our industrial growth is largely responsible for that. We have accustomed men to think of work that way. . . .

But something entirely outside the workshops of the nation has affected this hired employment very seriously. The word "unemployment" has become one of the most dreadful words in the language. The condition itself has become the concern of every person in the country. . . .

I do not believe in routine charity. I think it a shameful thing that any man should have to stoop to take it, or give it. I do not include human helpfulness under the name of charity. My quarrel with charity is that it is neither helpful nor human. The charity of our cities is the most barbarous thing in our system, with the possible exception of our prisons. What we call charity is a modern substitute for being personally kind, personally concerned and personally involved in the work of helping others in difficulty. True charity is a much more costly effort than money-giving. Our donations too often purchase exemption from giving the only form of help that will drive the need for charity out of the land. . . .

In the last analysis independence means self-dependence. Dependence on some one else for employment in busy times may too easily become dependence on some one else for support in slack times.

If it is right and proper to help people to become wise managers of their own affairs in good times, it cannot be wrong to pursue the same object in dull times. Independence through self-dependence is a method which must commend itself when understood.

Methods of self-help are numerous and great numbers of people have made the stimulating discovery that they need not depend on employers to find work for them—they can find work for themselves. I have more definitely in mind those who have not yet made that discovery, and I should like to express certain convictions I have tested.

The land! That is where our roots are. There is the basis of our physical life. The farther we get away from the land, the greater our insecurity. From the land comes everything that supports life, everything we use for the service of physical life. The land has not collapsed or shrunk in either extent or productivity. It is there waiting to honor all the labor we are willing to invest in it, and able to tide us across any dislocation of economic conditions.

No unemployment insurance can be compared to an alliance between a man and a plot of land. With one foot in industry and another foot in the land, human society is firmly balanced against most economic uncertainties. With a job to supply him with cash, and a plot of land to guarantee him support, the individual is doubly secure. Stocks may fall, but seedtime and harvest do not fail.

I am not speaking of stop-gaps or temporary expedients. Let every man and every family at this season of the year cultivate a plot of land and raise a sufficient supply for themselves or others. Every city and village has vacant space whose use would be permitted. Groups of men could rent farms for small sums and operate them on the co-operative plan. Employed men, in groups of ten, twenty or fifty, could rent farms and operate them with several unemployed families. Or, they could engage a farmer with his farm to be their farmer this year, either as employe or on shares. There are farmers who would be glad to give a decent indigent family a corner of a field on which to live and provide against next winter. Industrial concerns everywhere would gladly make it possible for their men, employed and unemployed, to find and work the land. Public-spirited citizens and institutions would most willingly assist in these efforts at self-help.

I do not urge this solely or primarily on the ground of need. It is a definite step to the restoration of normal business activity. Families who adopt self-help have that amount of free money to use in the channels of trade. That in turn means a flow of goods, an increase in employment, a general benefit.

4. A Participant Recalls the Ford Hunger March of 1932

The marchers proceeded across the Baby Creek Bridge and gathered at the corner of Fort Street and Miller Road in a dense throng around a waiting truck. They were still in Detroit. One of the marchers, Detroit Communist leader Albert Goetz, swung up on the truck and began to speak.

He restated the purpose of the march: to have a committee present their demands to the Ford Motor Company. He called on the workers to form an orderly and disciplined march. "We don't want any violence," he said sharply. "Remember, all we are going to do is to walk to the Ford employment office. No trouble. No fighting. Stay in line. Be orderly."

Goetz paused a moment. The crowd was silent. "I understand," he continued, "that the Dearborn police are planning to stop us. Well, we will try to get through somehow. But remember, no trouble."

A tremendous cheer greeted his remarks and the march began.

Eight abreast, singing and cheering, the marchers proceeded toward the Dearborn city limits, where about fifty Dearborn and Ford police in uniform were lined up across the road. The workers went forward.

An officer yelled, "Who are your leaders?"

"We are all leaders," the marchers shouted back.

"Stop or we'll shoot," threatened the cops, and immediately they fired large amounts of tear gas into the ranks of the workers.

The marchers hesitated. Blinded and choked by the gas, they retreated. Some ran up a railroad trestle on one side of the road. The officers now came forward and with their night sticks attacked others as they were standing, some alone, some in small groups.

The workers fought back. A group rescued one marcher from an officer on the trestle. One of the officers shot at the workers as they ran from the trestle.

By this time, the workers had scattered over a field covered with stones alongside the road. Desperate to fight back, they began throwing the stones at the oncoming police.

The officers continued to fire tear gas, but the swirling wind carried most of it away. The workers, filling the air with a hail of stones, pushed the police back, and when the tear gas gave out, the police turned and ran.

Reprinted with permission of the Meildejohn Civil Liberties Institute from *The Ford Hunger March* by Maurice Sugar, 1891–1974. Copyright © 1980, pp. 34–36.

For almost a half-mile the marchers continued down the highway toward the plant, the police retreating before them. Then they reached the first street intersection, where they were confronted with two fire engines equipped with ladders and hoses. The firemen were frantically attempting to make the hose connections. Before they had succeeded, the workers reached them, whereupon they joined the police in retreat. This retreat was continued for another half-mile, until the employment gate—Gate 3 of the plant—was reached.

At this point the fire department units made their water connections. About thirty feet above the road and extending across it, was a bridge used for the passage of workmen into the factory without interference by traffic. Stationed on the road below the bridge were a large number of police officers. From the top of the bridge the firemen poured powerful streams of icy water on the workers below. From the bridge and from the road below came a steady rain of tear gas bombs. According to the marchers, it was at this bridge that the Dearborn police were joined by a large number of Ford Motor Company private police, by a strong force of officers from the Detroit Police Department, and by the state police.

A regular siege developed. The workers, now grimy with sweat and dust, their eyes red from gas fumes, kept up a regular barrage with the stones they had carried from the field.

The police drew their pistols. Suddenly they began shooting into the crowd. It was here that nineteen-year-old Joe York was shot and killed, then Coleman Leny and Joe DeBlasio.

The police were shooting left and right. Besides the three fatalities, there were twenty-two workers known wounded by gunshot. Perhaps fifty more were hit, escaping to their homes or places of hiding for medical attention.

In the face of the downpour of icy water and the rain of bullets, almost all of the marchers withdrew. It was then that the leaders of the union and the Unemployed Council decided to call off the demonstration. A speaker mounted the back of a car and said that the tear gassing, clubbing, and shooting were "Ford's bloody answer to the demands of the employed and unemployed Ford workers."

He took a vote to start the return march in close formation. It passed.

5. A Participant Recalls the Bonus Army March of 1932

The soldiers were walking the streets, the fellas who had fought for democracy in Germany. They thought they should get the bonus right then and there because they needed the money. A fella by the name of Waters, I think, got up the idea of these ex-soldiers would go to Washington, make the kind of trip the hoboes made with Coxey in 1898, they would be able to get the government to come through. . . .

When we got to Washington, there was quite a few ex-servicemen there before us. There was no arrangements for housing. Most of the men that had wives and children were living in Hooverville. This was across the Potomac River—what was known as Anacostia Flats. They had set up housing there, made of cardboard and of all kinds. I don't know how they managed to get their food. Most other contingents was along Pennsylvania Avenue.

They were tearing down a lot of buildings along that street, where they were going to do some renewal, build some federal buildings. A lot of ex-servicemen just sort of turned them into barracks. They just sorta bunked there. Garages that were vacant, they took over. Had no respect for private property. They didn't even ask permission of the owners. They didn't even know who the hell the owners was.

They had come to petition Hoover, to give them the bonus before it was due. And Hoover refused this. He told them they couldn't get it because it would make the country go broke. They would hold midnight vigils around the White House and march around the White House in shifts.

The question was now: How were they going to get them out of Washington? They were ordered out four or five times, and they refused. The police chief was called to send them out, but he refused. I also heard that the marine commander, who was called to bring out the marines, also refused. Finally, the one they did get to shove these bedraggled ex-servicemen out of Washington was none other than the great MacArthur.

The picture I'll always remember . . . here is MacArthur coming down Pennsylvania Avenue. And, believe me, ladies and gentlemen, he came on a white horse. He was riding a white horse. Behind him were tanks, troops of the regular army.

This was really a riot that wasn't a riot, in a way. When these ex-soldiers wouldn't move, they'd poke them with their bayonets, and hit them on the head with the butt of a rifle. First, they had a hell of a time getting them out of the buildings they were in. Like a sit-in.

They managed to get them out. A big colored soldier, about six feet tall, had a big American flag he was carrying. He was one of the bonus marchers. He turned to one of the soldiers who was pushing him along, saying: "Get along there, you big black bastard." That was it. He turned and said, "Don't try to push me. I fought for this flag. I fought for this flag in France and I'm gonna fight for it here on Pennsylvania Avenue." The soldier hit him on the side of the legs with the bayonet. I think he was injured. But I don't know if he was sent to the hospital.

This was the beginning of a riot, in a way. These soldiers were pushing these people. They didn't want to move, but they were pushing them anyway.

As night fell, they crossed the Potomac. They were given orders to get out of Anacostia Flats, and they refused. The soldiers set those shanties on fire. They were practically smoked out. I saw it from a distance. I could see the pandemonium. The fires were something like the fires you see nowadays that are started in these ghettoes. But they weren't started by the people that live there.

The soldiers threw tear gas at them and vomiting gas. It was one assignment they reluctantly took on. They were younger than the marchers. It was like sons attacking their fathers. The next day the newspapers deplored the fact and so forth, but they realized the necessity of getting these men off. Because they were causing a health hazard to the city. MacArthur was looked upon as a hero.

And so the bonus marchers straggled back to the various places they came from. And without their bonus.

6. Leading Retailers Propose a Solution, 1934

Although the number of persons receiving relief under the Federal Emergency Relief Act varies from month to month, the most reliable figures indicate that nearly 18 million individuals are now in that class, a great proportion of whom are, of course, the unemployed and their dependents. To them, however, must be added approximately two million more who are disabled from earning a livelihood: dependent children, widows and aged, disabled veterans, the blind, the sick, those rendered dependent by injury and accident, and the defectives. These are supported by various funds, philanthropies, or in institutions, and are like the major group of 18 million, taking only a small part in the national economy as consumers. The effect of the withdrawal of this large body from the consuming line goes even farther. Their inability to operate as buyers of food diminishes immediate consumption, and therefore has an effect on daily commerce which, in turn, affects the productive industries. So that the longer this body of non-consumers exists, the more it tends to draw new recruits to itself, and the more insecure becomes the footing of those individuals who are still capable of earning and consuming. This means that the man still on the payroll is perpetually conscious of the 20 millions of non-earners whom he may at any moment have to join, and his fear of being swept away from his job acts as a check on his impulse to spend his earnings. On the other side, dividends and profits are also adversely affected, and the high rate of expenditure is checked there. The 20 millions who cannot buy are the central fact of the economic situation. . . .

The wage-earner's natural tendency to spend, which is spurred both by the general standard of living and advertising, is checked whenever he is temporarily out of employment, and whenever he feels insecure in his employment, on account of the hazards which we now analyze:

1. Unemployment

Even in normal times a certain number of men and women desiring work are unable to find work. Since 1920 this number has never fallen below a million and a half. From 1927 through 1929 it stood at two million. . . .

. . . It is estimated that in March, 1933, that number was between 12 and 14 million persons.

2. Insufficient Wages

No accurate statistics exist under this heading. It is known, however, that even before the depression certain families on the relief rolls were there because the income of the wage-earner in the family was insufficient for the bare necessities of life. This may have been due to the incapacity of the individual to find better paying

---

From "Retailers Economic Security Plan," Box 21, Papers of the Committee on Economic Security, RG 47, Records of the Social Security Administration, National Archives.

work, or to do the work if he found it; or it may have been due to the payment in the only available jobs of sub-standard wages.

A recent study of Federal Unemployment Relief cases shows that at one time more than 20% of families on relief had one or more wage-earners employed (not on relief work). It is assumed that these cases include part-time work for heads of families and employment of women and children.

3. Absence of Wage-Earners from Family

Where parents are separated or divorced, or where there is a widowed mother, the family group often lacks a qualified wage-earner. Of the 4 million 700 thousand widows in the United States in 1930, 82% were forty-five years of age or over.

4. Sickness and Disabilities

It is estimated that the average person is disabled for seven days in each year on account of illness. This not only reduces earnings, but if insurance is lacking, diverts expenditures to medical aid and drugs. Serious illness affects approximately one-fourth of the population in a given year, and the sufferers are disabled for periods ranging from a week to permanent disability. The chronically sick are not wanted on payrolls, and even the healthy who suffer a sudden protracted illness may find their jobs taken. The worker who can protect himself by savings and insurance, therefore, wants not only to cover the expenses of his illness but the expenses of the time during which he is hunting for another job.

5. Old Age

Old age is a disqualification for work in two unequal ways. There is the definite physical disqualification, through lack of stamina or failure of the faculties; there is the much less definite disqualification resulting from the policy of refusing jobs to the elderly when younger men are available. In 1930 there were $6\frac{1}{2}$ million persons over sixty-five years of age, and two-fifths of them were not gainfully employed. It has been estimated that at least one-third of those over sixty-five are dependent or in need.

6. Accidents and Injuries

The loss of 280 million working days and 420 million dollars in wages is the annual cost of over a million accidents in industry. Ten million industrial and non-industrial accidents in 1933 resulted in 90,000 deaths and 330,000 permanently disabled persons.

Summary

As any individual succumbs to one of the hazards noted above, his power of consumption is instantly reduced and in a short time almost completely nullified. Furthermore, he takes with him his dependents. Finally, the existence of these hazards if a permanent threat to the worker, against which he must protect himself; and a certain part of this protection is, again, money withdrawn from consumption.

E S S A Y S

In the first essay, Theodore Rosenof shows how different ways of understanding the causes of the Great Depression yielded a debate over appropriate political solutions. In the second essay, Roy Rosenzweig assesses efforts to rally the unemployed in the early years of the Depression, noting both the organizational and political constraints faced by unemployed workers, and the importance of their experience to the coming of industrial unionism and the welfare state.

Understanding the Crash

THEODORE ROSENOF

The roots of the debate over recovery centered on the concept of economic maturity, a concept derived from an analysis of America's economic past, a concept with far-reaching implications for America's economic future. Espoused by various New Dealers, progressives, and radicals, it led squarely to the purchasing power thesis. Implicitly it led beyond: radicals saw it as a basis for a new economic "system." Its epochal implications were sharply rejected by conservatives. The key departure from the "norm" in their view (based upon classical economy and confidence thesis assumptions) was the New Deal itself. Further concepts developed in this context included the idea of "artificial prosperity" and the idea that Americans historically had tried to find "easy" ways out of their hard dilemmas. The question posed was, would Americans now truly confront or again try to escape from their problems? In terms of the logic of those who espoused the mature economy theme (if not in terms of their practical applications), the time had now come at last for just such a confrontation.

    As the depression persisted through the years, as times became worse—culminating in the crisis of 1933—rather than better, the optimism of the first months following the crash gave way among some to a view that the depression was no mere crash or panic, that it marked an epochal stage in the history of capitalism, that it reflected deep-seated and organic changes in the economic order. This view was expressed both in economic theory and in the economic thinking of political leaders. Opposed to this view, which reflected the pessimism of the time, was a second, which reflected the pertinacity of the time. As economists and politicians of the left advanced the economic maturity thesis, economists and politicians of the right reaffirmed the verities of classical theory, steadfastly arguing that the downturn was but temporary and that its severity was due to factors external to the system itself.

Reprinted by permission of the author.

A basic cleavage, then, lay between those who saw the depression as the end of one era and the beginning of another in the nation's history, and those who denied the reality of such a sharp break with the past; between those who advanced the mature economy theme (given its most famous political expression in Franklin Roosevelt's 1932 Commonwealth Club address), and those who rejected it; between various radicals, progressives, and New Dealers, on the one hand, and conservatives on the other. In the past, the economic maturity argument went, an open frontier and a rapidly growing population had provided the basis for an expanding economy. Now the frontier had disappeared and the population was becoming stationary. Technological advance had brought unemployment. In the past external expansion of the economy was possible; now this possibility was rendered nugatory by the sweep of economic nationalism across the world.

The mature economy theme, this epochal view of the economic order, was expressed in at least some measure by such modern progressives as Senators Robert M. La Follette, Jr., and Bronson Cutting, and by such New Deal Democrats as Michigan Governor Frank Murphy and New York Congressman James Mead. Pennsylvania's New Deal Governor George Earle argued that during the nineteenth century economic expansion was so great "that labor-saving devices were not a problem. Then . . . our expansion began rapidly to slacken"; technological unemployment appeared. ". . . we had . . . exploited our resources. Our frontier days were over. There was no more room for expansion." New York Mayor Fiorello La Guardia sketched a striking picture of the implications of a mature economy: "We have no frontiers now. The country is built. There are no promising markets in the world awaiting our goods. What are we going to do?"

Such New Dealers as Alabama Senator Hugo Black and relief administrator Harry Hopkins also expressed representative versions of this theme. In the past, as Black saw it, "the rapid . . . growth of our population, the influx of immigrants, and the availability of new lands constantly opened new opportunities for employment and new and enlarged markets for the products of our farms and factories. But in more recent years the natural growth of our population has slackened, the flow of immigration has abated, the frontier of new lands has disappeared." These changed conditions, aggravated by the contagion of economic nationalism and the economic impact of technology, "have made it much more difficult . . . for workers to find a market for their labor and . . . for industry and agriculture to find a market for their products." The economy could now "be stabilized and strengthened only if we find . . . means of utilizing . . . productivity . . . to raise the standard of living of our existing population."

Harry Hopkins argued that "as a Nation we refused for many years to recognize basic changes which were taking place in our economic structure. . . . We seem to have assumed there was no end to anything. . . . Those who could find no economic place for themselves moved West until there were no more frontiers. Our foreign trade dropped off as . . . other nations strove for economic self-sufficiency. We built up our industrial plant until its machines could produce more than our income pattern would let us consume." To men such as Earle, La Guardia, Black, and Hopkins, the logic of a new stage led to the necessity of a New Deal—reforms and readjustments to revive and reorder the economy. It signaled the end of capitalism's expansionist phase, but not of capitalism itself; it called for a new emphasis on consumptive rather than on productive faculties, an "intensive" expansion in consumptive capacity to replace the "extensive" geographic expansion of the past.

To radicals, the new economic stage marked the collapse of capitalism and heralded the coming of a new socioeconomic order. This was the radical and socialist version—and use—of the mature economy theme. Milwaukee's Socialist Mayor Daniel Hoan, for example, argued that this depression was unlike its predecessors. In the past, he contended, "there was free land to absorb the unemployed," or new industries to absorb capital, or war. None of these were now present. ". . . Evidence that this is a permanent problem is obvious. . . ." Socialist party leader Norman Thomas held that the capitalist crisis was rooted in the frontier's closing, the stabilization of population, economic nationalism, income maldistribution, and the failure of a new industry to appear as in past depressions to lead the way to recovery. All these made it impossible for capitalism to function as it did when it was an expanding force.

Wisconsin's radical Congressman Thomas Amlie viewed capitalism as an organism which grew only as long as it had room for expansion. First the western frontier, and with its closing, other frontiers kept the system going: the construction of railroads and great industries in the late nineteenth century; imperialism, which permitted the investment of capital abroad; spending for war, which stimulated prosperity; the scientific frontier and the advent of the automobile; and foreign loans to finance American exports. But this depression, Amlie argued, was terminal. There were no longer any land frontiers into which to expand; the frontier of world trade was permanently closed to expansion because of trade restrictions; and even if some great new invention such as the automobile appeared, it would be of little avail given the maldistribution of wealth. To Amlie, the nation faced "the stern reality of a frontier that has permanently disappeared."

The frontier thesis constituted an integral part of the mature economy theme; it also provided a basis for related views of the American economic past and present. The idea that in times past the frontier had provided a haven to which the economically distressed could go to repair their fortunes played an important role in the views taken toward unemployment by a number of New Dealers, progressives, and radicals. . . .

While conservatives generally attributed the paucity of capital investment to a lack of business confidence, those on the left utilized the frontier thesis to fashion an alternative explanation. Bob La Follette, for example, based much of his analysis of American capitalism upon this adaptation of the thesis. In the nineteenth century, he argued, the expanding frontier had continually offered opportunities for profitable capital investment, including the inducement for the investment of those "huge blocks of capital" which drew the economy out of past depressions. But without the inducement of the frontier the old method of pulling the economy out of depression would not work. The incentive for private capital investment had been so reduced that it could no longer "take place in a large enough volume to prevent our economy from contracting." The only way the country could now recover was for "Government . . . to provide the capital for capital expenditure purposes. . . ."

Phil La Follette argued that the crucial economic change of the era was that "horizontal expansion" around the globe had been completed and the need now was to turn to "vertical development." Private capital investment worked only as long as

"frontiers still beckoned for development. . . . It is a failure when the great enterprises are in the realm of housing . . . and other phases of life here at home. Purely
private capital will invest horizontally, but it will not invest perpendicularly." The
frontier's closing marked the end of the "old capitalism" and produced a stagnation
of capital. That stagnation would continue until government acted to provide a new
mechanism for capital investment. "The issue is not capitalism versus socialism or
communism, but the solution of the problem produced by the disappearance of the
frontier."

A number of New Dealers argued that there was already an overexpansion of
plants and factories (at least relative to effective consumer demand); therefore to
put further capital into more factories would be to aggravate the problem. This argument was expressed by such men as Hugo Black, James Mead, Congressman
Maury Maverick, and Senators Claude Pepper and Lewis Schwellenbach. Franklin
Roosevelt's best-known statement in this vein came in the Commonwealth Club address, but it was not an isolated expression. During the early years of the New Deal
the President repeatedly asserted that in some lines—largely in the area of heavy industry—the country was overbuilt, the productive plant was greater than could be
balanced by existing demand. Roosevelt therefore rejected "the orthodox . . . view
that there is this flood of money waiting for investment" upon the restoration of
confidence. "The Lord only knows where that money would go, I don't."

Conservatives mounted an ideological attack upon the New Deal-progressive-
radical version of the frontier thesis and the economic maturity theme. It was, they
charged, inherently defeatist, inherently pessimistic. This element of alleged defeatism in the New Deal—the idea that America's historic expansion had ended,
that unemployment had become chronic—was rejected by such men as Herbert
Hoover, 1936 GOP vice-presidential candidate Frank Knox, veteran Illinois Republican Frank Lowden, and Senators Frederick Steiwer and L. J. Dickinson. Former
Treasury Secretary Ogden Mills declared, "We must scotch the pernicious notion
that the frontier is closed. Ours is still the land of opportunity. . . ." Senator Walter
George affirmed, "we are a young nation. . . . We are [not] always going to have unemployment. . . . In the future we will expand our industries to such an extent as
will make radio and automobile and other . . . industries of the present of minor
consequence. . . ."

Alf Landon, Kansas Governor and 1936 Republican presidential candidate,
particularly stressed this theme. The mature economy argument—that the economic
crisis marked the end of the expansionist era, that government must play an increasingly important economic role—was not new, Landon insisted. It had been heard
during the depression of the 1890s; it had not been true then; it was not true now.
The end of the western frontier did not—in the nineties or the thirties—mark the
end of the era of expansion; for in its place was the "new frontier" of new wants and
inventions spiralling the economy to evergreater levels of progress. American capitalism retained its dynamism and could be renewed again; the problem was not loss
of energy in the nation's economic system but loss of faith among its New Deal
leaders.

Lewis Douglas, one-time Roosevelt administration budget director, thereafter a
leading Democratic critic of the New Deal, argued that since the frontier did not
disappear suddenly and since the population's rate of growth did not slacken all at
once, the impact of these factors could easily be overestimated, "particularly since

other countries . . . maintained a fair degree of prosperity in the face of no frontier at all and a diminishing population." Douglas further challenged the idea that the country's industrial plant was overbuilt. This, he argued, was not a new idea; it had been expressed during depressions for over a century; it had been proven wrong in every case. Every past depression had been conquered by capital consumption. Even if no new industry now emerged, the continual need for replacement would still provide great activity in the area of capital goods.

To the assertion by adherents of the mature economy thesis that the disappearance of the physical frontier required the implementation of economic planning, conservative critics of the New Deal responded by pointing to the existence of other frontiers that could provide bases for further economic expansion. The roots of growth, they suggested, lay not in geography but in technology. This idea—that the new frontier of science was key—was particularly developed by Senator Henry Hatfield and by former President Hoover. Hatfield argued that chemical research and the industries based upon it offered "an unlimited field for new . . . activity." The creators of synthetic products through chemical research were today's pioneers, and there was "no geographical limit . . . for scientific pioneering." In contrast to the New Deal's adaptation of the frontier thesis, Hatfield stressed that the new employment created by chemical research "is . . . none of it . . . artificially stimulated." Science was thus the true frontier, government economic intervention an "artificial" one.

Herbert Hoover continually criticized the economic maturity theme as evidencing a lack of faith not only in the economic system's vigor but in that of America itself. In his 1932 response to Roosevelt's Commonwealth Club address, for example, he challenged "the whole idea that . . . this country has reached . . . the height of its development." What Roosevelt had "overlooked is the fact that we are yet but on the frontiers of development of science . . . and . . . invention. . . ." "Progress . . . was not due to the opening up of new agricultural land; it was due to . . . scientific research, the opening of new invention. . . . There are a thousand inventions . . . in the lockers of science . . . which have not yet come to light; all are but on their frontiers." Hoover repeated this argument again and again during the New Deal years, berating the economic maturity idea and the plans and paraphernalia based upon it.

Conservatives—mostly of the Republican variety—presented an alternative explanation to the rejected mature economy theme. Their argument had four main parts: that the depression was worldwide, that it had in large measure been a consequence of the World War, that it was not otherwise unique among depressions, and that it had persisted because of New Deal policies. The theme that the American depression was part of an international crisis of international origins was expressed by such conservative Republicans as Herbert Hoover, Congressmen James Beck and Bertrand Snell, and Senators David Reed and Warren Austin. Implicit in this view was the idea that the American economic system as such could not be held responsible for the depression, an idea embraced by such critics of the New Deal as Hoover, Republican Allen Treadway, and Democrat Joseph Ely.

Those who viewed the depression as worldwide in its origins often pointed to the World War as its basic underlying cause. The war provided an external and wholly reprehensible source for the depression, requiring change neither in the country's economic institutions nor in its ideology. Ogden Mills, for example, attributing the depression to the war, explicitly absolved the American economic system of culpability, adding that "once started . . . the pattern has not differed essentially from that of previous" crises. The corollary of the contention that this depression was otherwise basically like those that had gone before was equally clear. What, asked Frank Lowden, justified the New Deal's "revolutionary" changes in government? "We have had serious depressions before." Conservatives such as Henry Hatfield, Congressman Hamilton Fish, and Senator Josiah Bailey all similarly characterized the present crisis as only the latest in a long series of depressions.

The denial that this depression was epochal led easily to the assertion that the "natural" return of prosperity had been arrested by the New Deal. The country had conquered depressions before, the refrain ran; why did this depression—among all others—persist? Herbert Hoover was only one of the many conservative Republicans who argued that the United States along with other nations was coming out of the depression in 1932. Other countries continued to advance, the argument went, but America's progress was held back by the 1932 election and the advent of the New Deal. Among those expressing this theme, at least in part, were Mills, Beck, and Frank Knox. "The American system is not at fault," Knox asserted in 1936. "Recovery was on its way four years ago." The nations making the greatest strides toward recovery, Senator Simeon Fess added, were "those least affected by artificial remedies." "Recovery has come fastest," David Reed concluded, "in those lands . . . which have seen the futility of trying to legislate prosperity. . . ."

GOP House leaders Bertrand Snell and John Taber further argued that there had been a revival of prosperity in the United States in 1933—until the National Industrial Recovery and Agricultural Adjustment acts went into effect. Others insisted that such recovery as existed by 1936 dated from the Supreme Court's decision invalidating the NRA, among them Hoover, Landon, and Knox. Michigan Senator Arthur Vandenberg declared in 1936 that any economic advance had been due to the natural upswing of the business cycle; it had come in spite of rather than because of the New Deal. The New Deal's "planned economy" in each case was seen as the very preventive of recovery; in each case it was argued that the economy spurted toward recovery freed from the restraints of such intervention—or in spite of them. Landon, Knox, and Steiwer all echoed the charge that the New Deal had retarded recovery; Hoover, Beck, and Bailey all agreed that recovery would have come "naturally" had it not been for governmental interference.

Conservatives, then, provided an alternative to the idea that the depression marked a sharp break with the past and that government accordingly would be required to enlarge its economic role. Rejecting the radical implications of the frontier thesis, they stood solidly upon the traditions of classical economics and limited government. Contending that the processes of capitalism—unthwarted by those of government—would have spiralled the economy toward recovery, they stressed the reality of continuity in the past and the need for continuity in the present. By the later thirties some New Dealers had also fastened upon a version of a continuous past, but they used it for a very different purpose: as yet another rationale for government economic intervention. American capitalism, they now argued, had long been supported by governmental props. . . .

The concern over the lost geographic frontier, on the one hand, and over the decline of the export trade and the movement toward nationalism, on the other, were closely linked. Each posited, in effect, that the spurs or props or supports that had activated and enlarged and enriched American capitalism in the past—an expanding western frontier provided by the new lands of a young nation, and the expanding export trade provided by the debtor status of a young nation—had ceased to exist. The implications of this for the future of capitalism in America were obvious and enormous. The geographic frontier clearly could not be rediscovered; new exports frontiers seemed highly unlikely in the thirties; the logical concomitant of both factors seemed to many to be that the new frontier was at home.

To New Dealers and modern progressives, government intervention would now play the same role that the open frontier had played in the past: it would cushion the impact of depression, provide succor for the unemployed, and work to renew the economy. It would provide an institutional replacement for a vanished geographical phenomenon. But while New Dealers and progressives saw in the mature economy thesis a rationale for economic policies designed to readjust and revamp the existing system, radicals saw in the mature economy thesis proof that even such readjustments and revamping were doomed to fail, that they—much less the conservatives' policies based upon the very rejection of the mature economy assumptions—could not save the system which had lost its dynamic, which had reached its terminus.

Each group, on a wide range of issues, including the key question as to whether a lack of "confidence" or purchasing power lay behind the depression's persistence, utilized its view of the depression in historical perspective as a basis for its explanation of and rationale for present assumptions, attitudes, policies, and programs. To those who accepted the mature economy thesis, such phenomena as a redistribution of income, unemployment relief, and measures geared to social welfare would all seem in order. For some, the mature economy theme had implications for fiscal policy; government would have to act because of the stagnation of private capital. It also had implications for farm and labor policy; if distressed farmers and workers could no longer move west, new arrangements were now imperative.

To those who denied the validity of the mature economy thesis, who denied the western frontier a key role in America's economic past, who stressed the continuing role of expanding scientific rather than contracting geographic frontiers, who stressed that the crisis of the thirties was just another depression and not the end of a centuries-old era of capitalist expansion, and who moreover attributed the depression's severity to factors external to the "American system," all these mature economy assumptions could be and were rejected. To conservatives these ideas were merely knee-jerk reactions that occurred during times of depression—whether in the nineties or in the thirties—and could best be understood as gauges of pessimism rather than as measures of economic reality. They had been expressed before and had been proven wrong; the western frontier had disappeared years before in any case; other countries had prospered without geographical frontiers or growing populations.

Finally, some reformist leaders fashioned a continuous view of the past to fit the New Deal present. Such administration spokesmen as Robert Jackson and Harry Hopkins argued that New Deal economic intervention constituted a modernization of the American tradition: the government had always subsidized the economic system. To some the New Deal constituted a most beneficent modernization; if the New Deal had renewed prosperity, much as the spending for war and foreign loans of the twenties had, the New Deal's programs for "building up . . . America" (to use James Mead's phrase) were far superior to the havoc of the war or the folly of the loans. Whether they could secure a genuine and lasting rather than an artificial and ephemeral prosperity remained a central, continuing question of the era.

Organizing the Unemployed

ROY ROSENZWEIG

On March 7, 1930, President Herbert Hoover made his most detailed economic statement of the four months following the Wall Street Crash. "All the evidence," Hoover declared, "indicate that the worst effects of the crash upon unemployment will have passed during the next sixty days." Although Hoover's veneer of optimism remained untarnished during his next three years in office, unemployment mounted steadily. At the time of this very speech, even according to moderately conservative government estimates, joblessness had already increased almost tenfold from 492,000 to 4,644,000. By the following March it had almost doubled again, and before peaking in March 1933 it had practically doubled once more to 15,071,000.

Although virtually no industry or community escaped the scourge of unemployment, the impact was not uniform. Autos, textiles, and other durable-goods industries were particularly hard hit in the early years of the Depression. Between March 1929 and August 1931 the payroll of the Ford Motor Company dropped from 128,142 to 37,000 persons. Even within industries and communities, unemployment was selective. The poor, the unskilled, the young, and the foreign born suffered disproportionately. Managerial employees suffered least, and whites did much better than blacks. The unemployment rate for Harlem blacks, for example, was between one and a half and three times that of the whites in New York City. Yet, for all these variations, what was truly remarkable about '30s joblessness was its pervasiveness—one third of a nation was out of work.

How did these unprecedented millions of unemployed respond to their plight in the early years of the Great Depression? Although many observers on both the right and the left expected them to turn to radicalism, the jobless, of course, never composed the shock troops of revolution. Still, it is a serious mistake to conclude on this basis, as did one historian, that "most of the unemployed meekly accepted their lot." The jobless employed a number of spontaneous survival strategies such as informal and formal cooperative movements, family and neighborhood networks of assistance, individual and group looting of supermarkets, coal bootlegging, determined searches for work, and innovative stretching of income. At the same time, radical organizers helped stimulate more formal and political jobless actions such as sit-ins at relief stations, national and state hunger marches, demonstrations at City Halls, and direct resistance to evictions. Organized into a variety of groups under the leadership of several left-wing organizations, the unemployed compiled an impressive record in the early '30s. Not only did these radical organizations of the unemployed stop evictions and raise relief payments, they also helped to intensify the class consciousness of many of their members.

Excerpted from "Organizing the Unemployed: The Early Years of the Great Depression, 1929–1933" by Roy Rosenzweig. Copyright © 1978. Reprinted by permission of the author.

But we must be wary of exaggerating or romanticizing the past. While no one would deny the heroism, energy, and imagination of the radical leaders and rank-and-file militants active in the unemployed movement, we must realize that their organizations constituted neither a revolutionary force nor even a truly mass movement. The core, active membership of the unemployed movement—perhaps 100,000 in 1933—never included even one per cent of that third of a nation that was out of work at the height of the Depression. While the radical unemployed movement often succeeded in winning immediate concrete gains for the jobless on the local level, it was much less successful in its efforts to create a revolutionary movement based on the unemployed.

What were the barriers to the development of such a mass-based, revolutionary unemployed movement? Were the radicals themselves responsible, as many commentators of both the right and the left have argued? Or was the problem in external social, economic, and political conditions that made a jobless-based revolutionary movement an impossibility in the early '30s? . . .

. . . With the coming of mass unemployment in 1930, organizational activity accelerated and organization of the unemployed became a top priority for Communist activists. In March 1930 the Party's theoretical journal declared that "The tactical key to the present state of class struggle is the fight against unemployment." Organizational activities took very concrete and visible forms. In Chicago, for example, Communists led, organized, or participated in 2,088 mass demonstrations in the first five years of the Depression. Not just mass demonstrations, but also leafleting, personal contacts, and eviction protests were used to build a core of local activists around whom to organize a local unemployed council. Any issue of immediate concern to the jobless was seen as a potential organizing tool. "The Councils," writes one historian, "did not consider any issue too small or unimportant to fight for: brooms for housewives in Seattle, milk for a baby in Detroit, breaking down barriers against Negro relief in St. Louis, coffee instead of cocoa for welfare recipients in New York, . . . an anti-spaghetti crusade at a Minneapolis relief commissary."

The early successes of the Communist unemployed movement grew directly out of the spontaneous discontent that was sweeping through the urban unemployed. "So desperate were the unemployed," wrote two Chicago observers, "that protest was seething through the disadvantaged neighborhoods of the city." The Chicago CP was unable to fulfill all the requests for organizational assistance from protesting groups. The Communist unemployed associations, usually known as Unemployed Councils, built on a cooperative neighborhood solidarity that emerged in response to the disorganization and inadequacy of local relief. Consequently, the Communist Unemployed Councils were most effective when they seized upon potent neighborhood issues. Because of the unemployed movement's initial connection to the Trade Union Unity League, Communist organizers were told to form unemployed groups on a shop or factory basis. But, as unemployed leader Herbert Benjamin has recalled, "down below people weren't concerned with" these directives. They were "just concerned with finding any means they could of acting." Most often this meant local, ad hoc neighborhood councils mobilized around specific grievances.

Out of this combination of aggressive organizing and spontaneous discontent emerged a vital Communist-led unemployed movement beginning in January and

February 1930. These months saw demonstrations of the unemployed in such places as New Britain, Connecticut; Passaic, New Jersey; Buffalo, New York; Pontiac, Michigan; Detroit; Boston; Philadelphia; and New York City. These early stirrings climaxed dramatically on March 6, 1930. The Party mobilized all its resources behind nationally coordinated demonstrations on March 6, which it called International Unemployment Day. Within the first month of the campaign the Party distributed over one million leaflets. Chicago Communists distributed 200,000 leaflets, 50,000 stickers, and 50,000 shop papers in the last few days before the demonstration. These energetic efforts paid off. Throughout the United States huge numbers of unemployed workers, many of whom had never before taken part in radical demonstrations, took to the streets. Although precise figures are impossible to arrive at now, the Communist Party at the time claimed a nationwide mobilization of one and one-quarter million people.

The March 6 demonstrations awakened many to the existence of mass unemployment and large-scale unrest in America. In Detroit, where over 35,000 jobless workers had been mobilized by the Unemployed Council, business leaders "were shocked by the emergence of truly radical agitation, and by the support it received." Even local Communists were surprised by the size of the crowd. In many cases, government repression—a problem that was to bedevil the unemployed movement throughout its history—came immediately. The scene of carnage as the bloody Union Square Demonstration in New York prompted even the *New York Times* to strong description:

> Hundreds of policemen and detectives, swinging nightsticks, blackjacks and bare fists, rushed into the crowd, hitting . . . all with whom they came in contact, chasing many across the street and adjacent thoroughfares. . . . A score of men with bloody heads and faces sprawled over the square with policemen pummeling them.

The blood spilled on March 6 was only the beginning. In the next five months over 4,000 people were arrested at radical demonstrations. The battle lines were drawn.

Despite these repressive measures, the Unemployed Councils blossomed in the period immediately following the March 6 demonstrations. Unemployed workers around the country began constituting themselves as loosely-organized, neighborhood-oriented councils of the unemployed. By mid-Summer Chicago had twelve locals and Philadelphia seven. Minneapolis, Milwaukee, and Indianapolis also had strong groups.

Of particular significance was the emergence at this time of interracial unemployed councils. As early as December 1929 Party leader Earl Browder had stressed that the organization of black workers had to be a top priority of the unemployed councils. The March 6 demonstrations provided an opportunity to implement this call, and throughout the country they attracted large numbers of black participants. Black Communist leader Cyril Briggs felt that March 6 revealed "the successful breaking down of the wall of prejudice between white and Negro workers fostered by the employers and the substitution of working-class solidarity and fraternization." Not all unemployed groups cut across racial lines, but many, especially those in Southern cities like Chattanooga and Atlanta, were the first interracial organizations in their areas. Even in the North black and white solidarity threatened public officials. "Here was something new," black sociologists St. Clair Drake and Horace

Cayton have commented about the frightened reaction in Chicago: "Negroes and whites *together* rioting against the forces of law and order." "The beginnings of a breaking down of barriers between whites and Negroes," unemployed leader Aurelia Johnson has recalled, were among the central achievements of the unemployed movement.

In the spring of 1930 the CP [Communist Party] made its first efforts at national coordination of the unemployed movement. Out of a Preliminary National Conference on Unemployment in New York at the end of March and a Chicago Convention in early July emerged a new national organization—The Unemployed Councils of the U.S.A. Although officially under Trade Union Unity League control, the Unemployed Councils, in practice, remained a largely autonomous neighborhood movement based on the anger and confusion of the jobless. . . .

. . . The real effectiveness of the Councils rested not on their ability to occasionally force increased relief appropriations, but on their capacity to resolve *individual* relief grievances. By 1932 the Chicago Unemployed Councils had already handled several thousand individual cases, and in the process had helped establish important precedents on adequacy and quality of relief. Moreover, in many localities the Unemployed Councils successfully fought relief discrimination and liberalized administrative thinking regarding the right of clients to complain. It was this function of the Unemployed Councils as grievance representatives for the jobless that constituted their greatest attraction to the rank-and-file unemployed worker. A study of Cleveland Unemployed Council members confirmed that individual relief grievances were most often the "precipitating factor" in creating Unemployed Council members.

The prevention of evictions was another concrete service that the Unemployed Councils performed for the jobless in the early '30s. A variety of techniques came into play: blocking the sheriff's entrance; returning the furniture; packing the courts to pressure judges to stop evictions. As the Depression deepened in 1931 and 1932, eviction struggles occurred with increasing frequency. In March 1931 Edmund Wilson reported that the Unemployed Councils had "practically stopped evictions" in Detroit, and that one landlady had actually called the Unemployed Council to ask whether she could evict her tenant yet.

This new "bread and butter" focus implemented in the fall of 1930 proved particularly effective in black communities. Mark Naison, in his recent study of Communists in Harlem, notes a shift at that time from agitational work into practical organizational activity. According to Naison, this policy, combined with the aggressive leadership of a committed, interracial group of organizers, helped the Harlem Unemployed Council "develop into a mass movement with solid roots in the community, one of the major sources of Communist influence among the least privileged sectors of Harlem's population." The two major tactics employed by the Harlem Council were the relief-bureau sit-in and eviction resistance. Unemployed Council sit-ins, demonstrations, and disruptions at the home-relief bureaus sought—and sometimes won—immediate relief for hard-hit Harlem residents. These eviction struggles brought concrete results, not only in Harlem, but in other urban black communities as well. When Chicago blacks received eviction notices, "it was not unusual," according to Cayton and Drake, "for a mother to shout to the children, 'Run quick and find the Reds!' " These struggles persisted despite vicious police attacks which led, for example, to the killing of three black eviction protesters in August 1931.

The Unemployed Councils aimed for direct approaches to the immediate needs of the jobless. But, how direct? Soliciting food donations for the hungry or, alternatively, seizing food from the grocery store? The Councils briefly flirted with both of these tactics, but ultimately rejected them. In early 1931 directives from both the Comintern and the Trade Union Unity League urged that the Councils set up relief kitchens and undertake direct food collections. By July, however, the Party had reconsidered, and Browder had denounced communal charity schemes as an "open right-wing opportunist deviation." But this new policy sometimes caused problems on the local level. In Harlem, according to Naison's study, Council leaders concluded that the rejection of "spontaneous efforts of rank-and-file Council members to collect food, money, and clothing for starving neighbors, or to cook communal meals for the unemployed. . . . had isolated the Harlem Council from many sincere workers who saw no contradiction between taking a collection for their neighbors and resisting an eviction or marching on City Hall." Consequently, by the fall of 1931 the Harlem Council began to take up food collections, although such collections never became a central focus of the Council's work.

Unemployed Council participation in food seizures similarly reflected both an ambivalence at the top and a tendency of some local unemployed groups to set their own course in accordance with local conditions. In the early '30s individual and group looting of supermarkets was not an isolated phenomenon. "Grown men, usually in two's and three's, enter chain stores, order all the food they can possibly carry, and then walk out without paying," the *Nation* reported from Detroit in the summer of 1932. Although most such incidents took place outside of the organized unemployed movement, Unemployed Councils in Toledo and Oklahoma City joined in the food looting in early 1931. Such actions, however, frightened not only authorities, but also some top Communist leaders. In the summer of 1931 Browder condemned food seizures as "an effort to substitute an idealistic, 'heroic' action to 'inspire' the masses, in the place of the necessary Bolshevist organization and leadership." Unemployed Council leader Herbert Benjamin recalls that "those of us who were politically more responsible" continually advised against food riots, and he believes that more such rioting would have occurred without the Unemployed Councils. "It seems probable," conclude two academic writers unsympathetic to the left, "that the Communist Party exercised an important influence in restricting the amount of violence against persons and property during the depression."

While the CP helped to restrain the violence of the out-of-work, it could do little to restrain police violence directed against the jobless. As an examination of the dispatches of the *Federated Press* or even the *New York Times* shows, police violence against unemployed demonstrators was almost a daily occurrence. One of the most dramatic incidents came on March 7, 1932, when the Detroit Unemployed Councils led 3,000 in a march on Henry Ford's River Rouge Plant in Dearborn to demand jobs, fuel, and food. The Dearborn police responded with bullets. By the end of the day four marchers lay dead and over fifty had been seriously wounded. Such incidents were all too common in the '30s.

The successes of the Unemployed Councils as a local pressure organization between 1930 and 1933 were not equaled on the national level. The Unemployed Councils did not receive effective national leadership until the fall of 1931, when

Herbert Benjamin was assigned by the CP to direct this work. Even then the national office remained a "nominal sort of thing," as Benjamin has recalled. In fact Benjamin himself *was* the national organization—he initially had no supporting staff.

In the early '30s national Unemployed Council activity revolved around petition drives for the CP's unemployment-insurance bill and two national hunger marches in December 1931 and December 1932. The marches did much to publicize the unemployed cause, although neither was a dramatic success. The Communists limited participation in the marches to elected representatives of local Unemployed Councils, and as a result only 1600 marched in the first and 3200 in the second. More importantly, the marches failed to mobilize many jobless outside of those already in the Communist Party; over 70% of the 1932 hunger marchers, for example, belonged to the Communist Party or the Young Communist League.

The national organization of the Unemployed Councils strengthened and solidified in the years after 1933. Yet these same years saw the loss of much of the vitality and spontaneity of the unemployed movement, particularly on the local level. The local Councils settled down as a more orderly movement that sought to represent the unemployed in their dealings with relief authorities; they became in many areas the bargaining agent for both relief recipients and WPA [Works Progress Administration] workers. Large demonstrations of eviction resistance occasionally flared up, but more often the unemployed organizations quietly carried out their trade-union functions. In 1940 Irene Oppenheimer, a sociologist, noted that each year the unemployed organizations tended to have fewer sit-ins, strikes, and picket lines; she concluded that unemployed activity "has been characterized by a gradual evolution from the position of a purely conflict group to an organized and responsible relationship with the authorities."

Along with this decreasing activism on the local level came the nationalization and unification of the unemployed movement. By 1936 the Workers' Alliance of America, originally a federation of Socialist unemployed groups, encompassed most of the Communist, Musteite, and independent jobless leagues as well. Increasingly, the Workers' Alliance focused its attention on Washington (where it had its headquarters), and it developed into a relatively effective lobbying organization for national-relief and unemployment-insurance measures. Basically, the Workers' Alliance accepted the terms of the New Deal; it adopted the politics of the popular front—a left-wing New Deal liberalism—and developed a close symbiotic relationship with New Deal relief officials. In 1938, for example, Workers' Alliance locals campaigned actively for New Deal candidates. Both nationally and locally the unemployed movement after 1933 moved from insurgency to respectability. "The unorganized unemployed," wrote a *Saturday Evening Post* reporter in 1938, "are no longer merely an undecorative and troublesome fringe on the body politic." . . .

When Socialist organizing of the unemployed finally got underway in the early years of the New Deal, it tended to mirror both the organizing approach and constituency of the Communist Unemployed Councils. But the third major radical movement of unemployed workers, that led by the followers of A. J. Muste, the Dutch Reformed Minister turned labor educator and organizer, differed in organizing methods and support.

Beginning around 1932, the Musteites sought to transform their propaganda and educational organization—the Conference on Progressive Labor Action—into an independent working-class center competitive with the AFL [American Federation of Labor], CP, and SP [Socialist Party]. The unemployed offered a possible power base for this transformation, and in 1932 the Musteites began organizing Unemployed Leagues. The Musteites, like the Communists and Socialists, met with their greatest success when they pitched their efforts toward the bread-and-butter needs of the unemployed. But to this immediate-needs focus they added their own, unique "American Approach"—an effort to identify their Unemployed Leagues with popular patriotic symbols such as the Rattlesnake Flag and the slogan "Don't Tread on Me." This approach made the Musteites somewhat more tolerant and flexible in dealing with existing non-political unemployed groups than the Communists or Socialists. They worked closely and successfully with jobless self-help groups— organizations devised by the unemployed to meet their needs through barter and exchange of labor for produce and fuel. While other unemployed groups stigmatized self help as "collective picking in garbage cans," the Musteites initially condoned this approach, calling it "a cement . . . to keep the organization together . . . that would push the members into further action."

This flexibility and Americanism paid off: the Musteites were able to attract more native-born and less-politicized members, and to build a following in areas that the Communists and Socialists were unable to penetrate. From the small industrial and mining towns of Ohio, the steel mills of Pittsburgh, the coal fields of Eastern Pennsylvania and West Virginia, and the textile mills of North Carolina, thousands of unemployed enlisted under their banners. While the CP Unemployed Councils in Ohio were confined to the cities and towns with large immigrant populations, like Youngstown, the Musteite Leagues found support in much smaller and more rural towns.

The attractiveness of patriotic rhetoric for many Depression unemployed is further evidenced by the success of the Washington marches of Father James Cox and the Bonus Expeditionary Force. In January 1932 Father Cox, a round-faced, spectacled Pittsburgh radio priest active in the labor movement, led 15,000 unemployed from the Pittsburgh area to Washington to present their demands for immediate relief. The following summer the famous Bonus March gathered over 20,000 jobless World War I veterans in the capital.

Why were these marches able to attract many who were immune to the appeals of radical unemployed groups? One important reason was that the radicals had to recruit the jobless in the face of well-ingrained cultural assumptions that identified radical activity with anti-Americanism, alienism, and deviance. E. Wight Bakke, a Yale economist who made an extremely careful and sensitive study of the New Haven unemployed, found that "the identification of all radical ideas with Russia is all but universal." In New Haven, at least, these patriotic and anti-communist cultural assumptions militated against the success of radical groups. Father Cox and the Bonus Marchers, like the Musteites to a lesser degree, played effectively on this patriotism and anti-Communism. Cox's March was, in part, a reaction against the Communist Hunger March of 1931. In explaining his march, Cox said:

> Some weeks ago I read of the invasion of Washington by a Communistic group of marchers waving the red flag, singing the Internationale and demanding all sorts of fantastic things. This is repugnant to me, and I so stated casually over the radio. I remarked that, while I condemned these demonstrations, I believed a body of real American citi-

zens should go to Washington and protest against unemployment conditions which exist in the United States today.

This Americanist rhetoric carried through Cox's entire march. His followers arrived in Washington singing the Star Spangled Banner and waving American flags; they concluded their visit at the Tomb of the Unknown Soldier. The Bonus Marchers also manipulated patriotic symbols to cultivate an image of respectability.

This patriotic posturing apparently enabled Cox and the Bonus Army to attract followers who disdained the radical unemployed movements. Most workers were used to frequent periods of joblessness, but small entrepreneurs and white-collar workers were not. In the '30s, for the first time, unemployment was an experience shared by both the middle and working classes; but, it was the middle-class unemployed who experienced the greatest shock and attitude changes as a result of the Depression. Hence, although these middle-class jobless were important potential supporters for '30s protests, they were unlikely to join avowedly radical groups like the Unemployed Councils. The Bonus Army and Father Cox, with their patriotic rhetoric, could and did mobilize the middle-class unemployed. According to one recent historian, the "vast majority" of the Bonus Marchers were "middle-aged and middle-class—small businessmen, skilled tradesmen, white-collar workers, with a sprinkling of professionals, such as teachers, lawyers, and dentists." Although little is known about Father Cox's marchers, his financial backing came from the small store owners of the Allegheny County Retail Merchants Association.

Although to a lesser degree, the Musteites shared with Cox and the Bonus Army the ability to attract more middle-class, native-born, and "Middle American" unemployed. Yet, the Musteites Americanist rhetoric also brought its problems. At the Unemployed League's first national convention, held in Columbus, Ohio on July 4, 1933, the Musteites had to quell a revolt led by a "Stars and Stripes" faction over the Musteites' failure to open the Convention with a prayer and the National Anthem. In the long run, much of this native American and small-town support evaporated as the Musteites became more and more revolutionary in their gradual movement toward Trotskyism, and as the New Deal liberalism of Franklin Roosevelt competed for the allegiance of the out-of-work. . . .

We see, then, that between 1929 and 1933 the . . . unemployed movements varied in ideological assumptions, organizing personnel, geographic bases, and organizing strategies. Yet they shared some common achievements. First, they resolved the immediate individual grievances of their members with particular success: they won relief adjustments, blocked evictions, and reconnected the gas and electric for thousands of unemployed. Second, on a collective level, the unemployed organizations helped create pressure not only for higher levels of relief and larger relief appropriations, but also for more equitable and less degrading administrative procedures at relief stations. And, third, they were the first groups in the '30s to propagandize and agitate openly and actively for unemployment insurance. Although there were a number of elements involved, such as the pressure on FDR from Huey Long, their agitation did help to pave the way for the Social Security Act of 1935, which included provisions for unemployment insurance. The battle for unemployment insurance had a long history going back to the early 20th Century, but the radical unemployed movement can be credited with helping to revive it as a serious issue in the Great Depression. The psychological impact of the unemployed movement should, similarly, not be minimized. Jobless workers became convinced that thier condition was not their own fault, that larger economic forces had thrown them out of work.

Perhaps most importantly, the unemployed movement helped raise the political and social consciousness of the thousands of workers who passed through its ranks. For many the unemployed movement was their first experience in any sort of mass pressure organization, and through this affiliation many learned the power of organization as a weapon. Sam Brugos, a leader of a Cleveland Unemployed Council, had no contact with radicalism or trade unionism prior to the Depression. Yet, he told an interviewer of his determination to "join a union and organize a strike" as soon as he found a job. Obviously many jobless workers did just that in the late '30s. Many leaders of the CIO came directly out of the unemployed movement, and it appears that many in the rank and file had similar training. . . .

. . . The organizers of the radical unemployed movement confronted more than just police batons and tear gas. They sought to win the allegiance of the unemployed in the face of powerful ideological and cultural assumptions that militated against their success. Although the Depression did much to erode working-class faith in American capitalism, this breakdown had not led to a new consciousness, at least by the early '30s. As the Lynds found in Muncie, Indiana during the Depression, "fear, resentment, insecurity, and disillusionment were largely an *individual* experience for each worker, and not a thing generalized by him into a *'class'* experience." Workers had a culture of their own, of course, which rejected many of the values of middle-class American society. But many of the values of that very working-class culture—patriotism, distrust of politics, and a frequent anti-radicalism—also discouraged membership in radical unemployed groups. "In the face of Communism," Bakke found in talking to the New Haven jobless, "the most insecure American workman becomes a hero by defending American conditions."

Moreover, unemployed organizers had to try to mobilize an American working class that was divided within itself along ethnic, racial, religious, and geographic lines. Although occasionally the shock of unemployment did break down racial and ethnic barriers, the basic divisions remained. Homer Morris, an American Friends Service Committee worker, described the persistence of racial, national, religious, and family feuds in the impoverished coal-mining camps of West Virginia and Kentucky. Similarly, one New Haven worker blamed his unemployment on the "Jews in control who had no use for Italians." Among the Depression unemployed the problems in developing class consciousness were exacerbated by the presence of large numbers of jobless men and women from middle-class backgrounds. Given this context, most unemployed people in the early '30s did not come to see themselves as part of a common group united by their lack of work.

Finally, the jobless, as a group, were particularly difficult to organize for a number of reasons. As one '30s radical leader has commented: "I don't know of any task in the revolutionary movement more discouraging and disheartening than the task of trying to keep an unemployed organization . . . together." One problem was the continual churning of leadership and membership caused by the impermanence of unemployment. Another was the debilitating effects of unemployment: joblessness, for some, often led to despair, apathy, and listlessness, rather than rebellion. Because of the persistence of the work ethic throughout the Depression, many of those without work began to see themselves as worthless. Such men and women were more likely to withdraw from society than to actively protest against it; the last thing they wanted was to publicly identify themselves as "reliefers" by participating in jobless associations. Finally, there was the battle for survival itself: unemployed workers often were too absorbed in their own personal struggles for food and housing to concern themselves with political action. Not only individualist efforts, but also collective sharing and cooperation among kinship networks, neighbors, and ethnic groups absorbed the full energies of many unemployed workers.

Given these formidable barriers—persistent and often violent repression by government and business, the strength of cultural values which inhibited jobless political activity especially of the radical variety, and the inherent problems involved in basing a revolutionary movement on the unemployed—it becomes clear that the accomplishments of the '30s unemployed movement are more notable than its failure. It remains a significant example of a locally-based, grass-roots organization under radical leadership that worked creatively and militantly to meet the concrete, immediate needs of the unemployed.

SUGGESTED READING

Argersinger, Jo Ann E. *Toward a New Deal in Baltimore: People and Government in the Great Depression* (1988).

Barber, William J. *From New Era to New Deal: Herbert Hoover, the Economists, and American Economic Policy, 1921–1933* (1985).

Bernstein, Michael A. *The Great Depression: Delayed Recovery and Economic Change in America, 1929–1939* (1987).

Cohen, Lizabeth. *Making a New Deal: Industrial Workers in Chicago, 1919–1939* (1990).

Fearon, Peter. *War, Prosperity, and Depression: The U.S. Economy, 1917–45* (1987).

Galbraith, John Kenneth. *The Great Crash, 1929* (1972).

Hawley, Ellis, ed. *Herbert Hoover and the Crisis of American Capitalism* (1973).

Hearn, Charles. *The American Dream in the Great Depression* (1973).

Keller, Morton. *Regulating a New Economy: Public Policy and Economic Change in America, 1900–1933* (1990).

Lisio, Donald. *The President and Protest: Hoover, MacArthur, and the Bonus Riot.* 2d ed. (1994).

Lorence, James J. *Organizing the Unemployed: Community and Union Activists in the Industrial Heartland* (1996).

McElvaine, Robert. *The Great Depression: America, 1929–1941* (1993).

Olson, James. *Herbert Hoover and the Reconstruction Finance Corporation, 1931–1933* (1977).

Peeler, David. *Hope Among Us Yet: Social Criticism and Social Solace in Depression America* (1987).

Poppendieck, Janet. *Breadlines Knee Deep in Wheat: Food Assistance in the Great Depression* (1986).

Rosen, Elliot A. *Hoover, Roosevelt, and the Brains Trust: From Depression to New Deal* (1977).

Rosenof, Theodore. *Dogma, Depression, and the New Deal: The Debate of Political Leaders over Economic Recovery* (1975).

Sautter, Udo. *Three Cheers for the Unemployed: Government and Unemployment Before the New Deal* (1991).

Schwarz, Jordan A. *The Interregnum of Despair: Hoover, Congress, and the Depression* (1970).

Watkins, T. H. *The Great Depression: America in the 1930s* (1993).

Woodruff, Nan Elizabeth. *As Rare as Rain: Federal Relief in the Great Southern Drought of 1930–31* (1985).

CHAPTER
8

The Dilemmas of Liberal
Internationalism: Foreign
Policy Between the Wars

At the close of World War I, the United States was the preeminent economic power in the world. But in many respects, the country was ill prepared for the responsibility that accompanied its new international status. Woodrow Wilson's expansive liberal internationalism, crafted in part as an alternative to European colonialism and in part as a frantic response to the Russian Revolution of 1917, unraveled in the early 1920s. The United States did not have enough leverage to force France and Britain to accept U.S. conditions on free trade and European reconstruction. And the benefits of free trade and mutual security proved hard to sell in domestic politics. While many economic interests pressed for open international markets, many others fought to keep tariffs high and to protect the domestic market. Progressive and Conservative Senators (the former disappointed by Wilson's willingness to bargain his principles, the latter dismayed at the prospect of a multilateral veto of American foreign policy) united to prevent U.S. membership in the flagship of liberal internationalism, the League of Nations.

In the wake of Wilson's failure, the foreign policy of the 1920s stumbled from problem to problem and from crisis to crisis. Republican Administrations understood the benefits of free trade but shaped their foreign economic policies around the needs of specific industries—in some cases pursuing freer trade, in some cases maintaining high protective tariffs, in some cases blessing American participation in restrictive international cartels. The Administration and private investors scrambled throughout the decade to negotiate an escape from a tangle of reparations (German payments to France and England), war debts (owed by European Allies to the United States), and loans (American efforts to prop up Germany) that strangled European recovery. And the United States, on the outside of the League of Nations looking in, patched together a variety of arms control and neutrality agreements designed to maintain a tenuous peace. The fragility and disorganization of global commerce contributed to the coming of the Great Depression and the rapidity with which it spread around the world. As individual countries tumbled into depression, competitive currency depreciation, tariff retaliation, lack of central bank coopera- tion, and the absence of an international lender of last resort combined to make things much worse and recovery much more difficult.

If the Depression underscored the failures of the 1920s, it also rekindled the Wilsonian vision of liberal internationalism. In the early years of the crisis, the United States and others pursued nationalist economic solutions (including higher protective tariffs and inflationary spending programs), which further curtailed trade, eroded the gold standard, and deepened the Depression. But by the middle 1930s, many had come to view the Depression as a consequence of international eco- nomic disarray and the pursuit of freer trade as the only viable recovery strategy. It proved exceedingly difficult, however, to persuade either domestic interests or inter- national competitors to take the risk of opening markets under such dismal eco- nomic conditions. In the end, the international economic crisis would yield the harsher consequences of World War II, and the war would finally provide the op- portunity and the leverage to construct an international economic order under U.S. leadership.

D O C U M E N T S

In Document 1, President Wilson defends in vain the basic principles of international cooperation embodied in the League of Nations. Document 2, excerpted from a State Department press release, suggests the ways in which the United States struggled to maintain peace and prosperity from outside the League of Nations. Documents 3 and 4, the former written by a group of leading economists and the latter by President Hoover, stake out the debate over protectionism and free trade sparked by the Depression and the passage of the sharply protectionist Smoot-Hawley Tariff in 1930. In Document 5, Sec- retary of State Cordell Hull marks a renewed commitment to liberal internationalism.

1. President Woodrow Wilson Defends the League of Nations, 1919

What it is important for us to remember is that when we sent those boys in khaki across the sea we promised them, we promised the world, that we would not con- clude this conflict with a mere treaty of peace. We entered into solemn engagements with all the nations with whom we associated ourselves that we would bring about such a kind of settlement and such a concert of the purpose of nations that wars like this could not occur again. If this war was to be fought over again, then all our high ideals and purposes have been disappointed, for we did not go into this war merely to beat Germany. We went into this war to beat all purposes such as Germany enter- tained. . . .

. . . You have heard a great deal about Article X of the covenant of the league of nations. Article X speaks the conscience of the world. Article X is the article which

---

From Speech at Indianapolis (September 14, 1919). U.S. Senate. Doc. 120, 66th Congress, 1st session, 19–28.

goes to the heart of this whole bad business, for that article says that the members of this league (that is intended to be all the great nations of the world) engage to respect and to preserve against all external aggression the territorial integrity and political independence of the nations concerned. That promise is necessary in order to prevent this sort of war from recurring, and we are absolutely discredited if we fought this war and then neglect the essential safeguard against it. You have heard it said, my fellow citizens, that we are robbed of some degree of our sovereign, independent choice by articles of that sort. Every man who makes a choice to respect the rights of his neighbors deprives himself of absolute sovereignty, but he does it by promising never to do wrong, and I can not for one see anything that robs me of any inherent right that I ought to retain when I promise that I will do right, when I promise that I will respect the thing which, being disregarded and violated, brought on a war in which millions of men lost their lives, in which the civilization of mankind was in the balance, in which there was the most outrageous exhibition ever witnessed in the history of mankind of the rapacity and disregard for right of a great armed people.

We engage in the first sentence of Article X to respect and preserve from external aggression the territorial integrity and the existing political independence not only of the other member States, but of all States, and if any member of the league of nations disregards that promise, then what happens? The council of the league advises what should be done to enforce the respect for that covenant on the part of the nation attempting to violate it, and there is no compulsion upon us to take that advice except the compulsion of our good conscience and judgment. It is perfectly evident that if, in the judgment of the people of the United States the council adjudged wrong and that this was not a case for the use of force, there would be no necessity on the part of the Congress of the United States to vote the use of force. . . . There is in that covenant not only not a surrender of the independent judgment of the Government of the United States, but an expression of it, because that independent judgment would have to join with the judgment of the rest. . . .

When you look at the covenant of the league of nations thus, in the large, you wonder why it is a bogey to anybody. You wonder what influences have made gentlemen afraid of it. You wonder why it is not obvious to everybody as it is to those who study it with disinterested thought, that this is the central and essential covenant of the whole peace. As I was saying this forenoon, I can come through a double row of men in khaki and acknowledge their salute with a free heart, because I kept my promise to them. I told them when they went to this war that it was a war not only to beat Germany but to prevent any subsequent wars of this kind. I can look all the mothers of this country in the face and all the sisters and the wives and the sweethearts and say, "The boys will not have to do this again."

You would think to hear some of the men who discuss this covenant that it is an arrangement for sending our men abroad again just as soon as possible. It is the only conceivable arrangement which will prevent our sending our men abroad again very soon, and if I may use a very common expression, I would say if it is not to be this arrangement, what arrangement do you suggest to secure the peace of the world? . . . If the gentlemen who do not like what was done at Paris think they can do something better, I beg that they will hold their convention soon and do it now.

They can not in conscience or good faith deprive us of this great work of peace without substituting some other that is better.

So, my fellow citizens, I look forward with profound gratification to the time which I believe will now not much longer be delayed, when the American people can say to their fellows in all parts of the world, "We are the friends of liberty; we have joined with the rest of mankind in securing the guarantees of liberty; we stand here with you the eternal champions of what is right, and may God keep us in the covenant that we have formed."

2. A State Department Official on the Benefits of Disarmament, 1931

One of the greatest obstacles to the prosperity of all the nations is the existence of a competition to build armaments. In addition to the enormous expenditures which such a competition involves, it creates a feeling of insecurity which is reflected at once in the world's business.

Competition in the building of armaments is the result of thousands of years of fear, and we can not expect easily to allay that fear, for the idea of limiting and reducing armament by international agreement is very recent and the fear is very old. Of course all disputes have not always been settled by the sword. Far from it. Conciliation and arbitration have developed through the centuries concurrently with the science of war. In fact, as the world became more populous, as wars became more universal through extensive interlocking of national interests, as their consequences became more apparent to all nations, I think that the belief that recourse to war could be eliminated took a firm hold on the imagination of the world.

Of late years this belief has made great strides. The Pact of Paris is a true response to the aspirations of the people of this world. They have come to believe that their Governments can refrain from war and must find ways of eliminating the hazards of war from this modern world. They see war not only as a danger to the nations involved but as a menace to our whole fabric of civilization. The same instinct of self-defense which brings men to arms is at work to find ways of keeping them from taking up arms. . . .

I have touched upon the economic aspect of disarmament, but before leaving the subject, may I say just a few words more on this? Faced with one of the most serious of the world's economic crises, nearly all governments are struggling with the heavy burden of nonproductive armament expenditures. It has been estimated that the cost of armaments to the world approximates $5,000,000,000, and as the President stated in his address to the International Chamber of Commerce in May, this is an increase of about 70 per cent over that previous to the Great War. A study of the budgets of eight of the principal military and naval powers shows that the cost of armaments to them approximates $3,000,000,000, or over 16 per cent of their total budget expenditures. As Mr. Castle pointed out not so long ago, individual items in

From Address by Mr. Pierre De L. Boal, Department of State, *Press Releases* (October 17, 1931), pp. 318, 321–323.

this total give us cause for consideration; we may note that at a time when our national deficit exceeds $900,000,000 at the close of the last fiscal year, a single battleship of our fleet, for example, not only costs $40,000,000 to build but requires an annual outlay of $2,000,000 for its maintenance.

In addition there are enormous sums spent in modernizing parts and overhauling the vessel. Since at the end of 25 years the ship is scrapped, we can estimate its minimum cost to the nation at approximately $250,000,000, if we add all these sums and figure the compound interest for this period at 5 per cent. This, the cost of just one battleship, is more than sufficient to pay for several years costs of all the Foreign Offices of the world, those Departments whose principal function is the maintenance of friendly and pacific relations between countries. In mentioning a battleship it is not my intention to differentiate it from other items of armament. I use it merely as a convenient unit of cost for purposes of illustration.

I might add that these figures represent expenditures for national defense alone and do not take into consideration pensions or debts arising out of past wars, items which in themselves far exceed the costs I have quoted to you. Would it not seem obvious in view of the treaties negotiated renouncing war as an instrument of national policy and providing for pacific means for the settlement of international disputes that the self-defense of countries can effectively be insured by proportionally smaller military forces than these? The armaments of the world, unlimited as they are, constitute a menace not only to peace, but an excessive and unnecessary burden and a check to the economic rehabilitation of us all. . . .

When America is represented at the disarmament conference in February, its delegates will earnestly strive to effect a substantial limitation of armament which, while maintaining national security, will divert a vast proportion of the world's wealth away from destructive to constructive purposes and thus hasten the restoration of American and of general prosperity.

3. Leading Economists Argue for Lower Tariffs, 1930

The undersigned American economists and teachers of economics strongly urge that any measure which provides for a general upward revision of tariff rates be denied passage by Congress, or if passed, be vetoed by the President.

We are convinced that increased restrictive duties would be a mistake. They would operate, in general, to increase the prices which domestic consumers would have to pay. By raising prices they would encourage concerns with higher costs to undertake production, thus compelling the consumer to subsidize waste and inefficiency in industry.

At the same time they would force him to pay higher rates of profit to established firms which enjoyed lower production costs. A higher level of duties, such as is contemplated by the Smoot-Hawley bill, would therefore raise the cost of living and injure the great majority of our citizens.

Few people could hope to gain from such a change. Miners, construction, transportation and public utility workers, professional people and those employed

---

in banks, hotels, newspaper offices, in the wholesale and retail trades and scores of other occupations would clearly lose, since they produce no products which could be specially favored by tariff barriers.

The vast majority of farmers also would lose. Their cotton, pork, lard and wheat are export crops and are sold in the world market. They have no important competition in the home market. They cannot benefit, therefore, from any tariff which is imposed upon the basic commodities which they produce. . . .

They would lose through the increased duties on manufactured goods, however, and in a double fashion. First, as consumers they would have to pay still higher prices for the products, made of textiles, chemicals, iron and steel, which they buy. Second, as producers their ability to sell their products would be further restricted by the barriers placed in the way of foreigners who wished to sell manufactured goods to us.

Our export trade, in general, would suffer. Countries cannot permanently buy from us unless they are permitted to sell to us, and the more we restrict the importation of goods from them by means ever higher tariffs, the more we reduce the possibility of our exporting to them.

This applies to such exporting industries as copper, automobiles, agricultural machinery, typewriters and the like fully as much as it does to farming. The difficulties of these industries are likely to be increased still further if we pass a higher tariff.

There are already many evidences that such action would inevitably provoke other countries to pay us back in kind by levying retaliatory duties against our goods. There are few more ironical spectacles than that of the American Government as it seeks, on the one hand, to promote exports through the activity of the Bureau of Foreign and Domestic Commerce, while, on the other hand, by increasing tariffs it makes exportation ever more difficult.

We do not believe that American manufacturers, in general, need higher tariffs. The report of the President's Committee on Recent Economic Changes has shown that industrial efficiency has increased, that costs have fallen, that profits have grown with amazing rapidity since the end of the World War. Already our factories supply our people with over 96 per cent of the manufactured goods which they consume, and our producers look to foreign markets to absorb the increasing output of their machines.

Further barriers to trade will serve them not well, but ill. . . .

Many of our citizens have invested their money in foreign enterprises. The Department of Commerce has estimated that such investments, entirely aside from the war debts, amounted to between $12,555,000,000 and $14,555,000,000 on Jan. 1, 1929. These investors, too, would suffer if restrictive duties were to be increased, since such action would make it still more difficult for their foreign debtors to pay them the interest due them.

America is now facing the problem of unemployment. The proponents of higher tariffs claim that an increase in rates will give work to the idle. This is not true. We cannot increase employment by restricting trade. American industry, in the present crisis, might well be spared the burden of adjusting itself to higher schedules of duties.

Finally, we would urge our government to consider the bitterness which a policy of higher tariffs would inevitably inject into our international relations. The

United States was ably represented at the world economic conference which was held under the auspices of the League of Nations in 1927. This conference adopted a resolution announcing that "the time has come to put an end to the increase in tariffs and to move in the opposite direction."

The higher duties proposed in our pending legislation violate the spirit of this agreement and plainly invite other nations to compete with us in raising further barriers to trade. A tariff war does not furnish good soil for the growth of world peace.

4. President Hoover Argues for High Tariffs, 1932

As a matter of fact there never has been a time in the history of the United States when tariff protection was more essential to the welfare of the American people than at present. Prices have declined throughout the world but to a far greater extent in other countries than in the United States. Manufacturers in foreign countries which have abandoned the gold standard are producing goods and paying for raw materials in depreciated currency. They may ship their goods into the United States with great detriment to the American producer and laborer because of the differences in the value of the money they pay for their raw materials and the money they receive for their finished products. Under such conditions it is imperative that the American protective policy be maintained. If the intent or the effect of the proposed bill is to remove the possibility of executive action or to reduce tariff protection there never was a time more appropriate on account of widespread domestic unemployment and the possibilities which lie before us.

. . . The first legislative act of Washington's Administration was a tariff bill. From that day to this, one of our firm national policies has been that tariffs are solely a domestic question in protection of our own people. It is now proposed that an international conference should be called with view to "lowering excessive tariffs." The very implication of calling other nations into conference with view to changing our tariff duties is to subject our tariffs to international agreement.

For myself I hold that any inequalities or excessive duties in the American tariff can be corrected through the flexible provisions of the present tariff law. If other nations should adopt this principle and such an instrumentality it would automatically remove excessive duties and unequal treatment throughout the world without interference with domestic control of tariff policies.

If the meaning of the Congress is that such a conference should discover and negotiate the elimination of particular excessive duties throughout the world, then I do not need to elaborate upon the direction in which such action leads for it means simply attempting the futility of negotiating a world tariff amongst 60 or 70 nations subject to confirmation of their legislative bodies. If on the other hand what the Congress means is to undertake a general lowering of American tariffs in exchange

From President's Veto Act to Amend the Tariff Act of 1930 (May 11, 1932), Department of State, *Press Releases* (May 14, 1932), pp. 477, 479–481.

for lowering of tariffs elsewhere in the world, and if the Congress proposes to make such a radical change in our historic policies by international negotiation affecting the whole of American tariffs, then it is the duty of the Congress to state so frankly and indicate the extent to which it is prepared to go.

I am fully alive to the effect on our own and world commerce of the many arbitrary restrictions now in existence. The Departments of State and Commerce are actively engaged in protecting our export trade from unfair discriminations and infractions. If at any time circumstances are such as to permit the hope that such barriers to international trade and commerce may be removed through the medium of an international conference without sacrificing American interests or departing from the historic policies followed by our country, I shall not hesitate to take the lead in calling such a conference. . . .

Of high importance to us also in consideration of these matters is that the principal interest of a majority of the 60 or 70 other nations which might be approached for mutual tariff concessions would be to reduce the American agricultural tariffs. No concessions otherwise than those related to agricultural products would be of any importance to those particular nations. The effect of such a shift in the basis of our agricultural tariffs would be to make us large importers of food products, to demoralize our agricultural industry and render us more and more dependent upon foreign countries for food supply; to drive our farmers into the towns and factories, and thus demoralize our whole national economic and social stability.

5. Secretary of State Cordell Hull Promotes Reciprocal Trade, 1936

As time goes on, it becomes increasingly clear that no nation can achieve a full measure of stable economic recovery so long as international trade remains in the state of collapse into which it was plunged during the years of the depression. The whole post-war period has been characterized by an ever-increasing drift toward economic nationalism, which has expressed itself in a constant growth of barriers to international trade. This drift has become enormously intensified during the past 6 years, though responsible statesmen in many countries have never ceased to deplore it. Under its impact the international economic structure of the world has been all but shattered, and individual nations have sought economic improvement more and more by means of purely domestic measures, on the basis of a greater degree of self-containment than was ever before consciously attempted. . . .

A rapid and drastic contraction of international trade of the kind that the world has witnessed during the past few years constitutes a double attack upon the economic well-being of each nation's population. The necessary materials habitually obtained in other parts of the globe become more difficult to secure. The surplus national production habitually shipped to other countries becomes more difficult to sell. Output in

From Speech by Cordell Hull to Chamber of Commerce (April 1936), Department of State, *Press Releases,* No. 875.

the surplus-creating branches of production must be curtailed, or else accumulating surpluses force prices below the level of remunerative return to the producers. In either case, the whole economic structure becomes disrupted. Vast unemployment ensues, not only in the field of production, but also in such lines of activity as transportation, banking, merchandising, and the various avocations and professions. Financial investment and other forms of savings become impaired or are wholly destroyed. Distress spreads throughout the nation in ever-widening circles.

Economic distress quickly translates itself into social instability and political unrest. It opens the way for the demagogue and the agitator, foments internal strife, and frequently leads to the supplanting of orderly democratic government by tyrannical dictatorships. It breeds international friction, fear, envy, and resentment, and destroys the very foundations of world peace. Nations are tempted to seek escape from distress at home in military adventures beyond their frontiers. And as fear of armed conflict spreads, even peace-loving nations are forced to divert their national effort from the creation of wealth and from peaceful well-being to the construction of armaments. Each step in the armament race bristles with new menace of economic disorganization and destruction, multiplies fear for the future, dislocates normal constructive processes of economic life, and leads to greater and greater impoverishment of the world's population.

In the past few months we have witnessed a swift increase in international political tension; a recrudescence of the military spirit, which sees no goal in life except triumph by force; an expansion of standing armies; a sharp increase of military budgets; and actual warfare in some portions of the globe. Human and material resources are being shifted, on a truly alarming scale, in a military direction rather than in one of peace and peaceful pursuits. . . .

Through its trade-agreements program, this country is furnishing its fair share of leadership in the world movement toward a restoration of mutually profitable international trade and, as a consequence, toward an improvement in the employment of labor, a fuller measure of stable domestic prosperity, and the only sound foundation for world peace. And we, who are concerned with the execution of the program, find special gratification in the fact that our effort in this direction has widespread support in the Nation as a whole. The press of this country, in its vast majority, has been clear-sighted enough to recognize the vital importance of the program. Great business organizations, like yours, have given us invaluable encouragement. With such inspiration to guide us, we shall go forward in our effort to bring peace and prosperity out of political tension and economic distress.

☞ *E S S A Y S*

In the first essay, Frank Costigliola assesses the cultural impact of American internationalism. Despite its retreat from the League of Nations, as Costigliola stresses, the prominence of American consumer goods, tourism, and films yielded a European fascination with all things American. In the second essay, Emily Rosenberg traces the logic and institutions of Republican foreign policy in the 1920s, and the emergence of a new "internationalist" commitment in response to the contradictions of Republican policy, the onset of the Depression, and the futile recovery strategies of the early New Deal.

Foreign Policy and Cultural Expansion

FRANK COSTIGLIOLA

In the 1920s, American economic, political, and cultural influence washed over Europe. The first cultural wave came in 1917–19 with the two-million-man American Expeditionary Force [AEF], which brought Europeans face to face with the United States' power and creativity, the development of which they had watched for over two centuries. A second swell of cultural influence followed the Dawes Plan, Locarno, and the financial stabilizations. These achievements, the fruit of the peaceful change and economic reconstruction policy, opened Europe to American business and cultural penetration. Tourists, expatriates, and Hollywood films flooded Europe, serving as missionaries for American life-styles and products. The United States' rank as the world's most powerful nation induced Europeans to pay attention to American culture. That culture's vitality, and its appropriateness to the machine age, made it all the more attractive to Europeans struggling with modernization. American models influenced Europe's popular entertainment, its artistic development, and its thoughts about the future. In cultural matters as well as in economic and political ones, the United States was the engine, the leading nation whose independent and pioneering course Europe was compelled to follow.

Perhaps because Europeans were so fascinated by the United States' economic power, they interpreted aspects of American culture, whether literature or life-style, as the products of a machine-dominated society. Increased mechanization, they believed, was the central element of Americanization. For many Europeans, American culture was above all technological. *Americanism* suggested materialism, efficiency, largeness, mechanization, standardization, automation, mass production, mass consumption, mass democracy, technocracy, uniformity, pragmatism, reformism, optimism, spontaneity, generosity, and openness. *Americanization* had two overlapping meanings: the spread eastward of Yankee influence and the modernization indigenous to both continents but more advanced in America. Some Europeans favored the Americanization of their continent, others opposed it; but nearly all believed that the United States was setting the path along which they would have to follow.

After 1917 American culture penetrated Europe in various ways. The American Expeditionary Force prepared the way for post-war cultural exchange by introducing Europeans to jazz and doughboys to the charm of the Old World. The doughboy's machines, their efficiency, energy, and innovativeness, impressed Europeans. Exhausted by the war, disillusioned with their own societies, many Europeans wondered whether they should not adopt the methods of these highly successful Americans. After the war, many former soldiers returned to the Old World as artists, tourists, or businessmen, each in his own way spreading U.S. culture. Along with Herbert Hoover's American Relief Administration, smaller private aid teams initiated Progressive reforms. Hollywood films stimulated demand for America's products while exposing

Europeans to its speech, its manners (and mannerisms), and its values. Fads swept Europe as boxers and dance troupes pioneered this cultural and economic frontier.

Yankee popular culture excited many European artists, particularly avant-garde Germans of the *neue Sachlichkeit,* or new objectivity school, who sought modern cultural models to replace discredited imperial ones. Although many of these artists, like other Europeans, feared domination by the machine, they welcomed Americanism as a way to increase the Old World's economic productivity while re-solving its social and ideological conflicts.

America's mass culture seemed democratic and progressive, the wave of the fu-ture. Many German leftist artists saw little contradiction in paying simultaneous alle-giance to bolshevism and Americanism. Both creeds preached popular sovereignty, mass culture, and technological development. In the heyday of U.S. influence, such German artists as Bertolt Brecht decided that Americanism, not bolshevism, offered the surer and more comfortable road to progress.

The United States was not only Europe's competitor, creditor, and occasional political mediator, but also the leader of Western civilization; and what happened in America was of intense, often personal interest to many Europeans. They watched closely, and reacted with near-hysterical joy, to Charles Lindbergh's solo flight across the Atlantic and, only a few months later passionately repudiated the Massa-chusetts trial and execution of Nicola Sacco and Bartolomeo Vanzetti.

America's influence in Europe had great impact also on its own artistic devel-opment. American painters, writers, composers, and other artists made pilgrimages to Europe, looking for freedom and esthetic inspiration. There they found many artists fascinated with the technologically dominated culture they had scorned. Moreover, significant numbers of expatriate artists ended up financing their adven-tures by working for compatriot businessmen and tourists. In the Old World, then, many Yankee artists found both esthetic validation and financial support for devel-oping an indigenous American art.

Just as America's power led Europeans to heed American culture, so too did such prestige or moral power enhance the effectiveness of the United States' unoffi-cial economic diplomacy. Washington officials realized that America's reputation for success and efficiency, coupled with its lack of interest in most European political ri-valries, gave the nation a subtle but important moral authority in the Old World.

The State Department valued this asset because it yielded influence abroad with minimal cost or responsibility. Department officials tried to maximize Amer-ica's moral power by making sure their foreign policy initiatives would succeed. In 1927, the department countered European resentment of U.S. power by using Charles Lindbergh as a goodwill ambassador. Like the AEF a decade earlier, Lind-bergh riveted Europeans' attention on Yankee boldness and technology, and thus quickened the pace of Americanization.

. . . AEF soldiers did more than fight. They impressed allies and enemies with American motor vehicles and American know-how. In Germany the doughboys helped suppress bolshevism; in Poland they fought typhus. As good Progressives they believed that with enough "soap, clean towels, and above all clean underwear, we can wash Poland."

The first American troops paraded through Paris on July 4, 1917, a time when the French army faced mutiny and exhaustion. Prefects throughout France reported that arrival of these American "saviors" raised civilian morale. George Creel, director of the Committee on Public Information, tried to undermine German morale by dropping behind enemy lines pamphlets that promised American-sized rations for prisoners-of-war and pictured the huge AEF buildup in France.

The buildup made good propaganda, but it snarled traffic in the French ports allotted to American traffic, St. Nazaire and Nantes. AEF engineers tackled the difficulty by building new port facilities, stringing telephone lines, and constructing a reservoir. French newspapers admired the Americans' superior "boldness" and "initiative," and found French accomplishments wanting by comparison. Struggling to comprehend the invasion, journalists defined "Americanism" as a "method of procedure . . . more concerned to do things well and quickly than to follow old-fashioned regulations." Many argued that adoption of this attitude "will do us good." The AEF introduced the French to jazz as well as American methods, whetting appetites for the jazz bands that flocked to Paris in the twenties. Although not all Frenchmen and women liked jazz, most appreciated the doughboys' sense of humor, kindness to children, and generosity. Marriage statistics perhaps best convey the closeness of the personal ties between many Yankees and the French. In St. Nazaire, Franco-American nuptials in 1919 reached 21.7 percent of the total, climbing to 37 percent in June. Although most soldiers brought their wives back to America, some fifteen hundred remained with their spouses in France, forming a link between the two societies and a vanguard for the 1920s expatriates.

Less happy relations also foreshadowed the 1920s. Although trigger-happy soldiers and hostile French peasants caused incidents throughout the AEF's two-and-a-half-year stay, trouble worsened after the Armistice. Americans awaiting transport home were bored, and irked by gouging merchants; many French chafed at the foreigners' continued occupation. Local newspapers condemned Woodrow Wilson's stance at Versailles. On the second anniversary of Congress's declaration of war on Germany, street fighting broke out between AEF soldiers and natives of St. Nazaire. Anti-American demonstrations followed in other cities. In Nice a gang ambushed and killed American military police. Such hostility exposed the reverse side of French admiration for America and foreshadowed the difficulties between the two nations from 1919 to 1933. In 1919 as in later years, the United States' riches and efficiency excited envy and fear as well as adulation.

Specific complaints against the AEF paralleled later ones against American businessmen and tourists. Although Americans tried to improve transportation facilities, the heavy AEF vehicles angered natives by clogging traffic and damaging highways. Many French people later condemned the mass production methods, imported from America, that forced changes in their lives. The French complained of AEF requisitions and later war debt demands, even though the United States tardily paid for the requisitions and reduced the burden of the war debt. Proper Frenchmen and women deplored the doughboys' sometimes crude and violent behavior. Working-class Frenchmen charged that the free-spending Americans bid up the cost of living and corrupted the local women. In the 1920s, tourists and expatriates drew the same charges. Thus, the AEF's impact in the postwar era increased both cultural exchange and the tensions between Americans and French.

The American army's experience in occupied Germany was a happier one, and it too foreshadowed the 1920s. After initial hostility, soldiers of the American

Forces in Germany (AFG) and civilians of the Rhineland soon developed cordial relations. In mid-1919, the *New York Times* repeatedly criticized American soldiers who loudly compared German hospitality with French hostility. Doughboys found Fräulein even more attractive than Mademoiselle. Commanding General Henry Allen stated that one-third of his men had married German girls. The venereal disease rate hit 423 per 1000. Germans both welcomed and resented the free-spending Americans. In marks, an AFG private's pay exceeded that of some German bank presidents. Despite the Reich's technological achievements, AFG personnel demonstrated to the Germans superior methods for drilling wells, maintaining sanitation, building bridges, and repairing roads. American forces also maintained order, suppressing a strike and Communist agitation.

The Rhineland occupation from 1919 to 1923 underscored America's decisive role in the war and doubtless heightened Germany's receptivity to U.S. methods, ideas, and products. In 1931, a German observed: "Victors in war always become the unconscious ideal and model of the conquered: America, which has conquered the whole world, has stamped its childish version of mechanistic style on our era." Although Germans and other Europeans found it easy to criticize American culture, it was harder to deny that culture's pervasive influence in the Old World.

In 1917–19 other Americans influenced Europe. Convinced that "American theories" were essential to European reconstruction, American women formed the Committee for Devastated France, which undertook social work and reconstruction in the Aisne, one of the worst battlefield areas. André Tardieu (later prime minister) recalled that the committee molded much of the social reorganization of Aisne; it introduced community "public spirit." With the committee's guidance the French organized agricultural cooperatives, public libraries, Boy Scout troops, and nursing schools. These institutions offered services and, the Americans calculated, opened new career opportunities for French women. Local peasants and townspeople came to appreciate the new institutions, and maintained them after the Americans left in 1923. Although the French had at first resisted American social service techniques, the committee concluded, they had "bent to the contact of our methods." With similar Progressive idealism, the Young Women's Christian Association (YWCA) trained women of Czechoslovakia and Poland in recreation and social service work.

Other Americans set up schools and hospitals. Probably the most influential was the American Red Cross Albanian Vocational School (AVS) in Tirana, established upon completion of wartime medical relief. Under American direction, the AVS operated in English, which Albania had adopted as its second tongue. The school provided Tirana with electricity, operated a printing press for the government, improved agriculture, installed the nation's first indoor water tap, and trained hundreds of young Albanians. Oriented toward American ideas, methods, and products, AVS graduates challenged Italian domination of Albania. Despite the Americans' sincere protests about the "disinterested character" of their involvement in the school, such cultural influence had unavoidable political implications, which did not escape the Italians. In 1933 they insisted that the Americans leave.

As the AVS demonstrated, there was direct linkage between America's participation in the Great War and the subsequent economic and cultural penetration of Europe. The soldiers and social workers awakened Europeans to the advantages of American products. Observing the AEF's mobile antityphus campaign in Poland, the minister of health remarked, "One Doctor plus one Ford makes six Doctors." Some 10,000 AEF and AFG soldiers plus ARA veterans remained in Europe, and others returned in the 1920s as tourists and representatives of U.S. firms. The AFG newspaper called the troops "but a vanguard of millions of Americans who will . . . invade the several states of Europe. We are paving the way for the men who will enter the European markets of the future."

That invasion accelerated after the Dawes Plan and Locarno stabilized Europe. American tourists, expatriates, and movies broadened Europe's exposure to Yankee products, life-styles, and ideas. Along with the loans that flooded Europe after 1924–25, tourists provided Europeans with the dollars they needed to pay their debts and buy American exports. The annual pilgrimage of as many as a quarter of a million tourists, plus the presence of eighty thousand U.S. expatriates, stimulated consumption in Europe of American products. Tourists and expatriates demanded the same goods—cokes and chewing gum, typewriters and Ford—that they knew at home. Their example, highlighted by the consumption patterns portrayed in Hollywood films, aroused European desires for the same amenities. Tourists and expatriates who fled Main Street found much of the Old World entranced with Wall Street and Hollywood. The economic and cultural exchange was a dynamic process. As Europe became more Americanized, more tourists felt comfortable vacationing there. Similarly, Europe's Americanization stimulated demand for U.S. exports, which in turn enhanced the prosperity that financed tourists' trips to Europe.

. . . Tourists constituted the largest and economically most important American group in Europe. The number of United States visitors jumped from roughly 15,000 in 1912 to 251,000 in 1929. In the latter year, American citizens in Europe spent close to $323 million and immigrants visiting home expended an additional $87 million. By the end of the 1920s, foreign travel became possible for middle-class Americans.

Visits to Paris nightclubs and the Louvre seemed a painless answer to America's balance-of-payments dilemma. Tourists' dollars helped Europe pay its debts and the United States maintain its tariff. Herbert Hoover's Commerce Department noted happily that worldwide American tourist expenditures of $770 million in 1927 more than matched $714 million in war and private debt receipts. In addition to the financial dividend, tourism had a beneficial "political effect," American officials told the Germans, "leading to a normal resumption of relations" between the two nations.

The flood of travelers generated resentment as well as dollars. Always the tourists' favorite, France in 1926 attracted foreigners who picked up bargains as the franc fell. Americans commonly asked waiters and shopkeepers "How much is that in real money?" A few even papered their train compartments or luggage with franc notes. Such insensitivity aggravated tensions over the war debt, and in July Paris erupted in several antiforeign, and especially anti-American, demonstrations. Both French and American officials tried to calm emotions. Calvin Coolidge balanced a rebuke of "bumptious" tourists with a warning that badly treated Americans would stay home. But probably the majority of visitors had pleasant tours that never made newspaper headlines—in any case, France remained the number one American tourist attraction in Europe.

In 1929, the combined expenditure of American tourists and residents in France totaled over $137 million, creating an American economy in Paris. In the French capital one could be born in the American hospital, attend one of several

American schools and churches, belong to the American Legion, the YMCA, the Cornell, Harvard, or American Women's Club; read one of three Parisian-American newspapers, in a favorite café or at the American Library; sip whiskey in the many American bars, drink milk delivered by American milkmen, eat sweet corn and ice cream produced by local Americans; go to hockey games, boxing matches, and other imported sport events; receive care from American dentists and doctors and be buried by an American undertaker. With fewer United States tourists or permanent residents, Berlin still supported an American church, student association, newspaper and, intermittently, chapters of the American Medical Association, Daughters of the American Revolution, and the Harvard Club.

The forty thousand American residents in Paris created teaching, writing, and translating jobs that helped support expatriate artists. For American writers who matured in the decade after 1919, residence in Europe, especially on the Left Bank in Paris, was almost an initiation rite. The city was "our 'university,' " Matthew Josephson recalled. The "lost" generation was on a quest for personal freedom and revitalized American art. Although many American writers, painters, and composers mocked Main Street's materialism, these largely middle-class sons and daughters did not entirely abandon its values. Most artists who sailed to Europe were confident in their own capabilities and in America's esthetic potential. In Paris they found themselves, and they found European artists entranced by America's technocratic civilization. The fruit of this cultural cross-fertilization yielded, in such diverse artists as Ernest Hemingway, Gertrude Stein, and Virgil Thomson, a reaffirmation of their Yankee heritage and a recommitment to developing an indigenous American art of which they could be proud.

American artists in Europe seemed light-years away from the less colorful U.S. diplomats and bankers. Yet ties bound the two groups. Each was confident in the power of the individual and the potential of American development. Neither put much faith in political reform or politics generally, and this abnegation strengthened the status quo. The artists who left for Paris and the administration leaders who struggled for a policy of limited involvement in Europe each felt constrained by provincial America. Personal ties, not always harmonious, also linked artists with the business-governing elite. Writer and publisher Harry Crosby secured a position at Morgan et Cie. from Uncle J. P. Morgan and researched the poetic effects of hashish while guest of Cousin Joseph Grew, ambassador to Turkey. Another Crosby cousin, Walter Berry, won renown as an international lawyer and bibliophile and, as Edith Wharton's confidant and lover, inspired the novelist to new heights. Between his failed diplomacy of 1918–19 and ambassadorships to Moscow and Paris in the 1930s, William Bullitt married John Reed's widow and cultivated the friendship of artists. Banker Otto Kahn helped finance Hart Crane's *The Bridge*. Americans like reparations expert Fred Bate and International Chamber of Commerce official Lewis Galantière combined such Right Bank work with active encouragement of the artists on the Left.

In October 1918, Walter Damrosch, an officer in the AEF and former conductor of the New York Symphony, established a music school in France to train military band leaders. After the war, the Conservatoire américain continued to educate American composers. Damrosch hired Nadia Boulanger, a prominent French musician, who encouraged composers like Virgil Thomson to take pride in and develop their native musical traditions. Thomson was part of that generation of American composers, born between 1890 and 1910, which went to Paris in the 1920s. Like other artists, many were attracted by Europe's cheap prices.

Harold Loeb, the editor of a lavish literary magazine called *Broom* published inexpensively in Berlin, explained that "literature, as well as finance, is sensible to the trade balance." Encouraged by the United States government, Austria stabilized its currency in 1923, Germany in 1924, and France in 1926. While it reduced the dollar's extraordinary buying power, stabilization attracted American businessmen and tourists to Europe. This meant jobs for artists, especially in journalism. Warren Susman calculates that almost 70 percent of American expatriates in Paris gained at least a partial living from writing articles printed in the United States or Europe.

Loeb, Matthew Josephson, and other expatriates looked for inspiration from European artists. "Instead," Josephson recalled, I found "a young France that . . . was passionately concerned with the civilization of the U.S.A., and stood in fair way to be *Americanized*." Other expatriates sharpened Europe's image of America as the land of technology and business. Assisted by Ezra Pound, George Antheil composed and conducted in Paris the *Ballet Méchanique,* an orchestration of nine machine-played pianos, electric bells, and a whirring airplane propeller. Gerald Murphy, a wealthy painter and a leader of the expatriate colony, chose such themes as machines and smokestacks. Ernest Hemingway, whose writing in the 1920s was translated into French, German, and Italian, embodied a work ethic as strong as Herbert Hoover's. Jake's parsimonious outlook in *The Sun Also Rises,* Hemingway's novel on expatriate life, paralleled American leaders' moral view of debts and currencies. Anna Louise Strong, an American journalist in Moscow who helped establish the John Reed technical school for Russian youths, brought along her "Ford . . . electric toaster, percolator, etc. etc."—for her own convenience and to "show the folks here American stuff."

Although the expatriates' idiosyncrasies defied rigid categorization, most self-exiles were the figurative sons and daughters of General John Pershing, Henry Ford, and Herbert Hoover. America's business/machine civilization had provoked their rebellion, but America remained their cultural homeland just as surely as the culture of business suffused their art and thought.

Malcolm Cowley chronicled how these inadvertent "trade missionaries" stimulated, by their life-style, demand for American goods. A few expatriates urged more explicit ties between economic and cultural expansion. Walter Lowenfels argued that "American intellectuals must take their place beside the businessmen to guide the intellectual future of the world." F. Scott Fitzgerald also anticipated an imperial future. "Culture follows money," the novelist declared; "we will be the Romans in the next generation as the English are now."

The esthetic and business spheres intersected in other ways. Well-paying European audiences helped support black jazz bands. Europeans read American authors like Sinclair Lewis and Ernest Hemingway in part because they believed it essential to understand the giant across the Atlantic. In 1930, Lewis won the Nobel Prize in recognition both of his own abilities and America's coming of age.

Europeans often addressed American writing in terms of Yankee economic predominance. American poetry had "skyscraper creativity," a German reviewer wrote. A French analyst compared Hemingway's style to "modern buildings: girders and concrete"; another labeled it "the very essence of American genius . . . reaching the first rank by jostling one's way to the fore." Whatever the metaphor, young Europeans hastened to copy the American novelist. A German critic remarked in 1932, "Young European authors write like Hemingway."

. . . During the Great War, Hollywood invaded European and other world markets. YMCA representatives entertained Allied troops with American films, and the "movie habit" caught on among civilians and soldiers. In the 1920s, American films were an international box-office hit. Assured of the domestic market, which netted 60 percent of total world film revenue, Hollywood produced extravaganzas with which Europeans could not compete. By 1925, United States films made up 95 percent of the total shown in Britain, 60 percent of the total in Germany, 70 percent in France, 65 percent in Italy, and 95 percent in Australia and New Zealand. In Germany, the number of cinemas increased by 35 percent from 1920 to 1929, while the production dropped from 646 films to 175 films. Americans owned three-fourths of the most fashionable movie theatres in France. Hollywood's profits depended on foreign screenings, since domestic revenues covered only production costs, and frequently not even that.

"Trade follows the film," Americans and Europeans agreed. Greek appliance wholesalers and Brazilian furniture dealers found that their customers demanded goods like those pictured in the American movies. Although direct correlation between films and trade was hard to prove, Congress, parsimonious in most matters, established a Motion Picture Section in the Bureau of Foreign and Domestic Commerce in 1926. Bureau chief Julius Klein and his officials attested that the United States films "stimulat[ed] the desire to own and use such garments, furnishing, utensils, and scientific innovations as are depicted on the screen." Will H. Hays, Hollywood czar, boasted of the power of these "silent salesmen of American goods."

American films not only sold United States goods, but, many Europeans feared, threatened independent national identity. "America has colonized us through the cinema," one Frenchman complained. Another French critic testified to the secularization of John Winthrop's city upon the hill: "Formerly US preachers . . . deluged the world with pious brochures; their more cheerful offspring, who pursue the same ends, inundate it with blonde movie stars; whether as missionaries loaded with bibles or producers well supplied with films, the Americans are equally devoted to spreading the American way of life." Charles Pomaret, a member of the Chamber of Deputies, remarked that Europeans had become "galley-slaves" to American finance and culture—appropriately, an image taken from the Hollywood hit *Ben-Hur.* British groups worried that the many Hollywood films shown throughout the empire led to "American domination in the development of national character or characteristics." After a concerned speech by the Prince of Wales, the London *Morning Post* warned: "The film is to America what the flag was once to Britain. By its means Uncle Sam may hope some day, if he be not checked in time, to Americanize the world."

After 1925, Britain, Germany, and France tried to check the trend. Governments enacted measures to limit the number of imported Hollywood films and encourage domestic production. This policy diminished but did not eliminate Hollywood's dominance in Europe. Required by law to produce domestic films if they wanted to import the popular American ones, German and other European producers responded with "quota quickies," often subgrade efforts produced only to meet the letter of the law. American filmmakers circumvented the restrictions by investing in Europe, especially Germany. They imported European directors and performers and remained preeminent in world film exports. The State and Commerce departments vigorously supported Hollywood's diplomacy. In the late twenties film exporters faced a new danger, with talkies. How could they screen English-language movies in polyglot Europe? Hollywood responded with multilanguage production. In collaboration with a Berlin company, Paramount filmed *The Blue Angel* in English and German versions. In France, Paramount worked on an assembly-line basis: sixty-six features in twelve languages for the first year. Dubbed sound tracks helped, and by 1931 United States films had regained all but 10 percent of their 1927 market in England and Germany.

Hollywood films were a hit in Europe because they projected modern culture in a vivid and attractive light. Film embodied the era's emphasis on mechanical, simultaneous, and concentrated production. The message was mass entertainment. As Adolf Behne, a German avant-gardist, recognized, "Film is . . . democratic. . . . This ha[s] been recognized by the German masses, which flock to see Charlie Chaplin films." As the industry's global leaders, Hollywood producers had budgets large enough to pay for the casts of thousands and other spectacular effects calculated to please those masses. Finally, the films portrayed an image of life in fabulous America, the giant of the contemporary world and the pioneer of Europe's own future.

. . . From Switzerland to the Soviet Union, Europeans acknowledged America's cultural leadership. "Mrs. Lenin," Anna Louise Strong reported from Moscow, "wants . . . American ideas on education through doing; manuals about . . . various things." Jean Paul Sartre reflected, "Skyscrapers . . . were the architecture of the future, just as the cinema was the art and jazz the music of the future." André Siegfried, a French sociologist, concluded that America had replaced Europe as "the driving force of the world."

American cultural influence probably went deeper in Germany than anywhere else in Europe. "Berlin Goes American," a journalist reported from the German capital, where cafeterias offered "griddle cakes mit syrup" and theatres featured Broadway hits. Germans, especially Berliners, eagerly borrowed almost anything American: shorter hemlines and hairdos, flapper styles, soda fountains, prizefights, Hollywood films, the Charleston, jazz. In the business and technological fields, many German industrialists, particularly the larger and more successful ones, adopted the efficient techniques of Henry Ford and Frederick Taylor. Other small businessmen, unable to install or compete with mass assembly lines, protested Germany's transformation. Some intellectuals and members of the middle class sided with the smaller entrepreneurs and defended the virtues of *Volk, Kultur,* and *Heimat* against the invasion of foreignness, functionalism, and modernity. The mania for things American became an issue in the sharp debate over Germany's future.

In this controversy many left-wing intellectuals and artists, particularly those of the *neue Sachlichkeit* or new objectivity school, embraced the technocratic vision of Americanism, but not for the same reasons as the industrialists. The businessmen sought greater productivity and profits, most of which they were unwilling to pass on to workers. The intellectuals and artists viewed increased efficiency and productivity as a vehicle toward greater social justice. Struggling to throw off the constraints of the past in art and architecture, many Germans—like the Frenchmen observing the AEF—admired the Americans' success, inventiveness, and practicality. Avant-garde Germans welcomed American mass culture as democratic and appropriate for the machine age. In designing new structures, some of which were built with American loans, German architects incorporated efficient design elements also borrowed from the United States, such as wall closets, folding beds, and self-service restaurants. *Der Querschnitt,* an avant-garde journal, interpreted jazz in terms of machinery: "Man became mechanical, rigorously ruled by a strict, rhythmically syncopating present, which call itself the jazzband." Germans made similar analogies in describing the fad for American synchronized dance troupes, such as the Tiller Girls. Siegfried Krakauer, Berlin cultural editor for the *Frankfurter Zeitung,* explained: "The Girls were artificially manufactured in the USA and exported to Europe. . . . Not only were they American products; at the same time they demonstrated the greatness of American production. . . . When they formed an undulating snake, they radiantly illustrated the virtues of the conveyor belt; when they tapped their feet in fast tempo, it sounded like *business, business;* when they kicked their legs high with mathematical precision, they joyously affirmed the progress of rationalization." Whether intentionally or not, Krakauer parodied German fascination with that factory upon the hill.

The strength of this appeal was demonstrated by left-wing artists' simultaneous allegiance to Americanism and bolshevism. Both paths offered an alternative to the discredited past; both promised a democratic, technocratic, peaceful, and abundant future. Especially during the years of the quasi-capitalistic New Economic Policy in Russia, the two paths appeared to some Europeans to merge into a single road. Indeed, the contrast in the early twenties between Russia's distress and America's success led some left-wing Germans like Bertolt Brecht to pick the Western route: "I am now very much against Bolshevism . . . universal service . . . rationing of food, control. . . . I would like an automobile." Others adhered to bolshevism while also reaching for the Americanist dream. Maria Piscator recalled that her husband's Communist theatre group

> invented "America." Everything that was useful, effective, expedient, operative, performing properly and instrumental for productivity was called American. Even time had an American tempo. . . . None of them had seen America. . . . They admired what seemed real to them: the objective existence of the land of plenty, its material genius, with its prosperity, its slogans, and the great god—the machine. it is impossible to understand the complexity of Epic Theatre without taking into account this capture of the imagination by America, while, at the same time, the period was idealistically entangled with the new Russia. . . .

What happened in America affected the whole world. The United States had become John Winthrop's city upon the hill, though not for the religious reasons that he had expected, and Europeans could not avert their gaze. Whether they welcomed the prospect or dreaded it, most Europeans believed that American civilization portrayed the future course of their own societies. The United States was the metropolis, the hub of the modern cultural system, and Europe now figured as a satellite.

Stabilized by the Dawes Plan, Locarno, and the gold standard, Europe was a beckoning frontier for American business and cultural pioneers. Cultural and economic influence enhanced America's prestige and thus the effectiveness of its economic, unofficial diplomacy. Yet ironically, the very success of the peaceful change and economic reconstruction policy created conditions which, by the late twenties, were undermining the new order.

The Dilemmas of Interwar Foreign Policy

EMILY ROSENBERG

In the 1920s, United States private enterprise greatly expanded the nation's export trade and foreign investment, and the government, building on prewar trends, worked through private interests to guide United States participation in the international economy. But contradictions undermined cooperative notions. Conducting an economic policy through the private sector assumed an identity of interests between private enterprise and the national state. Often the interests did coincide, and then, as Hoover clearly understood, it greatly simplified government's tasks to have private citizens, rather than policymakers, involved in international economic details and negotiations. Not only did this private approach remove highly technical discussions from the political arena and put them into the hands of "experts"— bankers, businessmen, or economists—but it accorded with the liberal bias against large government. Often, however, the private sector could not or would not execute public policy. Private bankers were ultimately bound by their own standards of liquidity and their stockholders' expectations, not by government's prescriptions for international interest. Capital, particularly toward the end of the decade, did not always flow as officials desired. In addition, private chosen instruments acted in the name of American interests, but had no public accountability, or even much visibility, in the political process. The American public believed that the Republican Administrations were following a policy of disengagement from international affairs, yet the private sector was involving the United States in the intricate world system at government's behest and making enormous profits by this economic entanglement. The private approach to economic diplomacy ultimately made the public less able to understand their country's relationship with the rest of the world.

The liberalism of the cooperative state contained even more profound dilemmas. Republican Administrations of the 1920s made equal access, not free trade, their basic goal in commercial policy; Americans sought equality of opportunity abroad, yet enjoyed protectionism at home. Moreover, policymakers fought attempts by foreign governments to manipulate world prices, while they instituted "voluntary" restrictions on investment capital and acquiesced in price-setting cartels dominated by American companies in the oil, copper, and electrical industries. Hoover suggested that because American economic controls sprang voluntarily from the private sector, they were somehow more benign and acceptable. By such

From Emily Rosenberg, *Spreading the American Dream* (Hill and Wang, 1982), 159–164, 169–180.

policies, American liberalism of the 1920s actually distorted liberal, free-market-place doctrines. A liberalism that would not recognize that high tariffs and private cartels constituted restrictions within the world marketplace bore little similarity to the ideas of Adam Smith, who had warned against concentrations of private power, as well as against government interference. . . .

The central assumption behind the foreign policy of the pre-Depression era was that the United States could simultaneously enjoy great international economic power and limited government. But the cooperative state proved unable to halt the spiral of declining trade and rising default on debts that set in after 1929. During the 1920s, America's high-tariff policy had strengthened its position as a creditor; foreigners used American loans in part to meet previous debts and to purchase American exports. When American lenders slowed their extension of credit in late 1928 and then stopped foreign lending altogether after the stock-market crash of 1929, foreign trade declined, export inventories mounted, and debts went unpaid. America's combined imports and exports fell from $9.5 billion in 1929 to less than $3 billion in 1932; in September 1931, Great Britain left the gold standard, and forty other countries followed during the next six months; after 1931, there was large-scale international default on governmental war debts and on private securities. (By 1935, for example, Germany's default rate was 99.6 percent, Brazil's was 93 percent, China's was 100 percent.) The international system of trade, finance, and exchange was in collapse. It needed a massive infusion of capital to make up for the retreating investment and to reverse the downward trend, but there was no adequate governmental or international mechanism to provide it.

The private banks, experiencing their own liquidity crises, could not be expected to resume massive international lending. The Young Plan of 1929 tried to scale down war debts and reparations and to schedule German payments on private American loans; in 1931, Hoover declared a one-year moratorium on war debts. But neither measure arrested the crisis. The Young Plan, reflecting the views of the internationalist business community, proposed a Bank of International Settlements (BIS) that could coordinate international monetary policy through the central banks of the leading nations. But it was too late to construct institutions to stop the depressionary spiral; nationalist pressures were strong and the American public viewed with suspicion any proposal advanced by international business interests. Without strong American support, the BIS was useless. Hoover's inability to fashion any significant response to the crisis highlighted the inadequacy of a structure based on private capital.

If the private sector could not resuscitate the international economy, neither could the government save the private sector. Governmental institutions possessed few means of protecting the private businesses and chosen instruments that had ventured abroad during the 1920s at government's urging. Despite the cries of Americans that foreigners should be forced to repay their debts and despite business's appeal for greater governmental support of their foreign claims, the government was helpless to prevent massive defaults.

The cooperative ethic thus collapsed along with the international economy. The private sector was unable to work in the interests of international stability; the public sector was unable to protect the foreign stakes of its citizens. Franklin Delano

Roosevelt, who became President in 1933, gradually moved toward more governmental regulation and greater executive-branch power over foreign economic policy. The largest globally oriented corporations also hoped for a stronger governmental role in assuring a stable international system, but they did not wait for that. Most sought to secure their own international positions through greater geographical diversification or stronger monopolistic arrangements. Both government and private capital, then, moved to bring order out of international chaos; and both moved further and further away from a liberal marketplace model.

Depression gave birth to neomercantilist restrictions and political uncertainties. In 1930, Congress enacted the extraordinarily high Smoot–Hawley tariff. Nationalist business interests backed this tariff to preserve the dwindling domestic market for themselves. Despite the objections of a thousand American economists, pressure from internationalist business circles, and protests from more than thirty foreign countries, Hoover signed the bill, hoping that if domestic prosperity was restored, international health would also return. Yet, while Hoover futilely struggled to prove that nationalistic measures and international health were not at odds, in fact, the tariff was seen, as Dana F. Fleming has written, as a "declaration of economic war by the strongest economic power against the whole of the civilized world." Other nations responded with similar economic nationalism. By 1932, American traders and investors began to discover a radically changed international environment: higher tariffs; special trading agreements; import quotas; regulations on prices, exchange rates, and profit remittances; and, in some places, pressure to cooperate with national, government-sponsored cartels.

As they looked beyond America's borders in the early 1930s, most traders and investors felt alarm and pessimism. The rules of the international economic game were changing. In 1932, American financial journals advised against investments in firms with significant foreign holdings. From 1933 to 1940, statistics on direct investment revealed a net *inflow* for the first time since records had begun to be kept in 1900.

Extractive and agricultural investments suffered most. The great investments in raw materials that the American government had encouraged after World War I produced a surplus in most commodities during the 1920s. During the 1930s, these surpluses glutted the marketplace, and prices declined sharply. The Guggenheim's huge nitrate holdings in Chile went broke: the value of United Fruit's investment in Central America dropped sharply under the combined impact of depression and a new banana disease. As copper prices plummeted, the American-dominated copper cartel collapsed. American companies with foreign investments in copper, nitrates, tin, bananas, rubber, and sugar generally showed losses after 1930.

Price stabilization became the object of the private diplomacy carried on by the many international companies that had large stakes in raw materials. During the 1930s, some American companies joined in privately arranged cartels—the tactic of a producers' monopoly that, when practiced by foreign governments, had been anathema to Hoover. American investors signed price-setting agreements with other tin producers to boost their profits. Goodyear and U.S. Rubber Company, operating in Dutch and British colonies, participated in an international rubber agreement, even though the United States government had loudly denounced the British government's rubber controls in the 1920s. A similar private accord over the price of sugar, backed by significant American interests in Cuba, was also tried, though it failed because too many growers remained independent. All in all, international stabilization of prices, a principle that ran directly counter to liberal pricing by supply and demand, became one method of survival. By mid-decade, Franklin Roosevelt, reflecting the government's growing acceptance of a regulated international market, even came out in favor of government-enforced commodity agreements, at least those that would raise the price of America's major agricultural exports, wheat and cotton. . . .

As the Depression undermined the ethos of the cooperative state, government policymakers increasingly sought to fulfill national goals through direct involvement in the international economy. The United States government moved toward becoming an international regulatory state. Such a state, as this term must be understood, did not provide a set of controls over American business practices (though it did include a few); rather, it created a variety of government-operated mechanisms to promote economic recovery and to safeguard against the kind of breakdown experienced after 1929. It created significant new powers for the executive branch and allowed for direct governmental intervention in international economic and cultural realms. The international regulatory state developed slowly, not reaching its peak until the cold-war period, but its origins were in the crises of the 1930s.

Before policymakers really began to fashion a regulatory state, they had to define America's position in the world and to set particular goals. American economic and cultural expansion had long proceeded under the umbrella of liberal-developmental faiths that linked free enterprise, equal access, and free flow to a vision of international development and global progress. As nations threw up economic barriers during the 1930s and began to rearm, Americans debated what policies would be appropriate to the new, more restricted world order.

Many internationalists called on the government to take more vigorous action to restore an integrated, liberalized, and peaceful international system. Many urged the United States to join, or at least to act in concert with, the League of Nations in order to attack economic problems and punish military aggression. To these internationalists, spheres of interest and mercantilistic restrictions were characteristic of a less-enlightened past, and they could only breed international rivalries and, ultimately, wars. In his book *At the Rim,* James T. Shotwell wrote that civilization in the 1930s was at a turning point. "The issue before us is whether we shall have to turn back the march of progress and accept once more the anarchy of the old state system, with all its risks and dangers, its accentuation of conflict, and its acceptance of war as an instrument of policy. It is a contest of the future with the past." This internationalist group, of course, contained many factions. Some wished primarily to restore international stability, to accelerate a Pax Americana in which American economic might could expand without obstruction. Others, who would find a leader in Secretary of Agriculture Henry Wallace, urged Roosevelt to forge an international system that would support social reform and popular control worldwide. Both groups of internationalists favored an open world, but the first cared most that it was open to American business and the other that it was open to the New Deal's concern for social justice. This difference in emphasis, muted at first in the common effort to promote international recovery and to eliminate restrictive nationalism, would grow into a major split within the Roosevelt and Truman Administrations during and after World War II.

Other people, who considered themselves more nationalistic—more American—than the internationalists, embraced the concept of spheres of interest and advocated greater national self-sufficiency. They warned against the globalism inherent in policies of open-door liberalism. Expansionist policies, they believed, could only bring Americans into conflict with others; spheres of interest, they maintained, offered the surest road to peace. Like the internationalists, the advocates of greater American self-sufficiency were a diverse lot, and they did not see eye to eye on all issues. Some tended to be arch-protectionists, closely allied to domestic interests that resented the domination of international corporations and the competition of imported goods. Mining interests from Western states, for example, advocated developing domestic raw materials, rather than importing them, and strongly opposed the internationalists who sought further to integrate American and foreign economies. George Peek, a leading spokesman for agricultural interests, whom F.D.R. appointed administrator of the Agricultural Adjustment Act and special adviser on foreign trade, also argued in favor of protecting domestic markets and encouraging exports only of "those products we can best produce, particularly those agricultural products which are the backbone of our prosperity." Peek warned that increasing economic interconnections with the world in a liberalized order would continue to sacrifice agricultural interests for the well-being of industrial exporters, something he felt had happened during the 1920s. And the agricultural depression of the 1920s, he believed, was a major cause of the worldwide Depression of the 1930s. Peek's book *Why Quit Our Own?* (1936), written with economic isolationist Samuel Crowther, invoked the historical tradition of George Washington's Farewell Address and Henry Clay's American System to advocate a new "American program" that would boost agricultural exports without committing the United States to a general lowering of tariff barriers or to international economic cooperation. He also advocated extension of government credits to finance agricultural exports; he became the first president of the Export-Import Bank of 1934. Peek, like other business nationalists, wanted to halt (through protectionism)—not to accelerate—the integration of the United States into the world economy.

Charles Beard, one of the era's most prominent historians and a bitter foe of internationalism, developed a different formulation of the dangers of globalism and the advantages of self-reliance. In *The Idea of National Interest* (1934), Beard rejected the liberal faiths that had posited economic expansion as a means of achieving prosperity and world peace. War, not peace, he maintained, was the inevitable result of global economic aspirations. Like Peek, he called for a revival of Alexander Hamilton's vision of "national interest," that is, self-sufficiency in the nation's primary needs—the "means of subsistence, habitation, clothing, and defense." By invoking the economic philosophy of Hamilton, and even of Thomas Jefferson (the two political adversaries disagreed on many points, but not on their desire to break the new nation's economic dependence on Europe), Beard tried to elevate self-sufficiency into a strong and still-viable American historical tradition. As Beard explained in *The Open Door at Home* (1934), a companion volume to *The Idea of National Interest,* America should "substitute an intensive cultivation of its own garden for a wasteful, quixotic, and ineffectual extension of interests beyond the reach of competent military and naval defense."

But Beard's invocation of tradition and his unfortunate use of the nostalgic garden metaphor did not reflect a mindless desire to retreat into a simpler past. His vision of America's proper path looked to the future. New technology, Beard believed, made self-sufficiency more practical than ever before; technology could create substitutes for products hitherto supplied only from foreign lands. America could break its dependence on foreign sources of supply by development of synthetics (he provided the example of nitrates) and could, through careful social engineering, convert the economic surplus it currently exported into programs to achieve real social justice at home. Beard, in short, believed that international liberalism was expansionistic and ultimately militaristic; he wanted the term "national interest" once again to be identified with the strength of the national economy, rather than being defined by the business internationalists and other expansionists. The open door to new opportunities and profits could be found at home.

In retrospect, it may seem that Franklin Roosevelt, who took office in 1933, had to make a clear choice between nationalist and internationalist policies, but Roosevelt, without doubt, was a master of inconsistency. Initially at least, he tried to cultivate support from both groups. During the Presidential campaign of 1932, for example, he assailed the Republicans' high tariff but also emphasized the need to preserve domestic markets. (Given two contradictory drafts of a speech on tariff policy—one advocating protectionism and one favoring reciprocal lowering of tariffs—Roosevelt told an adviser to "weave the two together.") It was clear that the President favored both international cooperation toward a liberalized and more integrated world order and maximum national flexibility that might insulate Americans from international troubles. His earliest appointments included both prominent internationalists, such as Secretary of State Cordell Hull, and others, including George Peek, who believed that recovery had to come from purely domestic measures. Although there was much confusion, Roosevelt actually did follow both policies, emphasizing nationalism in the first year and internationalism thereafter.

During 1933, Roosevelt's actions had an ultranationalist tone. That year a World Economic Conference, which outgoing President Hoover strongly endorsed, convened in London. European leaders hoped to bring Americans into a cooperative effort to stabilize exchange rates (as a first step toward raising world price levels and restoring trade) and to counteract the nationalistic restrictions that were contracting world trade. Although Roosevelt's Secretary of State, Cordell Hull, who believed in trade liberalization as a primary means of recovery, received F.D.R.'s preliminary support for such measures, the President decided at the last minute not to go along with the London conference's internationalist approach. The President wanted to maintain maximum flexibility for domestic policy and announced that he was unwilling to stabilize the dollar. Roosevelt thus doomed, or at least delayed, cooperative attempts to restore the international economic order. In the process, he incurred the deep distrust of most European leaders. (A notable exception was John Maynard Keynes, a prominent British economist and treasury official who advocated the same sort of nationally contained capitalism envisioned by Beard.)

Most American internationalists lashed out against F.D.R.'s actions and warned that the President's narrow nationalism would only incur retaliation. Internationalists were even more horrified when Roosevelt announced his decision to begin massive gold purchases, a scheme that would inflate the dollar by manipulating the price of gold and thereby raise prices for American commodities. It was just such competitive inflation of national currencies that the Europeans (and Hoover) had hoped to prevent through international agreements. Internationalist critics also attacked the New Deal's Agricultural Adjustment Act (administered by George Peek), which temporarily banned all agricultural imports in order to reduce domestic farm surpluses. They charged that the AAA presented one more obstacle to the restoration of world trade and represented the kind of governmental restrictions that Americans had traditionally opposed.

A few months after the London conference, at a Pan-American gathering in Montevideo, Uruguay, the President once again showed his reluctance to liberalize trade. Cordell Hull, though feeling the sting that Roosevelt had handed him in London, continued to proselytize for free trade. He introduced a resolution calling for hemispheric efforts to reduce tariffs and to embrace most-favored-nation policies. But again Roosevelt undercut his Secretary of State. He summoned reporters to the White House to inform them that Hull's proposals were an independent action to which his Administration attached little importance. To underscore his reservations, Roosevelt used the occasion of Hull's absence in Uruguay to appoint protectionist George Peek as an adviser on foreign trade.

In Congress, where nationalist interests had always been strong, the suspicion of international economic ties brought new protective legislation supported by Roosevelt. In 1933 and 1934, lawmakers mandated formal regulation of the sale of foreign securities. The new laws required foreigners (as well as Americans) to file detailed prospectuses and information with the newly created Securities and Exchange Commission. When foreign governments were the sellers, their information had to describe existing indebtedness, itemize governmental receipts and expenditures, and list any defaults within the previous twenty years.

Congress also toughened its policy on war debts. Throughout the 1920s, the United States had taken a hard line, insisting on repayment while refusing to recognize that Europeans' ability to repay had any relationship to America's high tariffs or to Germany's payment of reparations. In response to the general economic collapse, Hoover in July 1931 accepted a year-long moratorium on debts; but, despite European pleas that cancellation of both reparations and war debts would serve the interests of recovery, the President rejected outright cancellation. After the moratorium expired in the summer of 1932, most countries defaulted, and Roosevelt's failure to try a cooperative approach to international economic difficulties at the London conference precluded any comprehensive solution to the war-debts problem. Angered by foreign defaults, Congress then took the initiative. In the Johnson Act of January 1934, Congress forbade private loans to any country that had defaulted on debts owed to the United States government. Realizing the Johnson Act's popular appeal, Roosevelt quietly supported the measure, though he also recognized how unpopular it was with foreign governments and with Americans who had favored international cooperation. He did manage to slip in an exception for *governmental* loans made to foreign nations so that the act would not hamstring operations of the new Export-Import Bank. The Johnson Act and Roosevelt's halting endorsement of its nationalistic approach reinforced the notions that countries too poor to pay their debts should be punished, rather than assisted in recovery, and that American lenders should go slow in their international dealings.

American policy in the first year of the New Deal, then, shaped by Roosevelt's nationalist advisers, by the President's desire to give himself maximum flexibility in international matters, and by Congress's response to nationally based special interests, was cautious toward foreign economic involvement and primarily addressed the problem of domestic recovery. Charles Beard and other advocates of nationalism or self-sufficiency applauded Roosevelt in early 1934 for his reluctance to embrace internationalist solutions. It looked as though Roosevelt might repudiate expansion and global economic integration. But nationalists mistakenly interpreted the President's actions as a reflection of his commitment to their position. In fact, however, as the historian Robert Dalleck has stressed, Roosevelt saw his early policy only as a response to short-term emergency conditions. He maintained a philosophical commitment to cooperative internationalism.

During 1934, Roosevelt began to emphasize how national security was dependent on a liberal world order that could be open to American goods, capital, and culture. More important, he began to develop new governmental mechanisms for making internationalism work. Because of the great domestic opposition to foreign entanglements, these efforts were sometimes halting; but their ultimate purpose was nonetheless clear. Under pressure from the unrelenting economic depression and the growth of Fascism's military challenge, F.D.R. devised new governmental powers to reinstate a liberal order that would supposedly benefit all nations, without some needing to pursue policies of aggressive territorial expansionism.

. . . The international turmoil of the 1930s arose, partly at least, out of the Anglo-American economic dominance of the 1920s. During that expansionary decade, Americans rolled up favorable trade balances and, together with Britain, came to monopolize three-fourths of the world's mineral resources. At the same time, America's balance of trade and position as a World War I creditor gave United States lenders predominant control over international purse strings.

Internationalists justified Anglo-American control over minerals and investments as efficient and advantageous to all, but other, less-favored industrial countries came to believe they were entrapped as second-rate powers. During the 1930s, writers and politicians in Germany, Italy, and Japan pointed out that their countries had insufficient raw materials to maintain their industrialized economies and complained that they could not depend on purchasing raw materials from others, because the breakdown of international lending and closure of foreign markets left them short of funds. Increasingly, political groups in Germany, Italy, and Japan turned away from international liberalism toward national self-sufficiency. To shield themselves from dependence on an unstable economic order dominated by others, they sought to acquire territory that would bring them both mineral wealth and a captive market. Japan's move into Manchuria in 1931, Italy's invasion of Ethiopia in 1935, and Germany's reoccupation of the Rhineland in 1936 were all designed to achieve a more viable and self-sufficient economic base.

Anglo-American dominance gave them the economic power to choke off the strategic raw materials needed for war and thus check these early signs of aggression. But after Japan absorbed Manchuria, the League of Nations placed no economic sanctions on Japan (despite the fact that Japan's move clearly violated the Washington Treaty and the Kellogg-Briand Pact), and the League's economic restrictions against Italy omitted the most important commodity of all—petroleum. In part, the League acted weakly because economic sanctions served little purpose without United States cooperation. And the Roosevelt Administration seemed ill-disposed to cooperate, because popular sentiment ran so strongly against involvement in foreign quarrels.

Congress balked at any Presidential effort to favor one side in a conflict. The revisionist historians of World War I and the Nye Committee's Senate hearings in 1934 had hardened beliefs that involvement in World War I had been the unfortunate result of pressures from international bankers and traders whose profits became tied to an Allied victory. In 1935, Roosevelt asked Congress to give him discretionary power to embargo war supplies to belligerents; he wanted to be able to deny arms to an aggressor while supplying them to a victim. But Congress refused. F.D.R.'s congressional critics charged that the grant of such authority would allow the President, at his own discretion, to act in harmony with members of the League of Nations and to become allied with one side in a foreign war. Roosevelt accepted, instead, Congress's Neutrality Act of 1935. Rather than giving the Executive discretionary power over commerce, the Neutrality Act specifically mandated an absolute embargo on the sale of munitions to all belligerents in a war. A few months later, Congress went further and forbade the purchase of securities issued by belligerent nations and created a new National Munitions Control Board to license all peacetime trade in "arms, ammunition, or implements of war." This neutrality legislation, passed during the Italian invasion of Ethiopia, seemed primarily concerned with barring practices that, in the name of neutral rights, had led America into a war to support the Allies in 1917.

After World War II, internationalists faulted Roosevelt for not fighting harder for economic sanctions to choke off aggression in its early stages. Yet the reluctance to jump conspicuously into economic warfare in the mid-1930s did not mean that Roosevelt employed no economic diplomacy in an effort to ameliorate international problems. Roosevelt, in fact, was increasingly listening to internationalist advisers such as Cordell Hull, who believed that if the machinery of world trade was lubricated, Germany, Italy, and Japan could once again make up their deficiencies through purchase rather than conquest. Roosevelt came to believe that measures to restore international prosperity would alleviate pressures for aggressive acts more effectively than isolating the aggressors economically. Economic weakness was, after all, the problem; the wisdom of further aggravating the deprivation was not at all clear, even from an internationalist point of view.

Roosevelt tackled the problem of international disorder by using economic measures that, unlike an embargo, did not attract the public spotlight. With surprisingly little public notice, he widened the Executive's authority over international economic policy and gradually accumulated substantial power to parcel out economic rewards and punishments. From 1934 on, the economic foreign policy of the New Deal—trying to reestablish an open, liberalized order without controversial entanglements—embraced two goals: trade liberalization through tariff policy, and an increase of discretionary power over loans and trade that could be exercised by the Executive largely outside the control of Congress.

In 1934, the President clearly endorsed Secretary Hull's beliefs and began to work seriously on Hull's dream of trade reform, producing what became the Trade Agreements Act of 1934. In stating his new internationalist approach to peace and prosperity, Roosevelt announced that his goal was to create a more equitable world order by seeking to restore "commerce in ways which will preclude the building up of large favorable trade balances by any one nation at the expense of trade debits on the part of other nations." Hull's assistant in the State Department was Francis Sayre, a law professor from Harvard and Woodrow Wilson's son-in-law. In elaborating the philosophy behind the Trade Agreements Act, Sayre offered this arch-internationalist analysis of the Depression:

> One of the important underlying causes of the existing financial difficulties which are so grievously delaying the return of prosperity is the failure of international trade, due to its diminished proportions, to offer a sufficiently broad base to support the volume of international debts and credits and thus to stabilize the financial situation of the various countries. Without an increased international trade it is difficult to see how to meet the problems of international finance which press in on every side.

The Trade Agreements Act of 1934 gave the President authority to raise or lower existing tariff rates by as much as 50 percent. Tariffs would be lowered against the products of nations that granted American goods reciprocal concessions, and because of America's adherence to most-favored-nation treatment, the reductions given to one government would then extend to all except those that continued to discriminate against American commerce. Countries that did not grant most-favored-nation status to Americans could still, under the 1922 tariff law, be penalized by an increase of 50 percent. The act had two purposes: to contribute to a general lowering of tariff and to effect the spread of the most-favored-nation doctrine of equal access. It represented a victory for the internationalists, who had long favored both equal access and freer trade, and a major setback for the business nationalists, who had always tried to merge equal access with protectionism. Reflecting the nationalists' anger, George Peek excoriated Roosevelt for becoming a tool of Carnegie Endowment, the World Peace Foundation, and other pro League, internationalist groups and soon resigned from the Administration. He charged F.D.R. and Hull with adopting trade policies that, in Peek's words, were "un-American" and "Internationalism Gone Wild."

Cuba became the first country to benefit from a reciprocal trade agreement under the new law. But, since tariff agreements with Cuba had been specifically exempted from most-favored-nation generalization, this was a special case. Lower duties on Cuban sugar would apply exclusively to Cuba, without automatically being accorded to others under the most-favored-nation policy. Such exemption obviously preserved markets in the United States for Cuban growers, most of whom were American investors. The special situation of Cuba meant that reciprocal lowering of duties with Cuba was more easily agreed upon, because reductions did not raise complications over their extension to others.

There were also pressing political reasons for rapidly lowering duties on Cuban sugar. In 1933, Cuban reformers had unseated the long-time dictator Gerardo Machado and established a government that American landowners in Cuba feared might embark on a program of agrarian reform. Roosevelt refused to send American marines to ward off the threat, but he made it clear that a trade agreement placing lower duties on sugar would not be negotiated with the existing government. He also promised Cuban army leaders, notably Fulgencio Batista, that the United States would support a coup against the reformist government and reward its leaders with a trade agreement that would bolster Cuba's depressed economy. After the coup, Roosevelt not only signed the trade agreement with Batista but also formally abrogated the Platt Amendment of 1902, the hated clause that had turned Cuba into a U.S. protectorate after the Spanish-American War. These actions made Batista appear to be an ardent nationalist, the hero who ended Cuba's demeaning status as a protectorate and alleviated its economic depression. The case of Cuba illustrated the great power that control of tariff duties could bring to the American Executive.

Elsewhere, however, Executive authority under the Trade Agreements Act of 1934 never became the formidable force in diplomacy or recovery that Hull and other champions had sought. Since each reduction had to apply to every other country, except those specifically under penalty for discrimination against American goods, the writing of reciprocal trade agreements became an intricate task. Instead of cutting through the tangle of trade and tariff policies to make trade less complicated, the Trade Agreements Act itself got lost in the morass. Although the Roosevelt Administration eventually signed agreements with eighteen governments, it found these of little help in boosting the overall volume of international trade.

The significance of the Trade Agreements Act of 1934 was less its impact on economic recovery than the fact that it made tariff negotiations a more direct tool of Executive diplomacy and that it made the U.S., for the first time, an advocate of both equal access and freer trade. In an article in *Foreign Affairs,* Henry F. Grady lauded the 1934 act: "This new policy is of an importance that can hardly be exaggerated. We are to a greater degree than ever before meshing our domestic economy into the world economy." The economic internationalists were in the ascendancy.

SUGGESTED READING

Adams, Frederick. *Economic Diplomacy: The Export-Import Bank and American Foreign Policy, 1934–1939* (1976).
Brandes, Joseph. *Herbert Hoover and Economic Diplomacy* (1962).
Cohen, Warren. *Empire Without Tears: America's Foreign Relations, 1921–1933* (1987).
Costigliola, Frank. *Awkward Dominion: American Political, Economic, and Cultural Relations with Europe, 1919–1933* (1984).
Dallek, Robert. *Franklin D. Roosevelt and American Foreign Policy.* 2d ed. (1995).
Eckes, Alfred. *The United States and the Global Struggle for Minerals* (1979).
Gardner, Lloyd. *Economic Aspects of New Deal Diplomacy* (1964).
———. *Safe for Democracy: Anglo-American Response to Revolution, 1913–1923* (1984).
Gardner, Richard. *Sterling-Dollar Diplomacy in Current Perspective.* Rev. ed. (1980).
Hogan, Michael. *Informal Entente: The Private Structure of Cooperation in Anglo-American Economic Diplomacy, 1918–1928* (1977).
Hull, Cordell. *The Memoirs of Cordell Hull* (1948).
Iriye, Akira. *The Globalizing of America, 1914–1945* (1993).
Jones, Kenneth Paul, ed. *U.S. Diplomats in Europe, 1919–1941* (1981).
Kindleberger, Charles. *The World in Depression.* Rev. ed. (1986).

Knock, Thomas. *To End All Wars: Woodrow Wilson and the Quest for a New World Order* (1992).

LaFeber, Walter. *Inevitable Revolutions: The United States in Central America* (1984).

Leffler, Melvyn. *The Elusive Quest: America's Pursuit of European Stability and French Security, 1919–1933* (1979).

———. "1921–1932: Economic Impulses and Domestic Constraints." In *Economics and World Power,* ed. William Becker and Samuel Wells, 227–256 (1984).

Levin, N. Gordon. *Woodrow Wilson and World Politics* (1968).

Link, Arthur, ed. *Woodrow Wilson and a Revolutionary World* (1982).

Nolan, Mary. *Visions of Modernity: American Business and the Modernization of Germany* (1994).

O'Brien, Thomas. *The Revolutionary Mission: American Enterprise in Latin America* (1996).

Parrini, Carl. *Heir to Empire: United States Economic Diplomacy, 1916–1923* (1969).

Pike, Frederick. *FDR's Good Neighbor Policy* (1995).

Randall, Stephen. *United States Foreign Oil Policy* (1986).

Rosenberg, Emily. *Spreading the American Dream* (1982).

Thorne, Christopher G. *The Limits of Foreign Policy: The West, the League, and the Far Eastern Crisis of 1931–1933* (1972).

Wilkins, Mira. *The Maturing of Multinational Enterprise* (1974).

Williams, William A. *The Tragedy of American Diplomacy* (1959).

Wilson, Joan Hoff. *American Business and Foreign Policy* (1971).

Hard Times and Harder Times: Agriculture Between the Wars

American agriculture stumbled through the 1920s. For most, high wartime demand was followed by a postwar slump that saw demand, prices, and farm incomes tumble. While much of the industrial economy recovered from the depression of 1920–1921, the agricultural economy settled into a persistent state of crisis. New fertilizers and mechanization increased farm productivity but, in the absence of significant new markets, only contributed to plummeting prices. For individual farmers, who needed to maintain income in order to pay off debts, the only response was to increase production and (inadvertently) drive prices down even further. These pressures were magnified in the largely tenant-based sharecropping system that persisted on the ruins of the South's plantation economy. In the decade after 1920, the number of farms shrank and the rate of debt and tenancy, for those who managed to remain on the land, rose sharply. Farmers organized sporadically, but could not recapture the scope of the late-nineteenth-century Populist movement. Before the crisis of the 1930s forced the issue, state and federal governments did little to support farm prices or relieve farm debt.

The Depression spread like a plague over the farm economy of the West and South. Collapsing agricultural prices were exacerbated by near-record production of most staples (despite the drought of 1930), which depressed prices further and eroded future markets. The pre-Depression average annual farm income of almost one thousand dollars fell to barely three hundred dollars by 1932. Expenditures on farm labor fell by half, and agricultural credit evaporated. Nearly one million farms were foreclosed between 1930 and 1934. By one estimate, one-quarter of the State of Mississippi went on the auction block on a single day in April 1932. In one of the saddest examples of irrational conditions during the Depression, farmers tried to keep crop prices up by plowing under harvests and destroying surpluses while millions were scavenging for food and suffering from starvation and malnutrition. In much of the South, especially among black sharecroppers, the crash did little more than confirm already dismal conditions; after 1929 it simply seemed that many others were doing as badly. As rural and urban economies

*collapsed, farmers, farm hands, and farm families joined a growing migrant com-
munity whose population, over two million by 1933, was greater than that of
most cities. In the first two years of the Depression the net migration from farms
ran at about four hundred fifty thousand a year; after 1931 this flow reversed,
and by 1933 almost six hundred thousand a year left the cities on a futile quest
for security. Generally, migrants were not heading for a specific place or job, but
heading south and west in search of occasional work, subsistence, and a climate
in which one could live without shelter. Dismal economic conditions were soon
matched by dismal environmental and weather conditions. A drought settled over
the Midwest from 1932 to 1941, and dust storms—a consequence of drought and
land exhausted by poor farming practices—became common occurrences. In
March 1935 a single storm carried off more dirt than had been excavated to build
the Panama Canal and destroyed half the wheat crop of Kansas and the entire
wheat crop in Nebraska.*

    *Farmers tried to counter these conditions, although the political isolation of
rural communities often meant that their protests—such as slowing production (or
destroying produce) in order to increase prices, and resisting foreclosures and farm
auctions—were spontaneous, informal, and short-lived. More broadly, groups such
as the Farmers' Union and the Share Cropper's Union demanded government help.
The Agricultural Adjustment Act (AAA), passed in 1933, committed the federal
government to debt relief (by 1940 the federal government had financed almost 40
percent of all farm debt) and to price supports through strict production limits,
although the spectacle of livestock being killed and crops being ploughed under did
not go over well in the depths of the Depression. Refined and redrafted again in
1935 and 1938, and supplemented by the Farm Security Administration in 1937,
the AAA did bring a modicum of stability to the farm economy. In practice, large
commercial farmers benefited the most from the program. Tenant farmers and
sharecroppers benefited the least because landowners often kept to production limits
by evicting tenants and croppers. Sharecroppers joined in organizations such as the
Southern Tenant Farmers' Union and the Share Croppers Union to counter the
oppressive practices of landowners and the effects of AAA policies, but the New Deal
(constrained by the influence of conservative Southern Democrats) proved ambivalent toward granting agricultural workers the same organizing and bargaining
rights being won by industrial workers.*

D O C U M E N T S

The first four documents trace the economic landscape of rural America in the 1920s
and 1930s. Document 1 testifies to the misery of the early Depression years; Document
2 focuses on the particular misery of the sharecropping system; Document 3 recalls the
conditions of the dust bowl; and Document 4 recounts resistance to farm foreclosures.
In Document 5, a noted farm leader lays out farmers' political demands. Document 6
excerpts the basic assumptions and terms of the New Deal's Agricultural Adjustment
Act (AAA). In Document 7, a report on the impact of the AAA in the South details the
ways in which agricultural policy was administered in the South to the disadvantage
of black sharecroppers. Also passed over by New Deal policy, as the novelist John
Steinbeck suggests in Document 8, were the migrant farm workers of the West and
Southwest.

1. Conditions in Rural America, 1932

My name is Oscar Ameringer. I am editor of the *American Guardian* and former editor of the *American Miner.* I live in Oklahoma City, Okla. . . .

During the last three months I have visited, as I have said, some 20 States of this wonderfully rich and beautiful country. Here are some of the things I heard and saw: In the State of Washington I was told that the forest fires raging in that region all summer and fall were caused by unemployed timber workers and bankrupt farmers in an endeavor to earn a few honest dollars as fire fighters. The last thing I saw on the night I left Seattle was numbers of women searching for scraps of food in the refuse piles of the principal market of that city. A number of Montana citizens told me of thousands of bushels of wheat left in the fields uncut on account of its low price that hardly paid for the harvesting. In Oregon I saw thousands of bushels of apples rotting in the orchards. Only absolute flawless apples were still salable at from 40 to 50 cents a box containing 200 apples. At the same time, there are millions of children who, on account of the poverty of their parents, will not eat one apple this winter.

While I was in Oregon the *Portland Oregonian* bemoaned the fact that thousands of ewes were killed by the sheep raisers because they did not bring enough in the market to pay the freight on them. And while Oregon sheep raisers fed mutton to the buzzards. I saw men picking for meat scraps in the garbage cans in the cities of New York and Chicago. I talked to one man in a restaurant in Chicago. He told me of his experience in raising sheep. He said that he had killed 3,000 sheep this fall and thrown them down the canyon, because it cost $1.10 to ship a sheep, and then he would get less than a dollar for it. He said he could not afford to feed the sheep, and he would not let them starve, so he just cut their throats and threw them down the canyon.

The roads of the West and Southwest teem with hungry hitchhikers. The camp fires of the homeless are seen along every railroad track. I saw men, women, and children walking over the hard roads. Most of them were tenant farmers who had lost their all in the late slump in wheat and cotton. Between Clarksville and Russellville, Ark., I picked up a family. The woman was hugging a dead chicken under a ragged coat. When I asked her where she had procured the fowl, first she told me she had found it dead in the road, and then added in grim humor, "They promised me a chicken in the pot, and now I got mine."

In Oklahoma, Texas, Arkansas, and Louisiana I saw untold bales of cotton rotting in the fields because the cotton pickers could not keep body and soul together on 35 cents paid for picking 100 pounds. The farmers cooperatives who loaned the money to the planters to make the crops allowed the planters $5 a bale. That means 1,500 pounds of seed cotton for the picking of it, which was in the neighborhood of 35 cents a pound. A good picker can pick about 200 pounds of cotton a day, so that the 70 cents would not provide enough pork and beans to keep the picker in the field, so that there is fine staple cotton rotting down there by the hundreds and thousands of tons.

From "Statement of Oscar Ameringer," U.S. House, Committee on Labor, *Hearings Before the House Committee on Labor,* 72d Congress, 1st session (February 1932), pp. 97–99.

As a result of this appalling overproduction on the one side and the staggering underconsumption on the other side, 70 per cent of the farmers of Oklahoma were unable to pay the interests on their mortgages. Last week one of the largest and oldest mortgage companies in that State went into the hands of the receiver. In that and other States we have now the interesting spectacle of farmers losing their farms by foreclosure and mortgage companies losing their recouped holdings by tax sales.

The farmers are being pauperized by the poverty of industrial populations and the industrial populations are being pauperized by the poverty of the farmers. Neither has the money to buy the product of the other, hence we have overproduction and underconsumption at the same time and in the same country.

I have not come here to stir you in a recital of the necessity for relief for our suffering fellow citizens. However, unless something is done for them and done soon, you will have a revolution on hand. And when that revolution comes it will not come from Moscow, it will not be made by the poor communists whom our police are heading up regularly and efficiently. When the revolution comes it will bear the label "Laid in the U. S. A." and its chief promoters will be the people of American stock.

2. Tenant Farmers Recall the Conditions of Sharecropping in the 1930s

"We never had a fair deal while we was wid Mr. Jones. Every time he settled wid us he took de inside track and 'lowed us what he pleased. We knowed it, but twa'n't no use to complain. Hattie Duncan use to have a row wid Mr. Jones all de time, but we never said nothin'. We knowed we wouldn't git nothin' dat way but cussin'. Dey tell me Mr. Jones is after de Duncans to go back wid him, but I bound dey ain't a-goin'. I don't mind workin' hard; I 'spects dat. But it is hard, after you done de best you can, to be cussed at and talked to like a dog. Aaron killed hisself a-workin' for Mr. Jones; he kept a-pluggin' away even after his blood got too high till dem strokes caught up wid him. I spent de best years o' my life on de Jones farm, and what has we got to show for it? Nothin'—nothin' but younguns!

"De most we cleared wid Mr. Jones was $600. Cotton was sellin' for 30 cents a pound, dey wa'n't no boll weevil much, and we made big crops 'long den. De average we cleared wid Mr. Jones was from $150 to $200 a year. De year we made 70 bales o' cotton and 971 bags o' peas we cleared round $500 or $600."

"What good did it do? . . ." [Aaron asks]. "Long den I put by $600 in de bank and bought me five mules dat cost $250 apiece. I was aimin' to buy me a piece o' land soon as I could 'cumulate enough. When Mr. Jones found out I had banked some money, he shut right down on us and refused to furnish us a dust o' flour or a strip o' meat till we had spent every cent I had put by. What can you do wid sech as dat? Mr. Jones's brother was in de bank, and dey wa'n't no way o' keepin' de money I banked a secret from Mr. Lem. Den next he got busy and worked us out'n de mules, one at a time. At de end o' de year he'd take 'em for debt, claimed we didn't pay out or owed him stuff we didn't know what for.

From "Aaron and Mary Matthews," in *Such As Us: Southern Voices of the Thirties,* ed. Tom Terrill and Jerrold Hirsch (Chapel Hill: University of North Carolina Press, 1978), 88–90.

"Soon as he got de mules in his hand, he furnished de team and made us pay half de fertilize. We never could git him to tell us what de fertilize 'mounted to. 'What in de hell is dat to you?' he'd holler at me when I'd ask him."

"It was de same way wid de books," Mary [adds] as Aaron pauses, . . . "I bought me a five-cent book and ask him to set down what he was chargin' us wid. He cussed at me, said I didn't have no sense, I was a fool, and to move out."

"He said nobody should keep no dam' books on his place, and if we didn't like it, Goddam' it, git out!" Aarons corrects. "He charged us wid stuff we didn't know what 'twas for and wouldn't explain nothin'. We had to pay for pickin' off all de peanuts, ours and his'n too, as well as de pea bags. He claimed to pay half de fertilize, but it was worked out in sech a way we ended up payin' it all, I reckon. He furnished us wid $6.00 a week de year round; dat had to take care o' rations and every string o' clothes. I don't know how much dat come to, but I know we'd ought to cleared more dan we did much as we made some years. Mr. Lem told me several times I had made enough on de farm to buy de Vasser place if I had took care o' my money. Took care o' my money! When he wouldn't let me have nothin' in de bank, wouldn't let me have no peace till I had drawed out every cent! If I had had justice, we'd be livin' on a farm o' our own right now. I tell you one thing: hell's gettin' het up right now for some folks. De devil's waitin' for 'em; dey're goin' jus' as straight—"

"Hush talkin' so bad 'bout de man, Aaron. Everybody's got some good in 'em if you can find it. Dis past gone year we made jus' 15 bales o' cotton and 223 bags o' peas and 75 or 80 barrels o' corn on a four-horse crop. I can't tell you how much it ought to come to—more 'n we got, I know. Mr. Jones furnished us de $6.00 a week like Aaron said and paid half de fertilize, while we paid all de labor for pickin' peas and de pea bags and one half de fertilize. We never got no rental checks. Some has got gov-ment money on dey crops, but ain't none come to us. I don't know how it works. We never had no help from de gov-ment; Aaron's old enough to draw de old pension, but he ain't ask for none yet. When we settled dis year, Mr. Jones took de whole crop and claimed we was in debt $218."

"If you want to know what de settlement is like I can tell you:

"'Aaron, come 'ere! You're behind dis year. De crop's all in, and you ain't paid out.'

"'How much did my part come to?'

"'Not 'nough to cover your account.'

"'What did you say de account is?'

"'For fertilize, de 'lowance by de week, de money I let you have—'

"'Which money you talkin' 'bout?'

"'You're a dam' fool. It's all booked here. You think you can keep it all in your dam' head?'

"'How much did de fertilize come to?'

"'What in de hell is dat to you? I ain't robbin' you o' nothing'. I carried you de whole dam' year, and now you owe me two hund'ed and eighteen dam' dollars. Looks like dey's no end to carryin' your dam' crowd o' dam' niggers.'

"'I know de crop ain't much, but—'

"'Goddam' you! Git out o' my dam' house, you and your dam' niggers, don't I'll put you in de dam' road—'"

"Hush, Aaron! Don't talk so bad! . . . It's bad as he says and has been for most o' nineteen years. Soon as settlement was over dis year, Mr. Jones locked up de co'n, nailed boa'ds across de door of de crib, and left us blank, not even no co'n for bread. Den he said git out. I wisht we could o' gone back to . . . Virginia and left from round here. Dey ain't never been nothin' but trouble in dis country.

3. From a Dust Bowl Diary, 1934

[*April 25, 1934, Wednesday*] Last weekend was the worst dust storm we ever had. Weve been having quite a bit of blowing dirt every year since the drouth started, not only here, but all over the Great Plains. Many days this spring the air is just full of dirt coming, literally, for hundreds of miles. It sifts into everything. After we wash the dishes and put them away, so much dust sifts into the cupboards we must wash them again before the next meal. Clothes in the closets are covered with dust.

Last weekend no one was taking an automobile out for fear of ruining the motor. I role Roany to Frank's place to return a gear. To find my way I had to ride right beside the fence, scarcely able to see from one fence post to the next.

Newspapers say the deaths of many babies and old people are attributed to breathing in so much dirt.

[*May 7, 1934, Monday*] The dirt is still blowing. Last weekend Bud [her brother] and I helped with the cattle and had fun gathering weeds. Weeds give us greens for salad long before anything in the garden is ready. We use dandelions, lamb's quarter, and sheep sorrel. I like sheep sorrel best. Also, the leaves of sheep sorrel, pounded and boiled down to a paste, make a good salve. . . .

[*May 21, 1934, Monday*] . . . Saturday Dad, Bud, and I planted an acre of potatoes. There was so much dirt in the air I couldn't see Bud only a few feet in front of me. Even the air in the house was just a haze. In the evening the wind died down, and Cap came to take me to the movie. We joked about how hard it is to get cleaned up enough to go anywhere.

The newspapers report that on May 10 there was such a strong wind the experts in Chicago estimated 12,000,000 tons of Plains soil was dumped on that city. By the next day the sun was obscured in Washington, D.C., and ships 300 miles out at sea reported dust settling on their decks.

Sunday the dust wasn't so bad. Dad and I drove cattle to the Big Pasture. Then I churned butter and baked a ham, bread, and cookies for the men, as no telling when Mama will be back.

[*May 30, 1934, Wednesday*] . . . The mess was incredible! Dirt had blown into the house all week and lay inches deep on everything. Every towel and curtain was just black. There wasn't a clean dish or cooking utensil. There was no food. Oh, there were eggs and milk and one loaf left of the bread I baked the weekend before. I looked in the cooler box down the well (our refrigerator) and found a little ham and butter. It was late, so Mama and I cooked some ham and eggs for the men's supper because that was all we could fix in a hurry. It turned out they had been living on ham and eggs for two days.

Mama was very tired. After she had fixed starter for bread, I insisted she go to bed and I'd do all the dishes.

It took until 10 o'clock to wash all the dirty dishes. That's not wiping them— just washing them. The cupboards had to be washed out to have a clean place to put them.

4. A Farmer Recalls a "Penny Sale" of the 1930s

It was our penny sale over there. A fellow by the name of Fry lived on a farm south of St. James, west of Truman. He was renting a farm and in the fall of the year the landlord decided he wanted to move him off. He had a son that got married and he wanted to put him on there. Mr. Fry had a contract that said if he had anything plowed at a certain date that he had the farm rented for another year. But the landlord insisted on moving Mr. Fry out, so he called on the Holiday Association. We met with him several times and tried to make some settlement, and we just couldn't get anywhere with him at all. The landlord was a Board of Director of the Truman Bank and Mr. Fry had his interests in the bank there. It got to be real exciting; we had meeting after meeting clear up to 2 o'clock on the day of the sale. They decided to have the sale . . . well they decided to foreclose him in order to get him off—that was the only way to get him off. They called on the Holiday Association from Iowa to come up. Mr. Fry had a brother-in-law that was an auctioneer who was very sympathetic to the Holiday Association, so we were pretty well set. It was agreed all though the Holiday Association that nobody could bid over a dime on the penny sales on any item. At 2 o'clock the owner of the land, he went out from a porch and said, "I'll take my chances with the Holiday Association." He said, "I've got as many friends out there as the Holiday has." It was estimated that 5,000 people came up from Iowa in order to take part in this sale. We had them all over the state of Minnesota that came in. One lady walked from way up around Madison, hitchhiked down for that particular sale.

The sheriff from Watonwan county, Mr. Brumel, I believe was his name, he came out there, of course, to protect the interest of the bankers, you might say. He set two machine guns up on his big car. This lady from Madison walked up to him and said, "You ain't got the guts to use them even if you had to."

The sale never got on the way until about 2 o'clock in the afternoon; they had sold about half of the machinery, everything selling for anywhere from three, four, five, six cents, somewhere in there. Finally, the banker realized that they were having a legal sale, so he asked to auctioneer, he said, "You mean to say that this is a legal sale?"

He said, "Yes, it is. We advertised it and we are selling to the highest bidder." So the sale went on.

I now want to get down to the horses, They were selling a team there and someone bid twenty cents or something and someone knocked him down that fast. [laughs] When the sale was over, everybody went in and paid up their bill and returned the property to Mr. Fry.

From "Ernest C. Johnson Interview" from *Holiday: Minnesotans Remember the Farmers' Holiday Association,* Plains Press, 1984, pp. 73–75. Reprinted by permission of Plains Press.

That evening after supper the sheriff from Watonwan County, he deputized all the employees in the highway department and as many people as he could get around town and they came out and took the property to St. James and put it in the fairgrounds. They set up their guards and their machine guns, and defied us to come and get it. Of course we knew better than to go and get it.

So then they decided, the Holiday Association, that they would make it a test case in the Supreme Court. They called on all the Holiday Associations around to contribute. Within two or three days we had the thousand dollars which it takes to enter a case in the Supreme Court. So they returned the property. We got a bill for $400 for deputy fees and feed, but we haven't paid it yet.

5. Milo Reno Suggests "What the Farmer Wants," 1934

The farmer asks for the privilege of serving society by producing food in abundance to sustain life, and the raw material from which the blessings and comforts of life are processed.

The farmer wants this government maintained and perpetuated in the spirit of its founders—a government for the people and not for the classes; a government that insures justice and equity, a justice that recognizes the right of the toiler, in whatever capacity he may be serving, to the abundance produced by his hands.

The farmer wants, and demands, that the present unthinkable condition, where people starve in the midst of super-abundance of food, go naked and freeze with an abundance of raw material to be processed into clothing, and with a multitude of laborers happy to perform the service of processing, be made impossible. . . .

The farmers demand that an American price be paid for that part of their products which is consumed in this country, and that production costs be recognized as a basis for price; and the farmers realize that, while production costs should be a basis for price in this country, any surplus produced should be the farmers' responsibility. Under the Swank-Thomas bill, which both the Farmers' Holiday and the Farmers' Union are backing, on that percentage of a farmer's production which is necessary for home consumption, he would receive production costs. The percentage above the amount necessary for home consumption, he could retain in his possession as a permanent surplus, to protect the public from lean years, or he could sell it on the open market for export purposes at whatever price the world market would justify. . . .

The farmers, who are the victims of the criminal program of deflation that destroyed thirty billions of farm values in a period of eighteen months, forcing millions to mortgage their farms and chattels, demand that the government refinance those farms and homes upon terms as advantageous as we conceded to our foreign debtors.

We demand that the departments of agriculture, both national and state, get entirely out of the game of politics, and perform their functions as was intended under the laws establishing Land Grant Colleges.

We ask that the farmers be permitted to select their own Secretary of Agriculture, making the Secretary responsible to the farmer instead of a political machine. . . .

From Milo Reno, "What the Farmer Wants," in *Challenge to the New Deal,* ed. Alfred Bingham and Selden Rodman (New York: Falcon, 1934), 68–72.

The farmer believes that the greatest protection to society, as a whole, is the independently owned farm of small units, that such farm homesteads constitute the moral and economic strength of the nation, and that if the present monopolization of the food producing lands of this nation, by powerful corporations and combinations of capital, be permitted to continue, it will mean the complete and final enslavement of, not only the American farmer, but all of the labor and those who serve society.

The farmers demand for themselves a right to live and enjoy the decent existence that our resources entitle us to, and we are ready to concede the same consideration to every other group that serves.

The Farmers' Holiday Association, which is representative of the militant, independent farm population, is just as ready to preserve the homes of the wage earners, that are today being confiscated by the financial pirates, as to preserve the ownership of their farms. In fact, the farmers and industrial laborers have a common interest. The industrial laborers constitute by far the greatest market for the products of the American farm, and the farmers are by far the greatest market for the things produced by labor. An injury to one is immediately reflected in the other. This is proven conclusively by the fact that the wage of the industrial laborer and the income of the farmer have been practically the same for many years. Any increase in industrial wages is immediately reflected in the farmer's income because of the wage earner's ability to buy. Any increase in the farmer's income is immediately reflected in the demand for the things that labor produces, consequently labor is employed and wages increase. When the wage earner is receiving a generous wage, that enables him to buy the products of our farms, it is immediately reflected in an increased demand for farm products at prices that permit the farmer in turn to buy the thousand things that labor produces. Such a condition contributes to the comforts and happiness of the industrial laborer and relieves the farmer of the distress of glutted markets and prices that mean his bankruptcy and desolation.

The distress of both farmer and laborer has been caused entirely by in-between factors chiseling in both directions, an uneconomic system of distribution that takes toll every step of the way from the farm to the laboring consumer and vice versa.

6. The Agricultural Adjustment Act, 1933

AN ACT

To relieve the existing national economic emergency by increasing agricultural purchasing power, to raise revenue for extraordinary expenses incurred by reason of such emergency, to provide emergency relief with respect to agricultural indebtedness, to provide for the orderly liquidation of joint-stock land banks, and for other purposes.

Be it enacted by the Senate and House of Representatives of the United States of America in Congress assembled,

---

From U.S., *Statutes at Large,* Vol. 48 (Washington: Government Printing Office, 1933), 31–32.

TITLE I—AGRICULTURAL ADJUSTMENT

Declaration of Emergency

That the present acute economic emergency being in part the consequence of a severe and increasing disparity between the prices of agricultural and other commodities, which disparity has largely destroyed the purchasing power of farmers for industrial products, has broken down the orderly exchange of commodities, and has seriously impaired the agricultural assets supporting the national credit structure, it is hereby declared that these conditions in the basic industry of agriculture have affected transactions in agricultural commodities with a national public interest, have burdened and obstructed the normal currents of commerce in such commodities, and render imperative the immediate enactment of title I of this Act.

Declaration of Policy

SEC. 2. It is hereby declared to be the policy of Congress—

(1) To establish and maintain such balance between the production and consumption of agricultural commodities, and such marketing conditions therefor, as will reestablish prices to farmers at a level that will give agricultural commodities a purchasing power with respect to articles that farmers buy, equivalent to the purchasing power of agricultural commodities in the base period. The base period in the case of all agricultural commodities except tobacco shall be the prewar period, August 1909–July 1914. In the case of tobacco, the base period shall be the postwar period, August 1919–July 1929.

(2) To approach such equality of purchasing power by gradual correction of the present inequalities therein at as rapid a rate as is deemed feasible in view of the current consumptive demand in domestic and foreign markets.

(3) To protect the consumers' interest by readjusting farm production at such level as will not increase the percentage of the consumers' retail expenditures for agricultural commodities, or products derived therefrom, which is returned to the farmer, above the percentage which was returned to the farmer in the prewar period, August 1909–July 1914.

7. Depression and New Deal Both Hit Black Farmers, 1937

The recent depression has been extremely severe in its effects upon the South. The rural Negro—poor before the period of trade decline—was rendered even more needy after 1929. Many tenants found it impossible to obtain a contract for a crop and were left stranded without any economic resources. It is also evident that many

---

Reprinted with the permission of Congressional Information Service, Inc. University Publications of America.

Negro as well as white farm owners lost their property. As the competition in earning a livelihood increased, social unrest grew and racial prejudice became more severe, to the extent that racial friction and lawlessness increased in many sections of the rural South. A study of lynching over a period of forty years reveals that as cotton prices go down, the number of lynchings increases. A study of racial relations during the depression verifies that conclusion. In addition, there are evidences of the breakdown of the plantation system during the years of depression. Many rural Negro schools have been closed during the last few years.

The most severe situation confronting the Negro farmer has been that facing the share cropper and farm tenant. The difficulties in the production of cotton involved losses to the landlords. These, in turn, were translated into greater dependence, less security and lower standards of living for the tenants. Since the share croppers were least powerful to resist the hardships of economic depression, they have suffered greatest from the chaos which has permeated southern agriculture.

A most instructive picture of the situation is reflected by the treatment of the Negro farmer under Federal aid offered prior to the initiation of the Recovery Program. There were many abuses in the administration of this aid which are instructive as indication of what can happen to colored farmers under any program of relief. . . .

When the New Deal was extended to agriculture, one of the most important features of the program was the plan for acreage reduction. In the case of cotton, there was to be a forty per-cent reduction. The cultivation of cotton gives rise, perhaps, to more employment among Negroes than the production of any other product. Naturally, therefore, a program which proposes to reduce materially the amount of this production affects Negroes. . . .

The displacement of Negro tenants (as was the case also for whites) began before, and grew throughout the depression. Thus, at the time of the announcement of crop reduction program, there were many families without arrangements for renting crops—some without shelter. Since the new program has been announced, there have been fewer opportunities for contracting for a crop and this condition has become more grave. Where landlords have kept their promise and have maintained the number of their families, they have often changed the families and substituted smaller families for their former tenants. Often managing share-tenants have been reduced to share croppers despite the fact that the Administrative Rulings and Instructions prohibit such action. This has allowed the owner of the farm to receive the full payments from the acreage reduction plan. It has also materially reduced the status of a large number of Negro cotton producers.

In instances where tenants have not been displaced, they have been given only shelter and fuel. They have no contract to make crops, no income and no certain means of supplying themselves with food and clothing. If they do receive these, it is because their landlord chooses to give them to the tenant and their continued supply rests entirely in the hands of the giver.

Although there has been but little increase in complete displacement of tenants in the South, the fact that they are remaining is not deeply significant. In many instances landlords are willing to allow their former tenants to live in houses and cabins (for which there are no other possible occupants at this time). The already

exploited Negro is rendered more impotent to resist unfair treatment by this peculiar situation. Thus, it is the inability to secure a crop—the contract which provides
for advances of seeds, subsistence and equipment, rather than physical displacement—that is most crucial. The tenant in the South—and the Negro tenant in particular—is being separated from his means of earning a living.

8. John Steinbeck on Migrant Labor in California, 1938

Thus, in California we find a curious attitude toward a group that makes our agriculture successful. The migrants are needed, and they are hated. Arriving in a district they find the dislike always meted out by the resident to the foreigner, the
outlander. This hatred of the stranger occurs in the whole range of human history,
from the most primitive village form to our own highly organized industrial farming. The migrants are hated for the following reasons, that they are ignorant and
dirty people, that they are carriers of disease, that they increase the necessity for police and the tax bill for schooling in a community, and that if they are allowed to organize they can, simply by refusing to work, wipe out the season's crops. They are
never received into a community nor into the life of a community. Wanderers in
fact, they are never allowed to feel at home in the communities that demand their
services.

Let us see what kind of people they are, where they come from, and the routes
of their wanderings. In the past they have been of several races, encouraged to come
and often imported as cheap labor; Chinese in the early period, then Filipinos,
Japanese and Mexicans. These were foreigners, and as such they were ostracized
and segregated and herded about.

If they attempted to organize they were deported or arrested, and having no advocates they were never able to get a hearing for their problems. But in recent years
the foreign migrants have begun to organize, and at this danger signal they have
been deported in great numbers, for there was a new reservoir from which a great
quantity of cheap labor could be obtained.

The drought in the middle west has driven the agricultural populations of Oklahoma, Nebraska and parts of Kansas and Texas westward. Their lands are destroyed
and they can never go back to them. Thousands of them are crossing the borders in
ancient rattling automobiles, destitute and hungry and homeless, ready to accept
any pay so that they may eat and feed their children. And this is a new thing in migrant labor, for the foreign workers were usually imported without their children
and everything that remains of their old life with them.

They arrive in California usually having used up every resource to get here,
even to the selling of the poor blankets and utensils and tools on the way to buy
gasoline. They arrive bewildered and beaten and usually in a state of semi-starva-
tion, with only one necessity to face immediately, and that is to find work at any
wage in order that the family may eat.

And there is only one field in California that can receive them. Ineligible for relief, they must become migratory field workers. . . .

From *The Harvest Gypsies: On the Road to the Grapes of Wrath* by John Steinbeck, pp. 20–21. (Migrant
Labor in California 1938.) Reprinted by permission of Heyday Books.

The earlier foreign migrants have invariably been drawn from a peon class. This is not the case with the new migrants. They are small farmers who have lost their farms, or farm hands who have lived with the family in the old American way. They are men who have worked hard on their own farms and have felt the pride of possessing and living in close touch with the land. They are resourceful and intelligent Americans who have gone through the hell of the drought, have seen their lands wither and die and the top soil blow away; and this, to a man who has owned his land, is a curious and terrible pain. . . .

And there is another difference between their old life and the new. They have come from the little farm districts where democracy was not only possible but inevitable, where popular government, whether practiced in the Grange, in church organization or in local government, was the responsibility of every man. And they have come into the country where, because of the movement necessary to make a living, they are not allowed any vote whatever, but are rather considered a properly underprivileged class.

. . . As one little boy in a squatters' camp said, "When they need us they call us migrants, and when we've picked their crop, we're bums and we got to get out."

E S S A Y S

In the first essay, Robin Kelley documents the experiences of sharecroppers in Depression-era Alabama, the range of their political responses (including individual resistance and the organization of the Share Croppers' Union) and the often violent reaction of Southern planters and politics. In the second essay, Theodore Saloutos argues that the New Deal accomplished a great deal for farmers, especially considering the long history of agricultural crises and the forbidding economic and political climate in which New Deal agricultural policy was forged.

The Share Croppers' Union

ROBIN D. G. KELLEY

Within the limited world of cotton culture existed a variety of production relations. Cash tenants, more often white than black, usually leased land for several years at a time, supplied their own implements, draft animals, seed, feed, and fertilizer, and farmed without supervision. Share tenants, on the other hand, might own some draft animals and planting materials, but the landowner provided any additional equipment, shelter, and if necessary, advances of cash, food, or other subsistence goods such as clothing. Verbal contracts were made annually and the landowner generally marketed the crop, giving the tenant between three-fourths and two-thirds of the price, minus any advances or previous debts. The most common form of tenancy in the South was sharecropping. Virtually propertyless workers paid with a portion of the crops raised, sharecroppers had little choice but to cultivate cotton—the landowner's choice of staple crops. The landowner supplied the acreage, houses, draft animals, planting materials, and nearly all subsistence necessities, including food and cash advances. These "furnishings" were then deducted from the share-cropper's portion of the crop at an incredibly high interest rate. The system not only kept most tenants in debt, but it perpetuated living conditions that bordered on intolerable. Landowners furnished entire families with poorly constructed one- or two-room shacks, usually without running water or adequate sanitary facilities. Living day-to-day on a diet of "fat back," beans, molasses, and cornbread, most Southern tenants suffered from nutritional deficiencies—pellagra and rickets were particularly common diseases in the black belt.

The gradations of tenancy must be understood in relation to both race and the geographic distribution of cotton production. The black belt, the throne of King Cotton in Alabama, with its rich, black, calcareous clay soil, still resembled its antebellum past in that blacks outnumbered whites four to one in some counties in 1930. As with other cotton growing areas, the plant's life cycle and seasonal needs determined the labor and living patterns of those who worked the land. In early spring, after the land had thawed and dried from winter, cotton farmers plowed and fertilized rows in preparation for planting, which followed several weeks later. When the young plants began to sprout, the cotton had to be "chopped"—grass and weeds were removed and the stalks separated so that they did not grow too close together. If this was not done regularly the crop could be lost. Picking time, the most intense period of labor involving all family members, began around September 1 and continued through October. Once the cotton had been picked, ginned, baled, and sold, accounts were settled between the tenant and the landowner. The tenants, who usually found themselves empty-handed after settling accounts, cultivated gardens to survive the winter, begged for food and cash advances, or spent several days without anything to eat. And throughout the entire year, particularly during the lean winters, tenants hauled firewood, cut hay, repaired their homes, fences, tools, and watering holes, cared for their stock, cleared trees, and removed stalks from the previous harvest.

Women's lives were especially hard in the world of cotton culture. Rising before dawn and the rest of family, wives and daughters of tenant farmers prepared meals over a wood stove or open fire; fetched water from distant wells or springs; washed laundry by hand in pots of boiling water; toted firewood; tended livestock; made preserves, dyes, clothes, and medicinal remedies; ground corn meal; gathered eggs; and tried to keep a house that generally lacked screens, windows, indoor plumbing, and electricity tidy. Women also worked in the fields, especially during picking and chopping time, and in the midst of physically exacting labor they bore and raised children. Many had little choice but to take in laundry or perform domestic work for meager wages, thus tripling their work load. Women choppers and pickers generally earned half as much as their male co-workers. To make matters worse, because husbands and elder sons occasionally migrated to nearby cities or mines to find work, escape family responsibilities, or avoid persecution in one form or another, many women and children in a variety of female-headed households and extended families were left to organize production without the benefit of adult male labor.

It was not unusual for a black woman to manage household finances and negotiate the year-end settlements with her landlord. On some plantations the woman's role as spokesperson was a defensive measure. When a black man appeared to settle his debts, the landlord's wife sometimes negotiated in her husband's place so that if the sharecropper objected to the final agreement, the landlord could accuse him of "insulting a white woman." The presence of the sharecropper's wife or eldest daughter in his place mitigated the landlord's desire to construe the dialogue as a violation of white womanhood. Black women were also more likely to be literate and have more formal education than black men. According to the 1940 Census, more black women than black men obtained formal education beyond five to six years. In the black belt counties where the illiteracy rate among African-Americans was as high as 35 to 40 percent in 1940, the ability to read and write could determine a sharecropper's success or failure. In several cases, women proved so important as managers that in some families their unexpected death or illness meant total ruin of an already precarious financial situation. "As long as mother lived," recalled a member of the Share Croppers' Union in Tallapoosa County, "she managed some way and kept us in school, but the boss took everything away from father until he would be so worried he would not know what to do."

It is tempting to characterize the black belt as a timeless, static, semifeudal remnant of the post-Reconstruction era, but such an idyllic picture ignores the history of rural opposition and does not take into account significant structural changes that have occurred since the 1890s. Black and white populists waged a losing battle against the expansion of tenancy, and in the wake of defeat, many landless farmers resisted debt peonage with their feet. Drowning in a sea of debt, tenants often broke their contracts, leaving an unsuspecting landowner at a critical moment in the planting cycle. Given the demography of the plantation, open collective rebellion was virtually impossible. Shacks were placed near the edge of the plantation, and two or three miles often separated tenant families from one another. Therefore, more individualized forms of resistance (theft, arson, sabotage, "foot dragging," slander, and occasional outbreaks of personal violence) were used effectively to wrest small material gains or to retaliate against unfair landlords. Such tactics were legitimated by folk cultures that celebrated evasive and cunning activities and, ironically, by the dominant ideology of racist paternalism that constructed an image of blacks as naturally ignorant, childlike, shiftless laborers with a strong penchant for theft.

Resistance, in some ways, altered the structure of production as well as the planters' ability to make a profit. With the onset of World War I, for example, large numbers of workers left the countryside altogether to take advantage of employment opportunities in the sprawling urban centers of the North and South. Areas most affected by the exodus were forced to adopt limited forms of mechanization to make up for the dwindling labor force and rising wages. The movement off the land was accompanied by improved roads and the availability of affordable automobiles, which increased rural mobility. The number of automobiles owned and operated by Alabama farmers increased from 16,592 in 1920 to 73,634 in 1930. Small holders and tenants who acquired vehicles were no longer beholden to the plantation commissary and could now purchase supplies at much lower prices in the nearby urban centers. The revolution in transportation compelled landowners to furnish tenants in cash in lieu of credit lines at plantation commissaries and county stores in an attempt to retain rural labor in the face of competitive wages offered in the cities. But after 1929, cash was a rare commodity, and landowners resurrected the commissary system, effectively undermining their tenants' newly acquired freedom and mobility.

By the time Birmingham Communists established links to the cotton belt early in 1931, tenancy seemed on the verge of collapse. Advances of food and cash were cut off, debts were piling higher, and the city offered fewer opportunities to escape rural poverty. Subterranean forms of resistance were by no means abandoned, but groups of black farmers now saw the logic in the CP's [Communist Party's] call for collective action.

The slogan demanding self-determination in the black belt did not inspire Birmingham's nascent Communist cadre to initiate a rural-based radical movement. The 1930 "Draft Program for Negro Farmers in the Southern States" expressed the Central Committee's doubt as to the ability of black sharecroppers and tenants to create an autonomous radical movement, and a few months later James Allen, editor of the *Southern Worker,* argued that only industrial workers were capable of leading tenants and sharecroppers because the latter lacked the collective experience of industrial labor. Aside from spouting rhetorical slogans, Party organizers all but ignored the black belt during their first year in Birmingham. Indeed, their first taste of rural organizing was in northern Alabama among a small group of white tenant farmers who had asked the TUUL [Trade Union Unity League] for help obtaining government relief.

Then, in January 1931, an uprising of some five hundred sharecroppers in England, Arkansas, compelled Southern Communists to take the rural poor more seriously. Birmingham Party leaders immediately issued a statement exhorting Alabama farmers to follow the Arkansas example: "Call mass meetings in each township and on each large plantation. Set up farmers Relief Councils at these meetings. Organize hunger marches on the towns to demand food and clothing from the supply merchants and bankers who have sucked you dry year after year. . . . Join hands with the unemployed workers of the towns and with their organizations which are fighting the same battle for bread."

The response was startling. The *Southern Worker* was flooded with letters from poor black Alabama farmers. A sharecropper from Waverly, Alabama, requested "full information on this Fight Against Starvation," and pledged to "do like the Arkansas farmers" with the assistance of Communist organizers. A Shelby County tenant made a similar request: "We farmers in Vincent wish to know more about the Communist Party, an organization that fights for all farmers. And also to learn us how to fight for better conditions." Another "farmer correspondent" had already made plans to "get a bunch together for a meeting," adding that poor farmers in his community were "mighty close to the breaking point.". . .

The CFWU [Croppers' and Farm Workers' Union] was eventually launched in Tallapoosa County, a section of the eastern piedmont whose varied topography ranges from the hill country of Appalachia in the north to the coastal-like plains and pine forests of the south. In 1930, almost 70 percent of those engaged in agriculture were either tenants or wage workers, the majority of whom were sharecroppers. Blacks comprised the bulk of the county's tenant and rural laboring population, and while they constituted roughly one-third of the total population, most blacks resided in the flat, fertile southeastern and southwestern sections of the county. As in the black belt counties further south, antebellum planter families in these two areas retained political and economic ascendancy, despite competition from textile and sawmill interests. Not surprisingly, the impetus to build a union came from local tenant farmers living primarily in southeastern Tallapoosa County. Estelle Milner, a young school teacher and the daughter of a black Tallapoosa sharecropper, was instrumental in establishing links between black farmers and Communist leaders in Birmingham. She laid the groundwork for the Party's activities by secretly distributing the *Southern Worker* and placing leaflets in strategic areas. Two brothers, Tommy and Ralph Gray, contacted the Party, persuaded several local sharecroppers to send letters to the *Southern Worker,* and in early spring invited a Communist organizer to help them build a union. . . .

. . . The nascent movement formulated seven basic demands, the most crucial being the continuation of food advances. The right of sharecroppers to market their own crops was also a critical issue because landlords usually gave their tenants the year's lowest price for their cotton and held on to the bales until the price increased, thus denying the producer the full benefits of the crop. Union leaders also demanded small gardens for resident wage hands, cash rather than wages in kind, a minimum wage of one dollar per day, and a three-hour midday rest for all laborers—all of which were to be applied equally, irrespective of race, age, or sex. Furthermore, they agitated for a nine-month school year for black children and free transportation to and from school.

By July 1931 the CFWU, now eight hundred strong, had won a few isolated victories in its battle for the continuation of food advances. Most Tallapoosa landlords, however, just would not tolerate a surreptitious organization of black tenant farmers and agricultural workers. Camp Hill, Alabama, became the scene of the union's first major confrontation with the local power structure. On July 15, Taft Holmes organized a group of sharecroppers near Camp Hill and invited Coad, along with several other union members, to address the group in a vacant house that doubled as a church. In all, about eighty black men and women piled into the abandoned house to listen to Coad discuss the CFWU and the Scottsboro case. After a black informant notified Tallapoosa County sheriff Kyle Young of the gathering, deputized vigilantes raided the meeting place, brutally beating men and women alike. The posse then regrouped at Tommy Gray's home and assaulted his entire family, including his wife who suffered a fractured skull, in an effort to obtain information about the CFWU. Only an agitated Ralph Gray, who had rushed into the house armed, saved them from possible fatal consequences. Union organizer Jasper Kennedy was arrested for possessing twenty copies of the *Southern Worker,* and Holmes was picked up by police the following day, interrogated for several hours, and upon release fled to Chattanooga.

Despite the violence, about 150 sharecroppers met with Coad the following evening in a vacant house southwest of Camp Hill. This time sentries were posted around the meeting place. When Sheriff Young arrived on the scene with Camp Hill police chief J. M. Wilson and Deputy A. J. Thompson, he found Ralph Gray standing guard about a quarter-mile from the meeting. Although accounts differ as to the sequence of events, both Gray and the sheriff traded harsh words and, in the heat of argument, exchanged buckshot. Young, who received gunshot wounds to the stomach, was rushed to a hospital in nearby Alexander City while Gray lay on the side of the road, his legs riddled with bullets. Fellow union members carried Gray to his home where the group, including Mack Coad, barricaded themselves inside the house. The group held off a posse led by police chief J. M. Wilson long enough to allow most members to escape, but the wounded Ralph Gray opted to remain in his home until the end. The posse returned with reinforcements and found Gray lying in his bed and his family huddled in a corner. According to his brother, someone in the group "poked a pistol into Brother Ralph's mouth and shot down his throat." The mob burned his home to the ground and dumped his body on the steps of the Dadeville courthouse. The mangled and lifeless leader became an example for other black sharecroppers as groups of armed whites took turns shooting and kicking the bloody corpse of Ralph Gray.

Over the next few days, between thirty-four and fifty-five black men were arrested near Camp Hill, nine of whom were under eighteen years of age. Most of the defendants were charged with conspiracy to murder or with carrying a concealed weapon, but five union members, Dosie Miner, T. Patterson, William Gribb, John Finch, and Tommy Finch, were charged with assault to murder. Although police chief Wilson could not legally act out his wish to "kill every member of the 'Reds' there and throw them into the creek," the Camp Hill police department stood idle as enraged white citizens waged genocidal attacks on the black community that left dozens wounded or dead and forced entire families to seek refuge in the woods. Union secretary Mack Coad, the vigilantes' prime target, fled all the way to Atlanta. But few Tallapoosa Communists were as lucky as Coad. Estelle Milner suffered a fractured vertebra at the hands of police after a local black minister accused her of possessing ammunition. . . .

The repression and the deteriorating economic conditions stunted the union's growth initially, but the lessons of Camp Hill also provided a stimulus for a new type of movement, reborn from the ashes of the old. On August 6, 1931, the fifty-five remaining CFWU members regrouped as the SCU [Share Croppers' Union] and reconstituted five locals in Tallapoosa County.

Throughout 1931 the SCU existed without an organizational secretary. Between August 1931 and early 1932, the SCU's only direct link to the Party was a nineteen-year-old YCL organizer from Springfield, Massachusetts, named Harry Hirsch, who adopted the pseudonym "Harry Simms." Simms's role was that of liaison, intermittently carrying information back and forth between district leaders and the SCU locals, which now began to operate with virtually no CP direction. As Simms observed, they were meeting every week in small groups and "carrying on the work on their own initiative even [though] we have not sent an organizer down there.". . .

After a year of rebuilding following Camp Hill, the union emerged stronger than ever. A threatened pickers' strike in 1932 won union members on at least one Tallapoosa plantation the right to sell their own cotton directly as well as a continuation of winter food advances. Days after the victory was announced, organizer Luther Hughley was arrested for vagrancy, but soon after he was placed in police custody, he was accused of kidnapping a white woman from Camp Hill. Before a mass campaign could be initiated, however, Hughley was released and threatened with rope and faggot if he did not leave the county. Aside from Hughley's arrest and the aborted pickers' strike, Camp Hill remained rather quiet and uneventful after the cotton had been picked. While most farmers prepared for the coming winter, five

SCU organizers joined Al Murphy as delegates to the National Farmers' Relief Conference in Washington, D.C., in December. The peace did not last very long. Exactly two weeks after the delegation left Alabama for the conference, the SCU in Tallapoosa County once again found itself embroiled in an explosive battle with local authorities.

It all started near Reeltown, an area about fifteen miles southwest of Camp Hill. The SCU's armed stand centered around a landlord's attempt to seize the property of Clifford James, a debt-ridden farmer who had been struggling desperately to purchase the land he worked. The story actually dates back to 1926, when James borrowed $950 to purchase the seventy-seven-acre plot he was working from Notasulga merchant W. S. Parker. The full cost of the land was $1,500. In addition to the borrowed money, James paid $250 in cash and sold $450 worth of timber from his property. Parker then absorbed James's debt by taking out a mortgage on the land. After advancing James money, food, and implements in 1927, Parker sold him three mules on credit, which then augmented James's debt to $1,500. James's friend and fellow SCU member, Ned Cobb, was also indebted to Parker. "[Parker] had it in for me," Cobb recalled. "He knew I had good stock and I was a good worker and all like that. He just aimed to use his power to break me down; he'd been doin to people that way before then."

When the SCU reorganized in Tallapoosa County, its approach to debt peonage attracted James and hundreds of other black farmers. As a result of debates within the Communist Party's National Negro Commission, the SCU added to its core program the abolition of all debts owed by poor farmers and tenants, as well as interest charged on necessary items such as food, clothes, and seed. The SCU's solution to indebtedness had appealed to so many black tenants and small landowners that even W. S. Parker felt the union's policies damaged relations between him and his tenants. "The reaction among James and several other Negroes," Parker admitted, "who before had shown a spirit of cooperation to the mentioning of foreclosures, seemed to point conclusively that there was some sort of sinister influence at work among them." James threw himself into the movement, becoming a Communist and a leader of an SCU local that included farmers from Reeltown and Lee County.

Parker blamed this "sinister influence" for his inability to reach an agreement with James concerning his debts. Unable to come to terms, Parker asked Deputy Sheriff Cliff Elder to serve a writ of attachment on James's livestock. When Elder arrived on December 19, 1932, about fifteen armed SCU members were already standing outside James's home prepared to resist or avert the seizure. Although the group challenged established property rights by protecting James's right to retain his livestock in contravention of the law, they tried to avoid a gun battle. Their collective stand differed from the individualized practice of hiding vulnerable items, but the first stages of confrontation remained clearly within the traditional boundaries of rural paternalism. Ned Cobb humbly pleaded with Elder: "Please sir, don't take it. Go to the ones that authorized you to take his stuff, if you please, sir, and tell em to give him a chance. He'll work to pay what he owes em." When Elder and his black assistant officer attempted to seize the animals, humility ceased. James and Cobb warned them against taking the animals, and Elder interpreted their warnings as death threats. Fearing for his life, he left James's farm, promising to return to "kill you niggers in a pile."

Elder returned a few hours later with three reinforcements—Chief Deputy Dowdle Ware, former sheriff J. M. Gaunt, and a local landlord named J. H. Alfred. Several SCU members barricaded themselves in James's home and others stood poised at the barn. Shots were exchanged almost as soon as the four men stepped onto the property, but when Elder's small posse "seed that crowd of niggers at the barn throw up their guns they jumped in the car" and fled from the vicinity. Unable to persuade Governor Miller to dispatch state troops, Sheriff Young proceeded to form his own posse, gathering men from Lee, Macon, Elmore, and Montgomery counties to scour the area for suspected SCU members.

When the shoot-out was over, SCU member John McMullen lay dead, and several others were wounded, including Clifford James, Milo Bentley, Thomas Moss, and Ned Cobb. Within the next few days, at least twenty union members were rounded up and thrown in jail. Several of those arrested were not involved in the shoot-out, but their names were discovered when the police returned to James's home and uncovered the SCU local's membership list along with "considerable Communistic literature." The violence that followed eclipsed the Camp Hill affair of 1931. Entire families were forced to take refuge in the woods; white vigilante groups broke into black homes and seized guns, ammunition, and other property; and blacks were warned that if they appeared in the Liberty Hill section of Reeltown they would be shot on sight. A blind black woman reported to be nearly one hundred years old was severely beaten and pistol whipped by a group of vigilantes, and one Tallapoosa doctor claimed to have treated at least a dozen black patients with gunshot wounds. . . .

The confrontation at Reeltown apparently did not discourage the union's recruitment efforts. By June 1933, Al Murphy reported a membership of nearly 2,000 organized in 73 locals, 80 women's auxiliaries, and 20 youth groups. New locals were formed in Dale and Randolph counties and in the border town of West Point, Georgia. The Communists also established 5 additional rural Party units, each composed of 30 to 35 members. In other parts of the rural South, those who stood their ground at Reeltown were celebrated in rural folklore, as exemplified in the following verses composed just a few months after the incident and sung by sharecroppers in Rock Hill, South Carolina:

> What you gwine do nigger, wit' the power dat's in yo' ahm?
> Git wipin' yo eye tear, 'till de strenff is dead an' gone?
> Bowed down on yo' knees, 'till turkey buzzard git through wit' you?
>
> Wa' cher gwine do nigger, ain' nothin' lak what ah said
> Do lak Alabamy boys an' win or be foun' dead.

National Communist leaders regarded the SCU as the finest contemporary example of black revolutionary traditions. The apparent militancy of the burgeoning movement was the proof Communist theoreticians needed to justify the slogan demanding self-determination in the black belt. But the union's rank-and-file, who had little time to theorize about the changes taking place in the rural South, found little to celebrate. Black farmers were organizing primarily for their own survival and for a greater share in the decaying system of cotton tenancy. They might have won the battle to exist, but by late 1933 the SCU faced an additional set of problems when the federal government decided to intervene in the production process.

Congress and President Roosevelt attempted to reinvigorate the country's dying cotton economy with the AAA. Conceived in 1933 as an emergency measure, the AAA was supposed to increase the purchasing power of landowning farmers by subsidizing acreage reduction. A year later the Cotton Control Act and the Gin Tax Act, both sponsored by Alabama senator John Bankhead, made cotton reduction programs compulsory and added a mandatory tax on the ginning of all cotton above the specified quota. Southern sharecroppers were supposed to receive one-ninth of the 1934–35 benefit checks, but in most cases they received nothing since local planters controlled distribution of parity payments. Moreover, landlords used the Gin Tax Act as a lever to obtain their tenants' cotton. In order to gin cotton without paying the tax, tenants had to obtain gin certificates from their landlords or from local planter-dominated AAA boards. If a tenant refused to give the cotton to his or her landlord to be ginned, the landlord would withhold the gin certificate until cotton prices dropped.

At first such abuses were commonplace, and a liberal section of the Agricultural Adjustment Administration tried to restructure the distribution process. However, most planters did not have to engage in fraud in order to benefit from New Deal policies. They merely reallocated land, evicted redundant tenants, and applied the cash subsidies to wages rather than sharing it with their tenants. New Deal policies, therefore, indirectly stimulated a structural change in the cotton economy— the mechanization of agriculture. Cotton production remained unmechanized for so long partly because most landlords lacked capital and because the units of production—plots farmed by tenants and sharecroppers—were too small to warrant adoption of expensive technology. Tenancy provided the cheap labor needed to make the transition to mechanization, but it limited production to small, segmented units. By farming larger units of production, landlords could apply the parity payments and savings derived from not furnishing tenants to tractors, fertilizers, and other implements needed for large-scale cotton farming. Local relief administrators helped the landlords by clearing the relief rolls during cotton picking and cotton chopping seasons, thus ensuring an abundant supply of cheap labor.

As large portions of the 1933 crop were being plowed under and the first wave of tenants was being evicted, the SCU called strikes on several cotton plantations in Chambers and Lee counties and demanded fifty cents per one hundred pounds. The union's first attempted strike since its founding three years earlier crumbled, however, when seven SCU leaders were arrested and posses forced pickers back into the fields. Although the strike failed, thousands of evicted tenants in Alabama began turning to the SCU for assistance. By March 1934, the union claimed 6,000 members and established locals in the black belt counties of Lowndes, Macon, Montgomery, and Dallas. The SCU's sudden growth in the black belt prompted Murphy to move the underground headquarters from Birmingham to Montgomery. The proliferation of black belt locals was directly linked to mass evictions and landlord abuses stemming from the AAA. As Murphy pointed out, nearly half of the SCU's membership was recruited between July 1933 and April 1934. According to one SCU leader in Camp Hill, because of the AAA, the union "is taking on new life. . . . The SCU in places where [it] has been slack [is] beginning to wake up and people don't wait for the comrades to come as they used to."

The SCU adopted a variety of methods to deal with landlords' abuses of the parity program. First, because hundreds of evicted tenants and sharecroppers were simultaneously removed from relief rolls and CWA [Civil Workers Administration] projects so that cheap wage labor would be available for cotton chopping, union organizers fought for immediate relief and tried to persuade federal authorities to investigate local CWA administrators. In February 1934, a group of black women organized a "Committee of Action," marched down to the CWA office in Camp Hill, and eventually won partial demands for relief. Tenants and sharecroppers who had not yet been evicted were instructed not to sign the joint parity checks unless the landlords paid their portion in cash rather than use the funds to settle debts. SCU members often refused to give up their rental share of cotton unless they received their portion of the AAA check. The union also convinced some day laborers and cotton pickers to boycott plantations that were considered "vicious in their treatment of tenants and sharecroppers." On one plantation in Chambers County, a boycott of this kind led to the arrests of eleven union members.

Late that summer the SCU prepared for another cotton pickers' strike in Lee and Tallapoosa counties. With a demand of one dollar per hundred pounds, the strike started in mid-September on B. W. Meadows's plantation in Tallapoosa County and soon spread to several large plantations in both counties, involving between seven hundred and one thousand pickers. The landlords' first response was to evict the strikers, but because it was the height of the cotton picking season, planters needed all available labor. With the support of local police, the planters turned to force to break the strike. In Lee County, police arrested seven union members for distributing strike leaflets, and in Tallapoosa vigilantes shot at least three strikers, including a woman Party organizer. Pinned to the doors of several suspected strikers' homes was the following message: "WARNING, TAKE NOTICE. If you want to do well and have a healthy life you better leave the Share Croppers' Union." Hooded night riders in Lee County kidnapped and beat SCU organizer Comit Talbert, and later in the evening two more Lee County sharecroppers were kidnapped, draped in chains, and taken to a nearby swamp where vigilantes threatened to drown them if they remained in the union. The local sheriff intervened but arrested the shackled black sharecroppers and held them on charges of attempted murder.

The Alabama Relief Administration also played a crucial role in undermining the strike. As soon as the SCU announced plans for a cotton pickers' strike. Thad Holt, director of the state relief administration, dropped from the relief rolls all "able bodied" workers who did not volunteer to pick cotton for wages. Even the state reemployment agency in Birmingham relocated several people with "farm experience" to the cotton fields.

In spite of repression, mass evictions, and the expanded pool of cheap labor, the SCU claimed some substantial victories. On most of the plantations affected, the union won at least seventy-five cents per one hundred pounds, and in areas not affected by the strike, landlords reportedly increased wages from thirty-five cents per hundred pounds to fifty cents or more in order to avert the spread of the strike. On Howard Graves's plantation, located on the border of Lee and Tallapoosa counties, union members not only won the sought-after one dollar per hundred pounds, but they forced Graves to raise monthly credit allowances from ten to fifteen dollars. Finally, the SCU claimed a small victory on General C. L. Pearson's plantation when about one thousand sharecroppers and tenants refused to gin their cotton at

Pearson's gin. By taking their cotton to an independent gin in Dadeville, they saved money and prevented Pearson from seizing their cotton to cover past debts.

The 1934 cotton pickers' strike marked the SCU's first major victory since its birth three years earlier. As tales of the union's stand in Tallapoosa County spread from cabin to cabin, so did the union's popularity; by October, Murphy reported a total membership of eight thousand. The celebration ended abruptly, however, as thousands of families found themselves landless during the harsh winter of 1934–35. The eight-thousand-strong union stood helpless in the face of New Deal–induced evictions, and no antifascist slogans or demands for self-determination could solve their quandary.

Evaluating New Deal Agricultural Policy

THEODORE SALOUTOS

New Deal farm policy included a series of complex and interrelated programs that aimed to elevate the long-range social and economic position of the farmers, rather than simply attain stated price objectives. The policy was as comprehensive in character as political considerations permitted, seemingly contradictory and inconsistent, and the product of many minds and influences at work outside and inside the Department of Agriculture before and after the Roosevelt administration took office. The Department of Agriculture was among the most prestigious of all federal government agencies of cabinet rank and played a crucial and dominant role in all this. But other agencies participated too; and since their actions had a definite bearing on the farmer, they and their programs must be considered a part of farm policy.

Agencies which liberal groups easily could believe were more constructive and creative in their approach than the Agricultural Adjustment Administration (AAA) included the Federal Emergency Relief Administration (FERA), which during the course of its existence provided many rural communities with relief; the Resettlement Administration (RA), which became an official part of the Department of Agriculture only after Rexford G. Tugwell stepped down at its director, and which in turn was absorbed by the newly created Farm Security Administration (FSA); the Rural Electrification Administration (REA), which did extensive work, before it became affiliated with the Department of Agriculture in 1939, in preparing the groundwork for the electrification of many farms; the Tennessee Valley Authority (TVA), whose influence on the agriculture of the South and many rural communities was incalculable; and the Farm Credit Administration (FCA), established as a private lending agency outside the government. . . .

An assessment of the New Deal in agriculture may well begin with AAA, which was the most publicized of the farm agencies. The philosophy behind AAA was that farmers, who were in a highly competitive business, could improve their financial position by employing the same methods that prudent businessmen used—that is by

Excerpts from "New Deal Agricultural Policy: An Evaluation" by Theodore Saloutos from *Journal of American History 61,* 1974, pp. 394–407, 408–412, 415–416. Used by permission of the Organization of American Historians and the author's estate.

adjusting their production to effective demand. The general objectives of the much heralded first AAA were to overcome the disparities between farm and nonfarm prices by granting benefit payments to producers who cooperated with the federal government to balance production with demand and thereby bring farmers a return more in line with their incomes for the years between 1909 and 1914.

Phase two began with the enactment of the Soil Conservation and Domestic Allotment Act of 1936, which placed emphasis on increasing the income of farmers, not through acreage controls and marketing agreements as had been the case with the first AAA, but through the adoption of land uses and farm practices that con served and built up the fertility of the soil. Phase three began with the adoption of a new AAA in 1938, which sought to steer "a middle course" between the programs of the first AAA and the Soil Conservation and Domestic Allotment Act of 1936. This was deemed necessary because of a conviction that the adjustment value of the program begun in 1933 had been obscured by the droughts of 1934 and 1936, which had a greater effect on acreage and marketing adjustments than had been planned.

The lesson learned from the droughts of 1934 and 1936 was that a more permanent solution to the price imbalance was likely to be found in conservation rather than in acreage reduction or marketing agreements. This belief was strongly reinforced by the Court decision declaring the first AAA unconstitutional. But then the unusually favorable growing conditions of 1937 and the prospects of excellent crops in 1938 exposed the administration and farmers to the inadequacy of the conservation approach in years of bumper crops and emphasized the need for a broader program based on the control of a larger reserves storage. AAA sought to meet these conditions by establishing an "ever-normal granary" to provide for larger reserves as added protection against drought and to substitute surplus control—that is through the control of marketing in interstate commerce—as a means of combating surpluses. The new AAA or phase three in addition provided for the beginnings of a federal crop insurance program for wheat. . . .

Opinions naturally differed over the goals of the New Deal in agriculture and how these goals were to be achieved. Men such as Henry A. Wallace, Milburn L. Wilson, Henry Tolley, Mordecai Ezekiel, and members of the Wisconsin school of agricultural economics recognized that resolving the farm dilemma depended on more than the attainment of higher prices and incomes, although all agreed that the primary objective of AAA was to raise farm prices to parity levels. This being the case, it can be said that the New Deal had achieved its objective only in part by 1939. The prices of most farm commodities in August 1939, the month before the Nazis invaded Poland, were low in comparison with parity and August 1929 price levels. Of the prices received for farm commodities, only one, that for beef cattle, had attained parity by August 1939. Corn was 59 percent of parity, cotton 66 percent, wheat 50, butterfat 59, hogs 60, chickens 93, and eggs 49. The income of the farm population, which had significant bearings on the purchase of farm products, after dropping to a low of $39,000,000,000 in 1933, had recovered to only $66,000,000,000 in 1939 but had not reached the $79,000,000,000 of 1929. . . .

The parity price formula did not create serious difficulties in the early New Deal years because it was employed as a broad, general directive to improve the economic status of agriculture and also because Congress had given the Department of Agriculture considerable latitude in applying the formula. But this period of grace came to an end. Beginning with the spring of 1941 Congress insisted on a more rigorous interpretation, as seen in the mandatory farm commodity loans of 85 percent of parity, the 90 percent loans, and the 110 percent ceilings that followed. The change that restricted the range of administrative decision came at a time when the economic effects of the war were beginning to be felt and made past price relationships unrealistic. The war and the violent changes that it brought in the values of goods and services exposed the weaknesses of parity prices.

Parity prices, in short, whether they took 1909–1914 or some other period as their base, whether they took regional and the quality differentials of a commodity into account—much as these refinements helped—were not suitable goals for a farm policy simply because the function of prices was to guide and direct economic activity. In the words of one farm economist parity prices were "backward looking" and represented "the dead hand of the past." It was difficult if not impossible to force agriculture into a set of price relationships that existed years ago.

The efforts of the New Deal to control production through the restriction of acreages and the adoption of conservation and adjustment practices can hardly be adjudged a success. The New Dealers had been inspired to some extent by American manufacturers and industrialists who had been able to slow down the volume of their production in periods of low consumer demand; but they soon discovered, if they had been unaware of it before, that restricting production in agriculture where there were millions of producers was far more difficult to achieve than in manufacturing or industry where the producers were fewer in number.

The farmer's instinct was to produce in order to feed, clothe, and otherwise furnish the world; he disliked cutting down his production deliberately. However expert he was in his work there was little that he could do to control the quality and the quantity of his wheat, raw cotton, leaf tobacco, and other crops. Proper seeding, spraying, and care in the harvest could and did help the bounty and character of the crop; but a great deal of this could be undone, sometimes overnight, by heavy storms, floods, droughts, untimely frost, or the ravages of crop pests—all beyond or largely beyond the control of man. The droughts of 1934 and 1936 demonstrated that the forces of nature often were more significant than human planning in affecting the volume of the crop. . . .

Soil conservation, which became a key objective during phase two of AAA, always had attracted the attention of the more concerned citizen, but the interest of the general public was not aroused until its attention was directed to the agricultural surpluses. The reduction in the acreage of the basic crops under AAA reduced the drain on soils which was recognized as being in the public interest. This phase of AAA had greater appeal to nonfarm people than the gaining of higher prices and income for farmers. Conservation specialists furthermore employed the drought in the Great Plains states and the resulting dust storms as a means of impressing farmers and the general public with the need for more effective measures. Under the stimulus of this new interest, research in conservation expanded rapidly and the more comprehensive surveys made from year to year added to knowledge of the problem. . . .

Another development encouraged by the New Deal was the cultivation of soil-improving crops such as legumes, lespedeza, and soybeans. The range of these crops was extended northward, and the production of soybeans became a major item. The growing of flax likewise spread into a number of states, and experiments with other crops, particularly minor ones, were carried on over most of the United States. Hybrid corn was used more extensively and yields double previous ones were reported in many areas. These changes and experiments were expected to have far-reaching effects on the economy.

The controversial ever-normal granary, which Wallace, its principal architect and exponent, defined as "a definite system whereby supplies following years of drought or other great calamity would be large enough to take care of the consumer, [and] under which the farmer would not be unduly penalized in years of favorable weather," also must figure in any evaluation of the New Deal. To avoid a repetition of the Farm Board experience of huge surpluses and sagging prices it became necessary, after the loan program had reached a certain point, "to keep the granary from running over by some practical program of production adjustment." Wallace considered storing grain in the soil instead of in the bin also a part of the ever-normal granary.

Something akin to the ever-normal granary had been in operation from the beginning. During the drought of 1934 corn stored on farms under the first corn loan in 1933 helped provide feed supplies for livestock. In 1939 a loan and storage program was in effect for wheat, the primary food crop, and for corn, the number one feed crop. Wheat reserves were held in the ever-normal granary through a federal crop insurance program under which the wheat growers put aside a portion of their crops as premiums to offset possible crop failures. By storing corn, a nonperishable potential supply of pork, beef, dairy products, eggs, and other products was carried over. . . .

Wallace insisted that the planning for larger reserves was a product of the earlier years and not a response to the immediate war or national defense needs. He stated repeatedly that the droughts of 1934 and 1936 and AAA of 1938 had prepared the groundwork. The supplies of wheat and corn in 1940, Wallace said, were at the levels considered desirable by AAA. The wheat reserve was about twice and the corn reserve about three times pre-AAA levels. Supplies of some types of tobacco were in excess of their goals, in part because growers in 1939 chose not to use marketing quotas and because of the war. The supply of cotton was excessive mainly because the war cut off most of the foreign market.

Passage of the Federal Crop Insurance Act of 1938 marked the start of a new, voluntary program, purely experimental in character, to apply initially only to wheat. Proponents viewed the crop insurance program as the agricultural counterpart of the Social Security Act, which furnished unemployment insurance for nonagricultural workers. During the first year of the program, 1939, about 56,000 farmers received in excess of 10,000,000 bushels of wheat or the cash equivalent in indemnities for crops destroyed by forces beyond their control; this provided them with income that otherwise would have been lost. About 94 percent of the losses paid on the insured crop in 1939 were paid in the principal wheat-producing counties of the nation, where wheat was the chief, and in many cases, the only source of income. By 1940 many requests were received for the extension of insurance protection to crops such as corn, cotton, tobacco, citrus fruits, and vegetables which from an insurance standpoint posed difficulties not posed by wheat. By 1941 the insurance program was extended to include cotton, a major commodity. . . .

The criticisms most frequently made of AAA and other programs of the New Deal were that they catered primarily to the commercial, wealthier, and more substantial members of the middle class; that they rendered little, if any, assistance to tenants and sharecroppers; and that AAA, in particular, reduced members of low-income groups from tenants and sharecroppers to farm laborers or pushed them off the land completely. . . . These criticisms were made especially by those who were not farmers and who did not live in farm communities or know much about farming. These apprehensions were not entertained by persons better acquainted with farming because of an underlying assumption on their part that AAA was temporary legislation, that prices were going to rise, that the Depression was going to end, and that the emergency legislation was going to disappear.

One can argue that these changes had been going on for years prior to the New Deal and continued after the New Deal ended. Most difficulties of the small farmers came from technological changes that increased output per worker and substituted capital for human labor. Mechanization and the need for more capital had far more to do with consolidation of farms and increasing their size than the organization of AAA. AAA undoubtedly hastened consolidation of small farms into larger ones, especially in the cotton industry and in those types of farming that employed migratory labor; and it also concentrated attention on a situation which existed for some time and to which very little attention had been given.

That AAA did little for tenants, sharecroppers, and farm laborers is beyond dispute, although an exception has to be made for those who came under the classification of managing farm tenants. Relief for farm laborers never was designed to become a part of AAA; consequently little, if anything, could have been expected from this direction. The failure of AAA to come to the aid of sharecroppers and tenants may be attributed to a way of thinking that prevailed in agricultural circles, including educators, farm lobbyists, farm journalists, congressional leaders, and other members of the so-called agricultural establishment.

The objective of the Department of Agriculture and the land-grant colleges all along had been to establish prosperous farm families through the application of practical research and science. The assumption had been that this assistant could be rendered most effectively to those farmers who were accustomed to the family farm system and had incomes from their operations that were sufficient to attain a satisfactory standard of living. Agricultural thinking, research, teaching, and extension work that concentrated almost exclusively on the well managed family farm strongly influenced AAA.

Strong attitudes also prevailed in rural areas as well as in the Department of Agriculture regarding poor farmers and what should be done for them. These attitudes were brought to bear on congressmen and senators through the farm organizations to which the more successful farmers belonged, and they influenced decisions on the kind of assistance provided to tenants and sharecroppers. The general feeling of many landlords and employers was that if the rural poor received too much assistance, they would become independent and difficult to deal with. "If they moved away, the labor market would be tightened. If they became owners they also became competitors. If something had to be done, the last of these alternatives was preferable." This probably would not affect many, and those who climbed the ladder to proprietorship soon would acquire the outlook of their fellow proprietors.

As a consequence persons associated with agricultural colleges, agricultural experiment stations, and the Department of Agriculture seldom bothered with sharecroppers, tenants, and other low-income farmers, largely from the belief that such people were not able to climb into "the good income group." Small wonder then that agricultural institutions of higher education and research were ill-informed or uninformed about the nature and extent of poverty in rural areas and unprepared to consider the problem. Had the Department of Agriculture chosen to face this problem directly, which was unlikely, it would have encountered a hardened resistance to it not merely from substantial and wealthier farmers, but from many others who believed that agriculture held a slim future for depressed elements. . . .

Despite limitations in the intentions and accomplishments of AAA in behalf of tenants, sharecroppers, and small farmers, and the acquiescence of rural public opinion toward such a policy, it would be a mistake to assume that the New Deal did as little for these elements as is sometimes imagined. There is much evidence to the contrary, especially when one looks at the work of agencies other than AAA. Between 1933 ad 1935, when the Resettlement Administration finally came into existence, at least four governmental agencies tried to deal with various phases of rural poverty. Insofar as immediate relief was concerned, the most significant of these was the Federal Emergency Relief Administration, whose work was not confined exclusively to farmers. . . .

After February 1935, when almost 1,000,000 farm families, including farmers and farm laborers, were receiving relief grants or rehabilitation loans, farm families began to leave the general relief rolls rapidly, especially after expansion of the rural rehabilitation program and a partial resumption of agricultural prosperity. Figures in June 1935 indicated that nearly three fourths of the heads of families on relief in June 1935 were farmers and that slightly more than one fourth were farm laborers. Tenants, other than sharecroppers, made up more than one half of the farm operators on relief; farm owners accounted for another one third and sharecroppers for nearly one eighth. In the cotton areas, sharecroppers were represented more heavily on the relief rolls than either owners or other kinds of tenants. . . .

Much has been made of the unwillingness of larger farmers and landlords under AAA to share the benefit payments fairly with their tenants. That many tenants—the exact number has never been known and probably never will be—were deprived of their just dues is beyond doubt. But even if these payments had been shared fairly, sharecroppers and tenants would not have experienced significant economic progress. These payments would have purchased a few more of the necessities of life and little else. The payments listed in the public record represent the landlord's share on land operated by a number of tenants, who in theory earned proportionate shares. Individual payments to the tenants do not appear in this record. Of significance is the fact that fully 46 percent of the almost 5,250,000 farmers receiving payments under AAA in 1938 received $40 or less for the year. Fully 33 percent received sums ranging from $40 to $100 annually, and less than 2 percent from $1,000 to $10,000. The numbers receiving sums of over $3,000 averaged a small fraction of 1 percent. These incentive payments were nothing more than their name suggests, designed primarily to introduce better farming methods for those who had a stake in the land and were going to stay on it. There was little in the program, fraud or no fraud on the part of landlords, that would have encouraged poorer farmers to remain on the land if they had alternatives other than farming.

The New Deal did show some response to the needs of tenants and farmers receiving small payments and to those who had been defrauded under AAA. An amendment to the Soil Conservation and Domestic Allotment Act sought to render greater assistance to tenants and farmers receiving small payments. The amendment protected tenants against lease changes that would increase the share of the landlord's payments; and they were assured a division of payments between landlords and tenants in proportion to the shares in the crop. Payments that amounted to less than $200 annually were to be scaled upward, according to a specific schedule. And beginning in 1939 all individual payments were limited to $10,000.

Some of the criticism leveled against AAA was unfair and the product of hindsight rather than foresight. It was expecting far too much of the New Deal to undo within a few years a system of tenancy and sharecropping that had been years in the making. To accomplish this, years of painstaking research and planning, a high degree of cooperation, a sympathetic Congress and generous financial outlays over a long period of time, endless patience and goodwill, and some good luck were needed. Unfortunately, these ingredients were not present in sufficient quantity. Ridding the nation of sharecropping and tenancy required something more, considerably more, than favorable decisions at the administrative level. . . .

FSA must rank as one of the most forward-looking as well as one of the most bitterly fought agencies sponsored by the New Deal. Apart from the tenant-purchase program it administered under the Bankhead-Jones Act, FSA left a very impressive statistical record of assistance. Including the work of the predecessor organization, RA, FSA as of May 1, 1941, through the voluntary farm debt adjustment committees established in every farming county, helped work out debt reductions totaling almost $100,000,000 for 145,000 indebted farmers. This represented a reduction of nearly 23 percent on debts that originally amounted to more than $445,000,000.

FSA discovered that many of the farmers who came for assistance were in difficulties because of illness and could not do a good day's work; and in cooperation with state and local medical societies, FSA worked out a special medical care program for borrowers. This proved so popular with both physicians and FSA clients that health associations were organized in 634 counties in thirty-one states during the late 1930s and early 1940s. By May 1, 1941, about 80,000 families or 300,000 people were obtaining medical care through these associations. In many cases FSA included enough money in its rehabilitation loans to enable the borrower to make his first annual payment to the county health association. This resulted in both swifter progress toward rehabilitation and, as the health and ability of the family to support itself improved, in larger repayment on the loans.

FSA further realized that small farmers could not compete on even terms with commercial farmers and encouraged borrowers to pool their resources to buy tractors, lime-spreaders, purebred bulls, seed fertilizer, and other farm and household supplies in large quantities at lower prices. Small farmers also began to sell their pigs, chickens, and truck crops cooperatively. Often FSA included enough money in a rehabilitation loan for a borrower to pay his share of the cost of a combine, feed mill, terrace, or other equipment he could use cooperatively with his neighbors. Originally the loan included a sum that enabled the borrower to join a long-established cooperative. More than 300,000 low-income farm families were taking part in about 16,000 small cooperatives started with FSA help.

From 1935, when the rehabilitation program was initiated, until 1941, FSA loaned more than $516,000,000 to 870,000 farm families, many of whom, judged by normal standards, were among the worst possible credit risks. By May 1, 1941, they had paid $182,000,000 into the federal treasury, and the expectations were that fully 80 percent of the money loaned would be repaid eventually with interest. The annual cost of the rehabilitation loans including losses, according to FSA sources, amounted to less than $75 for each family assisted. This sum was low for relief of any kind; estimated costs of work relief ranged from $350 to $800 per year.

As a result of FSA assistance many farm families made rapid gains in their net worth, standard of living, and ability to support themselves. A survey made at the end of the crop year of 1939 to determine the progress of 360,000 regular rehabilitation borrowers disclosed they had increased their net worth beyond and above all debts—including obligations to the government—by almost $83,000,000 since they had obtained their first FSA loan. This was an average increase of more than $230 per family which meant a gain in new purchasing power in their communities in a single year.

Obviously the efforts of FSA angered certain influential segments of the agricultural establishment, such as the leadership of the American Farm Bureau Federation and the Cooley Committee of the House of Representatives. FSA, it was evident, was seeking to help those who needed help the most to remain on the land, contrary to the beliefs of those who held that these impoverished elements, and farmers in general, would be better off if they left agriculture completely. . . .

Left-wing critics claim that the New Deal could have accomplished far more for farmers than it actually did. They further assert that the mood of the American people was such that the Department of Agriculture, Wallace, and all surrounding him and his department could have brought about long overdue fundamental reforms for low-income farmers. Just what these reforms were to be is unclear, unless they were nationalization of the land and establishment of cooperative or collective farms. There is little evidence to support the claim that the American people were receptive to such proposals. The farm holiday movement, which was at its peak in the initial stages of the New Deal, did not advocate this kind of change. Even if the farm holiday movement was supposed to represent farmer or public indignation with the New Deal for its failure to provide greater assistance for farmers, it had very little support behind it. At best the farm holiday movement represented a splinter group broken off the main branch of the Farmers' Union, the smallest of the general farmer organizations.

In attempting to summarize the effects of the New Deal on the American farmer one has to keep several things in mind. The New Deal happened in one of the most distressed periods of American history, one in which economies around the world were racked by comparable economic pains. The New Deal also sought to achieve relief, recovery, and reform in a set of economic conditions that had been years in the making, that could not possibly be undone in a short span of time under a system of government controlled by those who had faith in the capitalist system and political establishment and who depended on Congress, farmers, and the general public for continuation in office. Finally, the programs of FSA, the Bankhead-Jones Act, rural electrification, crop insurance, and the ever-normal granary were just beginning to get off the ground when the New Deal came to an end.

Still when all is said and done those farmers who were able to remain in agriculture, especially those with capital and resources, had more to gain from the New Deal than those who lacked capital and resources. The New Deal revived and maintained the morale of most farmers after it had fallen to the lowest depths in history. Farm prices failed to rise to the parity levels designated by the lawmakers, but they were lifted from the low levels of 1932 and 1933, and many of these gains can be attributed to the programs of the New Deal. Both farmers and the general public were made more aware of the need of conserving the soil; a laudable start was made in furnishing electricity for rural areas long neglected by private industry; the Shelterbelt Project helped make life on the Great Plains more bearable for more farmers; and statesmanlike measures, although unsuccessful in accomplishing their purposes, were adopted to improve international trade.

Whether Wallace had the future defense needs of the nation in mind when hostilities broke out may be a moot point. But beyond debate is the fact that "the peacetime programs of research, education, credit, rehabilitation, conservation, and adjustment carried on by the Land Grant Colleges and the Department of Agriculture were important factors contributing to agriculture's ability to respond to war needs. . . ." The New Deal with all its limitations and frustrations, by making operational ideas and plans that had been long on the minds of agricultural researchers and thinkers, constituted the greatest innovative epoch in the history of American agriculture.

SUGGESTED   READING

Burwood, Stephen, and Melvyn Dubofsky, eds. *Agriculture During the Great Depression* (1990).

Conrad, David. *The Forgotten Farmers: The Story of Sharecroppers in the New Deal* (1965).

Daniel, Cletus. *Bitter Harvest: A History of California Farmworkers, 1870–1941* (1981).

DeWitt, Howard. *Violence in the Fields: California Filipino Farm Labor Unionization During the Great Depression* (1980).

Fite, Gilbert. "The Farmers' Dilemma, 1919–1929." In *Change and Continuity in Twentieth-Century America: The 1920s,* ed., John Braeman, Robert H. Bremner, and David Brody (1968).

———. *Cotton Fields No More: Southern Agriculture, 1865–1980* (1984).

Gregory, James. *American Exodus: The Dust Bowl Migration and Okie Culture in California.* (1989).

Grubbs, Donald. *The Cry from the Cotton: The Southern Tenant Farmers' Union and the New Deal* (1971).

Hamilton, David. *From New Day to New Deal: American Farm Policy from Hoover to Roosevelt, 1928–1933* (1991).

Hurt, R. Douglas. *The Dust Bowl: An Agricultural and Social History* (1981).

Kelley, Robin D.G. *Hammer and Hoe: Alabama Communists During the Great Depression* (1990).

Kester, Howard. *Revolt Among the Sharecroppers* (1936).

Kirby, Jack. *Rural Worlds Lost: The American South, 1920–1960* (1987).

Linder, Marc. *Migrant Workers and Minimum Wages* (1992).

Lowitt, Richard. *The New Deal and the West* (1984).

McWilliams, Carey. *Factories in the Field* (1939).

Mooney, Patrick H. *Farmers' and Farm Workers' Movements* (1995).

Neth, Mary. *Preserving the Family Farm: Women, Community, and the Foundations of Agribusiness in the Midwest, 1900–1940* (1995).

Painter, Nell. *The Narrative of Hosea Hudson* (1979).

Perkins, Van. *Crisis in Agriculture* (1969).

Riney-Kehrberg, Pamela. *Rooted in Dust: Surviving Drought and Depression in Southwestern Kansas* (1994).

Rosengarten, Theodore. *All God's Dangers: The Life of Nate Shaw* (1974).

Saloutos, Theodore. *The American Farmer and the New Deal* (1982).

Shindo, Charles. *Dust Bowl Migrants in the American Imagination* (1997).

Shover, John. *Cornbelt Rebellion: The Farmers' Holiday Association* (1965).

Whayne, Jeannie. *A New Plantation South* (1996).

Worster, Donald. *Dust Bowl: The Southern Plains in the 1930s* (1979).

CHAPTER
10

Private Lives in Hard Times

The magnitude of the Great Depression can be measured not only in simple economic terms but also in the ways in which it challenged, uprooted, and complicated patterns of private life. Through the 1930s, the economic crisis indelibly shaped the roles and responsibilities of family members, the terms under which individuals contemplated or entered into relationships, and the larger tangle of social assumptions and premises. In a political culture that celebrated individualism and the ability of male breadwinners to provide for their families, the psychological toll of the Depression was tremendous. Unemployment was at once an economic calamity, a declaration of personal failure, and a blow to the masculinity of the male workers. This was reflected in the ways in which ordinary Americans would understand and respond to the Depression, and how they would frame their appeals to the state for assistance.

In many ways, the Depression exacted a harder toll on women, many of whom faced a situation in which their incomes made the difference between survival and starvation but in which they were pressured to step aside and let men have the available jobs. Popular assumptions and public policies both reflected the contemporary assessment (as put by the columnist Norman Cousins): "There are approximately ten million people out of work in the United States today. There are also ten million or more women, married and single, who are jobholders. Simply fire the women, who shouldn't be working anyway, and hire the men. Presto! No unemployment. No relief rolls. No Depression." Despite these pressures, female employment inched up slightly. Women moved into the labor force to supplement family incomes in a time of crisis. The jobs that were left after 1929–1930 were lower-paying, part-time, and concentrated in "female" industries. Many employers responded to the Depression by cutting costs and mechanizing (turning many "male" industrial jobs into "female" machine operative jobs). And industrial home work (such as garment piece work) expanded markedly. In addition to supplementing family incomes, women faced the task of slashing domestic expenditures. The "home economist" or consummate "consumer" of the 1920s was pressed in the 1930s to make do with less and to expand domestic labor to take up the slack.

The Depression also forced people to reassess their private lives and private relationships. For children and teenagers, hard times indelibly colored the terms and expectations of family life. For young people, the Depression meant putting off life decisions such as marriage or parenthood. For married couples, the economic crisis lent a new urgency to the desire to control family size—a fact reflected in abortion rates, contraceptive sales, and increased public acceptance of "family planning." For gay Americans, the Depression era proved a less tolerant climate than either the relatively carefree decade that had preceded it or the sexually tumultuous war years that would follow. Of course, the ways in which people responded, coped, and suffered varied by class, race, and region. Beyond the aggregate statistical measures and the common experience of uncertainty or unemployment, it is important to remember, the Depression was also a starkly personal event that shaped the personal lives of millions of Americans.

D O C U M E N T S

In Document 1, a working-class woman traces the economic and domestic pressures of living with less after 1929. The constraints of "making do," of course, were exaggerated by the consumer culture that had flourished in the 1920s. In Document 2, a doctor suggests the ways in which the Depression created new demands for contraceptive services and education. The interviews excerpted in Document 3 touch on the impact and importance of the economic crisis in the lives of children who lived through it. Document 4, drawn from a contemporary sociological study of the effects of unemployment, suggests the personal and psychological toll of losing a job. And a letter presented here as Document 5 provides an idea of the sorts of demands ordinary Americans—bred in a culture of individualism and self-help—made of their government in the early years of the crisis.

1. A Working Class Woman on "Making Do" in the 1930s

I stretched everything to make ends meet, but some of the ends just wouldn't meet. You can only stretch things so far.

My husband was a sheet metal worker. He'd been working steady, but when the hard times came he was just off and on, off and on.

I got a job helping out in a grocery store across from a school. Made sandwiches for the kids during their lunch hour. Made a little money that way, and got some good sandwiches for my own kids. Otherwise, my kids made bean sandwiches   just mashed up beans and put them between bread.

My aunt and uncle lived next door and used to help out with clothes for the kids. And sometimes when I was late with the payment—we was buying our house from them—why, they helped us out that way, by waiting for it. But we always made it up later. I saw to that.

Seems my house was always full to the rafters. What with our three kids and his dad and my mom and sometimes his brother—all not working. We had a long lot, 160 foot back, and he put the whole thing in garden—pole beans, squash, tomatoes, and even a few hills of potatoes.

From *Making Do: How Women Survived the 1930s* by Jeanne Westin, Follett, pp. 33–34.

I don't think we ate salads in those days. We had radishes or green onions right out of the garden, but we never seemed to have salad. I think he tried to raise lettuce, but it didn't turn out so good.

We ate lots of macaroni and spaghetti and I could make three pounds of hamburger go a long way. I used to mix a pound of butter with a pound of margarine and, if I didn't tell 'em, people didn't know the difference. And I didn't tell 'em.

I figured every which way I could to make ends meet—turned shirt collars, watched for specials—but some of them ends just wouldn't meet. They just couldn't be stretched far enough to meet.

The worst of it all was the kids. I wanted to give to them and help them more, but I just didn't have the money to do the little extras. You know, it made me feel terribly bad, but as I remember, they were very good about it.

I did what I had to do. I seemed to always find a way to make things work. I think hard times is harder on a man, 'cause a woman will do something. Women just seem to know where they can save or where they can help, more than a man. It's just a worry for him, and he feels so terrible when he can't take care of his family.

My husband got very despondent, you know. Oh, he'd say you can't have this and you're not getting that, and I don't want to hear about this; just fighting against it all the time. A woman, like I said, can take more. I always said that she can stand more pain. Take, for instance, when a man gets sick; why everybody within yelling distance has to wait on him. But a woman, now, will go along with pain and never say anything. Least that's how it seems to me.

2. Dr. Hilda Standish Recalls Efforts to Control Reproduction in the 1930s

Standish: After I came back from China, I was very fortunate. It was at a time when the movement in Connecticut had gotten to the point of not being able to get anywhere in the legislature. Therefore, the leaders decided that this law on the books probably would not hold anyway, so why not open a clinic and see. Mrs. Hepburn, who was the leader in the movement in Hartford, and a friend of Margaret Sanger's, decided to get a board of directors and actually open a clinic here. This was all taking place just as I came back from China. I don't remember through whom I heard about it, but at any rate I was asked if I would be interested in being the medical director of this new clinic that was forming. Well, I was. This was before I was married; the clinic was to be open only two or three days a week. We organized, found the place and all the things we needed and so forth, and opened on July ninth of 1935, which was little over a year after I came back. It was called the Maternal Health Center and was at 100 Retreat Avenue where the Medical Arts Building now stands. . . .

Reprinted from *Second to None: A Documentary History of American Women, Vol. II: From 1865 to the Present,* edited by Ruth Barnes Moynihan, Cynthia Russett, and Laurie Grumpacker by permission of the University of Nebraska Press. Copyright © 1993 by the University of Nebraska Press.

The office was on the first floor of a brownstone on Retreat Avenue, right across from the Hartford Hospital entrance to the clinic. This proved interesting, because while the Hartford Hospital could not sponsor us, nor could the Board of Health or anything else, openly, many of the nurses in the outpatient department, the postpartum department particularly, would say, "Well, you've just had a baby, and it would be wise to wait a while before you have another. If you just follow that white line across the street, and look up you'll see a sign there, and you might be interested in going in and talking with them." So, we really had quite a few referrals from the Hartford Hospital. [Laughs.] . . .

Nichols: All this was illegal, of course.

Standish: We didn't think it was, honestly. It was such a strange old law, because it was a law that would not permit you to *use* methods of birth control. Now, how do you know whether anybody's using them or not! But a doctor or a nurse by aiding and abetting a person to break a law is himself or herself responsible and liable to fine or imprisonment. So, it got back to us. But we thought that if the lawyers ever really judged this or the court did, that they would say, "This is simply ridiculous, and this law does not hold." We really thought that. . . .

Nichols: Did you ever feel that your own professional status was in any way threatened by what you were doing?

Standish: No, not in the least. Practically all of the doctors on the staff that I knew were very much for it. Many of them didn't dare say so, but this was true of our doctors in the public health group, too. They just dared not in their positions. Even the Catholic doctors were, many of them, in favor of it. They sent us patients. Of course, in those days we were very careful as to the patients we took. They had to be married. They had to have had one child. Now, as I think of it, it was just ghastly to have been so strict.

Nichols: They had to have had a child already?

Standish: Yes, and they had to be referred by a minister or a social worker or a doctor. These references, well, we had to have them. It was sad, for many of the women wanted to come and just didn't dare because they couldn't seem to feel it was right or find a sponsor. The priest, of course, couldn't send them or wouldn't send them, and yet they'd come sometimes on their own. We'd say, "There must be a sponsor somewhere." We didn't dare take people on their own. We had plenty of patients. The clinic ran 50 percent Catholic women. This has been true in most places, that you have the same percentage as you have in the population, and in those days Hartford was just about 50 percent Catholic. They'd say, "The priest doesn't know what we're up against. We just can't have more children. We love the ones we have, but we can't have any more. We can't support them." Or, "I'm just worn out." . . .

Nichols: Did you see many patients?

Standish: Yes, in the four years that we were there, we had over three thousand patients. . . .

Nichols: If you had to say what were the most common reasons why women came to you—because of finances? Or because of health? What were the reasons why they came to you?

Standish: Both.

Nichols: Even increased sexual pleasure? I would assume that these are all interrelated.

Standish: We didn't hear much of that. It was primarily, "I just can't have another child." "I'm tired." "I don't have enough money to support another child." "I can't take care of the ones I have in the way I want to." "We don't have a good enough home," etc. I would say for 99 percent these were the reasons.

3. Children Recall the 1930s

Slim Collier

My father was sort of a fancy Dan. A very little man, five feet two. He was a tool-and-die maker in addition to being a farmer. The kind of man that would get up in the morning and put on a white shirt and tie, suit, camel hair coat, gloves, get in his late model Chrysler, drive from the farm into the city, park his car in the parking lot, get out, take off his coat, put his suit in the locker and put on those greasy overalls to be a tool-and-die maker. He had a lot of pretensions. When the Depression hit him, it hit hard.

He was the kind of man that would put a down payment on a place, get a second mortgage, put a down payment on another place. The Depression wiped out his houses. The anger and frustration he experienced colored my whole life. He was the kind of man, if somebody went broke he was pleased. Now it happened to him. . . .

This short temper was a characteristic of the time. Men who were willing to work couldn't find work. My father was the kind of man who had to be active. He'd invent work for himself. A child who was playing irritated him. It wasn't just my own father. They all got shook up. . . .

Phyllis Lorimer

When it happened, I was in a boarding school which I loved. At Glendora. It was the best boarding school in California at that time. A beautiful school in the middle of orange trees. I was about to be president of the student body and very proud of myself. Suddenly I couldn't get any pencils and went to the principal to find out why. She was embarrassed because we were old friends. She said, "I'm sorry, the bills just haven't been paid." She complimented me, saying, "Were there scholarships, you could have it." And, "I couldn't be sorrier."

I was mortified past belief. It was hard for the principal. I called my mother and said, "Come and pick me up." Which she did. I went back home which wasn't much of a home because we were living with a stepfather whom I detested.

It was rough on me, the Thirties. I wasn't aware of it being with everyone else. I thought it was just personal. I was in no way aware that it was a national thing. Having grown up in some affluence, I was suddenly in a small court in Hollywood with a stepfather who was drunk and ghastly.

My brother was still at Dartmouth, where he was fortunate enough not to know what was going on at home. Whatever money there was went to keep brother at

Dartmouth. We were living on a form of relief. We had cans of tinned bully beef. And we had the gas turned off. My mother was an engaging lady who made everything a picnic. We cooked everything on an electric corn popper, so it was gay in certain aspects. (Laughs.) My mother had humor and charm, so I didn't know it was a desperate situation. When there wasn't any money, she'd buy me a china doll instead of a vegetable. (Laughs.) She was an eccentric, and everybody stared at her. I was the little brown mouse.

My father was still holding up his pride. He had been successful, and then things went. Two houses with everything in it. His own career had nothing to do with the Depression. He blew it. Lots of times bills weren't paid when there was no Depression.

I had come from this terribly wealthy family, with cousins who still had so much that, even during the Depression, they didn't lose it. Suddenly I had four great white horses. They were given to me by my cousins. I was a very good horsewoman. (Laughs.) I rode at all the shows and steeplechases and all that. And went home to canned bully beef at night. (Laughs.)

My brother was socially oriented, a tremendous snob. While we were eating bully beef, he was living extremely well at Dartmouth. Nobody told him how bad things were. He lived magnificently, with a socialite friend, in a house with a manservant. He came back and found the truth, and the truth was ghastly.

He was five years older, a male, facing the fact that he had to go out and do it. It set for him a lifelong thing: he was never going to be caught in the same trap his parents were—never, ever going to be the failure his father was.

4. The Plight of the Unemployed in the 1930s

Unemployment, in so far as it affected such families, has caused the concealed lack of respect for the husband to come into the open or, if the antagonistic sentiments were openly expressed prior to the depression, to increase the aggression toward the husband. The manifestations of the above changes were in increased conflicts, blaming the husband for unemployment, constant nagging, withdrawal of customary services, sharp criticism in front of the children, irritability at hitherto tolerated behavior, indifference to his wishes, and so on. The story of the Patterson family will illustrate the decline in the husband's status in families in which his position was low even prior to unemployment. . . .

. . . Prior to the depression Mr. Patterson was an inventory clerk earning from $35 to $40 a week. He lost his job in 1931. At the present time he does not earn anything, while his 18-year-old girl gets $12.50 a week working in Woolworth's, and his wife has part-time work cleaning a doctor's office. Unemployment and depression have hit Mr. Patterson much more than the rest of the family.

From "Mr. Patterson," in Mirra Komarovsky, *The Unemployed Man and His Family* (New York: The Dryden Press, 1940), pp. 25–28.

The hardest thing about unemployment, Mr. Patterson says, is the humiliation within the family. It makes him feel very useless to have his wife and daughter bring in money to the family while he does not contribute a nickel. It is awful to him, because now "the tables are turned," that is, he has to ask his daughter for a little money for tobacco, etc. He would rather walk miles than ask for carfare money. His daughter would want him to have it, but he cannot bring himself to ask for it. He had often thought that it would make it easier if he could have 25 cents a week that he could depend upon. He feels more irritable and morose than he ever did in his life. He doesn't enjoy eating. He hasn't slept well in months. He lies awake and tosses and tosses, wondering what he will do and what will happen to them if he doesn't ever get work any more. He feels that there is nothing to wake up for in the morning and nothing to live for. He often wonders what would happen if he put himself out of the picture, or just got out of the way of his wife. Perhaps she and the girl would get along better without him. He blames himself for being unemployed. While he tries all day long to find work and would take anything, he feels that he would be successful if he had taken advantage of his opportunities in youth and had secured an education.

Mr. Patterson believes that his wife and daughter have adjusted themselves to the depression better then he has. In fact, sometimes they seem so cheerful in the evening that he cannot stand it any more. He grabs his hat and says he is going out for a while, and walks hard for an hour before he comes home again. That is one thing he never did before unemployment, but he is so nervous and jumpy now he has to do something like that to prevent himself from exploding.

Mrs. Patterson says that they have not felt the depression so terribly themselves, or changed their way of living so very much.

. . . The wife thinks it is her husband's fault that he is unemployed. Not that he doesn't run around and try his very best to get a job, but he neglected his opportunities when he was young. If he had had a proper education and had a better personality, he would not be in his present state. Besides, he has changed for the worse. He has become irritable and very hard to get along with. He talks of nothing else, and isn't interested in anything else but his troubles. She and her daughter try to forget troubles and have a good time once in a while, but he just sits and broods. Of course that makes her impatient with him. She cannot sit at home and keep him company, so that during the past couple of years she and her daughter just go out together without him. It isn't that they leave him out—he just isn't interested and stays at home.

Mr. Patterson insists that his child is as sweet as ever and always tries to cheer him up, but the tenor of his conversation about his wife is different. She does go out more with the daughter, leaving him alone. He cannot stand it, worrying so and having them so lighthearted. "When you are not bringing in any money, you don't get as much attention. She doesn't nag all the time, the way some women do," but he knows she blames him for being unemployed. He intimates that they have fewer sex relations—"It's nothing that I do or don't do—no change in me—but when I tell her that I want more love, she just gets mad." It came about gradually, he said. He cannot point definitely to any time when he noticed the difference in her. But he knows that his advances are rebuffed now when they would not have been before the hard times.

5. An Ordinary American Appeals to Her Government, 1935

Troy, N.Y.
Jan. 2, 1935.

Dear Mrs. Roosevelt,

About a month ago I wrote you asking if you would buy some baby clothes for me with the understanding that I was to repay you as soon as my husband got enough work. Several weeks later I received a reply to apply to a Welfare Association so I might receive the aid I needed. Do you remember?

Please Mrs. Roosevelt, I do not want charity, only a chance from someone who will trust me until we can get enough money to repay the amount spent for the things I need. As a proof that I really am sincere, I am sending you two of my dearest possessions to keep as security, a ring my husband gave me before we were married, and a ring my mother used to wear. Perhaps the actual value of them is not high, but they are worth a lot to me. If you will consider buying the baby clothes, please keep them (rings) until I send you the money you spent. It is very hard to face bearing a baby we cannot afford to have, and the fact that it is due to arrive soon, and still there is no money for the hospital or clothing, does not make it any easier. I have decided to stay home, keeping my 7 year old daughter from school to help with the smaller children when my husband has work. The oldest little girl is sick now, and has never been strong, so I would not depend on her. The 7 year old one is a good willing little worker and somehow we must manage—but without charity.

If you still feel you cannot trust me, it is allright and I can only say I do not blame you, but if you decide my word is worth anything with so small a security, here is a list of what I will need—but I will need it very soon.

2 shirts, silk and wool. size 2

3 pr. stockings, silk and wool, $4\frac{1}{2}$ or 4

3 straight flannel bands

2 slips—outing flannel

2 muslim dresses

1 sweater

1 wool bonnet

2 pr. wool booties

2 doz. diapers 30 × 30—or 27 × 27

1 large blanket (baby) about 45" or 50"

3 outing flannel nightgaowns

From *Down and Out in the Great Depression: Letters from the Forgotten Man* edited by Robert S. McElvaine. Copyright © 1983 by the University of North Carolina Press. Used by permission of the publisher.

If you will get these for me I would rather no one knew about it. I promise to repay the cost of the layette as soon as possible. We will all be very grateful to you, and I will be more than happy.

Sincerely yours,

Mrs. H. E. C.

☞ E S S A Y S

In the first essay, Ruth Milkman suggests how the economic crisis bore heavily on the lives of working women by simultaneously forcing women to "make do" under difficult conditions, pressing them to increase their paid labor to supplement family incomes, yet (given the severity of male unemployment) withholding social and political support for working women. In the second essay, Leslie Reagan traces the subtle shift in the politics of reproduction during the Depression, including the increased demand for contraceptives and abortion services, and the response of physicians—many of whom proved willing to expand the practice of reproductive health in a context in which nontherapeutic abortions remained illegal. In the third essay, George Chauncey shows how the Depression narrowed the relatively permissive and tolerant sexual culture of the 1920s: in part, the end of Prohibition gave local authorities the opportunity to regulate nightlife and its Jazz Age excesses; in part, the crisis of masculinity that accompanied the collapse of the family wage economy sharpened gender distinctions and intolerance of "transgressors."

Women's Work in Hard Times

RUTH MILKMAN

... During the Great Depression ... women's unpaid household production became more important than it had been in earlier years. In a sense, the family "took up the slack" in the economy during the 1930s.

People who were unemployed naturally turned to their families for support. The work of women in physically and psychologically maintaining their families became tremendously difficult as family incomes declined and the psychological stresses attending unemployment took their toll. Women showed amazing resourcefulness in coping with the crisis on the family level. They used a wide variety of strategies, generally turning back toward "traditional" forms of family organization.

The most immediate problem facing the family struck by unemployment was the material hardship created by their lowered income. Women cut back family expenditures in many areas. Typical strategies were moving to quarters with lower rent, having telephones removed, and denying themselves many purchased goods and services to which they had become accustomed in the prosperity of earlier years. Clothing, prepared meals, domestic service, automobiles, magazine subscriptions

From "Women's Work and the Economic Crisis: Some Lessons from the Great Depression" by Ruth Milkman from *Review of Radical Political Economics* 8:1, © 1976, pp. 81–85. Reprinted by permission of Jai Press, Inc.

and amusements were among the many products and services which suffered declines in sales as optimists heralded the "live at home movement."

Many women managed to approximate their families' prior standard of living despite lowered incomes by substituting their own labor for goods and services they had formerly purchased in the marketplace, reversing the trend toward increased consumption in the preceding decades. Home canning was so widespread that glass jar sales were greater in 1931 than at any other point in the preceding eleven years. There was a corresponding drop in sales of canned goods, which had doubled in the decade from 1919–29. Similarly, the 1930s saw a revival of home sewing. People who had never sewed before attended night school classes to learn how to sew and remodel garments.

Women's efforts to cut back family expenses by substituting their own labor for purchasable commodities represented only one set of alternatives in the struggle to make ends meet. Many women engaged themselves in paid work in attempts to compensate for a reduction in family income. There was a revival of domestic industry: women took in laundry, ironing, and dressmaking; they baked cakes to sell; they took in boarders. Everywhere there were signs in yards advertising household beauty parlors, cleaning and pressing enterprises, grocery stores, and the like.

Women also sought paid jobs outside their home to increase the family income. They did this despite the strong cultural sanctions against married women working, sanctions which were strongly reinforced with the onset of mass unemployment. Women who thus defied the cultural prescription frequently justified their behavior as a response to the family emergency created by the unemployment of their husbands, and they generally planned to stop working for pay as soon as the situation improved. The following case is representative:

> Until 1930 Mr. Fetter was able to support the family. After that date his earnings from irregular work were supplemented by his wife's earnings of $9.00 per week in a restaurant. Both husband and wife disliked to have the wife work, but there seemed no other solution of the economic problem.

The last resort of families for whom none of these strategies succeeded—and there were many—was to go "on relief." Accepting this alternative, however, was widely viewed as an admission of failure of the family. Mr. Fetter's "reaction to the idea of relief was violent." In another case study, a husband and wife expressed their reluctance to accept any government assistance: "We are able people; we must keep on our feet." And in cases where the relief strategy was pursued, a great deal of resentment toward the social service agencies was expressed. Experienced wives and mothers often felt, not without reason, that the social workers they dealt with were too young and naive to understand the costs involved in raising a large family.

Added to the difficulties in maintaining families on a reduced income were the demands placed on the institution to reabsorb members who had been independent during the better times before the crash. Not only did unemployed husbands spend more time around the house, but old people, who frequently suffered from discrimination in employment, tended to "double up" with their sons' and daughters' families. The younger generation was likely to be relatively better off in terms of employment, but were less likely to have a securely owned dwelling. This strategy of pooling the resources of two generations represented a clear break with the long-term trend toward nuclearization.

Youth, who also faced discrimination in the labor market, returned home during the Depression. The dependence of this generation on the previous one caused delays, sometimes permanent ones, in new family formation. The marriage rate dropped sharply, from 10.1 marriages per thousand people in 1929 to 7.9, the low point in 1932. In 1938 it was estimated that 1.5 million people had been forced to postpone marriage because of the economic depression. Cohort data on ever-married rates reveals that many of these "postponements" were permanent. The proportion of single women (never married by 1970) ages 25–30 in 1935 is about 30 percent higher than the proportion in the cohort five years younger. One spinster of this generation recalls:

> There were young men around when we were young. But they were supporting mothers.
>
> It wasn't that we didn't have a chance. I was going with someone when the Depression hit. We probably would have gotten married. He was a commercial artist and had been doing very well. I remember the night he said, "They just laid off quite a few of the boys." It never occurred to him that he would be next. He was older than most of the others and very sure of himself. This was not the sort of thing that was going to happen to him. Suddenly he was laid off. It hit him like a ton of bricks. And he just disappeared.

The material tasks of family maintenance became extraordinarily challenging during the 1930s, as women struggled to stretch a decreased income to maintain the members of their nuclear family and, in many cases, the younger and older generations as well. However, this was but one aspect of the increased importance of women's unpaid labor in the home during the depression. The task of psychological maintenance was also made much more difficult in families affected by unemployment. The concrete fact of idleness, the declassment in the community which generally accompanied it, and a multitude of side effects associated with the various strategies pursued to maintain the family materially placed enormous strains on the family as an emotional support system, and on women's role in its maintenance.

Since his role as wage-earner is often the basis of the father's status within the family, that status tends to be lowered by his unemployment. The man without a job in the 1930s often felt superfluous and frustrated, "because in his own estimation he fails to fulfill what is the central duty of his life, the very touchstone of his manhood—the role of family provider." The strain attending unemployment was exacerbated in cases where other family members were earning money. A woman who replaced her husband as the "breadwinner" during the Depression recalls:

> In 1930, it was slack time. He didn't have a job, my husband. Even now, the painter's work is seasonal. So I went to work those times when he wasn't working, and he took care of the boy.
>
> Yah. He said he's walking upside down, if you know what that means. (Laughs.) You start walking on the floor, and then you put yourself upside down, how you feel. Because he couldn't provide for his family. Because when we got married, he actually said, "You're not gonna work."

To say that the unemployed father lost status in the family would seem to imply that women who assumed the role of "provider" gained somehow. But such a role reversal was not a simple exchange of power. Women's responsibility for providing emotional support to family members was not diminished during this period. On the contrary, the reversal of roles made this task much more difficult, for an unemployed husband demanded more support than ever before. If there was any increased recognition of women's economic role in the family, it did not represent a gain in status, for no one was comfortable with the new state of affairs, and the reversal of roles was resented by everyone involved.

The tension unemployment produced within the family was intensified by the general declassment accompanying lowered family income. As the status of the family in the community dropped there appeared alongside the tendency for families to strengthen their ties with relatives a general decrease in social contacts outside the family circle. Lacking appropriate clothing and money for dues or donations, many families stopped attending church and dropped their club memberships. In addition, many had sacrificed their telephones and there was little money for carfare, so it was more difficult to socialize with friends. People were ashamed of their lowered standard of living and hence reluctant to invite guests into their homes.

Further pressures on the psychological balance of the family were exerted by the various strategies women pursued to maintain its members materially. The simple fact of decreased income increased family discord over financial matters, and the crowding resulting from "doubling up," moving to less expensive quarters, or being unable to heat all the rooms in a house during the winter, produced much friction among family members. Moreover, they saw much more of each other than before, whether they wished to or not, simply because they were unemployed and spent more time at home.

Women in families affected by unemployment, then, were under incredible pressure from all sides. Their responsibility to maintain their families materially and psychologically became much more difficult to fulfill. Sociologists who studied the impact of the depression on families at the time noted that these strains generally resulted in an initial period of disorientation, which was ultimately resolved either through adjustment or "disintegration" of the family. Whether or not a family was able to adjust to the new situation depended on a variety of factors, but on the whole, these studies showed that the impact of the crisis was to exaggerate previous family patterns. "Well-organized" families became more unified, while the problems of unstable families were accentuated.

Families which survived the crisis intact certainly were more "unified" in the sense that they spent more time together than before, but it is not clear that this choice was freely made or that families were newly prized by their members. Indeed, the Lynds reported that "Each family seems to wish wistfully that the depression had not happened to *it,* while at the same time feeling that the depression has in a vague general way 'been good for family life.' " Families which broke under the strain did not always fall apart visibly. Although the frequency of desertion, the "poor man's divorce," rose, legal divorce was expensive, and its rate declined.

There is scattered evidence that in some families the strain was manifested in a decline in sexual activity. The most common reason given for such declines was fear of unwanted pregnancy. In a number of instances, however, women reported that they had lost respect for their unemployed husbands, and could no

longer love them as before. A psychiatrist observed of a group of long-term unemployed miners:

> They hung around street corners and in groups. They gave each other solace. They were
> loath to go home because they were indicted, as if it were their fault for being unem-
> ployed. A jobless man was a lazy good-for-nothing. The women punished the men for
> not bringing home the bacon, by withholding themselves sexually. . . . These men suf-
> fered from depression. They felt despised, they were ashamed of themselves. They
> cringed, they comforted one another. They avoided home.

There must have been many cases like these, in which the family simply could not
cope with all the strains which converged on it. The emergence of social services on
a large scale during the later 1930s probably represented, at least in part, a response
to these family failures, and supplied a bolster to the institution. But what is really
more remarkable than the record of failures is the amazing extent to which families
were able to successfully absorb all the new strains placed upon them.

In some cases there was organized resistance to the agents of dispossession. In
the country, there were "ten cent sales" in which neighbors would bid ridiculously
low prices for a farmer's property that was being auctioned off by creditors trying to
collect on a mortgage, and then return it all to the original owner. In the city, people
would move the furniture of an evicted family back into the tenement as soon as it
had been put out in the street, to the despair of the landlord.

While actions like these must often have represented the difference between
survival and disintegration of a family, most families seem to have depended even
more on their internal strengths. It was, to a great extent, women who took up the
increased burdens involved in maintaining the family—indeed, this was their traditional responsibility. The importance of their contribution to family maintenance
during the crisis was probably only seldom recognized. In Tillie Olsen's fictional
portrayal of a family's efforts to cope with the crisis, for example, the husband only
appreciates his wife's contribution after she is taken sick. "You useta be so smart
with money—make it stretch like rubber. Now it's rent week and not a red cent in
the house. I tell you we gotta make what I'm getting do . . ."

Some women were revitalized by the increased responsibility they acquired
during the Depression. One woman's hypochondria disappeared with the crisis:
"Now her mind is taken up with the problems of stretching her kitchen dollar further than ever and keeping the home up-to-date and clean without new furnishings
and the help of a cleaning woman." Another woman, a daughter, who would never
have looked for paid work if not for the decline in her once wealthy family's income, developed a whole new sense of self-respect from her experience as a wage-
earner. She recalls:

> Now it was necessary for me to make some money because the stepfather was drunk all
> the time and the father was pretending it hadn't happened. Having gone to a proper
> lady's finishing school, I didn't know how to do anything. I spoke a little bad French,
> and I knew enough to stand up when an older person came into the room. As far as any-
> thing else was concerned, I was unequipped.
>
> I heard there was a call for swimmers for a picture called *Footlight Parade*. At
> Warner Brothers. The first big aquacade picture. I went, terrified, tried out on the high
> diving thing and won. I couldn't have been more stunned. I truly think this is where I got

a life-long point of view: respect for those who *did,* no respect for those who *had* . . . just because their father had done something and they were sitting around.

I loved the chorus girls who worked. I hated the extras who sat around and were paid while we were endangering our lives. I had a ball. It was the first time I was better than anybody at something. I gained a self-respect I'd never had.

This kind of depression experience was, of course, limited to women of privileged social groups, those who would otherwise have spent their lives as more or less leisured symbols of their father's or husband's status. Hard work was nothing new to working class women, and their increased responsibilities could not have been welcomed so eagerly. For these women and their families, the experience of sex-role-reversal—either a complete shifting of responsibility for earning money from husband to wife, or simply an increased reliance on the wife's unpaid work and her strategies for survival—was a part of a very painful period in the family's history. The deviation from traditional sex roles was thus, to say the least, negatively reinforced by the accompanying experience of economic deprivation for most families. It did not generally mean that the husband-wife relationship became more egalitarian in the long run, rather the impact of the crisis was to define women in terms of the traditional female role even more rigidly than before.

Women "took up the slack" in the economy during the Great Depression, then, not by withdrawing from the paid labor force, . . . but in their family role. There was an increased economic dependence on their unpaid household labor, reversing the preDepression trend toward increased use of consumer goods. The process of nuclearization, similarly, reversed itself, as the unemployed turned to their kin for help. The family's role in maintaining people psychologically also became more difficult for women to fulfill.

The traditional family role of women was reinforced because of its increased material importance during the 1930s, then, although women did not "return to the home" in the way the "reserve army" theory suggests. On the contrary, role reversals between husband and wife were common, and precisely because of the *negative* reinforcement given to sex role reversal which resulted from its origin in economic deprivation, traditional sex roles were reinforced.

Reproductive Practices and Politics

LESLIE REAGAN

"My husband has been out of work for over six months and no help is in sight," wrote one mother to Margaret Sanger and the American Birth Control League; "I can't afford more children." Every year she performed two abortions upon herself, and she reported, "I have just now gotten up from an abortion and I don't want to repeat it again." The disaster of the Great Depression touched all aspects of women's lives, including the most intimate ones, and brought about a new high in the incidence of abortion. As jobs evaporated and wages fell, families found themselves

From *When Abortion Was a Crime: Women, Medicine, and Law in the United States, 1860s–1973* by Leslie Jean Reagan, pp. 132–147. Copyright © 1997 University of California Press. Reprinted by permission.

living on insecure and scanty funds. Many working people lost their homes; tenants had their belongings put out on the street. Married couples gave up children to orphanages because they could not support them.

As women pressured doctors for help, the medical practice of abortion, legal and illegal, expanded during the 1930s. Physicians granted, for the first time, that social conditions were an essential component of medical judgment in therapeutic abortion cases. Medical recognition of social indications reveals the ways in which political and social forces shaped medical thinking and practice. A handful of radical physicians, who looked to Europe as a model, raised the possibility of liberalizing the abortion law. During these years, abortion became more concentrated in the hands of physicians in both hospitals and private offices as a result of structural changes in medicine. . . .

The Depression years make vivid the relationship between economics and reproduction. Women had abortions on a massive scale. Married women with children found it impossible to bear the expense of another, and unmarried women could not afford to marry. As young working-class women and men put off marriage during the Depression to support their families or to save money for a wedding, marriage rates fell drastically. Yet while they waited to wed, couples engaged in sexual relations, and women became pregnant. Many had abortions.

During the Depression, married women were routinely fired on the assumption that jobs belonged to men and that women had husbands who supported them. Discrimination against married women forced single women to delay marriage and have abortions in order to keep their jobs. One such woman was a young teacher whose fiancé was unemployed. As her daughter recalled fifty years later, "She got pregnant. What were her choices? Marry, lose her job, and bring a child into a family with no means of support? Not marry, lose her job and reputation, and put the baby up for adoption or keep it?" As this scenario makes clear, she had no "choice." Furthermore, it points to the limitations of the rhetoric of "choice" in reproduction; social forces condition women's reproductive options. The teacher's boyfriend found a local physician who helped her in his office; then she went to a hotel to miscarry. Two years later she married a different man, who had a job, and eventually bore seven children.

That almost a thousand New Jersey women purchased a type of abortion "insurance" in 1936 demonstrates that abortion was a recurring and common need for many. New Jersey police uncovered a "Birth Control Club" of eight hundred dues-paying and card-carrying members. Membership in the club "entitled them to regular examinations and to illegal operations, when they needed them, at a further fee of $75 and upward." Most of the members were "girl clerks" who worked in Newark's downtown offices. Just as working people made small regular payments for life insurance and funeral coverage, these working women bought a form of health insurance through dues paid to this "club." These women *expected* to have abortions in the future. The club provided a means of blunting the expense of abortions and other gynecological care. When the *New York Times* covered this incident, birth control leaders immediately attacked the headline dubbing this a "birth control" club. The medical director of the American Birth Control League explained that the birth control movement "opposed" abortion and that the two were not the same.

The Depression helped legitimate contraceptives. American society increasingly accepted birth control during the 1930s. Condoms sold briskly in drug stores and gas stations. In 1930, the American Birth Control League had fifty-five birth control clinics in fifteen states; by 1938 there were over five hundred clinics. Hostility toward welfare payments and "relief babies" helped win support for providing birth control to the poor. The federal government quietly sponsored, for the first time, provision of birth control services in the late 1930s. As courts began to overturn the Comstock Laws on contraceptives, they allowed the medical profession to prescribe birth control devices. One 1937 poll found that nearly 80 percent of American women approved of birth control use. That year the AMA [American Medical Association] finally abandoned its official opposition to birth control. The medical profession had been pushed by the birth control movement into accepting responsibility for contraception. Contraceptives were not foolproof, however.

Greater availability of contraceptives could not alone meet the increased need for control over childbearing. The recognized expert on abortion, Frederick J. Taussig, reported that the number of abortions had grown "throughout the world." He believed it was "due less to [a] laxity of morals than to underlying economic conditions." A New Orleans physician who studied the septic abortion cases at the Charity Hospital found that the number of criminal abortions among poor, white patients rose 166 percent between 1930 and 1931. This surge reflected, he suggested, "the financial pressure . . . on this type of charity patient." Studies of Cincinnati, Minneapolis, New York, and Philadelphia showed that the use of abortion swelled in the early 1930s.

Medical studies and sex surveys demonstrated that women of every social strata turned to abortion in greater numbers during the Depression. Comparative studies by class and race appeared for the first time in the 1930s. Induced abortion rates among white, middle- and upper-class, married women rose during the Depression years. The Kinsey Institute for Sex Research, led by Paul H. Gebhard, analyzed data from over five thousand married, white, mostly highly educated, urban women. The researchers found that "the depression of the 1930's resulted in a larger proportion of pregnancies that were artificially aborted." For every age group of women, born between 1890 and 1919, the highest induced abortion rate occurred during "the depth of the depression." White, married women were determined to avoid bearing children during the Depression: they reduced their rate of conception as well.

In the early years of the Depression, married women aborted more of their first pregnancies than had women of earlier generations. Dr. Regine K. Stix discovered this pattern after interviewing almost a thousand women at a New York City birth control clinic in 1931 and 1932, all of whose incomes were severely reduced by the Depression. The young married woman who had an abortion did so "because she was the bread-winner in the family and could not afford to lose her job, much less produce another mouth to feed. A year or two later," Stix explained, "if her husband was working, she gave up her job and planned a baby or two." The findings of Kinsey researchers suggest that aborting first pregnancies early in marriage might have been a growing trend, particularly among more educated, urban white women.

Married black women, like their white counterparts, used abortion more during the Depression. Since African American women lost their jobs in disproportionate numbers, their need may have been greater than that of white women. Unfortunately, Kinsey researchers did not collect data from black women before 1950, but others documented black women's resort to abortion during the 1930s. Dr. Charles

H. Garvin, an esteemed black surgeon from Cleveland, commented in 1932 "that there has been a very definite increase in the numbers of abortions, criminally performed, among the married." The African American press reported on black women's use of abortion. In 1935, Harlem Hospital, which cared for mostly poor black patients, opened a separate ward, "The Abortion Service," to treat the women who came for emergency care following illegal abortions.

A number of studies showed that white and black married women of the same class had abortions at the same rate. A study of reproductive histories collected from forty-five hundred women at a New York clinic between 1930 and 1938 suggested that when class was controlled, working-class women, black and white alike, induced abortions at the same rate. The researchers found that "the incidence of pregnancies and spontaneous and induced abortion [among black women] was identical with that obtained for the entire group." A Houston study found that approximately equal properties of Mexican, African American, and white women had abortions. Studies like these of women of the same class suggest that any racial differences in overall abortion rates may be explained best by class differences.

The evidence on the practice of abortion by class is somewhat contradictory, but it seems that affluent women had higher abortion *rates* than did working-class women, but working-class and poor women actually had a greater *number* of abortions because they were pregnant more often. The Kinsey group of upper- and middle-class white women aborted 24.3 percent of their pregnancies in 1930 and 18.3 percent in 1935. In contrast, the working-class black and white women in the New York clinic study aborted at about half that rate, or 11.5 percent.

The key difference between black and white women was in their response to pregnancy outside of marriage, not their use of abortion. Unmarried white women who became pregnant were more likely to abort their pregnancies than were African American women in the same situation. Instead, more black women bore children out of wedlock and did so without being ostracized by their families and community. Dr. Virginia Clay Hamilton discovered important differences in abortion behavior between white and black single women during interviews with over five hundred low-income women who entered New York's Bellevue Hospital in 1938 and 1939 following the interruption of pregnancy, whether by miscarriage or induced abortion. Hamilton promised confidentiality and found that "the group showed surprisingly little reluctance to discuss the intimate questions which were put to them." Both white and black unmarried women had higher rates of induced abortion than did married women, but 64 percent of the unmarried white women told of having deliberately induced their abortions compared to only 40 percent of the unmarried black women. "Still more striking," commented Hamilton, was the racial difference in abortion behavior among the previously married. Divorced and widowed black women, "behav[ed] essentially like those still married," while divorced and widowed white women returned to the behavior of unmarried women when faced with illegitimate pregnancies. The level of induced abortions among previously married white women approached the high level of abortions among single white women. The Kinsey report found the same racial differences in the behavior of unmarried women.

The tolerance of illegitimacy among African Americans was tempered by class. As African Americans advanced economically, they held their unwed daughters and sons to more rigid standards of chastity. Similarly, by the time the Kinsey Institute interviewed black women in the 1950s, there were clear class differences in the use of abortion by unmarried black women: those with more education (and presumably more affluence) aborted at a higher rate than those with less education.

Women's religious background made little difference in their abortion rates, though religiosity did make a difference. A study of working-class women in New York in the 1930s found almost identical abortion rates among Catholic, Jewish, and Protestant women. However, researchers found striking differences in the reproductive patterns followed by women of different religious groups, a finding that seems to reflect class differences. Catholic and Jewish women tended to have their children earlier in their lives and began aborting unwanted pregnancies as they got older; Protestant women tended to abort earlier pregnancies and bear children later. The Kinsey Report found for both married and unmarried white women, the more devout the woman, the less likely she was to have an abortion; the more religiously "inactive" a woman, the more likely she was to have an abortion.

Access to physician-induced abortions and reliance upon self-induced methods for abortion varied greatly by class and race. Most affluent white women went to physicians for abortions, while poor women and black women self-induced them. Physicians performed 84 percent of the abortions reported by the white, urban women to Kinsey researchers. Fewer than 10 percent of the affluent white women self-induced their abortions, though black women and poor white women, because of poverty or discrimination in access to medical care, often did so. According to the Kinsey study on abortion, 30 percent of the lower-income and black women reported self-inducing their abortions. Sara Brooks, a black Alabama midwife, recalled her own attempt at abortion in the 1930s. A friend told her go visit "Annie" to get herself out of "trouble." Annie gave Brooks a mixture of camphor gum and nutmeg. When Brooks took it, she recalled, "It made me *so* sick." The doctor who was called gave her warm baking soda to force her to vomit. She believed she would have otherwise died, as her own mother had after taking turpentine to induce an abortion.

Low-income women's and black women's greater reliance upon self-induced methods of abortion meant that the safety of illegal abortion varied by race and class. Self-induced abortions caused more complications and hospitalization than did those induced by physicians or midwives. Since poor women and black women were more likely to try to self-induce abortions and less likely to go to doctors or midwives, they suffered more complications. Dr. Regine K. Stix learned from interviewing almost a thousand women in 1931 and 1932 that self-induced abortions, as compared to midwife- or physician-induced abortions, had the highest rates of infection and hemorrhage. Women reported having no complications after their abortions in 91 percent of the abortions performed by doctors and 86 percent of those performed by midwives. In contrast, only 24 percent of the self-induced abortions were without complications. Of the women who entered the county hospital in Portland, Oregon, after illegal abortions, more than two-thirds had induced their abortions themselves. It is worth noting that although the majority of complications occurred in self-induced abortions, physicians performed the majority of abortions.

As more women had abortions during the Depression, and perhaps more turned to self-induced measures because of their new poverty, growing numbers of women entered the nation's hospitals for care following their illegal abortions. The Depression deepened an earlier trend toward the hospitalization of women who had abortion-related complications in public hospitals. As childbirth gradually moved into the hospital, so too did abortion. Hospitals separated their abortion cases from other obstetrical cases because of the danger of spreading infection and devoted entire wards to caring for emergency abortion cases. At Cook County Hospital, physicians sent all patients with septic abortions or other obstetrical infections to Ward 41. One intern at Cook County Hospital recalled that in 1928 she saw at least thirty or forty abortion cases in the month and a half she worked there; or, one woman a day and several hundred women a year entered the hospital because of postabortion complications. In 1934, the County Hospital admitted 1,159 abortion cases, and reported twenty-two abortion-related deaths that year. Both black and white patients entered the nation's hospitals for care following illegal abortions.

Doctors and public health reformers began to realize the importance of illegal abortion as a contributor to maternal mortality. The maternal mortality study conducted by the Children's Bureau, first reported on in 1931, spotlighted the magnitude of maternal mortality due to illegal abortion. This study, of over seven thousand maternal deaths in fifteen states in 1927 and 1928, found that illegal abortion was responsible for at least 14 percent of the nation's maternal mortality. Another major study of maternal mortality in New York City by the New York Academy of Medicine found that 12.8 percent of maternal deaths were the result of septic abortion. The New York study also showed that abortion had increased as a cause of death both in absolute numbers and in proportion to other causes of maternal mortality. Taussig estimated that approximately fifteen thousand women died every year in the United States because of abortion.

A few physicians began to talk of reform, and even repeal, of the abortion laws. In 1933, two radical physicians published books favoring the decriminalization of abortion in the United States. Both of the physician-authors, Dr. William J. Robinson and Dr. A. J. Rongy, were Jewish immigrants from Russia who were active in politically radical circles as well as members of mainstream medical organizations. Both belonged to the AMA and the New York State and County Medical Societies. For over thirty years Robinson tried to persuade physicians to provide contraceptives. In 1911, he advocated the legalization of abortion, along with a few others, but the rest of the medical profession quickly dismissed such ideas. When Robinson published his book, he considered the time "ripe" for change. In *The Law against Abortion: Its Perniciousness Demonstrated and Its Repeal Demanded,* Robinson contrasted the poisonings, injuries, and deaths of women who had illegal abortions in the United States with the safety record of more than a decade of legal abortions performed by physicians in the Soviet Union.

Rongy offered a different tactic in his book, *Abortion: Legal or Illegal?* He advocated an expansion of the legitimate reasons for therapeutic abortions, which would come close to legalizing abortion. The American public, Rongy argued, already accepted abortion as a "social necessity." "No matter how callous the average physician appears to be," Rongy contended, "he is not left unaffected by the pathetic and often pitiful pleadings of the woman to whom a new pregnancy is a genuine cause of distress." Because of such experiences, most doctors, Rongy declared, privately supported liberalizing the abortion laws. Yet physicians feared to voice publicly their support for legal change. Rongy argued that the legal exception for therapeutic abortions set a precedent that could be used. The indications for abortions should be expanded.

Although Rongy's book "evoked a controversy," a serious public debate on the merits of liberalizing the abortion laws did not develop. One reason it did not was that it was censored. Rongy complained that "the august New York *Times* refused to allow the publisher to advertise" his book. Open discussion of abortion frightened publishers, some of whom opted for silence on the subject. One magazine had its staff of fourteen discuss whether an article on abortion should be published, then protected itself further by giving the article to "several hundred women" who were asked whether it was objectionable. None of the women objected, but before publishing the article, the editors deleted certain graphic paragraphs as a result of reader comments. Though the author of the article referred to Rongy's book, she did not say a word about his proposal to liberalize access to abortion. Instead, she emphasized the dangers of abortion and advised, "Have your baby!" Another reporter discovered that citizens who relied upon libraries for information would have a difficult time learning anything about abortion. The New York Public Library possessed no literature on abortion except the sections included in the Children's Bureau maternal mortality study, and the Academy of Medicine refused to allow nonphysicians to see books on contraception and abortion. American medical publications similarly avoided open debate on the question of reforming the criminal abortion laws. A *JAMA* reviewer described both books as "omens of an expansion in the United States of the demand for sex freedom" and criticized them for ignoring "the evils that may follow . . . repeal or relaxation" of the criminal abortion laws.

The reviewer may have feared that the United States would see, as Europe had, the rise of a feminist and socialist movement for legal abortion. The Soviet Union had legalized abortion in 1920, and socialists and feminists had made the legalization of abortion an issue in Germany, Austria, Switzerland, and England. In England, a movement for the legalization of abortion arose out of the organizing of leftist-feminists active in the birth control movement. In the 1920s these feminists learned that working-class women used abortion as their form of birth control. Furthermore, studies showed that deaths because of illegal abortion contributed greatly to maternal mortality. In 1936, a group of middle-class feminists committed to the interests of the working class and socialism formed an organization, the Abortion Law Reform Association (ALRA), to demand that abortion be made legal and accessible. The ALRA found support among working-class women in England and helped bring them to speak on their own behalf at parliamentary hearings on abortion. . . .

Popular abortion reform movements developed in Europe in the 1920s and 1930s; why not in the United States? In the U.S. as in England, working-class women constantly made it clear to birth controllers that they relied upon abortion, but no organization comparable to the ALRA formed to demand the decriminalization of abortion in the United States. The weakness of working class and socialist movements in this country—and the weak links between feminists, birth controllers, and socialists—hampered the development of a similar political movement around abortion. The red scare after World War I devastated the women's movement and the left, which had actively supported the early birth control movement and which, in Europe, nurtured the movement to legalize abortion. As the American birth control movement withdrew from the left and became a movement of middle-class professionals, the association of legal abortion with Soviet socialism surely tainted the notion among American birth control supporters, who were themselves under assault. The U.S. birth control movement maintained an antiabortion stance and argued for the legitimacy of contraceptives by arguing that birth control could eliminate illegal abortion (a position shared with the more mainstream birth control movement in England). The refusal of American birth controllers to engage in a discussion about liberalizing access to abortion ensured that a public discussion of the idea never developed. . . .

Although few physicians joined the political challenge of the laws, physicians nonetheless liberalized access to "therapeutic" abortion. During the 1930s, individual physicians and the profession as a whole accepted a de facto expansion of the accepted indications for therapeutic abortions. . . .

Therapeutic abortion for women who had tuberculosis illustrates how social conditions entered medical judgment. Tuberculosis of the lungs was the most frequent reason for therapeutic abortion, though there was disagreement over this indication. At the turn of the century, physicians observed that the condition of women who had tuberculosis declined with pregnancy. Physicians urged women with tuberculosis to avoid pregnancy and agreed that when a tubercular woman became pregnant, a therapeutic abortion should be performed to prevent her decline and death. . . .

As Taussig noted, the decision whether to abort the pregnant woman with tuberculosis "is intimately bound up with the social-economic status of the patient." Although doctors disagreed on when tuberculosis made an abortion necessary, they agreed each case had to be examined "from all angles, social as well as medical" before a decision could be made. Long-term bed rest and treatment in a sanatorium could bring a woman with active tuberculosis to a safe delivery. Few could pay for sanatorium care, however, and in those cases, Taussig believed that abortion was justified. He explained how the number of children, housework, and poverty entered into the physician's assessment of proper treatment in these cases. His explanation demonstrates how an affluent woman's desire for a baby, or a poor woman's distress at the prospect, could be incorporated into the physician's decision regarding the necessity of therapeutic abortion.

> In a poorly nourished woman with a large family, we must regard the saving of fetal life with less concern than in the woman who can and will carry out sanatorium treatment for the required period of time during and after her pregnancy, and for whom the saving of the child is a matter of great concern. In such women with but one or no children we may, even in active cases, refrain from intervention, while in those whose external conditions make the pregnancy and the subsequent care of the child a serious burden, we would incline more readily, even in latent cases, to an interruption.

The desperate poverty and hunger of many Americans during the Depression similarly entered medical diagnosis. Taussig rejected the Soviet policy of providing abortions for women who already had large families, but reached the same conclusion by medicalizing the problems of large, low-income families. A large family, he suggested, could be detrimental to the health of both a woman and her family. On that basis, an abortion could be medically justified. Abortions in cases of asthma, weight loss, and physical depletion were legitimate, according to Taussig, when the woman had "heavy household duties" and children whom she could not care for or feed adequately. Taussig admitted that conservatives would disagree and that American laws did not allow abortions until a woman's health had already declined, but he favored allowing physicians to perform therapeutic abortions in order "to preserve the health of the mother and the integrity and well being of the family.". . . .

Taussig's acceptance of broadening the medical indications for therapeutic abortions to include social and economic reasons helped legitimate what was already accepted practice among many doctors. Taussig explained that since the world war "there have been two movements running counter to each other" in terms of their medical and political views of therapeutic abortion: on the one hand, some advocated the liberalization of indications for therapeutic abortion to include social indications; on the other hand, socially conservative doctors argued that therapeutic abortion should be done rarely and never for social reasons. The latter group rejected looking to the circumstances of the patient as part of medicine. Taussig's belief in the necessity of considering the pregnant woman's social situation favored and strengthened one stream of medical thought. . . .

Even though Taussig believed social conditions, family need, and income should be considered by the doctor, he resisted addressing the question of what the patient herself wanted. Physicians who debated the indications for therapeutic abortion all shared the assumption that doctors would make decisions for patients. Radical physicians like Robinson and Rongy, in contrast, assumed that women themselves would determine when an abortion was necessary. Although mainstream medical thinking assumed that abortion decisions were under physicians' control, plenty of physicians listened to their patients and helped them obtain abortions. Allowing physicians to treat social reasons as legitimate medical reasons created some space in which women and their families could make their preferences known and physicians could listen.

Despite the objections of some, physicians did perform therapeutic abortions for economic reasons. An editorial comment in *JAMA* confirmed that physicians performed abortions out of sympathy for destitute patients. "Poverty," the editor asserted, "does not constitute an indication for abortion." Yet, he admitted, "there is no doubt that in the United States many abortions are performed for borderline cases in which there is a strong ethical indication plus a more or less minor medical ailment." The expansion of therapeutic abortions benefited women who wanted abortions and who found doctors who could, and would, justify them on combined medical and social grounds.

Because patients with complications from illegal abortions increasingly went to hospitals, the problem of illegal abortion became visible to doctors in an unprecedented way. The suffering that so many doctors witnessed made many willing to help women seeking abortions. In previous years many doctors had privately observed the horrible results of illegal abortion and tried to cope with them individually in patients' homes or their own offices. In the Depression decade, as interns, residents, staff, and specialists in hospitals, doctors observed, on a larger scale, the continuous stream of patients needing emergency care as a result of illegal abortions. From his days as a hospital intern, Dr. Rongy recalled a young woman who was hospitalized following her abortion and her mother who stayed by her side for ten days until her daughter died of septicemia. This "tragedy . . . left a profound impression." A physician who interned at Freedmen's Hospital in Washington, D.C., in the 1930s later recalled attending a hemorrhaging woman who "still had the straightened-out coat hanger hanging from her vagina." In hospital wards, doctors saw women with septic infections, perforations of the uterus, hemorrhages, and mutilation of intestines and other organs caused by self-induced abortions or ineptly performed operations.

The hospital atmosphere, one surmises, made more doctors aware of medical participation in underground abortion services and the stretching of indications to perform therapeutic abortions. In past decades, almost every general practitioner or specialist in obstetrics had been approached at least once by a woman seeking an abortion. The demand generated by the disaster of the Depression increased the number of women knocking on doctors' doors for help. Hospitals concentrated abortion and physicians in one place. In the hospital, doctors could observe each other, talk informally, and spread rumors about physicians' involvement in abortion. Such an atmosphere, I suspect, helped forge a liberal consensus within a section of the medical profession about the horrors of self-induced and poorly performed criminal abortions, together with an acceptance of performing abortions for needy patients or referring them to abortionists.

The Campaign Against Homosexuality

GEORGE CHAUNCEY

"The sudden featuring of the horticultural young man as a nightclub feature" was noted with distress by a New York nightclub insider at the height of the pansy craze in 1931. He quickly reassured his readers, though, that "recurrent though the vogue is for this type of entertainer, its popularity is short." The vogue in New York, however, had little time to run its course. After a decade in which gay men and a smaller number of lesbians had become highly visible in clubs, streets, newspapers, novels, and films, a powerful backlash to the Prohibition-era "pansy craze" developed. The anti-gay reaction gained force in the early to mid-thirties as it became part of a more general reaction to the cultural experimentation of the Prohibition years and to the disruption of gender arrangements by the Depression. As the onset of the Depression dashed the confidence of the 1920s, gay men and lesbians began to seem less amusing than dangerous. A powerful campaign to render gay men and lesbians invisible—to exclude them from the public sphere—quickly gained momentum.

Early in 1931 several of the city's newspapers began a campaign against clubs featuring female impersonators and "m.c.'s who boast of a lavender tinge in their make-up." The campaign gathered momentum when gunfire broke out at Jean Malin's venue, the Club Abbey, on the night of January 25, which sent its gangster proprietor, Dutch Schultz, into hiding, and his assailant, Charlie (Chink) Sherman, into a hospital. Although the Abbey managed to reopen the following night, it closed for good a few days later. Rumors abounded that the shootout marked the beginning of

---

a long-feared war between rival gangs to control the Broadway liquor trade, and pressure built for the police to restore order.

The police responded by launching a campaign of harassment against the remaining Times Square clubs featuring pansy acts. On the night of January 28, 1931, they raided the Pansy Club on West Forty-eighth Street and the Club Calais at 125 West Fifty-first Street. They charged both with liquor violations, even though city authorities had stopped enforcing the Volstead Act several years earlier. Police Commissioner Edward Mulrooney announced the next day: "There will be a shake-up in the night clubs, especially of those which feature female impersonators." True to his word, he sent plainclothesmen to the pansy clubs to make sure their paperwork was in order and that they had secured the proper cabaret licenses and certificates of occupancy. He also stationed uniformed officers at the door of each club, with orders to make sure it closed promptly at 3 A.M.—a curfew commonly violated—and he threatened to impose a 1 A.M. curfew. The policemen also endeavored to disturb the relaxed atmosphere and illegal liquor trade that were crucial to the clubs' profitability. "Cops spotted at the door of nite clubs are more inquisitive than ever," *Variety* reported. "All seekers after synthetic joy [that is, illegal liquor] are getting a Hawkshaw glance that is guaranteed to throw cheaters into a panic. This is scaring away the better wine-buyers." Two men entering a club "without a female in tow," the paper added, were subject to even greater scrutiny and intimidation. While the pansy acts had already begun to lose some of their popularity, the strict enforcement of the curfew and steady barrage of harassment left the clubs with no choice but to end their flirtation with such acts. "The 'temperamentals' who held sway on the main stem for a year," *Variety* reported in early February, "are about ready to concede they are slipping as nite draws."

Later that year the police moved to crack down on the city's drag balls as well. They forced the organizers to cancel one planned for September 26 at the New Star Casino at Park Avenue and 107th Street, where several had been held the previous year, and half a dozen policemen appeared the following week to prevent a smaller drag from being held in its stead at a West 146th Street hall. The suppression of Harlem's drag balls, at least, was short-lived. Within a few months, the police, having made their point, backed down and permitted the annual Hamilton Lodge ball, the largest drag ball of the year, to be held at the Rockland Palace. This ball continued to be held every February until the late 1930s and to receive extensive coverage from Harlem's leading paper, the *Amsterdam News*. But no more drag balls were held in Madison Square Garden or midtown hotels, just as no more pansy acts were produced there.

The retreat of the drag balls from Times Square was telling. "If the cops have their way," *Variety* reported as the campaign against pansy acts got under way, "the effeminate clan will hereafter confine its activities to the Village and Harlem." Prohibition culture had allowed gay visibility to move into the center of New York's most prestigious entertainment district, but in the early thirties, the authorities were determined to return it to the city's periphery. In addition to ending the Times Square pansy acts and drag balls, the police tried to eradicate pansies from the streets of the Square. In September 1931, for instance, they launched a "round-up . . . of apparent homosexuals" who gathered on Forty-second Street near Bryant Park. Their efforts were only partially successful. "The degenerates . . . gradually returned," as one social-hygiene society observed, "and [could be] seen in that section almost nightly." Bryant Park, portions of Forty-second Street and Sixth Avenue, and the streets of the Hell's Kitchen neighborhood to the west of the Square continued to serve as gathering places for young "painted queens," as well as for soldiers, seamen, hustlers, and the gay men who were attracted to them. But over the course of several years the police succeeded in forcing the majority of the most "obvious" gay men out of the rest of Times Square, especially the more "respectable" area north of Forty-second Street where the district's remaining theaters and nightclubs clustered. It was a commonplace among gay men that after Fiorello La Guardia, a man known for his moralism as well as his reformism, was elected mayor in 1933, he had issued orders forbidding the appearance of drag queens anywhere between Fourteenth and Seventy-second Streets. Whatever the cause, the disappearance of the "painted queens" from Times Square was noted by the less overt gay men who remained there. One of the Square's habitués remarked at the beginning of World War II that things had "changed since the decade of 1925–1935 when the flaming homosexual was a common sight on the streets of mid-town New York, and they are seldom to be encountered [there] nowadays."

The timing of the initial crackdown, in 1931, seems to have been determined only partially by the shooting at the Club Abbey. The declining political fortunes of Jimmy Walker's mayoral administration were more salient. An investigation into corruption in New York City's magistrates' courts and police force directed by the distinguished Tammany Hall foe Samuel Seabury had begun to pose a serious threat to Mayor Walker; his new appointed police commissioner, Edward Mulrooney, launched a highly publicized war on vice in an effort to divert attention from the investigation. The fact that the drag balls had become chic events for the social elite to attend doubtless had contributed to the inclination of the police under the laissez-faire Walker administration to tolerate them, but this provided tenuous security indeed. The prominence of the drags—along with gay club acts, burlesque, and other highly visible "moral evils"—made them an inviting target once the mayor needed to demonstrate his resolve to clean up New York.

Although the 1931 crackdown was precipitated by the newspaper campaign, the shooting at the Club Abbey, and the mayor's political crisis, it signaled a more fundamental shift in the cultural and political climate and was soon followed by more enduring measures that pushed "fairies" out of the clubs and back into the periphery of the city. Many Americans—including many New Yorkers—were appalled by the lawlessness of the speakeasies and nightclubs, and their fears only grew in the wake of the Depression, as battles broke out in the clubs between gangs struggling to claim a share of declining profits. Some worried that the cultural developments of the late Prohibition period had somehow contributed to the Depression by replacing a productionist ethic with a consumerist one, a regard for traditional American moral values with the flaunting of illicit desires. By the early thirties, a general revulsion had set in against the "excesses" of Prohibition, and the celebration of sexual perversity on the stages of the premier cultural district of the American cultural capital seemed the most galling expression of such excess. New York had been denounced as the Sodom and Gomorrah of the nation throughout the twenties, but Jean Malin's pansy act must have provided a more vivid demonstration of the accuracy of that charge than most critics could have anticipated. As many Americans came to believe that such excesses could no longer be tolerated, a more enduring campaign against the visibility of the gay world was launched in New York and cities throughout the nation.

The most significant step in the campaign to exclude the gay world from the public sphere was a counterintuitive one: the repeal of Prohibition. For rather than initiating a new era of laissez-faire tolerance in urban life, as is often imagined, Repeal inaugurated a more pervasive and more effective regime of surveillance and control. Repeal made it possible for the state to redraw the boundaries of acceptable sociability that seemed to have been obliterated in the twenties. This had enormous consequences for gay life, for those boundaries were drawn in a way that marginalized and literally criminalized much of gay sociability. Repeal resulted in the segregation and isolation of the gay social world from the broader social life of the city, in which it had played such a significant role in the 1920s. This new isolation, in turn, established the conditions that made it possible for gay men and the gay world to be demonized in the even more hostile climate of the postwar period. . . .

Prohibition had been a failure in New York. It had criminalized much of the city's nightlife, driven many entrepreneurs out of business, and resulted in the closing of numerous restaurants and several well-known hotels, as well as most of the city's saloons. But it had not stopped people from drinking or socializing in unrespectable ways. Instead, it had resulted in the growth of an underground economy controlled by criminal gangs, and it had precipitated a popular revolt against Prohibition enforcement that was so widespread it seemed to undermine the authority of the law itself. It had also created a speakeasy-based demimonde in which the boundaries of acceptable public sociability were significantly reconfigured by the "promiscuous" and unregulated intermingling of the classes and sexes. . . .

The alcoholic beverage control laws promulgated after Prohibition were designed, then, not only to control the consumption of liquor per se but also to regulate the public spaces in which people met to drink. Officials intended them to help reestablish the boundaries of respectable public sociability that had been eroded by the Prohibition ethos. To this end, state legislatures throughout the country enacted stringent rules to govern the conduct of taverns and put powerful new regulatory agencies in place to enforce them. The cornerstone of the power of the administrative agency established in New York, the State Liquor Authority (SLA), was its exclusive authority to license the sale of alcohol. If liquor would once again be sold legally, the state sought to ensure that it would be sold only by those duly licensed on the basis of their acquiescence to state regulations governing their behavior and that of their patrons. Licenses became a privilege, which the state could revoke if an establishment failed to conform to state standards. By offering state sanction and all the privileges it entailed to those drinking establishments that conformed to SLA regulations, the law severely discouraged proprietors from risking violations of them. . . .

. . . Repeal was essential to the relegitimization of nightlife in the 1930s because it enabled reputable entrepreneurs to reenter the business and create sanitized forms of entertainment. But the obverse was equally significant: Repeal served to draw new boundaries between the acceptable and the unacceptable, and to impose new sanctions against the latter. The most general rule designed to effect this project of normalization (or to "prevent a return to the conditions of the saloon") required that licensed establishments not "suffer or permit such premises to become disorderly."

The requirement that establishments be "orderly" proved to have a profound impact on gay bars. For while the legislature did not specifically prohibit bars from serving homosexuals, the SLA made it clear from the beginning that it interpreted the statute to mandate such a prohibition. The simple presence of lesbians or gay men, prostitutes, gamblers, or other "undesirables," it contended, made an establishment disorderly. An owner who tolerated their presence risked losing his or her license. . . .

The implications of the SLA's anti-gay policy for gay bars and gay sociability were made clear by its closing of Gloria's, a bar on Third Avenue at Fortieth Street, in 1939. The owners had made it apparent they wanted to run it as a gay bar by hiring Jackie Mason as its manager. Mason was a well-known figure in gay circles, who had run a gay speakeasy in Charles Street in the mid-1920s (where Jean Malin once worked), had organized the Madison Square Garden drag ball in 1930, and since then had regularly arranged drag shows for both gay and straight clubs. As one SLA investigator put it, Mason was "a fag and a leader of that element . . . where Jackie Mason is, fags are"; he was a popular man and a sure draw as a host. Gloria's was part of a gay bar circuit that included Benny's, a block to the south; Will Finch described both bars in the spring of 1939 as "very crowded, almost exclusively with homosexuals." Men felt free to camp it up at Gloria's. They "gabbed around in feminine voices," it seemed to one SLA investigator. "Some called others by feminine names. [They] acted, walked, and impersonated females, and [female] attitude and gestures.

It was precisely this openness that aroused the ire of the police and SLA. The SLA warned Gloria's management that they had endangered their license by "permit[ting] the premises to become disorderly in permitting homosexuals, degenerates and undesirable people to congregate on the premises." As the SLA indicated at a hearing, it based this judgment on its investigators' reports that the bar had hired Mason to attract a gay following and that the men they had seen at the bar behaved in a campy (or "feminine") manner. The SLA also specified two particular incidents of disorderly conduct witnessed by its agents: a man the agents had invited to the bar had, after a two-hour conversation in a booth, caressed (or "fondled," as they put it) one of the agents under the table; and the management had permitted two heterosexual couples to goose several homosexual men who had passed by them in the crowded bar. The SLA also alleged that two men had solicited the investigators and that one had offered to arrange a date between an investigator and two "degenerates." The SLA initially agreed to renew Gloria's license on the condition that it ban homosexuals from the premises. When the management failed to evict its homosexual patrons, the Authority not only revoked the owner's license, but prohibited the licensing of the premises to anyone else for a year, thus making it virtually impossible for the owner to recoup his original investment by selling his equipment.

Unlike most bars, Gloria's took the SLA to court and offered an exceptionally forthright challenge to the revocation of its license. It first tried to protect its license by denying that it had violated the SLA regulation. The SLA had not proved that homosexuals had been present at the bar, it argued, and, moreover, the investigators' lack of scientific training about homosexuality rendered them incompetent to identify homosexuals. But having implicitly acquiesced to the SLA's anti-gay policy as a safeguard, the bar then challenged the policy itself. So long as homosexuals were neither diseased nor engaging in conduct it agreed would be disorderly, such as making noise, soliciting, or the "annoying or accosting of people," the bar contended, the Liquor Authority could not require a bar's management to "refuse to serve such people." "There is no rule or regulation of the State Liquor Authority nor any section of the Alcoholic Beverage Control Law," Gloria's insisted, "which provides that a sex variant may not be served at a licensed premises."

The Liquor Authority successfully countered both arguments. It stood by the testimony of its investigators and insisted that it would be improper for the court to second-guess the Authority's own finding of fact. More significant is that while it continued to maintain that numerous specific acts of disorderly conduct had occurred, it argued that even if no such acts had taken place, it still had the power to close the bar simply because "lewd and dissolute" people such as homosexuals had congregated and been served there. In a brief order, the Appellate Division (the state's second-highest court) affirmed the decision of the Liquor Authority. It did not explain its reasoning and thus did not address the arguments made by either party, but the effect of its ruling was to uphold the Authority's policy of closing bars that served homosexuals.

The SLA made full use of that power. In the two and a half decades that followed, it closed literally hundreds of bars that welcomed, tolerated, or simply failed to notice the patronage of gay men or lesbians. As a result, while the number of gay bars proliferated in the 1930s, '40s, and '50s, most of them lasted only a few months or years, and gay men were forced to move constantly from place to place, dependent on the grapevine to inform them of where the new meeting places were. . . .

When the SLA launched a campaign against bars serving homosexuals as part of its effort to "clean up the city" in the months before the 1939 World's Fair opened, it quickly discovered just how effective that grapevine could be. The authorities were particularly concerned about the Times Square area, which remained a major tourist attraction and showcase for the city despite its rapid "deterioration" under the impact of the Depression. After closing several bars in the area patronized by homosexuals, including the Consolidated Bar & Grill on West Forty-first Street, the Alvin on West Forty-second, and more distant bars that were part of the same circuit, the SLA's investigators discovered that many of the patrons of those bars had simply converged on the Times Square Garden & Grill on West Forty-second Street and turned it into their new rendezvous. In late October 1938 an SLA investigator, sent to the bar after a police report that "about thirty . . . fairys [sic] and fags" had been noticed there, noted that several of the gay men he had previously noticed at the other bars were "now congregating" there, along with a large number of soldiers. The owner himself insisted that "we never looked for . . . this kind of business. . . . [The police] close some places; [the fairies] come over here. . . . It was the neighborhood—[the fairies] know what places . . . are [open to them]. The word passes so fast. They knew [when a bar] is a degenerate place.". . .

The enhanced role of the State Liquor Authority in the regulation of gay life marked an important transition in the policing of urban sociability. In the half-century before the Depression, the primary impetus for the policing of morality had come from private societies that organized to exert pressure on the metropolitan police to enforce moral codes and even used their influence at the state and federal level to acquire police powers for themselves. But the moral crisis generated by Prohibition had undermined their legitimacy, and the financial crisis generated by the Depression had undermined their private support. By 1931 the Committee of Fourteen, as noted before, had seen its cultural authority so diminished by the popular revolt against moral vigilantism that it was reduced to pleading to donors that it had never "been interested in regulating the conduct of individuals," an objective now evidently in some disrepute, but had only been concerned to attack the parties "who make money out of the exploitation of girls." When it lost the support of its major financial backers the next year, the most effective social-purity society in the city's history was forced to terminate its work. The state legislature established the State Liquor Authority the following year, however, and its agents took up the task previously performed by the Committee's agents: surveying bars and other sites of public sociability, threatening the livelihoods of entrepreneurs who sanctioned public disorder, defining such disorder even as they searched for it. . . .

Rather than eliminating gay bars, in fact, SLA regulations ironically served to foster the creation of exclusively gay bars. Before Repeal, most gay men had gathered at saloons, restaurants, and speakeasies also frequented by straight people. Gay men remained "discreetly" invisible at some, but were quite open at others. Restaurants and saloons had always risked trouble with the authorities if they allowed gay men to gather on their premises, and their patrons were subject to arrest for disorderly conduct. Actual interference from the authorities, however, was rare. But after Repeal, bar owners risked losing their entire business if they served a single homosexual. Given this danger, most bars became reluctant to let *any* gay people mix openly with their other patrons and sought to protect themselves by excluding from their premises anyone they suspected of being gay. Lesbians and gay men continued to covertly patronize bars and restaurants throughout the city. But the anti-gay SLA regulations served, as intended, to exclude homosexuals from the public sphere by preventing them from socializing *openly* in "straight" bars. The same ban also resulted in the establishment of exclusively gay bars, however, where men could be openly gay. Bars that saw profit in serving gay men usually committed themselves to them, knowing their tenure would likely be brief. Exclusively gay bars, a relatively rare phenomenon before the 1930s, proliferated after Repeal. Thus, while gay life continued to thrive in the 1930s, '40s, and '50s, it was hidden and more segregated from the rest of city life than it had been before.

SUGGESTED READING

Agee, James, and Walker Evans. *Let Us Now Praise Famous Men* (1941).

Bauman, John F. *In the Eye of the Great Depression: New Deal Reporters and the Agony of the American People* (1988).

Beneria, Lourdes, and Catherine Stimpson, eds. *Women, Households, and the Economy* (1987).

Berube, Allan. *Coming Out Under Fire: The History of Gay Men and Women in World War II.* (1990).

Bird, Caroline. *The Invisible Scar* (1966).

Chauncey, George. *Gay New York: Gender, Urban Culture, and the Making of the Gay Male World, 1890–1940* (1994).

D'Emilio, John, and Estelle Freedman. *Intimate Matters: A History of Sexuality in America* (1988).

Deutsch, Sara. *No Separate Refuge: Culture, Class and Gender on an Anglo-Hispanic Frontier in the American Southwest, 1880–1940* (1987).

Elder, Glen. *Children of the Great Depression* (1974).

Gonzalez, Rosalinda M. "Chicanas and Mexican Immigrant Families, 1920–1940." In *Decades of Discontent,* ed. Lois Scharf and Joan Jensen, 59–84 (1983).

Gordon, Linda. *Heroes of Their Own Lives: The Politics and History of Family Violence: Boston, 1880–1960* (1988).

Green, Harvey. *The Uncertainty of Everyday Life, 1915–1945* (1992).

Lange, Dorothea. *An American Exodus.* Rev. ed. (1969).

McElvaine, Robert. *Down and Out in the Great Depression: Letters from the "Forgotten Man"* (1983).

Mintz, Steven. *Domestic Revolutions: A Social History of American Family Life* (1988).

Reagan, Leslie. *When Abortion Was a Crime: Women, Medicine, and Law in the United States, 1867–1973* (1997).

Robinson, John. *Living Hard: Southern Americans in the Great Depression* (1981).

Sternsher, Bernard, ed. *Hitting Home: The Great Depression in Town and Country* (1970).

Sternsher, Bernard, and Judith Sealander, eds. *Women of Valor: The Struggle Against the Great Depression as Told in Their Own Life Stories* (1990).

Terkel, Studs. *Hard Times: An Oral History of the Great Depression* (1970).

Terrill, Tom, and Jerrold Hirsch. *Such As Us: Southern Voices of the Thirties* (1978).

Tone, Andrea. "Contraceptive Consumers: Gender and the Political Economy of Birth Control in the 1930s." *Journal of Social History* 29 (Spring 1996): 485–506.

Tone, Andrea, ed. *Controlling Reproduction* (1997).

Van Horn, Susan Householder. *Women, Work, and Fertility, 1900–1986* (1988).

Wandersee, Winifred D. *Women's Work and Family Values, 1920–1940* (1981).

Ware, Susan. *Holding Their Own: American Women in the 1930s* (1982).

Westin, Jeanne Eddy. *Making Do: How Women Survived in the '30s* (1976).

C H A P T E R
11

Shaping the New Deal: Recovery
and Reform Politics

Given the failure of Hoover's policies and the tremendous suffering throughout the country, the new Administration of Franklin Roosevelt plainly needed to respond politically to the Depression in new ways. Roosevelt's first flurry of legislation— including efforts to shore up the nation's banks and a balanced budget bill that cut veterans' benefits and federal salaries—showed little change in basic economic philosophy. But the Administration soon proved its willingness to experiment. Through the spring of 1933, the New Deal pressed through Congress an "alphabet soup" of regulatory, relief, and public works initiatives, including the Agricultural Adjustment Act (AAA), the Federal Emergency Relief Act (FERA), the Civilian Conservation Corps (CCC), the Tennessee Valley Authority (TVA), and the Public Works Administration (PWA). The most important initiative of this "hundred days" was the National Industrial Recovery Act, establishing the National Recovery Administration (NRA). In the NRA, Roosevelt embraced both business demands for freedom to set competitive standards and prices (without fear of antitrust prosecution) and Hoover's policy of encouraging trade association. But the NRA added a new twist: it not only encouraged the formation of trade associations but gave those trade associations the power to prosecute or penalize "cutthroat" competitors. Seen by most as a "business bill," the National Industrial Recovery Act also included a provision that protected (in very vague terms) the rights of workers to join unions and bargain collectively with their employers. In practice, the act proved extraordinarily complex and almost impossible to enforce. In the eyes of small firms facing extinction, consumers facing higher prices, and citizens facing the persistence of the Depression, the NRA was at best a failure and at worst counterproductive. Almost mercifully, the Supreme Court declared the entire experiment an unconstitutional federal invasion of the states' right to regulate commerce. Having made no progress toward recovery in its first two years, and having generated considerable opposition from the left and the right, the New Deal was forced to start from scratch in 1935.

The first six years of the Great Depression were marked by an increasingly desperate political scramble for economic recovery and relief with little appreciable result. While the Depression persisted, however, the Roosevelt Administration was forced to rethink its approach to the social and economic crisis. The Administration's new approach reflected two key considerations: first, its early experiments had been spectacular and unconstitutional failures; second, those most affected by the Depression—workers, the unemployed, farmers—were not waiting around for the New Deal to hit on the perfect political solution. Increasingly, they responded to the Depression and its conditions on their own. For the next five years, the New Deal would walk a tightrope between its own political agenda and the demands, aspirations, and political threat posed by the people. The immediate solution, marking the last great flurry of New Deal reform, was the passage of the Wagner (National Labor Relations) Act and the Social Security Act in 1935. These cornerstones of the "second" New Deal were built on long debates over labor law and social provision (stretching back to the Progressive Era) and on the immediate urgency of crafting an alternative or successor to the NRA. In some respects, these acts were revolutionary. The Wagner Act erased the legal vestiges of the open shop and set the stage for the unionization of mass production industry. The Social Security Act established for the first time a direct federal responsibility for the welfare of citizens. In other respects, these acts were less radical. The Wagner Act tied the fate of the labor movement to federal policy, which would retreat in the late 1930s and especially after 1945. And the Social Security Act organized the American welfare state around contributory entitlements for male workers, reflecting both the weakness of the federal government and the persistent ideology of the family wage.

While the launching of the "second" New Deal marked a turn from business-oriented recovery policy to more fundamental reform, it also underscored the limits of the New Deal order. Before and after 1935, the New Deal was always dependent upon the votes of conservative Southern Democrats. Federal spending captured these votes in the early New Deal, but Southerners saw the labor and welfare legislation of 1935 as a clear threat to Southern race relations and economic competitiveness. In many respects, Southern legislators were able to shape federal law (winning both the exemption of agricultural and domestic workers from Social Security and local control over its administration, for example). But after 1935, the South increasingly joined Republicans in opposition to the New Deal. By the late 1930s, the Administration faced not only stiff legislative opposition but a Depression that showed no sign of lifting. Achievements after 1935 were meager, highlighted perhaps by the passage of the first national minimum wage law, the Fair Labor Standards Act of 1938. For the most part, the New Deal drifted through the late 1930s, and the direction of reform was ultimately resolved by an economic and political crisis of a very different kind: the outbreak of World War II.

DOCUMENTS

The first three documents touch on varying assessments of the early New Deal. Business lobbied hard for the National Industrial Recovery Act but, as Document 1 suggests, often responded selfishly and cynically to the opportunity it presented. In Document 2, civil rights activists note the uneven and often discriminatory impact of the act, which some dubbed the "Negro Removal Act." In Document 3, a liberal journalist caustically assesses the entire program of the early New Deal. Document 4, excerpting Roosevelt's 1935 message to Congress, suggests the gravity of the New Deal's turn to the left. The final three documents suggest the logic and limits of the 1935 reforms. Document 5 traces the logic of organizing and financing the Social Security programs as contributory entitlements. In Document 6, one of the drafters of the Social Security Act explains how both political and administrative considerations led to the exemption of agricultural and domestic workers. Document 7, drawn from the meeting of an advisory committee charged with reforming Social Security in 1939, suggests how prevalent and powerful assumptions about men and women shaped social policy.

1. A Business Cynic on the NRA Codes, 1934

Dear Brother in the Chemical Manufacturing Industry:

After many months of battling with the N.R.A. for a Code of Fair Competition for our Industry, we are happy to advise that we have succeeded beyond all expectations. In order that you may know exactly what you may do under this Code we send you the following information and remarks covering article by article.

Preamble

Most all of the Sap Industries have got themselves in a hole right to start with in their codes by using the following words at the end of their Preamble, "and be binding upon every member thereof." We were too smart for that, however, as it was not our purpose to be bound by anything.

Article I—Definitions

We almost succeeded in obtaining a definition that a "chiseler" would be deemed to mean anyone who did not mind Mr. Alliance, but since the Code means that anyway, we did not insist.

Article II—Hours of Labor

Don't pay much attention to the 40 hours per week. If you wish to work 48 hours per week just keep on doing it, in this way establishing a 48 hour week in your plant. . . .

The main point is that by careful wording of our Code we have succeeded in establishing a 48 hour week, whereas a lot of stupid industries have allowed the N.R.A. to talk them into a 40 hour week and they are now worried about 32 hours a week.

Article III—Minimum Wages

Don't let the 40¢ per hour mentioned for the North and 35¢ for the South disturb you. This applies only to common labor, and only if you paid more on July 15, 1929, and if you will look over your payrolls as of July 15, 1929, all members of the Industry can probably find some subnormal employees who were working at a rate of 30¢ in the North or 25¢ in the South. This will establish your base rate.

From "Suggested Letter to Be Written by the Chemical Alliance, Incorporated to the Members of the Chemical Manufacturing Industry Giving Them the Lowdown on the Chemical Manufacturing Industry Code" (1934), File 19, Willis F. Harrington Papers, Hagley Museum and Library, Wilmington, DE.

Also note that you can call anyone who is just starting to work for you, an apprentice or a learner, and you may pay them 24¢ in the North and 20¢ in the South, for a period of six months.

. . . An excellent way to handle this is to hire a man for six months, then let him go, hire another man and call him a learner. This will establish definitely a 24¢ rate in the North and a 20¢ rate in the South for you. . . .

Article V—Administration

Believing as we do in rugged individualism—and every man for himself—we have set up the Alliance as the agency to administer the Code, but you will note under Paragraph (b) we were careful to state that the Alliance shall not have the power in any way to bind the Industry as regards the matters covered in this section (b).

We had quite a time with Section (c). The Administration wanted to name three members for the Code Authority and were so insistent we finally had to agree to let them name three representatives. . . . Mind you—they can do nothing—but we will have to tolerate them. . . .

Article VI

Since there were several of us on the Committee we had to agree we would all share the expenses of running the Code, otherwise we would have adopted the European plan and made old Uncle Sam pay the cost of our taking away his candy. However, we intend to take it out of the hide of Kid Consumer anyway.

Article VII

If for any reason you are foolish enough to think you are bound to do anything not good for your own pocketbook, merely pull out Article VII and call yourself a member of some other handy industry. (This may be dangerous because we are telling you no other industry is sitting as sweet as we are).

Article VIII—Employee Organization and Bargaining

We had to put in this Article because they had it obligatory under the Act but if it scares you any just look at the grandest piece of nullification that was ever done in Article IX hereinafter discussed.

Article IX

We can't begin to tell you what a time we had getting this in. We first attempted to include only the statement that the Industry shall not have deemed to have waived any of their constitutional rights, but we could not get away with this so we put a lot of boloney, some of which will no doubt be a great surprise to members of the Industry, particularly the statement that the main purpose and product of our Industry is the "extension of chemical knowledge in the public interest."

You may have thought you were in business to make money and to cover this, we carefully stated that this was a function of the Industry only as regards its "by-products." . . .

Conclusion

Now, boys, don't get too cocky. We have been smart, yes, but don't hesitate to learn from others. The Auto and Steel rackets pulled some slick tricks after their codes were adopted with trial periods. Their idea was good and we should follow it. In general the trick is to immediately start howling about how tough it is on you to live up to the Code, that you are giving your life blood, but that à la Frank Merriwell it is all for the cause and you will fight to the last ditch to keep the Blue Eagle flying, but you may fail. Then when the ninety days are up, the poor goofs in Washington will be glad to let you keep the fruits of this glorious victory.

Note: We hope that the bills which the lawyers will render will not eat up all that we have managed to steal by this Code.

2. The National Urban League Documents Discrimination Under the NRA, 1934

The report of the Joint Committee on National Recovery on Negro workers under the N.R.A. presents evidence that many provisions in the codes have been, in effect, discriminatory against black workers. It lists three major devices which have had that effect. The first is the occupational differential. "Proponents of Codes exempt from maximum hours provisions and minimum wage scales those occupations in which Negro workers are chiefly to be found." (Example: Outside crews and cleaners in cotton textiles; of 13,000 Negroes in Industry, 10,000 come with this category.) The second is the geographical differential. "Certain Industries employ large number of Negroes as unskilled labor in the South but not elsewhere." (Example: Lumber. Negro labor 60% in the South but only 37% in all United States.) The third is the "grandfather clause" appearing in 18 approved codes and providing minimum scales for identical classes of labor based on wages received July 15, 1929, obviously perpetuating colored and white differential.

If the indicated fact that completely complying companies have not reduced the racial differential except as compared with the first half of 1933 is combined with the strong evidences of discrimination against Negroes, both under code provisions and in spite of code provisions, two observations can be made:

1. Individual complying companies and industries with the less discriminatory provisions have suffered a competitive disadvantage.
2. The immediate effect of the N.R.A. decreasing the spread between the wages of white and colored labor has been nullified to an undetermined extent by

Reprinted with the permission of Congressional Information Service, Inc. University Publications of America.

discriminations against Negroes. If the comparison is made between the last half of 1933 and any recent year, the spread in total income—as distinct from wage rates—between southern white labor as a whole and southern Negro labor as a whole has been increased.

Two courses have been suggested to eliminate these conditions:

1. Increase the North-South differential spread for the industries which have suffered more due to their more favorable treatment to Negro labor, and
2. Eliminate and counteract those Code provisions which have discriminated against Negroes.

. . . Article 7A of the Act declares that "employees shall have the right to organize and bargain collectively through representatives of their own choosing" and shall not be restrained from joining any labor organization with which they wish to affiliate themselves. . . . If unions persist in discriminating and often excluding colored workers from their membership, the new trend of events will translate such action into the exclusion of Negro workers from all desirable jobs in areas where labor is well organized. Unless specific safeguards are set up, Negro wage earners will suffer.

3. The New Deal Is No Revolution, 1934

It must already be apparent, a brief nine months after its inauguration, that the New Deal is not a revolution. The plain truth is that the brave utterances of President Roosevelt on the one hand and the dark threats of certain of his aids on the other have not succeeded in making it so; and because the New Deal is not a revolution it may even now be written down as having been no more successful than those similar examples of wishful thinking in our recent American past, the Full Dinner Pail and the New Freedom. . . .

Obviously, the New Deal is neither revolutionary nor counter-revolutionary. Its rationale may be stated in the following group of propositions. The New Deal recognizes that our economy has slowed down and that the forces within it are no longer in equilibrium. Opportunities for capitalist enterprise have contracted—the population has ceased expanding by leaps and bounds, there are no new great industrial fields to be opened up, oversea outlets have been shut off by high tariff walls or are already being closely worked by hostile imperialist nations—and capitalism is confronted by a fall in the rate of profit. The world market for our agricultural products has disappeared and a decline in farm land values has set in. Not only have new jobs for white-collar and professional workers virtually become non-existent, but there is a surplus rather than a dearth of industrial labor as well. Class lines have been clearly drawn; the danger of class hostilities is no longer remote but just on the horizon. Under the conditions of a free market the owners of the means of production, because of their greater strength and organization, could continue to maintain themselves, perhaps for a long time; but their security would depend upon the steady debasement of the standards of living of the other classes in society.

This, it must be plain, would eventually lead to the creation of conditions favorable to either revolution or counter-revolution; but the philosophers of the New Deal, abhorring the thought of violence and having no conscious class interests of their own, have refused to agree that the mechanism has run down. They will wind it up again and, having done that, will suspend in balance and for all the years the existing class relations in American society. . . .

The New Deal, to put it baldly, has assumed that it is possible to establish a permanent truce on class antagonisms. The device it is going to use is the restoration of purchasing power through the application of an idea known to antiquity and the Middle Ages—the just price. . . .

The American farmer was to be restored to the capital and consumption markets by giving him a just price for his commodities on the basis of production limited to the home market. The details of the administration agricultural program are by this time familiar; nor is it necessary to examine at length the economic weaknesses of the scheme. Suffice it to say that the producers of the basic agricultural commodities of the country were to be induced to restrict their output on the promise of the payment of the proceeds of a series of taxes which were to be placed on the processors but actually passed on to the consumers. These taxes, when added to current prices, were to make the returns on wheat, cotton, corn, hogs, tobacco, rice, and dairying products equal to the prices received by farmers during 1909–14. . . .

Industry was to be revived in a somewhat different way, although again the just price was to be the specific. The New Deal was not prepared to guarantee directly to every large enterpriser and every rentier a fair return on his investment; but it moved toward this goal just the same if somewhat circuitously. Industry, which to some extent had been checked from assuming inevitable monopoly characteristics because of the existence of the antitrust laws, was now to be formed into cartels and, working through the agencies of its own trade associations, it was to devise codes of fair practice for the purpose of regulating methods of competition. . . .

The New Deal planned to save labor also through the just price. The industrial codes were to have a dual purpose: they were not only to protect industry from its own baser instincts but they were to provide further opportunities for the employment of labor through the establishment of basic maximum working hours and minimum wages and the elimination of child labor. The purchasing power of the working class was to be restored by increasing the total number of persons in industry and by raising the per capita wage of sweated workers to a subsistence level. While there was some talk of providing formally for the leveling upward of all wages so that the stipulated minimum rates would not in effect become the maximums, this idea was soon abandoned. . . .

The New Deal thus had turned out to be no revolution because it had effected no enduring changes in the class relations in American economic society. It had started out hopefully by attempting to allay class hostilities; it ended, ironically enough, by making the cleavage between classes more pronounced than it had been ever before. Agriculture was in revolt. An organized capital and an organized labor confronted each other, like two hostile armies, across the narrow no-man's land of governmental regulation.

What was President Roosevelt going to do next? Would it be further efforts at trying to keep the New Deal on an even keel: now by yielding to agricultural pressure and resorting to price fixing of farm products or even perhaps to licensing of processors in order to keep the prices of the things the farmers bought in line; now by giving in to labor and raising the wage minimums set in the codes, and now by heeding the complaints of industry and making an intensive drive to punish the violators of codes who cut prices, exceeded production quotas, and resorted to unfair practices generally? . . .

Looking a little farther into the future, would the United States try fascism, with the crushing of labor organizations and the frank utilization of the political state to preserve the position of capitalism and to depress the lot of the workers and farmers to meaner and meaner subsistence levels? Or should we seek our salvation in a reversion to imperialist oversea expansion: not, of course, to old-fashioned territorial aggression but to struggles with rival powers for foreign markets—even at the risk of war?

4. President Roosevelt Outlines Social Security for Congress, 1935

The detailed report of the Committee sets forth a series of proposals that will appeal to the sound sense of the American people. It has not attempted the impossible, nor has it failed to exercise sound caution and consideration of all of the factors concerned: the national credit, the rights and responsibilities of States, the capacity of industry to assume financial responsibilities and the fundamental necessity of proceeding in a manner that will merit the enthusiastic support of citizens of all sorts. . . .

Three principles should be observed in legislation on this subject. First, the system adopted, except for the money necessary to initiate it, should be self-sustaining in the sense that funds for the payment of insurance benefits should not come from the proceeds of general taxation. Second, excepting in old-age insurance, actual management should be left to the States subject to standards established by the Federal Government. Third, sound financial management of the funds and the reserves, and protection of the credit structure of the Nation should be assured by retaining Federal control over all funds through trustees in the Treasury of the United States.

At this time, I recommend the following types of legislation looking to economic security:

1. Unemployment compensation.
2. Old-age benefits, including compulsory and voluntary annuities.
3. Federal aid to dependent children through grants to States for the support of existing mothers' pension systems and for services for the protection and care of homeless, neglected, dependent, and crippled children.

From "Message to Congress" (January 17, 1935), in *The Public Papers and Addresses of Franklin Delano Roosevelt* (New York: Random House, 1938), Vol. 4, 43–46.

4. Additional Federal aid to State and local public-health agencies and the strengthening of the Federal Public Health Service.

I am not at this time recommending the adoption of so-called "health insurance," although groups representing the medical profession are cooperating with the Federal Government in the further study of the subject and definite progress is being made.

With respect to unemployment compensation, I have concluded that the most practical proposal is the levy of a uniform Federal payroll tax, 90 percent of which should be allowed as an offset to employers contributing under a compulsory State unemployment compensation act. The purpose of this is to afford a requirement of a reasonably uniform character for all States cooperating with the Federal Government and to promote and encourage the passage of unemployment compensation laws in the States. . . .

In the important field of security for our old people, it seems necessary to adopt three principles: First, noncontributory old-age pensions for those who are now too old to build up their own insurance. It is, of course, clear that for perhaps 30 years to come funds will have to be provided by the States and the Federal Government to meet these pensions. Second, compulsory contributory annuities which in time will establish a self-supporting system for those now young and for future generations. Third, voluntary contributory annuities by which individual initiative can increase the annual amounts received in old age. It is proposed that the Federal Government assume one-half of the cost of the old-age pension plan, which ought ultimately to be supplanted by self-supporting annuity plans. . . .

The establishment of sound means toward a greater future economic security of the American people is dictated by a prudent consideration of the hazards involved in our national life. No one can guarantee this country against the dangers of future depressions but we can reduce these dangers. We can eliminate many of the factors that cause economic depressions, and we can provide the means of mitigating their results. This plan for economic security is at once a measure of prevention and a method of alleviation.

We pay now for the dreadful consequence of economic insecurity—and dearly. This plan presents a more equitable and infinitely less expensive means of meeting these costs. We cannot afford to neglect the plain duty before us. I strongly recommend action to attain the objectives sought in this report.

5. The Committee on Economic Security Argues for Contributory Social Insurance, 1935

An adequate old-age security program involves a combination of noncontributory pensions and contributory annuities. Only noncontributory pensions can serve to meet the problem of millions of persons who are already superannuated or shortly will be so and are without sufficient income for a decent subsistence. A contributory annuity system, while of little or no value to people now in these older age groups,

From "Report to the Committee on Economic Security," pp. 25, 33–34. Box 1, Working Papers of the Committee on Economic Security, RG 47, Records of the Social Security Administration, National Archives.

will enable younger workers, with the aid of their employers, to build up gradually their rights to annuities in their old age. Without such a contributory system the cost of pensions would, in the future, be overwhelming. Contributory annuities are unquestionably preferable to noncontributory pensions. They come to the workers as a right, whereas the noncontributory pensions must be conditioned upon a "means" test. Annuities, moreover, can be ample for a comfortable existence, bearing some relation to customary wage standards, while gratuitous pensions can provide only a decent subsistence. . . .

Instead of Government subsidy to the contributory annuity system it may be advisable to supplement the earned annuities of people now old (and whose earned annuities are, therefore small) by granting them assistance under noncontributory old-age pension laws, on a more liberal basis than in the case of persons who have accumulated no rights under the contributory annuity system. Thus, one of the required provisions of a State old-age pension law might be that in no event, prior to the year 1960, shall an annuity to which a person is entitled under the contributory annuity system be taken into account in determining the need of such person for assistance.

In considering the costs of the contributory system, it should not be overlooked that old-age annuities are designed to prevent destitution and dependency. Destitution and dependency are enormously expensive, not only in the initial cost of necessary assistance but in the disastrous psychological effect of relief upon the recipients, which, in turn, breeds more dependency.

The contributions required from employers and employees have an equally good justification. Contributions by the employees represent a self-respecting method through which workers make their own provision for old age. In addition many workers themselves on the verge of dependency will benefit through being relieved of the necessity of supporting dependent parents on reduced incomes, and at the expense of the health and well-being of their own families. To the employers, contributions toward old-age annuities are very similar to the revenues which they regularly set aside for depreciation on capital equipment. There can be no escape from the costs of old age, and, since these costs must be met, an orderly system under which employers, employees, and the Government will all contribute appears to be the dignified and intelligent solution of the problem.

6. An Architect of Social Security Recalls the Southern Concession, 1935

In the congressional hearings and in the executive sessions of the Committee on Ways and Means, as well as in the House debate, the major interest was in old age assistance. Very important changes were made in this part of the bill, principally by the House committee.

Title I of the original bill was very bitterly attacked, particularly by Senator Byrd, on the score that it vested in a federal department the power to dictate to the

Witte, Edwin E. *The Development of the Social Security Act,* © 1962. Reprinted by permission of The University of Wisconsin Press.

states to whom pensions should be paid and how much. In this position, Senator Byrd was supported by nearly all of the southern members of both committees, it being very evident that at least some southern senators feared that this measure might serve as an entering wedge for federal interference with the handling of the Negro question in the South. The southern members did not want to give authority to anyone in Washington to deny aid to any state because it discriminated against Negroes in the administration of old age assistance.

It was my position in the prolonged questioning which I underwent from Senator Byrd that there was no intention of federal dictation. The fact is that it had never occurred to any person connected with the Committee on Economic Security that the Negro question would come up in this connection. After the first days of the committee hearings, however, it was apparent that the bill could not be passed as it stood and that it would be necessary to tone down all clauses relating to supervisory control by the federal government.

The principal changes which were made by the Ways and Means Committee to this end were the following:

1. The conditions for the approval of state plans for old age assistance were stated negatively, with the effect that states might impose other conditions for old age assistance than those dealt with in the bill. Under the original bill, states could not impose any income or property restrictions, nor bar from old age assistance persons with criminal records or any other group of persons. Under the House bill, states were free to impose any conditions they saw fit, with the limitation that if they prescribed conditions as to age, residence, citizenship, etc., their restrictions might not be more stringent than those stipulated in the bill.
2. The House bill eliminated the provision that states must furnish assistance sufficient to provide, "when added to the income of the aged recipient, a reasonable subsistence compatible with decency and health." This provision was copied from the Massachusetts and New York laws and was very objectionable to southern members of Congress. The elimination of this provision left the states free to pay pensions of any amount, however small, and yet recover 50 per cent of their costs from the federal government.
3. The provision that the methods of administration in the states must be satisfactory to the federal department was toned down by adding the qualification, "other than those relating to selection, tenure of office and compensation of personnel." This limitation was inserted because it was feared that the federal administrative agency would require the states to select their personnel on a merit basis, as had been done by the United States Employment Service. The members of Congress did not want any dictation by the federal government in this respect and inserted this limitation for the express purpose of allowing the states to appoint whomever they wished to administer old age assistance.
4. The provisions relating to the withdrawal of approval of state plans were somewhat toned down by inserting provisions to the effect that withdrawal of approval may occur only after notice to the state authorities, a fair hearing, and a finding that "in a substantial number of cases" the requirements of the federal act were being violated.

7. Social Security Advisers Consider Male and Female Pensioners, 1938

Mr. Myers One very good solution would be to require that the woman must be married to an annuitant for at least five years before she receives any benefits. If a man who is 65 retires and he has been married for three years, he receives 110% for the next two years and following that they will be married five years and they will receive 150% thereafter. Under the plan as it is here they are supposed to be married five years and would receive 100%. Under the plan she would have to be married five years before he retired. He would receive nothing for two years and after that he would receive 150%. Under this plan he would receive 100% for the two-year period and then 150%. . . .

Mr. Mowbray It seems to me that the restriction on the marital period and the period of waiting is only desirable to keep out the designing woman. That wouldn't affect things at all. I made the remark that I thought a two-year period was long enough in a life insurance policy, but I was not at all sure that a five-year period was long enough as a defense against a designing woman.

Mr. Brown How far should those in need be kept in need to protect the system against designing women and old fools? Do you think it ought to be longer than five years? . . .

Miss Dewson I am confused about one point. The single man or single person gets less than the married person. Supposing that the man who is married, say at 66, loses his wife and becomes a single man, would that change his annuity?

Mr. Brown He would drop back. He drops back to the 100%. He no longer gets wife allowance, whereas if the wife survives him it would drop back to the 75%.

Miss Dewson That is what makes it more for the married man?

Mr. Brown Yes, on the principle that it is more costly for the single man to live than for the single woman if she is able to avail herself of the home of the child. A woman is able to fit herself into the economy of the home of the child much better than the single man; that is, the grandmother helps in the raising of the children and helps in home affairs, whereas the aged grandfather is the man who sits out on the front porch and can't help much in the home. . . .

Mr. Brown Are there any other points? In regard to the widows' benefits at 75% of the base we could put in a corollary as to whether 75% of the base is proper.

Mr. Linton I wonder why we didn't make the widows' benefit the regular individual annuity without cutting it down 25%. . . . Why not cut it 50%. Why should you pay the widow less than the individual himself gets if unmarried?

Mr. Williamson She can look after herself better than he can.

Mr. Linton Is that a sociological fact?

Mr. Brown Can a single woman adjust herself to a lower budget on account of the fact that she is used to doing her own housework whereas the single man has to go out to a restaurant?

From Federal Advisory Council Minutes (April 29, 1938), morning session, 18. File 025, Box 12, Chairman's Files, RG 47, Records of the Social Security Administration, National Archives.

E S S A Y S

These essays suggest both the promises and limits of New Deal reform. In the first essay, Colin Gordon argues that New Deal labor policy was shaped by the demands of
workers' actions (see Chapter 12), by the desire of some business interests to regulate
wages and buttress consumption, and by the political and legal constraints imposed by
the Supreme Court when it struck down the National Recovery Act in 1935. In the second essay, Patricia Sullivan traces the ambivalent impact and intent of the New Deal in
the South. In some respects, as Sullivan suggests, the New Deal accommodated itself
to the demands of Southern conservatives and (through uneven standards and deference
to local authorities) countenanced continued discrimination; in other respects, the mere
fact of the federal presence in the South gave African Americans and Southern liberals
a powerful foundation from which to demand equity and full citizenship. In the third essay, Linda Gordon shows how the political and ideological influence of the family wage
pressed welfare reformers (and their opponents) to create a bifurcated welfare system;
the first, male, track was financed by the contributions of workers and granted pensions
and unemployment insurance as entitlements; the second, female, track relied on general
revenues and, as a consequence, supported a relatively meager and increasingly stigmatized range of assistance programs for single women and the elderly.

From the National Industrial Recovery Act to the Wagner Act

COLIN GORDON

In late May [1933], the Roosevelt administration sent the National Industrial Recovery Act [NRA] up the hill. . . .

The NRA was an ad hoc synthesis of disparate industrial or trade association
recovery plans, most of which were concerned less with strengthening the economy
than with long-standing patterns of competition and disorganization in their respective industries. Few seemed troubled by the act's economic inconsistencies, the
legal portent of its intentionally vague anticompetitive and labor provisions, or the
looming problem of administration—although one New Deal adviser wrote . . . that
the "multifarious authorship" of the NRA had produced "an omnibus enabling act"
which, "instead of a synthesis [seemed] a conglomeration of purposes, an obfusca-
tion of ends and a stultification of methods." The only common goal was antitrust
reform, although this was more a rallying cry than an end in itself. "We had widely
varying ideas as to the form and method" of trade regulation, admitted one trade
association official, but "to the average trade association secretary, having gone
through a period of membership starvation, the National Industrial Recovery Act
appeared as a gift from the gods."

The NRA, as one business lobbyist marveled, had "the most widespread and
splendid support from industrial groups throughout the country." Important proponents included trade associations in the steel, rubber, textile, paper, lumber, clothing,

From *New Deals: Business, Labor, and Politics in America, 1920–1935* by Colin Gordon, pp. 171–172,
174–189, 280–293, copyright © 1994 Cambridge University Press. Reprinted with permission of Cambridge University Press.

and leather industries; leading firms (already cooperating closely with the federal government) in oil and coal; and a wide array of larger firms that hoped (with some cause) that the NRA would make it possible to drive out marginal, cutthroat, and regional competitors. While the inconsistencies, failures, and vagaries of the NRA made it difficult to pin down industrial support once the codes were in place, most viewed the NRA as either a golden opportunity or a minor nuisance. "By enlisting the aid of the sheriff to control the other fellow," as Virgil Jordan noted, leading firms simply hoped "they could get some advantage for themselves." Those who had sought such regulatory innovation for the past decade were ecstatic. "The Lumber Code is not an edict handed us by Congress or the President," argued William Greeley of the West Coast Lumbermen's Association; "we went to Washington and asked for it." And those with little need for federal intervention were scarcely threatened. In such cases, as NRA officials admitted of the automobile industry, the code was invariably "very broad and one could do almost anything under it." . . .

All that distinguished the NRA's brand of industrial self-government from the voluntarism of the 1920s was the promise that competitive standards would be uniform and uniformly enforced. "It was felt that government should be minimized and limited to the acceptance or rejection of the proposals of business groups," reported an NRA study group, "but the Government was expected to enforce accepted rules with rigor." Business expected the NRA to provide a firm and impartial means of regulation that was not motivated or distracted by short-term market goals, ideally supplying a legal footing for trade association platforms and penalizing marginal or regional competitors. In practice, the NRA was unable to perform the only task that business demanded of it. The result, as a handful of laissez-faire cynics had warned in 1933, was the continuation of chaotic and unbridled competition, accompanied by unprecedented, haphazard, and ineffective government "regimentation."

Compliance was a riddle that the NRA was unable and, in many respects, afraid to solve. For business interests *nearly* complete compliance with code provisions was not enough; one chiseler could bring down price, wage, or trade practice standards like a house of cards. Economically, politically, and bureaucratically incapable of enforcing cooperation, the NRA based its policy on willfully optimistic assumptions about business conduct. Its failure to enforce the codes not only undermined its effectiveness and credibility but also pressed firms (or at least those not irretrievably discouraged by the NRA experience) to search for some other means of taming short-term motives for long-term stability and disciplining or destroying marginal competitors. . . .

Given the uneasy combination of cooperation, rationalization, and organization, the codes failed where they were needed most and succeeded where they were not needed at all. Monopolistic institutions and practices were strengthened in many industries that had historically "skirted the bounds of the antitrust laws." Many traditionally fragmented industries suffered continued murderous competition and often saw conditions deteriorate with the introduction of a code. "Without a general willingness in an industry to observe its own laws," antitrust lawyer Goldthwait Dorr cautioned, "a code becomes a Volstead Act. It penalizes the observers, [and] becomes an instrument of unfair competition." And because the NRA's tenure was limited to two years (actually much less, given the time it took to draft the codes), firms stalled implementation, abandoned codes early, or resisted the brief experiment altogether. . . .

The NRA had scrambled the competitive stakes but given firms little incentive to cooperate. Business was unable to enforce compliance (a fact that had encouraged it to support the NRA in the first place), and the NRA was unwilling to do so (a task for which it was ill-equipped and that threatened to open a hornet's nest of legal challenges). Reluctantly and belatedly, the NRA moved to revamp the entire process of following its directives. During the fall of 1933, compliance rested with code authorities, NRA deputies, and regional administrators. In late October, however, the NRA accepted that its early emphasis on "banners and ballyhoo" had worn thin and established a formal Compliance Division, which by the end of 1933, was backlogged with over 10,000 complaints. For the duration of the NRA, the Compliance Division faced the familiar conflict between self-government and coercive regulation that infused the recovery program as well as the constant disappointment of industries that expected rewards for cooperation matched with stiff penalties for recalcitrance.

Even with the creation of the Compliance Division, the NRA's ultimate legal authority was uncertain. Cases that clearly involved interstate commerce could be filed in federal courts, but a preponderance of Republican judges and pervasive fear of a constitutional test case discouraged even selective prosecution. Trade practice violations could also be passed on to the FTC [Federal Trade Commission], a process that duplicated paperwork and delayed and distracted enforcement. Labor violations were technically handled by the National Labor Board (NLB) and a few industrial labor boards, but their resolution was often a casualty of jurisdictional disputes between the NRA and NLB. Final authority was usually reserved for the NRA, which allowed firms to define labor violations as trade practice violations and bypass the NLB altogether. In most cases, the only penalty imposed by the NRA (usually for underpaying wages or code authority assessments) was restitution. This allowed employers to reap the rewards of noncompliance if they evaded the NRA and, if caught, only forced them to pay their share. With prosecution and punitive fines a distant threat, there was no compelling reason to cooperate. . . .

By late 1934, the NRA had lost all credibility. Although strengthened by the Compliance Division, its "crackdown" was too little and too late. As a midwestern regional office reported, "The general feeling is that it will only be a short time until [employers] can do as they please." The NRA was unlikely to garner much support by changing the rules or raising the stakes. "Without more enforcement," admitted [Donald] Richberg, "we would lose the support of those willing to comply. With more enforcement we would increase the number and vigor of our opponents." In industry after industry, the discrepancy between code rules and code compliance was identified as the NRA's signal flaw: "The great majorities . . . are, of course, willing as they have been from the beginning to continue compliance with the code," argued one lumber mill owner, "as soon as the Government is prepared and able and willing to enforce it." A tobacco merchant agreed that "the greatest drawback . . . has been a lack of procedure under which a code violator could be punished."

The NRA never served as the external regulatory force it pretended to be. It was unable either to define its objectives or to wield the power necessary to attain them. The codes retained some scattered credibility in those industries with their own means of forcing competitors to accept collective goals and continue to observe them under some tangible threat. But in most cases, NRA officials and code authorities assumed that codes would be self-enforcing because most firms wanted them enacted and were unable to escape the logical cul-de-sac of "self government." The public-spirited voluntarism of the Blue Eagle campaign collapsed as it became apparent that industries needed more than window stickers to put their houses in order. The Compliance Division never sorted out its judicial procedures or penalties. And sporadic or belated attempts to enforce the codes only underlined the perceptual and practical dilemmas of the entire recovery program: many firms wanted the restrictive regulations promised by the codes, but few wanted to shoulder the associated costs, and none were willing to play along if competitors were free to opt out of the game. . . .

Through 1934 and 1935, industry leaders looked increasingly to labor standards as the most local focus of regulation and to labor unions as the most effective means of ensuring compliance. "There has been no factor so disturbing in price competition within our industry," noted one lumber executive typically, ". . . as the fact that wages were not maintained at fair level." Although the NRA proved its inability to stand above competitive interests, many industries found their codes effectively policed by labor unions. As one NRA study concluded, "Basic labor terms did much to stabilize competition [and] strong labor organization in an industry was found to assure the most effective codes." Industries that had toyed with regulatory unionism in the 1920s were accustomed to unions playing such a role and welcomed the opportunity to strengthen the organizational bonds between workers, unions, and firms. Others viewed the labor provisions of the NRA more cynically but could not avoid comparing the dismal compliance record of open-shop industries with the relative success of unionized industries. Few firms welcomed the gains made by organized labor after 1933, but fewer still questioned the importance of industrial unionism to the competitive world of the 1930s.

For many in business and politics, unions filled an organizational void left by competitive anxiety and administrative disarray. The prospect of union-based enforcement encouraged many industries to frame collective goals as labor standards; restrictions on hours or shifts could ration production or restrain excess capacity, and minimum wages could support prices across an industry. Competitive, labor-intensive industries were well versed in this reasoning. As a lumber representative noted, if wages could be effectively regulated, "prices will ultimately take care of themselves." Industry-wide wage rates would "amount to running a knife through at a certain level," agreed Clay Williams; if "we cut off everything below that . . . we uncover immediately, and in a great many industries, some unit that is living on a take-out from the wage of the worker, and if you mark up the level so that there can't be a take-out it amounts to running a razor around the unit's throat." Wage standards also meshed with the "purchasing power" focus of recovery. Basing higher prices on higher wages (rather than vice versa) commanded greater public and political support. And unions made such standards enforceable without raising the hackles of die-hard progressives, antitrusters, or constitutional literalists.

Unions held a unique position in the battle over industrial regulation and recovery. Workers and unions together had a tremendous stake in the political warfare against depressed markets and cutthroat competition. For employers, after all, these were questions of prices, profits, and the specter of bankruptcy; for workers, these were questions of subsistence. Although closely concerned with the survival of firms in which organized labor thrived, unions had a greater ability and incentive to look beyond the competitive self-interest of many of those firms and strive for industry-wide stability of wages and employment. Unions possessed both an intimate, *internal* knowledge of industry conditions (which the NRA lacked) and an *external* collective rationality (which competing firms lacked). As retailer Edward Filene noted wryly, "Our labor unions have a better understanding of what is good for business today than our chambers of commerce have."

Industry and the NRA sporadically appreciated the regulatory role of unions before 1933, but the code experience opened many eyes. "In industries where labor was well organized . . . ," concluded one report, "enforcement was generally quicker and more satisfactory than that obtained through the complicated compliance machinery established by the NRA. The unions checked code compliance, educated workers in the meaning of the codes . . . and continually insisted upon improvements in compliance machinery." The same report went on to note that "of the three types of pressure used, the pressure of public opinion, pressure from within the industry itself, or pressure of organized groups of employees, the last was found to be most effective." This pattern of union-based compliance was both a reality of code administration and a lesson to be applied to regulatory politics after the NRA. An aide to Senator Wagner suggested "two ways in which code enforcement can be secured: one is by the techniques written into the codes themselves, and the other is through the policing of industry by organized labor." Arguing that NRA-enforced pricing, production, and trade standards were merely "a positive invitation to insincere industrialists to evade the provisions," Wagner's aide concluded that unions were "fighting the decent employer's battle . . . by forcing the undercutters to observe code provisions, or by forcing such employers out of business."

Many unionized, competitive industries used the NRA to nurture longstanding patterns of business unionism. In these industries, unions were the foremost proponents and enforcers of codes, and marginal firms complained repeatedly of strikes and organizing drives initiated by closely allied unions and code authorities. In the needle trades, manufacturers candidly relied on Sidney Hillman's Amalgamated Clothing Workers to discipline code chiselers. Indeed, as NRA officials complained, "Code authorities misdirected their efforts to compel small employers either to keep a closed shop or be driven from business." A report on the coat and suit code added that "the code authority offered all possible assistance to the unions . . . not for the purpose of obtaining members for those organizations [but] because the provisions of the code and the provisions of the collective agreement were in the main identical." Hosiery unionists noted "an exceptional degree of compliance in the hosiery industry . . . attribut[able] mainly to the fact that there has been an effective union in the industry and the union representatives on the code authority were able to secure cooperation." And, as leading shoe firms discovered, labor standards were virtually impossible to enforce *without* a union.

But business was scarcely united in its admiration of the unions' role under the NRA. Competitive, nonunion industries appreciated the regulatory potential of organized labor but feared radicalism and loss of managerial authority. Nonunion, noncompetitive industries saw little reason to qualify their rigid open-shop views, although many pragmatically courted conservative unions as insurance against shop-floor radicalism. GM [General Motors], for one, privately hoped to flush radicals out of its plants by "subscrib[ing] to the principle of collective bargaining" with a conservative American Federation of Labor (AFL) union but could (or would) only do so if the rest of the industry went along. Capital-intensive industries, such as oil or chemicals, paid little sincere attention to labor standards before or after the NRA. The Chemical Alliance even advised its members to ignore wage provisions and to take advantage of a six-month "learner" wage by hiring and firing on a biennial basis. And many industries split over the impact or role of unions. Smaller, marginal firms who resented the codes resented the threat of union enforcement even more. And among those who supported the codes, many preferred a return to competitive warfare to union-enforced competitive peace.

Business ambivalence reflected the range of interests and strategies among industries and firms and some doubt that even business unions could capture the cut-throat fringes of an industry. "Industry accepted the Recovery Act . . . [and] would stand for substantial [wage] increases and lower hours if they knew that *every* other competitive concern on the same day would be put to the same increases," argued a midwestern quarry operator, noting that "this only can be done by taking in the entire group of industries at one time in a new type of national union." Others echoed this sentiment, adding that business unions might "take some of wind out of the implacable type of organizer's sails" and "hold up the wages of the chiseler." While the prospect of union-enforced codes inspired mixed support for collective bargaining, it did force many to confront labor as a competitive and organizational factor. As Cyrus Ching of U.S. Rubber reasoned:

> If we in this room, representing a number of industries, advocate employee representation [company unions] or relationships built up around individual plants, we must depend on our industry through its code authority or some other agency to take care of the substandard conditions which exist . . . within a particular industry and if they are unable to do that, then they must depend on organized labor to keep the substandard units of an industry from tearing down the wage structure. I think that is one of the important things that we have to face in this whole code situation.

The NRA's view of labor's position in the codes closely reflected that of business. NRA officials celebrated union-enforced compliance in some industries while undercutting similar efforts in others. Despite this inconsistency, NRA officials were always attentive to instances of successful code compliance (which were rare) and broadly appreciated the regulatory power of unions within and beyond the code era. "It seems clear that if the labor provisions of the codes can thus be enforced," remarked William Davis of the Compliance Division, "such enforcement would greatly stabilize competitive conditions; so much so that industry would want to retain its codes for the labor provisions alone." Others agreed that compliance seemed possible only through massive litigation or the entry of industrial unions. In late 1934, Davis argued that unions were "the most effective instrument" of policing the codes and that noncompliance "will decrease in each industry in the same proportion that . . . efficient employee organization increases, thereby affording the conflicting interests in that industry an effective mechanism by which they can move along to a solution of their common problems."

By 1935, the NRA, industry, and organized labor had accepted that business-minded unions were the most logical and effective means of regulating industrial competition. "Compliance with code provisions can be secured," noted the AFL's William Green, "[and] the best means of securing compliance is through self-organization of workers." Conservative unionists and NRA administrators, of course, were inspired partly by other concerns; the former wished to rebuild after a decade of setbacks and knew that stable competition meant stable wages and employment as well, whereas the latter were interested in seeing the NRA succeed in its own right and hoped that unions would both provide the discipline necessary to make the codes work and effect a redistribution of income sufficient to renew mass-consumption.

Employers were less easily sold on union-driven regulation, but the NRA experience strengthened long-standing patterns of regulatory unionism in some industries and educated many others in the organizational potential of unionized labor markets. In the summer of 1935, Howell Cheney (a silk manufacturer and NICB director) wrote Roosevelt that "industry as a whole is coming to have a matured faith that the best part of the NRA cooperative scheme can be preserved under voluntary codes . . . and by labor agreements." Other employers noted that, with conservative unions keeping watch over competitive standards, "the worker [would] now share in the responsibility of a responsible industry." And as congressional hearings on a new collective bargaining law opened in 1935, Harry Millis of the NLB concluded simply that "many employers have found that they can conduct their business more satisfactorily on a union than a nonunion basis." . . .

By 1935, a legal challenge begun by Schecter Bros., a small New York poultry firm, had wound its way to the Supreme Court. In May, the court struck down the NRA as an unconstitutional exercise of federal power. Ongoing congressional hearings on the NRA's future were suddenly faced not only with well-documented failure but also with its dissolution. Days before the *Schecter* decision, Richberg had favored "killing the NRA while it is still respectable" rather than pushing through a qualified extension under which "trade and industry will have no confidence in enforcement and no fear of resisting government pressure." NRA stalwarts seemed, as the *New York Times* sneered, "like people who have a tired bear by the tail and are not sure whether it is safe to let go or not." Business interests and New Dealers scrambled to salvage politically, economically, and legally defensible remnants of the NRA. Some industries tried to maintain code standards but, shorn of federal enforcement, such warmed-over associationalism offered little but further legal troubles. As an alternative, many saw federal labor law, enforced by unions, as an end run around constitutional restrictions. In the wake of the *Schecter* ruling, Compliance Director Davis predicted "an immediate country-wide swing in support of minimum labor standards." Slowly and haphazardly, the Roosevelt administration moved in this direction.

For firms continuing to search for some means of compelling their market rivals (and themselves) to observe standards of competition, federal labor law was the logical course. Many industries objected to "the continuation of the NRA, *other than the part which applies to labor.*" Howell Cheney observed that "a majority of industrial employers have faith in the validity of establishing maximum hours and minimum wages and have experienced some of the very practical benefits of stabilized costs." The Roosevelt administration, corporate proponents of "business planning," and employers in competitive, labor-intensive code industries all traced the failure of the NRA to the weakness of a potentially regulatory labor movement. Reeling from a decade-long open-shop offensive in much of the industrial economy, organized labor spent the NRA era fighting for basic legal and political recognition. Only where these battles had been previously won were unions able and willing to police codes of fair competition. During the tenure of the NRA and its demise in 1935, industry and the New Deal turned the prevailing approach to anticompetitive and recovery policies inside out. Industrial regulation became less a matter of establishing competitive standards than of empowering those who were expected to enforce those standards: industrial unions.

If the implications and application of labor-centered regulation were contentious and complicated, its reasoning was deceptively simple: In a protected economy, labor standards served the same regulatory purpose as uniform prices or production quotas. The NRA experience had underlined the potential and (not incidentally) the constitutionality of union driven regulation. And quite aside from its regulatory promise, the labor strategy supported consumption by supporting wages and protected the administration's left flank by extending federal bargaining rights. This was the culmination of the NRA experience, although it was a logical leap that many employers were unprepared to make. As the "First New Deal" drew to a close, the prospects for competitive organization were less ambitious, and the stakes much higher. Industries and the NRA moved cautiously to adapt to the legal strictures of the post-*Schecter* era. Many pursued anew the phantom of "self-regulation." Some reformed their regulatory ties with the government along more limited and discretionary lines. And others, facing not only persistent and severe competition but also internal threats from an invigorated labor movement, turned to federal labor law as a last-bet reprieve from the tortures of the market.

The Southern Politics of New Deal Reform

PATRICIA SULLIVAN

The predominantly conservative southern bloc in Congress, coupled with the traditional emphasis on localism and volunteerism in the region, stood as the greatest obstacle to the New Deal aspirations toward a new, more equitable social order. As has been amply documented, the National Industrial Recovery Act (NIRA) and the Agricultural Adjustment Act, the cornerstones of the early New Deal, were easily tailored by local southern elites and their powerful representatives in Congress to fit the prevailing economic and political arrangements in the region.

But the persistence of old forms and old allegiances masked subtle shifts in the expectations and political consciousness of people who responded directly to the emergence of the federal government as a dominant force in the economic life of

From *Days of Hope: Race and Democracy in the New Deal Era* by Patricia Sullivan. Copyright © 1996 by the University of North Carolina Press. Used by permission of the publisher.

the nation. The unfair and racially inequitable administration of federal programs in the South became a focus of protest, an occasion for organized action. In August 1933 twelve hundred black Atlantans gathered in a mass meeting to denounce the discriminatory administration of the National Recovery Administration (NRA) wage codes. The assembly petitioned the Roosevelt administration to ensure that the benefits of the New Deal "be accorded to all citizens alike, irrespective of race." In 1934, black and white tenant farmers in Arkansas formed the Southern Tenant Farmers Union (STFU) to protest the rampant inequities in the New Deal farm program. For groups such as these, the New Deal offered a way to create "an avenue out of the political and economic wilderness."

Rather than try to diffuse such protests, many New Deal reformers encouraged them. White southern progressives and black New Deal administrators sought out and supported new constituencies stirred by federal initiatives, viewing them as essential to the vitality of the New Deal as a political process. As their efforts to secure fundamental reforms from within the Roosevelt administration met with frustration, they became more deliberate in their support and encouragement of political action and organization among traditionally disfranchised groups. They acted as catalysts in a long-term effort to institutionalize the democratic aspirations of Roosevelt's recovery program by appealing to the expectations of groups long on the margins of southern politics. Their efforts prepared the way for Roosevelt's 1938 attack on the unyielding dominance of conservative white southerners in the political life of the region and the nation.

The creation of a position to ensure the participation of black Americans in the recovery effort was emblematic of the new departure heralded by the New Deal. Commenting on Clark Foreman's appointment as "Special Adviser on the Economic Status of Negroes," the *New Republic* called it "an experiment . . . worth watching." The editorial observed that wage differentials based on race were the major contributing factor in "the appalling plight of the Negro, particularly in the South." Yet, the editorial explained, enforcement of an equal wage often led to the replacement of black workers by whites. "Of course," it was assumed that no government official could "compel employers to end this discrimination." Foreman could be most useful, the *New Republic* predicted, by helping to "create conditions under which the Negroes [could] organize and fight for their own rights."

The potentially disruptive nature of New Deal reform was most readily apparent in the implementation of the NIRA, which aimed to apply national standards to industry and labor. Southern manufacturers, desperate for regulation, swallowed their initial objections to this unwieldy piece of legislation. Clearly, however, NIRA provisions for an industry-wide minimum wage and NIRA protection of the right of labor to organize implicitly threatened the maintenance of a low-wage, nonunion labor force. Federal work relief and credit also challenged the culture of dependency that had secured an abundant, cheap labor supply. The principle of an equal wage for white and black workers under the NRA codes, and in government-funded work projects, struck at the very basis of the southern system. Efforts of industrialists and their southern political representatives to secure and maintain a racial wage differential inaugurated the first major contest over the New Deal in the South.

"Aside from the damage to the Negroes, prejudice complicates the working of our whole economic machinery, as was clearly evident when the NRA started the making of codes," Clark Foreman explained in a *New York Times* article. The National Industrial Recovery Act was primarily an enabling act that relied on the voluntary cooperation of business to set industry-wide codes that could stimulate recovery by providing for fair competition and a restoration of purchasing power. The codes, which regulated prices and set maximum hours and minimum wages, had federal sanction. Commenting on the implementation of the NIRA, black sociologist Ira DeA. Reid wryly observed, "One may safely give long odds that when the Economic Fathers set out to establish the present machinery for industrial recovery they had not the slightest idea that they would meet such a problem as that of a wage differential based on race." The obvious question concerning southern practices, however, quickly became apparent. Would southern workers, and most specifically black workers, be treated fairly and equitably under the New Deal, or would federal programs bend to the power of southern Democrats and reinforce the caste system.

Southern manufacturers, joined by the unmatched power of southern conservatives in Congress, were determined to maintain a racial differential under the NRA codes. Ira Reid reported that members of the Labor Advisory Board of the NRA "found themselves facing a most complicated array of statistics, inferences and assumptions of southern industrialists," data proving that it was "both necessary and expedient to permit a differential wage for Negro workers." Although no reputable labor-efficiency studies based on race were available, employers insisted that because of the inefficiency of black workers, they could not afford to pay black workers an equal wage. Furthermore, they warned that if such a policy was enforced, black workers would lose their jobs, and many of the affected businesses would shut down, thus undercutting the NRA's goal of stimulating production. Southern employers used this apparently grim fact in their effort to persuade southern black leaders to endorse a lower minimum wage, compelling them to weigh the short-term consequences of swelling the ranks of the black unemployed against the less-pressing but equally troublesome choice of sanctioning a federal endorsement of the southern caste system.

The code-making process, though technically democratic, reflected existing political realities in the nation's capital. All groups to be affected by a proposed code had a right to speak at public NRA code hearings in Washington. To streamline the procedure, however, NRA officials attempted to resolve major issues at prehearing conferences between representatives of the affected industry and the affiliated, all-white, trade unions. Foreman reported to Harold Ickes that his efforts to convince NRA officials of the need for special attention to the status of black workers were fruitless. Their ignorance of the racial dimension of economic dislocation was compounded by the political pressure exerted by southern manufacturing interests "determined to keep Negro labor cheap and amenable."

The swift convening of a system of NRA code hearings for nearly six hundred industries taxed the capacity of the established civil rights organizations like the National Association for the Advancement of Colored People (NAACP) and the National Urban League to respond quickly and effectively. Neither organization had a permanent representative in Washington, and the challenges and opportunities inherent in the inauguration of the New Deal were beyond the tactics and strategies perfected in the struggles of an earlier time. The negative program of protest that had served the NAACP well since its founding was inadequate to the vast social reordering spurred by economic collapse and national intervention. The implementation of a national recovery program would have immediate and long-term consequences for black Americans, the great majority of whom were disfranchised and denied basic citizenship rights. On resigning from the NAACP in 1934, W. E. B. Du Bois chided his associates: "We are called to formulate a positive program of construction and inspiration. We have been thus far unable to comply."

During the summer of 1933, Robert C. Weaver and John Preston Davis returned to their hometown of Washington determined to obtain a hearing for black workers. Weaver, a doctoral candidate in economics at Harvard, and Davis, a recent graduate of Harvard Law School, were deeply concerned that none of the major national black organizations appeared to be addressing the issue of black participation in the New Deal. With the assistance of Robert Pelham, a retired government worker who ran an independent news release operation, Weaver and Davis established themselves as the Negro Industrial League (NIL). Pelham provided them with free office space, a typewriter, and supplies. From this base, the two monitored the daily flow of NRA announcements, wrote testimonies, and became regular attendees at code hearings, where they lobbied for fair treatment of black workers and testified on the adverse effects of specific codes. They were, Weaver later recalled, "something of an oddity." He added, "No one expected us, we were literate and we were contentious." . . .

With the depression, the abysmal social conditions of black Americans emerged in sharp relief and completely engaged the intellectual ferment of the young men in Cambridge. "The impact of unemployment and dislocation . . . especially in the South" was "unbelievable," Weaver recalled. The depression had exposed "just how tenuous the economic base of blacks in America was. In fact, it wasn't even a base. It was a moving target down." The men sought out social science literature that might shed some light on this vast problem, finding little available. Discussions on how to meet the emergency and the deep structural problems it exposed dominated mealtime conversations and frequent discussion sessions in Cambridge and sometimes at Howard Law School with Charles Houston. "As we tried to look at what could be done," said Weaver, "it became crystal clear to Bill [Hastie], John Davis, Ralph [Bunche] and myself that the precedents were in the Reconstruction period and that you had to look to the federal government. This was the only way you were going to get meaningful activity because, of course, by this time all the states in the South had completely disfranchised blacks." The New Deal provided a new opportunity to get federal action that could counter the dual system that had brutally proscribed the opportunities of black Americans.

Davis and Weaver were moved by the potential inherent in the new administration's initiatives and by the expectations generated by these initiatives. But during the summer of 1933 they were driven more by a sense of urgency that was shared by other young black intellectuals. If the interests of black workers were not quickly and effectively represented in the national arena, in all likelihood federal policy would sanction existing arrangements. Lester Granger voiced a widely shared concern when he charged in *Opportunity,* the magazine of the National Urban League, that the depth of the economic crisis was aggravated by the "bankruptcy of effective leadership among American Negroes." He explained, "Few of the old line Negro 'intellectuals' have taken pains during the past decade to keep abreast of the increasingly intricate industrial problems which involve the fate of America's black working masses." Economic collapse had exposed the "rapidly widening gulf of misunderstanding between the masses of Negroes and that educated group who would be their spokesmen." But Granger predicted that the deep discontent simmering among the laboring classes, black and white, would seek and find a solution to their desperate plight, as evidenced in the appeal of Communist Party and other left-wing groups. "In this very state of confused despair and bitter disillusionment lay the seeds of a new racial attitude and leadership," he predicted.

Weaver and Davis typified the new political leadership that emerged from the dual impact of the depression and the federal initiatives of the New Deal. Dynamic and improvisational, they were guided by their determination to secure a voice in the process surrounding the development and implementation of the New Deal. Their effort to defeat the wage differential was joined to a broader and more far-reaching goal, which was to help facilitate the full and active participation of black Americans in the recovery effort. This included New Deal–sponsored programs and the newly invigorated labor movement, which, for the first time, enjoyed federal protection. Weaver, Davis, and their political associates acted on the assumption that, in addition to aiding those who had suffered the greatest economic hardships, such a policy was essential to the success of New Deal reforms. The maintenance of a substandard wage for one group inhibited the possibility of building a viable labor movement and would ensure that the South remained an economic backwater. Thus, in an effort to join black efforts to a larger political coalition, they sought out and joined with those individuals in the labor movement and from the South who recognized that racial discrimination and exclusion thwarted any effort to secure fundamental economic and political reform.

The NIL succeeded not only in focusing attention on the issue of racial discrimination in the administration of NRA codes but also in establishing a national organizational structure for representing the special economic conditions and concerns of black Americans. By September 1933 the NAACP, the National Urban League, and thirteen other black organizations had joined with the NIL to form the Joint Committee on Economic Recovery, with John Davis as executive secretary and Robert Weaver as director of research. Financial assistance from the NAACP and a small grant from the Rosenwald Fund provided for a five-thousand-dollar annual operating budget, which included a modest salary for Davis; the limited funding required Weaver to return, reluctantly, to a teaching position at A&T College in Greensboro. "My heart was in what was going on in Washington," he recalled.

Although it never approached the power of the better-organized, and well-funded, business groups and trade unions, the Joint Committee served multiple purposes. Largely as a result of its efforts, the NRA decided against providing federal sanction to lower wage and hour standards for black workers. In each case, requests by southern businessmen for racial differentials were denied. Nevertheless, discrimination against black workers under NRA codes was widespread. The Joint Committee opened the way for effective protest and political action by keeping the issue of racial discrimination in the national recovery effort before the public. The committee became a clearinghouse for hundreds of individual reports of code violations; Davis conducted numerous surveys and made several investigative tours through parts of the South. His published findings in the NAACP's *Crisis* magazine attracted the interest and concern of Eleanor Roosevelt, who passed his article, "NRA Codifies Wage Slavery," along to Donald Richberg, assistant to the administrator of the NRA.

Southern businessmen did succeed in writing a regional wage differential into NRA codes. Through regional codes and widespread local subterfuge, they were often able to achieve a racial wage differential in practice. Regional codes were applied to nearly one hundred industries, which employed more than half a million black workers. The code for the laundry trade, for example, contained six different wages based on geography, with the lowest, at fourteen cents an hour, in states where black women composed the great majority of laundry workers. In many cases, employers changed the job classification of black workers so that they would not be covered by the code; in other cases, employers simply ignored the code provisions.

At the Maid-Well Garment Company in Forrest City, Arkansas, 200 of the 450 women employed were black. The company was required to pay the workers $12 a week under the cotton code but persisted in paying the black women $6.16, with ten cents deducted for a doctor's fee. A complaint filed with the Labor Department by one of the black workers was referred to the Joint Committee on Economic Recovery. After further investigation, John Davis filed a complaint with the NRA on 13 January 1934. On 30 January Maid-Well dismissed all of its black employees. Davis's efforts to secure restitution of back wages for the women were frustrated by "constant malingering on the part of both local and national compliance officials entrusted with the enforcement of the National Industrial Recovery Act." . . .

. . . [T]he politics of NRA code-making underscored one of the defining issues of the New Deal in the South. "The current question is, in view of the fact that all of the southern states sanction a lower wage for Negro workers such as school teachers and other public employees, should this differential be given the legal sanction and approval of the recovery machinery of the Federal Government?" The threat of job displacement and of the further elimination of job opportunities was a real one, as Southland and other cases illustrated. This was, Weaver recalled, "a very tough issue." But he, Davis, Reid, and others started from the premise that there should be no discrimination, especially when public funds were involved. "Wherever the Federal government touches interracial life it should stand for the policy of interracial cooperation instead of separation," Davis argued. "Any measure that will place Negroes on a lower, segregated status should be opposed." This position was widely endorsed in the black press and in journals of black opinion, such as *Crisis* and *Opportunity.* The initiatives of the Joint Committee invited the exploration of tactics and strategies to secure a no-discrimination policy.

The struggle surrounding the NRA codes and wage differentials highlighted the racial stratification of the South's labor market, providing a focus for the thorough examination of the South's economic problems that had been sparked by the depression. Davis and Weaver's efforts won the support of sympathetic members of the Roosevelt administration and of a number of liberal white southerners who were prepared to look beyond the racial divide in their search for structural solutions to the region's impoverishment. The NRA's rejection of racial wage differentials established an important precedent. "For once," Will Alexander proclaimed, "the federal government has acted on the assumption that Negro laborers are American laborers." The government thus created new opportunities for black workers and the American labor movement to move beyond the debilitating tradition of racial exclusion and discrimination. Among black activists, southern progressives, and a new generation of labor organizers, there was a growing consensus that such a policy was essential not only to the security of black workers but also to the success of the newly revitalized labor movement. . . .

Nevertheless, the process surrounding the New Deal offered a unique opportunity to test strategies, establish new precedents, and stretch the boundaries of participation. As they engaged the social forces released by the depression and the New Deal, Foreman, Weaver, and other young progressives were participating in a broader movement. "More important than the factual representation of New Deal programs," Weaver advised the annual convention of the NAACP in 1937, "is the interpretive analysis of results and the evolution of techniques for the future. . . . Unless a group like ours is constantly developing, consciously or unconsciously, such techniques, it will not only fail to advance, but must rapidly lose ground." . . .

. . . Allowing for its deficiencies and inequities, the New Deal marked a decisive break with the past. New Deal legislation fundamentally altered the relationship between the government and the individual citizen and invested the newly revived labor movement with strength and confidence. Roosevelt made the 1936 election a referendum on the role of government in a modern society. Campaigning against those "economic royalists" who had come to see government "as a mere appendage of their own affairs," Roosevelt pledged an activist federal government, committed to the "establishment of a democracy of opportunity for all the people." He proclaimed, "Freedom is no half and half affair." Whereas his opponents would concede "that political freedom was the business of Government," they "maintained that economic slavery" was "nobody's business." Protection of political rights, Roosevelt insisted, must be joined by protection of "the citizen in his right to work and his right to live."

The 1936 election transformed the nation's political landscape. The unprecedented popular plurality of votes that Roosevelt commanded weakened old regional and state allegiances and created a new majority defined along class, rural-urban, and ethnic lines. The Roosevelt sweep embraced "ideologically compatible progressive Republicans or independents and converted Socialists." Rooted in its old base of urban machines and southern and border states, the Democratic Party emerged as a national party, incorporating new constituencies that had been drawn to the programs and party of Franklin Roosevelt. The base of Roosevelt's vote spread to 81 percent among the lowest income groups. A commentator observed, "He had waged his campaign against the minority at the top and the rest responded." . . .

The South, more than any other region, offered a striking dichotomy between mass popular support for New Deal initiatives and a stiffening opposition among its elected representatives in Congress. Indeed, the South was the one region where, according to a Gallup poll, a majority of the people backed the Court-packing plan. Lyndon Johnson's vigorous support of the president's plan won him a Texas congressional seat in 1937. Even though there were a notable number of young, southern supporters of the New Deal in the House and the Senate, supporters like Lyndon

Johnson and Claude Pepper, seasoned representatives of the South's landowners and industrialists had emerged as key opponents.

In February 1938, Lucy Randolph Mason, the southern director of public relations for the Congress of Industrial Organizations (CIO), reported to Eleanor Roosevelt on the precarious political situation in the region. She warned of a growing opposition to the Roosevelt administration "among the power holding group," regardless of the "lip service" they might be giving it. If a vote was taken among this group, she was confident the president would lose. "The only hope for progressive democracy in the South," she observed, "lies in the lower economic groups, particularly the wage earner." They adored Roosevelt. Yet most of these people did not vote. Mason advised that the poll tax be abolished and that a deliberate campaign be waged to enfranchise the great majority of nonvoting southerners, "a hope more likely filled if the mass production industries" could be organized to give the unions "real strength." Robert Weaver recalled that for people in Washington who were concerned with the situation in the South, one fact had become increasingly evident: "If you were going to make real basic changes, you had to do something about the electorate."

Men, Women, and the Assumptions of American Social Provision

LINDA GORDON

Black men and women were almost entirely excluded from welfare planning in the New Deal, and white women, despite their hard-won governmental positions, were marginalized. The center was occupied by an all-white and virtually all-male group that advocated social insurance. The social insurance vision of welfare was enacted in Social Security's old-age pensions and unemployment compensation, while the social work vision was expressed in Social Security's public assistance programs, such as ADC [Aid to Dependent Children]. An amalgam of these two models continues to shape American domestic policy, creating a two-track welfare system. What was previously called social insurance is now referred to as "entitlements" or just "Social Security"; the social work–inspired programs, such as ADC, are now called public assistance, or just "welfare."

Social insurance is a little used term today but in the first half of this century it denoted a distinct welfare vision: government provision to replace wages temporarily or permanently lost through illness, injury, unemployment, or retirement. Directed mainly at full-time wage earners, social insurance ideas had little direct influence on ADC; but they had great indirect influence, because the social insurance programs grew stronger in part by distinguishing themselves from public assistance. Indeed it is the relationship between the two types of programs that created the contemporary meaning of "welfare." That relationship was constructed in part as a sexual division of labor, because the two welfare models were to a large extent marked by gender. Social insurance was overwhelmingly a male vision, social work a deeply feminized one. Just as comparing white to black women's perspectives made it possible to identify the racial aspects of both visions, so now comparing social insurance and social work perspectives makes visible the gendered aspects of our welfare system: not only what was female in it but also what was male. This gendered reading will show some of the "deep structure" of our welfare system. . . .

Despite sharp, even bitter differences, a core of agreement about social insurance had developed by the 1920s. Its proponents were convinced that interruptions of income from circumstances beyond the control of individual workers were inevitable in a capitalist economy, and that public responsibility for the victims of such misfortunes was not only a matter of ethics but also necessary for a healthy economy. This new kind of welfare plan had a few agreed-upon principles: coverage of clearly defined causes of need, such as unemployment or illness, by government provision, with compulsory participation; automatic (that is, not means- or morals-tested) benefits among those covered without discretion on the part of administrators.

Today the distinction between social insurance and public assistance is understood mainly in terms of the "contributory" funding of the former, through special earmarked taxes, but this was not the primary meaning of that distinction before the New Deal. Many social insurance proposals called for funding from general tax revenues, just like public assistance, and proponents never counted on a strict actuarial relation between payments into a fund and payments out to an insured person. The social insurance advocates emphasized not how funds were raised but rather rationalizing and universalizing programs and spreading risk. "It fundamentally aims," wrote Paul Douglas, "to distribute the burden . . . which falls with such a crushing weight upon the minority . . . over a wider group who as a whole are able to bear it. This is indeed the real purpose of all insurance." They took models from private—capitalist or fraternal—insurance schemes and adapted them to state control. Perhaps the most important adaptation was making them compulsory, a decision taken very early and agreed to fairly unanimously.

Social insurance got its name by analogy to private insurance. Defining it a quarter-century earlier, John Commons pointed out that all insurance was really social insurance, since all insurance aimed at "the social distribution of individual loss." At first the notion of social insurance included nongovernmental insurance programs run by such nonprofit groups as unions or benevolent societies. By the 1930s "social" as a modifier of insurance had come to mean "public," as in insurance "made universal by governmental compulsion." Because social insurance would be dignified, advocates envisioned it as a vastly preferable alternative to older poor-relief traditions. And the Social Security Act soon gave social insurance programs, in addition, the status of entitlements as distinct from the discretionary, charitable standing of programs like ADC.

Unlike public assistance, social insurance was not exclusively directed at the poor but rather at wage-earners more generally. One of social insurance's selling points was its benefits to all classes. Its advocates proposed not to relieve but to prevent poverty. In an influential debaters' handbook on social insurance published in 1912, only one of thirty two articles mentioned poverty. (It was also the only one by a woman.) Indeed social insurance agitation gained critical support from big business when it became clear that private "welfare capitalism" was inadequate and too expensive; in this respect support for social insurance represented an attempt to shift some of the costs of maintaining a labor force to the public purse. . . .

Social insurance designers saw themselves as pioneers but they lacked clarity or unanimity about the desired results. Some believed that social insurance was a stage in the development of an increasingly responsible and beneficent state. Others believed that a few strategically placed social insurance programs would obviate the necessity for expanded state provision. None foresaw—or intended—that social insurance, rather than ending poverty, would intensify inequality and thus create greater need for additional welfare programs.

When welfare advocates sought to derive their arguments from fundamental principles, gender showed again, although not in a binary, male-female contrast. They used three types of complementary, not alternative, ethical claims—rights, needs, and compensation for services—and many writers used all three.

Men more often made *rights* claims, associating their welfarist ideas with principles of liberal thought about citizenship. Statistician Frederick Wines spoke of a "natural right" to relief came up as early as 1883. In 1920 social work educator Arthur James Todd found the origins of modern social work not in the church, the peasant moral economy, the paternal bond between lord and peasant, or anything of the English tradition, but rather in *The Declaration of the Rights of Man* and Tom Paine: "Modern social-reform movements and social work represent a series of concrete attempts to define and redefine the Rights of Man." Prefiguring Franklin Roosevelt's "Four Freedoms," Todd listed some new "rights": to a decent income, to organize for economic protection (unions), to leisure, to education, to recreation, to health (including sanitation, preventive hygiene, protection from impure and adulterated food), to decent habitation, to a childhood "untainted by unnecessary and preventable diseases or degeneracies" (a eugenics goal), and to women's rights.

In the nineteenth-century woman movement, rights talk was characteristic of the most radical—those we today call feminists—while women charity workers preferred the language of self-sacrifice. Women revived and expanded rights talk in the Progressive Era by announcing social rather than individual rights. Florence Kelley spoke of constitutional rights to childhood and leisure that "follows from the existence of the Republic." But they also relied on appeals to pity and compassion and did not surrender their confidence in altruism. Social insurance rhetoric, on the other hand, hinged on rational-choice assumptions that governing motivations were always self-interested and appealed to mutual advantage, implicitly denying altruism as a social motive.

As women extended their program from charity to welfare, asking that the state provide pity and compassion, they argued that *needs* themselves were a claim on the polity: that fulfilling human needs was necessary to the social order and therefore a public responsibility; in short, they were politicizing needs. Their arguments were explicitly ethical because they were simultaneously campaigning for specific policies and for changing fundamental premises about the boundaries of public responsibility. Child welfare work particularly emphasized needs. Homer Folks talked of children's need for family life, as opposed to institutional care, in the 1890s. Later child welfare workers spoke of children's needs for play and security and used these new diagnoses as the basis for new concepts of child abuse and neglect. The protracted struggle against child labor spread an authoritative discourse about "meeting" children's needs. Sometimes needs seemed to trump rights. In child protective services, for example, a widening variety of children's needs could outweigh parental rights.

The consciousness of needs and the whole casework structure—emphasis on personal, flexible approaches—flowed from a maternalist vision. Indeed, turn-of-the-century social workers often used the words "maternal" and "paternal" interchangeably, referring to an authority that directs, guides, and controls. But the social insurance orientation was not paternalist. It broke away from the personal, caretaking dimension of social work and moved toward a structural relation of social control between themselves and the poor—one that was distant, not individually supervisory.

Needs-based claims flourished as social work became professionalized. Casework, the dominant social work technique by the 1920s, required ascertaining the individual and social needs of clients. Social work begins, said Porter Lee in his 1929 presidential address to the NCSW [National Conference of Social Work], "by someone seeing an unmet need." Social workers became reformers, he argued, by rousing others to see the need. This is one of the ways in which casework skills could be said to be feminine, involving attentiveness, empathy, and asking the right questions. Social work leader Bertha Reynolds came to believe that casework was defined by "perceptiveness regarding needs." The variability of needs did not seem to these social workers to make determinations less exact; casework discourse sought to make needs scientific through empirical studies of the costs of living and the making of family budgets. Social insurance plans, by contrast, required no discretionary ascertainment of need. . . .

In additions to needs and rights, welfare reformers also promoted *compensation for service* as a principle of entitlement. Mothers'-aid advocates clung to the word "pension" precisely because its association with veterans imbued it with honor. For the women's reform network, however, its masculine overtones were both attractive and disadvantageous. The service for which veterans received pensions was not merely a man's work assigned by a conventional division of labor. Military service was a symbolic basis of citizenship and one particularly responsible for citizenship's traditional masculinity. Feminists consciously constructed a maternal citizenship in opposition, imagining a citizen mother who could stand as an equal beside the citizen soldier. In one prominent line of feminist theory and in the mothers'-aid campaign in particular, women reformers argued that women's work as reproducers (of culture as well as particular children) constituted a service of value to society equivalent to that of the soldier.

The compensation-for-service claim for welfare was a kind of comparable-worth argument about what counted as a "contribution" to society. The welfare advocates who used it saw that the valuation of various social contributions is not fixed or self-evident. For example, in 1935, the group most widely considered deserving of compensation for service was unemployed male heads of families with children, and all welfare proponents considered unemployment insurance the highest priority. The notion that the elderly deserved pensions in recognition of their years of service was not yet widely accepted; the ethical principle that previously enforced care for the elderly was not reward for contribution but filial obligation. The popular notion that the elderly had contributed, "paid their dues" in years of service, and thus deserved pensions from the state was constructed by an active social movement. (One problem with the emphasis on needy children inherent in the mothers'-aid campaigns was that children could not be said to have rendered service.)

Legally the service claim may have been the most important of all legitimations for state assistance. In defending state welfare legislation against legal attack, the most consistently effective arguments were based on remuneration for service. Before the New Deal, key appellate courts accepted no distinction between entitlement programs, pensions, and public assistance, between workmen's compensation, civil service pensions, and poor relief. A wide variety of programs were upheld on the grounds that government could confer benefits on groups of citizens who had served the state. This legal logic rejected rights as well as needs claims, because the public monies were not construed as rights inhering in individuals, even those who putatively earned them.

The emphasis on mothers' service to the state might have proved fruitful had it been systematically maintained. But state mothers'-aid advocates ultimately featured children, not mothers, and appealed to the public sympathy rather than to the sensibility that service deserved compensation. As a result mothers' aid laws were upheld on traditional poor-relief grounds—that states could assist indigents because doing so served a public purpose. This categorization weakened the possibility of claiming mothers' aid as an entitlement, because support of the indigent was an allowable state function but never an obligatory one. Mothers'-aid advocates also neglected opportunities to claim universal children's allowances, and this too was consequential: The means-testing of the programs was a red flag that placed it automatically in the category of poor relief. But women's reliance on need claims was not a "mistake"—the inferior position of programs for women was determined by many factors, most fundamentally poor women's lack of political power. Despite romantic rhetoric about motherhood, women were not able to establish mothering, and especially not single mothering, as honorable state service. In the growing social insurance discourse of the 1920s, men continued to dominate positions from which they could make rights and compensation-for-service claims.

Thus in three modes of claiming, two were predominantly male. Rights and claims on the basis of service to the state were male, if for no other reason than that men controlled the state. Both approaches gained strength from the law of contract in its irrevocability and universality. By contrast the needs tradition called up a female realm of nurturance, and of authority through the power to give. Similarly, the oppositional use of needs talk represented the bringing into public of a private logic, in the way in which family members ask for help because they need it, not because they deserve it or it is their share. . . .

Perhaps the ultimate difference was that social insurance aimed to prevent poverty, social work to prevent pauperism. Poverty is an economic condition—lack of money; pauperism is also an internal, moral, and/or psychological condition. Thus "prevention" in the social work tradition required environmental and character reform, not just economic tinkering. Both social insurance and social work reformers aimed to help the unfortunate achieve independence, but they defined it differently. For the former independence was a wage; for the latter it remained a matter of character and individual circumstances, and those required casework. Often called "differential casework," this technique required in-depth investigation of a client's background, circumstances, and attitudes. Individualization was in fact the essence of casework: Its guiding principle was "to treat unequal things unequally." The very premise of casework was antibureaucratic, in the pure sense of bureaucracy, since it insisted on the worker's discretion. The caseworker was emphatic that money alone was not enough. The deindividualization of social insurance alone was anathema to social workers. . . .

The irreduceable conflict, the difference that ultimately necessitated ADC's separation from the Social Security Act's social insurance program, came not from social work rejection of insurance or universal plans of provision, but from social insurance rejection of casework. Isaac Rubinow defined mothers' aid as incompatible with his social insurance principles because it was means-tested, entailed submitting to supervision, offered low stipends, and did not create an entitlement the recipient could enforce through the courts if necessary. Those who wrote ADC also opposed stinginess, but supervision lay at the heart of their welfare program. The contrast was sharp. The social insurance principle had become standard, across-the-board entitlements, while social work's chief diagnostic as well as rehabilitative tool remained differential casework, with individualized, nonstandard treatment at its heart. Even when women sought inspiration from European social insurance programs, they tended to "feminize" the plans, incorporating casework and moralism. Thus Katharine Coman, a Wellesley College economist, concluded, after a survey of European old-age pension programs, that the purpose of pensions for the elderly should be "not merely the comfort . . . of the individual . . . but the influence on the moral fibre of the community. . . . Thrift is an old-fashioned virtue, but it is still an essential element in race efficiency." Rubinow responded that she had confused two projects and that her view demonstrated that the "old ideas of asceticism" were still alive. . . .

If their commitment to casework was in some ways elitist, women reformers also had a democratic reason for disinterest in social insurance—the fact that it was premised on insuring wage earners, collecting taxes, and administering benefits through employers. The workplace location of social insurance was premised on the assumption that women were economic dependents of male breadwinners, and that women would therefore be taken care of by men's insurance. It is ironic that reformers so dedicated to empirical research would have been so loyal to this fiction in the face of so much contrary evidence.

The family-wage myth was still widespread in the 1930s, but it encompassed different interpretations. The social insurance advocates' family-wage view was a rather conservative version, based on the unexamined assumption that women's full-time domesticity was desirable for all concerned. It was patriarchal to the degree that it continued to view a family, for policy purposes at any rate, as an attribute of a male wage earner. It supported the trade unionist demand for a family wage high enough to allow a husband alone to support his family—a demand that working-class women had usually supported, not least as an escape from the drudgery of the double day. Social insurance proponents also shared the male workers' rhetoric that made the family wage a token of masculinity; aged or unemployed workers were said to need protection from the "impotence" of dependency, for example. It ignored all those whose economic distress was created by long-term lack of access to the steady wages on which they wanted to base social insurance. "What the widow needs is . . . sensible life insurance," Rubinow announced in 1934.

The social insurance advocates cemented the family wage into the fundamental structure of welfare benefits. In doing so they also walled out numerous men as well as women. They neglected what we would call today the "working poor," for they assumed that only the interruption of wages was problematic, while in fact low wages themselves were the problem for many men. Moreover, many workers were not wage earners at all but farmers, sharecroppers, or even small businessmen who also needed help. The social insurance advocates had an extremely urban, industrial view of need, one serving the new professional middle class and the aristocracy of the working class—those with steady jobs for major employers.

For the women the family-wage commitment not only informed their design of ADC but also justified leaving the task of designing an overarching welfare state to the men. While they exempted themselves in some ways from the conventional sexual division of labor, by remaining single and/or pursuing public careers, they accepted it in their deference to the social insurance men. They never challenged the men's ultimate responsibility and authority to take care of the whole, as they cared for the women and children. Women's welfare job, like that of women in families, was to care for the husbandless and their charges, dependents of dependents, conceived as a small residuum. Although they wanted to treat these single mothers and their families well, their continuing fear of pauperization made them oppose long-term public provision to establish female-headed families on a stable or permanent basis.

Their family-wage commitment was illogical in several respects. They knew the error of assuming that resources sent into a family through its male head would necessarily be shared fairly among family members. Many among them had worked for agencies dealing with family violence, desertion, and drunkenness, and they knew the fallacy of considering men the universal protectors of women and women the beneficiaries of male support. It is not surprising that the male social insurance advocates were uninterested in directing grants to women. Abraham Epstein argued, "Nor is it the mission of family allowances to usher in a new relationship between man and wife . . . no apparent reason why the alleviation of this particular form of insecurity should have to carry with it a general reformation of the world." But the women welfare advocates did want to reform the world, and the family in particular, and thought the state could do it. Nevertheless they refrained from challenging the family-wage principle.

If this shared gender system was inadequate to help the poor, it worked rather well for the welfare advocates themselves, and this helped keep it unchallenged for so long. Male-female relations among these activists were usually smooth and effective precisely because of their sexual division of labor. While economically many women reformers were condemning poor women to a life of dependence that they themselves had escaped, politically they were in the same position as their poor "clients." They designed programs that would benefit women directly when male wage earners failed them, but did not encourage women's independence from men.

Thus it arose that both tracks of the two-track welfare system were designed to maintain the family-wage system. (That they did not succeed is another matter.)

The very process of a gender analysis reveals the inaccuracy of dichotomizing men and women: The gender differences were actually part of a *shared* vision of the ideal gender structure of the society and family. Where the men and women differed was in analyses of the nature of poverty and how to help the poor. The social insurance advocates tended to assume that the damages of poverty would be cured by money and jobs. The social work advocates had a more complex view, in part a feminist one. They attempted the difficult and perhaps counterhistorical task of defending the value of women's traditional domestic labor in a capitalist industrial context. They also tried to integrate a social, psychological dimension into an economic theory of poverty. Influenced by the experience of social workers combating drinking and domestic violence, and particularly by their clients, they believed that the injuries of class were experienced through problems like alcoholism, defeatism, and violence as well as through inadequate food and shelter. They considered the social insurance definition of poverty partial, reductive, and naive. Despite the social distance between them and the objects of their concern, they identified with the women and children who were hurt by intrafamily abuse perhaps even more than with those hurt by societal abuse. But they did not, in this period, suppose that economic independence might be a precondition for the self-esteem and self-development they sought to give poor women. Nor did they develop a system of casework suitable to conditions in which public assistance took in millions of clients. Nevertheless their vision at its best—articulated most vividly not in their words but in, for example, their settlement-house work—foreshadowed more recent projects for the empowerment of the poor, such as community organizing, far more than did social insurance schemes.

SUGGESTED READING

Badger, Anthony. *The New Deal* (1989).

Barber, William. *Designs Within Disorder: Franklin D. Roosevelt, the Economists, and the Shaping of American Economic Policy* (1996).

Berkowitz, Edward. *America's Welfare State* (1991).

Bernstein, Irving. *A Caring Society* (1985).

Biles, Roger. *The South and the New Deal* (1994).

Brand, Donald. *Corporatism and the Rule of Law: A Study of the National Recovery Administration* (1988).

Brinkley, Alan. *The End of Reform: New Deal Liberalism in Recession and War* (1995).

Brock, William. *Welfare, Democracy, and the New Deal* (1987).

Fraser, Steve, and Gary Gerstle, eds. *The Rise and Fall of the New Deal Order* (1989).

Gordon, Colin. *New Deals: Business, Labor, and Politics in America, 1920–1935* (1994).

Gordon, Linda. *Pitied But Not Entitled: Single Mothers and the History of Welfare* (1994).

Hawley, Ellis. *The New Deal and the Problem of Monopoly* (1966).

Irons, Peter H. *The New Deal Lawyers* (1982).

Leff, Mark. *The Limits of Symbolic Reform: The New Deal and Taxation, 1933–1939* (1984).

Leuchtenberg, William. *Franklin D. Roosevelt and the New Deal* (1963).

Mink, Gwendolyn. *The Wages of Motherhood: Inequality in the Welfare State, 1917–1942* (1995).

Olson, James Stuart. *Saving Capitalism: The Reconstruction Finance Corporation and the New Deal, 1933–1940* (1988).

Patterson, James. *America's Struggle Against Poverty* (1981).

Quadagno, Jill. *The Color of Welfare* (1996).
Radford, Gail. *Modern Housing for America: Policy Struggles in the New Deal Era* (1996).
Romasco, Albert. *The Politics of Recovery* (1983).
Rosenof, Theodore. *Economics in the Long Run: New Deal Theorists and Their Legacies* (1997).
Schwarz, Jordan A. *The New Dealers* (1993).
Sitkoff, Harvard, ed. *Fifty Years Later: The New Deal Evaluated* (1985).
Sullivan, Patricia. *Days of Hope: Race and Democracy in the New Deal Era* (1996).
Vittoz, Stanley. *New Deal Labor Policy and the American Industrial Economy* (1987).
Ware, Susan. *Partner and I: Molly Dewson, Feminism, and New Deal Politics* (1987).
Witte, Edwin. *The Development of the Social Security Act* (1962).

CHAPTER
12

Race, Gender, and the Rise
of the CIO

The Depression and the New Deal sparked the emergence of the modern labor movement. By the early 1930s, union membership had shrunk to barely 10 percent of the labor force, and the American Federation of Labor (AFL) showed little interest in new organization or the concerns of the unemployed. As the crisis wore on, workers increasingly struck against the misery and uncertainty of Depression era employment: "We starve while we work," one coal miner noted, "we might as well strike while we starve." In the years 1930–1932, major strikes erupted in the southern coal industry and in the Pennsylvania hosiery industry. At the same time, an unprecedented organization of unemployed workers (see Chapter 7) began pressing employers, communities, and governments for relief and jobs. Organization and protest became more widespread and confident after 1933 when, at least to workers, it seemed that the National Industrial Recovery Act had granted them new legal rights and protections. While neither New Dealers nor business took the labor provisions of the act very seriously, workers took full advantage of the legal opening offered by the act's Section 7(a), and pressed employers and the government to honor the full meaning of the law. After 1933 a series of strikes and accompanying cases brought before the National Labor Board (formed to administer the act's labor provisions) forced the government to refine and define its labor policy. When the act was found unconstitutional in 1935, the New Deal lost little time in retrieving and strengthening its labor provisions with the passage of the National Labor Relations (Wagner) Act.

With the Wagner Act, workers again claimed a firmer legal standing and initiated a series of "representational" strikes aimed at establishing unions. After 1935 this strike activity was aimed directly at the mass production core of the economy: steel, auto, rubber, chemicals. These industries were traditionally hostile to labor, but their intransigence had (in many respects) been softened by the economic pressures of the Depression. Accordingly, while the strikes were bitter, they were settled fairly quickly: employers did not have the cash or patience to fight long battles. In the rubber and auto strikes, workers used a sit-down strategy of occupying

the plants until they were recognized. In turn, this organizational drive trans-
formed the shape and focus of the labor movement. Union activists, frustrated by
the conservatism of the AFL, created their own national union, the Congress of
Industrial Organizations (CIO). The CIO, led by John Lewis of the Mine Workers,
concentrated on the mass production industries. It owed its strength in part to
rank-and-file activists and in part to the legal protections of the Wagner Act. By
1940 the CIO had successfully organized the automobile industry, the rubber in-
dustry, most of the steel industry, and large portions of other industries. The rift
between the AFL and the CIO (which included numerous jurisdictional disputes
and competition for new members) would last into the 1950s, when the two
merged to form the modern AFL-CIO.

The CIO signaled the rise of industrial unionism, which embraced all workers
regardless of skill, as a clear alternative to the labor aristocracy perpetuated by
craft unionism and the AFL. To a lesser degree, the CIO also embraced the ideal
of social unionism, which saw unions not only as organizations of workers but as
community institutions, consumer organizations, civil rights organizations, and
players in local, state, and national politics. Indeed, much of the historical interest
in the CIO revolves around an assessment of the gap between its promise and per-
formance on these terms in the 1930s. Industrial unionism meant, at least in the-
ory, that African American workers would enter the labor movement on equal
terms, but the CIO's civil rights records was very uneven: in some settings, workers
were able to build strong interracial alliances; in others, the CIO conceded to pre-
vailing patterns of discrimination and segregation. Industrial unionism also
promised to bring women into the labor movement on equal terms, but again the
record was mixed: organization lagged in historically female industries (barely one
in fifteen female workers would claim union membership by 1940), and patterns
of job segregation and unequal pay persisted. More broadly, the CIO retreated
somewhat after its initial victories. After 1936 the declining political fortunes of
the New Deal and the intransigence of many employers (particularly smaller and
southern mass production firms) forced the CIO to rely increasingly on federal
arbitration of key national contracts. Reliance on the state (and alliance with the
Democratic party) narrowed the CIO's attention to the contractual details of battles
it had already won, and distanced the CIO leadership from the radical rank-and-
file activists responsible for its early successes and its expansive social and political
vision.

D O C U M E N T S

Document 1 reproduces the text of the National Labor Relations Act, as passed in
1935. Document 2 is a recollection of the Flint sit-down strike. In Document 3, a
veteran meatpacker and CIO pioneer recalls the task of organizing the packinghouses. Document 4, excerpted from a massive congressional investigation of the
late 1930s, suggests the violent means by which some employers were prepared to
resist the CIO. The civil rights implications of the CIO are underscored by Document 5, in which the *Chicago Defender* (an African American paper) urges black
Chicagoans to support the CIO. And the obstacles to the CIO in the South are suggested by Document 6, in which a southern worker betrays little sympathy (or hope)
for the CIO.

1. The National Labor Relations Act, 1935

An Act

To diminish the causes of labor disputes burdening or obstructing interstate and foreign commerce, to create a National Labor Relations Board, and for other purposes.

Be it enacted by the Senate and House of Representatives of the United States of America in Congress assembled,

Findings and Policy

SECTION 1. The denial by employers of the right of employees to organize and the refusal by employers to accept the procedure of collective bargaining lead to strikes and other forms of industrial strife or unrest, which have the intent or the necessary effect of burdening or obstructing commerce by (a) impairing the efficiency, safety, or operation of the instrumentalities of commerce; (b) occurring in the current of commerce; (c) materially affecting, restraining, or controlling the flow of raw materials or manufactured or processed goods from or into the channels of commerce, or the prices of such materials or goods in commerce; or (d) causing diminution of employment and wages in such volume as substantially to impair or disrupt the market for goods flowing from or into the channels of commerce.

The inequality of bargaining power between employees who do not possess full freedom of association or actual liberty of contract, and employers who are organized in the corporate or other forms of ownership association substantially burdens and affects the flow of commerce, and tends to aggravate recurrent business depressions, by depressing wage rates and the purchasing power of wage earners in industry and by preventing the stabilization of competitive wage rates and working conditions within and between industries.

Experience has proved that protection by law of the right of employees to organize and bargain collectively safeguards commerce from injury, impairment, or interruption, and promotes the flow of commerce by removing certain recognized sources of industrial strife and unrest, by encouraging practices fundamental to the friendly adjustment of industrial disputes arising out of differences as to wages, hours, or other working conditions, and by restoring equality of bargaining power between employers and employees.

It is hereby declared to be the policy of the United States to eliminate the causes of certain substantial obstructions to the free flow of commerce and to mitigate and eliminate these obstructions when they have occurred by encouraging the practice and procedure of collective bargaining and by protecting the exercise by workers of full freedom of association, self-organization, and designation of representatives of their own choosing, for the purpose of negotiating the terms and conditions of their employment or other mutual aid or protection. . . .

From *U.S. Statutes at Large,* Vol. 49 (Washington: Government Printing Office, 1935), pp. 449–450, 452–453.

Rights of Employees

Sec. 7. Employees shall have the right to self-organization, to form, join, or assist labor organizations, to bargain collectively through representatives of their own choosing, and to engage in concerted activities, for the purpose of collective bargaining or other mutual aid or protection.

Sec. 8. It shall be an unfair labor practice for an employer—

(1) To interfere with, restrain, or coerce employees in the exercise of the rights guaranteed in section 7.

(2) To dominate or interfere with the formation or administration of any labor organization or contribute financial or other support to it. . . .

(3) By discrimination in regard to hire or tenure of employment or any term or condition of employment to encourage or discourage membership in any labor organization. . . .

(4) To discharge or otherwise discriminate against an employee because he has filed charges or given testimony under this Act.

(5) To refuse to bargain collectively with the representatives of his employees, subject to the provisions of Section 9 (a). . . .

Representatives and Elections

Sec. 9. (a) Representatives designated or selected for the purposes of collective bargaining by the majority of the employees in a unit appropriate for such purposes, shall be the exclusive representatives of all the employees in such unit for the purposes of collective bargaining in respect to rates of pay, wages, hours of employment, or other conditions of employment: *Provided,* That any individual employee or a group of employees shall have the right at any time to present grievances to their employer.

2. A Recollection of the Flint Sit-Down Strike of 1936

The Flint sit-down happened Christmas Eve, 1936. I was in Detroit, playing Santa Claus to a couple of small nieces and nephews. When I came back, the second shift had pulled the plant. It took about five minutes to shut the line down. The foreman was pretty well astonished. (Laughs.)

The boys pulled the switches and asked all the women who was in Cut-and-Sew to go home. They informed the supervisors they could stay, if they stayed in their office. They told the plant police they could do their job as long as they didn't interfere with the workers.

We had guys patrol the plant, see that nobody got involved in anything they shouldn't. If anybody got careless with company property—such as sitting on an automobile cushion without putting burlap over it—he was talked to. You couldn't paint a sign on the wall or anything like that. You used bare springs for a bed. 'Cause if you slept on a finished cushion, it was no longer a new cushion.

Governor Murphy said he hoped to God he would never have to use National Guard against people. But if there was damage to property, he would do so. This was right down our alley, because we invited him to the plant and see how well we were taking care of the place.

They'd assign roles to you. When some of the guys at headquarters wanted to tell some of the guys in the plant what was cookin', I carried the message. I was a scavenger, too.

The merchants cooperated. There'd be apples, bushels of potatoes, crates of oranges that was beginnin' to spoil. Some of our members were also little farmers, they come up with a couple of baskets of junk.

The soup kitchen was outside the plant. The women handled all the cooking, outside of one chef who came from New York. He had anywhere from ten to twenty women washing dishes and peeling potatoes in the strike kitchen. Mostly stews, pretty good meals. They were put in containers and hoisted up through the window. The boys in there had their own plates and cups and saucers. . . .

We had a ladies' auxiliary. They'd visit the homes of the guys that was in the plant. They would find out if there was any shortage of coal or food. Then they'd maneuver around amongst themselves until they found some place to get a ton of coal. Some of them even put the arm on Consumer Power if there was a possibility of having her power shut off.

Any of the wives try to talk the guys into coming out?

Some of 'em would have foremen come to their homes: "Sorry, your husband was a very good operator. But if he don't get out of the plant and away from the union, he'll never again have a job at General Motors." If this woman was the least bit scared, she'd come down and cry on her husband's shoulder. He'd more than likely get a little disturbed, get a hold of his strike captain. . . . Maybe we'd send a couple of women out there. Sometimes you just had to let 'em go. Because if you kept them in there, they'd worry so damn much over it, that'd start ruinin' the morale of the rest of the guys.

Morale was very high at the time. It started out kinda ugly because the guys were afraid they put their foot in it and all they was gonna do is lose their jobs. But as time went on, they begin to realize they could win this darn thing, 'cause we had a lot of outside people comin' in showin' their sympathy.

Time after time, people would come driving by the plant slowly. They might pull up at the curb and roll down the window and say, "How you guys doin'?" Our guys would be lookin' out the windows, they'd be singin' songs and hollerin'. Just generally keeping themselves alive.

Sometimes a guy'd come up to you on the street and say, "How the guys doin'?" You say, "They're doin' all right." Then he'd give ya a song and dance: "I hear the boys at Chevrolet are gonna get run out tonight." I'd say, "Hogwash." He'd end with sayin': "Well, I wish you guys the best of luck because, God damn, when I worked there it was a mess." The guy'd turn around and walk away.

Nationally known people contributed to our strike fund. Mrs. Roosevelt for one. We even had a member of Parliament come from England and address us.

Lotta things worked for the union we hadn't even anticipated. Company tried to shut off the heat. It was a bluff. Nobody moved for half an hour, so they turned it back on again. They didn't want the pipes to get cold. (Laughs.) If the heat was allowed to drop, then the pipes will separate—they were all jointed together—and then you got a problem.

Some of the time you were scared, because there was all kinds of rumors going around. We had a sheriff—he came in one night at Fisher One and read the boys the riot act. He told 'em they had to leave. He stood there, looked at 'em a few minutes. A couple of guys began to curse 'im, and he turned around and left himself.

National Guard troops were there. Some from Pontiac, some from Detroit. I lived within a block where they camped. I would pass these young fellas every day. One boy, pretty young, he had a union button on. Was it his union button or was it his dad's? I walked up to him. "Your captain allow you to wear that button?" He says, "I don't know, but I'm gonna find out." (Laughs.) They were twenty-year-olds. Well-behaved boys. No rough stuff, nothing untoward happened.

The men sat in there for forty-four days. Governor Murphy—I get emotional over him (laughs)—was trying to get both sides to meet on some common ground. I think he lost many a good night's sleep. We wouldn't use force. Mr. Knudsen was head of General Motors and, of course, there was John L. Lewis. They'd reach a temporary agreement and invariably the Flint Alliance or GM headquarters in Detroit would throw a monkey wrench in it. So every morning, Murphy got up with an unsolved problem. . . .

There were a half a dozen false starts at settlement. Finally, we got the word: THE THING IS SETTLED. My God, you had to send about three people, one right after the other, down to some of those plants because the guys didn't believe it. Finally, when they did get it, they marched out of the plants with the flag flyin' and all that stuff.

You'd see some guys comin' out of there with whiskers as long as Santa Claus. They made a rule they wasn't gonna shave until the strike was over. Oh, it was just like—you've gone through the Armistice delirium, haven't you? Everybody was runnin' around shaking everybody by the hand, sayin', "Jesus, you look strange, you got a beard on you now." (Laughs.) Women kissin' their husbands. There was a lotta drunks on the streets that night.

When Mr. Knudsen put his name to a piece of paper and says that General Motors recognizes the UAW–CIO—until that moment, we were non-people, we didn't even exist. (Laughs.) That was the big one. (His eyes are moist.)

3. Stella Nowicki Recalls Organizing the Packinghouses in the 1930s

At first the women were afraid. It took quite a bit of courage to join. They were concerned about their jobs. Many of them were sole breadwinners. Also the Catholic Church said that the CIO was red: you join the CIO and you are joining a red organization. To talk about the CIO then was like talking about socialism to some people

Reprinted from Nowicki oral history in *Rank and File: Personal Histories by Working-Class Organizers* by Staughton Lynd and Alice Lynd. Copyright © 1973 Monthly Review Press, pp. 273–276. Reprinted by permission of Monthly Review Press.

today. Even to talk union, you talked about it in whispers. You had to trust the person and know the person very well because he could be a stool pigeon. . . .

When I was at the University of Wisconsin, John Lewis made his speech that he was breaking away the coal miners union from the AFL and they were going to set up the CIO. We set up an organizing committee for the stockyards. There were seventeen of us that met, three women and fourteen men. One of them was an Irishman by the name of McCarthy who became the acting chairman of the Packing-house Workers Organizing Committee. We met behind a tavern on Honore Street. The organizing of these seventeen people was on Communist Party initiative and we worked through contacts in the IWO, the International Workers Order. In this group of seventeen there were some Poles and some Slovaks who were indigenous to the community. . . .

The National Labor Relations Act had been passed, giving workers the right to organize. But this was not easy because people were laid off. I was laid off, for instance, in the gut shanty and they tried to break my seniority. We had departmental seniority and I would be shifted all around. Besides casing and sliced bacon, I got to work in wrap and tie (hams), soap, glue, fresh sausage, pork, ham, almost every department. By being shifted around I became acquainted with many more women. I kept the names and addresses of all the women because I knew that some day I would need them. When we started organizing I knew women all over the whole plant. I would call them and get information as to pro-labor union sentiment, problems and issues, and so forth. We would print it up in the CIO news—the *Swift Flashes* we called it. . . .

Women had an awfully tough time in the union because the men brought their prejudices there. The fellows couldn't believe that women in the union were there for the union's sake. They thought that they were there to get a guy or something else. Some thought that we were frivolous. I would be approached by men for dates and they would ask me why I was in the union, so I would tell them that I was for socialism and I thought that this was the only way of bringing it about.

Some of my brothers, who believed in equality and that women should have rights, didn't crank the mimeograph, didn't type. I did the shit work, until all hours, as did the few other women who didn't have family obligations. And then when the union came around giving out jobs with pay, the guys got them. I and the other women didn't. It was the men who got the organizing jobs. Men who worked in plants got paid for their time loss—women didn't. I never did. But we were a dedicated group. We worked in coolers and from there I would go to the union hall and get out leaflets, write material for shop papers, turn in dues, etc., get home and make supper, get back. These guys had wives to do this but there was nobody to do mine. Sometimes I'd be up until eleven, twelve, or one o'clock and then have to get up early and be punched in by quarter to seven and be working on the job by seven. . . .

The women felt the union was a man's thing because once they got through the day's work they had another job. When they got home they had to take care of their one to fifteen children and the meals and the house and all the rest, and the men went to the tavern and to the meetings and to the racetrack and so forth. The fellows were competing for positions and the women didn't feel that that was their role. They were brainwashed into thinking that this union was for men.

4. A Congressional Committee Documents Violence Against Labor, 1937

Employer resistance to organization has taken many forms. These vary from company unions and other types of "welfare" organizations through blacklisting and espionage down to open displays of force. Espionage is the most efficient method known to management to prevent unions from forming, to weaken them if they secure a foothold, and to wreck them when they try their strength. Its use by management is an entirely "natural growth" in the long struggle to keep unions out of the shop.

But while management defends its antiunion "policy" openly—in fact, advertises it—it is less willing to defend or explain the "methods" by which unions are kept at bay. Even more sensitive and reluctant were the officials of the detective agencies appearing before the committee. As the hired help of industry, engaged in fighting unions, they made every effort to conceal that this was their true function. They went even further than management in inventing a variety of "reasons" for the employment of spies by industry. The odium attached to the practice made even the practitioners squirm.

The chief reasons advanced by employers and detective agency officials for the use of labor spies were: (1) Protecting industry against radicalism and Communism; (2) preventing sabotage (closely linked to the first); (3) detecting theft; (4) improving efficiency in methods and workers; merging into (5) improving relations between employers and workers, or "human engineering." These "legitimate" reasons for the employment of labor spies were strenuously advanced by officials of the detective agencies and, with diminished enthusiasm, by representatives of industry. These "reasons" were of so little merit that after examination by the committee they were repudiated by the same officials who advanced them. They are, however, interesting to examine for the light they shed on the actual motive. . . .

The furtive and despicable character of the spy springs logically, as we have seen, from the nature of espionage and its objectives. What the spy, so formed and directed, does to organizations of labor in the interests of employers must now be examined. A few examples of the techniques practiced by spies in destroying unions, wrecking organizing efforts, and preventing workers from exercising their civil rights will suffice.

The spy's work centers in the union. In his quest for information he naturally seeks membership in the local union, if he is not already a member. Once a member, his activities take on a new direction and impetus. He is then in a position to become an active agent of destruction.

That the spy should be a regular attendant at union meetings and active in the union's work is not surprising. Indeed the union is of more importance to him than his work in the factory. Since success as a spy depends upon advancement in union confidences, the spy has every incentive to press forward as a unionist. In time, he

From U.S. Senate. Committee on Education and Labor. *Violations of Free Speech and the Rights of Labor.* Report No. 46, Pt 3, "Industrial Espionage" (Washington: Government Printing Office, 1937), pp. 9–10, 17–20, 61–65.

comes to make the union his chief business. In this he has the assistance and training of the agency officials who guide his career and have themselves been similarly educated in union affairs. He becomes an expert in labor matters, a professional parliamentarian, a tactician, and often obtains a position of leadership in the local union.

The first job is to ascertain, not only the names of union members but particularly those who are most active or who play a leading part. . . .

Ascertaining the names of union members is sometimes difficult. But in this, his initial task, the spy must not fail. If need be, therefore, he will bribe janitors or custodians, rifle files or desks, burglarize offices to secure access to union records. . . .

A position as a custodian or sergeant at arms in the union offers opportunity to purloin the necessary records, carry them to the agency office for copying, and return them undisturbed to the files, as was done in Atlanta and Cincinnati by Pinkerton agents. Election to the office of financial or recording secretary is naturally of even greater importance. In that capacity the spy learns of every applicant for membership. At least 38 Pinkerton spies held such union offices.

The betrayal of union membership to the employer is implemented by the spy's day to day observation of union members in the plant for the infraction of plant rules. The employer today seldom dares to discharge outright for union activity. He must wait until the active unionist has given some plausible excuse for dismissal. Here the spy is of invaluable assistance. If the intended victim's work is beyond criticism the spy watches for such offenses as stepping over the conveyor belt, or smoking in the toilet—offenses which are customarily condoned, except where they offer the excuse for discrimination against union men.

Within the ranks of the union, however, in addition to reporting men for discriminatory discharge, the spy can be even more effective in disrupting the organization. One of the favorite devices is to seek to discredit the union leaders or frame them on false charges. The experienced spy knows that weakening the members' confidence in their leaders often leads to loss of confidence in the union and impairing the morale of the rank and file. In one instance, George Lichtenberger, a National Metal Trades Association spy in the Morse Twist Drill & Machine Co. of New Bedford, Mass., and secretary of the local of the International Association of Machinists in the plant, brought charges of embezzlement of union funds against the organizers. These charges were eventually proved false, but not until the local had begun to disintegrate. With satisfaction this spy reported that, as a result of his activities, "the company is increasing the hours and in some cases cutting the prices on work.". . .

In the councils of the union the spy often assumes the role of the agent provocateur. He incites to violence, preaches strikes, inflames the hot-headed and leads the union to disaster. Spies attempt to call abortive and premature strikes which will result in crushing the union before it has become stronger. They seek to discredit the union by attempting to associate it with violence and sabotage. A Corporations Auxiliary Co. spy sat in the meetings of the strike strategy committee of the Dodge Local of the United Automobile Workers in 1936 and urged the use of force and violence. A Pinkerton spy in the International Association of Machinists in Atlanta sought to provoke a general strike. A National Metal Trades spy in the Black & Decker strike at Kent, Ohio, in 1936, urged his fellow unionists to dynamite the plant. The fact that strikes and violence increase the business of detective agencies is a contributing cause to this sort of conduct.

More subtle than the role of the open provocateur but no less damaging is that of the contentious dissenter who, under the cloak of plausibility, creates a breach in the ranks of the membership. He attempts to discredit leaders, particularly aggressive ones who are seeking to increase the strength of the union. An able spy may be able to create a following for ideas opposed to the best interests of the union. He readily shifts from one side to another in a local struggle, prolonging contention and dissuading from positive actions which will build the union.

5. The *Chicago Defender* Sees the CIO as a Civil Rights Organization, 1939

If Armour and company forces its thousands of workers throughout America to strike for a union contract, Negroes will not enlist themselves as scabs against the great labor organization which members of their race have helped build. Not as long as a single picket marches before any of the huge plants with their profits ground from the back-breaking, high-speed labor of black and white workers alike.

These emphatic statements were made last week by Hank Johnson, Arthell Shelton, Kenneth Collins, and other leaders of the CIO Packinghouse Workers Organizing Committee [PWOC] on what may be the eve of the grimmest labor conflicts in American history. The statements were backed by the thousands of CIO buttons worn by colored packinghouse workers at their labor, worn like shields against low wages and poor working conditions.

"The present conflict at Armour & Co. is more than a battle between a corporation and a labor union," Hank Johnson remarked to this writer. "It is also another chapter in the long epic of the Negro people—their struggle for work and security. America's 14,000,000 citizens of my color are more than passive observers in this fight which we have sought to avoid by urging Armour and company to obey the National Labor Relations Act and come to terms with us.

"A national contract, signed by Armour and company, will secure the jobs and better the conditions of the thousands of Negroes now employed in the industry, and stir our people from coast to coast into further action for all the rights guaranteed them under the American constitution." . . .

For black workers have learned to raise their heads and to act unitedly for their rights as free men and women since the PWOC came into that turbulent district known as "the Yards." The story of that three-year-old organization, sweeping across the industry with the strength of a young giant, is also the story of the successful fight waged by its Negro and white workers to abolish discrimination and terror in Packingtown, to establish seniority rights and the principle of equal employment for the colored group previously regarded as aliens and outcasts.

. . . It was no easy task to begin organization work three years ago in the vast district of Packingtown where lean months of poverty sometimes erupted into explosions of violent hate. Each drawing slim pay envelopes, each subject to the prolonged

From "What Goes on in Packingtown," *Chicago Defender,* September 23, 1939, pp. 13, 15.

agony of layoffs, black and white slaved side-by-side in mutual fear and mistrust. It was almost worth a Negro's life if he asked for service at a Packingtown tavern or restaurant, and that antagonism was expressed in what had come to be a proverb of the Yards: "No Negro had better show his face west of Ashland Avenue after dark."

Today, because the PWOC has planted the seed of unity in the stony soil of Packingtown, Negroes walk freely and in safety. Any public place which refused them service would be quickly put out of business by a boycott of the white union members. On the very streets where danger once lurked at every corner for Negroes, colored men stopped for long chats about baseball with Polish or Irish workers.

6. A Southerner Recalls the Limits of Labor's Rights, ca. 1938

... "That strike last summer when the mill shut down for a week was what got us behind. There's always a few to make trouble for the rest."

"Did many people join the labor union then?" I asked.

Clara laid down her scissors. The five feet two inches of her was instantly like a sentinel standing guard. "I don't know nothin' about labor unions except they cause a lot of trouble. I'm havin' nothin' to do with 'em and nothin' to say about 'em. . . .

"The first time I ever saw what labor unions done was in Danville. . . . What was the strikers doin'? Settin' out in the bitter cold weather around fires built in the street. I didn't like the looks of it and I've had no use for the union since. And they didn't get a God's thing to eat but pinto beans, I know, because that's what the folks had where I was stayin'. No, sir, no union for me.

"The folks here at the Cone Mills ought to know to leave the unions alone. Didn't old man Caesar Cone leave it in his will—well, I reckon it was his diary—anyhow, he wrote it down—that before he'd recognize a union he'd shut down all his mills? And Julius Cone has had it put down in black and white that he'll do the same thing. Folks can talk all they want to about their right to join a union but right don't count much when money is against you. The government can say it'll make the Cones let everybody that wants to join the union but the Cones is still totin' the keys to the mill. They'd be as good as their word too; they'd shut down. It wouldn't hurt them, they would live without the mills runnin'—they got millions saved up—but we couldn't. We've got to have wages to live on. . . .

"And besides . . . them Cones is awful good where big things is concerned. It wasn't long, not more'n six months, anyhow, before the cut [wage reduction] that they give us $14,000 on our new church. Yessir, all we had to raise was $6,000. One of the Cones come down there and make a talk, sayin' that he knowed they was more able to give than us, and they was glad of the opportunity to help build our church. They understand it ain't easy for us to get along on what they can pay us. I've got nothin' to say against the Cones, and I'll have nothin' to do with no labor union."

From *Such As Us: Southern Voices of the Thirties,* edited by Tom Terrill and Jerrold Hirsch. Copyright © 1978 by the University of North Carolina Press. Used by permission of the publisher.

E S S A Y S

These essays offer three very different case studies of the emergence of the Congress of Industrial Organizations (CIO). In the first essay, Roger Horowitz shows how the critical role of Communist organizers and the nature of employment in the meatpacking industry facilitated the emergence of a radical and interracial union movement in Chicago's packinghouses. In the second essay, Elizabeth Faue suggests that the CIO (in this case in Minneapolis) marginalized women when it abandoned the expansive idea of "community unionism" for a narrowly contractual and bureaucratic form of national organization. In the third essay, Michael Honey traces patterns of CIO organizing in Memphis and suggests the tremendous obstacles to unionization in the "Jim Crow" South, and the success and failures of the CIO in this context.

Organizing the Packinghouses

ROGER HOROWITZ

On Sunday, July 16, 1939, sixteen thousand workers from Chicago's mass-production industries jammed the Chicago Coliseum to support the organizing drive in the Chicago stockyards and pressure Armour and Company to sign a national contract. The racially integrated crowd sang union songs and gave a "pandemonious reception" to featured speakers John L. Lewis and Chicago Bishop Bernard J. Sheil as well as union leaders such as the black assistant national director of the PWOC [Packinghouse Workers Organizing Committee], Henry (Hank) Johnson. Lewis berated the packing companies for maintaining "industrial serfdom" in their plants and promised that "the CIO will stand behind the PWOC in their efforts to bargain collectively." Although Lewis's bellicose statements were to be expected, the stunning appearance of Sheil, the second-ranking member of Chicago's Archdiocese, magnified the rally's impact. Sheil emphatically supported the CIO's efforts in the stockyards by quoting at length from Pope Pius XI's "Quadragesimo Anno" encyclical that endorsed "working men's associations." Drawing on the language of the Declaration of Independence, Sheil declared that a wage that did not provide for sufficient food, clothing, and shelter was "an unjust invasion of fundamental, natural rights." Herb March, a packinghouse union organizer and an acknowledged Communist, added to the meeting's drama by drawing audible murmurs and cheers when he entered the hall, his arm in a sling because of a gunshot wound sustained two days earlier.

The rally, held at the height of the organizing campaign at Chicago's Armour plant, reflected the covalent forces that made up the union assault on company power. The presence of John L. Lewis and workers from other factories targeted by the CIO indicated how rank-and-file organizing in the packinghouses was embedded in a larger workers' movement. The respect accorded Bishop Sheil, March, and Johnson by an integrated audience reflected what was happening on the shop floor of the Armour plant. White ethnic Catholics were cooperating with committed Communists and black workers in the unionization of that facility. In an advertisement published a week after the rally and designed to counter its message, Armour asserted that a national agreement was unnecessary because it already was "continuously bargaining with the CIO" in its Chicago plant. In so doing, management admitted that, by July 1939, "they just had to deal with the union.". . .

Eventual union successes in the late 1930s and early 1940s rested on unity in action by white and black packinghouse workers in a city where members of different races rarely cooperated. Organizers consistently stressed that the only way all packinghouse workers could attain a better life was by working together, regardless of differences due to ethnicity, religion, race, or sex. Union pioneers reminded blacks of their exclusion from better jobs and pointed out, "You'll never fight your way out of this until you get a union that's going to speak up for you." To whites who harbored racist sentiments toward black co-workers, the PWOC emphasized that "the boss is your enemy. The fellow worker beside you is not the enemy." As in other packing centers, inter-racial unity rested on the union's ability to satisfy the aspirations of all packinghouse workers for material advancement, job security, and power over their workplace.

A carefully constructed "culture of unity" strengthened the inter-racial amity on the shop floor. The PWOC organized integrated social activities such as picnics, dances, and softball teams and desegregated many of the bars near the stockyards. To visually represent their ideology, Chicago PWOC activists adopted a logo of two hands, one white, one black, clasped in a handshake. This symbolism made a deep impression on blacks who the union tried to recruit. "When you joined this union, the first thing you see is a black hand and a white hand," Ercell Allen recalled. "We did things together, black and white.". . .

The crumbling of community and business-sponsored support systems in the early years of the Great Depression weakened traditional loyalties within both black and ethnic communities and placed packing companies on the defensive. . . .

The depression and tumult of protest provided both the atmosphere and the initial recruits for advocates of working-class collective action to once again make inroads in the stockyards. As one of the few inter-racial organizations in Chicago, the Communist Party helped bridge the divisions among packinghouse workers and also initiated the process of unionization. Communists were particularly influential among workers active in the unemployed protests of the early 1930s who then secured jobs in packing when employment increased in 1933. Leon Beverly, for example, was an important future black leader of the Armour union whom Communists contacted during protests organized out of the Washington Park forum. Two other Communist recruits from the unemployed demonstrations, Refugio Martinez and Jose Rodriquez, organized among Mexican packinghouse workers. In the Back of the Yards neighborhood, a small group of ethnics, also recruited out of the unemployed protests, methodically expanded their contacts by joining community organizations affiliated with the Catholic church, the YWCA, and the University of Chicago Settlement House.

Chicago Communists received an enormous boost with the arrival of Herb March in the spring of 1933. Only twenty years old, March already was a veteran of mass organizing activity. The son of a Jewish union activist, March grew up in a pro-Socialist Brooklyn, New York, neighborhood. He joined the Young Communist

League (YCL) in 1929, and his evident talents earned him a dubious reward. Appointed YCL midwestern organizer over seven states, March left New York City with $5 in his pocket. He hitched rides and rode railroad cars for five days to reach Kansas City, the center of the district. For the next three years, March helped organize unemployed protests in Kansas City and surrounding states and made initial contacts within the area's packinghouses. He met Jacinta (Jane) Grbac at a Communist Party convention in 1932, and the two soon married. Unable to support children on the YCL's "salary," March moved to his wife's neighborhood in 1933 and found work at the Chicago Armour plant.

March brought a practical, down-to-earth tone to Communist organizing in meatpacking. Under the tutelage of William Z. Foster and other experienced Communists, March learned that agitation should dwell on specific issues and grievances rather than ideology. "They even referred to how the Russians did it," he recalled. "First you fight for hot water for tea, then you fight for the tea for hot water, and then you fight for the sugar for the tea." Strikingly handsome, an "outstanding speaker" and "brilliant tactician," March would sink deep roots in Chicago's packinghouses and construct both a union and political organization that lasted for several decades. From a small nucleus of fewer than a dozen in 1933, the packinghouse section of the Chicago Communist Party grew to several hundred by 1939.

March's arrival in Chicago fortuitously coincided with passage of the National Industrial Recovery Act (NIRA). Because many packinghouse workers routinely labored for upward of fifty hours a week, the mandatory reduction to forty hours forced companies to hire more workers. Communists March, Vicky Starr (known at the time as Stella Nowicki), and Joe Zabritsky deliberately "colonized," respectively, the Armour, Swift, and Wilson packinghouses. They found, as March recalled, that despite the weakness of the NIRA's protection of unions, "Workers so much wanted to organize, that when they saw there was a law that you had a right to organize, this encouraged workers to stick their necks out and to begin to fight." The "illusion that they had rights," and the tangible increase in employment, dispelled some of the "fear" that had hung over the packinghouses since 1922. News of the successful November 1933 strike in the Austin, Minnesota, Hormel plant inspired stockyards activists, and some began to display union buttons openly at work.

By 1934 at least five different unions were operating in the stockyards. Communists initiated the Packing House Workers Industrial Union (PHWIU) and recruited several hundred workers, primarily blacks from the Armour plant's killing floors. Arthur Kampfert and other former members of the World War I-era Stockyards Labor Council (SLC) resuscitated the organization and appointed Martin Murphy, SLC president during World War I, to the same position with the revived union. The new SLC was strongest among Polish and white ethnic butchers at small plants, such as Reliable Packing and G. H. Hammond; many probably had been members of the first SLC. A small independent union formed at the Hygrade plant, and the AFL-affiliated Amalgamated Meat Cutters sent a dozen organizers into the stockyards and claimed eight thousand members. Eight hundred Irish stockhandlers joined the Amalgamated and won a 10 percent raise with a quick strike in November 1933. . . .

A series of reversals in 1934 and 1935 forced the scattered nuclei of union activists to unify. Union sympathizers were fired in several plants, and the large firms tried to refurbish the credibility of the old representation councils by attributing an October 1934 wage increase to their influence. Workers dismissed for union activity learned to their dismay that NIRA section 7(a) and the new Labor Relations Board had no power to compel reemployment. SLC and PHWIU activists responded by dissolving their organizations and entering the Amalgamated; no doubt the Communist Party's abandonment of "dual unionism" facilitated the shift in policy by March and his associates.

Former SLC and PHWIU members quickly found that membership in the Amalgamated would not advance organizing efforts among packinghouse workers. In July 1935, Amalgamated Secretary-Treasurer Patrick Gorman blamed the loss of momentum in the stockyards on workers who "are slow in grasping the necessity for organization to improve working conditions and wages." The Amalgamated concomitantly reduced its organizing efforts throughout the meatpacking industry, cut its Chicago stockyards staff in half, and used the money it had saved to increase salaries of vice presidents by 20 percent. Kampfert and March secured permission to form an organizing committee but received neither money nor organizers. They asked for help from the Chicago Federation of Labor (CFL), only to be rebuked by Amalgamated representative "Big Bill" Tate, who told CFL delegates that the best way to help packinghouse workers was to "refuse to patronize a [butcher] store that does not display the union card." Although CFL leaders were sympathetic, they could do nothing without the Amalgamated's consent.

"We found out that organization didn't want us," black union pioneer Jesse Vaughn remembered thinking after the Amalgamated pulled back from the Chicago stockyards in 1935. "And we didn't want them because they wasn't for the working class of people." Hence, Chicago packinghouse activists closely followed the progress of the newly formed CIO and tried to devise a way to entice it into the packing industry. While the Amalgamated dithered, March, Kampfert, and other activists struggled to bring pro-union workers into an organizing committee that could receive CIO sanction. Several small meetings culminated in the creation of a "Committee of Eighteen" in January 1937. Participants included former SLC leaders Arthur Kampfert and Stanley Srotowski, Communists Lee Orear, Vicky Starr, and Frank McCarty, Jesse Vaughn from the small Roberts and Oake plant, and Austin union founder Jack Sechrest, a boomer butcher now working at Armour. After a ritualistic visit to Amalgamated president Dennis Lane, who assured them the time was not right for organizing, the Committee of Eighteen lobbied the CIO to enter meatpacking at the same time as the Austin and Cedar Rapids unions were engaged in a parallel campaign. Asked for proof of their strength, Chicago activists quickly collected two thousand signed cards that said, "I want a CIO union in the meat packing industry." Their pressure was successful. By the fall of 1937 the CIO had issued charters to nine Chicago locals claiming a membership of 8,200.

The CIO's entry into meatpacking, capped by the formation of the PWOC on October 27, 1937, was an enormous boost to the diligent efforts of the stockyard's "militant minority." The credibility of the new industrial union federation was far more important than its financial assistance, which was limited to employing several packinghouse workers. In Chicago, the CIO-affiliated Steel Workers Organizing Committee (SWOC) lent enormous authority to the new PWOC. "The people in the yards waited a long time for the CIO," an Armour worker remembered. "When they began organizing in the steel towns and out in South Chicago, everybody wanted to know when the CIO was coming to the yards.". . .

The PWOC's most important target was Chicago's Armour plant, the largest in the stockyards with more than seven thousand workers, two thousand of them black. The union's strategy "was to build a strong network in the Armour plant," Arthur Kampfert later wrote, "to develop leaders in every department." The shop-floor strategy was designed to create a union apparatus that could foster unity between black, white ethnic, white native-born, and Mexican workers by engaging them in concerted activity at the point of production. Union leaders hoped that securing small victories against the company would break through the "fear" that made workers reluctant to join the union and also the "hatred" that had kept them divided.

The nucleus of the Armour union came from the killing and cutting departments, where hundreds of former PHWIU members continued to toil. The integrated group of union pioneers from these areas made the Armour union inter-racial from its very beginnings. Black union pioneers in the hog kill, Al Malachi and Leon Beverly, worked closely with several whites in the adjacent hog cut, including Jack Sechrest, Arthur Kampfert, and Polish butcher Walter Strabawa. Union pioneers in the beef kill included the Rev. Walter Childs, a floorsman and a black member of the SLC during World War I; Peter Davis, a black who risen from laborer to butcher since starting at Armour in 1925; and Jesse Perez, a Mexican. Perez worked with other Mexican packinghouse workers to recruit their countrymen to the union through an organization (probably influenced by the Communist Party) called the Vincent Tolledano Club. Support for the union among black killing-floor workers helped garner white support because it meant that there would be no repeat of the 1921–22 disaster.

Building inter-racial solidarity infused union strategy beyond the killing floors. After secretive meetings in late 1936 established a skeletal organization, union activity surfaced in February 1937 when killing-floor workers began dispatching racially integrated "flying squads" to other departments. In May, two thousand packinghouse workers attended the CIO's first public rally, and Armour unionists started holding meetings at a Polish bar a block from the stockyards, Sikora's Tavern, whose owner permitted integrated gatherings. The union immediately affected the racial practices of taverns near the stockyards as black PWOC members began to frequent establishments favored by white union members. The union maintained high visibility by holding lunch-time, racially integrated, open-air rallies at Forty-third Street and Packers Avenue in the heart of the yards. Herb March, laid off by Armour for his union activity, became a fixture at these gatherings, speaking from a sound system mounted on his car. For the next twenty years Chicago packing unions would regularly hold rallies at this location, popularly known as "CIO corner.". . .

Ethnic production workers and white skilled craftsmen extended the union organization into predominantly white areas of the plant. Joe Bezenhoffer, a Croatian and later president of 347 for many years, was a skilled sausage maker who had been fired for leading a strike at a North Side plant before finding work at Armour. Carpenter William Mooney, an Irishman hired by Armour in 1928, used his maintenance job to spread the union message throughout the plant. Young Polish workers

Sigmund Wlodarczyk and Joe Poshonka encouraged fellow ethnics to join. George Kovacovic, a Croatian who had migrated to Chicago from the coal fields of Iowa where he had been a United Mine Workers member, also helped build the union among the white ethnics.

Women were slower to join, and female union activists tended either to be Communist Party members, such as Anna Novack in the canning department, or single, such as Sophie Kosciowlowski in the dried beef area. Indeed, the recruitment of Kosciowlowski, who was Polish, to the union is instructive of both ethnic and gender dynamics in the organizing drive. The daughter of a packinghouse worker, she first found work at Armour in 1918 when she was only thirteen. A union member during World War I, she left work to get married, a decision she later called "the biggest mistake I ever made." Divorced after nine years (a difficult decision in her Catholic community), Kosciowlowski was able to get her old job back in 1931. She knew union activist Sigmund Wlodarczyk through family members who also worked at Armour, and through these ethnic networks she became a secret member of the PWOC in 1937.

Armour fought the PWOC drive through a mixture of cooptation and intimidation. The company encouraged former delegates to the Employee Representation Plan, rendered illegal under the Wagner Act, to form an "independent union" known as the Employees Mutual Association (EMA). With their efforts sanctioned and assisted by management, EMA representatives commenced organizing in May 1937. They approached Armour employees during working hours and quickly claimed more than four thousand members. With Armour's evident good will, the EMA secured exclusive collective bargaining rights with the company in September.

At the same time, Armour tried to slow the growth of the PWOC by dismissing leader activists. March and Kampfert had already been laid off in the spring, but they had little seniority and the union was unable to lodge a protest with the NLRB. In November, Armour fired long-time employee Jacob Byra, a Back of the Yards ethnic who had been a union member during World War I. Byra recently had become a steward and recruited most of his ethnic co-workers in the hog coolers. Three weeks later, Armour dismissed beef-kill worker Pete Davis, who was black, when he came to work wearing a huge PWOC steward's button. Inadvertently, the company's actions lent credence to the union argument that management was the "enemy" of all workers regardless of their race.

The CIO fought back tenaciously by using the legitimacy conferred by the law to validate a shop-floor organizing strategy. "The only thing we could do is take the position that [with] the law they had a right to organize," recalled March, the strategist for the Chicago Armour drive. The union recruited members with the stated objective of winning a certification election and took the discharge cases to the NLRB. At the same time, the union asserted rights allegedly guaranteed by the Wagner Act *prior* to actual decisions from the courts or government agencies. "We set up committees and demanded to meet with employers on grievances," recalled March. "When they wouldn't, when we got enough of the workers organized, we'd have work stoppages." The result of this unrelenting pressure may have seemed only "little concessions here and there." But the ability of the union to force the company "to deal with the union" steadily increased "courage" and "determination" among the workers. The union's artful use of the legitimacy of the law to build a stubborn and effective shop-floor apparatus created an organizing juggernaut which, as March recalled, "kept on going like a snowball going downhill."

Throughout 1938, conflict raged in the Armour plant as the CIO extended its steward organization to new departments. Job actions, usually over the pace of work or application of seniority in job assignments, erupted in the sausage, canning, sheep-kill, and beef-kill departments. Often the simple threat of a stoppage was enough to reverse the dismissal of a worker or resolve a small grievance, because the union "picked circumstances carefully where we felt they would be compelled to yield." Indeed, the very absence of discharge cases appealed to the NLRB after 1937 reflected the capacity of the Armour local to halt arbitrary dismissals. . . .

While the visible apogee to the Armour campaign was the dramatic Coliseum rally on July 16, 1939, an event of more lasting significance for packinghouse workers occurred with far less fanfare two days earlier. Representatives of churches, businesses, community organizations, and the PWOC formed the Back of the Yards Council on July 14 (March was shot on his way home from the founding meeting). Through the council, Catholic union members such as PWOC representative Sigmund Wlodarczyk helped to neutralize conservative religious figures and establish warm ties with younger clerics more open to cooperation with the reputedly left-wing CIO. Perceptive observers had noted the presence of young Catholic priests from Back of the Yards churches at the July 16 rally. Indeed, Bishop Sheil's endorsement of the PWOC at the rally reflected the sentiments of a younger generation of white ethnic clergy who had grown up near, and sometimes worked in, the stockyards. "I knew that the Catholic workers of our district would not join unless the priests said it was right," Ambrose Ondrek, a Back of the Yards priest, later recalled. "So we provided leadership and told our people to join the CIO." Overt support from Back of the Yards religious leaders probably swung wavering Catholic workers into the union camp.

Bolstered by the Coliseum rally and the formation of the Back of the Yards Council, the PWOC finally overcame Armour's resistance to the union. A December 1939 NLRB certification election (held because of Armour's rejection of the 1938 tally) gave Local 347 more than four thousand votes to the Amalgamated's one thousand. A month later, Armour signed a local contract with the Chicago union, providing a guaranteed work week of thirty-two hours, improved vacations, and a grievance procedure. The agreement also ended Armour's hated practice of removing an employee's seniority rights whenever they missed sixty days of work. From its even stronger position, Local 347 consolidated its strength by recruiting workers in remaining unorganized pockets. With a strong union behind them, stewards in the canning room (where four people died from heat exhaustion in 1934) used a job action to force the company to install a cooling system. "This was a big boost to the power of the union," remembered steward Todd Tate. "Guys said, if the union can do that, maybe I want to join." Local 347 had achieved almost 100 percent union membership in the Armour plant by the beginning of World War II. "You just didn't work in that plant unless you supported the union," recalled March. In a scant three years, the PWOC had established a significant degree of workers' power in Chicago's Armour plant.

Gender and Community in the Minneapolis
Labor Movement

ELIZABETH FAUE

The relationship between gender and unionism took new forms in the 1930s. In the community-based, grass-roots labor militancy that prevailed through 1937, both men and women played major roles. Further, the labor movement embraced an egalitarian rhetoric that was gender-neutral in its implications. Despite the masculinist tone of press, poster, and prose within the labor movement, it was understood that women as well as men were vital to the movement's survival. By the late 1930s the base of the labor movement had shifted from the community to the workplace. Concomitant with this shift was the marginalization of women within labor unions.

The Minneapolis labor movement of the 1930s provides a case study of these changes. Characterized by a communal vision, local labor activists linked the struggles of truckers, garment workers, ironworkers, and the unemployed in community-level tactics that unified workers across craft and industrial lines. Both women and men were involved in mobilizing workers through union, political, and auxiliary organizations. A central characteristic of these campaigns was the activism and leadership of women in local-level struggles—an activism that did not, however, percolate to the national level.

With the advent of a more bureaucratic unionism, the level and quality of worker participation in the labor movement changed dramatically. As conflict and competition intensified between the AFL and the CIO, unions centralized authority and rigorously repressed factionalism and dissent at the local level. Attempts to create alternative union structures were perceived as threats to the norms of union governance. While men were brought into the union bureaucracy through new channels of promotion, the role of women workers in local union leadership declined, much as it had at the national level. As the decade of the 1930s drew to a close, women's auxiliaries and community organizations waned in importance and in numbers, and grass-roots activists lost the battle for a democratic labor movement.

As a process that marginalized women and finally excluded them from union leadership, bureaucratization was not gender-neutral. The ways in which an organization or a social movement rationalizes procedures, creates and enforces rules, and makes legitimate channels of authority and communication build on societal assumptions about manhood and womanhood. In evaluating both men and women by ostensibly gender-neutral but in fact deeply gendered and male standards of leadership and achievement, bureaucratic labor unions helped to re-create and reinforce gender inequalities in their organizational structures. . . .

The community-based unionism that emerged in the 1930s drew on the configurations of gender and class embedded in local solidarities; it embraced familial and fraternal sanctions of activism for both men and women and legitimated struggle that was expressive of and rooted in the claims of community. It proceeded to

From "Paths of Unionization: Community, Bureaucracy, and Gender in the Minneapolis Labor Movement of the 1930s" by Elizabeth Faue. Reprinted by permission of the author.

unionize workers by recruiting through local networks and institutions and through the culture of solidarity that develops during protest. Championing the brotherly solidarity of men, it gave new and collective meaning to formerly individual violence, aggression, and struggle that in that context defined manhood for the working class. Celebrating a political role for women, it built on their social activism in both neighborhood and workplace. Women had a clear, aggressive role that was legitimized in the context of community and family.

In these ways a community-based labor movement reshaped the role of labor leader and downplayed the importance of ethnic, skill, and gender differences. On a structural level marginalized workers, women in particular, were less disadvantaged in the community arena, where formal rules were kept to a minimum. In the garment unions, for example, women were militant shop-floor leaders and officers at the local level. In the Hotel and Restaurant Employees' union women were disproportionately represented on committees and among officers at the national level. Their national strength was rooted in their visible activism on local and state culinary boards. Finally, through cultural activities, even more than in formal organizational campaigns, unions reconciled labor militancy with femaleness and sisterhood even as they remained expressive of brotherly solidarity.

The development of bureaucratic organization in the labor movement required that leaders control the political skill, information, and means of communication necessary to consolidate power and stabilize the organization. The routinized process of union democracy made the same assumptions as political democracy: that one have a knowledge of the rules, be skilled at coalition building at both local and national levels, possess the ideal characteristics of a leader, and be relatively unconstrained in participation in public life. Unequal levels of education, skills, and resources among men and women restricted women's access to leadership, and contradictory demands of work and family limited their participation.

Further, labor bureaucracies, as the formal voices of tradition in the labor movement, both reflected and constructed gendered expectations of leadership. A labor leader was expected to demonstrate the manly attributes required to confront employers and to exhibit brotherly camaraderie with fellow workers. These characteristics demonstrate the cultural encoding of any political behavior. As one organizing handbook had it, the goal of any union was to win the workers over and to defeat the employer. "The term 'strike' means to hit," the pamphlet explained, and violent struggle was a legitimate way for men to effect change. Thus, in acting militantly and sometimes violently to achieve collective goals, men were not acting improperly. But because violence was proscribed for women in the constricted public sphere of bureaucracy, women's militancy could not be sanctioned.

Moreover, in situations in which the women workers were young, inexperienced in unionism, or reticent, unions posited a male leader as a necessary antidote. In a union's published example of a meeting based on Robert's Rules of Order, the serious, older, and experienced male union leader sets straight the enthusiastic but misguided and often cranky women members. In the garment trades the tension was palpable between men, who dominated positions of skill and leadership, and the "young, pretty, inexperienced girls," who were "NRA babies" in the union movement. "The problem of raising the new locals is as difficult as raising children," wrote Meyer Perlstein, a regional director for the International Ladies Garment Workers Union (ILGWU). Workers, especially women, needed to be "nursed carefully." They suffered from "infantile disorders," such as gossip and jealousy. Perlstein and other union officials agreed that women workers needed to break their individualistic habits. Only if they were "whipped into shape" could they become "trained and loyal members of our great family, the ILGWU."

The ILGWU went to great pains to explain how women could be brought into the union and how the union hall could provide an atmosphere more conducive to women's participation, but it recognized the resentment of men toward the "damned skirts" who dared to "invade the sacred halls of masculinity." Bringing women into the union should not mean that men would be "forced to submit to an atmosphere of rose-tinted femininity." Though a woman organizer for the union "might help to overcome the girls' reluctance to join or to go on the picket line," a "personable man in a predominantly feminine group adds a certain piquancy to the situation."

Within the bureaucratic unionism of the 1930s, activism for men and women was re-formed. Democratic processes defined new and appropriate routines of action, solidarity, and dissent. Taken out of the context of community, women's activism was delegitimized at the same time that normative rules of order and due process translated men's activism and rerouted male aggressive behavior into bureaucratic struggles for dominance. Bureaucratization redefined the very meaning of the political and the public. No longer were the boundaries between workplace and community permeable; the private domain of community existed separate and apart from the public domain of the union. Disagreement and dissent thus took on the aura of private and illegitimate disputes. As the bearers of the private, women were perceived as the most troublesome of unionists, workers who could not understand the rules of collective action and who severely undermined the capacity of leaders to lead. . . .

The Strutwear strike of 1935–36 dramatically illustrates the permeability of the boundaries between shop floor and community in the 1930s. For many workers and activities the Strutwear campaign represented a coming of age for the Minneapolis labor movement. As in the truckers' strike of 1934, the forces of community were both vital and visible in the struggle. The culture of solidarity created by the strike promoted interunion cooperation, the coalition of political and workplace organizations, and the support of community and social activists. In this context the community of union workers struggled with the legacy of narrow trade unionism and its privileging of men craftworkers over women and young men on the production line. It organized the unorganized.

When workers at the Strutwear hosiery plant walked out in August 1935, they challenged one of the most viciously antiunion firms in the city. They were ill prepared for the exigencies of a strike. Supported by the American Federation of Hosiery Workers, the union of knitters had organized only skilled male workers in the industry. The majority of the plant labor force—580 women workers engaged in seaming, looping, mating, and mending socks—were not members of the local; neither were the nearly 100 "boys" who worked as toppers on the production line. . . .

Few workers crossed the picket line the first day. Most amazing, production workers refused to report for work. The knitters who called the strike had made no provision for the participation of the operatives, but their recruitment was essential to the success of the strike. In the earlier strike failure to recruit them had caused the union's defeat, as it had in the Robitshek-Schneider garment strike in 1933. A profile of Strutwear workers showed a labor force divided largely along gender and skill lines, with only the intermediary job category of topper open to both men and women. Moreover, skill lines masked inequality among workers. Knitters started at a wage nearly double that of production-line workers; and while even an experienced woman on the line could get only a few dollars above the NRA code minimum, knitters on average earned twice as much as women and boys training as toppers. Also, the company had a practice of hiring learners below the code minimum (for $6 to $8 a week) and firing them at the end of training.

A strike that began with the grievances of skilled workers eventually had to address the poor pay and working conditions of operatives, both men and women. After the shop committee called the strike, union organizers began to contact them; most operatives knew about the strike from co-workers or public rumor. On the day of the strike the divisions in the labor force seemed to make little difference. Production workers held the line; and knowing that they needed the support of all departments, union leaders urged them to attend union meetings after the strike began and actively sought their participation.

The union went beyond the shop door, into the neighborhoods where workers lived. When the company tried to open the plant on the fourth day, 3,000 workers and union supporters formed a massive picket line. Police clubbed several strikers, driving them from the pavement. Afterward picketers followed the fifty knitters who stayed with the company from the factory to a department store, where the police escort hoped to lose the company workers in the crowd. Pickets confronted disloyal male workers in the aisles of the store; some followed them home. Women who had returned to work, in contrast, were only approached in the store and asked to come to the union meeting.

The labor protests at Strutwear built on layers of meaning in the working-class community. As the funerals of workers had become massive demonstrations of commitment, unity, and mourning, so too did protests that mirrored other rites of passage, of death and rebirth. A funeral for the company union became one such ritual. On the fifth day of the strike union leaders organized a large picket line. At midday hundreds of workers from the plant and the community formed a funeral procession for the company union. They circled the plant with the casket several times and finally held funeral rites in a vacant lot across the street. Evoking the ties among family, community, and workplace, they buried the old union and made way for the new. . . .

The success of the prolonged strike marked a turning point for women workers at the plant. Craft unionism, a strategy that marginalized and excluded both men and women operatives and sanctioned the poor conditions of their labor, was at least temporarily in retreat. In April 1936 Strutwear agreed to most of the strikers' demands, and the strike was won. The eight-month protest had created an opportunity for the union to enlarge and broaden its scope. At the conclusion of the strike, membership had grown to more than 700, including nearly 500 women. The Hosiery Workers' union now rushed to recruit women. By the end of the following year, Strutwear workers signed for a closed shop. New contracts brought both higher wages and hope for greater occupational mobility within the plant.

For many women who sought an active role in the union movement, neither union membership nor its benefits were sufficient to meet all of their needs. Their solution was to form auxiliaries, organizations that directed the efforts of working women and workers' wives. As the history of the Minneapolis truckers' auxiliary and the Flint Women's Emergency Brigade demonstrates, women's role in strikes proved to be crucial. These organizations continued to play a political role in the labor movement by serving as a base of social support and an arena of activism for women workers.

Women workers at Strutwear organized a hosiery workers' auxiliary in May 1938. At an AFFFHW [American Federation of Full Fashioned Hosiery Workers] convention Wanda Pilot, the only woman organizer of the federation, suggested auxiliaries as arenas for women's activism. Sixteen women delegates had intended to form their own division of the union; but because the constitution did not permit a separate organization, they formed an auxiliary. Membership was open to union members and to the wives and daughters of members. Though it focused on social events, it expanded to organize classes in labor history and economics.

The coming of the union to Strutwear had reshaped not only the relation of women to unionism in the plant but also the relation of unionism to workers generally. James Tibbetts, chair of the Strutwear shop committee, understood that men in the Strutwear union, as a minority of the labor force, feared that women were going to take over the union. Competition between men and women over jobs could soon follow. Tibbetts argued that "in shops like ours where the majority of members are women, men are always fearful that the women will try to take control of the union. This fear is not justified. . . . Women are usually willing to fill the role that nature put them in, that of being the supposedly weaker sex." The auxiliary could make a necessary and important contribution to the union. Recent studies of the auto industry, he claimed, showed that "a woman on the picket line is worth two men." But in effect, Tibbetts still envisioned the auxiliary's role as supporting the union: "When shops are organized and picket lines seem a remote dream, [ladies' auxiliaries] have a different part to play. Their job is to spread the gospel of unionism into channels that otherwise wouldn't be penetrated." By support, the shop chair meant union consumerism and social organization. Finally, Tibbetts argued that auxiliaries could help women, who lacked a collective spirit and who traditionally were not good union members, to learn unionism. The mutuality of the women who had supported a narrowly conceived craft union strike in 1935 had been forgotten. . . .

The high tide of community-based unionism in Minneapolis was reached during the Strutwear strike. Cooperation of the local labor establishment with national unions, political groups, and community activists underscored the importance of local activism for defeating the open shop and organizing the unorganized. In 1937, however, as rivalry between the AFL and the CIO heightened, national unions increasingly began to intervene in the affairs of locals. The recession that year made organizing workers difficult. The National Labor Relations Board's prohibition of sympathy strikes and secondary boycotts defused local union solidarity by denying legitimacy, and jurisdictional battles between unions further undermined the cooperation that was the basis of community unionism.

The consequences for unions—and for their men and women members—were severe. Rank-and-file members of all unions were increasingly isolated from decision making. In the garment and textile unions, where the conflict between men and women members and leaders traditionally had been strong, women lost the fragile gains of the early 1930s. Sexual inequality in labor leadership reasserted itself as national networks, dominated by men with ties to the union movement, replaced local gender-integrated ones at the local level. General Drivers' Local 574, the union that led the drive to make Minneapolis a union town, was increasingly besieged with directives and interference from the international Teamsters' union. With these losses, the promise of an egalitarian, broad-based union movement faded. . . .

Changes in local union leadership came at the same time the Twin City Joint Board was gearing up for an organizing drive at Munsingwear. Munsingwear, a major hosiery and undergarments firm, was one of the largest employers in Minneapolis, with nearly 2,000 workers. Despite the early depression of the textile and garment industries, the company began to rehire substantial numbers of workers in 1932, and it seems to have made profits during most of the depression years.

Like Strutwear Knitting, Munsingwear had a long history of company paternalism and antiunion activity. Munsingwear officers were prominent members of the Citizens' Alliance, the local employers' association, and they had played a role in the Strutwear strike by agreeing to subcontract some work for the company. To fight unions within the company, it established a company union with the NRA. Further, its management played a key role in the regional labor board of the NRA, where some of its officers were able to circumvent independent actions by the company union.

Munsingwear had long been a target of the ILGWU local leaders. After signing Boulevard Frocks in 1936, they began to make contacts with workers at Munsingwear. In November 1936 Underwear and Lingerie Workers Local 65 of the ILGWU received a charter. Sam Schatz was appointed special organizer. Many women were also involved in the Munsingwear drive, including the educational director, Leah Schneider. By March 1937 officers had been elected, and 30 people had signed up, with the promise of more. At the ILGWU convention that year, 200 members were reported.

On the strength of membership growth, Meyer Perlstein sent a letter to the Munsingwear management stating that the "time is ripe for a collective bargaining agreement. Our union is eager to avoid any interruption of production and cessation of work." Despite Perlstein's optimism, the ILGWU campaign was not successful. It simply could not attract enough members to call for an election. After nine months of organizing, union members had managed to sign only a small fraction of a 1,200-member labor force.

At this time Munsingwear management began negotiating with the Textile Workers Organizing Committee (TWOC-CIO). In two mass meetings the workers voted to sign with the Textile Workers' union and to approve a contract that appears to have gained some wage increases and union recognition for Munsingwear workers. The effort was headed by the new local CIO committee, including the regional director, Sander Genis. He played a central role in persuading workers to join the Textile Workers' Local 66, CIO. The company had been negotiating with TWOC in Chicago, and its reception of union overtures may have encouraged the workers.

Distrust of the ILGWU also played a hand in the organization. A local labor unity meeting demonstrated that memories of the Boulevard Frocks contract remained intact. Despite the ILGWU's advocacy of direct appeal to the workers, "without the help of firm, foreladies, or shop facilities," and the creation of a militant membership, they did not convince the Munsingwear workers. With the signing of the contract, the Munsingwear Employees' Association dissolved, and the ILGWU members were forced to resign from their union (or, it was alleged, from the company).

The failure of the ILGWU to organize Munsingwear was rooted in trends toward a more corporate, industrial unionism that stabilized the labor force and provided a higher standard of living of semiskilled workers. At the same time, the Munsingwear campaign demonstrated the choices workers had between the two models of unionism in the 1930s—the ILGWU, dominated now by nationally appointed officers, and the new CIO union, whose claims were stronger and more immediate because of the participation of a familiar community organizer. Though the company union had been outwardly controlled by management, Munsingwear workers trusted its union officers enough to sign with the CIO.

After the failure of organizing at Munsingwear, there was a noticeable change in the local ILGWU. The business agent and regional director increasingly set the priorities of the union, first and foremost by controlling union meetings. Issues raised in the midst of organizational drives had more to do with employers' demands for wage concessions than with improving working conditions. The nationally appointed director and business agent were concerned largely with contract supervision and industrywide cooperation with management. The needs of the workers as women, as union members, and as workers were downplayed in the struggle to maintain a regional garment industry against national competition. In effect, the national union advised the women to accommodate the employer and proved intolerant of individual dissent. While many workers still experienced some improvement in hours and wages in union shops, the union became a required part of the job, a prerequisite for employment, not a refuge from the demands of management. Moreover, decisions to strike or stay in the shops were directed by the board, the business agent, and the regional director. Complaints against the nationally appointed business agent were dismissed as the work of troublemakers. . . .

The 1930s witnessed an upsurge of labor militancy and organization that became a turning point in the history of the U.S. working class. Rooted in a dynamic sense of community, unionism went beyond the boundaries of the workplace to encompass both craft and industrial workers; men and women; immigrants, ethnics, and native-born white and black workers. The inclusive rhetoric of community became a powerful force in giving sanction to configurations of labor organization and protest in which men and women played equal parts.

When the industrial unions in the late 1930s adopted new forms of industrial relations that emphasized national authority over local autonomy and stability over militancy, they alienated many of the rank-and-file members who were the heart of the drive to "organize the unorganized." Centralization and union support for the war changed the nature of both men's and women's labor activism as unions closed down possibilities for grass-roots leadership and direction of union affairs. This bureaucratic transformation regendered the labor movement by limiting the scope and meaning of protest and organization in which women had been involved; it also redirected the activism of men into bureaucratic channels of communication, action, and authority.

The movement away from community issues, organizations, and control toward a more corporate, workplace-oriented unionism took place in an atmosphere of increasing political antagonisms and continued economic crisis. Community-based unions had made possible the rise of labor in Minneapolis, but divisiveness in the distribution of union power and resources at the local level undermined their strength. By the late 1930s unionists at both the local and national levels came to believe that highly centralized, bureaucratic national unions could give locals the stability they needed. What they neglected to see was how this choice altered the nature of unionism and the relationship of women workers to the movement.

Race and Unionism: The CIO in the South

MICHAEL HONEY

To understand the achievements and the failures of the southern CIO, it is first necessary to consider what it had to overcome. The southern racial system, intertwined as it was with economics, politics, and class relations, played an overarching role in keeping Memphis industrial workers unorganized. First slavery and then segregation had rigidly divided working people socially and occupationally along lines of color and caste. Efforts to overcome the color cleavage between potential allies had thwarted the Knights of Labor, Populists, and every other movement for labor reform. In the name of white supremacy, the state adopted a poll tax, which continued to accumulate every year it was not paid, leading to widespread disfranchisement of poor whites and most blacks. And yet many if not most whites remained convinced that they stood to gain from white supremacy and participated in race riots, lynchings, and the daily forms of coercion required to keep blacks oppressed.

Employers, the news media, and politicians generally viewed the caste system as necessary for business prosperity. In the 1930s, the city's economic base rested heavily on the wholesaling and distribution of cotton and other agricultural goods, and on industries related either to agriculture, the area's lumber resources, or transportation. Black labor, which became a caste apart from white labor, played a critical role in these enterprises. Employers kept black labor cheap by using the plentiful supply of rural workers, refugees from the surrounding sharecropping and tenant-farming system, to break up unionization and depress wage levels. The historic social division of southern workers by color also undercut organizing efforts, thereby perpetuating low wages, terrible job conditions, bad housing, and high mortality rates for white as well as black industrial workers. For all but a handful of white craftsmen, wages remained half the depressed northern rates in the 1930s, and many white as well as black industrial workers in Memphis made as little as ten cents an hour.

Labor organization provided the only possible means for industrial workers to improve their conditions, yet any effective campaign would require breaching the walls of segregation. Forty percent of the city's population of 300,000 consisted of African-Americans, and they made up the majority of the work force in cotton compressing and

Excerpted from "Industrial Unionism and Racial Justice in Memphis," by Michael Honey from *Organized Labor in the Twentieth Century South,* edited by Robert Zieger, pp. 136–143. Copyright © 1991 University of Tennessee Press. Reprinted by permission.

cottonseed oil companies, in woodworking industries, and on the riverfront. Blacks also constituted a significant portion of the work force at the city's handful of mass production industries—one-third of the work force at Firestone Tire, half or more at Fisher Body, and a small fraction of the work force at Ford auto. Industrial workers for the most part could not be organized until whites became willing to join with blacks in the same unions, the very thing that employers and politicians counted on them not doing.

Racial divisions rested not just on the attitudes of white workers, however, but also on a repressive social order adopted over the years to enforce segregation and cheap wages. This repressive order originated in the pre–Civil War era, when citizens could be run out of town on a rail or worse merely for speaking against slavery. In the "progressive" era, entrepreneur and power broker E. H. Crump put a new face on old forms of intolerance. Crump improved municipal services, kept the streets clean, maintained strict segregation, and obtained practically unanimous support from the business classes. He also built a political machine unsurpassed in the South. Crump almost single-handedly controlled Tennessee's most populous voting district and thus wielded enormous power at the state and even the federal level. During the Democratic party's heyday in the 1930s, he became increasingly arbitrary and brutal in using his power, driving political opponents and civil rights organizations underground. He also guaranteed the open shop to industry, pledging that, unlike Chicago or New York, Memphis would tolerate no CIO "nigger unionism" in Memphis.

Crump accepted the business unionism of the American Federation of Labor as long as the craft unions did not try to organize mass production. In return, he gave craft unionists municipal jobs and positions on all the city's licensing boards, rewarded AFL labor leaders with judgeships, and placed union men in elected local and state offices. For the most part, white craft unionists faithfully supported the Crump regime, espoused a philosophy of labor-management cooperation, and succeeded in monopolizing a handful of high-wage occupations in the building trades and printing industries. In common with their craft-union counterparts throughout the country, they did this by using unions to exclude blacks from skilled labor markets and by limiting employment in the building trades to relatives and friends. The white "brotherhoods" of railroad workers went so far as to assassinate blacks in order to eliminate them as brakemen and firemen. Clearly, the existing craft unions provided a major barrier to interracial organizing, and therefore to industrial labor organizing as well.

The national CIO recognized that the color line helped to confer unchallenged power on employers and Democratic party politicians at the expense of the majority of the southern population and resolved to oppose racial discrimination, lynching, and the poll tax. The CIO also recognized that racial division had helped to destroy organizing drives in packinghouse, steel, and other major industries in the North. Hence CIO unions adopted an interracial organizing strategy, hired black organizers and radical interracialists of the Communist Party, and in numerous organizing drives made alliances with civil rights groups. This strategy of building bridges between the black community and white workers proved more successful in the North—where blacks exercised some degree of political and economic power—than in Dixie, however.

Hence, during the 1930s, in places such as Memphis, the longstanding social barriers to industrial unionism seemed overwhelming. Conservative forces within the AFL's Labor Council engulfed the earliest efforts of progressive trade unionists to organize among white workers, and AFL unions ignored blacks when they attempted to organize following the 1935 passage of the Wagner Act. White women in a few garment shops gained bargaining rights, but no breakthroughs occurred such as those in the North during the CIO sit-down strikes. Only the Southern Tenant Farmers Union, headquartered in Memphis, demonstrated that blacks and whites could join together effectively in unions. By 1936, however, plantation bosses and their political allies had used savage repression to decimate this initiative. And when the United Auto Workers union (CIO) sent Norman Smith to Memphis in 1937 to organize the Ford auto plant, paid thugs, possibly employed by the Crump machine, beat him nearly to death on two separate occasions. Thus, at the very time the northern CIO achieved its greatest victories in 1936 and 1937, police and mob violence turned back industrial union organizers in Memphis, as they did in community after community in the South.

Not until the spring of 1939 did any hope for industrial or interracial organizing appear in Memphis. An unusual alliance of black stevedores in the AFL's International Longshoreman's Association (ILA) and white riverboat men in the CIO's Inland Boatmen's union, which later became a division of the National Maritime Union (NMU), nourished CIO hopes. Some 4,000 black and white workers shared power in a cross-federation alliance called the Joint Council of River Workers, and together they shut down traffic on the Mississippi from St. Louis to New Orleans for over a month. The strike not only closed the city's commercial lifeline; in addition, it defied racial customs and challenged the AFL's determination to keep the CIO out of Memphis. Company supervisors, hired thugs, and local police attempted to intimidate strikers, and the AFL's Memphis Labor Council leader Lev Loring even brought in scabs to break the strike. Under the fiery leadership of black longshoreman Thomas Watkins, however, Memphis ILA workers defeated efforts to use Memphis as a port for strike-breaking. The strikers eventually gained recognition, bargaining rights, and a contract, sending a signal of hope to workers in other industries and establishing a beach head for the CIO.

None of this would have been possible, labor activists recognized, without the cooperation and unity of black and white workers. However, the dangerousness of adhering to this principle remained clear to everyone, most of all to blacks. Only days after the success of the riverfront strike, Memphis police arrested Watkins and took him down to the river to kill him. Watkins barely escaped Memphis with his life, never to return. Other black longshore leaders, one of whom was spotted floating face down in the Mississippi, disappeared in subsequent months, and thugs used lead pipes to attack a black community activist who had worked with Watkins to open up the building trades to blacks. Crump's town lacked middle-class support for workers' rights or civil liberties, leaving organizers and especially blacks vulnerable to such attacks.

When the CIO's United Rubber Workers union launched a 1940 effort to organize the city's largest factory, the Firestone Rubber Company, the city's overt use of racism and anti-union terrorism revealed the barriers still confronting the CIO. Supervisors brutally beat a white worker in the plant who supported the union, E. H. Crump issued a vitriolic attack on the CIO, and Firestone thugs constantly threatened URW organizer George Bass. In one incident, they trapped him in an overturned car and tried to set it on fire and in another clubbed him so brutally that he required thirty-seven stitches to close head and face wounds. For their part, the police arrested a number of white CIO members as "fifth columnists," made intimidating visits to black workers in their homes, and brought the city to the verge of a race riot, shaking down blacks on the streets and ruining the businesses of several black Republican leaders. The national NAACP and the Southern Conference for Human Welfare both called this campaign of harsh harassment, accurately, a "reign of terror" against anyone who spoke for change in Memphis.

The Firestone campaign also revealed the continuing racial split within the working class. Blacks, constituting 800 of Firestone's 3,000 workers, supported the CIO almost to a man, in part because Bass clearly upheld the principle of interracialism. In order to defeat the organizing drive, the Crump regime backed an all-white AFL local, which baited the URW as the "nigger-loving Communist union." In a labor board election in December, blacks voted massively for the CIO while white workers voted overwhelmingly to elect the AFL, which subsequently provided only a facade of unionization. Thus, in the period before the outbreak of World War II, a combination of racial hysteria and police state tactics blocked meaningful organization at Firestone, the jewel crowning the city's efforts to attract big companies to Memphis.

When other CIO organizers came into Memphis, they drew conflicting conclusions about the meaning of the defeat at Firestone. Forrest Dickenson, who came in after Bass to organize the rubber and wood industries, concluded that his predecessor had made a basic tactical mistake by accepting black support before winning a large white following. In subsequent organizing drives, it became a standard CIO strategy to win whites before blacks, in hopes that the "nigger unionism" label would be less damaging. Leaders of the CIO's all-white local of the American Newspaper Guild, part of an industry where blacks played only a menial role, made this strategy into a principle, concluding that unionists should avoid racial issues at all costs.

A different conception of the union's role on race questions emerged among leftists, who entered Memphis via the NMU and the United Cannery, Agricultural, Packing, and Allied Workers Union (UCAPAWA). Following the 1939 river strike, a handful of unionists associated with UCAPAWA and the NMU secretly formed the first functional Communist Party branch (the police had successfully suppressed CP organizing earlier in the 1930s). They began holding interracial meetings in the old working-class neighborhood of Fort Pickering, where many industrial workers lived or worked. This secret group of Communists and their associates became a nucleus for trade-union activism and provided a core of support for the national CIO principle of interracialism. Although the circle of leftists remained small, in the early years of the Memphis CIO they exercised decisive influence because they organized blacks, and blacks and whites together where possible, without reservation. At the very time the CIO lost its campaign in the Firestone plant, the Communist-led UCAPAWA achieved its earliest organizing victories among some of the city's lowest-paid workers in the cotton and food processing industries. UCAPAWA also aided the organization of the International Woodworkers of America (IWA) in sawmills and woodworking factories.

Blacks predominated in these locally owned industries, and they took hold of the CIO movement with a fervor that stunned some white observers. Lucy Randolph Mason, southern publicist for the CIO, felt moved to tears by the powerful prayers and speeches of the half-literate blacks wearing overalls at union meetings. Ed McCrea, Tennessee district organizer for the Communist Party (and later a UCAPAWA organizer), spoke at one of these gatherings, and later observed that "you didn't have any trouble explaining unionism to blacks, with the kinds of oppression and conditions they had. It was a question of freedom." Black cotton worker Hattie Walls made the connection between the traditions of the black freedom struggle and the union movement explicit during a 1940 Memphis UCAPAWA school, turning "Old Ship of Zion," the black hymn about spiritual deliverance, into "Union Train." Pete Seeger and Woody Guthrie later carried this organizing anthem to CIO unions across the country.

The spiritual intensity of the black working class indicated that something more than mere trade unionism was at stake in the movement to build the CIO. At a time when civil rights organizations remained almost nonexistent in Memphis and the Mississippi Delta, the CIO provided an equal-rights philosophy combined with a specific means to change social conditions. It offered blacks, in Mason's words, "the acknowledgement of themselves as persons entitled to democratic respect," a status relative to whites found nowhere else in the South. Industrial unionism also provided a means to alter one of the most constant sources of oppression in the daily lives of black workers, their relationship to their bosses. The CIO provided an avenue, legally recognized by the federal government, to improve wages and working conditions and to resist arbitrary and dictatorial white rule at work. Black workers seized this opportunity, and became the backbone for the new union movement. Based largely on black support, UCAPAWA became the CIO's fastest-growing Memphis local in 1940–1941, and its membership elected John Mack Dyson as the CIO's first black local president.

UCAPAWA, NMU, the Newspaper Guild, and a few other locals built the ground floor for the Memphis CIO, but World War II played the decisive role in precipitating and legalizing unionization. The economic growth caused by the war dramatically expanded the city's manufacturing base in cotton, woodworking, and rubber, and added new munitions, chemical, and aircraft industries. As a result, between 1940 and 1943, Memphis manufacturing employment doubled to a total of some 40,000 workers. The number of women industrial workers tripled, making them 31 percent of the industrial work force in 1943, while blacks remained at about one-third of the industrial work force. The massive influx of new workers coincided with a return to economic prosperity and a labor shortage that put labor in a vastly more advantageous position than during the 1930s.

As the national climate increasingly stressed the need for unity and production, and the War Labor Board and other federal agencies demanded that local employers recognize and bargain with unions in order to get federal contracts, the city government muted its antagonism to the CIO. The mayor even welcomed the 1942 meeting of the Tennessee State Industrial Union Council, held in Memphis. Disillusioned with the AFL, whites at Firestone now voted in the CIO, and the Crump machine could do little to stop them. By 1943 about half of the 40,000 industrial workers in Memphis belonged to the CIO, with the rubber workers' local being the largest, followed by UCAPAWA, and then the smaller steel, woodworking, furniture, packinghouse, and other locals. As the sit-down strikes had been a turning point for the CIO in the North, the war proved decisive in the South, with Memphis one of the CIO's largest southern centers.

The antagonism of most white industrial workers to the CIO collapsed in the face of this unprecedented opportunity to unionize. "By that time," the first president of the CIO local at Firestone recalled, "we didn't give a damn about black or white. We didn't care if they were polka-dot. We were tired of the sweatshop conditions." Once organized, white workers experienced the fact that, far from degrading them, biracial unionism improved wages and working conditions, caused foremen and bosses to treat them with greater respect, and offered the possibility of more dramatic improvements in the postwar era. It also remained clear that without biracial industrial organization the unions could again break down into competing units organized by color or craft.

Racial politics played an increasingly significant role in the CIO, but they also raised new questions about the organization's future. Organizers could for a time concentrate simply on bringing people into unions and finesse racial issues by appealing to the simple principle of biracialism as a necessary means to a larger end. But what was the larger end? Eventually the implications of *how* unions organized became evident, and here the various tendencies in the labor movement diverged.

SUGGESTED   READING

Bernstein, Irving. *The Turbulent Years: A History of the American Worker, 1933–1941* (1970).

Brody, David. *Workers in Industrial America: Essays on the Twentieth Century Struggle* 2d ed. (1993).

Chateauvert, Melinda. *Marching Together: Women of the Brotherhood of Sleeping Car Porters* (1998).

Clark, Paul, ed. *Forging a Union of Steel* (1987).

Cobble, Dorothy Sue. *Dishing It Out: Waitresses and Their Unions in the Twentieth Century* (1991).

Cohen, Lizabeth. *Making a New Deal: Industrial Workers in Chicago, 1919–1939* (1990).

Dubofsky, Melvyn. *The State and Labor in Modern America* (1994).

Faue, Elizabeth. *Community of Suffering and Struggle: Women, Men, and the Labor Movement in Minneapolis, 1915–1945* (1991).

Fraser, Steve. *Labor Will Rule: Sidney Hillman and the Rise of American Labor* (1991).

Freeman, Joshua. *In Transit: The Transport Workers Union in New York City, 1933–1966* (1989).

Friedlander, Peter. *The Emergence of a UAW Local, 1936–1939* (1975).

Gabin, Nancy. *Feminism in the Labor Movement: Women and the United Auto Workers* (1990).

Gerstle, Gary. *Working-Class Americanism: The Politics of Labor in a Textile City, 1914–1960* (1989).

Halpern, Rick. *Down on the Killing Floor: Black and White Workers in Chicago's Packinghouses, 1904–54* (1997).

Honey, Michael. *Southern Labor and Black Civil Rights* (1993).

Horowitz, Roger. *"Negro and White, Unite and Fight!": A Social History of Industrial Unionism in Meatpacking, 1930–90* (1997).

Keeran, Roger. *The Communist Party and the Auto Workers Unions* (1980).

Lichtenstein, Nelson. *The Most Dangerous Man in Detroit: Walter Reuther and the Fate of American Labor* (1995).

Lynd, Staughton, ed., *"We Are All Leaders": The Alternative Unionism of the Early 1930s* (1996).

Meier, August, and Elliot Rudwick. *Black Detroit and the Rise of the UAW* (1979).

Milton, David. *The Politics of U.S. Labor* (1982).

Nelson, Bruce. *Workers on the Waterfront* (1988).

Nelson, Daniel. *American Rubber Workers and Organized Labor, 1900–1941* (1988).

Newell, Barbara. *Chicago and the Labor Movement* (1961).

Rosswurm, Steve, ed. *The CIO's Left-Led Unions* (1992).

Schacht, John. *The Making of Telephone Unionism, 1920–1947* (1985).

Schatz, Ronald. *The Electrical Workers: A History of Labor at General Electric and Westinghouse, 1923–1960* (1983).

Tomlins, Christopher. *The State and the Unions: Labor Relations, Law, and the Organized Labor Movement in America, 1880–1960* (1985).

Vittoz, Stanley. *New Deal Labor Policy and the American Industrial Economy* (1987).

Zieger, Robert. *The CIO, 1935–1955* (1995).

CHAPTER
13

Contesting the New Deal

By the late 1930s, the New Deal was increasingly besieged by critics from across the political spectrum. In part, this simply reflected the persistence of the Depression. Despite the frantic pace of reform through 1935, recovery remained elusive, and indeed the economy stumbled again in what was quickly dubbed the "Roosevelt Recession" of 1937. Some urged the New Deal to redouble its efforts, others began to argue that the Administration's policies were themselves the principal obstacle to recovery. The New Dealers themselves were uncertain about which direction to take, and devoted most of their energy to mopping up around the edges of existing programs. To compound this, the Administration had lost considerable political support. An ill-conceived effort to "pack" the Supreme Court (in order to ensure the constitutionality of the 1935 reforms) backfired badly in a political culture already anxious about the rapid expansion of federal and presidential power. And Southern Democrats, increasingly anxious about federal interference in Southern race and labor relations, joined Republicans in a political and congressional alliance against the New Deal. More broadly, the New Deal increasingly confronted radical critics who claimed it was doing too little, conservative and business opponents who criticized it for doing too much, and populist critics who managed to argue that it was doing too much and too little.

The left was disappointed by the timidity of the early New Deal, and by the scope and administration of the 1935 reforms. Workers and farmers, especially those in the Congress of Industrial Organizations and the Southern Tenant Farmers Union, had been instrumental in pressing the New Deal to the left between 1933 and 1935, and continued to argue that the federal government was not living up to its responsibilities. At the same time, the New Deal faced an array of local and regional challenges, including Upton Sinclair's gubernatorial run in California under the EPIC ("End Poverty in California") banner and the revival of progressive and labor-farm parties in states such as Minnesota and Wisconsin. But what was remarkable, in the end, was that the left did not make greater organizational and intellectual gains during the prolonged economic crisis. In part, this reflected historic and practical obstacles to third-party competition in the United States. And in part, it reflected the official stance of the Communist party—which had been a vocal critic of the New Deal in 1933 and 1934 but increasingly supported the New Deal in a "popular front" against conservative reactionaries at home and (as World War II approached) fascists abroad.

Business sharpened its attacks on the New Deal after 1935. While the New Deal was by no means antibusiness (and, at least in the National Industrial Recovery Act, had given business everything it wanted), some firms and industries increasingly resented the scope and costs of new federal programs. The most strident anti–New Deal groups were the National Association of Manufacturers (representing small and Southern firms), and the American Liberty League (an antitax group organized by the Du Ponts). More broadly, business interests dug in against further reform because early efforts (which they had by and large supported) had failed miserably; because they resented the material and managerial costs of complying with the Wagner and Social Security Acts; because the New Deal had not (despite its promises) managed to erase the low-wage advantage enjoyed by Southern industry; and because they resented the tax burden that accompanied the new federal programs. Business voiced its opposition as a classically American defense of individualism, property rights, and limits on state power. But, for the most part, its approach was practical rather than philosophical, opposed not to the idea of federal intervention but to its failure and its costs.

Finally, the New Deal also faced a variety of "populist" critics who generally joined the left in assailing the inequity of New Deal programs and the right in assailing the rapid growth of federal power and bureaucracy. These critics typically offered up a mixture of simple solutions to the Depression and fiery denunciations of the Roosevelt Administration. Francis Townshend, a California doctor, proposed a national plan that would give unemployed senior citizens $200 each on the condition that they spur recovery by spending it right away. Father Charles Coughlin, a Roman Catholic radio priest (and early supporter of the New Deal) increasingly viewed the New Deal as part of an elaborate bankers' conspiracy against the American people. Huey Long, a Senator from Louisiana, argued that the New Deal was drifting off course by the mid-1930s and advocated a dramatic redistribution of income and wealth. Together, Townshend, Coughlin, Long, and others capitalized on popular doubts by offering attractively simple solutions to the Depression. Such solutions were, in part, a nostalgia for a preindustrial society of small business, small farmers, and small towns; and an attack on concentrations of both wealth (corporations, banks, chain stores) and political power.

D O C U M E N T S

The first three documents trace elements of the left's opposition to the New Deal. Document 1 summarizes radical doubts about early New Deal policy. Document 2 suggests the reconciliation of at least the Communist left with the "popular front" led by the Roosevelt Administration. In Document 3, Upton Sinclair lists the premises of the "End Poverty in California" movement. Documents 4 and 5 suggest the "populist" response to the New Deal. In Document 4, Huey Long promotes his "Share Our Wealth" campaign for confiscatory taxation and radical income redistribution. In Document 5, Father Charles Coughlin touches on some of the (often contradictory) themes that made him both a champion of social justice and an ardent critic of the New Deal. The final three documents capture the arguments of the anti-New Deal coalition of business, Republicans, and southerners. Document 6, penned by a prominent business journalist of the 1930s, suggests business anxieties about an increasingly activist federal government. In Document 7, former President Hoover sees the Roosevelt Administration's attempt to "pack" the Supreme Court as part of a broader threat to liberty. In Document 8, Southern legislators candidly stake out the racial boundaries of New Deal reform.

1. Communists Lament the Futility of the New Deal, 1934

There has been revolutionary talk among intellectuals for some time. There has been some revival of the Socialist and Communist movements, among groups chiefly that were not too much steeped in the American individualist tradition. The "farm revolt" is habitual in American politics. But now there seems to be something more than these, something incidentally far more dangerous to the powers-that-be in capitalist America.

Cogent understanding of the futility of the New Deal compromises is far more widespread than it was, not only among intelligent economists and writers, but among native political leaders. Technocracy's challenge has ceased to be a seven-day's wonder, and has become a part of the ordinary American's mind: "of course" we could abolish poverty and insecurity if we used a little more sense in taking advantage of the machine. A bright new Utopia is ahead for American idealism to reach after. And in the way of radical organization that promises effective action, much has been accomplished in the last year, and especially in the last few months. There is a more mature understanding of the direction of history.

Most encouraging sign of a really popular uprising is the growth of political revolt in the West. The frontier was long the American substitute for revolution. And as it closed up, and the western migrants found the long arm of the East—the East in the guise of railroads, monopoly, Wall Street—reaching out to rob them of the wealth they were creating—one political insurrection after another has come out of the West. But this time Populism and Bryanism and Progressivism have been outgrown, and the phenomenon now known as the Farmer-Labor movement bids fair to become what its spokesman in Minnesota, Governor Olson, says it must become, "revolutionary.". . .

. . . And with the continuing failure of the New Deal the movement is bound to grow to serious proportions; and more sharply than ever before it will be a movement against capitalism. . . .

There are two things to fear from such a movement. One is that timidity and ignorance in the local leadership will allow the movements to fritter themselves away on agrarian reform proposals and monetary panaceas, unable or unwilling to face the challenge of a system in collapse. The other is that the Fascist spirit of racial and national prejudice will rise to throw the movement into the hands of Fascist demagogues. It is because of these dangers that intelligent direction and leadership are so urgently called for. Organizations like the Farmer Labor Political Federation working on the outside, and New America, building a disciplined corps of younger convinced radicals that can work through a mass movement on the inside, are essential.

The danger of some sort of Fascism is the most serious. Whether it comes through the NRA and the Chamber of Commerce, or whether it comes through an organization of colored shirts, or, what is ultimately more likely, through both, it is a menace that can only be met by an intelligent evaluation of the genuinely American radical forces, and their fullest utilization.

From "Postscript," in *Challenge to the New Deal,* ed. Alfred Bingham and Selden Rodman (New York: Falcon, 1934), pp. 281–284.

2. The Communist Party Argues for a "Popular Front," 1938

Franklin D. Roosevelt is clearly the chief figure in the progressive or liberal camp. Regardless of who will be the 1940 candidate behind which the forces of the democratic front will unite, it is clear that Roosevelt has become the symbol which unites the broadest masses of the progressive majority of the people. The reactionary camp can be defeated in 1940 only if the Roosevelt following is firmly united to include the organized labor movement, the really progressive Republicans, and the Negro people; and only if the New Deal forces, firmly uniting their basic following, win back the vacillating groupings among the farmers and city middle classes. . . . This is the way to the organized single democratic front which will include the unions of the C.I.O. and A. F. of L., the farmers, the New Deal forces, the progressive followers of the Republican Party, and all independent progressive movements of the people. We are not interested at this time in discussing who that personality might be, or in debating the question whether Roosevelt himself will be the candidate. *We are interested only in the combination of forces which contains the guarantee of victory against the reactionaries.*

Such unity of all the progressive and democratic forces can only be secured by the further unfolding and development of the New Deal program. We fully discussed this program question at our Party's Tenth Convention last May, and embodied our fundamental opinions on the question in the main resolution there adopted. The views we then expressed remain fully valid for the next period leading up to 1940. We need to change nothing in our convention discussions and decisions. But we do need much more decisive and energetic progress in concretely developing that program among the masses and in registering the mass opinion in governmental policy. . . .

We cannot afford to forget for a moment that the Communist Party is itself our first and most effective instrument in the struggle for the most immediate and the most far-reaching demands and aims of the working class and of the majority of the people. Our Party, together with the Young Communist League, uniting itself with the broadest masses in their daily struggles, must learn better than ever how to build itself stronger and stronger within the democratic front. . . .

This policy is in the direct line of the best traditions of American history. The United States stood in the forefront of world progress and democracy in 1776, despite all difficulties and hardships, with a heroism that formed our basic national character. The United States stood up against world reaction in the War of 1812, and confirmed her democracy and national independence. The United States led world progress in the Civil War of 1861–65, when it wiped out the slave-power and opened the continent for democratic development.

The spirit of Jefferson, Jackson and Lincoln has not departed from the American people. In that spirit we will take our place in the forefront of progress today, facing all the storms aroused by the evil spirits of reaction, shoulder our responsibilities of organizing the world for peace and progress. And the Communist Party will be in the front ranks of the American people in this struggle.

From Earl Browder, *Social and National Security* (New York: Workers Library Publishers, 1938), pp. 19–21, 24, 46.

3. Upton Sinclair's Twelve Principles to "End Poverty in California," 1936

1. God created the natural wealth of the earth for the use of all men, not of a few.
2. God created men to seek their own welfare, not that of masters.
3. Private ownership of tools, a basis of freedom when tools are simple, becomes a basis of enslavement when tools are complex.
4. Autocracy in industry cannot exist alongside democracy in government.
5. When some men live without working, other men are working without living.
6. The existence of luxury in the presence of poverty and destitution is contrary to good morals and sound public policy.
7. The present depression is one of abundance, not of scarcity.
8. The cause of the trouble is that a small class has the wealth, while the rest have the debts.
9. It is contrary to common sense that men should starve because they have raised too much food.
10. The destruction of food or other wealth, or the limitation of production, is economic insanity.
11. The remedy is to give the workers access to the means of production, and let them produce for themselves, not for others.
12. This change can be brought about by action of a majority of the people, and that is the American way.

4. Huey Long and the Share Our Wealth Society, 1935

And, now, what of America? Will we allow the political sports, the high heelers, the wiseacres, and those who ridicule us in our misery and poverty to keep us from organizing these societies in every hamlet so that they may bring back to life this law and custom of God and of this country? Is there a man or woman with a child born on the earth, or who expects ever to have a child born on earth, who is willing to have it raised under the present-day practices of piracy, where it comes into life burdened with debt, condemned to a system of slavery by which the sweat of its brow throughout its existence must go to satisfy the vanity and the luxury of a leisurely few, who can never be made to see that they are destroying the root and branch of the greatest country ever to have risen? Our country is calling; the laws of the Lord are calling; the graves of our forefathers would open today if their occupants could see the bloom and flower of their creation withering and dying because the greed of the financial masters of this country has starved and withheld from mankind those things produced by his own labor. To hell with the ridicule of the wise street-corner politician. Pay no attention to any newspaper or magazine that has sold its columns to perpetuate this crime against the people of America. Save this country. Save mankind. Who can be wrong in such a work, and who cares what consequences

From Upton Sinclair, *I, Governor of California, and How I Ended Poverty: A True Story of the Future* (Los Angeles: Upton Sinclair, 1936), 7.

From *Congressional Record* (May 23, 1935), 74th Congress, 1st Session, vol. 87, pt. 7, pp. 8042–8043.

may come following the mandates of the Lord, of the Pilgrims, of Jefferson, Webster, and Lincoln? He who falls in this fight falls in the radiance of the future. Better to make this fight and lose than to be a party to a system that strangles humanity. . . .

Here is the whole sum and substance of the share-our-wealth movement:

1. Every family to be furnished by the Government a homestead allowance, free of debt, of not less than one-third the average family wealth of the country, which means, at the lowest, that every family shall have the reasonable comforts of life up to a value of from $5,000 to $6,000. No person to have a fortune of more than 100 to 300 times the average family fortune, which means that the limit to fortunes is between $1,500,000 and $5,000,000, with annual capital levy taxes imposed on all above $1,000,000.

2. The yearly income of every family shall be not less than one-third of the average family income, which means that, according to the estimates of the statisticians of the United States Government and Wall Street, no family's annual income would be less than from $2,000 to $2,500. No yearly income shall be allowed to any person larger than from 100 to 300 times the size of the average family income, which means that no person would be allowed to earn in any year more than from $600,000 to $1,800,000, all to be subject to present income-tax laws.

3. To limit or regulate the hours of work to such an extent as to prevent overproduction; the most modern and efficient machinery would be encouraged, so that as much would be produced as possible so as to satisfy all demands of the people, but to also allow the maximum time to the workers for recreation, convenience, education, and luxuries of life.

4. An old-age pension to the persons over 60.

5. To balance agricultural production with what can be consumed according to the laws of God, which includes the preserving and storage of surplus commodities to be paid for and held by the Government for the emergencies when such are needed. Please bear in mind, however, that when the people of America have had money to buy things they needed, we have never had a surplus of any commodity. This plan of God does not call for destroying any of the things raised to eat or wear, nor does it countenance wholesale destruction of hogs, cattle, or milk.

6. To pay the veterans of our wars what we owe them and to care for their disabled.

7. Education and training for all children to be equal in opportunity in all schools, colleges, universities, and other institutions for training in the professions and vocations of life; to be regulated on the capacity of children to learn, and not on the ability of parents to pay the costs. Training for life's work to be as much universal and thorough for all walks in life as has been the training in the arts of killing.

8. The raising of revenue and taxes for the support of this program to come from the reduction of swollen fortunes from the top, as well as for the support of public works to give employment whenever there may be any slackening necessary in private enterprise.

I now ask those who read this circular to help us at once in this work of giving life and happiness to our people—not a starvation dole upon which someone may live in misery from week to week. Before this miserable system of wreckage has destroyed the life germ of respect and culture in our American people let us save what was here, merely by having none too poor and none too rich. The theory of the Share Our Wealth Society is to have enough for all, but not to have one with so much that less than enough remains for the balance of the people.

Please, therefore, let me ask you who read this document—please help this work before it is too late for us to be of help to our people. We ask you now, (1) help to get your neighbor into the work of this society and (2) help get other Share Our Wealth societies started in your county and in adjoining counties and get them to go out to organize other societies.

To print and mail out this circular costs about 60 cents per hundred, or $6 per thousand. Anyone who reads this who wants more circulars of this kind to use in the work, can get them for that price by sending the money to me, and I will pay the printer for him. Better still, if you can have this circular reprinted in your own town or city.

Let everyone who feels he wishes to help in our work start right out and go ahead. One man or woman is as important as any other. Take up the fight! Do not wait for someone else to tell you what to do. There are no high lights in this effort. We have no State managers and no city managers. Everyone can take up the work, and as many societies can be organized as there are people to organize them. One is the same as another. The reward and compensation is the salvation of humanity. Fear no opposition. "He who falls in this fight falls in the radiance of the future!"

5. Father Coughlin Lectures on Social Justice, 1935

It is the primary duty of the government and of all good citizens to abolish conflict between classes and divergent interests. It is our duty to foster and promote harmony among the various ranks of society. No sane man believes in the possibility of creating harmony by bandaging the festered sores of modern industry. No intelligent person preaches effectively against radicalism if he does not first destroy the causes which create it.

Social justice cries aloud to heaven for the workingmen to unite together with the industrialist, not against him. Social justice cries just as loudly to heaven for the industrialist to unite with the workingmen, not against them. The industrialist must recognize that the laborers in his factory are not mere chattels, nor are they to be treated less and insured less against the destructive forces of poverty than are his machines, his lathes and his furnaces which are housed against the inclemencies of all weather and are insured, in season and out of season, against fire and destruction. Labor is not something that can be bought and sold like any piece of merchandise. Labor is something human, something sacred. When you employ a man you are not hiring his muscles or his skill. You are engaging the services of his very soul which gives life and activity to his skill; of a soul that was inspired by Almighty God to love and to bring little babies into the world; of a soul made to the image and likeness of God before Whose common court you will commonly stand. You are em-

From Charles E. Coughlin, *A Series of Lectures on Social Justice* (Royal Oak, Mich.: Radio League of the Little Flower, 1935), pp. 30–33.

ploying the soul of one who is little less than an angel. In one sense you are attempting to purchase the services of something that is unpurchasable, of something that is immortal. The protection of that human life which, leaving all things else, surrenders itself to your just commands, imposes a duty upon you to care for its just rights even more sacredly than you care for your property rights. By all the precepts of social justice, you are forbidden to exclude the laborer from a share in the profits just as much as is this same social justice violated by a propertyless earning class who, in the excesses of communism, perhaps, would demand for themselves not only a share in the use of your produce but a total ownership of your private property.

While we uphold the doctrine of private ownership we will not permit you industrialists to forget the equally sacred doctrine of stewardship. One cannot exist without the other. Destroy the stewardship doctrine and your doctrine of private propertyism is as empty as a sucked egg. The doctrine of stewardship means this: That the earth and the fulness thereof belongs to God; that you who acquire private property have done so only under God; that you cannot exclude from its just usage your fellowmen. Never forget that from the natural resources about us and from the unremitting toil of our citizens springs all wealth. It is a toil that is expended upon either one's own private property or the private property belonging to some other person where capital and labor unite. When labor is willing to supply its brawn and its brain to work at your property, Mr. Industrialist, that same labor cannot be denied a just and living wage which enables it to share reasonably in the produce of American inventions, of American conveniences as well as in decent necessities of life. That is God's doctrine, not mine. You who fight against it are fighting against the Omnipotence of the hand that created you.

I ask you industrialists, if and when you arrive at that point in production where it is necessary to shut down your factories, do you cancel the insurance on your machinery, do you let it become a prey to rust and to destruction? Foolish question for anyone to entertain when, at this very moment—when tomorrow morning, because of these words which I have spoken—you will go running to insurance agencies to purchase riot insurance. Your United States Chamber of Commerce and your other organizations which you have so ably built up for yourselves never had the sagacity and the intelligence to estimate the superior value of the hands, the horned hands, that worked your machines in your factory without which your private property would be worth no more than a scrap heap. You can get along without machinery but you cannot get along without men. More than that, you can get along without advice from your bankers and their outworn philosophy but you dare not attempt to get along without advice from your laborers upon whose purchasing power and good-will you depend.

I am not excoriating you industrialists, nor casting upon you the burden of blame altogether for this condition in which we find ourselves. You, too, have been victimized. But I do castigate you because, like parrots, you have repeated the sophistry of your bankers, your competing manufacturers, if you will, because they manufacture money. You have been foolish enough to let them get away with it. I do blame you for refusing to face facts and for attempting to dwell in realms of fancy. Today your only salvation is identified with the establishment of social justice. Today your only redemption is for capital to join labor instead of perpetuating its harlotry with finance. . . .

See what has occurred in our midst when capital and industry permitted the bankers to dictate the policy of labor. Twelve million unemployed; seven million part time employed; seventeen million Americans living on doles; debts multiplying, taxation mounting—all because you industrialists have conspired with the so-called sound money manufacturers against the farmer and the laborer—and against your own best interests. At this moment these same financiers who wrecked our country are emerging from their hiding places to plead recognition for their plans of restoration.

Do we plan to be placid and apathetic and not unite against them? Are the just and living wage and the rights of labor subjects only to be discussed and not reduced to practice? If you believe in these principles which I have unfolded, I ask you to join the NATIONAL UNION FOR SOCIAL JUSTICE.

6. W. P. Kiplinger Argues "Why Businessmen Fear Washington," 1934

"The indefiniteness of Washington" is a subject of complaint by three out of four business men. They say business itself contains enough natural hazards, and on these are now superimposed a whole new set of political hazards. The objection is not so much to any single policy by itself. The objection is rather to a hodge-podge of policies which are sometimes conflicting, which are explained in different ways by different sets of officials, and which create in business minds the impression that the government is in a great state of indefiniteness and confusion.

This confusion makes fear—not fear of any one policy, but fear that the government mechanism isn't capable of administering all the ramifications of the new order. It's a vague fear, but it is more potent than any tangible situation.

Here are typical comments: "If the government would decide what to do, adopt a course and stick to it, business wouldn't mind and would adjust itself. But the continual changing of policies and the indefiniteness of the future make it hard to run business." "There seems to be no certainty. . . ." "It's hard to have confidence in the continuity of many government policies."

The uncertainties which business men feel about Washington may be broken down into a few major classes:

Inflation: It isn't the *fact* of inflation which is responsible for the worries. It is, rather, the uncertainty of the *time* and the *degree* and the *nature* of it when it comes. Most business men have come to regard inflation as inevitable. Many don't mind it; at least they are prepared to enjoy it while it is on the upgrade for a few years. But so long as they can't foresee when it will be evident, or how fast it will go, or how far, they can't easily plan ahead. Thus they play their cards close, take no chances, fear to expand.

Taxation: It's simple arithmetic to figure that taxpayers must pay the bills for current billions of emergency expenditures. The question is, Which taxpayers? Under this administration the answering finger points pretty much in the direction of business interests. Thus higher taxes of the future will eat into profits, especially "excessive profits."

NRA: Most business men accept the *theory* of government regulation of private industry, but they resent many of the clumsy methods of *application.* Fine schemes thought out at the top don't work well at the bottom. Changes are made from month to month. Different treatments are accorded different lines—different principles. Enforcement of codes is not yet provided in many lines. The heavy hand, the crack-down, is mixed with laxity. Too much has been attempted in too short a time, with too little system at the top to supervise all the intricacies at the bottom.

Toward the agricultural end, the AAA [Agricultural Adjustment Act], the feelings are similar to those toward NRA. There's rather general acceptance by business men of the principle of regulation of production, but there's distrust of the methods. There's fear that the magnitude of the problem is too great for solution by a few minds in Washington.

Labor: The government favors collective bargaining. A majority of business men asset in principle, but want to do it in their own ways, don't want "outside unions," which means A. F. of L. unions. The government doesn't specify "outside unions," but it insists on unions independent of the influence of employers. This naturally plays into the hands of the A. F. of L., because it is the principal organizer of unions. Thus employers are apt to think the government is "pro A. F. of L.," and that it will not protect employers against unreasonable attitudes by unions. . . .

If all the views of all the business men could be condensed into a brief address to Washington, perhaps the address would be something like this:

We know you have a hard job. We recognize the necessity for reforms, some of which must affect us. But you are forcing reforms on us faster than we can digest them. You seem to be experimenting, without knowing what it is that you are trying to find by experimentation. We accept your general leadership in the emergency, but we find your orders vague, and we don't know just what to do. Can't you reduce your program to something a little more definite, and tell us what it is, so that we may know how to plan ahead? If you will do this, we in turn will immediately increase our business, and provide more jobs than you are providing, and end the depression more quickly than you are ending it.

But the government shows few signs of heeding the pleas of business. Consequently from month to month business sentiment is becoming more restive, more impatient, more disposed to abandon its previous timidity. The movement will come to a head some time late this year. It will have nothing to do with the elections. It will not be partisan. It will be evident in a burst of "plain speaking" from various business groups. Some people will call it a "business revolt." Almost any observer can see it coming.

7. Herbert Hoover Comments on the New Deal, 1936

Through four years of experience this New Deal attack upon free institutions has emerged as the transcendent issue in America.

All the men who are seeking for mastery in the world today are using the same weapons. They sing the same songs. They all promise the joys of Elysium without

Excerpts from speech in Denver, October 30, 1936 from the Herbert Hoover Papers, Public Statements File.

effort. But their philosophy is founded on the coercion and compulsory organization of men. True liberal government is founded on the emancipation of men. This
is the issue upon which men are imprisoned and dying in Europe right now . . . centralized personal government disturbs only thinking men and women. But surely
the NRA and the AAA alone, should prove what the New Deal philosophy of government means even to those who don't think.

In these instances the Supreme Court, true to their oaths to support the Constitution, saved us temporarily. But Congress in obedience to their oaths should never have
passed these acts. The President should never have signed them. But far more important than that, if these men were devoted to the American system of liberty they never
would have proposed acts based on the coercion and compulsory organization of men.

Freedom does not die from frontal attack. It dies because men in power no
longer believe in a system based upon Liberty. . . .

. . . will Mr. Roosevelt reply in plain words?

Does he propose to revive the nine acts which the Supreme Court has rejected
as invasions of the safeguards of free men?

Has he abandoned his implied determination to change the Constitution? Why
not tell the American people before election what change he proposes? Does he intend to stuff the Court itself? . . .

Does Mr. Roosevelt not admit all this in his last report on the state of the Union:
"We have built up new instruments of public power" which he admits could "provide
shackles for the liberties of the people." Does freedom permit any man or any government any such power? Have the people ever voted for these shackles? . . .

The conviction of our fathers was that all these freedoms come from the Creator
and that they can be denied by no man or no government or no New Deal. They were
spiritual rights of men. The prime purpose of liberal government is to enlarge and not
to destroy these freedoms. It was for that purpose that the Constitution of the United
States was enacted. For that reason we demand that the safeguards of freedom shall
be upheld. It is for this reason that we demand that this country should turn its direction from a system of personal centralized government to the ideals of liberty.

8. Southern Democrats Erode the New Deal Coalition, 1938

Mr. Wilcox I regard the wage and hour bill, in its present form as reported to the
House, the most serious threat to representative democracy which has been proposed in this generation. It proposes a bureaucratic control of business and industry
and a dictatorship over labor which, if enacted, must ultimately result in a destruction of the right of collective bargaining and which may easily reduce labor to a
state of economic slavery.

It proposes the establishment of a Federal bureau or board with autocratic and
dictatorial power beyond any ever attempted in any government of free people. It
would place in the hands of a little group of Federal bureaucrats the power to regulate the earnings of millions of American citizens. And since, in the words of one of

From "Debate on the Fair Labor Standards Act," *Congressional Record* (December 13, 1938), 75th Congress, 2d session, vol. 88, pp. 1387–1389, 1402, 1404.

its sponsors, the bill, as drawn, is only a modest beginning, the Federal bureau once established will soon be extended to cover every business, every industry, and every man who works for a living in America. . . .

Then there is another matter of great importance in the South, and that is the problem of our Negro labor. There has always been a difference in the wage scale of white and colored labor. So long as Florida people are permitted to handle the matter, this delicate and perplexing problem can be adjusted; but the Federal Government knows no color line and of necessity it cannot make any distinction between the races. We may rest assured, therefore, that when we turn over to a Federal bureau or board the power to fix wages, it will prescribe the same wage for the Negro that it prescribes for the white man. Now, such a plan might work in some sections of the United States but those of us who know the true situation know that it just will not work in the South. You cannot put the Negro and the white man on the same basis and get away with it. Not only would such a situation result in grave social and racial conflicts but it would also result in throwing the Negro out of employment and in making him a public charge. There just is not any sense in intensifying this racial problem in the South, and this bill cannot help but produce such a result.

Many of our northern friends may honestly think that by forcing a uniform wage scale upon the South they are doing the Negro a real service. But those who know the facts know that when employers are forced to pay the same wage to the Negro that is paid to the white man the Negro will not be employed. This in turn will mean that he will be thrown onto the relief roll to be fed in idleness. This is just another instance of the well-intentioned but misguided interference of our uninformed neighbors in a delicate racial problem that is gradually being solved by the people of the South. This bill, like the antilynching bill, is another political gold brick for the Negro, but this time the white laborer is also included in the scheme.

ESSAYS

These essays touch on important sources of opposition to the New Deal. In the first essay, Alan Brinkley suggests that the arguments of Long and Coughlin drew on contemporary concerns about state and corporate power, and on broader anxieties about the coming of urban industrial society that reached back to the nineteenth century. In the second essay, Colin Gordon argues that business opposition to the New Deal reflected not so much philosophical or ideological objections to political intervention as it did shortsighted and pragmatic reactions to the costs of failures of New Deal programs.

Dissidents and Demagogues

ALAN BRINKLEY

The sudden rise of [Huey] Long and [Charles] Coughlin to national prominence raised many questions among their contemporaries, but none so frequent or compelling as a simple one: why? Why did so many Americans find these two men appealing? What

From *Voices of Protest* by Alan Brinkley. Copyright © 1982 by Alan Brinkley. Reprinted by permission of Alfred A. Knopf, Inc.

did their political power represent? Certain answers were obvious. Long and Coughlin were flamboyant, charismatic personalities who seemed to invite notice whatever they were doing. They exercised rare skill and imagination in using the media—and particularly the radio—to make themselves known. They were, in short, hard to ignore. And their style and visibility were prerequisites to their power.

But style and visibility alone were not enough. Many public figures manage to draw attention to themselves. Only a few move from there to the creation of powerful, sustained national movements. Personality, eloquence, media skills: all were for Long and Coughlin only the most obvious sources of a popularity that rested ultimately on a far deeper and broader set of concerns—on the evocation of a distinctive ideology.

The ideological content of the Long and Coughlin messages was often muddled and simplistic, at times nearly incoherent. Neither man was a careful or sophisticated thinker, and neither had much patience with complexities or ambiguities. Perhaps it should not have been surprising that, of all aspects of their movements, it was ideology that received the least serious attention from their critics. To their supporters, however, Long and Coughlin offered a message of real meaning. They provided, first, an affirmation of threatened values and institutions, and a vision of a properly structured society in which those values and institutions could thrive. They suggested, second, an explanation of the obstacles to this vision, a set of villains and scapegoats upon whom it was possible to blame contemporary problems. And they offered, finally, a prescription for reform, resting upon a carefully restricted expansion of the role of government. Some observers dismissed it all as meaningless and, as such, ominous: a demagogic attempt to delude the public with empty, impractical promises. They were not entirely incorrect. But the Long and Coughlin ideologies were not simply creations of the moment, designed to exploit current concerns. They rested on some of the oldest and deepest impulses in American political life. . . .

The most troubling feature of modern industrial society, Long and Coughlin maintained, was the steady erosion of the individual's ability to control his own destiny. Large, faceless institutions; wealthy, insulated men; vast networks of national and international influence: all were exercising power and controlling wealth that more properly belonged in the hands of ordinary citizens. These same forces had created the economic crisis of the 1930s and threatened, if left unchecked, to perpetuate it. Out of such concerns emerged the central element of the messages of both men: an affirmation of the ideal of community. Power, they argued, should not reside in distant, obscure places; the individual should not have to live in a world in which he could not govern or even know the forces determining his destiny. Instead, the nation should aspire to a set of political and economic arrangements in which authority rested securely in the community, where it could be observed and, in some measure, controlled by its citizens. Concentrated wealth and concentrated power had damaged the nation's social fabric; a system of decentralized power, limited ownership, and small-scale capitalism could restore it.

Neither Long nor Coughlin offered any precise definition of what a proper community should look like: how large it should be, how it should be structured. That was not the point. A community, they suggested, was less a particular place than a network of associations, a set of economic and social relationships in which the individual played a meaningful role and in which each citizen maintained control of his own livelihood and destiny. Such a community could exist in a small town, in an agricultural region, within a large city. What was important was that its essential institutions remain small and accessible enough to prevent abuses of power and excessive accumulations of wealth.

The community ideal had, to be sure, certain collective implications. Not only did Long and Coughlin explicitly denounce untrammeled self-interest—what Coughlin called the "outworn and impractical" doctrines of " 'free competition,' and 'rugged individualism' and 'laissez-faire.' " They asked, as well, for a redefinition of the concept of property ownership. No individual, they argued, should be allowed to accumulate so much wealth that his ownership of it became injurious to the rest of the community; nor shall he be permitted to use his wealth in ways that were harmful to his neighbors. The rights of ownership were not absolute. "We can allow our people to accumulate and grow prosperous," Long said in 1934. But "beyond that point where the accumulation of [property] becomes a menace to our society and the well-being of others no one should be permitted to go." Coughlin was even clearer. "Private ownership of private fortunes does not argue their unrestrained, uncurtailed and unlimited private use," he said in one of his first political sermons. "To put it in a way so that the humblest in this audience can understand," he later explained, "by the fact that I own an automobile, it does not argue that I may drive it on the wrong side of the street or park the car on your front lawn."

But if the vision smacked of collectivism, it was a collectivism of a decidedly unradical kind. Though Long and Coughlin denounced the tyrannical excesses of modern capitalism, they remained committed to a determinedly capitalist, middle-class vision. What, after all, was Long promising to those who supported his Share Our Wealth Plan but a guarantee to every family of "a home and the comforts of a home, including such conveniences as automobile and radio," all "free of debt"? As if material acquisitions were a part of Catholic religious dogma, Coughlin told his radio audience that "The Church is anxious for the workingman and the farmer to own his own home." "To multiply private ownership and not impede it," he explained, was a "sensible, socially just and American" approach to economic problems.

Essential to the survival of the community, therefore, was an economy of small-scale, local enterprise. How important such an economy was to Long and Coughlin was apparent in the frequency with which both men lamented its disappearance. One by one, they complained, the autonomous local institutions that sustained a meaningful community life were vanishing in the face of distant, impersonal forces. Small farmers, for example, had been transformed, as Coughlin put it, "from a happy, prosperous army of God-fearing men" to pitiful figures who must "throw themselves at the feet of the Government and beg for relief." Local financial institutions—what Long described as "the little banks in the counties and the parishes" and what Coughlin termed the "small bankers outside the great ring of Wall Street"—were in dire peril. So were the "small industrialists," who had, Coughlin claimed, "been bought out or . . . destroyed by questionable competition." Similarly troubling was the erosion of the local press. Coughlin spoke darkly of "the mounting tide of direct bank ownership of the nation's daily newspapers," while Long's *American Progress* charged that the "money powers" had come to "control the editorial policy of almost every publication in the United States." They were "only allowed to give us such information as the big fellows want us to have." The implications of this change were particularly ominous: without an independent press, freedom itself was in jeopardy. "The small rural newspapers," one Long supporter argued, "have the greatest opportunity today that they have ever had."

Nothing, however, more clearly symbolized the decline of meaningful community life than the plight of the local merchant. No institution had been more central to the community than the small, independently owned store; and none created greater anxiety when it began to flounder and disappear. It was a problem that concerned residents of rural and urban areas alike. In agricultural communities, the small merchant had traditionally been more than a supplier of goods. He had served, too, as a crucial instrument of credit, a banker, a purchaser of farm produce; his store had been a gathering place, at times a community's only social center. In larger towns and cities, neighborhood shops often catered to the tastes of particular racial or ethnic groups, to members of certain occupations, to residents of homogeneous urban enclaves. They reinforced a sense of community within the impersonal urban world. The arrival of the chain store, the mail-order house, and the other institutions of modern merchandising were, therefore, a source of particular alarm, one that Long, Coughlin, and their supporters cited repeatedly. "Where is the corner groceryman?" Long cried in a Senate speech. "He is gone or going. . . . [The] little independent businesses operated by middle class people . . . have been fading out . . . as the concentration of wealth grows like a snowball.". . .

When Long and Coughlin railed against the decline of the local merchant, therefore, they were doing more than appealing to a particular interest group. They were expressing a concern with which even the least politically sensitive American could identify; they were describing a visible threat to the survival of a meaningful local existence, a danger to what one supporter of Father Coughlin called "the foundation so welded together by the independent merchants, forming the foundations of boroughs and towns, and cities." They were evoking, in short, the most compelling symbol of the debilitation of the community. . . .

General concerns about the erosion of community life and the concentration of wealth and power in distant places did not alone, however, constitute a political ideology. Only by fusing such images with specific explanations of the problem could Long and Coughlin hope to translate the vague anxieties of their audiences into active political commitments. To accomplish that, they offered—with great vigor and relish—a cast of clearly identifiable villains. There was nothing surprising about whom and what they chose. If centralized wealth and power were the problems, then it was those in possession of that wealth and power who were to blame.

Their messages were not identical. They did not, for example, always attack the same people. Coughlin, for the most part, directed his hostility toward the bankers and financiers whom he believed to be in control of the monetary system, men such as J. P. Morgan, Andrew Mellon, Bernard Baruch, Eugene Meyer, Ogden Mills. Long denounced them too, but, far more often than Coughlin, he added to his litany men identified less with finance than simply with great wealth: John D. Rockefeller (who was perhaps his most frequent target), the du Ponts, the Vanderbilts, the Astors.

They differed, too, in the style and tone of their attacks. Coughlin's descriptions of his enemies tended to remain fuzzy and abstract, more ominous, perhaps, for their lack of personal detail. He ridiculed his targets for their arrogance. "The divine intelligence of the international bankers," he proclaimed scornfully, "has found its deserved place with the theory of the divine right of kings. Both are putrid corpses." He denounced their deviousness and malignity. "Like grinning devils," he cried, "there stand at the gates of this Eden of plenty the protectors of privately manufactured money." But even when he mentioned villains by name, he seldom discussed personalities.

Long, by contrast, reveled in vivid personal abuse. At times savagely, at times almost whimsically, he assailed his targets not just for their power, but for their personal habits, their appearances, and their life-styles. They were, as he described them, fat, slothful, profligate, at times even ridiculous men, "pigs swilling in the trough of luxury," who were too concerned with their own "ease and comfort" to take notice of the plights of others. Cartoons in the *American Progress* time and again presented graphic illustrations of this image. Florid men with puffy cheeks, heavy eyelids, and enormous bellies served as visual symbols of excess. Dressed in flamboyant vested suits (usually with gold watch chains and diamond tie pins), they sat smugly counting their money and chuckling over their nefarious victories.

When J. P. Morgan traveled to Europe for the hunting season, Long's newspaper ran a biting front-page account of "poor Mr. Morgan . . . hard at work over in Scotland" ruthlessly shooting down "little birds." When Huey sought to illustrate how even the wealthy could live comfortably within the limits envisioned by his wealth redistribution plan, he presented a preposterous "annual budget" for a family of four to prove that survival was possible on an income below one million dollars a year. Among the "essential" items it listed were "1 new suit a day at $100," "new set of jewelry per season at $10,000," "upkeep of doggy . . . $17,405," and "1 suit of B.V.D.'s a day at $10.". . .

The contrast was unmistakable. Coughlin evoked an image of cunning, manipulative, miserly men working carefully and artfully to maintain their power. Long . . . spoke of bloated and sybaritic plutocrats wallowing in sensual luxury. The one picture was of pinched, haughty, cold-blooded schemers, an Irish-Catholic image of puritanical Protestants or Jews. The other was of self-indulgent hedonists, a vaguely fundamentalist view of the sinful excesses of modern urban life.

Whatever their differences, however, Long and Coughlin shared a central concern. These "plutocrats" were dangerous chiefly for the remoteness and inaccessibility of their power. Local problems were not usually the fault of local people or institutions, they were suggesting; the blame more properly lay with what Long described as the "distant power centers," or what Coughlin termed "the hidden forces which have conspired against the common people of the world." Oppressed factory workers, for example, were engaged in a struggle not with their immediate superiors, the local factory owners and managers; their real enemies were the remote financial moguls who were exploiting workers and managers alike. "Your actual boss, Mr. Laboring Man, is not too much to blame," Coughlin advised workers in his audience. "If you must strike, strike in an intelligent manner not by laying down your tools but by raising your voices against a financial system that keeps you today and will keep you tomorrow in breadless bondage." From Long came a similar message. "Neither the owners of the factories nor the men who work in them are responsible for this trouble which impends in your home city," he told laborers in

Akron, Ohio. The real enemies were the wealthy tyrants of Wall Street, before whom, as an *American Progress* reader complained, "the small manufacturer is suffering both depression and suppression."

The problem did not, however, stop at Wall Street. As if to give even more forceful expression to their warnings about distant, inaccessible forces, Long and Coughlin emphasized, too, a dangerous link between the American financial establishment and the larger and stronger international banking community. The flow of power from local organizations to national institutions in New York was only the first step. From these Eastern establishments, power flowed on to London, Paris, and other European capitals, where it was exercised with even greater callousness.

The influence of the international bankers, like the influence of their American counterparts, stretched far back into the nineteenth century, as Coughlin in particular often explained. As early as 1816, he claimed, the "international Rothschilds" had been subtly directing the monetary policies of Great Britain; and by the 1860s, the Bank of England had become a mere tool of the great banking families of Europe. At the same time, these plutocrats had begun to extend their control to America. Their influence had been responsible for the tragic deflation of the currency after the Civil War. ("It will not do to allow the greenback, as it is called, to circulate as money," explained a circular Coughlin claimed they had distributed at the time, "as we cannot control that.") And the same international bankers had helped suppress every effort to reform the currency system for decades thereafter. . . .

It was hardly surprising, therefore, that the 1935 controversy over American entry into the World Court, in which both Long and Coughlin played prominent roles, crystallized in the minds of many of their followers a host of resentments—against the war, against international bankers, against the British, against Wall Street, against the whole process by which power was flowing into distant and malevolent institutions. "America is being betrayed by the Administration," one angry Long supporter charged during the World Court debate, "and promoted by the evil influence of the Proenglish. The American people don't want any entanglement with Europe. If we could drop all exports to and imports from Europe we would soon climb out of the Depression."

As the World Court controversy suggested, there was another disturbing aspect to the problem of centralized power. American government itself, Long and Coughlin charged, was becoming subservient to the great financial interests. The problem was not a new one. Ever since Alexander Hamilton, they argued, selfish plutocrats had battled the defenders of the people for control of political institutions. At times, they had succeeded—in 1873, for example, when they pressured Congress to agree to "the illegal outlawing of silver," as Coughlin put it; or in 1896, when they had combined to defeat William Jennings Bryan. Even greater blows had occurred in more recent years. In 1913, Woodrow Wilson had steered the Federal Reserve Banking Act to passage; few institutions more clearly symbolized unwanted concentration of power than the Federal Reserve Board the act had created. It was, Coughlin claimed, "the Temple of the moneychangers . . . the Temple which ruins the lives of millions who came as devotees to worship at its altar but remained its slaves in the courtyard of its misery." Most cruelly of all, the Great Depression, a result of centralized wealth and power, was spawning government policies that served to reinforce them. Herbert Hoover had been a willing tool of the plutocrats throughout his Administration, Long and Coughlin charged, establishing as his principal agent for recovery the Reconstruction Finance Corporation, through which the government loaned money not to the common citizens who needed it but to the great financial and industrial interests whose only concern was the preservation of their own hegemony.

Nor had the financial parasites loosened their grip in the first years of the Roosevelt Administration. Whatever Long and Coughlin thought of the President himself, they were not pleased with some of the men he had invited to participate in his Administration. Roosevelt had not been in office a month before Long began charging on the floor of the Senate that the Treasury Department had fallen under the control of "members of the Morgan House." Coughlin, similarly, denounced Secretary of the Treasury William Woodin as "the beneficiary of the Morgan blood money." Particularly offensive to Long and Coughlin was the apparent influence of financier Bernard Baruch—"the heeled henchman of Wall Street," Long called him; "fullback Barney," Coughlin described him, "whose agile legs had sidestepped the conventions of democracy from the days of Harding to those of Hoover." The new Administration had pledged itself to protect the influence of the common man; but the "gamblers of Wall Street aided by our great banks," a Virginia man wrote the *American Progress* early in 1934, were still "trying to enmesh our government." As a Coughlin supporter from Chicago warned Harold Ickes in 1933: "THE MONEY CHANGERS ARE STILL ON THE JOB, FIGHTING WITH THE IMMENSE POWER THEY STILL WIELD IN EVERY AVENUE OF LIFE. These forces of darkness are using every subtle influence to undermine . . . President Roosevelt.". . .

Government was not only part of the problem, however; it was central to the solution. Only government was powerful enough to provide the needed counterforce to the "financial plutocracy." Only government could protect the community and the individual against the menacing institutions of the modern economy.

Yet those committed to a decentralization of wealth and power were no more eager to see the state encroach upon their lives than they were to accept the influence of the great private interests. The picture Long and Coughlin presented of an active, responsible government was, therefore, carefully drawn to eliminate such concerns. Public institutions could, they claimed, be both forceful and unobtrusive; they could protect the individual and the community from the threatening financial powers without becoming intrusive powers themselves.

This idea of government power as both expansive and strictly limited found its clearest expression in the economic proposals of both Long and Coughlin—simple, self-sustaining reforms that would, they insisted, require no large bureaucratic structures. Long's Share Our Wealth Plan called for a clean, clear set of tax codes that would alone destroy concentrated wealth and erect no menacing power center in its place. Coughlin, similarly, based his hopes for change on what he considered simple, unobtrusive monetary reforms. Government would change the composition of the currency and the structure of the banking system. It would then permit the natural workings of the economy to produce and maintain a proper distribution of power, so that the wealth of America, as he often said, would "flow freely into every home." Each plan, in other words, envisioned a substantial increase in the power of government. But it was to be a largely negative, almost passive power. Government was to protect the individual, enhance the vitality of the community. It was not to become an intrusive behemoth.

Indeed, both men were outspoken in denouncing the expansion of federal power that they detected during the first years of the Depression. Coughlin decried "the harrowing growth of bureaucracy for the maintenance of which . . . the national liberty has been jeopardized." The "age-old curse" of such growth, he warned, was "the tendency of bureaucracy to become a law unto itself. The very nature of its development makes inroads upon the rights and liberties of citizens; its ultimate goal is inevitably some type of tyranny." Long, similarly, argued that the proliferation of government agencies and commissions was "contrary to the American system," was "tangling up the people's business to where they did not know how to handle it."

Such concerns were crucial in shaping the apparently conflicting attitudes of Long and Coughlin toward Franklin Roosevelt and his New Deal. Both men attacked Roosevelt constantly for not doing enough: for not acting to curb the power of the rich, for not reconstituting the currency, for not redistributing wealth. But they denounced him equally vigorously for doing too much: for creating programs of overbearing intrusiveness, for constructing a ponderous bureaucracy to meddle in what were properly local and individual matters. The National Recovery Administration, for example, had failed to act forcefully enough to curb corporate abuses, had become a tool of the moneyed interests. But perhaps even more disturbing, Long and Coughlin agreed, was the very concept of the NRA and other New Deal programs, which gave to the government dangerously excessive powers. The NRA, Long charged, was a plan "to regiment business and labor much more than anyone did in Germany and Italy. . . . The Farleys and Johnsons combed the land with agents, inspectors, supervisors, detectives, secretaries, assistants, etc., all armed with the power to arrest and send to jail whomever they found out not living up to some rule in one of these 900 catalogues." Coughlin found similarly disturbing the activities of the Public Works Administration, whose authority to acquire property and employ workers, he claimed, suggested "a radical leaning toward international socialism or sovietism."

Even when other criticisms of the New Deal evoked only a lukewarm public response, attacks upon its intrusiveness produced passionate agreement. "N.R.A. and A.A.A. are tyranny," a Long supporter complained to Harold Ickes. "I have lost my status as a free man. I must obey laws not made by any representative of mine." A Pennsylvania man, a self-proclaimed "conservative," reminded the President in a letter, "At least Huey Long and Father Coughlin are not advocates of the Government going into business in competition with its citizens." A disgruntled Mississippi reader of the *American Progress* moaned, "Now hasn't our new DICTATOR President, Mr. Roosevelt, kind of messed things up . . . in putting in effect all the wide Mussolini powers the congress gave him?" (Long's reputation as "dictator" of his home state made such statements seem sharply incongruous. But the contradictions appeared not to bother him and seemed to be lost on most of his supporters.)

It was not only individuals who were threatened by the expanding federal presence, but state and local governments. The rapid growth of the national bureaucracy imperiled the very basis of the Constitutional system. "A definite plan is afoot," the *American Progress* warned, "to end the sovereign powers of the states and to destroy the republic and substitute a social democracy." Coughlin spoke approvingly of "a very deep and growing feeling which is gaining headway constantly that the States should not be interfered with by the Federal Government in working out their own social welfare and educational programs." Roosevelt, a Coughlin supporter in Chicago charged, "radically is changing our form of government, usurping Federal power and obliterating state boundaries." Warned an *American Progress* reader, "A blueprint for the new form of government abolishing States Rights has been drawn up and published by Henry A. Wallace."

The imagery of these concerns was striking. The government bureaucracy was ominous because of its "craftiness," its cunning and "deceit." It was jeopardizing the citizen's "status as a free man." It was threatening to produce "tyranny," "slavery," "dictatorship." It was, in short, behaving exactly like the great private financial interests that oppressed the common man. An overbearing government, no less than a tyrannical plutocracy, endangered the individual and the community. Only by carefully defining and limiting the role of the state in any program of reform could the nation escape replacing one oppressive centralizing force with another.

Business vs. the New Deal

COLIN GORDON

By most estimates, business either opposed the Roosevelt administration from the outset or at least came to bitterly resent its policies by the late 1930s. Colorful illustrations of this theme are sprinkled throughout contemporary and historical accounts: Hanna Coal executive George Humphrey always spelt Roosevelt with a lowercase "r"; dinner guests of banker J. P. Morgan were forbidden to mention the "R" word at all. The easy assumption that (as contemporary magazine articles announced) "Businessmen Fear Washington" or "They Hate Roosevelt," however, makes for poor and inexact history. . . . New Deal policies were essentially business-friendly measures in progressive clothing. Yet at each turn of the New Deal, some business interests were vocal and insistent in their opposition. This basic contradiction, inconsistency, or fickleness deserves explanation. Generally, scholars have confused the question of whether the New Deal served business needs with the question of whether the New Deal did so *successfully*, and they have assumed (in narrowly functional reasoning) that any business opposition can be taken as evidence that New Deal policies were antibusiness. As I argue below, business-driven political programs simply failed, in large part because "business" rarely agreed on the benefits of such programs and almost always agreed that such programs were too costly.

In its broadest sense, business opposition to politics is generated not by a natural antagonism but by the fact that business and the state share the task of economic governance so closely. . . . Of course, the culture of the American political economy is largely an exercise in denying this close and dependent relationship. Even as politics infuse every level of economic activity, business interests and government officials guard the myth that such intervention is intended only to "level the playing field," to restrain "unfair competition," or to ensure that free markets have room to operate. In this atmosphere, business support for the New Deal could not survive long. Those whom the New Deal disappointed suddenly saw federal power as a threat rather than a solution; those whom the New Deal helped were inclined to take credit themselves and see politics as a costly obstacle to further growth and prosperity.

The economic conditions of the 1930s and the political stakes of the New Deal magnified these tensions. The New Deal's inconsistencies and cross-purposes reflected the disparate demands of different interests, all of whom championed their own pet panaceas and opposed or misunderstood others. Consumerist strategies designed to inflate purchasing power collided with productionist strategies that inflated prices. Federal wage and welfare standards encouraged inflation rather than redistribution. And conservative fiscal policy and anticompetitive regulation pulled the dollar in opposite directions. These dilemmas confounded policymakers, who had neither the institutional experience nor the practical inclination to deal coherently with problems of demand management, industrial regulation, labor law, and fiscal policy. In all, business opposition to the New Deal was only peripherally concerned with the abstract issues of limited government, free markets, or constitutional fealty in which such opposition was invariably couched. Business counted among its ranks political realists, ideological cynics, inveterate optimists, and shortsighted opportunists—an unsettling combination that magnified expectations and frustrations.

Endemic contradictions and changing conditions constantly shifted the balance of business support and opposition. New Dealers were willing to accept a degree of business discontent (which, after all, girded populist images and mass support at election time) but were by no means willing to write off the patronage of important industrial interests. . . . And although its policies were staunchly (if not always effectively) probusiness, the Roosevelt administration did not always seek or receive backing from the same firms and industries, which went through cycles of political solicitation, confusion, disenchantment, and accommodation. Many who supported or opposed particular policies made a virtue out of necessity and elaborated or justified their positions with (often misleading) rhetorical flourish. And on the heels of particularly difficult or compromising political decisions, business support often narrowed considerably only to expand or regroup around new issues or realities.

In all, business response to the New Deal was shaped by the uneven impact of New Deal policies, changes in the conditions under which early political deals were first made, and a growing appreciation of the costs of political solutions. More specifically, business opposition to the New Deal can be traced to four sources. First, business-minded regulatory policies failed consistently. Because such experiments entailed financial and managerial sacrifices, few were willing to prolong them if they proved unproductive. Second, as the focus of the National Recovery Act (NRA) narrowed to a more coercive and costly emphasis on labor policy, many firms balked at the implicit threat to managerial power. This was true of those who entirely rejected the premises of New Deal labor policy and of those who accepted the logical link between the NRA and the Wagner Act but resented the subsequent loss of discretion and flexibility. Third, the regional jealousies that inspired New Deal federalism were not easily erased. New federal powers altered but did not erase patterns of interstate and regional competition. And fourth, the central premise of labor-driven regulation—that labor costs would increase across an industry at the expense of marginal producers and consumers—was undermined by the reality and threat of international competition. . . .

The New Deal did not age well. Most applauded it initially (although few went so far as one executive, who dubbed Roosevelt "the greatest leader since Jesus Christ"). But almost immediately, the economic and administrative chaos of the NRA began to make enemies. As Hoover predicted bitterly and accurately in 1933, support for the New Deal would collapse "when the scared business man beg[an] to see . . . that his high hopes of escape from the Sherman Act into the heaven of assured high profits [was] illusory." Firms and industries had a contingent faith in the NRA and sharply different stakes in its success. While few objected outright to the act, as J.P. Morgan partner Russell Leffingwell noted, most were "subject to repeated disappointments." Business resented the failures rather than the premises of recovery policy. "Business wants the codes, in spite of all the complaining one hears," reasoned a furniture manufacturer in late 1934, adding that "men really want what the codes promise, and kick because the promises have not been kept." Although played up in contemporary and historical accounts as a revolt of oppressed consumers and small businesses, this shift in attitude reflected little more than an end to the delusion that business would voluntarily shoulder the costs necessary to bring order to their respective corners of the industrial economy.

Business doubts also reflected fundamentally different political demands and aspirations within and among industries and the increasingly onerous (in light of its absent or elusive benefits) burden of federal regulation. The NRA was an attempt, as Ellis Hawley notes, "to give 'something' to everyone, institutionalize the divisions, and avoid, at least for the time being, a definite commitment." But superficially common goals obscured substantial disagreement. In naive isolation, each NRA code satisfied the demands of leading firms in a particular industry. But together the codes created innumerable problems, including increased prices, contradictory jurisdiction, and inconsistent interpretation. As a chemical executive noted typically, "I have only sympathy for NRA to the extent of the chemical code." The codes also generated opposition within industries. New Deal programs benefited some interests at the expense of others and left the price of organization to be paid by regional or marginal competitors. "Under cover of the national emergency," admitted Teagle of Standard Oil, "interested parties have tried to impose on other members of their industry additional costs and other restrictions to do away with advantages previously held by competitors."

In the long run, both marginal and leading firms balked at the coercion implicit in New Deal policies. The former resented the intent of federal regulation; the latter resented its failures. Business, as Hawley notes, "worried constantly about creating an apparatus that might be used against them." Acceptance of the price of federal regulation was always a short-term strategy; as an oil executive explained to Interior Secretary Wilbur in 1929, "What [business interests] want is something of a temporary nature that will pull them out of the hole and then they want to be left alone." Neither Hoover nor Roosevelt, both of whom appreciated the inherent fickleness of business politics, were able to satisfy those who continued to demand regulatory compulsion and those who had tired of federal intervention. In 1933, most accepted Chamber of Commerce Director Silas Strawn's observation that "a planned economy cannot be effective unless the executive is vested with the power to enforce it." Over the next few months, many came also to agree with Strawn's warning that the costs of such power might resemble a "dictatorship such as they have in Russia, Italy and Germany." Business wanted a superhero to swoop down and set things right. What they got was a police force that was neither particularly effective nor likely to abandon the beat in the near future.

The New Deal had a few consistent supporters and a few consistent critics, but most business sentiment reflected a short-term jumble of opportunism, anxiety, and disillusion. . . .

In the end, even those who were not slighted or disappointed by the New Deal were likely to add their voices to the chorus of opposition. After scrambling for political solutions to the Depression, those interests that showed any recovery after 1932 and 1935 were quick to disavow political assistance and to accuse the New Deal of obstructing further gains. Like a drunk rescued from the gutter, suggested Robert LaFollette, business resented both the implication that they had needed any help and the fact that their rescuer had found them in such a degraded condition. "As soon as the businessman sees a slight improvement," complained another senator, "he keeps shouting 'the government must get out of business.' Businessmen do nothing but bellyache." The boundary between politics and markets was easily shifted in such a way that successful political solutions were seen as triumphs of the market and market failures were ascribed to political interference. Such willful delusion allowed business and its sympathizers to see the crash as the culmination of political errors, the early NRA as the capstone of self-regulation, and the later NRA as the leading edge of socialism.

As glimmers of recovery broke through in 1936 and 1937, the legislative innovations of 1933–35 were cast aside as relics of a desperate time. "The life preserver which is so necessary when the ship is sinking," observed Harper Silbey of the Chamber of Commerce, "becomes a heavy burden when man is back on dry land." The most tangible target of business outcry was the cost of New Deal programs, including union wages and taxes. After 1935, organized business made a fetish of "limited government" and "balanced budgets" (catch phrases that served as useful political abstractions for more belligerent positions on social security or workers' rights and obscured the persistence of a regressive tax system). This fiscal conservatism was transparently self-serving; it masked a spate of more specific objections to New Deal policy and a general unwillingness to pay for programs whose benefits were elusive or insufficient. In all, it was the inefficacy of politics, rather than any intellectual objection to political intervention, that caused the hiccup of fierce libertarianism after 1935. . . .

. . . Of the costs associated with New Deal policies, the most troubling for business was the problem of labor and labor organization.

New Deal labor law supplemented the NRA's anticompetitive policies with the "police" power of industrial unions. Although many industries and firms supported the Wagner and Social Security Acts, their reasons for doing so were dissimilar and often contradictory. Competitive, labor-intensive firms saw federal labor law as a means of flushing out marginal and regional cutthroat competitors. Less competitive mass-production firms weighed their antagonism toward any form of organized labor against the real threat of genuinely radical unionization and unhappily encouraged efforts to direct the labor movement into business-minded channels. Capital-intensive (often internationalist) firms, which stood to bear little increase in labor costs, saw higher wages and union recognition as practical solutions to industrial conflict and the disappearance of mass purchasing power. Others clung to the last point as well, albeit with some cynicism. "The thinking of the employer group," noted one labor economist drily, ". . . might be summarized by saying that they believed strongly in other employers paying high wages."

With starkly different reasons for supporting or opposing elements of the New Deal's stance on labor, employers were extremely sensitive to the form and administration of collective bargaining and welfare law. Because the direct and managerial costs of labor policy were so great, any hint that its various benefits might not be forthcoming provoked a vehement response. And many employers who were threatened by either uniform industry standards or the increased power of labor within their gates objected to labor-driven regulation from the outset. "Loss of control over labor relations [under Section 7a of the NRA] . . . was a bitter pill to swallow," as the editors of *Fortune* observed, "but the coating of price regulation was thick and sweet and the pill went down." After the NRA, with labor policy the sole source of regulation, the pill was even harder to digest.

Even sympathetic employers based their acceptance of New Deal labor policy on different goals, perceptions, and horizons. Few who accepted the immediate utility of union wages as a means of quelling competitive pressures or spurring consumption also accepted any longer-term commitment to workers' rights. As the weight of the Depression began to lift, employers began to rethink their concessions to organized labor. By the later 1930s (and certainly after 1945), the threats of chronic underconsumption, radical unionism, and competitive chaos were less urgent. Yet as employers soon realized, the political and economic power that made it possible for unions to rationalize or organize labor costs also made it difficult to remove or restrain those unions once their organizational utility was exhausted. In the longer run, regulatory policies premised on high labor costs would not survive economic internationalization, and only in instances where the equalization of costs among rival firms overwhelmed issues of global competitiveness were such policies seriously pursued.

A few industries, such as coal (which until very recently faced no international competitive pressures) continued to pursue unionization as a guard against regional competition and as a substitute for the organization of firms. Some, notably steel and autos, integrated CIO unions into the competitive ethos of their respective industries and pragmatically embraced the regulatory and antiradical potential of conservative industrial unionism. Others, including paragons of corporate liberalism such as GE, followed their superficially conciliatory policies of the 1920s and 1930s with brutal antiunion offensives. Regionally, union strength remained uneven, and unionism in regionally competitive industries (such as textiles) did little to even out state-to-state disparity in labor costs. Accordingly, states moved to unify costs not by supporting federal law but by chipping away at its authority at the state level. In turn, the federal government was pressed to prevent states from jockeying for competitive advantage by undermining the Wagner Act; in 1947, the federal government leveled the playing field again with the Taft-Hartley Act.

In short, many business interests accepted the immediate organizational and regulatory logic of federal labor policy but failed to appreciate its ultimate costs and inflexibility. Many underestimated the impact of unionization on managerial power and, when labor strategies either failed or became unnecessary, found it difficult to backtrack to the golden years of the open shop. And many lost faith in strategies centered on high and uniform labor costs as economic regionalism persisted in the national economy and global competition intruded on nationalist regulation. The competitive and social circumstances under which business accepted the logic of collective bargaining did not last past the late 1930s; the legal and organizational framework of collective bargaining, much to the dismay of business, remained intact well into the postwar era. . . .

For a variety of reasons, . . . New Deal federalism fell short of expectations. While the *Schecter* decision (which reaffirmed state prerogative over intrastate commerce) was a major blow, the coercive economic nationalism pursued by the New Deal and its (primarily northern) business patrons was on shaky legs long before any legal punches were landed. Competition between states and regions encompassed vast differences in economic development; the varying degrees of influence of race, migrant labor, and agriculture on regional labor markets; and a wide range of short- and long-term relationships between business interests and local or state politics. These differences, particularly acute between North and South, could not be erased by legislative fiat. The Roosevelt administration found it exceedingly difficult (indeed impossible) to administer the NRA or its successors in the South without either accepting persistent and flagrant noncompliance or brokering regulatory provisions for southern Democrats in such a way that federal uniformity was abandoned.

Although New Deal policies, including the Wagner, Social Security, and Fair Labor Standards (1938) Acts, closed much of the gap between North and South, states were still free to compete in other areas. State income and consumption taxes undermined the regulatory and redistributive intent of federal law, while state business taxes (or their absence) perpetuated regional competition. In turn, the whims of local politicians, judiciary officials, and police made the sincere enforcement of federal laws (especially those concerning civil and union rights) less than certain. And the South and Southwest, where supply-side military federalism displaced social federalism in the postwar era, continued to hold out open arms for union-busting emigrés from the North. After flirting with national standards, industry returned to exploiting regional disparity and using the threat of migration to "whipsaw" union demands or wring concessions from northern workers and politicians.

In politics, the New Deal's offensive against the "colonial economy" of the South was unhappily endured by southern politicos only as long as their immediate political and financial dependence on federal relief exceeded their longer-term regional economic strategies. After 1936, the rapprochement between southern congressional Democrats and the Roosevelt administration fell apart, in part because the Congress of Industrial Organizations (CIO) had turned its attention to the mills, factories, and refineries of the industrial South and in part because, at the first hint of recovery, the benefits of federal relief paled beside the threat of federal intervention in southern labor and race relations. New Deal policies were also confounded by the relative health of the South's agricultural industries (textiles and tobacco), which made them less eager to accept federal regulation and its ancillary costs. And World War II erased the fiscal crisis of state and local governments that had made their concession to New Deal federalism necessary and possible.

The persistence of political and economic regionalism sparked growing opposition. Regions, industries, and firms targeted by federal recovery and labor legislation objected to regulatory and fiscal federalism from the outset. Those that stood to gain from the New Deal's economic nationalism resented the ability of regional competitors to maintain political and economic advantages and turned their backs on policies that had not delivered as promised. In the postwar era, business proved willing to overlook the occasional inconvenience of regulatory disparity and inconsistency and fell back to older patterns of legislative competition, tax mongering, and jurisdictional shopping. . . .

Beneath the surface of the New Deal system lay a single, dormant fault line: the threat of international competition. New Deal policies, especially those concerned with labor, were premised on isolation from global markets; with competition confined to domestic markets, regulatory policy simply raised costs for all competing firms and passed the extra burden on to consumers. This reasoning reflected a tradition of industrial policy that had always offered high protective tariffs or quotas to any industry with the time or inclination to ask for them, and it infused New Deal regulatory and labor policies. The Roosevelt administration echoed its Republican forerunners by espousing an international economic platform that encouraged the export of loans and manufactured goods, promoted restrictive international cartels in basic commodities, and resisted the import of anything but cash.

International pressures did not seriously challenge the New Deal's implicit nationalism in the 1930s, but there were hints of future problems. While the Depression (which brought with it a destructive pattern of tariff retaliation and competitive currency depreciation) underscored the contradictions of protectionism, the triumph of internationalism was still a decade away. During the Hoover years, a smattering of internationalists favored the rapid reconstruction of European industry, lenient reparation demands on Germany, and various institutional safeguards for the free flow and convertibility of currencies. But the manufacturing economy remained overwhelmingly protectionist and leery of European competition. Even those who were internationally active preferred the sanctuary of multinational cartels. Hoover echoed this position, dismissing Wall Street internationalism as a "mental annex to Europe" and doing little to challenge the power of protectionist sentiment in Congress. The Democrats (reflecting both prevailing nationalism and the DuPonts' heavy investment in the party's National Committee) chimed in with a high-tariff platform in 1928.

Few appreciated the complex connections between protectionism and the pursuit of high-wage, inflationary recovery policies. High tariffs made costly regulatory experimentation possible; the possibility of future tariff revision (let alone full-blown free trade) made it risky. The sentiments of John Raskob of GM (perhaps the least dogmatic of the high-tariff Democrats) were typical:

> I believe we must work out a different policy under which American manufacturers will be forced to compete with the world for American as well as export trade, however, giving to those manufacturers the protection necessary to enable them to pay the high

wages established in this country, as against the low wages in other countries, and also to protect them against "dumping" and any other advantages which foreignors [sic] may possess and which are beyond the control of American manufacturers to meet without governmental help. If we could get such a tariff policy. I would be in favor of abolishing the Sherman law entirely.

This approach overflowed with contradictions. In its purest form, the internationalist position concentrated on efficient patterns of capital exchange and investment and betrayed little concern for U.S. labor standards or jobs. But the "whatever protection is necessary" notion left the tariff mired in interest-group politics and perpetuated the shortsighted simplicity of the "Open Door," which espoused the virtues of free trade as long as the United States held a clear competitive advantage but closed doors whenever and wherever this advantage was absent or lost.

In all, internationalism was a future problem. The sentiments of Cordell Hull and a few high-tech and banking internationalists did little to encourage global expansion or the political concessions upon which that expansion depended. The U.S. response to the Depression was decidedly protectionist, and the Reciprocal Trade Agreement Act of 1934 formalized collective inaction without any palpable influence on exports or imports. Only the outbreak of World War II gave U.S. planners the opportunity to infuse wartime diplomacy with the conditions for a postwar economic order. Once in place, internationalism clearly undermined the premises of New Deal nationalism. An executive of Vick Chemical complained that although taking wages out of competition and girding aggregate demand had a superficial appeal, "the logical extension of this theory is that you have to carry it all over the world and force every nation to set a floor [under wages]." International competition left employers unable to pass on the costs of mandatory welfare and unionized labor, a condition that had been central to business support for the Wagner and Social Security Acts. Protectionists (no longer able to bury labor costs in tariffs) and internationalists (less and less concerned with domestic conditions) turned their backs on policies they had previously supported.

S U G G E S T E D   R E A D I N G

Beito, David. *Taxpayers in Revolt: Tax Resistance During the Great Depression* (1989).
Best, Gary Dean. *The Critical Press and the New Deal* (1993).
Brinkley, Alan. *Voices of Protest: Huey Long, Father Coughlin, and the Great Depression* (1982).
Buhle, Paul. *Marxism in the United States* (1987).
Cohen, Robert. *When the Old Left Was Young, 1929–1941* (1993).
Hair, William Ivy. *The Kingfish and His Realm* (1992).
Hawley, Ellis. "The New Deal and Business." In *The New Deal: The National Level,* ed. David Brody, John Braeman, and Robert Bremner, 50–82 (1975).
Jeansonne, Glen. *Gerald L.K. Smith, Minister of Hate* (1988).
Kelley, Robin D.G. *Hammer and Hoe: Alabama Communists During the Great Depression* (1990).
Klehr, Harvey. *The Heyday of American Communism* (1984).
Lawson, R. Alan. *The Failure of Independent Liberalism, 1930–1941* (1971).
McIntosh, Clarence. "The Significance of the End Poverty in California Movement." *Pacific Historical Review* 27 (1983), 21–25.

Naison, Mark. *Communists in Harlem During the Depression* (1983).

Ottanelli, Fraser. *The Communist Party of the United States from the Depression to World War II* (1991).

Patterson, James T. *Congressional Conservatism and the New Deal* (1967).

Pells, Richard. *Radical Visions and American Dreams: Culture and Social Thought in the Depression Years* (1973).

Ribuffo, Leo. *The Old Christian Right* (1983).

———. *Left, Center, Right* (1992).

Valelly, Richard M. *Radicalism in the States: The Minnesota Farmer-Labor Party and the American Political Economy* (1989).

Warren, Donald. *Radio Priest: Charles Coughlin, the Father of Hate Radio* (1996).

Warren, Frank. *An Alternative Vision: The Socialist Party in the 1930s* (1976).

———. *Liberals and Communism: The Red Decade Revisited* (1966).

Weed, Clyde. *Nemesis of Reform: The Republican Party During the New Deal* (1994).

Williams, T. Harry. *Huey Long* (1969).

Wolfskill, George. *The Revolt of the Conservatives: A History of the American Liberty League* (1962).

C H A P T E R
14

The Social Impact of World War II

Historians have just begun to explore the enormous social impact of the Second World War. Its effects exaggerated by the preceding decade of the Depression, the war unleashed a frenzy of economic mobilization, political adjustment, social upheaval, and demographic change. Centers of wartime industry, particularly established industrial cities like Detroit and Chicago and the shipbuilding cities of the coastal South and West, saw their populations change and grow dramatically as the economy mobilized for war. While rapid growth and the demand for labor swept away the last vestiges of the Depression, they also sparked prolonged (and occasionally violent) confrontations over housing, public services, and employment opportunities.

Wartime race relations were shaped not only by the pace of wartime change (the war marked another wave of African American migration to the urban North) and reaction to it, but by the heady democratic rhetoric of the war effort itself. Indeed, many African Americans entered the war determined to fight for a "Double Victory," over racism at home and fascism abroad. "Our war is not against Hitler in Europe," as one civil rights activist argued, "but against Hitler in America. Our war is not to defend democracy but to get a democracy we have never had." Such expectations stood in stark contrast to the racial mood of the wartime cities. Confrontations over housing and urban space erupted in full-blown riots in Detroit and New York City in 1943. "Hate strikes" by white workers protesting the employment or promotion of blacks were a common occurrence. For its part, the federal government was torn between the democratic and egalitarian rhetoric of the war effort and its hope that race relations (especially the issue of a segregated military) could be put on the back burner until the war was over.

The war also shook gender roles and relations. A wartime labor shortage pulled women into the labor force in record numbers, but the mobilization of "Rosie the Riveter" led to few lasting gains. Employers, organized labor, and the state took great pains to portray women's war work as an exceptional and temporary extension of domestic tasks: the home front. And reconversion saw a retreat to essentially prewar patterns of income, union representation, and occupational segregation. But the war shattered the sexual reticence of the Depression years. The draft and overseas service made it necessary to confront issues of premarital sex, family planning, and disease prevention. The combination of military service and increased employment lessened the parental supervision of young adults and sparked a national anxiety about juvenile delinquency that would spill into the 1950s. And while the war

(marked by substantial same-sex environments in the military and war work) was
something of a "coming-out" experience for many homosexual Americans, it also
hardened political and public anxieties about gay life and relationships.

While the war itself was fought in Europe and the Pacific, the fight for and
about democracy was also fought at home. In this sense, the home front (marked
by ambivalence about women in the workforce, deteriorating race relations, intol-
erance of racial and sexual minorities, and the constitutional blemish of the "re-
location" of over one hundred thousand Japanese Americans) was an important
theater of the war—one that would remain active long after the fighting stopped
in 1945.

DOCUMENTS

In Document 1, President Roosevelt delivers his famous interpretation of American
war aims as the "four freedoms." In Document 2, a woman war worker recalls the
promise, and the limits, of economic and occupational progress made by women
during the war effort. In Document 3, a war columnist counsels women on the art of
writing to their boyfriends and husbands overseas. The letter reprinted as Document 4
suggests the emotional strains of the war. In Document 5, the African American union
leader A. Philip Randolph argues that the federal government should use its wartime
clout to fight for civil rights, including an end to employment discrimination and de-
segregation of the armed forces. In Document 6, an ordinary soldier makes a similar
case and points out the "strange paradox" of fighting a war for democratic rights that
so many African Americans did not enjoy.

1. President Franklin Roosevelt Identifies the "Four Freedoms" at Stake in the War, 1941

. . . There is nothing mysterious about the foundations of a healthy and strong
democracy. The basic things expected by our people of their political and economic
systems are simple. They are:

Equality of opportunity for youth and for others.

Jobs for those who can work.

Security for those who need it.

The ending of special privilege for the few.

The preservation of civil liberties for all.

The enjoyment of the fruits of scientific progress in a wider and constantly rising
standard of living.

These are the simple, basic things that must never be lost sight of in the turmoil
and unbelievable complexity of our modern world. The inner and abiding strength

From *The Public Papers and Addresses of Franklin D. Roosevelt* (New York: Macmillan, 1941), Vol. 9,
pp. 671–672.

of our economic and political systems is dependent upon the degree to which they fulfill these expectations.

Many subjects connected with our social economy call for immediate improvement.

As examples:

We should bring more citizens under the coverage of old-age pensions and unemployment insurance.

We should widen the opportunities for adequate medical care.

We should plan a better system by which persons deserving or needing gainful employment may obtain it.

I have called for personal sacrifice. I am assured of the willingness of almost all Americans to respond to that call.

A part of the sacrifice means the payment of more money in taxes. In my Budget Message I shall recommend that a greater portion of this great defense program be paid for from taxation than we are paying today. No person should try, or be allowed, to get rich out of this program; and the principle of tax payments in accordance with ability to pay should be constantly before our eyes to guide our legislation.

If the Congress maintains these principles, the voters, putting patriotism ahead of pocketbooks, will give you their applause.

In the future days, which we seek to make secure, we look forward to a world founded upon four essential human freedoms.

The first is freedom of speech and expression—everywhere in the world.

The second is freedom of every person to worship God in his own way—everywhere in the world.

The third is freedom from want—which, translated into world terms, means economic understandings which will secure to every nation a healthy peacetime life for its inhabitants—everywhere in the world.

The fourth is freedom from fear—which, translated into world terms, means a world-wide reduction of armaments to such a point and in such a thorough fashion that no nation will be in a position to commit an act of physical aggression against any neighbor—anywhere in the world.

That is no vision of a distant millennium. It is a definite basis for a kind of world attainable in our own time and generation. That kind of world is the very antithesis of the so-called new order of tyranny which the dictators seek to create with the crash of a bomb.

To that new order we oppose the greater conception—the moral order. A good society is able to face schemes of world domination and foreign revolutions alike without fear.

Since the beginning of our American history, we have been engaged in change—in a perpetual peaceful revolution—a revolution which goes on steadily, quietly adjusting itself to changing conditions—without the concentration camp or the quicklime in the ditch. The world order which we seek is the cooperation of free countries, working together in a friendly, civilized society.

This nation has placed its destiny in the hands and heads and hearts of its millions of free men and women; and its faith in freedom under the guidance of God. Freedom means the supremacy of human rights everywhere. Our support goes to those who struggle to gain those rights or keep them. Our strength is our unity of purpose.

To that high concept there can be no end save victory.

2. A Woman Worker Reflects on the "Good War" at Home During the 1940s

That women married soldiers and sent them overseas happy was hammered at us. We had plays on the radio, short stories in magazines, and the movies, which were a tremendous influence in our lives. The central theme was the girl meets the soldier, and after a weekend of acquaintanceship they get married and overcome all difficulties. Then off to war he went. Remember Judy Garland and Robert Walker in *The Clock?*

I knew Glenn six weekends, not weeks. They began on Saturday afternoon. We'd go out in herds and stay up all night. There was very little sleeping around. We were still at the tail-end of a moral generation. Openly living together was not condoned. An illegitimate child was a horrendous handicap. It was almost the ruination of your life. I'm amazed and delighted the way it's accepted now, that a girl isn't a social outcast any more. . . .

I had one of those movie weddings, because he couldn't get off the base. My parents approved. My mother had a talk with the head of the army base. She wanted to know why the guy I was to marry was restricted to quarters. He said they were having nothing but trouble with this guy. The major advised her to think twice before permitting her daughter to marry a man like this: he was totally irresponsible. My mother told me this, and we both laughed about it. He was a soldier. He could not be anything but a marvelous, magnificent human being. I couldn't believe for one minute what this major had said. He was given a weekend pass and we were married.

Shortly after that he was thrown out of the air force. This was my first doubt that he was magnificent. So he became a sergeant, dusting off airplanes. He was sent to various parts of the country: Panama City, Florida; Ypsilanti, Michigan; Amarillo, Texas. I followed him.

That's how I got to see the misery of the war, not the excitement. Pregnant women who could barely balance in a rocking train, going to see their husbands for the last time before the guys were sent overseas. Women coming back from seeing their husbands, traveling with small children. Trying to feed their kids, diaper their kids. I felt sorriest for them. It suddenly occurred to me that this wasn't half as much fun as I'd been told it was going to be. I just thanked God I had no kids. . . .

I ran across a lot of women with husbands overseas. They were living on allotment. Fifty bucks a month wouldn't support you. Things were relatively cheap, but then we had very little money, too. It wasn't so much the cost of food as points. I suspected the ration system was a patriotic ploy to keep our enthusiasm at a fever pitch. If you wanted something you didn't have points for, it was the easiest thing in the world . . . Almost everybody had a cynical feeling about what we were told was a food shortage.

When it started out, this was the greatest thing since the Crusades. The patriotic fervor was such at the beginning that if "The Star-Spangled Banner" came on the radio, everybody in the room would stand up at attention. As the war dragged on and on and on, we read of the selfish actions of guys in power. We read stories of the generals, like MacArthur taking food right out of the guys' mouths when he was in the Philippines, to feed his own family. Our enthusiasm waned and we became cynical and very tired and sick of the bloodshed and killing. It was a completely different thing than the way it started. At least, this is the way I felt. . . .

There were some movies we knew were sheer bullshit. There was a George Murphy movie where he gets his draft induction notice. He opens the telegram, and he's in his pajamas and bare feet, and he runs around the house and jumps over the couch and jumps over the chair, screaming and yelling. His landlady says, "What's going on?" "I've been drafted! I've been drafted." Well, the whole audience howled. 'Cause they know you can feed 'em only so much bullshit.

If a guy in a movie was a civilian, he always had to say—what was it? Gene Kelly in *Cover Girl?* I remember this line: "Well, Danny, why aren't you in the army?" "Hell, I was wounded in North Africa, and now all I can do is keep people happy by putting on these shows." They had to explain why the guy wasn't in uniform. Always. There was always a line in the movie: "Well, I was turned down." "Oh, tough luck." There were always soldiers in the audience, and they would scream. So we recognized a lot of the crap. . . .

The good war? That infuriates me. Yeah, the idea of World War Two being called a good war is a horrible thing. I think of all the atrocities. I think of a madman who had all this power. I think of the destruction of the Jews, the misery, the horrendous suffering in the concentration camps. In 1971, I visited Dachau. I could not believe what I saw. There's one barracks left, a model barracks. You can reconstruct the rest and see what the hell was going on. It doesn't take a visit to make you realize the extent of human misery. . . .

There was *one* good thing came out of it. I had friends whose mothers went to work in factories. For the first time in their lives, they worked outside the home. They realized that they were capable of doing something more than cook a meal. I remember going to Sunday dinner one of the older women invited me to. She and her sister at the dinner table were talking about the best way to keep their drill sharp in the factory. I had never heard anything like this in my life. It was just marvelous. I was tickled.

But even here we were sold a bill of goods. They were hammering away that the woman who went to work did it temporarily to help her man, and when he came back, he took her job and she cheerfully leaped back to the home. . . .

I think a lot of women said, Screw that noise. 'Cause they had a taste of freedom, they had a taste of making their own money, a taste of spending their own money, making their own decisions. I think the beginning of the women's movement had its seeds right there in World War Two.

3. Ethel Gorham Advises "How to Write a Letter to Your Man Overseas," 1942

One of the best rules to remember, if you want to spare yourself the unhappiness of wishing you hadn't sent yesterday's letter, is to leave out all personal upheavals. Did you run into a bit of in-law trouble? You have before, you know, and will again. Why mention it? Are you feeling lonely and upset and vaguely suicidal? Don't put it into written words unless you're prepared to jump out of the window and this is your last message on it all.

You've felt that way before. This hasn't been an easy time and some days are worse than others. But on paper it has a permanence that lasts until your next letter arrives, and even though your "blue" mood has long since passed, you're inflicting it on someone as if it were a thing of the present, filled with present concern.

It is so easy to sit down after a long day of conflict and penny pinching and lonesomeness and pour out all of it on paper. You feel you want someone you love to share your trouble. After all, he writes all the details about his military life, doesn't he, and he makes no bones about the food, the routine, the constant complaining. Ah, but that's different!

Your letters arrive as the only link he has with his outside life. In your letters he feels the pulse of normalcy. From your letters he draws the small details that go into building a continuity between his past and his future. . . .

Don't get involved in domestic details and don't labor them. If the children are a chore they always are. Don't take the attitude of here I am in my steaming hot kitchen while there you are in your nice cool barracks. Nothing is funnier and more unfair.

Leave out all reference, if you can, to the high cost of living. He probably feels troubled enough about your financial state and it is better to settle your problems in silence than to use valuable letter space to do it in. Besides, what can he do about it five hundred miles or a thousand miles or perhaps three thousand miles from home?

Presumably both of you knew that war made a mess of the facts of life. If you didn't, you should have consulted Sherman. And one of the minor messes is the need for women to stay home and wait and work and keep things going. There is no use fidgeting in a letter about it. . . .

Letters should be as warm and intimate as you yourself have been with the man to whom you are writing.

Incidentally, if he is not your husband you know what he is. Friend, companion, the boy next door. Treat him as such in your letters and don't be afraid of the effect. This is no time for coy girlish reticence. If everybody misses him, say so. If you miss him, say so too. You may never have another chance. . . .

What part of yourself you can put in your letters, that part he will have. Make it the most charming, most informative, most truly feminine part. It is hard to practice seduction a thousand miles away, but that's what your letters should do. A kind of mental, spiritual, companionable seduction. Thus you will get him to depend on your reactions,

---

From *So Your Husband's Gone to War* by Ethel Gorham. Used by permission of Doubleday, a division of Bantam Doubleday Dell Publishing Group, Inc.

your news, your understanding. If you give him this kind of letter, filled with the life you live, he will feel, each time he answers you, that he has never gone away. . . .

Do avoid at all times the statement that you are having such a riotous good time back home that of course you can't find time to write. It brands you as callous, shallow. If true, you probably don't care. If not true, it shows you haven't been writing often or consistently enough. And can you blame him if, brave soldier though he may be, he breaks his heart about it?

4. An Anxious Letter Home from the Western Front, 1944

Paris, France, 15 November 1944

My Dearest Darling:

. . . I have no idea what my boys are doing tonight, but they are fighting like hell and I am a damn yellow so-and-so to be here and not with them. After all, an officer is not supposed to be ill or ever feel bad. Guess I should have more intestinal fortitude so as to be able to have a sick headache and still do my duty as a machine gun platoon leader, don't you think? Why do I have to get sick and at a time that they need me, too. . . . I don't guess I have told you enough of why I am here, have I? Well, before I came overseas and a month after I came over, I had a bad headache nearly every month, then they began to come twice, then, three or four per month, and now, from one to two each week. The only thing that seems to relieve them is for me to lose all I have eaten and sleep it off. Also in the past month I have had frequent stomach aches and a tremendous amount of gas on my stomach. We had a few dull days so I came back to get checked over. The day I came back I had a bad headache and that nite I lost all I had eaten. Soo, that started it, they have taken x-rays of my sinus, my stomach, both negative and this a.m. they took one of my skull—you should see my skull, it sure is pretty, no brains at all—ha! Anyway, this is my fourth hospital, I hope they get on the ball and do one thing or the other, fix me up or tell me to get the hell back to the front. I am not sick, so don't get to doing any worrying—they are just trying to trace down the headaches which was sinus and now is migraine. One doc says one thing—another says another. . . .

If there was ever anything that you had done that you knew was not right while I've been away, you would be decent enough to tell me, wouldn't you, Barbie? Answer that. You would tell me those things even though you knew I'd hate you, wouldn't you? had you failed me. We are so far apart and I know how all the stories get to the soldiers about how their wives back in the States are roving around, too, I know what all the people back there think about the boys over here. Either one of us has a bad thing in us called jealousy, and we are too often doing too much wondering about each other's actions while we are apart.

Now, let's just stop and face this sexual situation for a minute: we are both very passionate and you might say always ready to do something when we are together, but I am quite certain we, neither one, could ever think of sexual relations or any other type relations as long as we are apart. No one could fill your sexual station with me. Sexual relations are no good unless you feel that the person you do them with is clean, above reproach, and to me you are the only clean woman in the whole wide world. I am true to you because I want to be, not because you want me to be. I love you because I want to love you, not because you want me to. I hope you are the same way, I mean, I hope you are true to me because you want to, not because you think I'd want you to be true. You know I'd want you to be true, but you get what I mean, don't you? . . .

Your Charlie

P.S. Give Miss T. a big hug and a kiss from her Dad.

5. A. Philip Randolph Argues for a March on Washington, 1942

Though I have found no Negroes who want to see the United Nations lose this war, I have found many who, before the war ends, want to see the stuffing knocked out of white supremacy and of empire over subject peoples. American Negroes, involved as we are in the general issues of the conflict, are confronted not with a choice but with the challenge both to win democracy for ourselves at home and to help win the war for democracy the world over.

There is no escape from the horns of this dilemma. There ought not to be escape. For if the war for democracy is not won abroad, the fight for democracy cannot be won at home. If this war cannot be won for the white peoples, it will not be won for the darker races.

Conversely, if freedom and equality are not vouchsafed the peoples of color, the war for democracy will not be won. Unless this double-barreled thesis is accepted and applied, the darker races will never wholeheartedly fight for the victory of the United Nations. That is why those familiar with the thinking of the American Negro have sensed his lack of enthusiasm, whether among the educated or uneducated, rich or poor, professional or nonprofessional, religious or secular, rural or urban, north, south, east or west.

That is why questions are being raised by Negroes in church, labor union and fraternal society; in poolroom, barbershop, schoolroom, hospital, hair-dressing parlor; on college campus, railroad, and bus. One can hear such questions asked as these: What have Negroes to fight for? What's the difference between Hitler and that "cracker" Talmadge of Georgia? Why has a man got to be Jim-Crowed to die for democracy? If you haven't got democracy yourself, how can you carry it to somebody else?

What are the reasons for this state of mind? The answer is: discrimination, segregation, Jim Crow. Witness the navy, the army, the air corps; and also government services at Washington. In many parts of the South, Negroes in Uncle Sam's uniform are being put upon, mobbed, sometimes even shot down by civilian and military police,

From A. Philip Randolph, "Why Should We March?" *Survey Graphic* (November 1942): pp. 488–489.

and on occasion lynched. Vested political interests in race prejudice are so deeply entrenched that to them winning the war against Hitler is secondary to preventing Negroes from winning democracy for themselves. This is worth many divisions to Hitler and Hirohito. While labor, business, and farm are subjected to ceilings and floors and not allowed to carry on as usual, these interests trade in the dangerous business of race hate as usual.

When the defense program began and billions of the taxpayers' money were appropriated for guns, ships, tanks and bombs, Negroes presented themselves for work only to be given the cold shoulder. North as well as South, and despite their qualifications, Negroes were denied skilled employment. Not until their wrath and indignation took the form of a proposed protest march on Washington, scheduled for July 1, 1941, did things begin to move in the form of defense jobs for Negroes. The march was postponed by the timely issuance (June 25, 1941) of the famous Executive Order No. 8802 by President Roosevelt. But this order and the President's Committee on Fair Employment Practice, established thereunder, have as yet only scratched the surface by way of eliminating discriminations on account of race or color in war industry. Both management and labor unions in too many places and in too many ways are still drawing the color line.

It is to meet this situation squarely with direct action that the March on Washington Movement launched its present program of protest mass meetings. . . .

The March on Washington Movement is essentially a movement of the people. It is all Negro and pro-Negro, but not for that reason anti-white or anti-Semitic, or anti-Catholic, or anti-foreign, or anti-labor. Its major weapon is the non-violent demonstration of Negro mass power. Negro leadership has united back of its drive for jobs and justice. . . .

By fighting for their rights now, American Negroes are helping to make America a moral and spiritual arsenal of democracy. Their fight against the poll tax, against lynch law, segregation, and Jim Crow, their fight for economic, political, and social equality, thus becomes part of the global war for freedom.

6. An African American Soldier Notes the "Strange Paradox" of the War, 1944

33rd AAF Base Unit (CCTS(H))
Section C
DAVIS-MONTHAN FIELD
Tucson, Arizona
9 May 1944.

President Franklin Delano Roosevelt
White House
Washington, D. C.

Dear President Roosevelt:

It was with extreme pride that I, a soldier in the Armed Forces of our country, read the following affirmation of our war aims, pronounced by you at a recent press conference:

From *Taps for a Jim Crow Army: Letters from Black Soldiers in World War II*, ABC-CLIO, © 1983, pp. 134–139. Reprinted by permission of ABC-CLIO.

"The United Nations are fighting to make a world in which tyranny, and aggression cannot exist; a world based upon freedom, equality, and justice; a world in which all persons, regardless of race, color and creed, may live in peace, honor and dignity.". . .

But the picture in our country is marred by one of the strangest paradoxes in our whole fight against world fascism. The United States Armed Forces, to fight for World Democracy, is within itself undemocratic. The undemocratic policy of jim crow and segregation is practiced by our Armed Forces against its Negro members. Totally inadequate opportunities are given to the Negro members of our Armed Forces, nearly one tenth of the whole, to participate with "equality" . . . "regardless of race and color" in the fight for our war aims. In fact it appears that the army intends to follow the very policy that the FEPC [Fair Employment Practices Commission] is battling against in civilian life, the pattern of assigning Negroes to the lowest types of work.

Let me give you an example of the lack of democracy in our Field, where I am now stationed. Negro soldiers are completely segregated from the white soldiers on the base. And to make doubly sure that no mistake is made about this, the barracks and other housing facilities (supply room, mess hall, etc.) of the Negro Section C are covered with black tar paper, while all other barracks and housing facilities on the base are painted white.

It is the stated policy of the Second Air Force that "every potential fighting man must be used as a fighting man. If you have such a man in a base job, you have no choice. His job must be eliminated or be filled by a limited service man, WAC, or civilian." And yet, leaving out the Negro soldiers working with the Medical Section, fully 50% of the Negro soldiers are working in base jobs, such as, for example, at the Resident Officers' Mess, Bachelor Officers' Quarters, and Officers' Club, as mess personnel, BOQ orderlies, and bar tenders. Leaving out the medical men again, based on the section C average only 4% of this 50% would not be "potential fighting men."

It is also a fact that ". . . the employment of enlisted men as attendants at officers' clubs, whether officially designated as "Officers' Mess" or "Officers' Club" is not sanctioned by . . ." the Headquarters of the Army Air Forces.

Leaving out the medical men again, at least 50% of the members of the Negro Section C are being used for decidedly menial work, such as BOQ orderlies, janitors, permanent KP's and the like.

Let us assume as a basis for discussion that there are no civilians or limited service men to do the menial work on the base. The democratic way, based upon "equality and justice" would be to assign this work to both Negro and white. Instead the discriminatory and undemocratic method is used whereby all of this work is assigned to the Negro soldiers. . . .

About 15% of the soldiers of Section C are in fighting jobs, and about another 5% are receiving "on-the-job-training" in Vehicle Maintenance. Thus we see that the maintenance of the ideology of "white supremacy" resulting in the undemocratic practices of jim-crow and segregation of the Negro members of the Armed Forces brings about the condition on Davis-Monthan Field whereby 80% of the whole Section is removed from the fighting activities on the base. . . .

How can we convince nearly one tenth of the Armed Forces, the Negro members, that your pronouncement of the war aims of the United Nations means what it says, when their experience with one of the United Nations, the United States of America, is just the opposite? . . .

With your issuance of Executive Order 8802, and the setting up of the Fair Employment Practices Committee, you established the foundation for fighting for democracy in the industrial forces of our country, in the interest of victory for the United Nations. In the interest of victory for the United Nations, another Executive Order is now needed. An Executive Order which will lay the base for fighting for democracy in the Armed Forces of our country. An Executive Order which would bring about the result here at Davis-Monthan Field whereby the Negro soldiers would be integrated into all of the Sections on the base, as fighting men, instead of in the segregated Section C as housekeepers.

Then and only then can your pronouncement of the war aims of the United Nations mean to *all* that we "are fighting to make a world in which tyranny, and aggression cannot exist; a world based upon freedom, equality and justice; a world in which all persons, regardless of race, color and creed, may live in peace, honor and dignity."

Respectfully yours,

Charles F. Wilson, 36794590
Private, Air Corps.

E S S A Y S

In the first essay, Robert Westbrook shows how wartime service was perceived and portrayed as a private obligation to one's family rather than as a public obligation to the state. On these terms, as Westbrook argues, the American war effort did not lead to substantial new state programs (as it did in other countries) and indeed paved the way for the domesticity of the 1950s. In the second essay, Ruth Milkman traces the occupational, economic, and social forces that combined to erase many of the wartime gains made by working women.

Fighting for the Family

ROBERT WESTBROOK

Americans during World War II were not called upon to conceive of their obligation to participate in the war effort as an obligation to work, fight, or die for their country as a political community. The contention of some critical philosophers that liberalism lacks a coherent conception of *political* obligation seems to be reflected in wartime discourse. By and large, the American state and other propagandists relied on arguments—such as those in the Atlantic Charter or Franklin Roosevelt's "Four Freedoms" speech—positing moral obligations that transcended those to a particu-

Excerpted from "Fighting for the American Family", pp. 198–215, in *Power of Culture* edited by T. J. Jackson Lears and Richard W. Fox. Copyright © 1993 University of Chicago Press, reprinted by permission.

lar political community. Or more interestingly, they appealed to Americans both as individuals and as families to join the war effort in order to defend *private* interests and discharge *private* moral obligations. Moreover, the more elusive evidence I have examined thus far of the felt obligations of Americans suggests that it was the latter sort of appeals that were most compelling and coincided most often with their own notions of "what we are fighting for."

In the discourse of obligation during World War II, no private interest outranked that of the family, and it is the place of the family in the prescriptions Americans were offered for "why we fight" that I would like to address here. But before I do so, I should say a bit more about the difficulties that liberalism and the liberal state have with political obligation in order to better indicate the questions and hypotheses I have taken from my reading in contemporary political philosophy. . . .

It is fair to say that the liberal theory of political obligation is in deep trouble these days. Arguing from a variety of perspectives, a number of philosophers have offered a powerful critique of the efforts of the philosophical giants of the liberal tradition from Hobbes to Rawls to provide an adequate basis for political obligation and have concluded that, as Carole Pateman puts it, "political obligation in the liberal democratic state constitutes an insoluble problem; insoluble because political obligation cannot be given expression within the context of liberal democratic institutions."

This critique of the liberal theory of political obligation has advanced on at least two fronts. On the one hand, such philosophers as John Simmons have used the tools of analytic philosophy to demonstrate that such traditional foundations for the liberal theory of political obligation as the tacit consent of citizens to the authority of the state or the reciprocal exchange of benefits between citizens and the state cannot provide an adequate account of or justification for obligation. On the other hand, such communitarian critics of liberalism as Michael Walzer have slighted these difficulties in favor of raising doubts about whether the liberal theory can be said to be an account of *political* obligation, that is, of obligations that men and women have as citizens. It is this latter critique that is most pertinent to my discussion here of the centrality of familial obligations and interests in the thinking of Americans about their commitment to the war effort in World War II.

In an essay on "The Obligation to Die for the State," Walzer addresses the problem of obligation in the context of war and raises the question of whether the obligation citizens have to the state can be made the motive for risking their lives. The answer to this question, he suggests, depends in critical respects on the nature of the state, and, in the case of the liberal state, the answer is no. The reason for this, he argues, is that the end of the liberal state, as conceived in the social contract tradition of Hobbes, Locke, and their successors, is the security of the life of the individuals who form it, and, consequently, "a man who dies for the state defeats his only purpose in forming the state: death is the contradiction of politics. A man who risks his life for the state accepts the insecurity which it was the only end of his political obedience to avoid: war is the failure of politics. Hence there can be no political obligation either to die or to fight."

When a war begins, political authorities in a liberal society may, as Hobbes put it, invite their subjects to "protect their protection," but this is an admission on the part of these authorities to a failure to hold up their end of the bargain on which the state rests. Peculiar in any case as a call to men and women to risk their lives for their instrument, the invitation is doubly peculiar as one to defend an instrument that has failed its function. As Walzer says, when individuals "protect their protection they are doing nothing more than defending themselves, and so they cannot protect their protection after their protection ceases to protect them. At that point, it ceases to be their protection. The state has no value over and above the value of the lives of the concrete individuals whose safety it provides. No man has a common life to defend, but only an individual life." The liberal state at war is like a bodyguard hired to protect the lives and property of a family who then gets into a fight with a gang threatening that family and turns to his clients and asks them to protect him. They have no obligation to do so since they hired the bodyguard precisely to avoid this kind of situation. If they fight the gang, they do so because of obligations they have to protect themselves and one another and not out of any political obligation to the bodyguard-state.

Walzer links this difficulty liberalism has with political obligation to its atomistic individualism and largely negative view of liberty, which make for a conception of the citizen as an individual who is protected by the state from interference by other individuals or by the state itself. The liberal position suggests "an indefinite number of distinct and singular relations between the individual citizens and the authorities as a body—a pattern that might best be symbolized by a series of vertical lines. There are no horizontal connections among citizens as citizens." The state is thought of "as an instrument which serves individual men (or families) but not or not necessarily as an instrument wielded by these men themselves" as constituents of a political community. Walzer concludes that any theory like liberalism which "begins with the absolute independence of freely willing individuals and goes on to treat politics and the state as instrumental to the achievement of individual purposes would seem by its very nature incapable of describing ultimate obligation."

It is important to add, as Walzer does, that this difficulty in liberal theory does not mean that citizens will not go to war and fight and die on behalf of ethical, if not political, obligations. As he says:

> Moved by love, sympathy, or friendship, men in liberal society can and obviously do incur ultimate obligations. They may even find themselves in situations where they are or think they are obliged to defend the state which defends in turn the property and enjoyment of their friends and families. But if they then actually risk their lives or die, they do so because they have incurred private obligations which have nothing to do with politics. The state may shape the environment within which these obligations are freely incurred, and it may provide the occasions and the means for their fulfillment. But this is only to say that, when states make war and men fight, the reasons of the two often are and ought to be profoundly different.

The fact that an argument is a bad one does not mean that it will not be made, and during World War II the American state did occasionally call upon its citizens to protect their protection, as if this amounted to something more than a plea to protect themselves. Less often, it "poached" on other nonliberal traditions in search of more persuasive grounds for political obligation. More frequently, it invoked commitments to such abstract, universal values as "freedom" that Americans shared with others not as citizens but as fellow human beings. Yet what is most striking about propaganda for the "Good War" is the degree to which, as if acknowledging that these were not compelling arguments for political obligation in a liberal society chastened by the failure of an earlier war to make the world safe for democracy, proponents of the war openly attempted—as Walzer's arguments suggest they might—to exploit private obligations in order to convince Americans to serve the cause of national defense. As I can only begin to suggest here, such obligations—to families, to children, to parents, to friends, and generally, to an "American Way of Life" defined as a rich (and richly commodified) private realm of experience—were tirelessly invoked in the campaign to mobilize Americans for World War II and formed the centerpiece of the propaganda produced by the state and its allies in Hollywood, the War Advertising Council, and elsewhere. . . .

The study of popular political theory will often find it in some unusual places, and I would like to begin my discussion of the mobilization of familial obligations in World War II with a story about the work of an American not usually numbered among the nation's great political philosophers: Norman Rockwell.

Sometime in 1942 Rockwell and his friend, neighbor, and fellow illustrator, Mead Schaeffer, decided to contribute to the war effort by offering their services as painters to the American government, but they were delayed initially by Rockwell's inability to come up with any ideas for posters that he really liked. "I wanted to do something bigger than a war poster," he wrote in his autobiography, "make some statement about why the country was fighting the war."

Rockwell thought the idea he was looking for might be found in Franklin Roosevelt's proclamation of the "four essential human freedoms"—freedom of speech, freedom of worship, freedom from want, and freedom from fear—that Americans hoped to secure abroad, but he was deterred by Roosevelt's language which he found "so noble, platitudinous really, that it stuck in my throat": "No, I said to myself, it doesn't go, how am I to illustrate that? I'm not noble enough. Besides, nobody I know is reading the proclamation either, in spite of the fanfare and hullabaloo about it in the press and on the radio." One night, while tossing and turning in bed with this problem, the solution struck him:

> I suddenly remembered how Jim Edgerton had stood up in town meeting and said something that everybody else disagreed with. But they had let him have his say. No one shouted him down. My gosh, I thought, that's it. There it is. Freedom of Speech. I'll illustrate the Four Freedoms using my Vermont neighbors as models. I'll express the ideas in simple, everyday scenes. Freedom of Speech—a New England town meeting. Freedom from Want—a Thanksgiving dinner. Take them out of the noble language of the proclamation and put them in terms everybody can understand.

Rockwell and Schaeffer then set out for Washington armed with rough sketches of their ideas. Here they met with little success. The Office of War Information, one administrator told them, intended to use only the work of "real artists."

On the way back to Vermont, a discouraged Rockwell stopped off in Philadelphia to meet with Ben Hibbs, the editor of *The Saturday Evening Post,* and happened to show him his sketches for *The Four Freedoms.* Hibbs found the sketches very exciting, pledged to publish them in the *Post,* and urged Rockwell to drop everything else he was doing. Early in 1943 the illustrations were published in four consecutive issues of the magazine.

The illustrations elicited an enormous response. Requests to reprint them poured into the *Post* offices, including many from government agencies that now found a use for them. Millions of reprints were made, and they were distributed all over the world. Subsequently, the Treasury Department used the original paintings as part of a war-bond tour that garnered nearly $133 million in bonds. "Those four pictures," Hibbs wrote, "quickly became the best known and most appreciated paintings of that era. They appeared right at a time when the war was going against us on the battle fronts, and the American people needed the inspirational message which they conveyed so forcefully and so beautifully."

What was the message that these pictures conveyed so forcefully and beautifully? It was, with one notable exception . . . that Americans were fighting World War II to protect essentially private interests and discharge essentially private obligations. And, in two of the four paintings, the message was that the people of the United States were fighting for the family.

Freedom from Fear was the only one of the four paintings that made a direct reference to the war. In this painting a concerned mother and father look in on their sleeping children. Their concerns on this occasion are, however, extraordinary (perhaps, this is indicated by the fact that both are in the children's room simultaneously), for they have been reading of the bombing of London in the newspaper that the father holds in his hand. As Rockwell said, the painting is supposed to say: "Thank God we can put our children to bed with a feeling of security, knowing they will not be killed in the night." The threat of bombing conveyed in the illustration, as Stephen Vincent Benét said in the essay accompanying it in the *Post,* is a threat that the geographical isolation of the United States cannot withstand, and hence children must rely on the courage of their parents to protect them from death and the fear of death. Freedom from fear, Benét intoned, "goes to the roots of life—to a man and a woman and their children and the home they can make and keep."

Familial interests and obligations were also central to Rockwell's vision of *Freedom from Want.* This painting portrayed a Thanksgiving dinner for which an extended family has gathered (and to which the viewer is invited). This was intended to convey the message that Americans are fighting to protect the opportunities they had, as Americans, to provide for the material needs of themselves and their families. Here Roosevelt's most controversial "freedom" was rendered not, as Henry Wallace would have had it, as the foundation of a Global New Deal in which every child was guaranteed a quart of milk a day, but rather as the defense of the familial surfeit of a peculiarly American holiday. . . .

Rockwell's translation of Roosevelt's noble, platitudinous, abstract, and universalist moral language into a more concrete, particular moral language centering on private obligations and interests was far from idiosyncratic. Indeed, I would maintain that this sort of translation is one of the most significant features of American propaganda during World War II. Again and again, propagandists explicitly or implicitly contended, as an advertisement for U.S. Rubber put it, that "words like *freedom* or *liberty* draw close to us only when we break them down into the *homely fragments of daily life."* And, more often than not, those fragments were literally "homely," that is, familial.

Like Norman Rockwell, the American state and private corporations interpreted the obligations of Americans to support the war effort as a duty owed to the family in which they were raised, the family they were themselves raising, the family they would someday raise, and/or, somewhat more abstractly, to the family as a social institution. The war, one ad said, was "this fight to keep our country a safe place for the wives we love, a place where our children can grow up free and un-afraid," and no obligation ranked higher in American war propaganda than the obligation to protect the family.

The enemy was repeatedly portrayed in posters and ads as a threat to the family, particularly its weaker members. The state, in turn, was seen in good liberal fashion as the protector of the family. In one very illuminating example of this argument, we find the Axis powers portrayed as Halloween vandals on a rampage. They have burned a family farm, an essentially private icon tied to "Our Democratic Institutions." Behind a tree Uncle Sam (literally "Uncle" Sam)—the American state—waits to foil their fur-ther mischief, armed with the rifle of American industrial might. In ads such as this, private corporations like Philco announced their eagerness to be a part of the family's arsenal, emphasizing that the sacrifices made in converting to war production would, as another ad put it, "help Daddy lick" the enemy.

The Philco ad is interesting not only because it clearly indicates that it was home and family that Americans were fighting for when they came to the defense of democratic institutions. It is also a nice example of the way the liberal state could use the representation of itself as a family relative, "Uncle Sam," to obscure the fact that a declaration of war marked its failure to hold up its end of the bargain struck with its citizens to protect them from death in exchange for their obedience. It was not "Uncle Sam" that was protecting the family during the war but fathers, mothers, and other relatives who went to war to keep Hitler, Mussolini, and Tojo from the door, and it was their private obligation to do so that the American state mobilized. Thus, to be true to the character of obligation in World War II, one would have to say that "Uncle Sam," as depicted in this ad, represents not the American state but the host of real Uncle Sams organized by the state to fight for their families. The gun he wields is a representation of the others, "our soldiers of production," who went to work in war plants in order to protect their homes.

Americans were instructed that they might discharge their obligation to pro-tect home and family in a number of ways. Soldiers, of course, were called upon to risk their lives in combat for their loved ones, and their mothers—who, according to *Life,* stood for "home, love, faith, all the things they are fighting for"—were presented with blue stars to signify this commitment and gold stars to signify that their sons had made the ultimate sacrifice. Hollywood portrayed soldiers fighting for mothers, chil-dren, brides, and brides-to-be back home. For example, in the most poignant scene in one of the best combat films, *Guadalcanal Diary* (1943), a marine captain lying fa-tally wounded on the beach reaches in death for his helmet and the photograph of his family tucked in its webbing. For those who had no personal pin-ups of wives or girl friends to plaster to the machines of war, the studios in cooperation with the state pro-vided surrogates like Betty Grable. Grable, far and away the most popular pin-up of the war, was offered to soldiers less as an exotic sex goddess than as a symbol of the kind of woman for whom American men were fighting. Grable, as Jane Gaines has said, was "model girlfriend, wife, and finally mother," and her popularity increased after she married bandleader Harry James in 1943 and had a child later that year.

On the home front, civilians were urged to aid their soldier-protectors in the war for the family by working in defense plants, supporting the Red Cross, conserving vital materials, and buying war bonds. One life insurance company warned that men deferred in 1942 because they were fathers should be aware that "upon victory rests everything that means most to you as a father . . . the security of your home . . . the safety and freedom of your children . . . the very *way of life* that America stands for" and recommended that these men supplement the protection victory afforded with the added fortification of a new insurance policy. Women who worked in factories to provide their protectors with the weapons they needed to protect them were assured that in so doing they were "fighting for freedom and all that means to women everywhere. You're fighting for a little house of your own, and a husband to meet every night at the door. You're fighting for the right to bring up your children without the shadow of fear."

Some corporations argued that the war was not only being waged to protect the family, but that it was a blessing in disguise that would actually enhance family welfare. Restraints on consumer spending coupled with high wages and savings invested in war bonds had provided consumers with the opportunity to engage in "installment buying in reverse" that would enable them to have the home of their dreams. "After the war," Revere Copper declared, "youth has a new world to look forward to. For today's young men and women can plan instead of dream, can be sure that the homes their parents merely wished for can become a reality for them. . . . In this war, we are fighting not only against our enemies, but *for* a better way of life for many more of us." The homes pictured in its ad were an example of what American families could have "by fighting, and sacrificing, and winning."

A few companies like furniture manufacturers W. & J. Sloane urged consumers not to wait for war's end to begin living this dream but to invest immediately in at least one major purchase that "can mean home . . . the root, the core, the propulsion of our lives." The better way of life, the "American Way of Life" that these ads and other propaganda described had little to do with citizenship. It was above all a rewarding domestic life for which Americans were fighting, a private sphere filled with goods and services provided by those who had for the duration halted production in order that their customers might effectively defend homes that would in the wake of victory be even more densely cluttered with commodities.

I could easily multiply these examples of "why we fight" documents that argue that "we fight for the family." All this is evidence, it should be said, of *prescriptions* about obligation and provides little direct evidence about the *felt* obligations of Americans during the war. But one can at least say that American propagandists—especially those working for private corporations—appealed to attitudes and convictions they believed (or their research told them) were widespread in their audiences. Moreover, the widespread popularity of Rockwell's paintings suggests that he struck a nerve as well. . . .

If the only theory Americans lived in World War II was liberalism and if they only thought about their obligations to the war effort in liberal, nonpolitical terms, the story would be neat and probably wrong. Historians no longer contend that liberalism is the only American political tradition, even if few doubt its hegemony, and though I am less disposed than some to stress the persistence in the United States of an adversarial republican ideology, one can now and again hear its faint echoes in World War II. Moreover, theory—especially lived theory—is rarely consistent. We shore up the weak flanks of our thinking with arguments to which our most cherished premises may not entitle us, preferring a jerry-built structure of thought that covers all the bases to a logical masterpiece that leaves us without benefits that logic would deny. I would like to conclude then with a look at two documents that reflect nonliberal perspectives that occasionally crept into the discourse about obligation during the war.

In a 1942 Birds Eye Foods advertisement one can see an attempt at a nonliberal argument that imparts a quite different meaning to "fighting for the family" than what I have discussed. Occasionally, to borrow some terms from political philosopher Amy Gutmann, Americans tried to think of themselves during the war not as a "state of families" but as a "family state" or, as a General Electric ad put it, "just one fighting family . . . 130,000,000 of us!" In the Birds Eye ad, which offers a nice contrast to Rockwell's later use of the Thanksgiving theme, the nation is portrayed as a family sitting down to Thanksgiving dinner at a table headed by Uncle Sam. Expressions such as this, it seems to me, grew out of anxieties about the capacity of a nation of "individualists" or even individual families to achieve the level of cooperation and solidarity necessary to win a total war. If the nation was to win the war, the ad suggests, its citizens must think of themselves as members of a single family, bound together by affective ties akin to those they shared with their closest relatives.

Yet arguments such as this were rare, for they presented a grave difficulty: they came perilously close to the theories of political obligation advanced by the enemy, particularly the Japanese, who justified dying for the state (the emperor) on the grounds that its state was (quite literally) a family state. This theory was widely attacked by Americans and perceived by many as evidence that the Japanese were a subhuman race. Americans were urged, in effect, to see themselves as defending liberalism and its thin conception of citizenship from the evil of a nation wedded to a much thicker and thereby oppressive conception of citizenship and political obligation. Yet a note of grudging admiration for the family state sometimes snuck into these denunciations, and it is evident as well in this ad.

But what the ad perhaps suggests best is the difficulty of coherently reconciling stronger theories of political obligation with liberal premises. The representations of the American state as an uncle and not a father (or mother) made it difficult to effectively depict the family state because it was not at all clear what avuncular authority amounted to. On the other hand, placing Uncle Sam at the head of the table rather than portraying a father-surrogate deflected too close an approximation of the ideology of the enemy. Had the artist put the carving knife in the hands of, say, FDR, howls of protest against creeping dictatorship would have gone up from the precincts of the Republican party if not elsewhere. Hence this ad stands less as a statement of collective than of aggregate purpose and, at most, a description of wished-for social rather than political bonds.

Nonliberal theories of political obligation need not be undemocratic, and sometimes during the war Americans were offered a glimpse of this alternative. Perhaps the best example of such a democratic theory was *Freedom of Speech,* the exceptional painting in Rockwell's series to which I alluded above. It is the only picture of the four to portray a public scene, and it envisions a political community and a democratic, participatory politics. It would not be stretching too far, I think, to say the painting provides a celebration of public life and speech akin to that later eulogized by Hannah Arendt: "a way of life in which speech and only speech made sense and where the central concern of all citizens was to talk with each other." Yet, unlike Arendt, Rockwell imagined the *polis* as a socially egalitarian community in which a working-class man (modeled on a filling station attendant) speaks as an equal among men with white collars and in which even women are allowed to participate. He thus painted a moment in the politics of the sort of state that some democratic philosophers have contrasted to the liberal state as one in which the state is not a bodyguard or insurance company for the private interests of citizens but a political community providing a common life for citizens as citizens.

Rockwell's portrait of this sort of political community was, I think, unwitting. As the anecdote about the origins of *The Four Freedoms* indicates, what impressed him about his meeting was the fact that Jim Edgerton was allowed to voice his objections on a proposed policy without being shouted down by his neighbors. It was not political community that Rockwell saw himself celebrating here, but tolerance of individual dissent, the use of free speech to protect private conscience from the state. This is also the meaning Booth Tarkington gave to free speech in his accompanying essay, a fable about a meeting of Hitler with Mussolini in the Alps in 1912 in which each plots to become dictator of his respective country by means of the destruction of free speech. However, the painting eluded Rockwell's intentions, principally because he happened to live in a part of the country where a remnant of participatory democracy survived, and he placed his dissenter (who it is difficult to recognize as such) in the midst of this remnant.

Such a participatory democracy would be one for which citizens would be obliged to die in order to protect the common life they share; such a state could lay claim to *political* obligations. Walzer finds this conception of the state in Rousseau's republican version of the social contract in which individuals undergo a qualitative transformation in moving from nature into civil society, a move that makes all the difference. Here the citizen receives from his active participation in a political community "a second life, a moral life, which is not his sole possession, but whose reality depends upon the continued existence of his fellow-citizens and of their association." From this perspective:

> A good society is one in which the new man, a moral member of a moral body, achieves his fullest development. The very instincts of pre-social man are overwhelmed and above all the instinct for self-preservation. When the state is in danger, its citizens rush to its defense, forgetful of all personal danger. They die willingly for the sake of the state . . . because the state is their common life. So long as the state survives, something of the citizen lives on, even after the natural man is dead. The state, or rather the common life of the citizens, generates those "moral goods" for which, according to Rousseau, men can in fact be obligated to die.

This is obviously a quite different conception of the state and of citizenship, one in which the citizen had "the lively sense of oneself as a participant in a free state, concerned for the common good" rather than "a lively longing for private pleasure." Walzer is obviously attracted to this nonliberal alternative, though he admits that it makes for a "hard politics" and is an ideal that "fails to describe any reality we know or can project for the future." Moreover, one cannot completely discount the worries liberal critics have expressed about the harmonies one finds between Rousseau's descriptions of this hard democratic politics and the organic ideologies legitimating the even harder politics of authoritarian states. For my purposes, what is most important is Walzer's contention that this democratic ideal does inhere in the feeling that some Americans have that citizenship must amount to more than liberalism allows and in the sense that these citizens (now a bare majority of registered voters) have that they should continue to participate in the minimal public life that the liberal state has conceded to democracy. Important as well is his suggestion that this participatory ideal plays a very important role in the liberal state as an *ideology* designed to counteract the absence in the liberal theory of obligation to a "horizontal" political community. "This imposing and difficult ideal," he notes, "becomes an ideology whenever we are told that we are already citizens, men at or near our very best, and that our country is a nation of citizens." This is "mystification of the worst sort," yet it serves a useful purpose in that it keeps the ideal alive: "ideology is the social element within which ideals survive."

Freedom of Speech was Rockwell's favorite painting in the series and the favorite of much of his audience as well, and I suspect this may be because it argued for a communitarian and thoroughly political conception of obligation that many found an attractive alternative to the liberal conception of fighting for the family and other private obligations and interests, though these obligations and interests were no less moral than those represented in the portrait of the town meeting. This was also the most thoroughly ideological of the illustrations, for it portrayed the hard politics of a nonliberal, democratic state unavailable to most yet appealing to many Americans; contended that it was their politics; and asked that they risk their lives for it. Yet *Freedom of Speech* also served to keep alive the ideal it represented. And those who remain wedded to this difficult and distant ideal may take some comfort in its appearance in a painting by Norman Rockwell, for this, one would think, would guarantee that it cannot be dismissed as un-American simply because it is not liberal.

Redefining Women's Work

RUTH MILKMAN

The economic mobilization for World War II dramatically transformed women's relationship to the labor market. They poured by the millions into jobs previously done only by men. As military conscription reduced the ranks of available workers and war production generated rapid economic expansion, the labor surplus of the 1930s was quickly replaced by a labor shortage—especially a shortage of male labor. Suddenly there was deep uncertainty about where the boundaries between "men's" and "women's" work should be drawn. Not only were women integrated into "men's jobs" on an unprecedented scale, but also, with conversion to war production, many entirely new occupations emerged—with no clear sex labels.

The war is often viewed as a period when job segregation by sex was broken down, albeit temporarily. Yet what is most striking about the wartime transformation is the way *new* patterns of occupational segregation developed in the industries opened to women. The boundaries between "women's" and "men's" work changed location, rather than being eliminated. If the most remarkable aspect of the sexual division of labor in the depression was its stability in the face of dramatic economic and political change, the wartime experience highlights something even more

Excerpt from *Gender at Work: The Dynamics of Job Segregation by Sex During World War II.* Copyright 1987 by Ruth Milkman. Used with the permission of the author and the University of Illinois Press.

fundamental: the reproduction of job segregation in the context of a huge influx of women into the work force and a massive upheaval in the division of labor.

Rather than hiring women workers to fill openings as vacancies occurred, managers explicitly defined some war jobs as "suitable" for women, and others as "unsuitable," guided by a hastily revised idiom of sex-typing that adapted prewar traditions to the special demands of the war emergency. As married women and mothers joined the labor force in growing numbers during the war, occupational segregation and the sex-typing of war jobs helped to reconcile women's new economic position with their traditional family role. Wartime propaganda imagery of "woman's place" on the nation's production lines consistently portrayed women's war work as a temporary extension of domesticity. And jobs that had previously been viewed as quintessentially masculine were suddenly endowed with femininity and glamour for the duration. . . .

. . . In 1940, on the eve of U.S. entry into the war, women factory workers made up only 20 percent of the female labor force, and most of them were employed in older, low-wage industries like textiles and clothing. In the war boom, however, the industries that had traditionally employed the fewest women drew on them most extensively. Although women's employment grew by 50 percent between 1940 and 1944 in the economy as a whole, it increased by 140 percent in manufacturing. And in major war industries (metal-working, chemical, and rubber), women's employment rose 460 percent in that four-year period.

Electrical manufacturing and auto were among the industries most affected: women's employment increased by 600 percent in auto and by 350 percent in electrical manufacturing in the mobilization period. The curtailment of civilian production, the vast expansion of employment, and the conscription of prewar workers into the military compelled both industries to completely overhaul their production processes as well as their labor utilization policies. Employers' views about what kinds of work were and were not appropriate for women had to be drastically modified. . . .

The longstanding tradition of extensive female employment in electrical manufacturing made the process of incorporating women into "men's jobs" in that industry relatively smooth. In auto, however, neither management nor labor was accustomed to women's employment in production work, except in parts plants and a few small enclaves of assembly plants like the cut-and-sew or wiring departments. The introduction of women into the all-male preserves of the auto industry was therefore a dramatic break with past practice. In addition, the process of conversion to military production was far more disruptive to the *status quo ante* in auto than in electrical manufacturing. While consumer goods production was curtailed in both industries, the changeover from car production to the manufacture of tanks, aircraft, and ordnance required more extensive retooling than conversion of the electrical industry involved. Electrical manufacturing was less capital-intensive to begin with, and there was far more overlap between its wartime and peacetime products.

If incorporating female labor into the auto industry was relatively difficult, it was also avoided longer than in electrical manufacturing and other war industries, thanks to the major auto corporations' procrastination in converting their plants to military production. In the first half of 1942, when the rest of the nation already had a labor shortage, Michigan was grappling with severe "conversion unemployment." The problem was particularly pronounced among women auto workers. Indeed, both the absolute number and the proportion of women among auto production workers dropped between April 1941 and April 1942. Not until late 1942, when conversion was complete and the prewar labor force had been reabsorbed into defense work, did the proportion of women in auto begin to rise. While the slow conversion process initially delayed the influx of women into the industry, it also made for an especially sudden shift in the sexual division of labor. In April 1942, only one of every twenty auto production workers was female; eighteen months later, one out of every four workers in the industry's plants was a woman.

The growth in female employment was more gradual in the electrical industry. Initially, it seemed like a marginal change in an industry that had always employed large numbers of women, and everyone concerned adjusted relatively easily. A U.S. Women's Bureau survey in mid-1942 found that only 7 percent of the women employed in New Jersey's electrical plants were "substitutes" for men, with the vast majority of them employed in "occupations that have always been women's." And as late as July 1943, only 14 percent of the production jobs in the Erie GE plant were considered "men's jobs" being performed by women. As the war-converted electrical industry expanded during the mobilization period, many of the new jobs that women filled closely resembled positions routinely occupied by females in the prewar years. Of course, the fact that women were also employed during the war in a range of jobs previously considered appropriate only for men did create tensions. But because female labor was a familiar presence in electrical manufacturing, and the sexual division of labor in the industry was relatively flexible, the wartime transition was much smoother there than in auto.

Although women were incorporated into electrical manufacturing more easily, and the wartime increase in total employment was much greater in that industry, the ratio of female to total employment increased far more in auto. This was primarily because of the geographical concentration characteristic of automotive production during this period. In 1939, the city of Detroit alone accounted for 48 percent of the nation's auto workers, and no other American city contributed more to the nation's military production during the war. Michigan, with 4 percent of the U.S. population, obtained more than 10 percent of the war contracts awarded by the government. Most of the work was carried out in the Detroit area, where employment doubled between 1940 and 1943. Not for nothing was the Motor City dubbed the "Arsenal of Democracy.". . .

There was substantial wartime migration to Detroit, whose population grew by 15 percent between 1940 and 1943. Most of the newcomers came from southern states where well-paid war jobs were not available. Despite the community's inability to accommodate more in-migrants, employers continued to recruit workers in the South. As the situation deteriorated, families who came to the city found it impossible to secure housing, and many simply left after a few months. Well before the problem reached this point, government officials recognized that the solution to the city's labor shortage was the employment of women who already lived in the area. In mid-1942, the War Production Board (WPB) threatened to withhold additional war contracts from Detroit manufacturers, and even to cancel existing contracts, if in-migration was not stemmed. The Detroit regional director of the WPB wrote to the Michigan Manufacturers' Association in July 1942, urging that the alternative to continued in-migration was "the recruiting of large numbers of women who do not ordinarily consider themselves a part of the industrial labor supply." As the WPB noted, "The recruitment of local women who are not now in the labor market is free from the disadvantages or limitations of the other methods of meeting the labor deficit. Local women workers will not require new housing, transportation or other facilities. They do not create a possible future relief burden. Each woman who is recruited will reduce the necessary in-migration correspondingly and thus reduce or eliminate the need for transferring contracts elsewhere." The same logic led the government to encourage employment of blacks as well as older and handicapped workers, groups that (like women) had always been shunned by most auto manufacturers.

Ultimately the Detroit labor shortage would be met in exactly this way. But employers refused to go along with the plan until the supply of male labor had been exhausted. "As long as the employers can hire men," Ernest Kanzler, the head of the Detroit WPB, pointed out at a meeting on the labor supply problem held in June 1942, "they don't talk about hiring women." The automotive management representatives at the meeting agreed. "They are used to talking in terms of men," acknowledged H. J. Roesch, of the Briggs Manufacturing Company. "In our plant," said the Industrial Relations Manager of Packard, "we have 3,000 applications for women right now that we can't use. I doubt if there isn't a plant in Detroit with the same predicament." It was not because auto industry employers were more flexible than their counterparts in electrical manufacturing, but because they were left with no choice in the matter that the wartime change in the sexual division of labor in auto was so much more extensive.

Although management recognized early on that unprecedented numbers of women would probably have to be employed in the auto industry during the war, they showed little interest in hiring women as long as the labor surplus created by conversion unemployment persisted. Initially, women war workers were employed only in jobs that had long before been established within the industry as "women's work." Although a U.S. Employment Service survey of war work in early 1942 found that women could capably perform the tasks required in 80 percent of the job classifications, UAW [United Automobile Workers] plants that employed women had, on average, women in only 28 percent of the classifications in July of that year. "The chief classifications on which they were employed," the UAW reported, "were assembly, inspection, drill press, punch press, sewing machines, filing, and packing." Such positions had often been filled by women before the war.

Even as the labor supply dwindled, auto employers were loath to forsake their prewar hiring preferences for white males. Ultimately, the federal government intervened, setting male employment allocation ceilings and giving the War Manpower Commission (WMC) the power to enforce them. "Over our strenuous objections," Detroit WMC director Edward Cushman recalls, "the Ford Motor Company began hiring 17, 18 and 19 year-old men. And we kept drafting them!"

The pressures that increased female representation in auto also led to growth in black employment during the war. In the industry's Detroit plants, black representation rose from about 4 percent of the work force in the prewar period to 15 percent in 1945. Before the war, auto employers (with the partial and eccentric exception of Ford) had refused to hire blacks. John L. Lovett, secretary of the Michigan Manufacturers' Association, believed that "Negroes do not have the 'speed and rhythm' to do this type of work," according to a 1941 government report. Lovett assured the investigator that "most Michigan employers have the same belief." As late as July 1943, after black employment had begun to increase in many automotive plants, employers complained that blacks "leave the job easily and are absent a lot." Management's objections to hiring blacks, while cast in a different idiom, paralleled their opposition to female employment.

Employers in electrical manufacturing were even more resistant to hiring blacks—in contrast to their willingness to employ women in greater numbers during the war. In 1940, blacks made up less than 1 percent of the electrical manufacturing work force, and only 3 percent at the wartime employment peak. Those blacks who did get jobs in electrical plants during the war, significantly, were concentrated in areas with tight labor markets. A 1943 government report on the radio and radar industry, which had a higher proportion of blacks than other branches of electrical manufacturing at the time, noted that "very few firms expect to increase their employment of nonwhites significantly unless forced to by greatly increased labor stringencies or by compulsory labor market controls." Because government intervention focused on "congested" war production areas like Detroit, the geographical decentralization of the electrical industry saved it from the political pressures that increased black employment in auto.

In addition to the geographical factor, the low level of black employment in wartime electrical manufacturing was related to the extensive participation of white women in the industry. "Those industries which delayed longest the employment of Negroes," Robert Weaver pointed out in his authoritative 1946 study, *Negro Labor,* "were usually light and clean manufacturing. They were the industries in which women (white) were used in the largest proportions." The electrical manufacturers relied primarily on the reserves of white female labor to meet their requirements, and introduced blacks only in localities where they had no alternative. In auto, on the other hand, management wanted neither women nor black workers so long as white men were available; but black men were often preferred over white women for unskilled "heavy" jobs.

The least favored group of workers in both industries was black women. "The [black] men are o.k. on unskilled jobs," reported one government representative in mid-1943, summarizing the attitude of auto industry employers toward black workers, "but the women are a drug on the market." In Detroit, Geraldine Bledsoe of the U.S. Employment Service complained publicly in October 1942 that more than one thousand black women had completed vocational training courses, "and yet they go day after day to the plants and are turned down." By mid-1943 the WMC estimated that twenty-eight thousand black women were available for war work in Detroit, but most war plants would employ them only as janitors, matrons, and government inspectors. Auto manufacturers began to hire black women in substantial numbers only after all other sources of labor had been fully exhausted. No data are available on the sex breakdown among the small group of blacks employed in electrical manufacturing during the war, but the much larger number of "women's jobs" in this industry may have made for less disparity between women and men. By 1950, black representation among women electrical workers was slightly greater than among men. . . .

Women were not evenly distributed through the various jobs available in the war plants, but were hired into specific classifications that management deemed "suitable" for women and were excluded from other jobs. Some employers conducted special surveys to determine the sexual division of labor in a plant; probably more often such decisions were made informally by individual supervisors. Although data on the distribution of women through job classifications in the wartime auto and electrical industries are sketchy, there is no mistaking the persistence of segregation by sex. A 1943 survey of the auto industry's Detroit plants, for example, found more than one-half of the women workers clustered in only five of seventy-two job classifications. Only 11 percent of the men were employed in these five occupations.

Jobs were also highly segregated in the electrical industry during the war. A 1942 study of electrical appliance plants (most of which had already been converted to military production when surveyed) found women, who were 30 percent of the workers, in only twenty-one job classifications, whereas men were spread across seventy-two of them. Nearly half of the women (47 percent) were employed in a single job category, and 68 percent were clustered in four occupations. Only 16 percent of the men were in these four job classifications. Another study of radio, radio equipment, and phonograph plants, conducted in early 1945, told the same story. Women were 58 percent of the workers surveyed, but half of them were found in four occupations, although these four categories accounted for only 6 percent of the male minority.

Job segregation by sex was explicitly acknowledged in many war plants: Jobs were formally labeled "male" and "female." The two largest electrical firms, GE and Westinghouse, continued this practice until the end of the war. And in 45 percent of the auto plants with sexually mixed work forces responding to a survey conducted in mid-1944 by the UAW Women's Bureau, jobs were formally categorized as "male" or "female." Available records suggest that sex segregation also existed elsewhere, even if it was not formally acknowledged. A case in point is the Ford River Rouge plant. The available data do not offer a very detailed breakdown, yet a great deal of segregation is apparent. In December 1943, when women's employment in the industry was at its wartime peak, women made up 16 percent of the Rouge work force. More than one-half of the job groups listed in the company's internal "factory count" included women, but 62 percent of the women workers were clustered in just 20 of the 416 job categories. And nearly two-thirds of the occupational groups were at least 90 percent male. . . .

Whatever the sexual division of labor happened to be at a given point in time, management always seemed to insist that there was no alternative. When a War Department representative visited an airplane plant where large numbers of women were employed, he was told that the best welder in the plant was a woman. "Their supervisors told me that their work is fine, even better than that of the men who were formerly on those jobs," he reported. "In another plant in the same area, I remarked on the absence of women and was told that women just can't do those jobs—the very same jobs. It is true, they can't do that type of work—as long as the employer refuses to hire and train them."

Although the specifics varied, everywhere management was quick to offer a rationale for the concentration of women in some jobs and their exclusion from others, just as it had in the prewar era. "Womanpower differs from manpower as oil fuel differs from coal," proclaimed the trade journal *Automotive War Production* in

October 1943, "and an understanding of the characteristics of the energy involved was needed for obtaining best results." Although it was now applied to a larger and quite different set of jobs, the basic characterization of women's abilities and limitations was familiar. As *Automotive War Production* put it:

> On certain kinds of operations—the very ones requiring high manipulative skill—women were found to be a whole lot quicker and more efficient than men. Engineering womanpower means realizing fully that women are not only different from men in such things as lifting power and arm reach—but in many other ways that pertain to their physiological and their social functions. To understand these things does not mean to exclude women from *the jobs for which they are peculiarly adapted,* and where they can help to win this war. It merely means using them as women, and not as men.

The idiom of women's war work in the electrical industry closely paralleled that in auto. "Nearly every Westinghouse plant employs women, especially for jobs that require dexterity with tiny parts," reported an article in *Factory Management and Maintenance* in March 1942.

> At the East Pittsburgh plant, for instance, women tape coils. The thickness of each coil must be identical to within close limits, so the job requires feminine patience and deft fingers.
>
> Another job that calls for unlimited patience is the inspection of moving parts of electric instruments. . . .
>
> Thirty-one pieces are assembled into a thermostat control for refrigerators at the Mansfield works. Westinghouse finds that women can handle these minute parts, and are willing to perform the highly repetitive operations that this type of assembly requires.

Repeatedly stressed, especially in auto, was the lesser physical strength of the average woman worker. "Woman isn't just a 'smaller man,' " *Automotive War Production* pointed out. "Compensations in production processes must be made to allow for the fact that the average woman is only 35 percent muscle in comparison to the average man's 41 percent. Moreover, industrial studies have shown that only 54 percent of woman's weight is strength, as against man's 87 percent, and that the hand squeeze of the average woman exerts only 48 pounds of pressure, against man's 81 pounds."

Accompanying the characterization of women's work as "light" was an emphasis on cleanliness. "Women can satisfactorily fill all or most jobs performed by men, subject only to the limitations of strength and physical requirements," a meeting of the National Association of Manufacturers concluded in March 1942. "However . . . jobs of particularly 'dirty' character, jobs that subject women to heat process or are of a 'wet' nature should not be filled by women . . . despite the fact that women could, if required, perform them."

The emphasis in the idiom of sex-typing on the physical limitations of women workers had a dual character. It not only justified the sexual division of labor, but it also served as the basis for increased mechanization and work simplification. "To adjust women's jobs to such [physical] differences, automotive plants have added more mechanical aids such as conveyors, chain hoists, and load lifters," reported *Automotive War Production.* A study by Constance Green found job dilution of this sort widespread in electrical firms and other war industries in the Connecticut Valley as well. "Where ten men had done ten complete jobs, now . . . eight women and two, three, or possibly four men together would do the ten split-up jobs," she noted. "Most often men set up machines, ground or adjusted tools, and generally 'serviced' the women who acted exclusively as machine operators."

Although production technology was already quite advanced in both auto and electrical manufacturing, the pace of development accelerated during the war period. Management attributed this to its desire to make jobs easier for women, but the labor shortage and the opportunity to introduce new technology at government expense under war contracts were at least as important. However, the idiom that constructed women as "delicate" and, although poorly suited to "heavy" work, amenable to monotonous jobs, was now marshaled to justify the use of new technology and work "simplification." At Vultee Aircraft, for example, a manager explained:

> It definitely was in Vultee's favor that the hiring of women was started when production jobs were being simplified to meet the needs of fast, quantity production. . . . Special jigs were added to hold small tools, such as drills, so that women could concentrate on employing more effectively their proven capacity for repetitive operations requiring high digital dexterity.
>
> Unlike the man whom she replaced, she as a woman, had the capacity to withstand the monotony of even more simplified repetitive operations. To have suspended the air wrench from a counterbalanced support for him would have served merely to heighten his boredom with the job. As for the woman who replaced him, she now handles two such counterbalanced, air-driven wrenches, one in each hand.

Of course, such changes led to greater efficiency regardless of the sex of the workers. But the potential for resistance to job dilution was substantially undercut by the claim, cast in the patriotic idiom of "production for victory," that the changes were necessary in order to facilitate women's employment. The significance of this is suggested by the fact that more than one-half the plants employing women in "men's jobs" that the Conference Board surveyed in 1943 had "simplified" the operations involved.

There was a contradiction in the management literature on women's war work. It simultaneously stressed the fact that "women are being trained in skills that were considered exclusively in man's domain" and their special suitability for "delicate war jobs." These two seemingly conflicting kinds of statements were reconciled through analogies between "women's work" at home and in the war plants. "Note the similarity between squeezing orange juice and the operation of a small drill press," the Sperry Gyroscope Company urged in a recruitment pamphlet. "Anyone can peel potatoes," it went on. "Burring and filing are almost as easy." An automotive industry publication praised women workers at the Ford Motor Company's Willow Run bomber plant in similar terms. "The ladies have shown they can operate drill presses as well as egg beaters," it proclaimed. "Why should men, who from childhood on never so much as sewed on buttons," inquired one manager, "be expected to handle delicate instruments better than women who have plied embroidery needles, knitting needles and darning needles all their lives?" The newsreel *Glamour Girls of '43* pursued the same theme:

> Instead of cutting the lines of a dress, this woman cuts the pattern of aircraft parts. Instead of baking cake, this woman is cooking gears to reduce the tension in the gears after use. . . .

They are taking to welding as if the rod were a needle and the metal a length of cloth to be sewn. After a short apprenticeship, this woman can operate a drill press just as easily as a juice extractor in her own kitchen. And a lathe will hold no more terrors for her than an electric washing machine.

In this manner, virtually any job could be labeled "women's work."

Glamour was a related theme in the idiom through which women's war work was demarcated as female. As if calculated to assure women—and men—that war work need not involve a loss of femininity, depictions of women's new work roles were overlaid with allusions to their stylish dress and attractive appearance. "A pretty young inspector in blue slacks pushes a gauge—a cylindrical plug with a diamond-pointed push-button on its side—through the shaft's hollow chamber," was a typical rendition. Such statements, like the housework analogies, effectively reconciled woman's position in what were previously "men's jobs" with traditional images of femininity.

Ultimately, what lay behind the mixed message that war jobs were at once "men's" and "women's" jobs was an unambiguous point: Women *could* do "men's work," but they were only expected to do it temporarily. The ideological definition of women's war work explicitly included the provision that they would gracefully withdraw from their "men's jobs" when the war ended and the rightful owners returned. Women, as everyone knew, were in heavy industry "for the duration." This theme would become much more prominent after the war, but it was a constant undercurrent from the outset.

Before the war, too, women had been stereotyped as temporary workers, and occupational sex-typing had helped to ensure that employed women would continue to view themselves as women first, workers second. Now this took on new importance, because the reserves of "womanpower" war industries drew on included married women, even mothers of young children, in unprecedented numbers. A study by the Automotive Council for War Production noted that of twelve thousand women employed during the war by one large automotive firm in Detroit, 68 percent were married, and 40 percent had children. And a 1943 WPB study found that 40 percent of the one hundred fifty thousand women war workers employed in Detroit were mothers. "With the existing prejudice against employing women over forty, the overwhelming majority of these women workers are young mothers with children under 16."

This was the group of women least likely to have been employed in the prewar years. "In this time of pressure for added labor supply," the U.S. Women's Bureau reported, "the married women for the first time in this country's history exceeded single women in the employed group." Married women were especially numerous in the auto industry, probably because of the vigorous effort to recruit local female labor in Detroit. Although comparable data are not available for the electrical industry, the major companies did lift their longstanding restrictions on the employment of married women during the war mobilization.

Some firms made deliberate efforts to recruit the wives and daughters of men whom they had employed before the war. A 1942 study by Princeton University's Industrial Relations Section reported on the reasons given by employers for this policy: "(1) It increases the local labor supply without affecting housing requirements;

(2) it brings in new employees who are already acquainted with the company and who are likely to be as satisfactory employees as their male relatives; and (3) it may help to minimize postwar readjustment since wives of employed men are not looking for permanent employment." Similarly, the Detroit Vickers aircraft plant had a policy of hiring "members of men's families who have gone to forces so that when these men come back there will be less of a problem in getting the women out of the jobs to give them back to the men."

The dramatic rise in married women's employment during the war raised the longstanding tension between women's commitment to marriage and family and their status as individual members of the paid work force to a qualitatively different level. Before the war, the bulk of the female labor force was comprised of unmarried women; young wives with no children; and self-supporting widowed, divorced, and separated women. When married women and mothers went to work during the war, the occupational sex-typing that linked women's roles in the family and in paid work, far from disintegrating, was infused with new energy.

The wartime idiom of sex segregation combined such prewar themes as women's dexterity and lack of physical strength with an emphasis on the value of women's multivaried experience doing housework and an unrelenting glamourization of their new work roles. That "woman's place" in wartime industry was defined so quickly and effectively owed much to the power of this sex-typing. Although the initiative came from management, neither unions nor rank-and-file workers—of either gender—offered much resistance to the *general* principle of differentiation of jobs into "female" and "male" categories. Nor was the ideology of "woman's place" in the war effort ever frontally challenged. There was a great deal of conflict, however, over the location of the boundaries between the female and male labor markets in wartime industry, and over wage differentials between these newly constituted markets. . . .

SUGGESTED READING

Adams, Michael. *The Best War Ever: America and World War II* (1994).
Albrecht, Donald, ed. *World War II and the American Dream* (1995).
Anderson, Karen. *Wartime Women: Sex Roles, Family Relationships and the Status of Women During World War II* (1981).
Bailey, Beth, and David Farber. *The First Strange Place: The Alchemy of Race and Sex in World War II Hawaii* (1992).
Berube, Allan. *Coming Out Under Fire: The History of Gay Men and Women in World War II* (1990).
Black, Gregory D., and Clayton R. Koppes. *Hollywood Goes to War* (1987).
Campbell, D'Ann. *Women at War with America: Private Lives in a Patriotic Era* (1984).
Capeci, Dominic. *Race Relations in Wartime Detroit* (1984).
Capeci, Dominic, and Martha Wilkerson. *Layered Violence: The Detroit Rioters of 1943* (1991).
Clive, Alan. *State of War: Michigan in World War II* (1979).
Daniels, Roger. *Prisoners Without Trial* (1993).
D'Emilio, John. *Sexual Politics, Sexual Communities* (1983).
Dower, John. *War Without Mercy: Race and Power in the Pacific War* (1986).
Gluck, Sherna Berger. *Rosie the Riverter Revisited: Women, the War, and Social Change* (1987).
Hartmann, Susan. *The Home Front and Beyond: American Women in the 1940s* (1982).

Hirsch, Susan, and Lewis Erenberg, eds. *The War in American Culture* (1996).

Honey, Maureen. *Creating Rosie the Riveter: Class, Gender, and Propaganda During World War II* (1984).

Jeffries, John W. *Wartime America: the World War II Home Front* (1996).

Johnson, Marilynn S. *The Second Gold Rush: Oakland and the East Bay in World War II* (1993).

Leff, Mark. "The Politics of Sacrifice on the American Home Front in World War II." *Journal of American History* 77 (March 1991): 1296–1318.

Lipsitz, George. *Rainbow at Midnight: Labor and Culture in the 1940s* (1994).

Mazon, Mauricio. *The Zoot-Suit Riots* (1984).

Meyer, Leisa D. *Creating GI Jane: Sexuality and Power in the Women's Army Corps During World War II* (1996).

Milkman, Ruth. *Gender at Work: The Dynamics of Job Segregation by Sex During World War II* (1987).

O'Brien, Kenneth Paul, and Lynn Hudson Parsons, eds. *The Home-Front War: World War II and American Society* (1995).

Okihiro, Gary Y. *Whispered Silences: Japanese Americans and World War II* (1996).

Reed, Merl. *Seedtime for the Modern Civil Rights Movement* (1991).

Roeder, George H. *The Censored War* (1993).

Rupp, Leila. *Mobilizing Women for War: German and American Propoganda, 1939–1945* (1978).

Sugrue, Thomas J. *The Origins of the Urban Crisis: Race and Inequality in Postwar Detroit* (1996).

Tateishi, John, ed. *And Justice for All: An Oral History of the Japanese-American Detention Camps* (1984).

Terkel, Studs. *"The Good War": An Oral History of World War II* (1984).

Tuttle, William. *"Daddy's Gone to War": The Second World War in the Lives of America's Children* (1993).

Wynn, Neil A. *The Afro-American and the Second World War.* Rev. ed. (1993).

The Political Economy

of World War II

For the United States, World War II was both an economic escape from the Great Depression and a political opportunity to ensure that such a crisis did not recur. The mobilization for war forced the Roosevelt Administration to sort out the future of the New Deal. And the international alliance against fascism allowed the Administration to sort out the terms of international trade and finance for the postwar era. The political economy of the postwar era would retain many of the features of the New Deal, but the promise and assumption of sustained economic growth displaced the contentious politics of the Depression years.

    The foundation of wartime planning was American leadership of an open global economy, what would become known (after the site of a late war economic conference) as the Bretton Woods system. American goals reflected a renewed commitment to the ideals and institutions of liberal internationalism, and a conviction that the political failures of 1919–1920 had hastened the crash, prolonged the Depression, and contributed to the outbreak of war in the late 1930s. Accordingly, American planners used their participation in the war to leverage the postwar cooperation of their allies and shape the terms of the peace around a single goal: sustained domestic and international economic growth based on free trade and investment.

    The booming war economy and the promise of postwar internationalism also called into question the very premises of the New Deal. Many economic and political interests assumed that postwar growth would render much of the New Deal obsolete. Others hoped that a healthy economy could support an even more expansive set of social programs and workers' rights. In the end, the results were mixed. For many, the war economy underscored the political and economic importance of government spending. This marked a concession to the persistence of a large and active federal government, but it also narrowed the government's role to stimulating and regulating the private sector through taxes and fiscal policy. In labor policy, the federal government's role was similarly both accepted and constrained. Under the peculiar conditions of the war, the labor movement concentrated on cementing the gains it had already made. And in welfare policy, the federal government avoided new programs and looked increasingly to private employment and employment-based benefits (especially health insurance) to build on the foundation laid by the Social Security Act.

In postwar debates over the future of the New Deal, not surprisingly, both New Deal liberals and laissez-faire conservatives were outflanked by "the politics of growth." This new political synthesis turned the attention of the New Deal state to the maintenance of economic growth through international trade. The necessity of meeting international responsibilities and managing the domestic economy made it impossible to return to the small government of 1929. At the same time the over-arching importance of private employment and private economic growth seemed to make a return to the reformist policies of 1935 equally untenable.

D O C U M E N T S

The first three documents chart American thinking about the postwar international order. In Document 1, the "Atlantic Charter" American planners use their early support of the British (prior to American entry into the war) to establish the basic terms for postwar commerce. In Document 2, drawn from congressional hearings on the 1944 Bretton Woods Agreement, legislators discuss the American postwar role. Document 3, excerpted from the Yalta Agreements of 1945, underscores both the fragility of the wartime alliance with the Soviet Union and the ways in which the Soviet threat would magnify the stakes and the costs of postwar leadership. The final two documents touch on the domestic economic debate. In Document 4, the New Deal–inspired National Resources Planning Board suggests how the promise of postwar growth might trump the debates about scarcity and stagnation that had marked the Depression era. In Document 5, the radical journalist I. F. Stone notes the political anxieties and dilemmas that accompany the end of the war and of the war-induced economic boom.

1. The Atlantic Charter, 1941

First, their countries seek no aggrandizement, territorial or other;

Second, they desire to see no territorial changes that do not accord with the freely expressed wishes of the peoples concerned;

Third, they respect the right of all peoples to choose the form of government under which they will live; and they wish to see sovereign rights and self-government restored to those who have been forcibly deprived of them;

Fourth, they will endeavor, with due respect for their existing obligations, to further the enjoyment by all States, great or small, victor or vanquished, of access, on equal terms, to the trade and to the raw materials of the world which are needed for their economic prosperity;

Fifth, they desire to bring about the fullest collaboration between all nations in the economic field with the object of securing, for all, improved labor standards, economic advancement, and social security;

Sixth, after the final destruction of the Nazi tyranny, they hope to see established a peace which will afford to all nations the means of dwelling in safety within their own boundaries, and which will afford assurance that all the men in the lands may live out their lives in freedom from fear and want;

From Message of Roosevelt to Congress (August 21, 1941), in *Peace and War: United States Foreign Policy, 1931–1941* (Washington, Government Printing Office, 1942), p. 107.

Seventh, such a peace should enable all men to traverse the high seas and oceans without hindrance;

Eighth, they believe that all of the nations of the world, for realistic as well as spiritual reasons, must come to the abandonment of the use of force. Since no future peace can be maintained if land, sea or air armaments continue to be employed by nations which threaten, or may threaten, aggression outside of their frontiers, they believe, pending the establishment of a wider and permanent system of general security, that the disarmament of such nations is essential. They will likewise aid and encourage all other practicable measures which will lighten for peace-loving peoples the crushing burden of armaments.

2. Debating the Bretton Woods Agreement, 1945

Mr. Luxford . . . [N]o country has signed this document in a way that would bind its government. Rather, when they signed the document at Bretton Woods, they were certifying to the fact that the conference felt that this was the way to do it. When they actually sign the agreements, that is going to be just the same as what Congress is now considering. If this Congress were to approve it, they may say "yes" or "no" to the Bretton Woods agreements, or again, they may say "yes, with a reservation." If they insist on that reservation at that point, then there will be no agreement among the countries. That means we will have to go back and try to make a new agreement.

The parliaments of the countries that have made these reservations will have to decide whether this reservation is vital to their acceptance, and, therefore, they must stay out or try to get other countries to accept that reservation. They may say, however, "Well, we would have liked it this way, but since all the other countries did not agree with us on it, we will take it the other way."

It is a question of taking three-quarters of a loaf when you cannot get the whole loaf.

Mr. Patman In effect, they signed without any qualifications, restrictions, limitations, or reservations; did they not?

Mr. Luxford That is what they are called upon to do?

Mr. Patman Yes.

Mr. Luxford Yes.

Mr. Patman All right. I will not go into that any further. Dr. White, if we had adopted something like the Bretton Woods agreements back in the early twenties, and it had worked as you expect this to work, would that have had any effect on preventing the war that we are in now?

Mr. White I think it would very definitely have made a considerable contribution to checking the war and possibly it might even have prevented it. . . .

Mr. Smith Do you believe the adoption of the fund proposal, Mr. White, would be a fine thing for the United States?

Mr. White I definitely do, Dr. Smith.

Mr. Smith Do you believe it would contribute to world peace?

Mr. White I certainly do.

From U.S. House, Committee on Banking and Currency. *Bretton Woods Agreement Act.* Hearings on HR 2211, 79th Congress, 1st Session (March/April 1945), vol. 1, pp. 139, 155.

Mr. Smith Do you believe that it would create confidence among industrialists to go ahead and plan for the future?

Mr. White I should think it would be a great help in that direction.

Mr. Smith Do you believe it would create employment and bring prosperity?

Mr. White I do.

Mr. Smith How much employment do you think it would bring?

Mr. White What was that last question, sir?

Mr. Smith How much employment do you think this fund would create?

Mr. White I could not answer that question. It will help substantially to create a higher level of business activity. It would run into millions.

Mr. Smith I have seen claims to the effect that, with the fund, our export trade would be increased so as to bring the total number of jobs producing exports up to five or six million.

Mr. White I would say that is not unreasonable.

Mr. Smith Do you think that we must have this fund?

Mr. White I think we would make a very serious error if we do not have it. I think history will look back and indict those who fail to vote the approval of the Bretton Woods proposals in the same way that we now look back and indict certain groups in 1921 who prevented our adherence to an international organization designed for the purpose of preventing wars.

Mr. Smith Broadly speaking, you think that this is necessary to create employment, prosperity, here at home, and to help the peoples of other countries to get on their feet?

Mr. White Let us put it this way: Bretton Woods proposals are essential to help move in the direction of those three objectives which you have named.

3. The Yalta Conference, 1945

The following statement is made by the Prime Minister of Great Britain, the President of the United States of America, and the Chairman of the Council of People's Commissars of the Union of Soviet Socialist Republics on the results of the Crimean Conference:

The Defeat of Germany

We have considered and determined the military plans of the three allied powers for the final defeat of the common enemy. . . .

The Occupation and Control of Germany

We have agreed on common policies and plans for enforcing the unconditional surrender terms which we shall impose together on Nazi Germany after German armed resistance has been finally crushed. These terms will not be made known until the final defeat of Germany has been accomplished. Under the agreed plan, the forces

From "The Crimea Conference; Report of the Conference," *Department of State Bulletin* 12 (February 18, 1945), pp. 213–215.

of the three powers will each occupy a separate zone of Germany. Coordinated administration and control has been provided for under the plan through a central control commission consisting of the Supreme Commanders of the three powers with headquarters in Berlin. It has been agreed that France should be invited by the three powers, if she should so desire, to take over a zone of occupation, and to participate as a fourth member of the control commission. The limits of the French zone will be agreed by the four governments concerned through their representatives on the European Advisory Commission.

It is our inflexible purpose to destroy German militarism and Nazism and to ensure that Germany will never again be able to disturb the peace of the world. We are determined to disarm and disband all German armed forces; break up for all time the German General Staff that has repeatedly contrived the resurgence of German militarism; remove or destroy all German military equipment; eliminate or control all German industry that could be used for military production; bring all war criminals to just and swift punishment and exact reparation in kind for the destruction wrought by the Germans; wipe out the Nazi Party, Nazi laws, organizations and institutions, remove all Nazi and militarist influences from public office and from the cultural and economic life of the German people; and take in harmony such other measures in Germany as may be necessary to the future peace and safety of the world. It is not our purpose to destroy the people of Germany, but only when Nazism and militarism have been extirpated will there be hope for a decent life for Germans, and a place for them in the comity of nations.

Reparation by Germany

We have considered the question of the damage caused by Germany to the allied nations in this war and recognized it as just that Germany be obliged to make compensation for this damage in kind to the greatest extent possible. A commission for the compensation of damage will be established. The commission will be instructed to consider the question of the extent and methods for compensating damage caused by Germany to the allied countries. The commission will work in Moscow.

United Nations Conference

We are resolved upon the earliest possible establishment with our allies of a general international organization to maintain peace and security. We believe that this is essential, both to prevent aggression and to remove the political, economic and social causes of war through the close and continuing collaboration of all peace-loving peoples.

We have agreed that a conference of United Nations should be called to meet at San Francisco in the United States on April 25, 1945, to prepare the charter of such an organization, along the lines proposed in the informal conversation at Dumbarton Oaks. . . .

Declaration on Liberated Europe

The Premier of the Union of Soviet Socialist Republics, the Prime Minister of the United Kingdom, and the President of the United States of America have consulted with each other in the common interests of the peoples of their countries and those of liberated Europe. They jointly declare their mutual agreement to concert during the temporary period of instability in liberated Europe the policies of their three governments in assisting the peoples liberated from the domination of Nazi Germany and the peoples of the former Axis satellite states of Europe to solve by democratic means their pressing political and economic problems.

The establishment of order in Europe and the rebuilding of national economic life must be achieved by processes which will enable the liberated peoples to destroy the last vestiges of Nazism and Fascism and to create democratic institutions of their own choice. This is a principle of the Atlantic Charter—the right of all peoples to choose the form of government under which they will live—the restoration of sovereign rights and self-government to those peoples who have been forcibly deprived of them by the aggressor nations. . . .

By this declaration we reaffirm our faith in the principles of the Atlantic Charter, our pledge in the declaration by the United Nations, and our determination to build in cooperation with other peace-loving nations world order under law, dedicated to peace, security, freedom and general well being of all mankind.

4. Postwar Hopes for Full Employment, 1942

I. There must be work for all who are able and willing to work. We all accept this principle. In our industrial society the limits to what one individual can do by himself are circumscribed. The day when individuals and small businesses completely dominated the economic scene is gone. The great centers of initiative and work creation are found in corporate or government enterprises. Such enterprises are private, quasi public, and public. The governments (cities, counties, States and Federal bureaus and courts), in addition to their job as suppliers of services, perform integrating and regulating functions in the field of employment.

We can have work for all, and we can have much higher levels of income, particularly for the lowest income groups. Full employment makes possible these higher income levels, and without full employment such levels are impossible. . . .

But full employment and high national income can be achieved only if national and international policies are followed which will make for these objectives. For example, it is sometimes stated that our international trade creates such a small percentage of our national income that we could forego it without serious damage. But a "small percentage" of our national income is of the magnitude of several billions of dollars. And roughly speaking it takes a million workers to produce a billion and a quarter or a billion and a half dollars of national income. So a reduction of a "small percentage" of the national income as a result of our international trade policy may cut the national income by several billions and result in related reductions in the volume of employment. Readjustments affecting employment and income for millions of people are not easy to achieve.

As a further example, it should be noted that fiscal policies are of major significance in achieving and maintaining full employment. A shift of a billion dollars in the Federal budget can mean employment or unemployment for a million workers whose jobs are dependent on government initiative. A shift in the burden of

From National Resources Planning Board, *Security, Work, and Relief Policies* (Washington, 1942), pp. 2–3.

taxes from low-income groups to high-income groups can mean the difference between continuous activity and interruption of activity; it can mean employment or unemployment.

As still another example of the many-sided problem of establishing full employment and high levels of income, we might refer to some of the issues in labor relations policy. What can be done to encourage the types of policies which will stimulate employment? Statesmanlike union leaders and managers have studied their joint problems from this standpoint. But too often the struggle for power between management and labor or between rival labor organizations has pushed these major problems of income and employment into the background. . . .

II. While full employment is necessary to high levels of national income, even full employment does not establish that continuity of income which individuals and families must have. A considerable number of our people reach advanced years unable to work and in need of income. Nearly all have time "between jobs" for which they are unable to provide. Sickness or disability from various causes interrupts the steady flow of income of others.

Military service has long been recognized as establishing a claim against the Government, and pensions and special insurance rights have been a part of our system for many years. More recently we have come to recognize that any person who makes his contribution to our national life is entitled to protection against the necessary interruptions of income. Thus, the establishment of the social insurances through the Social Security Act provides an orderly system by which workers will receive income in their old age. It provides for income during involuntary unemployment. The great blank in the present system which remains to be filled has to do with invalidity or health insurance. Some scheme for taking care of this need is necessary to maintain high levels of working efficiency. . . .

III. The machinery of the social insurances, however, is not suited to all situations and persons. For some the income from the insurance system will always be inadequate by any standard. Others will fail through no fault of their own to establish eligibility for insurance. Still others will require personal care and rehabilitation which only an adequate system of individualized public aid can provide.

In the present state of affairs it would seem that such a system can be made available only if a Federal grant-in-aid for general public assistance is made to local governments. But it cannot too strongly be stated that individualized aid need not be allowed to degenerate into a form of dole. Neither is it a substitute for work or insurance. It is a necessary complement to provide for those gaps which occur in any system. Furthermore, it protects the special programs from abuse. It must be administered as a complement to and not as a substitute for other parts of a comprehensive program. . . .

IV. . . . Full economic activity and full employment are our first need. Stabilizing of the income flow through a social insurance system is a second. The third requirement is that an adequate general public assistance system provide for those accidental and incidental needs which neither a work program nor an insurance system can supply. But a fourth element is closely related. We have become aware of the need of low-income persons for higher levels of services: access to education, to medical care, to recreational and cultural facilities, to adequate housing and other community facilities. While the insistent needs of some of our poorest citizens have made the provision of these services part of a public aid program, they are of great importance to all members of our society. The truth is that the levels of national income which we seek can apparently not be achieved unless these untapped services can be unlocked and made available to all. High national productive efficiency can be achieved only by wide diffusion of these services. They are no longer relief. They are the necessities of a people mobilizing their strength for a struggle which calls for their utmost in capacity; or for a people which need no longer divert its energies to destruction. . . .

Some may urge that such a program must be set aside until the war emergency is ended. But to postpone until the war is over will be too late. We should move now on the major changes needed to set our house in order.

It is easier to make these changes when employment is high, and it is easier to keep employment high than to lift it once it has declined. Furthermore, we cannot be blind to the fact that national morale is mightily influenced by consideration of what will come when a warring world will be replaced with one more devoted to the arts of peace. Shall that period be a return to the inequities of the past, or a forward movement toward the promise of the future?

5. I. F. Stone on Washington's Anxieties About the Peace, 1945

By the time these lines appear in print the war will almost certainly be over. The prospect of sudden victory has created anxiety here as well as jubilation. For with the coming of peace, the classic crutch of war is kicked out from under American capitalism. The United States faces not only the same old problem but the same old problem in a more intense and exacerbated form. We emerge from the war the Midas of nations. While other countries rise from the ruins appalled by their poverty, we are baffled by our wealth. Our power to produce has increased by 50 per cent since 1940, and the task of raising living standards to match that output is of such magnitude that only government, and business men willing to cooperate with government, can accomplish it. . . .

In a sardonic sense, the sudden surrender of Japan may well be regarded as its reprisal for atomic bombing. We were poorly enough prepared for a slow and comfortable period in which we could devote half our energies to the war in the Pacific and half to the resumption of large-scale civilian output. We are completely unprepared for a Japanese collapse, and unless we act quickly and wisely may face an economic collapse ourselves. The President's letter last night to Chairman J. A. Krug of the War Production Board has already been overtaken by events. There is immediate need for a program which will smooth the transition from war to peace, and a longer-range, if hardly less urgent, need for a program which will insure that industry reconverts to a full-employment level. No government agency has been authorized to tackle the second job, though some headway is being made in Congress by the full-employment bill. But even the simpler and more immediate task of reconversion has yet to be mapped out adequately. Mr. Krug, an ex-TVA man with

Reprinted with permission from the August 18, 1945 issue of *The Nation* magazine.

an N. A. M. mind, believes that the problem can be met by hoopla; he would remove all restrictions as rapidly as possible and let industry scramble back to civilian output pretty much on a hit-or-miss basis. The OPA [Office of Price Administration], the War Labor Board, and the Office of Economic Stabilization feel that controls must be retained and used during the transitional period if it is to be negotiated successfully.

Mr. Truman, whose Senatorial experience made him conversant with the problems of industrial mobilization for war and peace, had to decide between these two points of view, and his letter is a victory for those who fear too quick a removal of restrictions. But unfortunately it leaves Krug and the WPB [War Production Board] crowd at the controls, and they are already interpreting the President's letter to suit themselves. The WPB is as much big-business as ever and cannot be trusted to handle reconversion on a basis fair to the smaller business man and the consumer. The big fellows would like to grab off materials quickly at the expense of the smaller. There is quick profit to be made in turning swiftly to production of higher-price items. The health of business enterprise requires a fair distribution of scarce materials during the transition, and the welfare of the consumer requires the allocation and channelling of materials into badly needed low-cost goods. The nation's economic safety depends on continued price controls during the transition and planning on a unprecedented scale for a higher level of output.

All this is repugnant to the WPB crowd, and Mr. Truman should know from past experience that it will handle these problems its own sweet way, irrespective of White-House directives. New agencies, new men, new ideas, new directions are necessary—and quickly—if we are not to suffer a relapse into chronic mass unemployment now that war's blood transfusions will no longer be available to an ailing capitalism.

ESSAYS

In many ways, the war both entrenched and challenged the basic premises of the New Deal. In the first essay, Michael Sherry shows that the mobilization for war permanently magnified and militarized federal economic and fiscal policies. In the second essay, Alan Brinkley traces the ways in which the war effort shifted the premises and priorities of both the New Deal and the larger American liberal tradition.

Mobilization and Militarization

MICHAEL SHERRY

At the height of the American war effort, the British observer D. W. Brogan summed up "the American way of war," which he thought "bound to be like the American way of life." It was "mechanized like the American farm and kitchen (the farms and kitchens of a lazy people who want washing machines and bulldozers to

Reprinted from *In the Shadow of War: The United States Since the 1930s* by Michael Sherry. Copyright © 1995 Yale University Press, pp. 69, 71–80, 84–86. Reprinted by permission.

do the job for them"). It was practiced by "a nation of colossal business enterprises, often wastefully run in detail, but winning by their mere scale." To Americans, Brogan concluded, "war is a business, not an art; they are not interested in moral victories, but in victory. No great corporation ever successfully excused itself on moral grounds to its stockholders for being in the red; the United States is a great, a very great, corporation whose stockholders expect . . . that it will be in the black. Indeed the great corporation did run "in the black," promoting victory abroad, affluence at home, and militarization in the long run.

However dusty, the measures of American productive triumph remain dazzling. Manufacturing output doubled between 1940 and 1943. Armaments production increased eightfold between 1941 and 1943, to a level nearly that of Britain, the Soviet Union, and Germany combined. Output of ships, often by remarkable assembly-line methods, was staggering. Most telling was success in technically advanced fields: aircraft production zoomed from 5,856 in 1939 to 96,318 in 1944—more than double what any ally or enemy produced, even though the United States made bigger planes. Under Lend-Lease, it also supplied its allies: 400,000 motor vehicles and 2,000 locomotives to the Soviets, and over a fourth of Britain's military equipment by 1944. . . . America's insulation from attack and enormous resources—half the world's manufacturing took place in the United States by 1945—partly accounted for its superiority. But American triumph was not a simple one of "mere scale," as Brogan put it. In aviation (despite German breakthroughs in jet aircraft and rockets), in electronics, and in atomic weapons, American inventive supremacy (with Allied and refugee assistance) was unrivaled. Making the American triumph doubly gratifying, the production of nonwar goods also increased—a luxury no other major combatant enjoyed—despite the cessation of some products (automobiles) and the rationing of others (gasoline, for example). . . .

In turn, that success set in motion vital changes in the American political economy, including the regional redistribution of power and wealth. The war transformed the American West, where federal defense dollars flowed because of its proximity to the Pacific war, its presumably favorable climate, and its sparsely inhabited lands suitable for testing new technologies like jet aircraft and the atomic bomb. The big winner was the West Coast, especially California, which received 12 percent of all war orders and saw its aircraft and shipbuilding facilities reaching from San Diego to Los Angeles become "the nation's largest urban military-industrial complex." The inland West was less favored by the boom in manufacturing (although Denver, oddly enough, churned out submarine-chasing ships), but it prospered through the growth of military bases and the expansion of agricultural and extractive industries. The war effort "transformed a colonial economy" into a "diversified" economic powerhouse paced by advanced technologies and elements of what came to be called a "post-industrial" system. Despite the West's lingering dependence on federal monies, its subordination to the North and the East rapidly faded. In the wake of that grand change came others: a new image, as companies like Hughes Aircraft and Douglas Aviation emerged as heroic enterprises of technological victory; national preeminence for institutions like the University of California and the Caltech Jet Propulsion Laboratory, where prominent American and émigré scientists flocked; a hastened, though hardly complete or effortless, entry into the mainstream of American life for Hispanic Americans; and a massive population shift into parts of the

West. "It was as if someone had tilted the country: people, money, and soldiers all spilled west."

The West's gains were not necessarily other regions' losses. The South's coastal areas saw a "staggering" transformation, initiating the "Sunbelt" prosperity noticed in the 1970s and 1980s; and for southerners "the war challenged their provincialism," drawing them more fully into an American identity and bringing federal power more forcefully to their region. Those sectors suffering economic or population loss belonged to no single region but instead were scattered among rural areas and small towns (interior northern New England, for example). Wartime prosperity in other sectors, however, sometimes masked long-term shifts aggravated by the war. Farm output and income soared, but the farm population continued to shrink. In older industrial states like Michigan (only New York exceeded its share of prime defense contracts), "the shape, if not the size, of [the] economy emerged from the war relatively unchanged." Those states prospered for the moment but lacked the new industries that would fuel continued prosperity.

The war accelerated regional shifts of a grander sort as well, those on an international scale. Large American corporations emerged from the war flush with capital and expertise, eager to exploit markets abandoned by weakened European competitors, more maneuverable as a result of newly decentralized structures, and backed by the world's most powerful government. Once more concerned with domestic markets, those corporations became multinational firms and reached the zenith of their international power in the two decades after 1945. Although that development was largely on hold until the war was over, it was assisted by changes during the war. America's economic leverage allowed it to arm-twist allies dependent on American assistance into accepting tariff and monetary agreements that pried open much of the world, especially Europe's colonial empires, to American trade and investment. Soviet power, revolution and chaos in much of the decolonizing Third World, and other factors would limit the American achievement. And it was dubious indeed to claim, as Secretary of State Cordell Hull once did, that American principles of free trade and democracy were "beneficial and appealing to the sense of justice, of right and of the well-being of free peoples everywhere." But Hull and others did much to realize an old vision of an open economic world dominated by American capitalism.

Most telling, however, were changes internal to the American political economy. The war effected a partnership between big government and big business, after decades of erratic and sometimes strained relations, which largely held for the half-century to follow. Both conscious policy and inadvertent consequence forged the partnership, which "successively mobilized big business, aggrandized it, and linked it to the military establishment." National leaders decided that only generous cooperation with corporate giants could win the war—in the oft-quoted comment of Secretary of War Stimson, when a capitalist country goes to war, "you have to let business make money out of the process or business won't work." Since men like Stimson dominated mobilization—three-fourths of the WPB [War Production Board] executive staff were "dollar-a-year" men who remained on their company payrolls—their views prevailed.

As a result, mobilization enhanced both the immediate profits and the lasting power of larger corporations. Procurement flowed to them; by 1943, one hundred companies held contracts for 70 percent of defense production. Wartime policy guaranteed them profits, freedom from competition and antitrust action in most cases, and government capital or other incentives for plant expansion. Newer industries like aviation, synthetic rubber, and atomic energy were almost wholly financed by government capital. For many companies, the bonanza went far beyond wartime profits: they gained by "squeezing out marginal competitors, forging permanent links with the national government, gaining the inside track on research into new technologies, and absorbing state-financed capital expansion at highly favorable rates after the war." Among companies not doing essential war work, smaller firms often folded, but larger ones with clout in Washington and money to advertise often succeeded in identifying with the cause: Coca-Cola accompanied the troops overseas and a stick of Wrigley's gum went into each soldier's K-ration package. Tough proposals to cap or tax individual salaries and corporate profits were beaten back or watered down, while federal policies on reconversion to a peacetime economy were also beneficial to the interests of big business. . . .

Tentative terms for a lasting business-government partnership were set by the war. Government (especially the executive branch) and business (especially large corporations) would be the senior partners in the firm. Congress would help set policy and broker disputes but would function more as an arena for conflict than as a decisive force itself. Junior partners would be organized labor, agricultural interests, and small business, all of which gained a measure of security—union membership soaring to nearly fifteen million by 1945—at the price of abandoning ambitions for a dominant role. Even their status as junior partners was often in doubt. The aircraft industry, for example, remained notoriously antilabor, thanks to the illegal anti-union tactics of some of its leaders, to southern California's antilabor culture, and to the abundance of "celery pickers" and "country boys" who, at least as long as the Depression's effects lingered, felt "nigger rich" on eighteen dollars a week and proved difficult to unionize. . . .

Partnership involved policy as well as relations of power. In this regard too, war delineated possibilities without fixing them firmly, above all suggesting how to reconcile conflicting visions of the role of government and business in securing the nation's future prosperity and power. Among champions of activist government, the war marked a retreat from designs for government coercion of economic enterprise in favor of federal fiscal policy: the spigot of government spending rather than the hammer of the state's regulation would guide economic energies. The astounding prosperity produced by wartime spending, corporate capture of the governmental apparatus of regulation and mobilization, and the baleful example of totalitarian coercion all promoted this shift among liberals, who also began to abandon Depression-era assumptions of chronic economic stagnation. They could readily see the war as a triumph of John Maynard Keynes's principles of government investment and deficit financing: only about half of the wartime federal budget (which rose from 9 billion dollars in 1939 to 100 billion in 1945) came from taxes, the rest from war bonds and other borrowing. As Robert Lekachman archly put it in the 1960s, "The war pointed a sharp Keynesian moral. As a public works project, all wars (before the nuclear era) are ideal. Since all war production is sheer economic waste, there is never a danger of producing too much." At the same time, corporate leaders also increasingly set aside their reflexive suspicions of federal authority—some had done so long before the 1940s—to accept a major role for fiscal policy in promoting prosperity. The common ground of fiscal policy defined the means by which government could stimulate the economy without coercing its private institutions.

To be sure, that common ground remained ill defined and contested—just how much government spending, focused on what activities, backed by what tax and monetary policies? Looking beyond the war, some liberals favored a "social Keynesianism" emphasizing social welfare and public projects; corporate leaders tended to prefer a "business Keynesianism" harnessing private enterprise by lowering its taxes or buying its goods; economic conservatives, still powerful in business and both political parties, found either approach offensive, even immoral. Less clearly articulated was the "military Keynesianism" that would partly prevail, in which defense spending would be a major lever of stability and growth. . . .

Forging links among government, business, science, and other partners, the war effort demonstrated the temporary attractions of militarization—prosperity, power, victory—and hinted at more permanent ones. But Americans could hardly be faulted for failing to debate those attractions fully during the war. They were, after all, on a course only partly of their choosing. Europe had been "the center of the process of militarization," setting in motion "a militarization of the world" in which Europe itself became the "first and main casualty." Americans were relative newcomers to this historical process. Their future course was neither easily foreseen nor fully set, contingent as it was on decisions yet to be made and on a sustaining ideology yet to be completed.

Most Americans did see some connection between war spending and the return of prosperity. It was driven home to them in their daily lives, trumpeted in the media, and analyzed by economists. The necessity of government action to avert a postwar depression was a staple of wartime commentary, while advertising and political rhetoric instructed Americans to regard prosperity and affluence as not only a reward for victory but as the core of that "American way of life" for which they were fighting. Wartime affluence also raised expectations by improving living standards: even with rationing, per capita food consumption increased (annual meat consumption rose from 134 pound to 162 pounds).

Despite the war-induced prosperity, the urgency to extend it after the war, and the widespread assumption that government would be responsible for it, Americans rarely addressed the future relationship between national security and national prosperity. Instead, debate stalled largely at the point reached in 1942, stuck on the danger of a return to the 1930s and the alternatives posed by New Dealers and their opponents. The U.S. Chamber of Commerce simply noted in 1944 that a postwar depression "would be rooted ultimately in the cessation of governmental demand for armaments." Its stance was typical during and after the war, according to two historians: "Missing from the political discourse of this period was sustained discussion of the long-run implications for business of these momentous changes [wrought during the war] in the federal government's role in the economy." Even among heads of the largest corporations, who had gone farthest "toward accommodation with the newly enlarged national state," such discussion was slight, just as expectations of a postwar military market were generally low. . . .

In short, those worried about the postwar economy paid little attention to spending on national security (except to assume its virtual cessation), while those worried about national security rarely probed the economics involved (except to worry about what monies they could get). Two streams of wartime imagination thus ran parallel to but largely separate from each other, one striving for postwar abundance and economic security, the other for postwar power and military security. . . .

During the war, and among many historians after it, the most significant struggle seemed to have been over the fate of New Deal efforts at social welfare and economic regulation. That contest was indeed important, sharply fought, and substantially won by the New Deal's opponents, whose bitterness toward FDR scarcely abated during the war. Republicans were emboldened by big gains in the 1942 congressional elections, led by the intelligent conservative senator Robert Taft, and often joined by Southern Democrats upset by the urban priorities and racial liberalism of many New Dealers—those "social gainers, do-gooders, bleeding-hearts and long-hairs," as southern conservatives regarded them. Together, these forces scuttled or scaled back New Deal relief agencies, although insurance programs like Social Security remained intact. Roosevelt put up little fight, regarding some programs as temporary or made unnecessary by the war, viewing victory in war as more urgent than domestic legislation, and envisioning new initiatives once the war ended. Liberals, disillusioned as in 1918 that war failed to promote social reform, took some hope from those initiatives and from FDR's 1944 election victory over Thomas Dewey, who promised to keep the welfare state but run it better.

But the wartime campaign against the New Deal threw a smokescreen of symbolic antistatism over deepening government responsibility for social welfare and economic prosperity. Along with other forces, that campaign did not so much diminish such responsibility as redirect it into new channels carved out by the preeminent concern with national security. The failure to secure national health insurance, and the contrasting success of the GI Bill for veterans' assistance—certainly a welfare program, and an expensive one at that—illustrated the shift.

So too did Roosevelt, as he continued to link an older liberalism with national security. Urging an "economic bill of rights" for Americans, he suggested that wartime morale and efficiency required new federal guarantees of economic security: "Our fighting men abroad—and their families at home—expect such a program and have the right to insist upon it." He also implied that such guarantees would serve America in the future, "for unless there is security here at home there cannot be lasting peace in the world." Indeed, his use of "security"—a resonant word for Americans in the wake of depression and in the midst of war—linked its various meanings. "The one supreme objective for the future," he announced, is "Security. And that means not only physical security . . . from attacks by aggressors. It means also economic security, social security, moral security—in a family of Nations." He followed a similar line on specific measures like federal aid to impoverished school districts: "Nothing can provide a stronger bulwark [against war] in the years to come than an educated and enlightened and tolerant citizenry, equipped with the armed force necessary to stop aggression and warfare in this world." Similarly, he supported compulsory service for young men after the war as simultaneously serving defense, social welfare, and reform, goals linked in his 1944 campaign rhetoric, in which FDR compared the war effort to the New Deal just as he had earlier compared the New Deal to mobilization in World War I. Just as Americans had "joined in a common war against economic breakdown and depression," they now "joined in a common war against the Fascist ruthlessness," FDR proclaimed. New Deal programs were "fortifications . . . built to protect the people." The "coming battle for America and for civilization" resembled earlier "battles against tyranny [the fascists] and reaction [the New Deal's foes]." FDR's rhetoric hardly gained him all the legislation he wanted, and it soared above the possibility of military-business linkages to sustain power and prosperity, but it showed how liberalism was directed into the new channels of national security.

In such ways, the politics and economics of wartime mobilization strengthened the forces of militarization without yet guaranteeing them victory. War taught Americans to associate defense spending with prosperity, even if they did not think much about how the connection might be sustained, and it taught them to regard their industrial and technological muscle as the key to prosperity at home and power abroad, even if they could not anticipate how much they would flex it. It enhanced the power of large corporations, accommodated them to national government, and encouraged them to pioneer advanced technologies for military markets, even if few businessmen foresaw how the wartime bonanza might be sustained after the war. It redirected liberals, and key intellectual elites like scientists, toward the needs and opportunities of national security, even if they did not abandon older visions. It coopted alternative power bases like organized labor, even as wartime prosperity seemed to make the bargain acceptable. And amid all those changes, the drama of older issues—the danger of a return to the Depression, the venerable struggles among capital and labor and government, and the demands of war itself—obscured the possibility that temporary changes might become permanent fixtures. Up for election again in 1944, Roosevelt "realized that there was no more effective way for him to run than again to make the race against the memory of Herbert Hoover." Such pardonable political expediency hardly directed attention to the critical changes underway during the war. . . .

By 1944, too, American planning for the postwar era was in full swing. For decades after 1945, many historians, Cold Warriors, and Roosevelt-haters argued that the administration, fixated on victory and oblivious to American interests and Soviet intentions, failed in such planning. But their charges were essentially wrong, inspired by frustration that America's preeminent power had failed to secure all its ambitions after World War II. Granted, wartime planning for the postwar was chaotic, deprived of FDR's close attention, and unevenly articulated to the American people, but it hardly lacked content and purposefulness.

It was shaped in part by the view of recent history now prevailing among American leaders. In that view, the calamities of economic depression and world war had been avoidable, caused by the abdication of leadership by the United States and by the failures of the world's democracies. The victorious powers of World War I, in this reading, imposed a punitive peace that poisoned German politics, disrupted the global economy, and helped to usher in a global depression, which in turn bred the conditions that dictators exploited. They squandered the chance to use the League of Nations to control economic chaos and military aggression, in part because the United States had refused to join it. Instead, the Western democracies tried policies of appeasement, disarmament, and isolationism that emboldened the aggressors—"an invitation to Mussolini, Hitler and the Japanese war lords to run the world," according to Navy Secretary Forrestal in 1944. And they failed to grasp the dangers posed by new technologies and ideologies operating in a closed world system. For many Americans, the Versailles Treaty ending World War I symbolized the start of these follies, Munich their apogee, Pearl Harbor their consequences for Americans, and German V-2 rockets the future that such foolishness could bring.

Soon Hiroshima and the Holocaust would join the litany of symbols. It was a strikingly dark and self-castigating view of the past for a triumphant nation to adopt.

It was a past that must not and need not be repeated, Americans were told. Now loomed a "second chance" for them to lead the world. This emphasis on a second chance obscured any American drive for power. Americans were, it seemed, looking backward more than forward, atoning for sins of the past more than seeking domination of the future. Just as they saw war as forced upon them in 1941 by aggressors (emboldened by the democracies' weakness), so they now saw postwar power and responsibility as simple necessities. If a measure of American domination ensued, it involved no lust for power and would be welcomed by all nations seeking liberation from the traumas of depression and war. "No one charges us with wanting anything of anybody else's," Marshall asserted, and "no one is fearful of our misuse" of military power.

Several versions of second-chance thinking emerged among elites, including plans for a new world organization to promote economic recovery and collective security, and unilateral efforts to promote global capitalism under American auspices. Among these versions, however, the ideology of national preparedness was especially influential. Brogan noticed that "Americans have long been accustomed to jest at [their] repeated state of military nakedness. 'God looks after children, drunkards, and the United States.'" Those days now seemed gone. As Walter Lippmann put it, Americans "have come to the end of our effortless security" (and of "limitless opportunities," he added). Advocates of preparedness stressed the political and technological imperatives for replacing indifference to military power with a new "state of mind, so firmly imbedded in our souls as to become an invincible philosophy," as one scientist said. Future aggressors would only be deterred by military force. As one admiral put the commonplace argument, if the United States had shown its military might "*before, and not after,* a series of Munich conferences, . . . the personal following of any future Hitler would be limited to a few would-be suicides." Preparation to deter or wage war could not again await the onset of a crisis, not for "a nation grown so large in a world that has shrunk so small," not for an age when an enemy could strike with "a sudden devastation beyond any 'Pearl Harbor' experience or our present power of imagination to conceive." For those aware of the atomic bomb project, peril loomed even larger: "Every center of the population in the world in the future is at the mercy of the enemy that strikes first," advised the scientist Vannevar Bush. Advancing such arguments, advocates of preparedness codified and projected forward the new conception of national security outlined on the eve of World War II.

World War II and American Liberalism

ALAN BRINKLEY

Few would disagree that World War II changed the world as profoundly as any event of this century, perhaps any century. What is less readily apparent, perhaps, is how profoundly the war changed America—its society, its politics, and . . . its

Reprinted from *The War in American Culture* by Brinkley, Erenberg, & Hirsch. Copyright © 1996 University of Chicago Press, pp. 314–323, 326–327. Reprinted by permission of University of Chicago Press and the authors.

image of itself. Except for the combatants themselves, Americans experienced the war at a remove of several thousand miles. They endured no bombing, no invasion, no massive dislocations, no serious material privations. Veterans returning home in 1945 and 1946 found a country that looked very much like the one they had left— something that clearly could not be said of veterans returning home to Britain, France, Germany, Russia, or Japan.

But World War II did transform America in profound, if not immediately visible, ways. Not the least important of those transformations was in the nature of American liberalism, a force that would play a central role in shaping the nation's postwar political and cultural life. Liberalism in America rests on several consistent and enduring philosophical assumptions: the high value liberals believe society should attribute to individual rights and freedoms and the importance of avoiding rigid and immutable norms and institutions. But in the half century since the New Deal, liberalism in America has also meant a prescription for public policy and political action; and in the 1940s this "New Deal liberalism" was in a state of considerable uncertainty and was undergoing significant changes. Several broad developments of the war years helped lay the foundations for the new liberal order that followed the war.

Among those developments was a series of important shifts in the size, distribution, and character of the American population. Not all the demographic changes of the 1940s were a result of the war, nor were their effects on liberal assumptions entirely apparent until well after 1945. But they were a crucial part of the process that would transform American society and the way liberals viewed their mission in that society.

Perhaps the most conspicuous demographic change was the single biggest ethnic migration in American history: the massive movement of African Americans from the rural South to the urban North, a migration much larger than the "great migration" at the time of World War I. Between 1910 (when the first great migration began) and 1940, approximately 1.5 million blacks moved from the South to the North. In the 1940s alone, 2 million African Americans left the South, and 3 million more moved in the twenty years after that. The migration brought substantial numbers of them closer to the center of the nation's economic, cultural, and institutional life. The number of blacks employed in manufacturing more than doubled during the war. There were major increases in the number of African Americans employed as skilled craftsmen or enrolled in unions. There was a massive movement of African American women out of domestic work and into the factory and the shop. Much of this would have occurred with or without World War II, but the war greatly accelerated the movement by expanding industrial activity and by creating a labor shortage that gave African American men and women an incentive to move into industrial cities.

This second great migration carried the question of race out of the South and into the North, out of the countryside and into the city, out of the field and into the factory. African American men and women encountered prejudice and discrimination in the urban, industrial world much as they had in the agrarian world; but in the city they were far better positioned to organize and protest their condition, as some were beginning to do even before the fighting ended. World War II therefore began the process by which race would increase its claim on American consciousness and, ultimately, transform American liberalism.

Just as the war helped lay the groundwork for challenges to racial orthodoxies, so it contributed to later challenges to gender norms. Three million women entered the paid workforce for the first time during the war, benefiting—like black workers—from the labor shortage military conscription had created. Many women performed jobs long considered the exclusive province of men. Women had been moving into the workforce in growing numbers before the war began, to be sure, and almost certainly they would have continued to do so even had the United States remained at peace. Many of their wartime gains, moreover, proved short lived. Female factory workers in particular were usually dismissed as soon as male workers returned to take their places, even though many wanted to remain in their jobs.

Still, most women who had begun working during the war continued working after 1945 (if not always in the same jobs). And while popular assumptions about women's roles (among both women and men) were slow to change, the economic realities of many women's lives were changing dramatically and permanently—in ways that would eventually help raise powerful challenges to ideas about gender. The war, in short, accelerated a critical long-term shift in the role of women in society that would produce, among other things, the feminist movements of the 1960s and beyond.

Similar, if less dramatic, changes were affecting other American communities during the war. Men and women who had long lived on the margins of American life—because of prejudice or geographical isolation or both—found their lives transformed by the pressures of war. Asian Americans, Latino Americans, Native Americans, and others served in the military, worked in factories, moved into diverse urban neighborhoods, and otherwise encountered the urban-industrial world of the midtwentieth century. Life was not, perhaps, much better for many such people in their new roles than it had been in traditional ones. For Japanese Americans on the West Coast, who spent much of the war in internment camps, victims of popular and official hysteria, it was considerably worse. But for many such communities the changes helped erode the isolation that had made it difficult to challenge discrimination and demand inclusion.

No one living in the era of multiculturalism will be inclined to argue with the proposition that the changing composition of the American population over the past fifty years—and the changing relations among different groups within the population—is one of the most important events in the nation's recent history. Those changes have reshaped America's economy, its culture, its politics, and its intellectual life. They have forced the nation to confront its increasing diversity in more direct and painful ways than at any time since the Civil War. They have challenged America's conception of itself as a nation and a society. And they have transformed American liberalism. In the 1930s, most liberals considered questions of racial, ethnic, or gender difference of distinctly secondary importance (or in the case of gender, virtually no importance at all). Liberal discourse centered much more on issues of class and the distribution of wealth and economic power. By 1945 that was beginning to change. One sign of that change was the remarkable reception among liberals of Gunnar Myrdal's *An American Dilemma,* published in 1944. Myrdal identified race as the one issue most likely to shape and perplex the American future. The great migration of the 1940s helped ensure that history would vindicate Myrdal's prediction and that American liberals would adjust their outlook and their goals in fundamental ways in the postwar years.

Perhaps the most common and important observation about the domestic impact of World War II is that it ended the Great Depression and launched an era of unprecedented prosperity. Between 1940 and 1945 the United States experienced the greatest expansion of industrial production in its history. After a decade of depression, a decade of growing doubts about capitalism, a decade of high unemployment and underproduction, suddenly, in a single stroke, the American economy restored itself and—equally important—seemed to redeem itself. Gross national product in the war years rose from $91 billion to $166 billion; 15 million new jobs were created, and the most enduring problem of the depression—massive unemployment—came to an end; industrial production doubled; personal incomes rose (depending on location) by as much as 200 percent. The revival of the economy is obviously important in its own right. But it also had implications for the future of American political economy, for how liberals in particular conceived of the role of the state in the postwar United States.

One of the mainstays of economic thought in the late 1930s was the belief that the United States had reached what many called "economic maturity": the belief that the nation was approaching, or perhaps had reached, the end of its capacity to grow, that America must now learn to live within limits. This assumption strengthened the belief among many reformers that in the future it would be necessary to regulate the economy much more closely and carefully for the benefit of society as a whole. America could not rely any more on a constantly expanding pie; it would have to worry about how the existing pie was to be divided.

The wartime economic experience—the booming expansion, the virtual elimination of unemployment, the creation of new industries, new "frontiers"—served as a rebuke to the "mature economy" idea and restored the concept of growth to the center of liberal hopes. The capitalist economy, liberals suddenly discovered, was not irretrievably stagnant. Economic expansion could achieve, in fact had achieved, dimensions beyond the wildest dreams of the 1930s. Social and economic advancement could proceed, therefore, without structural changes in capitalism, without continuing, intrusive state management of the economy. It could proceed by virtue of growth.

Assaults on the concept of economic maturity were emerging as early as 1940 and gathered force throughout the war. Alvin Hansen, one of the most prominent champions in the 1930s of what he called "secular stagnation," repudiated the idea in 1941. "All of us had our sights too low," he admitted. The *New Republic* and the *Nation,* both of which had embraced the idea of economic maturity in 1938 and 1939, openly rejected it in the 1940s—not only rejected it, but celebrated its demise. The country had achieved a "break," exulted the *Nation,* "from the defeatist thinking that held us in economic thraldom through the thirties, when it was assumed that we could not afford full employment or full production in this country."

But along with this celebration of economic growth came a new and urgent fear: that the growth might not continue once the war was over. What if the depression came back? What if there was a return to massive unemployment? What could be done to make sure that economic growth continued? That was the great liberal challenge of the war years—not to restructure the economy, not to control corporate behavior, not to search for new and more efficient forms of management, but to find a way to keep things going as they were.

And in response to that challenge, a growing number of liberal economists and policymakers became interested in a tool that had begun to attract their attention in the 1930s and that seemed to prove itself during the war: government spending. That was clearly how the economy had revived—in response to the massive increase in the federal budget in the war years, from $9 billion in 1939 to $100 billion in 1945. And that was how the revival could be sustained—by pumping more money into the economy in peacetime. What government needed to do, therefore, was to "plan" for postwar full employment.

Those who called themselves "planners" in the 1940s did not talk much anymore, as planners had talked in earlier years, about the need for an efficient, centrally planned economy in which the government would help direct the behavior of private institutions. They talked instead about fiscal planning—about public works projects, about social welfare programs, about the expansion of the Social Security system. The National Resource Planning Board, the central "planning" agency of the New Deal since 1933, issued a report in 1942 called *Security, Work, and Relief Policies.* In the past, the NRPB had been preoccupied largely with older ideas of planning—regional planning, resource management, government supervision of production and investment. Now, in their 1942 report, the members turned their attention to the new kind of planning. The government should create a "shelf" of public works projects, so that after the war—whenever the economy showed signs of stagnating—it could pull projects off the shelf and spend the money on them to stimulate more growth. The government should commit itself to more expansive Social Security measures so that after the war—if the economy should slow down—there would be welfare mechanisms in place that would immediately pick up the slack and start paying out benefits, which would increase purchasing power and stimulate growth.

All of this reflected, among other things, the increasing influence in American liberal circles of Keynesian economics. The most important liberal economist of the war years—Alvin Hansen of Harvard, who contributed to many NRPB reports—was also the leading American exponent of Keynesianism. Keynesianism provided those concerned about the future of the American economy with an escape from their fears of a new, postwar depression. Economic growth, it taught them, did not require constant involvement in the affairs of private institutions—which the 1930s (and the war itself) had shown to be logistically difficult and politically controversial. Growth could be sustained through the *indirect* manipulation of the economy by fiscal and monetary levers.

The wartime faith in economic growth led, in other words, to several developments of great importance to the future of American liberalism. It helped relegitimize capitalism among people who had, in the 1930s, developed serious doubts about its viability. It helped rob the "administrative" reform ideas of the late 1930s—the belief in ever greater regulation of private institutions—of their urgency. It helped elevate Keynesian ideas about indirect management of the economy to the center of reform hopes. And it made the idea of the welfare state—of Social Security and public works and other social welfare efforts—come to seem a part of the larger vision of sustaining economic growth by defining welfare as a way to distribute income and stimulate purchasing power. It helped channel American liberalism into a new, less confrontational direction—a direction that would produce fewer clashes with capitalist institutions; that tried to define the interests of capitalists and the interests of the larger public in identical terms; that emphasized problems of consumption over problems of production; that shaped the liberal agenda for more than a generation and helped shape the next great episode in liberal policy experiments: the Great Society of the 1960s.

World War II had other important and more purely ideological effects on American liberalism—some of them in apparent conflict with others, but all of them important in determining the permissible range of liberal aspirations for the postwar era. First, the war created, or at least greatly reinforced, a set of anxieties and fears that would become increasingly central to liberal thought in the late 1940s and 1950s. It inflamed two fears in particular: a fear of the state and a fear of the people. Both were a response, in large part, to the horror with which American liberals (and most other Americans as well) regarded the regimes the United States was fighting in World War II. Both would be sustained and strengthened by the similar horror with which most Americans came to view the regime the nation was beginning to mobilize against in peacetime even before the end of the war: the Soviet Union.

The fear of the state emerged directly out of the way American liberals (and the American people generally) defined the nature of their enemy in World War II. During World War I many Americans had believed the enemy was a race, a people: the Germans, the beastlike "Huns," and their presumably savage culture. In World War II racial stereotypes continued to play an important role in portrayals of the Japanese; but in defining the enemy in Europe—always the principal enemy in the 1940s to most Americans—the government and most of the media relied less on racial or cultural images than on political ones. Wartime propaganda in World War II did not personify the Germans and Italians as evil peoples. It focused instead on the Nazi and fascist states.

The war, in other words, pushed a fear of totalitarianism (and hence a general wariness about excessive state power) to the center of American liberal thought. In particular, it forced a reassessment of the kinds of associational and corporatist arrangements that many had found so attractive in the aftermath of World War I. Those, after all, were the kinds of arrangements Germany and Italy had claimed to be creating. But it also created a less specific fear of state power that made other kinds of direct planning and management of the economy or society seem unappealing as well. "The rise of totalitarianism," Reinhold Niebuhr noted somberly in 1945, "has prompted the democratic world to view all collectivist answers to our social problems with increased apprehension." Virtually all experiments in state supervision of private institutions, he warned, contained "some peril of compounding economic and political power." Hence "a wise community will walk warily and test the effect of each new adventure before further adventures." To others the lesson was even starker. *Any* steps in the direction of state control of economic institutions were (to use the title of Friedrich A. Hayek's celebrated antistatist book of 1944) steps along "the road to serfdom." This fear of the state was one of many things that lent strength to the emerging Keynesian–welfare state liberal vision of political economy, with its much more limited role for government as a manager of economic behavior.

Along with this fear of the state emerged a related fear: a fear of "mass politics" or "mass man"; a fear, in short, of the people. Nazi Germany, facist Italy, even the Soviet Union, many liberals came to believe, illustrated the dangers inherent in trusting the people to control their political life. The people, the "mass," could too easily be swayed by demagogues and tyrants. They were too susceptible to appeals to their passions, to the dark, intolerant impulses that in a healthy society remained largely repressed and subdued. Fascism and communism were not simply the products of the state or of elite politics, many liberals believed; they were the products of mass movements, of the unleashing of the dangerous and irrational impulses within every individual and every society.

This fear of the mass lay at the heart of much liberal cultural and intellectual criticism in the first fifteen years after World War II. It found expression in the writings of Hannah Arendt, Theodor Adorno, Richard Hofstadter, Lionel Trilling, Daniel Bell, Dwight Macdonald, and many others. Like the fear of the state, with which it was so closely associated, it reinforced a sense of caution and restraint in liberal thinking; a suspicion of ideology, a commitment to pragmatism, a wariness about moving too quickly to encourage or embrace spontaneous popular movements; a conviction that one of the purposes of politics was to defend the state against popular movements and their potentially dangerous effects.

There were, in short, powerful voices within American liberalism during and immediately after World War II arguing that the experience of the war had introduced a dark cloud of doubt and even despair to human society. A world that could produce so terrible a war; a world that could produce Hiroshima, Nagasaki, the Katyn Forest, Auschwitz; a world capable of profound evil and inconceivable destruction: such a world, many American liberals argued, must be forever regarded skeptically and suspiciously. Humankind must move cautiously into its uncertain future, wary of unleashing the dark impulses that had produced such horror.

Some liberal intellectuals went further. Americans, they argued, must resist the temptation to think of themselves, in their hour of triumph, as a chosen people. No people, no nation, could afford to ignore its own capacity for evil. Reinhold Niebuhr spoke for many liberals when he wrote of the dangers of the "deep layer of Messianic consciousness in the mind of America" and warned of liberal culture's "inability to comprehend the depth of evil to which individuals and communities may sink, particularly when they try to play the role of God in history." Americans, he said, would do well to remember that "no nation is sacred and unique. . . . Providence has not set Americans apart from lesser breeds. We too are part of history's seamless web."

But Niebuhr's statements were obviously written to refute a competing assumption. And as it suggests, there was in the 1940s another, very different ideological force at work in America, another form of national self-definition that affected liberal thought and behavior, at home and in the world, at least as much as the somber assessments of Niebuhr and others. Indeed even many liberal intellectuals attracted to Niebuhr's pessimistic ideas about human nature and mass politics were simultaneously drawn to this different and, on the surface at least, contradictory assessment of the nation's potential. For in many ways the most powerful ideological force at work in postwar American liberalism, and in the postwar United States generally, was the view of America as an anointed nation; America as a special moral force in the world; America as a society with a unique mission, born of its righteousness. This is an ideological tradition that is often described as the tradition of American innocence. But innocence is perhaps too gentle a word for what has often been an aggressive and intrusive vision, a vision that rests on the belief that America is somehow insulated from the sins and failures and travails that affect other nations, that America stands somehow outside of history, protected from it by its own strength and virtue.

World War II did not create those beliefs. They are as old as the nation itself. But the American experience in the conflict, and the radically enhanced international stature and responsibility of the United States in the aftermath of the war, strengthened such ideas and gave them a crusading quality that made them as active and powerful as they had been at any moment in the nation's history. . . .

The war left other ideological legacies for American liberalism as well. In the glow of the nation's victory, in the sense of old orders shattered and a new world being born, came an era of exuberant innovation, an era in which, for a time, nothing seemed more appealing than the new. The allure of the new was visible in the brave new world of architectural modernism, whose controversial legacy is so much a part of the postwar American landscape. It was visible in the explosive growth of the innovative and iconoclastic American art world, which made New York in the 1940s and 1950s something of what Paris had been in the nineteenth century. It was visible in the increased stature and boldness of the American scientific community, and in the almost religious faith in technological progress that came to characterize so much of American life.

Above all, perhaps, it was visible in the way it excited, and then frustrated, a generation of American liberals as they imagined new possibilities for progress and social justice. That is what Archibald MacLeish meant in 1943 when he spoke about the America of the imagination, the society that the war was encouraging Americans to create:

> We have, and we know we have, the abundant means to bring our boldest dreams to pass—to create for ourselves whatever world we have the courage to desire. . . . We have the tools and the skill and the intelligence to take our cities apart and put them together, to lead our roads and rivers where we please to lead them, to build our houses where we want our houses, to brighten the air, to clean the wind, to live as men in this Republic, free men, should be living. We have the power and the courage and the resources of good-will and decency and common understanding . . . to create a nation such as men have never seen. . . . We stand at the moment of the building of great lives, for the war's end and our victory in the war will throw that moment and the means before us.

There was, of course, considerable naïveté, and even arrogance, in such visions. But there was also an appealing sense of hope and commitment—a belief in the possibility of sweeping away old problems and failures, of creating "great lives." Out of such visions came some of the postwar crusades of American liberals—the battle for racial justice, the effort to combat poverty, the expansion of individual rights. And although all of those battles had some ambiguous and even unhappy consequences, they all reflected a confidence in the character and commitment of American society—and the possibility of creating social justice within it—that few people would express so blithely today. Postwar liberalism has suffered many failures and travails in the half century since 1945. But surely its postwar faith in the capacity of America to rebuild—and perhaps even redeem—itself remains one of its most appealing legacies.

SUGGESTED READING

Atleson, James. *Labor and the Wartime State* (1998).

Bernstein, Barton. "America in War and Peace: The Test of Liberalism." In *Toward a New Past,* ed. Barton Bernstein (1968).

Brinkley, Alan. *The End of Reform: New Deal Liberalism in Recession and War* (1995).

Brody, David. "The New Deal and World War II." In *The New Deal: The National Level,* ed. David Brody, John Braeman, and Robert H. Bremner, 267–309 (1975).

Daniel, Pete. "Going Among Strangers: Southern Reactions to World War II." *Journal of American History* 77 (December 1990): 886–911.

Gardner, Richard. *Sterling-Dollar Diplomacy in Current Perspective.* Rev. ed. (1980).

Glaberman, Martin. *Wartime Strikes* (1980).

Griffith, Barbara. *The Crisis of American Labor: Operation Dixie and the Defeat of the CIO* (1988).

Gropman, Alan. *Mobilizing U.S. Industry in World War II* (1996).

Harris, Howell. *The Right to Manage: Industrial Relations Policies of American Business in the 1940s* (1982).

Hooks, Gregory. *Forging the Military-Industrial Complex* (1991).

Jacobs, Meg. " 'How About Some Meat?': The Office of Price Administration, Consumption Politics, and State Building from the Bottom Up, 1941–1946." *Journal of American History* 84 (December 1997) 910–941.

Janeway, Eliot. *The Struggle for Survival* (1951).

Koistinen, Paul. *The Military-Industrial Complex: An Historical Perspective* (1980).

Kolko, Gabriel. *The Politics of War* (1968).

Lichtenstein, Nelson. *Labor's War at Home* (1982).

Maier, Charles. *In Search of Stability* (1987).

Nash, Gerald. *The American West Transformed* (1985).

Ross, Davis. *Preparing for Ulysses: Politics and Veterans During World War II* (1969).

Sherry, Michael. *In the Shadow of War: The United States Since the 1930s* (1995).

Skopol, Theda, and Edwin Amenta. "Redefining the New Deal: World War II and the Development of Social Provision in the United States," in *The Politics of Social Policy in the United States,* ed. Theda Skocpol, 81–122 (1988).

Smith, C. Calvin. *War and Wartime Changes: The Transformation of Arkansas* (1986).

Sparrow, Bartholomew. *From the Outside In: World War II and the American State* (1996).

Vatter, Harold. *The U.S. Economy in World War II* (1985).

White, Gerald T. *Billions for Defense* (1980).

Winkler, Allen. *The Politics of Propaganda* (1978).